Professor of Romance Languages 512-2684

MAR CARIBE
OCÉANO ATLÁNTICO
Maracaibo
Barranquilla
Caracas
PANAMÁ
GUYANA
VENEZUELA
Georgetown
Medellín
Paramaribo
Río Orinoco
Panamá
Cayena
Bogotá
Cali
SURINAME
GUYANA FRANC
COLOMBIA
Quito
Río Amazonas
ECUADOR
Belém
Manaus
Guayaquil
PERÚ
BRASIL
CORDILLERA DE LOS ANDES
Recife
Cuzco
Lima
Brasília
La Paz
Arequipa
BOLIVIA
Sucre
PARAGUAY
Antofagasta
Río de Janeiro
Asunción
Trópico de Capricornio
CHILE
San Miguel de Tucumán
São Paulo
OCÉANO PACÍFICO
La Serena
Córdoba
OCÉANO ATLÁNTICO
Rosario
URUGUAY
Valparaíso
Santiago
ARGENTINA
Montevideo
Buenos Aires
Concepción
Río de la Plata
N
Bahía Blanca
Puerto Montt
Bariloche
Chiloé
AMÉRICA DEL SUR
Islas Malvinas
0
1500 kilómetros
Estrecho de Magallanes
Punta Arenas
Tierra del Fuego
0
1000 millas
Cabo de Hornos

ESPAÑA
0 200 kilómetros
0 100 millas
N
MAR CANTÁBRICO
Bahía de Vizcaya
FRANCIA
CANTABRIA
San Sebastián
Santander
La Coruña
Oviedo
ASTURIAS
Bilbao
PAÍS VASCO
LOS PIRINEOS
ANDORRA
Golfo de León
Santiago de Compostela
GALICIA
Pamplona
NAVARRA
Burgos
Vigo
León
Logroño
LA RIOJA
CASTILLA-LEÓN
CATALUÑA
Valladolid
Zaragoza
Lérida
Costa Brava
Zamora
ESPAÑA
Río Ebro
Oporto
Río Duero
Tarragona
Barcelona
SIERRA DE GUADARRAMA
Segovia
ARAGÓN
Salamanca
Ávila
Guadalajara
PORTUGAL
MADRID
El Escorial
Menorca
Madrid
Castellón
Mallorca
Río Tajo
Toledo
Cáceres
CASTILLA-LA MANCHA
Valencia
Palma
Lisboa
EXTREMADURA
COMUNIDAD VALENCIANA
Ibiza
ISLAS BALEARES
Ciudad Real
Badajoz
Mérida
Albacete
Almadén
Formentera
Alicante
Río Guadiana
SIERRA MORENA
MAR MEDITERRÁNEO
Murcia
Linares
Río Guadalquivir
MURCIA
Costa Blanca
Córdoba
Jaén
Lorca
Sevilla
ANDALUCÍA
Cartagena
SIERRA NEVADA
Huelva
Granada
Almería
Golfo de Cádiz
Jerez de la Frontera
Málaga
Cádiz
OCÉANO ATLÁNTICO
Costa del Sol
Gibraltar (R.U.)
Tánger
Ceuta (Esp.)
Orán
ISLAS CANARIAS
Santa Cruz de Tenerife
Lanzarote
Fuerteventura
La Palma
Tenerife
Las Palmas
Hierro
Gomera
Las Palmas de Gran Canaria
0 200 kilómetros
0 100 millas

¿Qué tal?

An Introductory Course

Sixth Edition

INSTRUCTOR'S EDITION

Thalia Dorwick

Ana María Pérez-Gironés
Wesleyan University

Marty Knorre

William R. Glass

Hildebrando Villarreal
California State University, Los Angeles

Contributing Writers:

Manuel Cortés-Castañeda
Eastern Kentucky University

Hope Doyle D'Ambrosio
American University

Becky S. Jaimes
Austin Community College

Talía Loaiza
Austin Community College

Boston Burr Ridge, IL Dubuque, IA Madison, WI New York San Francisco St. Louis
Bangkok Bogotá Caracas Kuala Lumpur Lisbon London Madrid Mexico City
Milan Montreal New Delhi Santiago Seoul Singapore Sydney Taipei Toronto

McGraw-Hill Higher Education

A Division of The ***McGraw-Hill*** *Companies*

This is an  book.

¿Qué tal?
An Introductory Course

Published by McGraw-Hill, an imprint of The McGraw-Hill Companies, Inc., 1221 Avenue of the Americas, New York, NY 10020.

This book is printed on acid-free paper.

1 2 3 4 5 6 7 8 9 0 VNH VNH 0 9 8 7 6 5 4 3 2

ISBN 0-07-249641-X (Student's Edition)
ISBN 0-07-253517-2 (Instructor's Edition)

Vice President and Editor-in-chief: *Thalia Dorwick*
Publisher: *William R. Glass*
Sponsoring editor: *Christa Harris*
Director of development: *Scott Tinetti*
Senior marketing manager: *Nick Agnew*
Senior production editor: *David M. Staloch*
Senior production supervisor: *Richard DeVitto*
Senior supplements producer: *Louis Swaim*
Interior and cover designer: *Violeta Díaz*
Photo researcher: *Alexandra Ambrose*
Art editor: *Robin Mouat*
Compositor: *TechBooks*
Typeface: *10/12 Palatino*
Printer and binder: *Von Hoffmann Press*

Cover image: *Detail from a mosaic mural at the San Antonio Convention Center by Carlos Mérida, commissioned for the 1967 Hemisfair. Copyright © Estate of Carlos Mérida/SOMAAP, México/VAGA, New York, NY. Photograph by David Walden, San Antonio, TX.*

Because this page cannot accommodate all the copyright notices, credits are listed after the index and constitute an extension of the copyright page.

LIBRARY OF CONGRESS CATALOGING-IN-PUBLICATION DATA

¿Qué tal? An Introductory Course / Thalia Dorwick . . . [et al.]—6th ed.
p. cm
English and Spanish.
Includes index.
ISBN 0-07-249641-X
1. Spanish language—Textbooks for foreign speakers—English. I. Dorwick, Thalia , 1944–

PC4129.E5 Q4 2002
468.2'421—dc21

2002016696

http://www.mhhe.com

CONTENTS

En la universidad 29

La familia 53

De compras 80

En casa 102

CAPÍTULO 5

Las estaciones, el tiempo y un poco de geografía 123

CAPÍTULO 6

¿Qué le gusta comer? 149

CAPÍTULO 7

De vacaciones 173

CAPÍTULO 8

Los días festivos 197

Capítulo 9

El tiempo libre 217

Capítulo 10

La salud 237

Presiones de la vida moderna 257

La calidad de la vida 279

CAPÍTULO 15

La vida social y la vida afectiva 342

CAPÍTULO 16

¿Trabajar para vivir o vivir para trabajar? 360

CAPÍTULO 17

En la actualidad 383

En el extranjero 401

PREFACE

"... to help students develop proficiency in the four language skills essential to truly communicative language learning..."

from the preface to *¿Qué tal?,* first edition, 1983

Welcome to the sixth edition of *¿Qué tal? An Introductory Course.* It has been twenty years since the publication of the first edition, and the coauthors are grateful to the instructors and students who have responded so positively to the goals and approach of *¿Qué tal?*.

In those twenty years, much has changed and much has remained constant in *¿Qué tal?*. *¿Qué tal?* has remained true to the goals of the first edition, as cited above. The approach, however, has evolved and kept pace with technological advances and our increasing knowledge of how languages are learned. The ancillary package for the first edition of *¿Qué tal?* was excellent for its time but seems small in comparison to the plethora of materials available to instructors and students today. Particularly noteworthy are the wide variety of new technologies that enhance language learning in ways not yet dreamed of twenty years ago.

In addition to these new technologies, instructors will find in the sixth edition those features that they have come to know and trust over the years. These features include:

- the popular, four-part chapter structure that facilitates lesson planning and organization
- grammar, vocabulary, and culture that work together as interactive units
- an abundance of practice materials, ranging from form-focused to communicative
- an emphasis on the meaningful use of Spanish
- a positive portrayal of Hispanic cultures around the world
- supplementary materials carefully coordinated with the core text and that actually 'work' with it

Here are some of the exciting, new features of the sixth edition:

- new text-integrated **En contexto** video segments that focus on high-frequency functional situations such as purchasing train tickets and visiting a pharmacy
- a new **Cultura en contexto** cultural feature that highlights a cultural topic illustrated in the text-integrated video segments
- **Notas culturales** and **En los Estados Unidos y el Canadá** cultural readings have been thoroughly revised and updated to reflect current student interests
- new chapter-culminating communicative activities (**A conversar**) that underscore the four-skills development featured in **Paso 4: Un paso más**
- a completely revised interactive Student CD-ROM that provides outstanding practice and review of vocabulary and grammar, interactive listening and speaking practice, and cultural video and activities.
- a new self-scoring, self-grading Electronic Workbook/Laboratory Manual that offers students and instructors an enhanced, interactive alternative to the traditional Workbook/Laboratory Manual
- a new Online Learning Center that offers a wide variety of practice and study materials, including flashcards, self-quizzes, Internet cultural activities, crossword puzzles, and much more

Please turn the page for a fully illustrated Guided Tour of the sixth edition of *¿Qué tal?*.

GUIDED TOUR

The sixth edition of *¿Qué tal?* features a uniquely clear and user-friendly organization. Each of its eighteen regular chapters is divided into four **pasos**, highlighted with color tabs for easy reference, with a cultural feature in the middle. Thus, each regular chapter has the following structure:

Paso 1: Vocabulario
Paso 2: Gramática
Enfoque cultural
Paso 3: Gramática
Paso 4: Un paso más

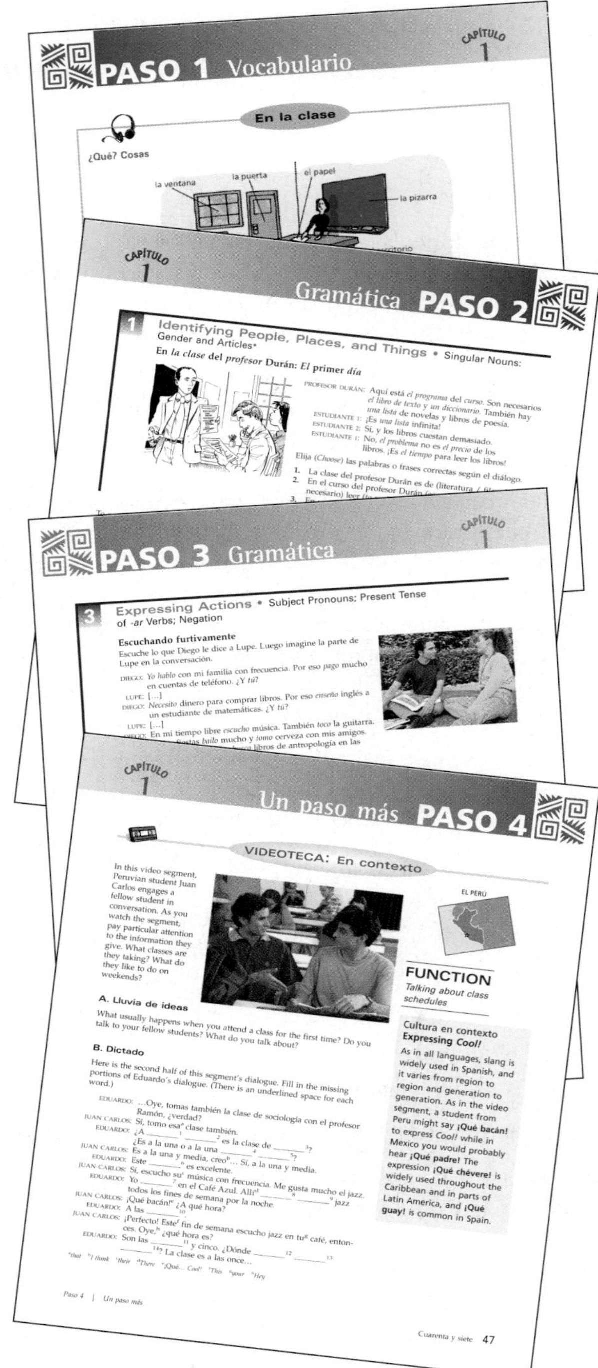

Paso 1: Vocabulario

This section presents and practices the chapter's thematic vocabulary. The lexical lists in these sections are read on the Listening Comprehension Audio CD and are signaled by a headphone icon. Each new lexical list is followed by a **Conversación** section that practices the new vocabulary in context.

Pasos 2 and 3: Gramática

These sections present one to two grammar points each. Each grammar point is introduced by a minidialogue, a cartoon or drawing, realia, or a brief reading that presents the grammar topic in context. Grammar explanations, in English, appear in the left-hand column of the two-column design; paradigms and sample sentences appear in the right-hand column. Each grammar presentation is followed by a series of contextualized exercises and activities that progress from more controlled (**Práctica**) to more open-ended (**Conversación**).

Paso 4: Un paso más

This section integrates the vocabulary and grammar from the first three **pasos** in a rich and stimulating selection of skill-building activities: **Videoteca: En contexto** (video comprehension and discussion questions); **A leer** (readings and pre-reading strategies); **A escribir** (brief writing assignments based on the chapter theme); and **A conversar** (chapter-culminating communicative activities). The **A leer** and **A escribir** sections are found in odd-numbered chapters; **A conversar** activities are found in even-numbered chapters.

Enfoque cultural

The cultures of the Spanish-speaking world are an integral part of every section of *¿Qué tal?,* but they take central stage in the **Enfoque cultural** section of each chapter. Located between **Pasos 2** and **3**, **Enfoque cultural** brings to life the richness and variety of Spanish-speaking cultures in a single, at-a-glance presentation. Each **Enfoque cultural** section focuses on a distinct country or region and includes interesting facts about people, places, and events in that geographical area. A video icon refers to corresponding cultural footage on the Video Program.

Also featured on this page is a unique Internet icon, which directs students to visit the *¿Qué tal?* website. Among other things, the *¿Qué tal?* website contains links to authentic web pages from the Spanish-speaking world that provide more information about the people, places, and events featured in the **Enfoque cultural** sections.

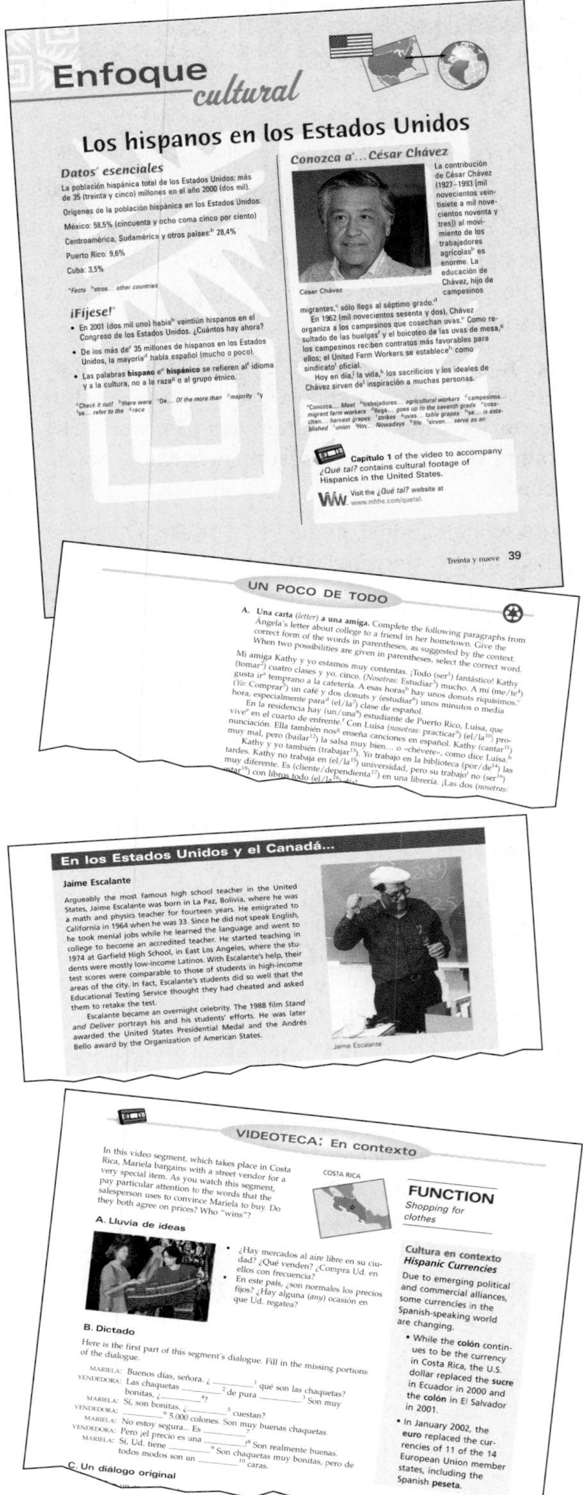

Additional features

- **Un poco de todo** activities, found in **Paso 3: Gramática**, combine and review grammar presented in the chapter as well as important grammar from previous chapters. Major topics that are continuously spiraled in this section include **ser** and **estar**, preterite and imperfect, gender and gender agreement, and indicative and subjunctive.
- **Nota cultural** features highlight an aspect of Hispanic cultures throughout the world.
- **En los Estados Unidos y el Canadá** are brief sections that focus on U.S. and Canadian Hispanics and institutions. Key words and phrases are highlighted in these sections in order to facilitate comprehension.
- **Nota comunicativa** sections provide additional information about communication in Spanish.
- **Vocabulario útil** boxes give additional vocabulary that may be necessary to work through a chapter's activities.
- **Cultura en contexto** sidebars in the **Videoteca: En contexto** section highlight a cultural point illustrated in the **En contexto** video segment.

For more information on these and other features of *¿Qué tal?,* please visit the text-specific website at **www.mhhe.com/quetal**.

VIDEO AND INTERACTIVE MULTIMEDIA

The Video

The Video Program that accompanies the sixth edition of *¿Qué tal?* offers a variety of video materials for use both in and out of class. There are three components to the Video Program, which comprise almost three hours of video material:

- **Minidramas** situational episodes: The **Minidramas**, linked by theme to each chapter of the textbook, follow the story of three different groups of people. The minidramas were filmed on location in Mexico, Spain, and Ecuador.
- **En contexto** functional vignettes: These vignettes, integrated directly into the textbook in **Paso 4** of every chapter, illustrate high-frequency functional language exchanges such as purchasing train tickets, bargaining for handcrafted items, shopping for produce, and visiting a post office. The **En contexto** vignettes were filmed on location in Peru, Mexico, and Costa Rica.
- **Enfoque cultural** segments: The **Enfoque cultural** segments provide cultural overview footage for every Spanish-speaking country and are integrated with the **Enfoque cultural** sections of the textbook.

Instructors will find all three of these video components, available on the Video Program, organized by chapter for easy access. Additionally, the Video Program is available to students on the Video on CD, packaged free with every new copy of the textbook, making the video materials completely accessible to students at all times and providing additional flexibility to the instructor.

The **Videoteca: En contexto** section of each chapter's **Paso 4: Un paso más** includes comprehension and discussion questions along with additional activities appropriate for use in the classroom. Additional activities are available in the Instructor's Manual and Resource Kit.

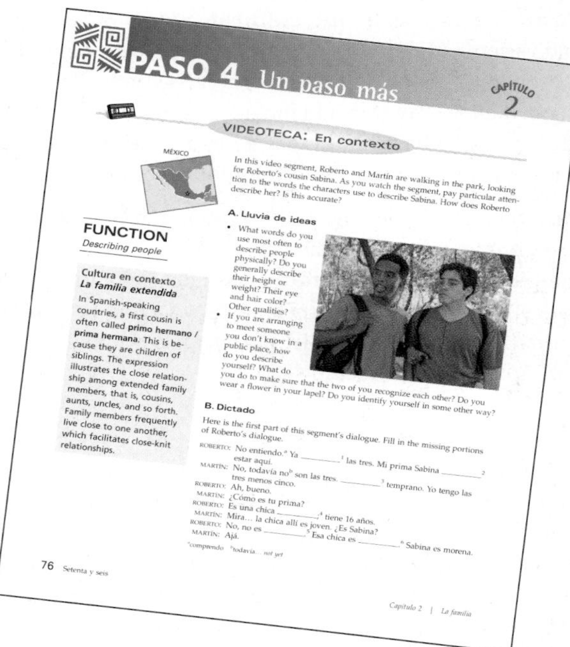

PASO 4 Un paso más

CAPÍTULO 2

VIDEOTECA: En contexto

MÉXICO

In this video segment, Roberto and Martín are walking in the park, looking for Roberto's cousin Sabina. As you watch the segment, pay particular attention to the words the characters use to describe Sabina. How does Roberto describe her? Is this accurate?

A. Lluvia de ideas

- What words do you use most often to describe people physically? Do you generally describe their height or weight? Their eye and hair color? Other qualities?
- If you are arranging to meet someone you don't know in a public place, how do you describe yourself? What do you do to make sure that the two of you recognize each other? Do you wear a flower in your lapel? Do you identify yourself in some other way?

FUNCTION
Describing people

Cultura en contexto
La familia extendida

In Spanish-speaking countries, a first cousin is often called **primo hermano / prima hermana**. This is because they are children of siblings. The expression illustrates the close relationship among extended family members, that is, cousins, aunts, uncles, and so forth. Family members frequently live close to one another, which facilitates close-knit relationships.

B. Dictado

Here is the first part of this segment's dialogue. Fill in the missing portions of Roberto's dialogue.

ROBERTO: No entiendo.[a] Ya ________[1] las tres. Mi prima Sabina ________[2] estar aquí.
MARTÍN: No, todavía no[b] son las tres. ________[3] temprano. Yo tengo las tres menos cinco.
ROBERTO: Ah, bueno.
MARTÍN: ¿Cómo es tu prima?
ROBERTO: Es una chica ________;[4] tiene 16 años.
MARTÍN: Mira... la chica allí es joven. ¿Es Sabina?
ROBERTO: No, no es ________.[5] Esa chica es ________.[6] Sabina es morena.
MARTÍN: Ajá.

[a]comprendo [b]todavía... *not yet*

76 Setenta y seis

Capítulo 2 | La familia

Here are some of the people and places featured in the Video Program:

Manuel and Lola, a couple from Seville, celebrate their anniversary.

Mariela, a computer lab director from San José, Costa Rica, purchases vegetables from her local greengrocer.

Juan Carlos, a student in Lima, Peru, purchases medication at a Lima pharmacy.

Roberto, a young man from Mexico City, asks a passerby for directions.

Elisa and her son José Miguel, who live in Quito, Ecuador, help a passing motorist find a mechanic.

Diego, a student from California, meets Antonio, a student in Mexico City, on the campus of the **Universidad Nacional Autónoma de México**.

The Online Learning Center Website

The new Online Learning Center (OLC) Website brings the Spanish-speaking world directly into students' lives and their language-learning experience through a myriad of resources and activities. Resources for students include vocabulary and grammar activities for each chapter, Internet cultural links and activities, and vocabulary flashcards. For instructors, the OLC provides grammar PowerPoint slides, online transparencies, additional A leer, A escribir, and A conversar activities, and links to professional organizations and other resources. The *¿Qué tal?* OLC can be accessed at **www.mhhe.com/quetal**.

The CD-ROM

Available in multiplatform format, the CD-ROM continues the emphasis on the meaningful use of Spanish that characterizes the student text. Correlated with the textbook by chapter, the CD-ROM offers multiple opportunities for learners to review and practice vocabulary and grammar in a meaningful, interactive format. A video segment in each lesson invites learners to "participate" in a dialogue with a native speaker of Spanish and further practice the language functions presented in the **En contexto** video. In addition, learners continue their development of reading, writing, listening, and speaking skills through interaction with textual passages and other engaging content. Cultural themes introduced in the textbook are further discussed in the CD-ROM, and a link from the CD-ROM takes the user directly to the *¿Qué tal?* Online Learning Center Website. The inclusion of additional learning resources, including the McGraw-Hill Electronic Language Tutor program, a "talking" glossary of terms, and verb reference charts, makes the *¿Qué tal?* CD-ROM a unique multimedia learning tool for the student of Spanish.

¿QUÉ TAL?: A SHORTER COURSE

As with all previous editions of *¿Qué tal?,* the sixth edition is based on the highly successful *Puntos de partida* first-year Spanish text. Responding to the wishes of many instructors across the country, *¿Qué tal?* retains the methodology and functionality of the *Puntos* program but in a shorter version, which can be ideal for classes meeting three or fewer times per week.

In order to create *¿Qué tal?* from *Puntos,* the coauthors reduced the amount of activities and exercises in the *Puntos* main text and supplements as well as the actual number of grammar points presented in *Puntos.* Additional points are subsumed within related structures or within other parts of the text (Instructor's Edition annotations, **Nota comunicativa** features, and so on).

The *Puntos* grammar points that were modified or removed for the sixth edition of *¿Qué tal?* are:

- Asking Yes/No Questions
- Relative Pronouns
- **Hace… que** + *present* and *preterite*
- Summary of the Subjunctive
- Stressed Possessives
- Hypothetical Situations

With one to three grammar points per chapter, we feel *¿Qué tal?* to be a very manageable book for you and your students. Above all, we believe *¿Qué tal?* to be a *flexible* program, one that can be adapted to suit different teaching and learning styles.

SUPPLEMENTARY MATERIALS FOR THE SIXTH EDITION

The supplements listed here may accompany the sixth edition of *¿Qué tal?.* Please contact your local McGraw-Hill Higher Education representative for details concerning policies, prices, and availability, as some restrictions may apply.

Workbook / Laboratory Manual and ***Audio Program***, by Alice Arana (formerly of Fullerton College), Oswaldo Arana (formerly of California State University, Fullerton), and María Sabló-Yates. The two volumes of the Workbook / Laboratory Manual provide a wealth of activities, both aural and written, that reinforce chapter content. Audio Program CDs are free to adopting institutions and are also available for student purchase upon request. An Audioscript is also available.

The ***Electronic Workbook / Laboratory Manual***, Vols. 1 and 2 provide an enhanced alternative to the print ***Workbook / Laboratory Manual***. Available for student purchase, these enhanced versions offer even more practice than the print *Workbook / Laboratory Manual,* in an electronic environment that offers immediate feedback, self-grading activities, and activity tracking for instructors. The laboratory portion includes the entire Audio Program on the same CD-ROM.

The ***Instructor's Manual and Resource Kit*** offers an extensive introduction to teaching techniques, general guidelines for instructors, suggestions for lesson planning in semester and quarter schedules, and additional pre- and post-viewing activities for the video. Also included are a wide variety of interactive and communicative games for practicing vocabulary and grammar.

The ***Testing Program*** reflects the revisions in the student text for the sixth edition. It also includes sections for testing reading and listening comprehension, as well as tests for oral proficiency and sections designed to test cultural material presented in the program.

Packaged with every new student text is a free ***Listening Comprehension Audio CD*** that provides additional vocabulary practice for the **Paso 1: Vocabulario** sections of the text. This audio supplement was designed to meet the needs of individual students and can be used to review and practice vocabulary as well as to practice pronunciation.

Packaged with every new student text is a free ***Video on CD*** that provides students with the complete Video Program for *¿Qué tal?*. It also includes a transcript of all video segments. Comprehension activities for the video segments are available on the *¿Qué tal?* Online Learning Center Website.

A set of ***Overhead Transparencies***, most in full color, contains drawings from the text and supplementary drawings for use with vocabulary and grammar presentation. An electronic online version of the Transparencies is available to instructors on the *¿Qué tal?* Online Learning Center Website.

The ***McGraw-Hill Electronic Language Tutor (MHELT)***, available in both PC and Macintosh formats, offers most of the more controlled exercises from the student text as well as some supplementary mechanical practice. A parsing tool provides students with guided feedback while they complete the exercises and keeps track of their work.

A ***training/orientation manual*** for use with teaching assistants, by James F. Lee (Indiana University), offers practical advice for beginning language instructors and language coordinators.

Also available for use with *¿Qué tal?* is a software program called ***Spanish Partner***, developed by Monica Morley and Karl Fisher (Vanderbilt University). This user-friendly program helps students master first-year vocabulary and grammar topics. Available for student purchase, Spanish Partner also offers clear feedback that helps students learn from their errors.

The ***Destinos Video Modules*** are also available for use with the sixth edition of *¿Qué tal?*. Containing footage from the popular "Destinos" telecourse series, as well as from original footage shot on location, the modules offer high-quality video segments that enhance learning of vocabulary, functional language, situational language, and culture.

A ***Practical Guide to Language Learning***, by H. Douglas Brown (San Francisco State University), provides beginning foreign-language students with a general introduction to the language-learning process. This guide is free to adopting institutions, and it can also be made available for student purchase.

Ultralingua en español, a Spanish-English bilingual dictionary on CD-ROM, is available for student purchase. This dual-platform CD-ROM contains 180,000 words and expressions, a special wild-card search function, an extensive hyperlinked grammar reference, and other valuable reference tools.

The ***¡A leer! Easy Reader Series*** features two short readers, ***Cocina y comidas hispanas***, on regional Hispanic cuisines; and ***Mundos de fantasía***, which contains fairy tales and legends. These readers can be used as early as the second semester.

The ***El mundo hispano*** reader features five major regions of the Hispanic world as well as a section on Hispanics in the United States.

ACKNOWLEDGMENTS

The suggestions, advice, and work of the following friends and colleagues are gratefully acknowledged by the authors of the sixth edition.

- Dr. Bill VanPatten (University of Illinois, Chicago), whose creativity has been an inspiration to us for a number of editions and from whom we have learned so very much about language teaching and how students learn.
- María Sabló-Yates, whose extensive research provides the basis for many of the **Enfoque cultural** sections.
- Dr. Manuel Cortés-Castañeda (Eastern Kentucky University), whose engaging and creative **A conversar** activities provide wonderful chapter-culminating communicative tasks and projects.
- Dr. Hope Doyle D'Ambrosio (American University), whose new **Cultura en contexto** cultural notes enrich the video-viewing experience for students and provide excellent topics for in-class discussion.

- Becky S. Jaimes and Talía Loaiza (both of Austin Community College), whose extensively revised and completely new **Notas culturales** offer students a series of outstanding cultural readings on a wide range of high-interest topics.
- Dr. A. Raymond Elliott (University of Texas, Arlington) whose contributions to the Instructor's Edition and Instructor's Manual and Resource Kit have served to make those supplements even more invaluable teaching resources.
- Laura Chastain (El Salvador), whose invaluable contributions to the text range from language usage to suggestions for realia.
- Ruth Ordás and Dr. Theodore V. Higgs, whose contributions to previous editions are still evident in the sixth edition.

In addition, the publishers wish to acknowledge the suggestions received from the following instructors and professional friends across the country. The appearance of their names in this list does not necessarily constitute their endorsement of the text or its methodology.

Joseph M. Amable
Cañada College
Geraldine Ameriks
University of Notre Dame
Catherine L. Angell
Austin Community College
Louise C. Barbaro-Medrano
Western Illinois University
Sandra Livingston Barboza
Trident Technical College
Julia Caballero
Duke University
Cecelia J. Cavanaugh
Chestnut Hill College
William David Cooper
Shasta College
Pilar del Carmen Tirado
State University of New York at Plattsburgh
Guillermina Elissondo
Worchester State College
Angélica Fernández
Front Range Community College
Janet D. Foley
Eastern Kentucky University
Frank Gangler
Dawson Community College
John G. Gladstein
Hanover College
Ying Han
Savannah State University
Lora Hittle
Western Wyoming Community College
Danielle Holden
Oakton Community College
Lisa Huempfner
Illinois State University
Susan M. Keener
Forsyth Technical Community College
Constance Kihyet
Saddleback College
Ellen Leeder
Barry University
Domenico Maceri
Allan Hancock College
Lourdes Manyé
Furman University
Bryan C. McBride
Eastern Arizona College
David Michels
Cardinal Stritch College
Constance Montross
Clark University
Judith Némethy
New York University
MacGregor O'Brien
Frostburg State University
Kathy A. Ogle
Pacific Lutheran University
Dale Edward Omundson
Anoka Ramsey Community College
Sue Pechter
Illinois Institute of Technology
Amanda R. Plumlee
LaGrange College
Rhea Rehark-Griffith
West Hills College
Karen L. Robinson
University of Nebraska at Omaha
Regina F. Roebuck
University of California, Santa Barbara
Karen Rose
Collin County Community College
Lynne C. Rushing
Collin County Community College
Jack Shreve
Allegheny Community College
Marguerite Solari
Oakton College
Amy E. Zink
Indiana University Southeast
Begoña Zubiri
Thomas More College

Within McGraw-Hill, we would like to acknowledge the contributions of the following: Linda Toy, Diane Renda, and the McGraw-Hill production group, especially Violeta Díaz for her work on the design of the sixth edition, David Staloch for his invaluable assistance as Production Editor, Rich DeVitto and Louis Swaim for their work on various aspects of production, Alexandra Ambrose for her contributions as Photo Researcher, and Robin Mouat for her work as Art Editor. We would also like to thank Jennifer Chow and Fionnuala McEvoy for their invaluable editorial assistance. Special thanks are due to Eirik Børve, who originally brought some of us together, and to Nick Agnew, Rachel Amparo, and the McGraw-Hill marketing and sales staff for their constant support and efforts. Our thanks also go to Scott Tinetti, our Director of Development, and Christa Harris, our Sponsoring Editor, for their guidance and their contributions to the development of this edition. Finally, we would like to thank the development editor, Dr. Pennie Nichols-Alem, for her patient and knowledgeable editorial talents that are seen in the textbook and other parts of the *¿Qué tal?* package.

The only reasons for publishing a new textbook or to revise an existing one are to help the profession evolve in meaningful ways and to make the task of daily classroom instruction easier and more enjoyable for experienced instructors and teaching assistants alike. Foreign language teaching has changed in important ways in the twenty years since the publication of the first edition of *¿Qué tal?*. We are delighted to have been—and to continue to be—one of the agents of that evolution. And we are grateful to McGraw-Hill for its continuing creative support for our ideas.

¿Qué tal?

AN INTRODUCTORY COURSE

Sixth Edition

CAPÍTULO PRELIMINAR

Primeros pasos

Chapter Opening photo Note

Every chapter begins with a photo and introduces the chapter theme.

Point out chapter opening photo and have students talk about the ethnic makeup of their campus. Encourage them to consider whether the proportion of students of diverse backgrounds is ideal. Ask what opportunities the campus offers for language learners to meet and talk to heritage speakers from the U.S. and abroad. Request and offer information about available Spanish clubs and Spanish "houses" or "tables" where participants speak only Spanish.

¿Qué tal? means *Hi, how are you doing?* in Spanish. This textbook, called *¿Qué tal?,* will help you to begin learning Spanish and to become more familiar with the many people here and abroad who use it.

With *¿Qué tal?,* you will begin to learn Spanish and to communicate with Spanish speakers in this country and in Spanish-speaking countries. To speak a language involves much more than just learning its grammar and vocabulary; to know a language is to know the people who speak it. For this reason, *¿Qué tal?* will provide you with cultural information to help you understand and appreciate the traditions and values of Spanish-speaking people all over the world.

Are you ready for the adventure of learning Spanish? **Pues, ¡adelante!** (*Well, let's go!*)

Resources

You and your students may find the following *¿Qué tal?* supplements helpful as you teach this chapter:

For the Instructor

- *Instructor's Manual and Resource Kit,* "Chapter-by-Chapter" Supplementary Materials
- Testing Program
- Overhead Transparencies 1–10
- Video (VHS or CD)
- *¿Qué tal?* Online Learning Center Website
- Audioscript
- Instructor's Resource CD

For Students

- Workbook/Laboratory Manual and Audio Program or Electronic Workbook/ Laboratory Manual
- Video on CD
- Interactive CD-ROM
- *¿Qué tal?* Online Learning Center Website
- Listening Comprehension Audio CD
- McGraw-Hill Electronic Language Tutor (MHELT)

¡Hola! ¿Qué tal? San Antonio, Texas ▶

PRIMER PASO

Saludos y expresiones de cortesía
See detailed supplementary materials and a model for vocabulary presentation in the *Primeros pasos* "Chapter-by-Chapter Supplementary Materials," IM.

Point out that the headphones icon indicates material included on the Listening Comprehension Audio CD packaged free with every new copy of the text.

Saludos° y expresiones de cortesía

° *Greetings*

1. Sevilla, España

2. Quito, Ecuador

3. La Ciudad de México, México

Here are some words, phrases, and expressions that will enable you to meet and greet others appropriately in Spanish.

1. MANOLO: ¡Hola, Maricarmen!
MARICARMEN: ¿Qué tal, Manolo? ¿Cómo estás?
MANOLO: Muy bien. ¿Y tú?
MARICARMEN: Regular. Nos vemos, ¿eh?
MANOLO: Hasta mañana.

2. ELISA VELASCO: Buenas tardes, señor Gómez.
MARTÍN GÓMEZ: Muy buenas, señora Velasco. ¿Cómo está?
ELISA VELASCO: Bien, gracias. ¿Y usted?
MARTÍN GÓMEZ: Muy bien, gracias. Hasta luego.
ELISA VELASCO: Adiós.

¿Qué tal?, ¿Cómo estás?, and **¿Y tú?** are expressions used in informal situations with people you know well, on a first-name basis.

¿Cómo está? and **¿Y usted?** are used to address someone with whom you have a formal relationship.

3. LUPE: Buenos días, profesor.
PROFESOR: Buenos días. ¿Cómo te llamas?
LUPE: Me llamo Lupe Carrasco.
PROFESOR: Mucho gusto, Lupe.
LUPE: Igualmente.

¿Cómo se llama usted? is used in formal situations. **¿Cómo te llamas?** is used in informal situations—for example, with other students. The phrases **mucho gusto** and **igualmente** are used by both men and women when meeting for the first time. In response to **mucho gusto**, a woman can also say **encantada**; a man can say **encantado**.

Follow-up: Saludos...
Have students work in pairs to practice the 3 dialogues using their own names. Use *trabajen en parejas* to cue students.

❖ **Transparencias 1–3**
Note: Transparencies 1–3 are maps of the Spanish-speaking world. Use these now to identify countries where dialogues take place.

1. MANOLO: Hi, Maricarmen! MARICARMEN: How's it going, Manolo? How are you? MANOLO: Very well. And you? MARICARMEN: OK. See you around, OK? MANOLO: See you tomorrow.
2. ELISA VELASCO: Good afternoon, Mr. Gómez. MARTÍN GÓMEZ: Afternoon, Mrs. Velasco. How are you? ELISA VELASCO: Fine, thank you. And you? MARTÍN GÓMEZ: Very well, thanks. See you later. ELISA VELASCO: Bye.
3. LUPE: Good morning, professor. PROFESSOR: Good morning. What's your name? LUPE: My name is Lupe Carrasco. PROFESSOR: Nice to meet you, Lupe. LUPE: Likewise.

PRIMER PASO

NOTA COMUNICATIVA

Otros saludos y expresiones de cortesía

buenos días	good morning (*used until the midday meal*)
buenas tardes	good afternoon (*used until the evening meal*)
buenas noches	good evening; good night (*used after the evening meal*)
señor (Sr.)	Mr., sir
señora (Sra.)	Mrs., ma'am
señorita (Srta.)	Miss (**¡OJO!*** *There is no Spanish equivalent for Ms. Use* **Sra.** *or* **Srta.** *as appropriate.*)
gracias	thanks, thank you
muchas gracias	thank you very much
de nada, no hay de qué	you're welcome
por favor	please (*also used to get someone's attention*)
perdón	pardon me, excuse me (*to ask forgiveness or to get someone's attention*)
con permiso	pardon me, excuse me (*to request permission to pass by or through a group of people*)

Suggestions: Nota comunicativa

- Model phrases in brief exchanges with students, using *señor, señorita,* or *señora;* help students use appropriate title for you.
- Model phrases of thanks, creating situations in which expressions are appropriate. For example, give student a book and elicit *gracias.* Respond *de nada,* and so on.
- Provide optional vocabulary, *permiso* (without *con*); model use of *con permiso* to take leave of someone, *cómo no* (as a rejoinder), *perdone* (in addition to *perdón*), *perdón* to request permission to pass by or through, *disculpe, oiga.*

Heritage speakers

Los títulos *don* y *doña* no tienen equivalente en inglés. Cuando se traduce, por ejemplo, *don Tomás,* se dice simplemente *Tomás* o *Mr. Tomás.* Pídales a los estudiantes hispanohablantes que le den ejemplos a la clase de algunas personas a las cuales ellos se refieren con estos títulos.

Conversación

A. Cortesía. How many different ways can you respond to the following greetings and phrases?

1. Buenas tardes.
2. Adiós.
3. ¿Qué tal?
4. Hola.
5. ¿Cómo está?
6. Buenas noches.
7. Muchas gracias.
8. Hasta mañana.
9. ¿Cómo se llama usted?
10. Mucho gusto.

Suggestion A

Conduct rapid response drill with students' books closed. See "Teaching Techniques," IM.

B. Situaciones. If the following persons met or passed each other at the times given, what might they say to each other? Role-play the situations with a classmate.

1. Mr. Santana and Miss Pérez, at 5:00 P.M.
2. Mrs. Ortega and Pablo, at 10:00 A.M.
3. Ms. Hernández and Olivia, at 11:00 P.M.
4. you and a classmate, just before your Spanish class

Note B

More than 1 answer is possible for some items.

Extension B

5. you and your Spanish professor, at 11 A.M. **6.** you and your cousin, at 10 P.M. **7.** you and the president of your college or university, at 4 P.M.

Watch out!, Careful!* **¡OJO! will be used throughout *¿Qué tal?* to alert you to pay special attention to the item that follows.

PRIMER PASO

❖ Transparency 4

C. **Más** (*More*) **situaciones.** Are these people saying **por favor, con permiso,** or **perdón**?

Suggestion D
- Model an interview with 2–3 students before asking others to form pairs and follow your example.
- Remind students to use informal expressions in student exchanges, but formal expressions when addressing you, the instructor.

D. **Entrevista** (*Interview*). Turn to a person sitting next to you and do the following.

- Greet him or her appropriately, that is, with informal forms.
- Find out his or her name.
- Ask how he or she is.
- Conclude the exchange.

Now have a similar conversation with your instructor, using the appropriate formal forms.

El alfabeto español

There are twenty-eight letters in the Spanish alphabet (**el alfabeto**)—two more than in the English alphabet. The two additional letters are the **ñ** and **rr** (considered one letter even though it is a two-letter group). The letters **k** and **w** appear only in words borrowed from other languages.

Until recently, the **Real Academia Española** (*Royal Spanish Academy*), which establishes many of the guidelines for the use of Spanish throughout the world, considered the **ch** (**che**) and **ll** (**elle**) to be separate letters of the Spanish alphabet. In *¿Qué tal?,* you will not see them listed as separate letters. However, the **ch** and **ll** *do* maintain a distinct pronunciation.*

Listen carefully as your instructor pronounces the names listed with the letters of the alphabet.

Notes: El alfabeto...
- *El abecedario* (ABCs) is synonym for *el alfabeto.*
- *Ch* and *ll* do not appear as separate letters in vocabulary lists in the sixth edition of *¿Qué tal?.*

*The **ch** is pronounced with the same sound as in English *cherry* or *chair,* as in **nachos** or **muchacho**. The **ll** is pronounced as a type of *y* sound. Spanish examples of this sound that you may already know are **tortilla** and **Sevilla**.

PRIMER PASO

Note: El alfabeto...
Common Hispanic first names and place names are used as examples of letters.

Letters	Names of Letters	Examples		
a	a	Antonio	Ana	(la) Argentina
b	be	Benito	Blanca	Bolivia
c	ce	Carlos	Cecilia	Cáceres
d	de	Domingo	Dolores	Durango
e	e	Eduardo	Elena	(el) Ecuador
f	efe	Felipe	Francisca	Florida
g	ge	Gerardo	Gloria	Guatemala
h	hache	Héctor	Hortensia	Honduras
i	i	Ignacio	Inés	Ibiza
j	jota	José	Juana	Jalisco
k	ca (ka)	(Karl)	(Kati)	(Kansas)
l	ele	Luis	Lola	Lima
m	eme	Manuel	María	México
n	ene	Nicolás	Nati	Nicaragua
ñ	eñe	Íñigo	Begoña	España
o	o	Octavio	Olivia	Oviedo
p	pe	Pablo	Pilar	Panamá
q	cu	Enrique	Raquel	Quito
r	ere	Álvaro	Clara	(el) Perú
rr	erre *or* ere doble	Rafael	Rosa	Monterrey
s	ese	Salvador	Sara	San Juan
t	te	Tomás	Teresa	Toledo
u	u	Agustín	Lucía	(el) Uruguay
v	ve *or* uve	Víctor	Victoria	Venezuela
w	doble ve, ve doble, *or* uve doble	Oswaldo	(Wilma)	(Washington)
x	equis	Xavier	Ximena	Extremadura
y	i griega	Pelayo	Yolanda	(el) Paraguay
z	ceta (zeta)	Gonzalo	Esperanza	Zaragoza

Suggestion: El alfabeto...
Point out that
- *ce, ci* produce an [s] sound; *ca, co, cu* produce a [k] sound.
- *ga, go, gu* produce a [g] sound; *ge, gi* are pronounced like Spanish *j*.
- *r* at beginning of a word is pronounced like trilled (double) *r*.
- letter *v* is pronounced like Spanish *b;* to distinguish *b* and *v*, Spanish speakers sometimes call the letter *b* *be grande* or *be de burro,* and the letter *v* *ve chica* or *ve de vaca.* In Spain *v* is called *uve*.
- letter *x* is sometimes pronounced like [ks], sometimes like [s], and sometimes like Spanish *j* (*México, Texas*).
- In Castilian Spanish *ce, ci,* and *z* produce an English *th* sound [Θ].
- In most dialects of Spanish, there is no difference in the pronunciation of the letters *ll* and *y;* however, from 1 area to another dialectal variation in *ll/y* is great. Teach pronunciation of your dialect and allow for variation. When possible, point out dialectal variation such as lateral pronunciation of the *ll* in northern Peninsular Spanish or strong palatal fricative from Argentina [zh].

Variation: El alfabeto...
Use common Hispanic last names: *Álvarez, Hernández, Fernández, Gómez, Pérez,* and so on.

Heritage speakers
- Invite a sus estudiantes hispanohablantes a pronunciar estas palabras. Pregúnteles a los otros estudiantes si ellos oyen alguna diferencia entre el modo en que los hispanohablantes pronuncian los sonidos, especialmente la *j* y la *ll*.
- Anime a los estudiantes hispanohablantes a que les pidan a varios parientes y conocidos que pronuncien estas palabras mientras ellos graban sus voces. Luego pueden tocar sus grabaciones en clase y comentar sobre las diferencias en la pronunciación de personas de países de habla hispana.

Práctica

A. ¡Pronuncie! The letters and combinations of letters listed on the following page represent the Spanish sounds that are the most different from English. You will practice the pronunciation of some of these letters in upcoming chapters of *¿Qué tal?*. For the moment, pay particular attention to their pronunciation when you see them. Can you match the Spanish letters with their equivalent pronunciation?

PRIMER PASO

Notes B
- For use of *Pasos* organization, see "Using *Pasos* Activities," IM.
- *Paso* in headers *Paso 1* and *Paso 2* means "step." *Paso* in place name *El Paso* refers to a pass or a passageway.

Suggestions B
- Introduce *¿Cómo se deletrea... ?*
- Explain that *acentuada* means "stressed" and that in Spanish the stressed vowel in some words must carry a written accent mark so that the word can be read correctly. Accent marks are presented in *Capítulos 2* and *3* of the Workbook/Laboratory Manual.

EXAMPLES/SPELLING	PRONUNCIATION
1. mucho: **ch**	a. like the *g* in English *garden*
2. Geraldo: **ge** (also: **gi**) Jiménez: **j**	b. similar to *tt* of *butter* when pronounced very quickly
3. hola: **h**	c. like *ch* in English *cheese*
4. gusto: **gu** (also: **ga, go**)	d. like Spanish **b**
5. me llamo: **ll**	e. similar to a "strong" English *h*
6. señor: **ñ**	f. like *y* in English *yes* or like the *li* sound in *million*
7. profesora: **r**	g. a trilled sound, several Spanish **r**'s in a row
8. Ramón: **r** (to start a word) Monterrey: **rr**	h. similar to the *ny* sound in *canyon*
9. nos vemos: **v**	i. never pronounced

Follow-up B
Have students think of other U.S. place names of Hispanic origin and spell them aloud in Spanish as other students pronounce them.

B. Deletreo (*Spelling*)

Paso (*Step*) **1.** Pronounce these U.S. place names in Spanish. Then spell aloud the names in Spanish. All of them are of Hispanic origin: **Toledo, Los Ángeles, Texas, Montana, Colorado, El Paso, Florida, Las Vegas, Amarillo, San Francisco.**

Paso 2. Spell your own name aloud in Spanish, and listen as your classmates spell their names. Try to remember as many of their names as you can.

MODELO: Me llamo María: **M** (eme) **a** (a) **r** (ere) **í** (i acentuada) **a** (a).

Los cognados

 **Los cognados**
See detailed supplementary materials for this section in IM.

Many Spanish and English words are similar or identical in form and meaning. These related words are called *cognates* (**los cognados**). Spanish and English share so many cognates because a number of words in both languages are derived from the same Latin root words—and also because Spanish and English are "language neighbors," especially in the southwestern United States. Each language has borrowed words from the other and adapted them to its own sound system.

Cognados
leader → **el líder**
el lagarto (*the lizard*) → *alligator*

Many cognates are used in **Primeros pasos**. Don't try to memorize all of them—just get used to the sound of them in Spanish.

Here are some Spanish adjectives that are cognates of English words. These adjectives can be used to describe either a man or a woman.

adjectives = words used to describe people, places, and things

arrogante	importante	pesimista
cruel	independiente	realista
eficiente	inteligente	rebelde
egoísta	interesante	responsable
elegante	liberal	sentimental
emocional	materialista	terrible
flexible	optimista	valiente
idealista	paciente	vulnerable

Notes
- This section offers opportunities for pronunciation practice as well as being a vehicle to make students comfortable with Spanish and to encourage self-expression.
- Formal practice for *Los cognados* is found in the next section, *¿Cómo es usted?*

PRIMER PASO

Suggestions
- Tell students that they need not try to memorize all words in this section.
- Model pronunciation of adjectives in brief sentences about yourself: *cruel... No soy cruel* (pointing to yourself), and so on.

The following adjectives change form. Use the **-o** ending when describing a man, the **-a** ending when describing a woman.

extrovertido/a	religioso/a	serio/a
generoso/a	reservado/a	sincero/a
impulsivo/a	romántico/a	tímido/a

Suggestions: ¿Cómo es usted?
- Introduce forms of *ser* in brief sentences using adjectives just presented in *Los cognados.*
- Make sure students connect *eres/es* forms with informal/formal concepts already discussed for greetings.

¿Cómo es usted?°

¿Cómo... *What are you like?*

You can use these forms of the verb **ser** (*to be*) to describe yourself and others.

(yo)	**soy**	I am
(tú)	**eres**	you (*familiar*) are
(usted)	**es**	you (*formal*) are
(él, ella)	**es**	he/she is

—¿Cómo es usted?
—Bueno...° Yo soy moderna, urbana, sofisticada...

Well . . .

Conversación

A. Descripciones

Paso 1. With a classmate, describe the famous Hispanic people in these photos, using cognate adjectives (see page 6 and above). **¡OJO!** Remember that some adjectives can end in **-o** or **-a**, such as **romántico/a, serio/a, tímido/a.** Use the **-o** ending when describing a male and the **-a** ending when describing a female.

MODELOS: ESTUDIANTE 1: ¿Cómo es Ricky Martin?
ESTUDIANTE 2: (Ricky Martin) Es importante, romántico y serio.

ESTUDIANTE 1: ¿Cómo es Cameron Díaz?
ESTUDIANTE 2: (Cameron Díaz) Es elegante y extrovertida.

Note A
- All practice for previous *Los cognados* feature is in this *Conversación* section.
- This is only a preliminary introduction to *ser.* There is no need to contrast *ser* with *estar* at this point.
- There is no need to emphasize subject pronouns at this point.

1. Ricky Martin es cantante (*a singer*).

2. Sammy Sosa es beisbolista con los Chicago Cubs.

3. Cameron Díaz es actriz.

4. Jennifer López es cantante y actriz.

National Standards: Community
Poll students to see who has heard of the following famous U.S. Hispanics: Edward James Olmos, Selena, Raúl Julia, Rosie Pérez. Celia Cruz, Gloria Estefan, Andy García, Jimmy Smits, and Carlos Santana. Invite students to add other famous personalities to list.

PRIMER PASO

Heritage speakers
Varios grupos de hispanohablantes de este país usan palabras adaptadas del inglés en el habla cotidiana. Muchas veces los hispanohablantes de países latinoamericanos o de España no conocen estas palabras, lo cual puede impedir la comprensión. Algunas de estas palabras son *elevador* en vez de *ascensor, aplicación* en vez de *solicitud; bonche* en vez de *montón, grados* en vez de *notas, lonche* en vez de *almuerzo,* entre otras.

Follow-up A
Paso 2. Encourage students to listen to each other by having them repeat what another student says about him- or herself: *¿Susie es ______? ¿Cómo es Bob?*

Suggestion B
- Model activity with 2–3 students before having others try it in pairs.
- Invite students to start this activity by introducing themselves and greeting each other.
- Explain that *muy* means *very* and is an adverb that precedes the adjective.

Follow-up B
Ask students information about their partners: *¿Cómo es María? ¿Es simpática?*

Paso 2. Now describe yourself to your classmate.

MODELO: Yo soy muy sentimental y sincero/a. Yo no soy pesimista.

B. Reacciones

Paso 1. Use the following adjectives, or any others you know, to create one sentence about a classmate. You can begin with **Creo que…** (*I think that . . .*). Your classmate will listen to your sentences, then tell you if you are right.

Adjetivos: eficiente, emocional, generoso/a, inteligente, impulsivo/a, liberal, sincero/a

MODELO: ESTUDIANTE 1: Alicia, (creo que) eres generosa.
ESTUDIANTE 2: Sí, soy generosa. (Sí, soy muy generosa.) (No, no soy generosa.)

Paso 2. Now find out what kind of person your instructor is, using the same adjectives. Use the appropriate formal forms.

MODELO: ¿**Es usted** optimista (generoso/a…)?

Spanish in the United States and in the World

Although no one knows exactly how many languages are spoken around the world, linguists estimate that there are between 3,000 and 6,000. Spanish, with over 410 million native speakers, is among the top five languages. It is the primary language spoken in Spain, in Mexico, in all of South America (except Brazil and the Guianas), in most of Central America, in Cuba, in Puerto Rico, and in the Dominican Republic—in twenty countries in all. It is also spoken by a great number of people in the United States and Canada.

Like all languages spoken by large numbers of people, modern Spanish varies from region to region. The Spanish of Madrid is different from that spoken in Mexico City, Buenos Aires, or Los Angeles, just as the English of London differs from that of Chicago or Toronto. Although these differences are most noticeable in pronunciation ("accent"), they are also found in vocabulary and special expressions used in different geographical areas. In Great Britain one hears the word *lift,* but the same apparatus is called an *elevator* in the United States. What is called an **autobús** (*bus*) in Spain may be called a **guagua** in the Caribbean. Although such differences are noticeable, they result only rarely in misunderstandings among native speakers, since the majority of structures and vocabulary are common to the many varieties of each language.

You don't need to go abroad to encounter people who speak Spanish on a daily basis. The Spanish language and people of Hispanic descent have been an integral part of U.S. and Canadian life for centuries. In fact, the United States is now the fifth largest Spanish-speaking country in the world!

Note: Spanish…
Islas Canarias and *Islas Baleares* are shaded but not labeled on the map on p. 9 because they are part of Spain. Belize and Andorra are *not* Spanish speaking. This is not obvious on this map.

Suggestion: Spanish…
Have students give examples of uses of Spanish in the U.S.: place and street names, restaurants, advertising, music, friends of Hispanic descent, television programs about Hispanics or with Hispanic characters, and so on. Explain derivations of terms, if you know them.

PRIMER PASO

Follow-up: Spanish...
Use place names on map to continue pronunciation practice. Write names of countries on board as students say them, then use list as a basis for choral repetition drill.

❖ **Transparency 5**

EL CANADÁ
LOS ESTADOS UNIDOS
MÉXICO
CUBA
LA REPÚBLICA DOMINICANA
PUERTO RICO
GUATEMALA
HONDURAS
EL SALVADOR
NICARAGUA
COSTA RICA
PANAMÁ
VENEZUELA
COLOMBIA
EL ECUADOR
EL PERÚ
BOLIVIA
EL PARAGUAY
EL URUGUAY
CHILE
LA ARGENTINA
ESPAÑA
LA GUINEA ECUATORIAL

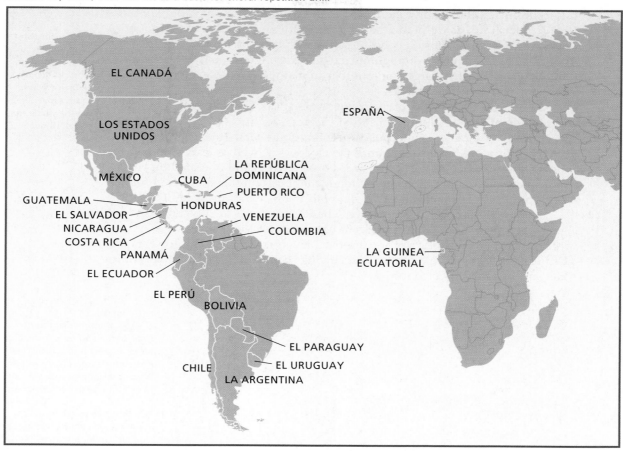

Who are the over 35 million people of Hispanic descent living in the United States today? For one thing, not all Hispanics are similar. They are characterized by great diversity, the result of their ancestors' or their country of origin, socio-economic and professional factors, and, of course, individual talents and aspirations.

There is also great regional diversity among U.S. Hispanics. Many people of Mexican

Comparing origins of U.S. Hispanic population
Total population based on U.S. census, 2000 estimates* 35.3 million

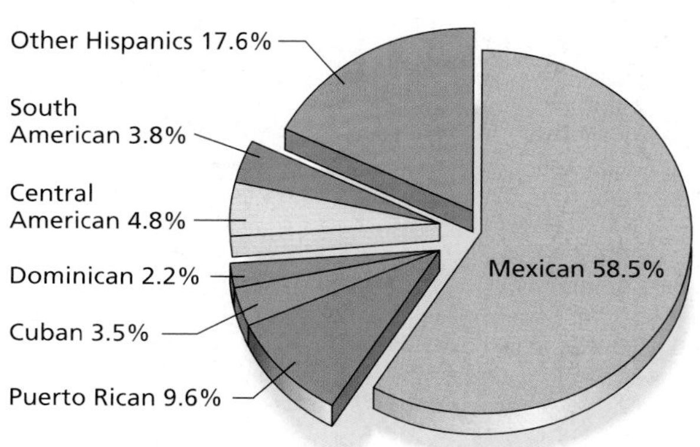

* Source: Census Bureau. The Hispanic Population: Information from the 2000 Census.

descent inhabit the southwestern part of the United States, including populations as far north as Colorado. Large groups of Puerto Ricans can be found in New York, while Florida is host to a large Cuban and Central American population. More recent immigrants include Nicaraguans and Salvadorans, who have established large communities in many U.S. cities, among them San Francisco and Los Angeles.

Although not all people of Hispanic origin speak Spanish, many are in fact bilingual and bicultural. This dual cultural identity is being increasingly recognized by the media and business community. Many major U.S. cities have one or more Spanish-language newspapers as well as television and radio stations. A wide variety of businesses are owned and operated by Hispanics, and major corporations in the food, clothing, entertainment, and service fields appeal to Hispanic clients . . . in both English and Spanish!

As you will discover in subsequent chapters of *¿Qué tal?*, the Spanish language and people of Hispanic descent have been and will continue to be an integral part of the fabric of this country. Take special note of **En los Estados Unidos y el Canadá...**, a routinely occurring section of *¿Qué tal?* that profiles Hispanics in these two countries.

Suggestions: Spanish...

- Point out that mural art has been popularized by Hispanic arts. Programs were initiated in the U.S. by Mexican muralists, among others.
- Have students research and make pie charts that illustrate ethnic makeup of their community.

Mural de la Pequeña Habana, el barrio cubano de Miami

WW. Multimedia: Internet
Have students find information on Internet about murals in the U.S. They can also search for community programs that foster mural-making, for example, the Precita Eyes Mural Arts Center in San Francisco.

Heritage speakers
Anime a los estudiantes hispanohablantes a que les pregunten a sus parientes y conocidos de origen hispánico los nombres por los cuales se refieren a sí mismos, nombres tales como *nica* o *boricua*. Luego invítelos a compartir esta información con sus compañeros de clase.

National Standards: Community
Chicano is another term for Mexican-American. Although it is not as popular today as it was in the 1970s and early 1980s, it is still used by many Mexican-Americans to refer to themselves and also to literature, art, and dialect of their community. Emphasize that students should be aware of different terms and expect individual preferences from members of the Mexican-American community.

SEGUNDO PASO

Notes: Más cognados

- The term *tira cómica* means cartoon. The little girl in this *tira cómica* is Mafalda, the main character in a famous Argentine comic strip by cartoonist Quino. Mafalda cartoons often poke fun at human foibles as well as offer pointed criticisms of social and political issues.

Más cognados

[a]Su… (*Here is*) *Your dinner* (literally, *little piece of lettuce*).

- In this Mafalda cartoon, which uses a cognate students can recognize, the artist pokes fun at bureaucracy by anthropomorphizing it. The pet turtle's name is *Burocracia*. The suggestion is that any bureaucracy is as slow as a turtle.

Although some English and Spanish cognate nouns are spelled identically (*idea, general, gas, animal, motor*), most will differ slightly in spelling: *position*/**posición,** *secret*/**secreto**, *student*/**estudiante**, *rose*/**rosa**, *lottery*/**lotería**, *opportunity*/**oportunidad**, *exam*/**examen**.

The following exercises will give you more practice in recognizing and pronouncing cognates. Remember: Don't try to learn all of these words. Just get used to the way they sound.

noun = person, place, or thing

Práctica

A. Categorías. Pronounce each of the following cognates and give its English equivalent. You will also recognize the meaning of most of the categories (**Naciones, Personas…**). Based on the words listed in the group, can you guess the meaning of the categories indicated with a gloss symbol (°)?

Naciones: el Japón, Italia, Francia, España, el Brasil, la China, el Canadá, Rusia
Personas: líder, profesor, actriz, pintor, político, estudiante
Lugares:° restaurante, café, museo, garaje, bar, banco, hotel, oficina, océano, parque
Conceptos: libertad, dignidad, declaración, cooperación, comunismo
Cosas:° teléfono, fotografía, sofá, televisión, radio, bomba, novela, diccionario, dólar, lámpara, yate
Animales: león, cebra, chimpancé, tigre, hipopótamo
Comidas y bebidas:° hamburguesa, cóctel, patata, café, limón, banana
Deportes:° béisbol, tenis, vólibol, fútbol americano
Instrumentos musicales: guitarra, piano, flauta, clarinete, trompeta, violín

OJO

In **Práctica B**, note that Spanish has two different ways to express *a* (*an*): **un** and **una**. All nouns are either masculine (*m.*) or feminine (*f.*) in Spanish. **Un** is used with masculine nouns, **una** with feminine nouns. You will learn more about this aspect of Spanish in **Capítulo 1**.

Suggestion: Más cognados

Expand cognate study with a presentation of predictable categories of cognates. Present them as a listening or pronunciation activity.

- -tion, -sion → *-ción, -sión*
  conversación, educación
- -ty → *-dad, -tad*
  identidad, libertad
- -ive → *-ivo, -iva*
  motivo, activo, pasivo
- -ure → *-ura*
  literatura, arquitectura

Follow-up A

Give students this cognate pattern; then have them invent additional cognates in the category of *Filosofía y política:* -ism → *-ismo,* for example, communism → *comunismo.* (Possibilities: *marxismo, materialismo, pesimismo, optimismo, capitalismo.*) Review other categories and proceed the same way.

- -tion → *-ción, -sión*
  sensación, repetición, visión, opción
- -ty → *-dad, -tad*
  universidad, sinceridad, comunidad
- -ure → *-ura*
  cultura, temperatura, pintura

Note A

Give students meaning and usage of **¡OJO!** These sidebars appear throughout *¿Qué tal?* and give important information to students. Most **¡OJO!** boxes and sidebars emphasize contrast between vocabulary and grammar points in Spanish and English.

SEGUNDO PASO

Suggestion B
Introduce *¿Qué es... ?* and do this activity as a brief dialogue.

Note B
Some traditional names for sandwich are *bocadillo* (Spain) and *torta* (Mexico).

Extension B
Cuba, turista, rancho, serpiente, chocolate, basquetbol, democracia, capitalista, millonario/a, vicepresidente/a, la República Dominicana

Follow-up B
Bring in magazine or newspaper ads that feature cognates. Have students guess meaning of most obvious cognates; encourage contextual guessing with less obvious ones.

Variation B
Dictate a few new cognates; have students complete a definition for each. They can do this in pairs, in which one writes the word provided by the other. **1.** *una estación* **2.** *un oboe* **3.** *un planeta* **4.** *la física* **5.** *un compañía* **6.** *una actriz* **7.** *un tenista* **8.** *una exploradora*

Notes: Pronunciación
- Point out different pronunciations of the English vowel *a: far, fat, fate, fail, sofa;* and of silent letter *e: make, mate, crate.*
- Remaining chapters of *¿Qué tal?* present pronunciation practice in the *Pronunciación y ortografía* sections of the Workbook/Laboratory Manual.

OJO Don't try to learn the gender of nouns now. You do not have to know the gender of nouns to do **Práctica B**.

B. **¿Qué es esto?** (*What is this?*) Being able to tell what something is or to identify the group to which it belongs is a useful conversation strategy. Begin to practice this strategy by pronouncing these cognates and identifying the category from **Práctica A** to which they belong. Use the following sentences as a guide.

Es **un** lugar (concepto, animal, deporte, instrumento musical).*
Es **una** nación (persona, cosa, comida, bebida).*

MODELO: béisbol → Es un deporte.

1. calculadora
2. burro
3. sándwich
4. golf
5. México
6. actor
7. clase
8. limonada
9. elefante
10. refrigerador
11. universidad
12. fama
13. terrorista
14. acordeón
15. democracia

Conversación

Identificaciones. With a classmate, practice identifying words, using the categories given in **Práctica A**.

MODELO: ESTUDIANTE 1: ¿Qué es un hospital?
ESTUDIANTE 2: Es un lugar.

1. un saxofón
2. un autobús
3. un rancho
4. un doctor
5. Bolivia
6. una Coca-Cola
7. una enchilada
8. una jirafa
9. una turista

Pronunciación

You have probably already noted that there is a very close relationship between the way Spanish is written and the way it is pronounced. This makes it relatively easy to learn the basics of Spanish spelling and pronunciation.

Many Spanish sounds, however, do not have an exact equivalent in English, so you should not trust English to be your guide to Spanish pronunciation. Even words that are spelled the same in both languages are usually pronounced quite differently. It is important to become so familiar with Spanish sounds that you can pronounce them automatically, right from the beginning of your study of the language.

*The English equivalent of these sentences is *It is a place* (*concept, . . .*); *It is a country* (*person, . . .*).

Suggestion: Pronunciación
- Emphasize diphthongized pronunciation of English *a* and *o* in *ate, make, same, oh, gold,* and *note*. Pronounce each word slowly, calling attention to movement of your lips. Contrast with Spanish *me, te, de, lo, no.*

Las vocales (*Vowels*): *a, e, i, o, u*

Unlike English vowels, which can have many different pronunciations or may be silent, Spanish vowels are always pronounced, and they are almost always pronounced in the same way. Spanish vowels are always short and tense. They are never drawn out with a *u* or *i* glide as in English: **lo** ≠ *low;* **de** ≠ *day.*

- **a:** pronounced like the *a* in *father,* but short and tense
- **e:** pronounced like the *e* in *they,* but without the *i* glide
- **i:** pronounced like the *i* in *machine,* but short and tense*
- **o:** pronounced like the *o* in *home,* but without the *u* glide
- **u:** pronounced like the *u* in *rule,* but short and tense

OJO The *uh* sound or schwa (which is how most unstressed vowels are pronounced in English: c**a**n**a**l, w**ai**t**e**d, **a**t**o**m) does not exist in Spanish.

Preliminary exercises: Las vocales…

• Pronounce these words in random order and have students tell whether each word is *español* or *inglés*. You may wish to translate unfamiliar words for students.

Eng.	Sp.	Eng.	Sp.	Eng.	Sp.
me	*mi*	dose	*dos*	lay	*le*
Fay	*fe*	sea	*si*	two	*tú*
ace	*es*	may	*me*	say	*se*
cone	*con*	no	*no*	day	*de*
tea	*ti*	Sue	*su*	Kay	*que*
low	*lo*				

• Write the following 2 columns on board. Read aloud one word at a time. Students will decide if the word you read was from column A or B. You may wish to translate unfamiliar words for the students.

A	B	A	B
1. *mesas*	*meses*	4. *emite*	*imite*
2. *señoras*	*señores*	5. *pelar*	*polar*
3. *calor*	*color*	6. *legar*	*lugar*

A. Sílabas. Pronounce the following Spanish syllables, being careful to pronounce each vowel with a short, tense sound.

1. ma fa la ta pa
2. me fe le te pe
3. mi fi li ti pi
4. mo fo lo to po
5. mu fu lu tu pu
6. mi fe la tu do
7. su mi te so la
8. se tu no ya li

B. Palabras (*Words*)**.** Repeat the following words after your instructor.

1. hasta tal nada mañana natural normal fascinante
2. me qué Pérez Elena rebelde excelente elegante
3. sí señorita permiso terrible imposible tímido Ibiza
4. yo con como noches profesor señor generoso
5. uno usted tú mucho Perú Lupe Úrsula

C. Naciones

Paso 1. Here is part of a rental car ad in Spanish. Say aloud the names of the countries where you can find this company's offices. Can you recognize all of the countries?

Paso 2. Find the following information in the ad.

1. How many cars does the agency have available?
2. How many offices does the agency have?
3. What Spanish word expresses the English word *immediately?*

ai Ansa International

RENT A CAR

Si necesita un coche para su trabajo o placer, nosotros tenemos el adecuado para Vd.

Con una flota de 40.000 coches y 1.000 oficinas, estamos a su servicio en los siguientes países;

- ALEMANIA
- ARABIA SAUDITA
- ARGENTINA
- AUSTRIA
- BELGICA
- BRASIL
- CHIPRE
- DINAMARCA
- ESPAÑA
- FINLANDIA
- FRANCIA
- GRAN BRETAÑA
- GRECIA
- HOLANDA
- IRLANDA
- ISLANDIA
- ITALIA
- JAMAICA
- LUXEMBURGO
- MALASIA
- MARRUECOS
- MARTINICA
- PARAGUAY
- PORTUGAL
- SUECIA
- SUIZA
- URUGUAY
- U.S.A.

En la mayoría de los casos, podemos confirmar su reserva inmediatamente.

Cuando esto no sea posible, su reserva le será confirmada en un plazo máximo de 48 horas.

*The word **y** (*and*) is also pronounced like the letter **i**.

Suggestions C

• Model names of countries, followed by choral and individual repetitions.

• Have students identify other cognates in ad.

Notes C

• When it appears in a Spanish text, "U.S.A." is pronounced as a single word.

• Another abbreviation of "United States," preferred in some countries, is *EE.UU.* (repeated letters stand for the plural noun *Estados Unidos*).

SEGUNDO PASO

Los números 0–30; *hay*

Canción infantil

Dos y dos son cuatro,
cuatro y dos son seis,
seis y dos son ocho,
y ocho dieciséis.

- Point out written accents on 16, 21 (shortened masculine form), 22, 23, 26; final *-e* of *veinte* and final *-a* of *treinta.*
- Write numbers on board and identify them (sometimes incorrectly). Students indicate their comprehension with *sí* or *no*. Encourage them to correct your "mistakes."

2+2=4
4+2=6
6+2=8
8+8

0	cero	10	diez	20	veinte		
1	uno	11	once	21	veintiuno	30	treinta
2	dos	12	doce	22	veintidós		
3	tres	13	trece	23	veintitrés		
4	cuatro	14	catorce	24	veinticuatro		
5	cinco	15	quince	25	veinticinco		
6	seis	16	dieciséis*	26	veintiséis		
7	siete	17	diecisiete	27	veintisiete		
8	ocho	18	dieciocho	28	veintiocho		
9	nueve	19	diecinueve	29	veintinueve		

The number *one* has several forms in Spanish. **Uno** is the form used in counting. **Un** is used before masculine singular nouns, **una** before feminine singular nouns: **un señor, una señora**. Also note that the number **veintiuno** becomes **veintiún** before masculine nouns and **veintiuna** before feminine nouns: **vein-ti*ún* señores, veinti*una* señoras**.

OJO

uno, dos, tres,... veinti**uno**, veintidós,...
but
un señor, veinti**ún** señores
una señora, veinti**una** señoras

- Say these pairs of numbers; have students repeat larger one; *dos / doce; once / uno; treinta / veinte; tres / trece; cuatro / catorce; quince / cinco; diez / once.*
- Point out that *hay* means both *there is* and *there are.*
- Model question form. *¿Hay ______?* with rising intonation.

Use the word **hay** to express both *there is* and *there are* in Spanish. **No hay** means *there is not* and *there are not*. **¿Hay... ?** asks *Is there . . . ?* or *Are there . . . ?*

hay = there is / there are

—¿Cuántos estudiantes **hay** en la clase? *How many students are there in the class?*
—(**Hay**) Treinta. *(There are) Thirty.*

—¿**Hay** pandas en el zoo? *Are there any pandas at the zoo?*
—**Hay** veinte osos, pero **no hay** pandas. *There are twenty bears, but there aren't any pandas.*

A children's song Two and two are four, four and two are six, six and two are eight, and eight (makes) sixteen.

*The numbers 16 to 19 and 21 to 29 can be written as one word (**dieciséis... veintiuno...**) or as three (**diez y seis... veinte y uno...**).

Suggestions: Los números...
- Practice *Canción infantil.*
- Practice numbers 0–10: count forward; count by 2s in evens and odds; count backwards from 10–0.
- Practice numbers 11–20: evens 0–20.
- Practice numbers 21–30: odds 0–30.
- Count from 0 to 30 by 3s; by 5s; by 10s.

SEGUNDO PASO

Reciclado: Los números
Using magazine or newspaper ads or photos, ask *¿Hay ______?* questions with previous cognate vocabulary.

Práctica

A. Los números. Practique los números según (*according to*) el modelo.

MODELO: 1 señor → Hay un señor.

1. 4 señoras
2. 12 pianos
3. 1 café (*m.*)
4. 21 cafés (*m.*)
5. 14 días
6. 1 clase (*f.*)
7. 21 ideas (*f.*)
8. 11 personas
9. 15 estudiantes
10. 13 teléfonos
11. 28 naciones
12. 5 guitarras
13. 1 león (*m.*)
14. 30 señores
15. 20 oficinas

B. Problemas de matemáticas. Do the following simple mathematical equations in Spanish. *Note:* + (**y**), − (**menos**), = (**son**).

MODELO: 2 + 2 = 4 → Dos y dos son cuatro.
4 − 2 = 2 → Cuatro menos dos son dos.

1. 2 + 4 = ?
2. 8 + 17 = ?
3. 11 + 1 = ?
4. 3 + 18 = ?
5. 9 + 6 = ?
6. 5 + 4 = ?
7. 1 + 13 = ?
8. 15 − 2 = ?
9. 9 − 9 = ?
10. 13 − 8 = ?
11. 14 + 12 = ?
12. 23 − 13 = ?

Conversación

Preguntas (*Questions*)

1. ¿Cuántos estudiantes hay en la clase de español? ¿Cuántos estudiantes hay en clase hoy (*today*)? ¿Hay tres profesores o un profesor?
2. ¿Cuántos días hay en una semana (*week*)? ¿Hay seis? (No, no hay…) ¿Cuántos días hay en un fin de semana (*weekend*)? Hay cuatro semanas en un mes. ¿Qué significa **mes** en inglés? ¿Cuántos días hay en el mes de febrero? ¿en el mes de junio? ¿Cuántos meses hay en un año?
3. Hay muchos edificios (*many buildings*) en una universidad. En esta (*this*) universidad, ¿hay una cafetería? ¿un teatro? ¿un cine (*movie theater*)? ¿un laboratorio de lenguas (*languages*)? ¿un bar? ¿una clínica? ¿un hospital? ¿un museo? ¿muchos estudiantes? ¿muchos profesores?

Suggestion A
Have students read aloud, practicing pronunciation.

Variation A
Use this or a similar activity for in-class dictation. See "Teaching Techniques: Dictation," IM.

Variation B
- Do as a pair activity in which 1 partner reads the equation and the other provides the answer.
- Write additional problems on large flash cards. Have students read problems aloud and give answers.
- Teach *¿Cuántos son?* Give additional problems orally.

Follow-up B
- *Un problema para Einstein:* 10 − 5 + 7 − 4 + 12 − 15 + 9 − 11 + 17 + 24 + 16 = ? (Answer: 22)
- Explain that × = *por.* Have students read and solve these equations orally.
  1. 2 × 2 = ?
  2. 2 × 6 = ?
  3. 18 × 1 = ?
  4. 3 × 7 = ?
  5. 4 × 4 = ?
  6. 11 × 0 = ?
  7. 3 × 8 = ?
  8. 2 × 15 = ?

Note: Conversación
A double *no* (*No, no…*) is used in complete sentences that express negative answers.

Extension: Conversación
3. Use same items, but ask questions about your campus, using *muchos/as* plus plural forms of nouns.
4. *Hay muchos animales en un zoo. ¿Hay un zoo en* (your city) *o en una ciudad cercana? ¿Cuántos elefantes hay? ¿Cuántas jirafas? ¿Hay muchos animales exóticos?*

Gustos° y preferencias

°*Likes*

¿Te gusta el fútbol? →

- Sí, me gusta mucho el fútbol.
- No, no me gusta el fútbol.
- Sí, me gusta, pero me gusta más el fútbol americano.

Gustos y preferencias
See detailed supplementary materials for this section in IM.

Do you like soccer? → • Yes, I like soccer very much. • No, I don't like soccer. • Yes, I like soccer, but I like football more.

SEGUNDO PASO

To indicate that you like something in Spanish, say **Me gusta** ______. To indicate that you don't like something, use **No me gusta** ______. Use the question **¿Te gusta** ______**?** to ask a classmate if he or she likes something. Use **¿Le gusta** ______**?** to ask your instructor the same question.

In the following conversations, you will use the word **el** to mean *the* with masculine nouns and the word **la** with feminine nouns. Don't try to memorize which nouns are masculine and which are feminine. Just get used to using the words **el** and **la** before nouns.

You will also be using a number of Spanish verbs in the infinitive form, which always ends in **-r**. Here are some examples: **estudiar** = *to study;* **comer** = *to eat.* Try to guess the meanings of the infinitives used in these activities from context. If someone asks you, for instance, **¿Te gusta *beber* Coca-Cola?**, it is a safe guess that **beber** means *to drink.*

verb = a word that describes an action or a state of being

En español, **fútbol** = *soccer* y **fútbol americano** = *football.*

Preliminary exercise: Gustos
Ask the following questions. *¿Qué te/le gusta más, el fútbol o el fútbol americano? ¿el tenis o el vólibol? ¿Qué le gusta a* (name of classmate)*?* Do not emphasize or expect students to produce *a* (*al*).

Notes: Vocabulario útil
- The *Vocabulario útil* boxes and sections occur throughout *¿Qué tal?* when additional vocabulary is needed to complete an activity.
- Students need not memorize this vocabulary. It is provided to help them complete activities in the text.
- When *Vocabulario útil* features appear, model new vocabulary for students in context of brief sentences, if possible, before letting them continue activity.
- In Latin America, rap is sometimes called *el cotorreo* (*cotorrear* means to talk without saying anything interesting) or *la música rap.*

Extension A
Use other names of currently famous people and cognates for sports and games: *el béisbol, el vólibol, el basquetbol, hacer jogging, jugar al bingo, practicar deportes,* and so on.

Conversación

A. Gustos y preferencias

Paso 1. Make a list of six things you like and six things you don't like, following the model. If you wish, you may choose items from the **Vocabulario útil** box below. All words are provided with the appropriate definite article.

MODELO: Me gusta *la clase de español.* No me gusta *la clase de matemáticas.*

Vocabulario útil*

el café, el té, la limonada, la cerveza (*beer*)
la música moderna, la música clásica, el rap, la música *country*
la pizza, la pasta, la comida mexicana, la comida de la cafetería (*cafeteria food*)
el actor ______, la actriz ______
el/la cantante (*singer*) ______ (**¡OJO! cantante** is used for both men *and* women)
el cine (*movies*), el teatro, la ópera, el arte abstracto

Paso 2. Now ask a classmate if he or she shares your likes and dislikes.

MODELO: ¿Te gusta la clase de español? ¿y la clase de matemáticas?

*The material in **Vocabulario útil** lists is not active; that is, it is not part of what you need to focus on learning at this point. You may use these words and phrases to complete exercises or to help you converse in Spanish, if you need them.

B. Más (*More*) **gustos y preferencias**

Follow-up B
Paso 1: Have students expand each interview to 3 sentences by adding rejoinders like *a mí* and *también: A mí me gusta tocar el violín también.*

Paso 1. Here are some useful verbs and nouns to talk about what you like. For each item, combine a verb (shaded) with a noun to form a sentence that is true for you. Use context to guess the meaning of verbs you don't know.

MODELO: Me gusta ____. → Me gusta estudiar inglés.

1. beber — café té limonada chocolate
2. comer — pizza enchiladas hamburguesas pasta
3. estudiar — español matemáticas historia computación (*computer science*)
4. hablar — español con mis amigos (*with my friends*) por teléfono (*on the phone*)
5. jugar — al tenis al fútbol al fútbol americano al béisbol al basquetbol
6. tocar — la guitarra el piano el violín

Paso 2. Ask a classmate about his or her likes.

MODELO: ¿Te gusta comer enchiladas?

Paso 3. Now ask your professor if he or she likes certain things. **¡OJO!** Remember to address your professor in a formal manner.

MODELO: ¿Le gusta jugar al tenis?

A LEER

El mundo hispánico (Parte 1)

Estrategia:° Recognizing Interrogative Words and *estar*

°Strategy

Note: A leer
This reading introduces *está* for location. Point out this usage but do not present *ser/estar* contrast at this time.

In the following brief reading, note that the word **está** means *is located;* **está** and other forms of the verb **estar** (*to be*) are used to tell where things are. You will learn more about the uses of **estar** in **Capítulo 5**.

The reading also contains a series of questions with interrogative words. You are already familiar with **¿cómo?, ¿qué?**, and **¿cuántos?** (and should be able to guess the meaning of **¿cuántas?** easily). The meaning of other interrogatives may not be immediately obvious to you, but the sentences in which the words appear may offer some clues to meaning. You probably do not know the meaning of **¿dónde?** and **¿cuál?**, but you should be able to guess their meaning in the following sentences.

Cuba está en el Mar Caribe. ¿Dónde está la República Dominicana?
Managua es la capital de Nicaragua. ¿Cuál es la capital de México?

Note that the reading has been divided into four very short parts. Each part corresponds to a map that offers geographical and population information about the countries of the Spanish-speaking world. Use the statements in the short parts as models to answer the questions.

SEGUNDO PASO

Notes: Las naciones...
- Explain meaning of *millones* ***de*** *habitantes.*
- Population figures for Mexico, Colombia, Argentina, and Spain cannot be produced by students, who know only numbers 0–30. Make sure to clarify meaning without expecting them to generate those numbers independently.

Suggestion: Las naciones...
Have students look at the maps while you use reading as a script to improvise listening comprehension material and questions on maps.

Las naciones del mundo hispánico

❖ **Transparencies 6–8**

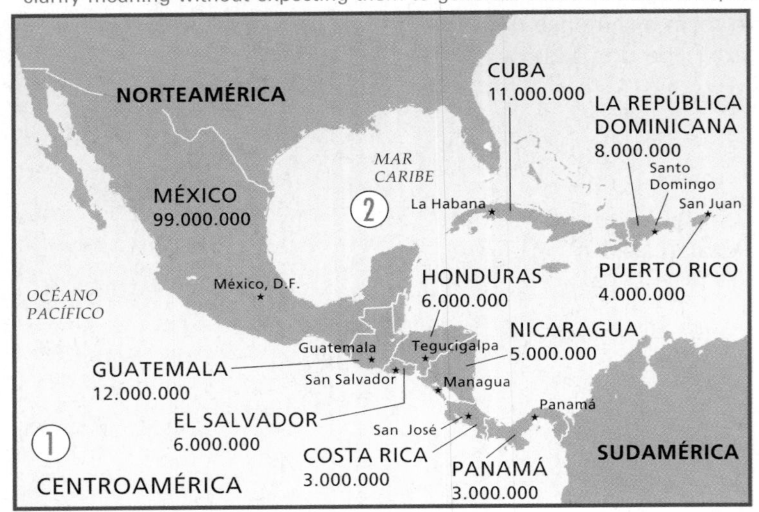

Parte 1 México y Centroamérica

Hay noventa y siete (97) millones de habitantes en México. ¿Cuántos millones de habitantes hay en Guatemala? ¿en El Salvador? ¿en las demás[a] naciones de Centroamérica? ¿En cuántas naciones de Centroamérica se habla español? México es parte de Norteamérica. ¿En cuántas naciones de Norteamérica se habla español? ¿Cuál es la capital de México? ¿de Costa Rica?

Parte 2 El Caribe

Cuba está en el Mar Caribe. ¿Dónde está la República Dominicana? ¿Qué parte de los Estados Unidos está también[b] en el Mar Caribe? ¿Dónde está el Canal de Panamá?

Parte 3 Sudamérica

¿En cuántas naciones de Sudamérica se habla español? ¿Se habla español o portugués en el Brasil? ¿Cuántos millones de habitantes hay en Venezuela? ¿en Chile? ¿en las demás naciones? ¿Cuál es la capital de cada[c] nación?

[a]las... *the other* [b]*also* [c]*each*

Follow-up: Las naciones...
Ask students *sí/no* questions about countries and cities or capitals: *¿Quito está en el Perú?* → *No, no está en el Perú; está en el Ecuador.*

Parte 4 España

España está en la Península Ibérica. ¿Qué otra nación está también en esa[d] península? ¿Cuántos millones de habitantes hay en España? No se habla español en Portugal. ¿Qué lengua se habla allí[e]? ¿Cuál es la capital de España? ¿Está en el centro de la península?

[d]*that* [e]*there*

WWW Multimedia: Internet
Students can find reference sources relating to Hispanic countries on the Internet. You may wish to expand activity by having students find additional information and later ask questions similar to those presented here; for example: *¿Cuántos habitantes hay en la capital de Guatemala?* They can then write correct answer on board.

Heritage speakers

Pregúnteles a los hispanohablantes de la clase si ellos mismos dicen o si conocen a personas que dicen *¿Qué horas son?* en vez de *¿Qué hora es?* No critique, sino repita que esta forma se oye en muchas partes de Latinoamérica.

¿Qué hora es?

Es la una. | **Son** las dos. | **Son** las cinco.

¿Qué hora es? is used to ask *What time is it?* In telling time, one says ***Es* la una** but ***Son* las dos** (**las tres, las cuatro**, and so on).

Es la una **y** { **cuarto.** / **quince.** }

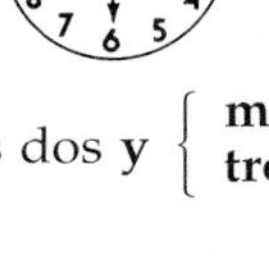

Son las dos **y** { **media.** / **treinta.** }

Son las cinco **y diez.**

Son las ocho **y veinticinco.**

Suggestions: ¿Qué hora es?

- Use clock made from paper plate to introduce telling time, and follow step-by step progression of explanation in the text.
- Remind students that *Es la una* but *Son las dos* (*las tres,* and so on).
- Point out that *son* is plural form of *es.*
- In Mexico and some parts of Central America, one frequently hears *¿Qué horas son?*
- Practice telling time with most basic forms before presenting *Nota comunicativa.*

Note that from the hour to the half-hour, Spanish, like English, expresses time by adding minutes or a portion of an hour to the hour.

Son las dos **menos** { **cuarto.** / **quince.** }

Son las ocho **menos diez.**

Son las once **menos veinte.**

From the half-hour to the hour, Spanish usually expresses time by subtracting minutes or a part of an hour from the *next* hour.

Son las cuatro de la tarde **en punto.**	*It's exactly 4:00 P.M.*
¿A qué hora es la clase de español?	*(At) What time is Spanish class?*
Hay una recepción **a las once** de la mañana.	*There is a reception at 11:00 A.M.*

OJO Don't confuse **Es/Son la(s)...** with **A la(s)...** The first is used for telling time, the second for telling at what time something happens (at what time class starts, at what time one arrives, and so on).

TERCER PASO

Suggestions: Nota comunicativa

- Model expressions with various times shown on your clock.
- Point out that *de la mañana* is used until lunch and *de la tarde* until the evening meal. Make sure students associate this information with greetings *buenos días* and *buenas tardes/noches.*
- Emphasize difference between *es/son* vs. *A la(s).*
- Ask *¿A qué hora es la clase de español?* After students respond, repeat answer, adding *en punto.* Repeat the question for a number of shared experiences: *la sesión de laboratorio, la clase de historia,* and so on.

❖ **Transparency 9**

Suggestion A

You might present the items in this order: *Son las nueve y media de la mañana.* **(6)** *Son las dos de la tarde.* **(2)** *Son las seis y dieciséis de la tarde.* **(8)** *Son las doce menos veinte de la noche.* **(1)** *Son las cinco y cuarto de la noche (mañana).* **(5)** *Son las diez y veintidós de la noche.* **(3)** *Son las dos y diecinueve de la tarde.* **(4)** *Es la una y cinco de la noche (mañana).* **(7)**

Follow-up A

Have students respond *sí* or *no* to the following statements. Vary time as needed for students. This is an opportunity to review infinitives from p. 17. Pantomime as needed to convey meanings. **1.** *Son las once de la noche. Es hora de estudiar.* **2.** *Son las siete de la mañana. Es hora de hablar español.* **3.** *Son las ocho de la mañana. Es hora de beber café en la cafetería.* **4.** *Son las seis y media de la tarde. Es hora de comer en un restaurante elegante.*

Suggestions B

- Ask students at what time they like to . . . *tocar (un instrumento musical), comer, estudiar (español), practicar deportes,* and so on.
- Introduce interrogative *¿cuándo?*
- Emphasize that students must include phrase *a la(s): Me gusta (comer) a las (doce en punto).*

Note B

This activity helps students prepare for *Conversación A.*

NOTA COMUNICATIVA

Para expresar° la hora — Para... *To express*

de la mañana	A.M., in the morning
de la tarde	P.M., in the afternoon (*and early evening*)
de la noche	P.M., in the evening
en punto	exactly, on the dot, sharp
¿a qué hora?	(at) what time?
a la una (las dos...)	at 1:00 (2:00 . . .)

Práctica

A. **¡Atención!** Listen as your instructor says a time of day. Find the clock or watch face that corresponds to the time you heard and say its number in Spanish. (Note the sun or the moon that accompanies each clock to indicate whether the time shown is day or night.)

1.

2.

3.

4.

5.

6.

7.

8.

B. **¿Qué hora es?** Express the time in full sentences in Spanish.

1. 1:00 P.M.
2. 6:00 P.M.
3. 11:00 A.M.
4. 1:30
5. 3:15
6. 6:45
7. 4:15
8. 11:45 exactly
9. 9:10 on the dot
10. 9:50 sharp

TERCER PASO

Conversación

A. Entrevista

Paso 1. Ask a classmate at what time the following events or activities take place. He or she will answer according to the cue or will provide the necessary information.

MODELO: la clase de español (10:00 A.M.) →
ESTUDIANTE 1: ¿A qué hora es la clase de español?
ESTUDIANTE 2: A las diez de la mañana... ¡en punto!

1. la clase de francés (1:45 P.M.)
2. la sesión de laboratorio (3:10 P.M.)
3. la excursión (8:45 A.M.)
4. el concierto (7:30 P.M.)

Paso 2. Now ask what time your partner likes to perform these activities. He or she should provide the necessary information.

MODELO: cenar (*to have dinner*) →
ESTUDIANTE 1: ¿A qué hora te gusta cenar?
ESTUDIANTE 2: Me gusta cenar a las ocho de la noche.

1. almorzar (*to have lunch*)
2. mirar (*to watch*) la televisión
3. ir (*to go*) al laboratorio de lenguas
4. ir al cine
5. desayunar (*to eat breakfast*)
6. hacer la tarea (*to do homework*)
7. salir con amigos (*to go out with friends*)
8. hacer ejercicio (*to exercise*)

Variation A
Expand exchange in *Paso 2* with *a mí* and *también: A mí me gusta estudiar español a las ocho de la noche también.*

Follow-up A
Put the following television schedule on board. Read incomplete sentences and have students respond with *a la(s)... : Hay un programa cómico (romántico, dramático, de animales, de música, para toda la familia, interesante) a ____.*
7:00—*Los Simpson*
7:30—*El Zoo de Barcelona*
8:00—*¡Festival de música!*
8:30—*Dibujos animados*
9:00—*E.R.*
10:00—*Cine Club: Historia de amor*

B. Situaciones. How might the following people greet each other if they met at the indicated time? With a classmate, create a brief dialogue for each situation.

MODELO: Jorge y María, a las once de la noche →
JORGE: Buenas noches, María.
MARÍA: Hola, Jorge. ¿Cómo estás?
JORGE: Bien, gracias. ¿Y tú?
MARÍA: ¡Muy bien!

1. el profesor Martínez y Gloria, a las diez de la mañana
2. la Sra. López y la Srta. Luna, a las cuatro y media de la tarde
3. usted y su (*your*) profesor(a) de español, en la clase de español

Suggestion B
Have several pairs of students present brief dialogues to class. Encourage others to listen to skits and ask brief comprehension questions based on them.

TERCER PASO

Palabras interrogativas

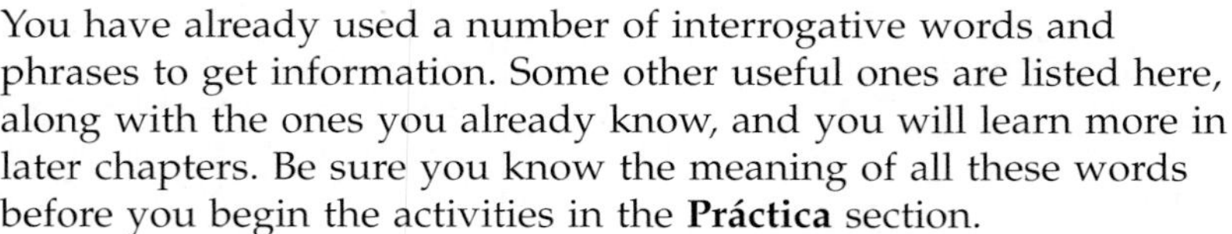

You have already used a number of interrogative words and phrases to get information. Some other useful ones are listed here, along with the ones you already know, and you will learn more in later chapters. Be sure you know the meaning of all these words before you begin the activities in the **Práctica** section.

¿a qué hora?	¿A qué hora es la clase?
¿cómo?	¿Cómo estás? ¿Cómo es Gloria Estefan? ¿Cómo te llamas?
¿cuál?*	¿Cuál es la capital de Colombia?
¿cuándo?	¿Cuándo es la fiesta?
¿cuánto?	¿Cuánto es?
¿cuántos?, ¿cuántas?	¿Cuántos días hay en una semana? ¿Cuántas naciones hay en Sudamérica?
¿dónde?	¿Dónde está España?
¿qué?*	¿Qué es un hospital? ¿Qué es esto? ¿Qué hora es?
¿quién?	¿Quién es el presidente?

Note that in Spanish the voice falls at the end of questions that begin with interrogative words.

¿Qué es un tren? ¿Cómo estás?

Suggestion: Palabras interrogativas
As a whole-class activity, invent a brief story about drawing by having students respond *sí* or *no* to these statements:
- *Las personas están… en casa* (draw a house on the board), *en un hospital, en una cafetería, en un hotel,* and so on.
- *El hombre a la izquierda* (pantomime) *es… terrorista, profesor, fotógrafo, turista,* and so on.
- *El hombre a la derecha* (pantomime) *es… policía, estudiante, recepcionista,* and so on.
- *El recepcionista es… impaciente, paciente, sincero…*
- Point out that *¿Cómo?* is used to indicate noncomprehension, not *¿Qué?* or *¿Cuál?*

Notes: Palabras interrogativas
- This section is a review. Students have probably seen and heard all of these forms already.
- Plural forms of most interrogatives are not presented until *Capítulo 9.*

*Use **¿qué?** to mean *what?* when you are asking for a definition or an explanation. Use **¿cuál?** to mean *what?* in all other circumstances. See also Grammar Section 28 in **Capítulo 9**.

TERCER PASO

Práctica

Preguntas y respuestas (*Questions and answers*)

Paso 1. What interrogative words do you associate with the following information?

1. ¡A las tres en punto!
2. En el centro de la península.
3. Soy profesor.
4. Muy bien, gracias.
5. ¡Es muy arrogante!
6. Hay 5 millones (de habitantes).
7. Dos pesos.
8. (La capital) Es Caracas.
9. Es un instrumento musical.
10. Mañana, a las cinco.
11. Son las once.
12. Soy Roberto González.

Paso 2. Now ask the questions that would result in the answers given in **Paso 1**.

Extension: Práctica
Paso 1. **13.** *En la clase.* **14.** *Son las tres y media.* **15.** *Es inteligente.* **16.** *Es un animal.*

Conversación

Más preguntas. What questions are being asked by the indicated persons? More than one answer is possible for some items. Select questions from the following list, or create your own questions.

PREGUNTAS

¿A qué hora es el programa sobre (*about*) México?
¿Cómo estás?
¿Cuál es la capital de Colombia?
¿Cuándo es la fiesta?
¿Cuántas personas hay en la fiesta?
¿Dónde está Buenos Aires?
¿Dónde está el diccionario?
¿Qué es esto?
¿Qué hay en la televisión hoy?
¿Quién es?

Suggestions: Conversación
- Use drawings as springboard for questions that reenter all of *Primeros pasos* material. Encourage students to listen to questions for meaning only and to respond with 1 word or phrase. Top drawing: *¿Quién es el hombre? ¿Quién es la mujer? ¿Cuántos niños* (pantomime) *hay?*, and so on.
- Have students form questions about drawings. Then have them answer questions asked by others, inventing details. Coach them to keep sequence of questions going.

❖ **Transparency 10**

TERCER PASO

Suggestions: A leer

- Before students begin reading, review definite and indefinite articles (for recognition) with them. Emphasize *un* → *el* and *una* → *la*. Present plural definite articles (*los, las*).
- Point out that students should guess underlined words from context, and discuss the first such word (*pampas*) with them.
- Have students point out or underline words in text that they recognize as cognates. This practice will be useful in future *A leer* sections, where they will have to understand meaning of sentence by referring to whole context.

Note: A leer

The underlining system for words to guess will continue in all *A leer* sections.

A LEER

El mundo hispánico (Parte 2)

Estrategia: Guessing Meaning from Context

You will recognize the meaning of a number of cognates in the following reading about the geography of the Hispanic world. In addition, you should be able to guess the meaning of the underlined words from the context (the words that surround them); they are the names of geographical features. The photo captions will also be helpful. You have learned to recognize the meaning of the word **¿qué?** in questions; in this reading, **que** (with no accent mark) means *that* or *which*.

Note also that a series of headings divides the reading into brief parts. It is always a good idea to scan such headings before starting to read, in order to get a sense of a reading's overall content.

La geografía del mundo hispánico

Introducción

La geografía del mundo hispánico es impresionante y muy variada. En algunas[a] regiones hay de todo.[b]

En las Américas

En la Argentina hay pampas extensas en el sur[c] y la cordillera de los Andes en el oeste. En partes de Venezuela, Colombia y el Ecuador, hay regiones tropicales de densa selva. En el Brasil está el famoso Río Amazonas. En el centro de México y también en El Salvador, Nicaragua y Colombia, hay volcanes activos. A veces[d] producen erupciones catastróficas. El Perú y Bolivia comparten[e] el enorme Lago Titicaca, situado en una meseta entre los dos países.[f]

La cordillera de los Andes, Chile

Una selva tropical en Colombia

[a]*some* [b]de... *a bit of everything* [c]*south* [d]A... *Sometimes* [e]*share* [f]naciones

TERCER PASO

La isla de Caja de Muertos, Puerto Rico

En las naciones del Caribe

Cuba, Puerto Rico y la República Dominicana son tres islas situadas en el Mar Caribe. Las bellas playas[g] del Mar Caribe y de la península de Yucatán son populares entre[h] los turistas de todo el mundo.

En la Península Ibérica

España, que comparte la Península Ibérica con Portugal, también tiene[i] una geografía variada. En el norte están los Pirineos, la cordillera que separa a España del[j] resto de Europa. Madrid, la capital del país, está situada en la meseta central. En las costas del sur y del este hay playas tan bonitas como las de[k] Latinoamérica y del Caribe.

¿Y las ciudades?

Es importante mencionar también la gran[l] diversidad de las ciudades del mundo hispánico. En la Argentina está la gran ciudad de Buenos Aires. Muchos consideran a Buenos Aires «el París» o «la Nueva York» de Sudamérica. En Venezuela está Caracas, y en el Perú está Lima, la capital, y Cuzco, una ciudad antigua de origen indio.

Una meseta de La Mancha, España

La ciudad de Montevideo, Uruguay

Conclusión

En fin,[m] el mundo hispánico es diverso respecto a la geografía. ¿Y Norteamérica? ■

[g]bellas... *beautiful beaches* [h]*among* [i]*has* [j]*from the* [k]tan... *as pretty as those of* [l]*great* [m]En... *In short*

Suggestions: A leer

- Have students bring images from magazines, books, and Internet that illustrate different aspects of Hispanic geography. You might assign specific topics to students or groups, and have them give brief oral presentations based on their findings.
- Have students give examples of geographical features from Hispanic world that are not found in reading. Accept answers in English, and give Spanish equivalents if you know them.
- Have students write short sentences with the following words, based on information provided in *Lectura* (*Parte 2*) or in their own knowledge of world geography. You can provide them with these examples: *ciudad* → *Buenos Aires es una ciudad de la Argentina* / *lago* → *En el Canadá hay lagos.* **1.** *ciudad* **2.** *capital* **3.** *lago* **4.** *volcán* **5.** *playa* **6.** *isla* **7.** *nación* **8.** *península* **9.** *río* **10.** *mar*

TERCER PASO

Follow-up: A leer
Practice new vocabulary from this reading passage and review interrogatives by asking: *¿Dónde hay pampas? ¿Dónde hay volcanes? ¿Qué forman España y Portugal? ¿Qué ciudad sudamericana es como París y Nueva York? ¿Qué son Cuba, Puerto Rico y la República Dominicana? ¿Dónde están?* and so on.

Comprensión

Demonstrate your understanding of the words underlined in the reading and other words from the reading by giving an example of a similar geographical feature found in this country or close to it. Then give an example from the Spanish-speaking world.

MODELO: un río → *the Mississippi,* el Río Grande

1. un lago
2. una cordillera
3. un río
4. una isla
5. una playa
6. una costa
7. un mar
8. un volcán
9. una península

VIDEOTECA: En contexto

FUNCTION

Greetings and leave-takings

 **Videoteca: En contexto Notes**

- Introduce this section if you are planning to work regularly with the video series throughout the course.
- See the IM for suggestions and follow-up activities to accompany the video series.
- Function boxes provide at-a-glance information on a functional use of language demonstrated and used in the dialogue.
- The *Lluvia de ideas* section will offer questions in Spanish beginning with *Capítulo 3.*

The **En contexto** segments represent highly functional contexts and language that you are likely to encounter in your interactions with Spanish speakers. The scenes have been filmed in San Jose, Costa Rica; Lima, Peru; and Mexico City, Mexico.

In this chapter's episode, Mariela Castillo, who is moving to a new apartment, meets her neighbors. Pay attention to the greetings and introductions used in the segment.

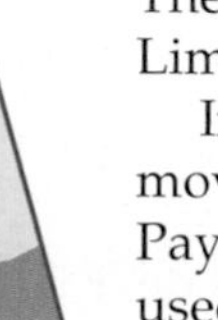

A. Lluvia de ideas (*Brainstorm*)

This recurring activity will direct your attention to a topic or topics featured in the **En contexto** video segment in order to help you understand it more fully.

- How would you introduce yourself to a new neighbor? What if the neighbor were older than you? What if the neighbor were younger than you?
- How do these greetings differ in English and Spanish?

B. Dictado (*Dictation*)

This recurring activity requires that you complete part of the dialogue in the video in order to help you focus on the specific language used by the video characters.

Fill in the missing portions of the dialogue. (There is an underlined space for each word.)

MARIELA: ¿Cómo te llamás?*
RICARDO: Me llamo Ricardo. ¿Cómo ___se___ [1] ___llama___ [2] usted?
MARIELA: Yo ___me___ [3] ___llamo___ [4] Mariela Castillo. Mucho ___gusto___, [5] Ricardo.
RICARDO: ___Igualmente___, [6] Sra. Castillo.
MARIELA: ___No___ [7] soy señora; soy ___señorita___. [8] Por el momento.[a]

[a]Por… *At this time.*

C. Un diálogo original

Paso 1. In groups of three, re-enact the situation between Mariela, Ricardo, and his mom (**mamá**). Don't forget to say **bienvenido** or **bienvenida** (*welcome*) to the new neighbor!

Paso 2. With a different classmate, role-play a situation similar to the one in the video. Each of you should choose one of the following two roles:

ESTUDIANTE 1: You are a new student moving into a dormitory.
ESTUDIANTE 2: You are a returning student at the dormitory. You want to greet and welcome the new student.

*Note that Mariela says **llamás** instead of **llamas**, with the stress on the last syllable of the word. This is known as **voseo**, a common dialectical feature of Spanish in Costa Rica and other Spanish-speaking countries. **Voseo** forms will not be actively taught or practiced in *¿Qué tal?*. For now, you just need to know that Mariela is asking the young boy's name.

Suggestion
Define *dictado* (dictation), and explain that this section is an activity designed for focused listening and writing practice. It provides students with model for communication.

Cultura en contexto *¿Usted o tú?*

The formal *you* form, **usted** (abbreviated **Ud.**), is more widely employed in Latin America than in Spain. In Spain, the use of **usted** is diminishing in general. In social settings, the use of **tú** is most common among young people even if they don't know each other. In some countries, such as Colombia, Chile, and Peru, **usted** is the pronoun of choice in the same context.

Note: Cultura en contexto
This feature highlights a functional use of the Spanish language within the cultural context presented by the video segment. You may wish to point this feature out to students prior to watching the segment as a comprehension aid.

En resumen

VOCABULARIO

Although you have used and heard many words in this preliminary chapter of *¿Qué tal?*, the following words are the ones considered to be active vocabulary. Be sure that you know all of them before beginning **Capítulo 1**.

Saludos y expresiones de cortesía

Buenos días. Buenas tardes. Buenas noches. Hola.
(Muy) Buenas. ¿Qué tal? ¿Cómo está(s)?
Regular. (Muy) Bien.
¿Y tú? ¿Y usted?
Adiós. Hasta mañana. Hasta luego. Nos vemos.

¿Cómo te llamas? ¿Cómo se llama usted?
Me llamo _______.

señor (Sr.), señora (Sra.), señorita (Srta.)

(Muchas) Gracias.
De nada. No hay de qué.
Por favor. Perdón. Con permiso.
Mucho gusto. Igualmente. Encantado/a.

¿Cómo es usted?

soy, eres, es

Los números

cero, uno, dos, tres, cuatro, cinco, seis, siete, ocho, nueve, diez, once, doce, trece, catorce, quince, dieciséis, diecisiete, dieciocho, diecinueve, veinte, treinta

Gustos y preferencias

¿Te gusta _______? ¿Le gusta _______? Sí, me gusta _______. No, no me gusta _______.

¿Qué hora es?

es la... , son las... y/menos cuarto (quince), y media (treinta), en punto, de la mañana (tarde, noche), ¿a qué hora?, a la(s)...

Note: Vocabulario
Students are *not* expected to know every word they have used in *Primeros pasos*. Only active vocabulary is listed here.

Palabras interrogativas

¿cómo?	how?; what?
¿cuál?	what?, which?
¿cuándo?	when?
¿cuánto?	how much?
¿cuántos/as?	how many?
¿dónde?	where?
¿qué?	what?, which?
¿quién?	who?, whom?

Palabras adicionales

sí	yes
no	no
está	is (located)
hay	there is/are
no hay	there is not / are not
hoy	today
mañana	tomorrow
y	and
o	or
a	to; at (*with time*)
de	of; from
en	in; on; at
pero	but
también	also

Suggestions: Vocabulario

- Use material from the inside front cover to familiarize students with frequently used classroom commands and other useful phrases.
- To practice question words, draw the following images on board: a house (where?), a clock face (what time?, at what time?), a calendar page (when?), numbers (how much/many?), a box with a question mark (what?), a stick person (who?), and so on. Ask information questions. Students respond by indicating or pointing to corresponding image.

Suggestion: Chapter Opening photo
Point out the chapter opening photo and have students talk about whether your institution may be similar to or different from the one pictured. To broaden the theme of university life, have students also talk about their own experiences interacting with Hispanic students studying in the U.S. or as exchange students. Encourage them to focus on the individual characteristics of the people they talk about, rather than any generic "national traits."

En la universidad

Reciclado:
Encourage students to generate cognate adjectives by asking:
¿Cómo son los estudiantes en ______ (name of university)*? ¿Son inteligentes? ¿elegantes? ¿idealistas? ¿interesantes? ¿pesimistas? ¿responsables? ¿serios? ¿extrovertidos?* You can also call on individual students to provide additional adjectives describing the students at your university.

Resources
You and your students may find the following *¿Qué tal?* supplements helpful as you teach this chapter:

For the Instructor
- *Instructor's Manual and Resource Kit,* "Chapter-by-Chapter" Supplementary Materials
- Testing Program
- Overhead Transparencies 11–16
- Video (VHS or CD)
- *¿Qué tal?* Online Learning Center Website
- Audioscript
- Instructors' Resource CD

Hay estudiantes de muchas nacionalidades en las universidades de este país (*this country*), como esta (*this one*) en Boston, Massachusetts. ¿Cómo son los estudiantes en su (*your*) universidad?

VOCABULARIO

- In the classroom
- University subjects

GRAMÁTICA

1 Singular Nouns: Gender and Articles
2 Nouns and Articles: Plural Forms
3 Subject Pronouns; Present Tense of **-ar** verbs; Negation

CULTURA

- **Enfoque cultural:** Los hispanos en los Estados Unidos
- **Nota cultural:** The Hispanic Educational System
- **En los Estados Unidos y el Canadá:** Jaime Escalante
- **Cultura en contexto:** Expressing *Cool!*

Multimedia

You will learn about discussing classes and schedules in the **En contexto** video segment.

Review vocabulary and grammar and practice language skills with the interactive CD-ROM.

WWW. Get connected to the Spanish-speaking world with the *¿Qué tal?* Online Learning Center: **www.mhhe.com/quetal**.

For Students
- Workbook/Laboratory Manual and Audio Program or Electronic Workbook/Laboratory Manual
- Video on CD
- Interactive CD-ROM
- *¿Qué tal?* Online Learning Center Website
- Listening Comprehension Audio CD
- McGraw-Hill Electronic Language Tutor (MHELT)

PASO 1 Vocabulario

CAPÍTULO 1

Paso 1: Vocabulario
See detailed supplementary material and a model for vocabulary presentation and other material in the *Capítulo 1 Vocabulario* section of "Chapter-by-Chapter Supplementary Materials," IM.

En la clase

Multimedia: Audio
Students can listen to and practice this chapter's vocabulary on their *Listening Comprehension Audio CD.*

¿Qué? Cosas

❖ **Transparency 11**

¿Dónde? Lugares en la universidad

la biblioteca	the library
la cafetería	the cafeteria
la clase	the class
el edificio	the building
la librería	the bookstore
la oficina	the office
la residencia	the dormitory

¿Quién? Personas

el bibliotecario	the (male) librarian
la bibliotecaria	the (female) librarian
el compañero de clase	the (male) classmate
la compañera de clase	the (female) classmate
el compañero de cuarto	the (male) roommate
la compañera de cuarto	the (female) roommate
el consejero	the (male) advisor
la consejera	the (female) advisor
el estudiante	the (male) student
la estudiante	the (female) student
el hombre	the man
la mujer	the woman
el profesor	the (male) professor
la profesora	the (female) professor
el secretario	the (male) secretary
la secretaria	the (female) secretary

Note
In most Hispanic countries, there is no equivalent of a U.S. academic or guidance counselor.

❖ Transparency 12

Suggestions A
- Point out the use of *están* for location.
- Give statements about drawings. Have students tell whether your statements are true or false. For example: *Hay un consejero en la clase.* (*falso*)

Variation A
- Present *el* → *un, la* → *una* before doing this variation. Then have students identify persons and objects, using short complete sentences: *Hay un profesor / una profesora. Hay un(a)...*
- Have students tell where individual objects and persons are, using short complete sentences: *La estudiante está en la biblioteca.*

Conversación

A. ¿Dónde están ahora (*are they now*)**?** Tell where these people are. Then identify the numbered people and things: 1 = **la mesa**, 3 = **el consejero**, and so on. Refer to the drawing and lists on page 30 as much as you need to.

1. Están en _____.

2. Están en _____.

3. Están en _____.

4. Están en _____.

Follow-up B
Have students give male counterparts of *la profesora, la secretaria, la estudiante, la consejera, la compañera de cuarto.* Then have them give female counterparts of *el profesor, el consejero, el compañero de cuarto.*

B. Identificaciones. ¿Es hombre o mujer?

MODELO: ¿La consejera? → Es mujer.

1. ¿El profesor?
2. ¿La estudiante?
3. ¿El secretario?
4. ¿El estudiante?
5. ¿La bibliotecaria?
6. ¿El compañero de cuarto?

Follow-up B
Introduce *estudias/estudio* and ask students what they study and whether they like it: *Sue, ¿estudias matemáticas? ¿Te gusta estudiar matemáticas?*

Las materias

The names for most of these subject areas are cognates. See if you can recognize their meaning without looking at the English equivalent. You should learn in particular the names of subject areas that are of interest to you.

la administración de empresas	business
el arte	art
la computación	computer science
las comunicaciones	communications
la economía	economics
el español	Spanish
la filosofía	philosophy
la física	physics
la historia	history
el inglés	English
la literatura	literature
las matemáticas	mathematics
la química	chemistry
la sicología	psychology
la sociología	sociology
las ciencias	sciences
las humanidades	humanities
las lenguas extranjeras	foreign languages

Universidad Nacional Autónoma de México (UNAM), México, Distrito Federal (D.F.)

Extension A
Hold up various books that students have at their desks and have them identify by the titles the subjects for which they use the books. Then have students identify the classes for which they might need the following books: *Introducción a Pascal, La revolución de los zares,* Mein Kampf, *La familia, Cómo usar el telescopio, Los microbios.*

Conversación

A. Asociaciones. ¿Con qué materia(s) asocia usted a… ?

1. Louis Pasteur, Marie Curie
2. la doctora Joyce Brothers, B. F. Skinner
3. Barbara Walters, Peter Jennings
4. Aristóteles, Confucio
5. Mark Twain, Toni Morrison
6. Frida Kahlo, Pablo Picasso
7. Microsoft, IBM
8. Isaac Newton, Stephen Hawking

B. ¿Qué te gusta estudiar (*to study*)**?**

Paso 1. Make a list with subjects you like to study and another list with subjects you don't like.

Me gusta estudiar… No me gusta estudiar…

Suggestion: Nota cultural
Emphasize difference between *la escuela primaria* or *el colegio* and *la escuela secundaria,* and elaborate on *los títulos universitarios* (*licenciatura, maestría y doctorado*).

Paso 2. In pairs, ask and answer questions about what you like and don't like to study.

MODELO: —¿Te gusta estudiar matemáticas?
—No, no me gusta estudiar matemáticas.

NOTA CULTURAL

The Hispanic Educational System

The educational system in Hispanic countries differs considerably from that of this country. Elementary school (**la escuela primaria**) can last five to eight years, depending on the country. After that, secondary school (**la escuela secundaria, el colegio**) may last four to seven years.

Hispanic universities have a long and respected history. At the university (always called **la universidad** and never **el colegio** or **la escuela**), students begin specialized programs (**la carrera**) in areas such as law, medicine, engineering, literature, and so on, immediately upon admission. The courses and standards for these university-level programs are generally established by national ministries of education, and their academic curricula are not very flexible; they usually offer only a few elective courses.

University students in Hispanic countries may be required to take up to eight different subjects in a single academic term. Academic performance is evaluated on a scale of one to ten, with five or six considered passing, depending on the country. In Spain, it is common to have one cumulative test at the end of the term. In other countries like Ecuador, students may have one or two partial tests in addition to a comprehensive final.

Esta estatua de Fray Luis de León está en la Universidad de Salamanca. La Universidad, que (*which*) data del año 1220 (mil doscientos veinte), es una de las más antiguas (*oldest*) de España.

 **Paso 2 Gramática**
See detailed supplementary materials for these grammar sections in IM.

1 Identifying People, Places, and Things • Singular Nouns: Gender and Articles*

En *la clase* del *profesor* Durán: *El* primer *día*

PROFESOR DURÁN: Aquí está *el programa* del *curso*. Son necesarios *el libro de texto* y *un diccionario*. También hay *una lista* de novelas y libros de poesía.
ESTUDIANTE 1: ¡Es *una lista* infinita!
ESTUDIANTE 2: Sí, y los libros cuestan demasiado.
ESTUDIANTE 1: No, *el problema* no es *el precio* de los libros. ¡Es *el tiempo* para leer los libros!

Elija (*Choose*) las palabras o frases correctas según el diálogo.

1. La clase del profesor Durán es de (literatura / filosofía).
2. En el curso del profesor Durán (es necesario / no es necesario) leer (*to read*) mucho.
3. En un curso de literatura (es lógico / no es lógico) usar un diccionario.

To name persons, places, things, or ideas, you need to be able to use nouns. In Spanish, all *nouns* (**los sustantivos**) have either masculine or feminine *gender* (**el género**). This is a purely grammatical feature of nouns; it does not mean that Spanish speakers perceive things or ideas as having male or female attributes.

Since the gender of all nouns must be memorized, it is best to learn the definite article along with the noun; that is, learn **el lápiz** rather than just **lápiz**. The definite article will be given with nouns in vocabulary lists in this book.

Note: Singular Nouns . . .
Minidialogue introduces material from both Grammar Sections 1 and 2. Continue to use previous guidelines for the presentation of minidialogues.

Follow-up: Singular Nouns . . .
1. *¿Dónde están las personas del diálogo?* **2.** *¿Quiénes son?* **3.** *¿Hay profesor o profesora en esta clase?* **4.** *¿Cuántos estudiantes hay en la clase?*

Note
Spanish equivalents for English grammatical terms will be given throughout this text.

	Masculine Nouns		Feminine Nouns	
Definite Articles	**el** hombre **el** libro	*the man* *the book*	**la** mujer **la** mesa	*the woman* *the table*
Indefinite Articles	**un** hombre **un** libro	*a (one) man* *a (one) book*	**una** mujer **una** mesa	*a (one) woman* *a (one) table*

*The grammar sections of *¿Qué tal?* are numbered consecutively throughout the book. If you need to review a particular grammar point, the index will refer you to its page number.

In Professor Durán's class: The first day PROFESSOR DURÁN: Here's the course syllabus. The textbook and a dictionary are required. There is also a list of novels and poetry books. STUDENT 1: It's an immense list! STUDENT 2: Yes, and the books cost too much. STUDENT 1: No, the problem isn't the price of the books. It's the time to read the books!

GENDER

A. Nouns that refer to male beings and most nouns that end in **-o** are *masculine* (**masculino**) in gender.	**sustantivos masculinos:** hombre, libro
B. Nouns that refer to female beings and most nouns that end in **-a, -ción, -tad**, and **-dad** are *feminine* (**femenino**) in gender.	**sustantivos femeninos:** mujer, mesa, nación, libertad, universidad
C. Nouns that have other endings and that do not refer to either male or female beings may be masculine or feminine. The gender of these words must be memorized.	el lápiz, la clase, la tarde, la noche
D. Many nouns that refer to persons indicate gender	
1. by changing the last vowel	el compañero → la compañer**a** el bibliotecario → la bibliotecari**a**
2. by adding **-a** to the last consonant of the masculine form to make it feminine	un profesor → una profesor**a**
E. Many other nouns that refer to people have a single form for both masculine and feminine genders. Gender is indicated by an article.	**el** estudiante (*the male student*) → **la** estudiante (*the female student*) **el** cliente (*the male client*) → **la** cliente (*the female client*) **el** dentista (*the male dentist*) → **la** dentista (*the female dentist*)
However, a few nouns that end in **-e** also have a feminine form that ends in **-a**.	el presidente → la president**a** el dependiente (*the male clerk*) → la dependient**a** (*the female clerk*)

Heritage speakers

- Pídales a los estudiantes hispanohablantes que mencionen otros sustantivos que no cambian al referirse a hombres o mujeres, como *turista, artista* o *dentista.*
- Pregúnteles si usan *clienta, presidenta* o *dependienta.*
- Señáleles que en algunos países hispanohablantes se dice *la presidente* o *la jefe* en vez de *la presidenta* o *la jefa. La presidenta* también puede significar *la esposa del presidente.*
- Pídales a los estudiantes hispanohablantes que investiguen los géneros de los nuevos términos tecnológicos (por ejemplo, *el impresor* y *la impresora, el grabador* y *la grabadora*).

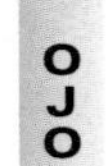

A common exception to the normal rules of gender is the word **el día**, which is masculine in gender. Many words ending in **-ma** are also masculine: **el problema, el programa, el sistema**, and so on. Watch for these exceptions as you continue your study of Spanish.

ARTICLES

A. In English, there is only one *definite article* (**el artículo definido**): *the.* In Spanish, the definite article for masculine singular nouns is **el**; for feminine singular nouns it is **la**.

definite article: *the*
m. sing. → **el**
f. sing. → **la**

B. In English, the singular *indefinite article* (**el artículo indefinido**) is *a* or *an*. In Spanish, the indefinite article, like the definite article, must agree with the gender of the noun: **un** for masculine nouns, **una** for feminine nouns. **Un** and **una** can mean *one* as well as *a* or *an*. Context determines meaning.

indefinite article: *a, an*
m. sing. → **un**
f. sing. → **una**

Preliminary exercise
As a gender quiz, give students these words and have them tell whether each is *femenina* or *masculina:* **1.** *artista* **2.** *mujer* **3.** *noche* **4.** *programa* **5.** *comedia* **6.** *hombre* **7.** *estudiante* **8.** *día* **9.** *compañero* **10.** *ciudad*

Práctica

A. Artículos

Dé (*Give*) el artículo definido apropiado (**el, la**).

1. escritorio
2. biblioteca
3. bolígrafo
4. mochila
5. hombre
6. diccionario
7. universidad
8. dinero
9. mujer
10. nación
11. bibliotecario
12. calculadora

Ahora (*Now*) dé el artículo indefinido apropiado (**un, una**).

1. día
2. mañana
3. problema
4. lápiz
5. clase
6. noche
7. papel
8. condición
9. programa

Follow-up A
Have students give feminine or masculine counterparts for the following words (ask for articles with answers). **1.** *el hombre* **2.** *la compañera* **3.** *el secretario* **4.** *un cliente* **5.** *una presidenta* **6.** *un turista*

B. Escenas de la universidad

Paso 1. Haga una oración con las palabras (*words*) indicadas.

MODELO: estudiante / librería → Hay un estudiante en la librería.

1. consejero / oficina
2. profesora / clase
3. lápiz / mesa
4. cuaderno / escritorio
5. libro / mochila
6. bolígrafo / silla
7. palabra / papel
8. oficina / residencia
9. compañero / biblioteca

Paso 2. Now create new sentences by changing one of the words in each item in **Paso 1**. If you do this with a partner, try to come up with as many variations as possible.

MODELO: Hay un estudiante en *la residencia*. (Hay *una profesora* en la librería.)

Variation B
Vary **Paso 1** of this activity by using the following model to form sentences: *estudiante/librería* → *El estudiante está en la librería.*

Suggestion A
Use place and person names from your campus and city as cues.

Extension A
10. *la librería* **11.** *el profesor* **12.** *la historia* **13.** *el cuaderno* **14.** *el libro* **15.** *el dinero* **16.** *la compañera de clase* **17.** *la física* **18.** *el manual de laboratorio* **19.** *el laboratorio de lenguas* **20.** *el profesor / la profesora* (name)

Note B
Clase means both *class* and *classroom.* The context of the sentence differentiates them.

Extension B
5. *el laboratorio de lenguas* **6.** *la capital de los Estados Unidos (del Canadá)* **7.** *la universidad* **8.** *Puerto Rico*

Follow-up B
Have students compare their lists. What items are similar? What items are different?

Note
Review minidialogue that precedes Grammar Section 1 before presenting material in this section.
- Have students form small groups to translate the main points of the ad.
- Have students read ad out loud to practice pronunciation of vowels.

Conversación

A. Definiciones. Con un compañero / una compañera, defina estas palabras en español según el modelo.

MODELO: biblioteca / edificio → ESTUDIANTE 1: ¿La biblioteca?
ESTUDIANTE 2: Es un edificio.

Categorías: cosa, edificio, materia, persona

1. cliente / persona
2. bolígrafo / cosa
3. residencia / edificio
4. dependiente / ¿ ?
5. hotel (*m.*) / ¿ ?
6. calculadora / ¿ ?
7. computación / ¿ ?
8. inglés / ¿ ?
9. ¿ ?

B. Asociaciones. Identifique dos cosas y dos personas que usted asocia con los siguientes lugares.

MODELO: la clase → la silla, el libro de texto
el profesor, el estudiante

1. la biblioteca
2. la librería
3. una oficina
4. la residencia

2 Identifying People, Places, and Things • Nouns and Articles: Plural Forms

Cursos de Idiomas en el Extranjero

Financiación
SIN INTERESES
en 3, 6 ó 12 meses

- Cursos para jóvenes de 7 a 17 años
- Cursos para adultos a partir de 18 años
- Cursos en Universidades: Idioma general y/o técnico
- Minimasters en Universidades
- USA, Inglaterra e Irlanda
- Programa residencial en Sevilla y/o Madrid con inglés
- Preparación para TOEFL, GMAT, SAT, GRE, USMLE
- Cursos de idiomas en Madrid

Instituto ProLengua ofrece pagar su curso aplazado en 3, 6 ó 12 meses

INSTITUTO PROLENGUA

Infórmate
902-253 797

- You can find many nouns in this ad. Can you guess the meaning of most of them?
- Some of the nouns in the ad are plural. Can you tell how to make nouns plural in Spanish, based on these nouns?
- Look for the Spanish equivalent of the following words.

  adult preparation offers course

- **Idioma** is another word for *language,* and it is a false cognate. It never means *idiom.*
- Using the vocabulary in the ad, guess what **en el extranjero** means.

Heritage speakers
- Anime a los estudiantes a ayudar a sus compañeros monolingües a traducir el anuncio.
- Invite a un estudiante hispanohablante a leer el anuncio en voz alta para que la clase oiga la pronunciación de las vocales.

	Singular	Plural	
Nouns Ending in a Vowel	**el** libro	**los** libro**s**	*the books*
	la mesa	**las** mesa**s**	*the tables*
	un libro	**unos** libro**s**	*some books*
	una mesa	**unas** mesa**s**	*some tables*
Nouns Ending in a Consonant	**la** universidad	**las** universidad**es**	*the universities*
	un papel	**unos** papel**es**	*some papers*

A. Spanish nouns that end in a vowel form plurals by adding **-s**. Nouns that end in a consonant add **-es**. Nouns that end in the consonant **-z** change the **-z** to **-c** before adding **-es: lápiz** → **lápices**.

Plurals in Spanish:

- vowel + **s**
- consonant + **es**
- **-z** → **-ces**

B. The definite and indefinite articles also have plural forms: **el** → **los, la** → **las, un** → **unos, una** → **unas**. **Unos** and **unas** mean *some, several,* or *a few.*

- **el** → **los**
- **la** → **las**
- **un** → **unos**
- **una** → **unas**

C. In Spanish, the masculine plural form of a noun is used to refer to a group that includes both males and females.

los amig**os**
the friends (both male and female)

unos extranjer**os**
some foreigners (both male and female)

Práctica

A. Singular → plural. Dé la forma plural.

1. la mesa
2. el papel
3. el amigo
4. la oficina
5. un cuaderno
6. un lápiz
7. una universidad
8. un bolígrafo
9. un edificio

B. Plural → singular. Dé la forma singular.

1. los profesores
2. las calculadoras
3. las bibliotecarias
4. los estudiantes
5. unos hombres
6. unas tardes
7. unas residencias
8. unas sillas
9. unos escritorios

Preliminary exercise
Have students listen to the following words and tell whether they are singular or plural. **1.** *el diccionario* **2.** *la librería* **3.** *los papeles* **4.** *el lápiz* **5.** *unos bolígrafos* **6.** *las clases* **7.** *una profesora* **8.** *las universidades*

Follow-up A
Have students give the plural of the following. **1.** *Juana, una estudiante; Juana y Elena...* **2.** *Ramón, un extranjero; Ramón y Ricardo...* **3.** *Ramón, un extranjero; Ramón y Raquel...* **4.** *David, un amigo; David y Cecilla...* **5.** *David, un amigo; David y Roberto...*

Extension B
Have students provide examples of certain nouns (some plural, some singular). Use names in class or at university (name of the instructor, names of 2–3 students together, name of president, names of professors, and so on).

❖ Transparencies 13–14

Suggestion A

- Encourage students to speak further about people, places, and things by asking questions such as: *¿Quién es?* (*¿Quiénes son?*) *¿Qué es? ¿Cuántos/as ____ hay? ¿Dónde está(n)?*
- Introduce *muchos/as.*

Reciclado A

Combine your review of numbers and questions with practice of singular and plural forms, by asking questions such as: *¿Cuántos/as estudiantes / mesas / sillas / libros hay en la clase?* Remind students to use *hay* in answers.

Extension B

Ask questions and pantomime keywords to elicit chapter vocabulary, for example, *¿Qué hay en nuestra* (pantomime) (*sala de*) *clase?*

Reciclado B

Have students form pairs to review cognates presented in the explanations and activities in *Primeros pasos* and scan realia and drawings in that chapter and in *Capítulo 1.* Then invite them to give as many nouns as they can that fit into the following categories: **1.** *lugares de la universidad* **2.** *cosas en una librería* **3.** *personas en una librería* **4.** *problemas de los estudiantes.*

Follow-up B

As whole-class activity, ask students what things they associate with certain places, for example: *¿Qué hay en una oficina típica de la universidad? ¿Qué hay en una clase que no hay en una oficina? ¿y en la biblioteca?*

Conversación

A. Identificaciones. Identifique las personas, las cosas y los lugares.

MODELO: Hay ____ en ____. → Hay unos estudiantes en la clase.

Palabras útiles: la computadora, el experimento, la planta, el teléfono

B. Semejanzas (*Similarities*) **y diferencias**

Paso 1. ¿Cuáles son las semejanzas y las diferencias entre los dos cuartos? Hay por lo menos (*at least*) seis diferencias.

MODELO: En el dibujo A, hay ____.
En el dibujo B, hay sólo (*only*) ____.
En el escritorio del dibujo A, hay ____.
En el escritorio del dibujo B, hay ____.

Palabras útiles: la cama (*bed*), la computadora, el estante (*bookshelf*), la lámpara, la planta

Paso 2. Ahora indique qué hay en su propio (*your own*) cuarto. Use palabras del **Paso 1**.

MODELO: En mi cuarto hay ____. En mi escritorio hay ____.

Enfoque cultural

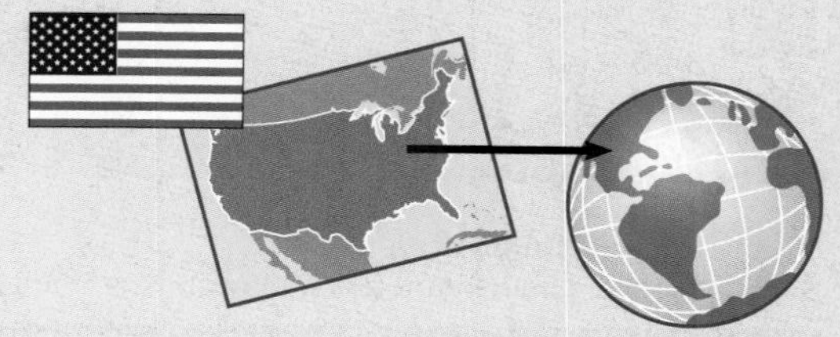

Enfoque cultural
See follow-up activities for this section in chapter by chapter materials in IM.

Los hispanos en los Estados Unidos

Datos[a] esenciales

La población hispánica total de los Estados Unidos: más de 35 (treinta y cinco) millones en el año 2000 (dos mil).

Orígenes de la población hispánica en los Estados Unidos:

México: 58,5% (cincuenta y ocho coma cinco por ciento)

Centroamérica, Sudamérica y otros países:[b] 28,4%

Puerto Rico: 9,6%

Cuba: 3,5%

[a]*Facts* [b]otros... *other countries*

¡Fíjese![a]

- En 2001 (dos mil uno) había[b] veintiún hispanos en el Congreso de los Estados Unidos. ¿Cuántos hay ahora?
- De los más de[c] 35 millones de hispanos en los Estados Unidos, la mayoría[d] habla español (mucho o poco).
- Las palabras **hispano** e[e] **hispánico** se refieren al[f] idioma y a la cultura, no a la raza[g] o al grupo étnico.

[a]*Check it out!* [b]*there were* [c]De... *Of the more than* [d]*majority* [e]y [f]se... *refer to the* [g]*race*

Conozca a[a]... César Chávez

César Chávez

La contribución de César Chávez (1927–1993 [mil novecientos veintisiete a mil novecientos noventa y tres]) al movimiento de los trabajadores agrícolas[b] es enorme. La educación de Chávez, hijo de campesinos migrantes,[c] sólo llega al séptimo grado.[d]

En 1962 (mil novecientos sesenta y dos), Chávez organiza a los campesinos que cosechan uvas.[e] Como resultado de las huelgas[f] y el boicoteo de las uvas de mesa,[g] los campesinos reciben contratos más favorables para ellos; el United Farm Workers se establece[h] como sindicato[i] oficial.

Hoy en día,[j] la vida,[k] los sacrificios y los ideales de Chávez sirven de[l] inspiración a muchas personas.

[a]Conozca... *Meet* [b]trabajadores... *agricultural workers* [c]campesinos... *migrant farm workers* [d]llega... *goes up to the seventh grade* [e]cosechan... *harvest grapes* [f]*strikes* [g]uvas... *table grapes* [h]se... *is established* [i]*union* [j]Hoy... *Nowadays* [k]*life* [l]sirven... *serve as an*

Capítulo 1 of the video to accompany *¿Qué tal?* contains cultural footage of Hispanics in the United States.

Visit the *¿Qué tal?* website at www.mhhe.com/quetal.

PASO 3 Gramática

Paso 3 Gramática
See detailed supplementary material for this grammar section in IM.

3 Expressing Actions • Subject Pronouns; Present Tense of *-ar* Verbs; Negation

Escuchando furtivamente

Escuche lo que Diego le dice a Lupe. Luego imagine la parte de Lupe en la conversación.

DIEGO: *Yo hablo* con mi familia con frecuencia. Por eso *pago* mucho en cuentas de teléfono. ¿Y *tú*?
LUPE: [...]
DIEGO: *Necesito* dinero para comprar libros. Por eso *enseño* inglés a un estudiante de matemáticas. ¿Y *tú*?
LUPE: [...]
DIEGO: En mi tiempo libre *escucho* música. También *toco* la guitarra. En las fiestas *bailo* mucho y *tomo* cerveza con mis amigos. Los fines de semana, *busco* libros de antropología en las librerías. ¿Y *tú*?
LUPE: [...]

Note
Minidialogue introduces material that will appear in Grammar Section 3. You may prefer to focus on subject pronouns alone before introducing the minidialogue. Continue to use the previous guidelines for minidialogue presentation.

Comprensión: ¿Cierto o falso?

1. Diego no habla mucho con su familia.
2. Es estudiante de ciencias.
3. No le gusta la música.
4. Es una persona introvertida y solitaria.
5. Habla francés.

Suggestion
Model Lupe's possible responses to Diego's questions; encourage student repetition and expansion. Translate unfamiliar vocabulary on board as you proceed. **1.** *No, no pago mucho en cuentas de teléfono. ¿Trabajas?* **2.** *No, ahora* (translate on board) *no trabajo. ¿Qué te gusta hacer* (translate)*?* **3.** *Yo también bailo los fines de semana. Pero no busco libros de antropología. Busco libros de arte moderno.*

Follow-up
Ask students if these statements are true for them (*¿sí o no?*): **1.** *Yo hablo francés* (*inglés*). **2.** *Nosotros hablamos español* (*francés*) *en esta clase.* (Suggestion: Introduce *un poco*). **3.** *Nosotros bailamos en esta clase.* **4.** *Yo bailo muy mal* (*muy bien*).

Subject Pronouns

Singular		Plural	
yo	I	**nosotros / nosotras**	we
tú	you (*fam.*)	**vosotros / vosotras**	you (*fam. Sp.*)
usted (Ud.)*	you (*form.*)	**ustedes (Uds.)***	you (*form.*)
él	he	**ellos / ellas**	they
ella	she		

Preliminary exercises
Have students answer the following questions.
- What subject pronoun would you use in English to speak about the following persons? **1.** yourself **2.** two men **3.** a female child **4.** yourself (male) and your sister **5.** yourself (female) and your mother **6.** your uncle
- What subject pronoun would you use in Spanish to speak to the following persons? **1.** *una profesora* **2.** *unos consejeros* **3.** *un estudiante* **4.** *unas amigas* **5.** *tu mamá* **6.** *un dependiente*
- What subject pronoun would you substitute in Spanish for each of the following persons? **1.** *tu amiga Eva* **2.** *Luis* **3.** *Fausto y yo* (male) **4.** *tú* (female) *y Cecilia* **5.** *tú* (male) *y Cecilia* **6.** *Vicente y David* **7.** *la señora Álvarez y tú*

Eavesdropping *Listen to what Diego is saying to Lupe. Then imagine Lupe's part in the conversation.* DIEGO: I speak often with my family. That's why I pay a lot in telephone bills. And you? LUPE: [...] DIEGO: I need money to buy books. That's why I teach English to a math student. And you? LUPE: [...] DIEGO: In my spare time I listen to music. I also play the guitar. At parties I dance a lot and drink beer with my friends. On weekends, I look for anthropology books in bookstores. And you? LUPE: [...]

*Usted and ustedes are frequently abbreviated in writing as **Ud.** or **Vd.**, and **Uds.** or **Vds.**, respectively.

PASO 3

A. Several *subject pronouns* (**los pronombres personales**) have masculine and feminine forms. The masculine plural form is used to refer to a group of males as well as to a group of males and females.

pronoun = a word that takes the place of a noun

Ted → *he*

Martha and Ted → *they*

ellos = *they* (all males; males and females)

ellas = *they* (all females)

B. Spanish has different words for *you*. In general, **tú** is used to refer to a close friend or a member of your family, while **usted** is used with people with whom the speaker has a more formal or distant relationship. The situations in which **tú** and **usted** are used also vary among different countries and regions.

tú → close friend, family member

usted (Ud.) → formal or distant relationship

C. In Latin America and in this country, the plural for both **usted** and **tú** is **ustedes**. In Spain, however, **vosotros/vosotras** is the plural of **tú**, while **ustedes** is used as the plural of **usted** exclusively.

Latin America, North America

tú } ustedes
usted }

Spain

tú → vosotros/vosotras

usted (Ud.) → ustedes

D. Subject pronouns are not used as frequently in Spanish as they are in English and may usually be omitted. You will learn more about the uses of Spanish subject pronouns in **Capítulo 2**.

VERBS: INFINITIVES AND PERSONAL ENDINGS

A. The *infinitive* (**el infinitivo**) of a verb indicates the action or state of being, with no reference to who or what performs the action or when it is done (present, past, or future). In Spanish all infinitives end in **-ar, -er,** or **-ir**. Infinitives in English are indicated by *to: to* speak, *to* eat, *to* live.

-ar:	habl**ar**	*to speak*
-er:	com**er**	*to eat*
-ir:	viv**ir**	*to live*

B. To *conjugate* (**conjugar**) a verb means to give the various forms of the verb with their corresponding subjects: *I speak, you speak, she speaks,* and so on. All regular Spanish verbs are conjugated by adding *personal endings* (**las terminaciones personales**) that reflect the subject doing the action. These are added to the *stem* (**la raíz** or **el radical**), which is the infinitive minus the infinitive ending.

hablar → habl-

comer → com-

vivir → viv-

C. The right-hand column shows the personal endings that are added to the stem of all regular **-ar** verbs:

Regular **-ar** verb endings:

o, -as, -a, -amos, -áis, -an

PASO 3

Preliminary exercises
- Explain purpose of rapid response drill. Have students give corresponding forms. ***yo:*** *bailar, estudiar, tocar, escuchar* ***tú:*** *buscar, hablar, pagar, tomar* ***Ud./él/ella:*** *cantar, necesitar, regresar, enseñar* ***nosotros:*** *comprar, pagar, estudiar, escuchar* ***vosotros:*** *desear, regresar, cantar, bailar* ***Uds./ellos/ellas:*** *practicar, tomar, desear, tocar*
- Have students give subject pronouns for *enseño, cantamos, estudian, paga, trabajan, desean, buscas, compra, habláis, regresas, bailan, tomo, escucha, necesitamos, toco.*

- Explain purpose of pattern practice (see "Teaching Techniques: Drills" in *IM*), and tell students how you want them to do it. ***En la clase de español:*** **1.** *Ud. estudia mucho. (nosotros, yo, ellos, Juan, tú, vosotras)* **2.** *Sara necesita un diccionario. (yo, Carlos y tú, tú, nosotras, Ada, vosotros)*, ***En una fiesta en la residencia:*** **1.** *Clara toma Coca-Cola. (tú, Ud., él, Uds., Elena y yo, vosotras)* **2.** *Tú cantas y bailas. (nosotros, los amigos, Uds., Eva y Diego, yo, vosotros)*

hablar (*to speak*): habl-

	Singular			Plural	
(yo)	habl**o**	*I speak*	(nosotros) (nosotras)	habl**amos**	*we speak*
(tú)	habl**as**	*you speak*	(vosotros) (vosotras)	habl**áis**	*you speak*
(Ud.) (él) (ella)	habl**a**	*you speak; he/she speaks*	(Uds.) (ellos) (ellas)	habl**an**	*you/they speak*

Some important **-ar** verbs in this chapter include those on the right.

OJO Note that in Spanish the meaning of the English word *for* is included in the verbs **buscar** (*to look for*) and **pagar** (*to pay for*); *to* is included in **escuchar** (*to listen to*).

bailar	to dance	**hablar**	to speak; to talk
buscar	to look for	**necesitar**	to need
cantar	to sing	**pagar**	to pay (for)
comprar	to buy	**practicar**	to practice
desear	to want	**regresar**	to return (*to a place*)
enseñar	to teach	**tocar**	to play (*a musical instrument*)
escuchar	to listen (to)	**tomar**	to take; to drink
estudiar	to study	**trabajar**	to work

D. As in English, when two Spanish verbs are used in sequence and there is no change of subject, the second verb is usually in the infinitive form.

Necesito llamar a mi familia.
I need to call my family.

Me gusta bailar.
I like to dance.

E. In both English and Spanish, conjugated verb forms also indicate the *time* or *tense* (**el tiempo**) of the action: *I speak* (present), *I spoke* (past).

Some English equivalents of the present tense forms of Spanish verbs are shown at the right.

hablo	*I speak*	Simple present tense
	I am speaking	Present progressive (indicates an action in progress)
	I will speak	Near future action

NEGATION

In Spanish the word **no** is placed before the conjugated verb to make a negative sentence.

El estudiante **no** habla español.
The student doesn't speak Spanish.

No, **no** necesito dinero.
No, I don't need money.

Notes A
- See *IM* for a discussion of input activities such as this one.
- Generally, the subject pronoun is not used before the verb in a sentence except for clarity or emphasis. The conjugated verb informs the listener as to the identity of the subject.

Práctica

A. Mis compañeros y yo

Paso 1. Read the following statements and tell whether they are true for you and your classmates and for your classroom environment. If any statement is not true for you or your class, make it negative or change it in another way to make it correct.

MODELO: Toco el piano → Sí, toco el piano. (No, no toco el piano. Toco la guitarra.)

1. Necesito más (*more*) dinero.
2. Trabajo en la biblioteca.
3. Tomo ocho clases este semestre/trimestre (*this term*).
4. En clase, cantamos en francés.
5. Deseamos practicar español.
6. Tomamos Coca-Cola en clase.
7. El profesor / La profesora enseña español.
8. El profesor / La profesora habla el alemán (*German*) muy bien.

Paso 2. Now turn to the person next to you and rephrase each sentence, using **tú** forms of the verbs in all cases. Your partner will indicate whether the sentences are true for him or her.

MODELO: ¿Tocas el piano? → Sí, toco el piano. (No, no toco el piano.)

Follow-up A
Paso 1. Convert students' statements into questions addressed to other students: *¿Necesita dinero (Jim)? ¿(Jim) Cree que tomamos cerveza en la clase? ¿Bailas tú en las fiestas?*

Suggestions A
- **Paso 2.** Encourage students to create their own questions.
- Encourage student partners to write a summary of their similarities and differences, using *nosotros* forms: *(Nosotros) Necesitamos mucho dinero y no tomamos cerveza en las fiestas.*

B. En una fiesta.

B. En una fiesta. The following paragraphs describe a party. Scan the paragraphs first, to get a general sense of their meaning. Then complete the paragraphs with the correct form of the numbered infinitives.

Esta noche[a] hay una fiesta en el apartamento de Marcos y Julio. Todos[b] los estudiantes (cantar[1]) y (bailar[2]). Una persona (tocar[3]) la guitarra y otras personas (escuchar[4]) la música.

Jaime (buscar[5]) un café. Marta (hablar[6]) con un amigo. María José (desear[7]) enseñarles a todos[c] un baile[d] de Colombia. Todas las estudiantes desean (bailar[8]) con el estudiante mexicano —¡él (bailar[9]) muy bien!

La fiesta es estupenda, pero todos (necesitar[10]) regresar a casa[e] o a su[f] cuarto temprano.[g] ¡Hay clases mañana!

[a]Esta... *Tonight* [b]*All* [c]enseñarles... *to teach everyone* [d]*dance* [e]a... *home* [f]*their* [g]*early*

Comprensión: ¿Cierto o falso?

1. Marcos es un profesor de español.
2. A Jaime le gusta la cerveza.
3. María José es de Colombia.
4. Los estudiantes desean bailar.

Note B
The majority of the items in comprehension activities of this kind are inferential: Students need to apply their knowledge of the paragraph to the individual items in order to decide if item is *cierto* or *falso*.

Suggestion B
Have students explain their answers in simple sentences. For example, **1.** *Falso. Marcos está en el apartamento con los estudiantes.* Students might disagree about and discuss items of this kind. For example, another student might say: *¡Sí! Hay profesores en las fiestas de los estudiantes,* and so on.

Follow-up B
Do orally or as dictation.
Cambie por el plural: **1.** *Él no desea tomar una cerveza.* **2.** *Ud. baila con un estudiante.* **3.** *¿Compro el lápiz mañana?* **4.** *Hablas con la dependienta.* **5.** *¿Hay sólo una extranjera en la clase?*
Cambie por el singular: **6.** *Ellas no buscan el dinero.* **7.** *¿Enseñan Uds. sólo dos clases de español?* **8.** *Necesitamos unos libros de texto.* **9.** *Las mujeres estudian sicología.* **10.** *¿Pagan Uds. sólo 30 pesos?*

En los Estados Unidos y el Canadá...

Jaime Escalante

Argueably the most famous high school teacher in the United States, Jaime Escalante was born in La Paz, Bolivia, where he was a math and physics teacher for fourteen years. He emigrated to California in 1964 when he was 33. Since he did not speak English, he took menial jobs while he learned the language and went to college to become an accredited teacher. He started teaching in 1974 at Garfield High School, in East Los Angeles, where the students were mostly low-income Latinos. With Escalante's help, their test scores were comparable to those of students in high-income areas of the city. In fact, Escalante's students did so well that the Educational Testing Service thought they had cheated and asked them to retake the test.

Escalante became an overnight celebrity. The 1988 film *Stand and Deliver* portrays his and his students' efforts. He was later awarded the United States Presidential Medal and the Andrés Bello award by the Organization of American States.

Jaime Escalante

Preliminary exercises: A
Have students use cues to form sentences.

- *¿Cómo están Uds.?* **1.** *yo / muy bien* **2.** *tú bien / ¿no?* **3.** *el profesor* (*la profesora*) */ muy bien* **4.** *nosotros / no / enfermo* (pantomime) **5.** *Julio / mal* **6.** *Uds. / bien / también*
- *¿Dónde están las siguientes ciudades?* **1.** *Amarillo, Los Ángeles, San Agustín, Toledo, Santa Fe, Reno* **2.** *Managua, Guadalajara, Buenos Aires, La Habana, Quito, La Paz, Bogotá*

Suggestions: Nota comunicativa

- Point out irregular *yo* form and accents on other forms.
- Emphasize use of *estar* for (1) condition or state of health, (2) location. Students have used *estar* to express both concepts since *Primeros pasos.*
- At this time, avoid explaining differences between *ser* and *estar*. If students ask, just tell them more than one verb translates as *to be* in Spanish.

 **Reciclado**
Emphasize interrogative words, presented in *Primeros pasos.*

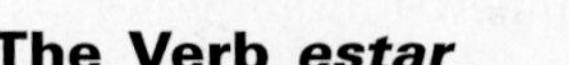

NOTA COMUNICATIVA

The Verb *estar*

Estar is another Spanish **-ar** verb. It means *to be*, and you have already used forms of it to ask how others are feeling or to tell where things are located. Here is the complete conjugation of **estar**. Note that the **yo** form is irregular. The other forms take regular **-ar** endings, and some have a shift in the stress pattern (indicated by the accented **á**).

yo	**estoy**	nosotros/as	**estamos**
tú	**estás**	vosotros/as	**estáis**
Ud., él, ella	**está**	Uds., ellos, ellas	**están**

You will learn the uses of the verb **estar**, along with those of **ser** (the other Spanish verb that means *to be*), gradually, over the next several chapters. For now, just answer the following questions, using forms of **estar**.

1. ¿Cómo está Ud. en este momento (*right now*)?
2. ¿Cómo están sus (*your*) compañeros de clase?
3. ¿Dónde está Ud. en este momento?

Note A
Emphasize use of definite article with titles when talking about persons, as in *El Sr. Ramírez habla español.* Contrast this with *Buenos días, Sr. Ramírez.* No article is used when speaking directly to a person.

❖ Transparency 15

Conversación

A. ¿Qué hacen? (*What are they doing?*) Tell where these people are and what they are doing. Note that the definite article is used with titles when you are talking about a person: **el señor, la señora, el profesor, la profesora**.

MODELO: La Sra. Martínez ______. →
La Sra. Martínez está en la oficina. Busca un libro, trabaja...

Frases útiles: hablar por teléfono, preparar la lección, pronunciar las palabras, tomar apuntes (*to take notes*), usar una computadora

1. Estas (*These*) personas ______.
La profesora Gil ______.
Casi (*Almost*) todos los estudiantes ______.
Unos estudiantes ______.

2. Estas personas están ______.
El Sr. Miranda ______.
La bibliotecaria ______.
El secretario ______.

3. Estas personas ______.
El cliente ______.
La dependienta ______.

Variation A
Bring illustrations to class. Using *¿quién(es)?*, ask questions based on them, for example, *¿Quién busca el libro?*, and so on. Students respond with name of person only.

B. Entrevista. Use the following questions as a guide to interview a classmate, and take notes on what he or she says. (Remember to write down the answers to your partner's questions using the **él/ella** form of the verbs.) Your instructor may want you to hand in your notes so that he or she can get to know the students better.

MODELO: ESTUDIANTE 1: Karen, ¿estudias filosofía?
ESTUDIANTE 2: No, no estudio filosofía. Estudio música.
ESTUDIANTE 1: (escribe [*writes*]): Karen no estudia filosofía. Estudia música.

1. ¿Estudias mucho o poco (*a lot or a little*)? ¿Dónde estudias, en casa (*at home*) o en la biblioteca? ¿Cuándo estudias, por la mañana (*in the morning*), por la tarde (*afternoon*) o por la noche (*at night*)?
2. ¿Cantas bien o mal (*poorly*)? ¿Tocas un instrumento musical? ¿Cuál es? (el piano, la guitarra, el violín...)
3. ¿Trabajas? ¿Dónde? ¿Cuántas horas a la semana (*per week*) trabajas?
4. ¿Quiénes pagan los libros de texto, tú o los profesores? ¿Qué más (*more*) necesitas pagar? ¿diccionarios? ¿la matrícula (*tuition*)? ¿el alquiler (*rent*)? ¿ ?

Notes B
- There are two kinds of questions: information questions and yes/no questions. In Spanish, the latter are marked either by rising intonation at the end of a statement or inverting subject and verb order: *Ud. trabaja aquí.* → *¿Trabaja Ud. aquí?*
- In Spanish, there is no equivalent for *do* or *does* when asking questions.
- The inverted question mark (¿) is obligatory in Spanish.

Variation B
Make the following statements. If students believe you, they respond with *Es verdad.* If they think you are lying, they say *Es falso.* 1. *Hablo español, inglés y francés.* 2. *Bailo muy bien.* 3. *No regreso a casa hoy.* 4. *Por la noche, enseño a estudiantes extranjeros.* 5. *Toco la guitarra.* Encourage students to make up original statements of their own to say to the class.

Follow-up B
Ask a sample question of several individual students, then have them report answers to others, for example, *Juan, ¿Ana estudia mucho o poco?* → *Ana estudia mucho.*

Note A
Chévere means *muy bien* (in Puerto Rican Spanish).

Suggestion A
Using Ángela's letter as a springboard, have students guess when she does things: *¿A qué hora le gusta ir a la cafetería?, ¿A qué hora es la clase de español?,* and so on. Follow up with questions directed to students in class. *Susie, ¿te gusta ir a la cafetería por la mañana? ¿A qué hora?*

Answers A
1. es **2.** toma **3.** Estudiamos **4.** me **5.** Compro **6.** estudio **7.** la **8.** una **9.** practicamos **10.** la **11.** canta **12.** baila **13.** trabajamos **14.** por **15.** la **16.** es **17.** dependienta **18.** estamos **19.** día

Preliminary exercise B
Have students respond *lógico* or *ilógico.*
1. *Cuando estoy en el cine, fumo.* **2.** *Descanso generalmente por la mañana.* **3.** *Los estudiantes tocan la batería en mis clases.* **4.** *Uds. escuchan música cuando estudian.* **5.** *Ud. mira películas en el laboratorio de lenguas.*

Note B
Escuchar means *to listen to:* The Spanish verb does not need a preposition in front of the object.

Variation B
- Describe the scene shown in the illustration and have students draw what they hear in your description.
- Have several students draw on board what other classmates describe for them.

In the *Capítulo 1* segment of "Chapter-by-Chapter Supplementary Materials" in the IM, you will find a chapter-culminating activity. You can use this activity to consolidate and review the vocabulary and grammar skills the students have acquired.

National Standards: Communication
Have a student volunteer his or her email address. Then, encourage other students to write an email to a classmate—from a friend or roommate's address—describing themselves, telling what classes they take, and listing three things they like to do during the weekend. They should not, however, reveal their names. During the next class period, students can survey their classmates in order to guess who wrote the email they received. You may wish to have students send you a signed version of the email to be treated as homework.

UN POCO DE TODO

A. Una carta (*letter*) **a una amiga.** Complete the following paragraphs from Ángela's letter about college to a friend in her hometown. Give the correct form of the words in parentheses, as suggested by the context. When two possibilities are given in parentheses, select the correct word.

Mi amiga Kathy y yo estamos muy contentas. ¡Todo (ser[1]) fantástico! Kathy (tomar[2]) cuatro clases y yo, cinco. (*Nosotras:* Estudiar[3]) mucho. A mí (me/te[4]) gusta ir[a] temprano a la cafetería. A esas horas[b] hay unos donuts riquísimos.[c] (*Yo:* Comprar[5]) un café y dos donuts y (estudiar[6]) unos minutos o media hora, especialmente para[d] (el/la[7]) clase de español.

En la residencia hay (un/una[8]) estudiante de Puerto Rico, Luisa, que vive[e] en el cuarto de enfrente.[f] Con Luisa (*nosotras:* practicar[9]) (el/la[10]) pronunciación. Ella también nos[g] enseña canciones en español. Kathy (cantar[11]) muy mal, pero (bailar[12]) la salsa muy bien… o «chévere», como dice Luisa.[h]

Kathy y yo también (trabajar[13]). Yo trabajo en la biblioteca (por/de[14]) las tardes. Kathy no trabaja en (el/la[15]) universidad, pero su trabajo[i] no (ser[16]) muy diferente. Es (cliente/dependienta[17]) en una librería. ¡Las dos (*nosotras:* estar[18]) con libros todo (el/la[19]) día!

[a] *to go* [b]A… *At that time* [c]*extremely delicious* [d]*for* [e]que… *who lives* [f]de… *in front (of us)* [g]*us* [h]como… *as Luisa says* [i]su… *her work*

Comprensión: ¿Cierto o falso? Which of these statements do you agree with after reading Ángela's letter? Change incorrect statements to make them true.

1. Ángela toma Español 1 en la universidad.
2. A Ángela no le gusta el español como materia.
3. Ángela no estudia con frecuencia.
4. Todos los amigos de Ángela son de habla inglesa (*English-speaking*).

B. ¿Qué pasa (*What's happening*) **en la fiesta?**

Paso 1. With a classmate, briefly describe what's going on in the following scene.

Paso 2. Now compare the scene above with parties *you* go to. You can use the **nosotros** form of verbs to describe what you and your friends do at these parties.

❖ Transparency 16

Vocabulario útil: descansar (*to rest*), escuchar, fumar (*to smoke*), mirar una película/la tele (*to watch a movie/TV*), tocar el piano/la guitarra, tomar cerveza/vino/refrescos (*beer/wine/soft drinks*)

Un paso más PASO 4

Optional section
This and all subsequent *Paso 4: Un paso más* sections are optional.

See IM for suggestions and follow-up activities to accompany video segment.

Suggestion: En contexto
After seeing video but before engaging in *Lluvia de ideas* activity, ask questions in Spanish: *En la primera* (write on board) *clase, ¿hablan Uds. con otros estudiantes en la clase? ¿De qué hablan? ¿De las materias?*

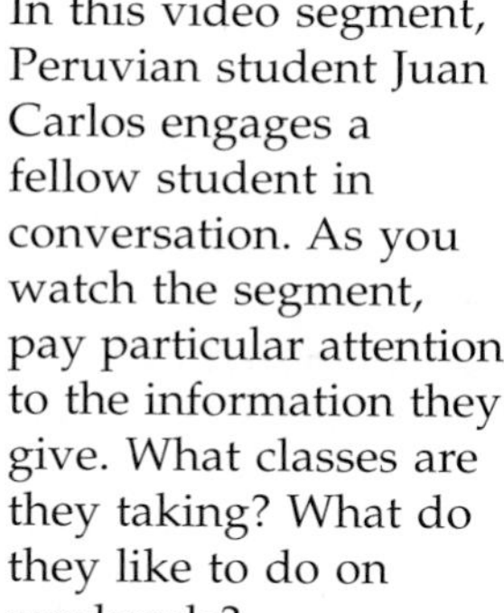

VIDEOTECA: En contexto

In this video segment, Peruvian student Juan Carlos engages a fellow student in conversation. As you watch the segment, pay particular attention to the information they give. What classes are they taking? What do they like to do on weekends?

FUNCTION
Talking about class schedules

A. Lluvia de ideas

What usually happens when you attend a class for the first time? Do you talk to your fellow students? What do you talk about?

B. Dictado

Here is the second half of this segment's dialogue. Fill in the missing portions of Eduardo's dialogue. (There is an underlined space for each word.)

EDUARDO: …Oye, tomas también la clase de sociología con el profesor Ramón, ¿verdad?
JUAN CARLOS: Sí, tomo esa[a] clase también.
EDUARDO: ¿A qué 1 hora 2 es la clase de sociología 3? ¿Es a la una o a la una y 4 media 5?
JUAN CARLOS: Es a la una y media, creo[b]… Sí, a la una y media.
EDUARDO: Este grupo 6 es excelente.
JUAN CARLOS: Sí, escucho su[c] música con frecuencia. Me gusta mucho el jazz.
EDUARDO: Yo trabajo 7 en el Café Azul. Allí[d] tocan 8 música 9 jazz todos los fines de semana por la noche.
JUAN CARLOS: ¡Qué bacán![e] ¿A qué hora?
EDUARDO: A las diez 10.
JUAN CARLOS: ¡Perfecto! Este[f] fin de semana escucho jazz en tu[g] café, entonces. Oye,[h] ¿qué hora es?
EDUARDO: Son las once 11 y cinco. ¿Dónde está 12 la 13 profesora 14? La clase es a las once…

[a]*that* [b]*I think* [c]*their* [d]*There* [e]*¡Qué… Cool!* [f]*This* [g]*your* [h]*Hey*

Cultura en contexto
Expressing *Cool!*

As in all languages, slang is widely used in Spanish, and it varies from region to region and generation to generation. As in the video segment, a student from Peru might say **¡Qué bacán!** to express *Cool!* while in Mexico you would probably hear **¡Qué padre!** The expression **¡Qué chévere!** is widely used throughout the Caribbean and in parts of Latin America, and **¡Qué guay!** is common in Spain.

Note B
The *Dictado* feature encourages students to recall vocabulary used in the *En contexto* dialogue they have just watched. Explain to them that they will see one underlined space for each missing word. This activity may be completed orally or in writing.

Suggestion B
Have students view video segment for a second time after they have completed their responses to correct their own work.

C. Un diálogo original

Paso 1. With a classmate, re-enact the situation between Eduardo and Juan Carlos.

Paso 2. With a different classmate, role-play a situation similar to the one in the video. Here are the roles:

ESTUDIANTE 1: You are a student coming into the classroom the first day of classes. You want to start a conversation with a classmate. As you sit down, you let your classmate see a CD (pronounced as the letters **c d** [**ce de**]), which you like a lot.

ESTUDIANTE 2: You are already sitting in class. You are also interested in making a new friend. One of your classmates has a CD of one of your favorite bands.

PASO FINAL

Note: A leer
In the Hispanic world there is no tradition of going away to study, unless there is no university in one's hometown or in nearby cities. Most students live with their families throughout their education. Students who live in dormitories, pensions, and private homes are from out of town. However, an increasing number of these students rent and share their apartments with other students, like many American students.

Old universities are typically in the downtown area of large, important cities. Therefore, they are surrounded by downtown life, with lots of bars and cafés. Many university buildings have their own *bar-cafetería.* Such bars and cafés are the equivalent of U.S. cafeterias and dining facilities in that they bring students together outside the classroom. These bars and cafés have traditionally provided an intense university and intellectual life for students. It is normal for students to meet with each other and even with their professors after classes and chat over a beer or coffee.

A LEER

Estrategia: More on Guessing Meaning from Context

As you learned in **El mundo hispánico** (**Primeros pasos**), you can often guess the meaning of unfamiliar words from the context (the words that surround them) and by using your knowledge about the topic in general. Making "educated guesses" about words in this way will be an important part of your reading skills in Spanish.

What is the meaning of the underlined words in these sentences?

1. En una lista alfabetizada, la palabra **grande** aparece antes de **grotesco**.
2. El edificio no es moderno; es viejo.
3. Me gusta estudiar español, pero detesto la biología. En general, odio las ciencias como materia.

Some words are underlined in the following reading (and in the readings in subsequent chapters). Try to guess their meaning from context.

Like the passages in **Primeros pasos** and some others in subsequent chapters, this reading contains section subheadings. Scanning these subheadings in advance will help you make predictions about the reading's content, which will also help to facilitate your overall comprehension. Another useful way to manage longer passages is to read section by section. At this point, don't try to understand every word. Your main objective should be to understand the general content of the passage.

Sobre la lectura... This reading was written by the authors of *¿Qué tal?* for students of Spanish like you. Later on in this text, you will have the chance to read more "authentic" selections.

Las universidades hispánicas

Introducción

En el mundo hispánico —y en los Estados Unidos y el Canadá— hay universidades grandes[a] y pequeñas; públicas, religiosas y privadas; modernas y antiguas. Pero el concepto de «vida[b] universitaria» es diferente.

El campus

Por ejemplo, en los países[c] hispánicos la universidad no es un centro de actividad social. No hay muchas residencias estudiantiles. En general, los estudiantes viven en pensiones[d] o en casas particulares[e] y llegan a la universidad en coche o en autobús. En algunas[f] universidades hay un *campus* similar a los de[g] las universidades de los Estados Unidos y el Canadá. En estos casos se habla[h] de la «ciudad[i] universitaria». Otras universidades ocupan sólo un edificio grande, o posiblemente varios edificios, pero no hay zonas verdes.[j]

Estudiantes de Medicina en Caracas, Venezuela

Los deportes

Otra diferencia es que en la mayoría de las universidades hispánicas los deportes no son muy importantes. Si los estudiantes desean practicar un deporte —el tenis, el fútbol o el béisbol— hay clubes deportivos, pero estos[k] no forman parte de la universidad.

Las diversiones[l]

Como se puede ver,[m] la forma y la organización de la universidad son diferentes en las dos culturas. Pero los estudiantes estudian y se divierten[n] en todas partes.[o] A los estudiantes hispanos —así como[p] a los estadounidenses* y canadienses[q] les gusta mucho toda clase de música: la música moderna —la nacional[r] y la importada (y hay para todos: Madonna, 'N Sync, R.E.M....)— la música clásica y la música con raíces[s] tradicionales. Otras diversiones preferidas por los estudiantes son las discotecas y los cafés. Hay cafés ideales para hablar con los amigos. También hay exposiciones de arte, obras de teatro y películas[t] interesantes.

Conclusión

Los días favoritos de muchos jóvenes[u] hispánicos son los fines de semana. ¿Realmente son muy distintos los estudiantes hispanos? ■

[a]*large* [b]*life* [c]naciones [d]*boarding houses* [e]*private* [f]*some* [g]los... *those of* [h]se... *one speaks* [i]*city* [j]*green* [k]*they* (literally *these*) [l]Las... *Entertainment* [m]Como... *As you can see* [n]se... *have a good time* [o]en... *everywhere* [p]así... *like* [q]estadounidenses... *people from the U.S. and Canada* [r]la... *(music) from their own country* [s]*roots* [t]*movies* [u]*young people*

Suggestion: A leer
Have students describe photo, using as many words from *Vocabulario* as possible. Elicit some sentences using questions.

*Although, technically, **norteamericano** refers to all North Americans, the term is sometimes used to refer solely to people from the United States of America. In this book, **estadounidenses** will refer to people of the United States and **norteamericanos** to North Americans.

Comprensión

Suggestion A
For items 1–3, have students substitute *en este país* and *de/en este país,* for *hispánico/a(s)*, and respond *cierto* or *falso* to the new statement. Then, have them restate each sentence with themselves (*yo*) as the subject (*Yo vivo en una residencia*) and also respond *cierto* or *falso.*

A. **¿Cierto o falso?** Indique si las siguientes oraciones son ciertas o falsas.

1. En los países hispánicos, la mayoría de los estudiantes vive en residencias.
2. En las universidades hispánicas, los deportes ocupan un lugar esencial en el programa de estudios del estudiante.
3. En una universidad hispánica, no hay mucho tiempo para asistir a (*time for attending*) conciertos y exposiciones de arte.
4. No hay mucha diferencia entre (*between*) una universidad hispánica y una universidad norteamericana con respecto al *campus*.
5. La música es una diversión para los estudiantes en todas partes.

B. **¿Qué universidad?** Indique si las siguientes oraciones son de un estudiante de la Universidad de Sevilla o de un estudiante de la Universidad de Michigan… ¡o de los dos!

	SEVILLA	MICHIGAN	LOS DOS
1. «Me gusta jugar al Frisbee en el *campus*.»	☐	☐	☐
2. «La casa es muy cómoda (*comfortable*) y tengo derecho a usar la cocina (*I have kitchen privileges*).»	☐	☐	☐
3. «Después de mi clase, ¿qué tal si tomamos un café?»	☐	☐	☐
4. «El sábado (*Saturday*) hay un partido de basquetbol. ¿Deseas ir (*to go*)?»	☐	☐	☐

A ESCRIBIR

Suggestion: A escribir
If students created charts comparing individuals, collate and analyze results on board. Ask: Can you account for any differences based on age? gender? national origin? and so on. After discussing the comments as a class, have students write a brief report on findings.

WWW Multimedia: Internet
After students have finished the *A escribir* section, have them visit the Website for *Universidad Iberoamericana* in Mexico City. Then have students write a brief description of the *Universidad Iberoamericana* campus, based on the interactive map (*mapa del plantel*).

In light of what you now know about some differences and similarities between universities in this country and in Hispanic countries, what information do you think would be important to share with a Hispanic student planning on studying at *your* university? In a brief paragraph, describe your university to such a student. Include information such as: **el número de residencias; si la universidad es grande/pequeña, pública/privada; el edificio más grande** (*biggest*); and so on.

Mi universidad…

En resumen

GRAMÁTICA

To review the grammar points presented in this chapter, refer to the indicated grammar presentations. You'll find further practice of these structures in the Workbook/Laboratory Manual, on the CD-ROM, and on the website.

1. Singular Nouns: Gender and Articles

Do you understand the gender of nouns and how to use the articles **el, la, uno**, and **una**?

2. Nouns and Articles: Plural Forms

Do you know how to make nouns plural and use the articles **los, las, unos**, and **unas**?

3. Subject Pronouns; Present Tense of *-ar* Verbs; Negation

You should be able to use subject pronouns, conjugate regular **-ar** verbs in the present tense, and form negative sentences.

VOCABULARIO

Los verbos

bailar to dance
buscar to look for
cantar to sing
comprar to buy
desear to want
enseñar to teach
escuchar to listen (to)
estar (*irreg.*) to be
estudiar to study
hablar to speak; to talk
  hablar por teléfono to talk on the phone
necesitar to need
pagar to pay (for)
practicar to practice
regresar to return (*to a place*)
  regresar a casa to go home
tocar to play (*a musical instrument*)
tomar to take; to drink
trabajar to work

Suggestions: Vocabulario

- Have students create word puzzles that they can exchange and solve.
- Have students play charades, using nouns from list, for example, *profesor* (student stands and pantomimes teaching class).
- Have students use adverbs from *¿Cuándo?* and verbs from *Los verbos* to make a chart that plots when and how often they do some things.

Los lugares

el apartamento apartment
la biblioteca library
la cafetería cafeteria
la clase class
el cuarto room
el edificio building
la fiesta party
la librería bookstore
la oficina office
la residencia dormitory
la universidad university

Las personas

el/la amigo/a friend
el/la bibliotecario/a librarian
el/la cliente client
el/la compañero/a (de clase) classmate
el/la compañero/a de cuarto roommate
el/la consejero/a advisor

el/la dependiente/a clerk
el/la estudiante student
el/la extranjero/a foreigner
el hombre man
la mujer woman
el/la profesor(a) professor
el/la secretario/a secretary

Las lenguas (extranjeras)

el alemán German
el español Spanish
el francés French
el inglés English
el italiano Italian

Otras materias

la administración de empresas, el arte, las ciencias, la computación, las comunicaciones, la economía, la filosofía, la física, la historia, las humanidades, la literatura, las matemáticas, la química, la sicología, la sociología

Las cosas

el bolígrafo pen
la calculadora calculator
el cuaderno notebook
el diccionario dictionary
el dinero money
el escritorio desk
el lápiz (*pl.* **lápices**) pencil
el libro (de texto) (text)book
la mesa table
la mochila backpack
el papel paper
la pizarra chalkboard
la puerta door
la silla chair
la ventana window

Otros sustantivos

el café coffee
la cerveza beer
el día day
la matrícula tuition

¿Cuándo?

ahora now
con frecuencia frequently
el fin de semana weekend
por la mañana (tarde, noche) in the morning (afternoon, evening)
tarde/temprano late/early
todos los días every day

Pronombres personales

yo, tú, usted (Ud.), él/ella, nosotros/nosotras, vosotros/vosotras, ustedes (Uds.), ellos/ellas

Palabras adicionales

aquí here
con with
en casa at home
mal poorly
más more
mucho much; a lot
muy very
poco little; a little bit
por eso therefore
sólo only

CAPÍTULO

2

La familia

For the Instructor
- *Instructor's Manual and Resource Kit,* "Chapter-by-Chapter" Supplementary Materials
- Testing Program
- Overhead Transparencies 17–21
- Video (VHS or CD)
- *¿Qué tal?* Online Learning Center Website
- Audioscript
- Instructor's Resource CD

For Students
- Workbook/Laboratory Manual and Audio Program or Electronic Workbook/Laboratory Manual
- Video on CD
- Interactive CD-ROM
- *¿Qué tal?* Online Learning Center Website
- Listening Comprehension Audio CD
- McGraw-Hill Electronic Language Tutor (MHELT)

Resources
You and your students may find the following *¿Qué tal?* supplements helpful as you teach this chapter:

Suggestion: Chapter Opening photo
Point out the chapter opening photo and have students talk about their own family experiences and ideas about Hispanic families. Encourage them to describe the people in the photo. Then ask students questions about the individuals in the photo. Pantomime descriptive adjectives. *¿Cómo son las personas en la foto? ¿Son jóvenes? ¿viejas? ¿Cuántas generaciones hay en esta foto?*

Los fines de semana, muchas familias mexicanas pasan la tarde en Xochimilco. **Xochimilco** significa «jardín de flores» (*garden of flowers*) en el idioma de los aztecas.

VOCABULARIO

- Family and relatives
- Adjectives
- Numbers 31–100

GRAMÁTICA

4 Present Tense of **ser**; Summary of Uses
5 Possessive Adjectives (Unstressed)
6 Adjectives: Gender, Number, and Position
7 Present Tense of **-er** and **-ir** Verbs; More about Subject Pronouns

CULTURA

- **Enfoque cultural:** México
- **Nota cultural:** Hispanic Last Names
- **En los Estados Unidos y el Canadá:** Los Sheen, una familia de actores
- **Cultura en contexto:** La familia extendida

Multimedia

You will learn more about describing other people in the **En contexto** video segment.

Review vocabulary and grammar and practice language skills with the interactive CD-ROM.

WWW. Get connected to the Spanish-speaking world with the *¿Qué tal?* Online Learning Center: **www.mhhe.com/quetal**.

PASO 1 Vocabulario

Paso 1: Vocabulario
See detailed supplementary materials and exercises and a model for vocabulary presentation and other material in the *Capítulo 2 Paso 1: Vocabulario* section of "Chapter-by-Chapter Supplementary Materials," IM.

❖ **Transparencias 17–19**

La familia y los parientes°

relatives

Multimedia: Audio
Students can listen to and practice this chapter's vocabulary on their Listening Comprehension Audio CD.

Heritage speakers
- El concepto de la familia para los hispanos no solamente incluye a la familia nuclear sino también a la familia extendida. Cuando llega un nuevo miembro a la familia, como el marido de una hermana, el concepto de la familia crece para incluir a consuegros, consuegras, cuñados, los concuños o concuñados, etcétera.
- Pregúnteles a los hispanohablantes de la clase qué términos de cariño se usan con frecuencia en sus familias.

la madre (mamá)	mother (mom)
el padre (papá)	father (dad)
los padres	parents
la hija	daughter
el hijo	son
los hijos	children
la hermana	sister
el hermano	brother
la esposa	wife
el esposo	husband
la abuela	grandmother
el abuelo	grandfather
los abuelos	grandparents
la nieta	granddaughter
el nieto	grandson
la prima	cousin (*female*)
el primo	cousin (*male*)
la tía	aunt
el tío	uncle
la sobrina	niece
el sobrino	nephew

Las mascotas°

Las... Pets

el gato	cat
el pájaro	bird
el perro	dog

Vocabulario útil

el padrastro / la madrastra	stepfather/stepmother
el hijastro / la hijastra	stepson/stepdaughter
el hermanastro / la hermanastra	stepbrother/stepsister
el medio hermano / la media hermana	half-brother/half-sister
el suegro / la suegra	father-in-law/mother-in-law
el yerno / la nuera	son-in-law/daughter-in-law
el cuñado / la cuñada	brother-in-law/sister-in-law
...(ya) murió	... has (already) died

Suggestions A

- Introduce your own or a fictitious family with a family tree on board or overhead transparency. Start with recognizable cognates *padre* (*papá*) and *madre* (*mamá*); add 2 family members at a time, assigning names and defining relationships as you go along; students just listen during this phase. Use family photographs to personalize.
- After several generations are written on board, check comprehension, asking questions with alternatives: *¿Quién es él, mi abuelo o mi padre?*
- Model names or integrate them in tree on board. Ask students if they have those particular relations. You may also introduce related vocabulary such as: *soltero/a, casado/a, la familia nuclear,* and *la familia extendida.*
- To follow up, have students use your presentation as a guide when presenting their own family members to class.

Conversación

A. ¿Cierto o falso? Look at the drawing of the family tree that appears on page 54. Decide whether each of the following statements is true (**cierto**) or false (**falso**) according to the drawing. Correct the false statements.

1. José Jaime es el hermano de Marta.
2. Luisa es la abuela de Patricia.
3. Marta es la sobrina de Jaime y Elena.
4. Patricia y José Jaime son primos.
5. Elena es la tía de Manolo.
6. Jaime es el sobrino de José Jaime.

Answers A

1. *F: Es el hermano de Patricia.* **2.** *C* **3.** *C* **4.** *F: Son hermanos.* **5.** *F: Es la hermana de Manolo.* **6.** *F: Jaime es el padre de José Jaime.*

B. ¿Quién es?

Paso 1. Complete las oraciones lógicamente.

1. La madre de mi (*my*) padre es mi abuela.
2. El hijo de mi tío es mi primo.
3. La hermana de mi padre es mi tía.
4. El esposo de mi abuela es mi abuelo.

Paso 2. ¿Quiénes son? Siga (*Follow*) el mismo (*same*) modelo.

1. prima **2.** sobrino **3.** tío **4.** abuelo

Suggestions B

- Do as listening comprehension activity, with students providing completion.
- Have students identify the members of each group: *los hijos* → *el hijo y la hija.* **1.** *los abuelos* **2.** *los padres* **3.** *los hermanos* **4.** *los nietos* **5.** *los tíos* **6.** *los sobrinos*

C. Entrevista. Find out about the family of a classmate using the following dialogue as a guide. Use **tengo** (*I have*) and **tienes** (*you have*), as indicated. Use **¿cuántos?** with male relations and **¿cuántas?** with females.

MODELO: E1:* ¿Cuántos hermanos tienes?
E2: Bueno (*Well*), tengo seis hermanos y una hermana.
E1: ¿Y cuántos primos?
E2: ¡Uf! Tengo un montón (*bunch*). Más de veinte.

Suggestion C

Model dialogue with several students before allowing class to work in pairs. Model options for a small family.

*From this point on in the text, ESTUDIANTE 1 and ESTUDIANTE 2 will be abbreviated as E1 and E2, respectively.

❖ Transparency 20

Adjetivos

guapo handsome, good-looking
bonito pretty
feo ugly

grande pequeño

casado married
soltero single

simpático nice, likeable
antipático unpleasant

rubio moreno

joven nuevo viejo

alto bajo

corto short (*in length*)
largo long

bueno good
malo bad

listo smart, clever
tonto silly, foolish

trabajador perezoso

rico rich
pobre poor

delgado thin, slender
gordo fat

To describe a masculine singular noun, use **alt*o*, baj*o***, and so on; use **alt*a*, baj*a***, and so on for feminine singular nouns.

Suggestion A
Have students make similar comparisons of classmates and people they know.

Answers A
1. *Es tonto.* **2.** *Es perezoso.* **3.** *Es alto.* **4.** *Es malo, antipático y feo.* **5.** *Paco es soltero y joven.* **6.** *Es nuevo y largo.*

Conversación

A. Preguntas. Conteste según los dibujos. ❖ Transparency 21

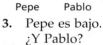

1. Einstein es listo.
¿Y el mono (*monkey*)?

2. Roberto es trabajador.
¿Y José?

3. Pepe es bajo.
¿Y Pablo?

4. El ángel es bueno y simpático. También es guapo. ¿Y el demonio?

5. Ramón Ramírez es casado. También es viejo. ¿Y Paco Pereda?

6. El libro es viejo y corto. ¿Y el lápiz?

B. **¿Cómo es?** Describe a famous personality using as many adjectives as possible so that your classmates can guess who the person is. Use cognate adjectives that you have seen in **Primeros pasos** and **Capítulo 1**.

MODELO: Es un hombre importante; controla una gran compañía de *software*. Es muy trabajador y muy rico. (Bill Gates)

Reciclado B
Use cognates (*optimista, inteligente,* and so on) learned in *Primeros pasos.*

Extension B
Have students describe themselves.

Los números 31–100

Reciclado
- Review numbers 1–30 with counting drills and math games.
- Remind students of the *-e* ending in *veinte* vs. the *-a* in *treinta, cuarenta, cincuenta,* and so on.

Continúe la secuencia:

treinta y uno, treinta y dos…
ochenta y cuatro, ochenta y cinco…

31	treinta y uno	36	treinta y seis	50	cincuenta
32	treinta y dos	37	treinta y siete	60	sesenta
33	treinta y tres	38	treinta y ocho	70	setenta
34	treinta y cuatro	39	treinta y nueve	80	ochenta
35	treinta y cinco	40	cuarenta	90	noventa
				100	cien, ciento

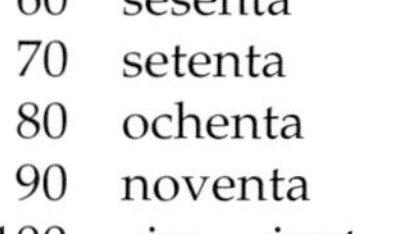

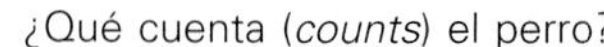
¿Qué cuenta (*counts*) el perro?

Beginning with 31, Spanish numbers are *not* written in a combined form; **treinta y uno,*** **cuarenta y dos, sesenta y tres**, and so on must be three separate words.

Cien is used before nouns and in counting.

cien casas	*a (one) hundred houses*
noventa y ocho, noventa y nueve, **cien**	*ninety-eight, ninety-nine, one hundred*

*Remember that when **uno** is part of a compound number (**treinta y uno, cuarenta y uno**, and so on), it becomes **un** before a masculine noun and **una** before a feminine noun: **cincuenta y *una* mesas; setenta y *un* coches**.

NOTA CULTURAL

Hispanic Last Names

In many Hispanic countries, people are given two last names (**apellidos**) such as in the case of **Amalia *Lázaro Aguirre***. The first last name (**Lázaro**) is that of Amalia's father; the second (**Aguirre**) is her mother's. This system for assigning last names is characteristic of all parts of the Spanish-speaking world, although it is not widely used by Hispanics living in this country. When Hispanic women marry, they might formally replace their second (maternal) last name with that of their husband's first (paternal) last name.

Follow-up: Nota cultural
Have students say what their full names would be if they were Latin American or Spanish.

Heritage speakers
Pregúnteles a los hispanohablantes qué apellidos tienen. Si son estudiantes de la segunda o tercera generación, ¿siguen usando este sistema?

National Standards: Comparisons
Have students look up telephone books for different Spanish-speaking cities online. Some phone books allow you to look at multiple listings, and others will search specific names and last names. In some cases, searches of last names require the 2 last names.

Conversación

A. Más problemas de matemáticas. Recuerde: + **y,** − **menos,** = **son.**

1. 30 + 50 = ? 80	**4.** 77 + 23 = ? 100	**7.** 84 − 34 = ? 50
2. 45 + 45 = ? 90	**5.** 100 − 40 = ? 60	**8.** 78 − 36 = ? 42
3. 32 + 58 = ? 90	**6.** 99 − 39 = ? 60	**9.** 88 − 28 = ? 60

NOTA COMUNICATIVA

Expressing Age

NIETA: ¿Cuántos años tienes, abuela?
ABUELA: Setenta y tres, Nora.
NIETA: ¿Y cuántos años tiene el abuelo?
ABUELA: Setenta y cinco, mi amor (*love*). Y ahora, dime (*tell me*), ¿cuántos años tienes tú?
NIETA: Tengo tres.

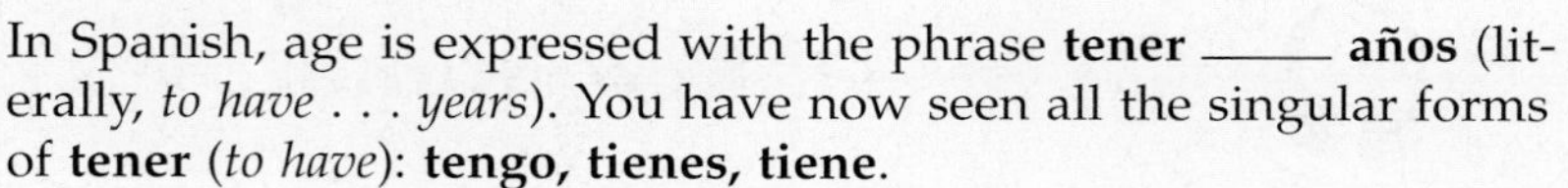

In Spanish, age is expressed with the phrase **tener ____ años** (literally, *to have . . . years*). You have now seen all the singular forms of **tener** (*to have*): **tengo, tienes, tiene.**

B. ¡Seamos (*Let's be*) **lógicos!** Complete las oraciones lógicamente.

1. Un hombre que (*who*) tiene noventa años es muy ____.
2. Un niño (*small child*) que tiene sólo un año es muy ____.
3. La persona más vieja (*oldest*) de mi familia es mi ____. Tiene ____ años.
4. La persona más joven de mi familia es mi ____. Tiene ____ años.
5. En mi opinión, es ideal tener ____ años.
6. Cuando una persona tiene ____ años, ya es adulta.
7. Para (*In order to*) tomar cerveza en esta ciudad (*city*), es necesario tener ____ años.
8. Para mí (*For me*), ¡la idea de tener ____ años es inconcebible (*inconceivable*)!

Suggestions: Nota comunicativa
- Introduce singular forms of *tener*. (Review them if you introduced them in the context of the family tree.)
- Model age dialogue with several students, asking about ages of some of their relatives.

¿Recuerda Ud.?

Before beginning Grammar Section 4, review the forms and uses of **ser** that you have already learned by answering these questions.

1. ¿Es Ud. estudiante o profesor(a)?
2. ¿Cómo es Ud.? ¿Es una persona sentimental? ¿inteligente? ¿paciente? ¿elegante?
3. ¿Qué hora es? ¿A qué hora es la clase de español?
4. ¿Qué es un hospital? ¿Es una persona? ¿una cosa? ¿un edificio?

Paso 2: Gramática
See detailed supplementary materials for these grammar sections in the IM.

Reciclado
Before teaching conjugations of *ser*, review subject pronouns. Review differences between *tú* and *Ud.* Have students tell you the difference between *nosotros/as* and *vosotros/as.* Ask where *vosotros* is used most.

4 Expressing *to be* • Present Tense of *ser;* Summary of Uses

Presentaciones

—Hola. Me llamo Manolo Durán.

- *Soy* profesor en la universidad.
- *Soy* alto y moreno.
- *Soy* de Sevilla, España.

—¿Y Lola Benítez, mi esposa? Complete la descripción de ella.

Es _____ (profesión).
Es _____ y _____ (descripción).
Es de _____ (origen).

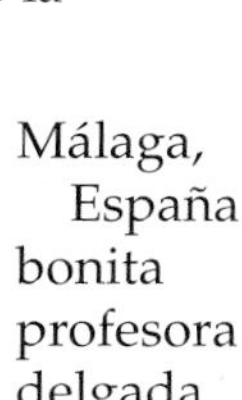

Málaga, España
bonita
profesora
delgada

As you know, there are two Spanish verbs that mean *to be:* **ser** and **estar**. They are not interchangeable; the meaning that the speaker wishes to convey determines their use. In this chapter, you will review the uses of **ser** that you already know and learn some new ones. Remember to use **estar** to express location and to ask how someone is feeling. You will learn more about the uses of **estar** in **Capítulo 5**.

PASO 2

A. Here are some basic language functions of **ser**. You have used or seen all of them already in this and previous chapters.

Reciclado
Review *ser* for telling time (from *Primeros pasos*).

National Standards: Communication
Point out different things you can express with *ser:* who someone/something is, whom something is for, and so on.

ser (*to be*)

yo	**soy**	nosotros/as	**somos**
tú	**eres**	vosotros/as	**sois**
Ud. / él / ella	**es**	Uds. / ellos / ellas	**son**

- To *identify* people and things [Práctica A]

OJO When you see a note in brackets **[Práctica A]** here, it refers you to that exercise for the grammar point. In this case, Exercise A (page 61) in the next **Práctica** section will allow you to practice this point.

Yo soy **estudiante**.
Alicia y yo somos **amigas**.
La doctora Ramos es **profesora**.
Esto (*This*) es **un libro**.

- To *describe* people and things*

Soy **sentimental**:
I'm sentimental (a sentimental person).

El coche es **muy viejo**.
The car is very old.

- With **de**, to express *origin* [Práctica B–C]

Somos **de los Estados Unidos**, pero nuestros padres son **de la Argentina**. ¿**De dónde** es Ud.?
We're from the United States, but our parents are from Argentina. Where are you from?

- To express *generalizations* (only **es**) [Conversación B]

Es **importante** estudiar, pero no es **necesario** estudiar todos los días.
It's important to study, but it's not necessary to study every day.

*You will practice this language function of **ser** in Grammar Section 6 in this chapter and in subsequent chapters.

B. Here are two basic language functions of **ser** that you have not yet practiced.

- With **de**, to express *possession* [Práctica D]

OJO Note that there is no **'s** in Spanish.

The masculine singular article **el** contracts with the preposition **de** to form **del**. No other article contracts with **de**.

Es el perro **de Carla**.
It's Carla's dog.

Son las gatas **de Jorge**.
They're Jorge's (female) cats.

Es la casa **del** profesor.
It's the (male) professor's house.

Es la casa **de la** profesora.
It's the (female) professor's house.

OJO de + el → del

- With **para**, to tell for whom or what something *is intended* [Conversación A]

¿Romeo y Julieta? Es **para** la clase de inglés.
Romeo and Juliet? It's for English class.

— ¿**Para** quién son los regalos?
— (Son) **Para** mi nieto.
Who are the presents for?
(They're) For my grandson.

Reciclado A
Review classroom vocabulary and practice *ser* + noun. Hold up or point to classroom objects, asking *¿Qué es esto?* Elicit plural forms by holding up 2 books, pencils, and so on.

Práctica

Preliminary exercise A
Do a chain drill: *Ana es estudiante. yo → Yo soy estudiante.* (*Mario y Juan, Uds., Lilia y yo, tú, vosotros, Teresa*)

A. Los parientes de Manolo. Look back at the family tree on page 54. Then tell whether the following statements are true (**cierto**) or false (**falso**) from Manolo's standpoint. Correct the false statements.

1. Lola y yo somos hermanos.
2. Mi esposa es la prima de Patricia.
3. Manuel y Luisa son mis (*my*) padres.
4. José Jaime es mi sobrino.
5. Mi hermana es la esposa de Jaime.
6. Mi padre no es abuelo todavía (*yet*).
7. Mi familia no es muy grande.

Answers A
1. *F: esposos* 2. *F: sobrina* tía 3. *C* 4. *C* 5. *C* 6. *F: Es abuelo de Marta, José Jaime y Patricia.* 7. *C*

Suggestions A
- Do as listening activity. Have students assume that you are Lola or Manolo. Adjust items 1 and 2 as needed.
- Ask personalized questions based on statements: *¿Tiene Ud. un esposo* (*una esposa*)*? ¿Tiene abuelos/as? ¿Cuántos? ¿Tiene primos? ¿De quién es sobrino? ¿Es tío/a?* and so on.

B. Nacionalidades. ¿De dónde son, según los nombres y apellidos?

Países (*Countries*): Francia, México, Italia, los Estados Unidos, Inglaterra (*England*), Alemania (*Germany*)

1. John Doe
2. Karl Lotze
3. Graziana Lazzarino
4. María Gómez
5. Claudette Moreau
6. Timothy Windsor

Answers B
1. *los Estados Unidos* 2. *Alemania* 3. *Italia* 4. *México* 5. *Francia* 6. *Inglaterra*

Extension B
- Review languages and have students tell what language the people speak.
- Imagine that you are a friend of persons listed in *Práctica B*. Tell where both of you are from: *John y yo somos de _____. Hablamos _____.*

Suggestions B
- Model pronunciation of names and countries.
- Have students answer: *¿De dónde es Ud.? ¿De este estado? ¿de una metrópoli? ¿de un área rural? ¿Es Ud. de una ciudad que tiene un nombre hispano? ¿Es de otro* (another) *país?*

Follow-up B
¿Es Ud. del norte de los Estados Unidos / del Canadá? ¿del oeste? ¿del este? ¿del sur?

Follow-up C
Have students create sentences about famous Hispanics. Put information on board in columns to help students form sentences or ask cue questions: *¿De dónde es ___?*

C. Personas extranjeras. ¿Quiénes son, de dónde son y dónde trabajan ahora?

MODELO: Teresa: actriz / de Madrid / en Cleveland →
Teresa es actriz. Es de Madrid. Ahora trabaja en Cleveland.

1. Carlos Miguel: médico (*doctor*) / de Cuba / en Milwaukee
2. Maripili: profesora / de Burgos / en Miami
3. Mariela: dependienta / de Buenos Aires / en Nueva York
4. Juan: dentista* / de Lima / en Los Ángeles
5. un amigo o pariente suyo (*of yours*) / ¿ ? / ¿ ?

Suggestion D
Have students give simple explanations using *porque, por eso.*

Follow-up D
Have students answer based on what they consider to be a typical family. *¿De quién es el coche* (*son los coches*)*? ¿A quién escucha más el hijo / la hija, al padre o a la madre? ¿De quién son los discos compactos? ¿De quién son las herramientas* (tools)*? ¿De quién es la cocina* (kitchen)*?*

D. ¡Seamos (*Let's be*) **lógicos!** ¿De quién son estas cosas? Con un compañero/una compañera, haga y conteste preguntas (*ask and answer questions*) según el modelo.

MODELO: E1: ¿De quién es el perro?
E2: Es de...

Personas: las estudiantes, la actriz, el niño, la familia con diez hijos, el estudiante extranjero, los señores Schmidt

¿De quién es/son... ?

1. la casa en Beverly Hills
2. la casa en Viena
3. la camioneta (*station wagon*)
4. el perro
5. las fotos de la Argentina
6. las mochilas con todos los libros

Reciclado: Nota comunicativa
Por eso (expression with *por*) was presented in *Capítulo 1.*

NOTA COMUNICATIVA

Explaining Your Reasons

In conversation, it is often necessary to explain a decision, tell why someone did something, and so on. Here are some simple words and phrases that speakers use to offer explanations.

porque because | **para** in order to

—¿Por qué necesitamos un televisor nuevo?	*Why do we need a new TV set?*
—Pues . . . **para** mirar el partido de fútbol... ¡Es el campeonato!	*Well . . . (in order) to watch the soccer game . . . It's the championship!*
—¿Por qué trabajas tanto?	*Why do you work so much?*
—¡**Porque** necesitamos el dinero!	*Because we need the money!*

Note the differences between **porque** (one word, no accent) and the interrogative **¿por qué?**

*A number of professions end in **-ista** in both masculine and feminine forms. The article indicates gender: **el/la dentista, el/la artista**, and so on.

Conversación

A. El regalo ideal. The first column below lists gifts that Diego would like to give to certain members of his family, listed in the second column. For him, money is no object! Decide who receives each gift, and explain your decisions by using the additional information included about the family members.

MODELO: _____ es para _____ →
El dinero es para Carmina, la hermana. Ella desea estudiar en otro (*another*) estado. Por eso necesita el dinero.

REGALOS

1. la calculadora
2. los libros de literatura clásica
3. los discos compactos de Andrés Segovia
4. el televisor
5. el radio
6. el dinero

MIEMBROS DE LA FAMILIA

a. José, el padre: Le gusta escuchar las noticias (*news*).
b. Julián y María, los abuelos: Les gusta mucho la música de guitarra clásica.
c. Carmen, la madre: Le gusta mirar programas cómicos.
d. Joey, el hermano: Le gustan mucho las historias viejas.
e. Carmina, la hermana: Desea estudiar en otro estado.
f. Raulito, el primo: Le gustan las matemáticas.

Suggestions A
- Provide several additional models with simple explanations, using *porque* and *por eso.*
- Have students interview each other to find out what some of their classmates would like for their next birthday, anniversary, or Christmas. After students have completed interviews, have them report their findings back to the class. As a group, you might want to review numbers by discussing how much each gift may cost. Introduce words such as *caro/a* and *barato/a.*

Follow-up A
¿Qué son buenos/malos regalos para las madres? ¿Y para los padres? ¿Qué les regala Ud. a sus hermanos?

Answers A
1. f **2.** d **3.** b **4.** c **5.** a **6.** e

B. ¿Qué opinas? Exprese opiniones originales, afirmativas o negativas, con estas palabras.

(No) { Es importante / Es muy práctico / Es necesario / Es tonto (*foolish*) / Es fascinante / Es una lata (*pain, drag*) / Es posible }

mirar la televisión todos los días
hablar español en la clase
tener muchas mascotas
llegar (*to arrive*) a clase puntualmente
tomar cerveza en clase
hablar con los animales / las plantas
tomar mucho café y fumar cigarrillos
trabajar dieciocho horas al día
tener muchos hermanos
ser amable con todos los miembros de la familia
estar en las fiestas familiares
pasar mucho tiempo con la familia

Follow-up B
- Have students present information about themselves, their families, and where they are from. Remind them not to overuse *yo: Yo soy Phillip. Soy de Garfield Heights. Tengo tres hermanos y una hermana. Mis abuelos son de Rusia.*
- Have students present information about themselves in a brief composition, which you correct before they present it to the class.

Suggestions B
- Have students guess meaning of *fumar cigarrillos* from context.
- Present phrases such as *¿Ah sí? No me digas. ¿De veras? No, hombre,* and so on, for students to use to respond to answers given by others.
- Have students imagine that they are at a family party in their parent's house. Have them answer these questions: *¿A qué hora llegan todos? ¿Quién(es) llega(n) tarde? ¿Quién(es) no llega(n)? ¿Qué toman Uds.? ¿Es posible bailar? ¿cantar? ¿hablar con muchos parientes? ¿Es necesario ser amable con todos? ¿A qué hora termina la fiesta?*

5 Expressing Possession • Possessive Adjectives (Unstressed)*

La familia de Carlos IV (cuarto)

La familia de Carlos IV, un rey español del siglo XVIII. En el cuadro están *su* esposa, *sus* hijos… ¿y *sus* padres y *sus* abuelos? ¿Quiénes son las personas a la izquierda del rey?

¿Tiene Ud. una foto reciente de *su* familia? ¿Quiénes están en la foto?

La familia de Carlos IV, por Francisco de Goya (español)

You have already seen and used several possessive adjectives in Spanish. Here is the complete set.

Possessive Adjectives

my	**mi** libro/mesa **mis** libros/mesas	*our*	nuestr**o** libro nuestr**os** libros	nuestr**a** mesa nuestr**as** mesas
your	**tu** libro/mesa **tus** libros/mesas	*your*	vuestr**o** libro vuestr**os** libros	vuestr**a** mesa vuestr**as** mesas
your, his, her, its	**su** libro/mesa **sus** libros/mesas	*your, their*	**su** libro/mesa **sus** libros/mesas	

In Spanish, the ending of a possessive adjective agrees in form with the person or thing possessed, not with the owner or possessor. Note that these possessive adjectives are placed before the noun.

Son {mis / tus / sus} cuadernos.

The possessive adjectives **mi(s), tu(s),** and **su(s)** show agreement in number only with the nouns they modify. **Nuestro/a/os/as** and **vuestro/a/os/as,** like all adjectives that end in **-o**, show agreement in both number and gender.

Es {nuestra / vuestra / su} casa.

The possessive adjectives **vuestro/a/os/as** are used extensively in Spain, but are not common in Latin America.

Reciclado
Have students describe people they know using adjectives from this chapter and *Primeros pasos* (*Mis tíos son ricos.*).

Carlos IV's Family The family of Carlos IV, an 18th-century Spanish king. In the painting are his wife, his children . . . and his parents and grandparents? Who are the people to the left of the king?

*Another set of possessives are called the *stressed possessive adjectives.* They can be used as nouns. For information on them, see Appendix 2, Using Adjectives as Nouns.

OJO

Su(s) can have several different equivalents in English: *your* (*sing.*), *his, her, its, your* (*pl.*), and *their*. Usually its meaning will be clear in context. When context does not make the meaning of **su(s)** clear, **de** and a pronoun are used instead, to indicate the possessor.

el coche, la casa, los libros, las mesas } de él (de ella, de Ud., de ellos, de ellas, de Uds.)

¿Son jóvenes los hijos **de él**?
Are his children young?

¿Dónde vive el abuelo **de ellas**?
Where does their grandfather live?

Práctica

A. Posesiones. Which nouns can these possessive adjectives modify without changing form?

1. su: problema primos dinero tías escritorios familia
2. tus: perro idea hijos profesoras abuelo examen
3. mi: ventana médicos cuarto coche abuela gatos
4. sus: animales oficina nietas padre hermana abuelo
5. nuestras: guitarra libro materias lápiz sobrinas tía
6. nuestro: gustos consejeros parientes puerta clase residencia

typo

B. ¿Cómo es la familia de Carlos IV?

Paso 1. Mire la ilustración de Carlos IV y su familia en la página 64. Conteste según el modelo.

MODELO: familia / grande → Su familia es grande.

1. hijo pequeño / guapo
2. esposa / fea
3. retrato (*portrait*) / bueno
4. hijas / solteras
5. familia / importante y rica

Paso 2. Imagine que Ud. es Carlos IV. Cambie las respuestas (*answers*) del 1 al 3.

MODELO: hijo pequeño / guapo → Mi hijo pequeño es guapo.

Preliminary exercises A
- Have students give the forms orally: **1.** *Dé la forma singular: nuestras abuelas, sus universidades, tus amigos, vuestros consejeros.* **2.** *Dé la forma plural: nuestro profesor, nuestra clase, vuestro compañero, vuestra actividad, tu familia, su perro.*
- Have students relate possessives to their respective subject pronouns: *mi* → *yo* (*sus, tus, mi, nuestras, vuestros, su, tu*)

Answers A
1. *problema, dinero, familia* **2.** *hijos, profesores* **3.** *ventana, cuarto, coche, abuela* **4.** *animales, nietas* **5.** *materias, sobrinas* **6.** —

Variation B
Have students work in pairs to think of famous families, like presidents' families or those from TV programs, and to describe each member until classmates guess them correctly.

Answers B
- **Paso 1: 1.** *Su hijo es guapo.* **2.** *Su esposa es fea.* **3.** *Su retrato es bueno.* **4.** *Sus hijas son solteras.* **5.** *Su familia es importante y rica.*
- **Paso 2: 1.** *Mi...* **2.** *Mi...* **3.** *Mi...*

Conversación

Entrevista. This interview will help you gather more information about the families of your classmates and instructor. Use the questions as a guide to interview your instructor or a classmate (use **tú[s]**) and take notes on what he or she says. Then report the information to the class.

1. ¿Cómo es su familia? ¿Grande? ¿pequeña? ¿Cuántas personas hay?
2. ¿Son simpáticos sus padres? ¿generosos? ¿cariñosos (*caring*)?
3. ¿Cuántos hijos tienen (*have*) sus padres? ¿Cuántos años tienen?
4. ¿Cómo son sus hermanos? ¿Inteligentes? ¿traviesos (*mischievous*)? ¿trabajadores? ¿Estudian o trabajan? ¿Dónde?
5. ¿Tiene Ud. (*Do you have*) esposo/a (compañero/a de cuarto)? ¿Cómo es? ¿Trabaja o estudia?

Suggestion: Conversación
Remind students to use *tu* forms with classmates and *su* forms with the instructor. Also, students will need to use *su* forms to report information to the class about someone else (his/her/their).

Follow-up: Conversación
Have students make sentences using as many words and phrases as possible with the following nouns. MODELO: *nuestro país* → *Nuestro país es ______. (En nuestro país hay ______. En nuestro país uno puede* [can] *______.).* **1.** *nuestro país* **2.** *nuestra clase de español* **3.** *nuestra universidad (librería)* **4.** *nuestra ciudad (nuestro estado)* **5.** *el centro de nuestra ciudad*

Enfoque cultural

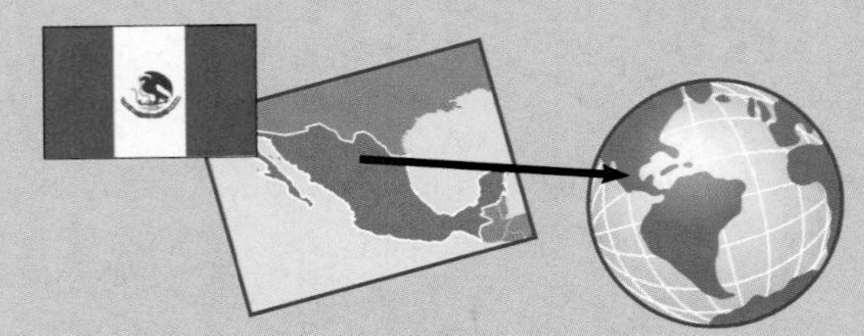

México

Enfoque cultural
See follow-up activities for this section in chapter-by-chapter materials in the IM.

Datos esenciales

Nombre oficial: Estados Unidos Mexicanos

Capital: la Ciudad de México, o México, Distrito Federal (el D.F.)

Población: 97.000.000 de habitantes

Moneda:[a] el nuevo peso

Idiomas:[b] el español (oficial), el zapoteca, el mixteca, el náhuatl, varios dialectos mayas

[a]*Currency* [b]*Languages*

¡Fíjese!

- México tiene 31 estados y el Distrito Federal.
- La población de México es aproximadamente: 25% indígena, 15% blanca y 60% mestiza (que se refiere a las personas de padres de razas indígena y blanca).
- Los indígenas mexicanos pertenecen a[a] grupos diversos: aztecas, mayas, zapotecas, mixtecas, olmecas y otros. La influencia de estas culturas indígenas contribuye a la diversidad y la riqueza de la cultura mexicana actual.[b]
- La ciudad de México ocupa el lugar del antiguo[c] Lago Texcoco. En el centro del lago estaba[d] Tenochtitlán, la capital del imperio azteca. Tenochtitlán era[e] una de las ciudades más grandes del mundo en el siglo XVI.[f]
- La Universidad Autónoma de México es una de las universidades más antiguas[g] de las Américas: es del año[h] 1551 (mil quinientos cincuenta y uno).

[a]pertenecen... *belong to* [b]*current* [c]*old, ancient* [d]*was* [e]*was* [f]siglo... *16th century* [g]más... *oldest* [h]es... *it dates from the year*

Multimedia: Internet
Have students search the Internet for more information and images of the ancient city of Tenochtitlán as well as on the Mexican muralists.

Conozca a... los grandes muralistas mexicanos

The Epic of American Civilization es un mural de Orozco. Está en Dartmouth College.

El muralismo es el estilo de pintura[a] que decora las paredes[b] de edificios públicos. Con su obra,[c] los muralistas desean enseñar la historia y la cultura de su país, y con frecuencia sus murales representan sus ideales políticos también.

Tres pintores mexicanos —Diego Rivera (1886–1957 [mil ochocientos ochenta y seis a mil novecientos cincuenta y siete]), José Clemente Orozco (1883–1949 [mil ochocientos ochenta y tres a mil novecientos cuarenta y nueve]) y David Alfaro Siqueiros (1898–1974 [mil ochocientos noventa y ocho a mil novecientos setenta y cuatro])— son probablemente los muralistas más famosos de hoy. Hay muchos murales de estos tres grandes muralistas por todo México.

[a]*painting* [b]*walls* [c]*work*

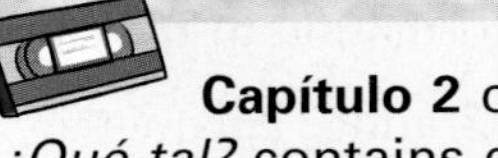

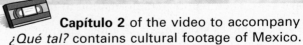

Capítulo 2 of the video to accompany *¿Qué tal?* contains cultural footage of Mexico.

Visit the *¿Qué tal?* website at www.mhhe.com/quetal.

Paso 3: Gramática

See detailed supplementary material for these grammar sections in IM.

6 Describing • Adjectives: Gender, Number, and Position

Un poema sencillo

Amigo
Fiel
Amable
Simpático
¡Lo admiro!

Amiga
Fiel
Amable
Simpática
¡La admiro!

According to their form, which of the adjectives below can be used to describe each person? Which can refer to you?

Marta: / Mario: { fiel   amable   simpática   simpático

Adjectives (**Los adjetivos**) are words used to talk about nouns or pronouns. Adjectives may describe or tell how many there are.

You have been using adjectives to describe people since **Primeros pasos**. In this section, you will learn more about describing the people and things around you.

adjective = a word used to describe a noun or pronoun

large *desk*   ***few*** *desks*
tall *woman*   ***several*** *women*

ADJECTIVES WITH *ser*

In Spanish, forms of **ser** are used with adjectives that describe basic, inherent qualities or characteristics of the nouns or pronouns they modify.

Tú **eres amable**.
You're nice. (*You're a nice person.*)

El diccionario **es barato**.
The dictionary is inexpensive.

A simple poem Friend Loyal Kind Nice I admire him/her!

FORMS OF ADJECTIVES

Spanish adjectives agree in gender and number with the noun or pronoun they modify. Each adjective has more than one form.

A. Adjectives that end in **-o** (**alto**) have four forms, showing gender and number.*

	Masculine	Feminine
Singular	amigo alt**o**	amiga alt**a**
Plural	amigos alt**os**	amigas alt**as**

B. Adjectives that end in **-e** (**inteligente**) or in most consonants (**fiel**) have only two forms, a singular and a plural form. The plural of adjectives is formed in the same way as that of nouns.

[Práctica A–C]

	Masculine	Feminine
Singular	amigo inteligente amigo fiel	amiga inteligente amiga fiel
Plural	amigos inteligente**s** amigos fiel**es**	amigas inteligente**s** amigas fiel**es**

C. Most adjectives of nationality have four forms.

The names of many languages—which are masculine in gender—are the same as the masculine singular form of the corresponding adjective of nationality **el español, el inglés, el alemán, el francés**, and so on.

[Práctica D]

OJO Note that in Spanish the names of languages and adjectives of nationality are not capitalized, but the names of countries are: **español, española**, but **España**.

	Masculine	Feminine
Singular	el doctor mexican**o** español alemán inglés	la doctor**a** mexican**a** español**a** aleman**a** ingles**a**
Plural	los doctor**es** mexican**os** español**es** leman**es** ingles**es**	las doctor**as** mexican**as** español**as** aleman**as** ingles**as**

PLACEMENT OF ADJECTIVES

As you have probably noticed, adjectives do not always precede the noun in Spanish as they do in English. Note the following rules for adjective placement.

A. Adjectives of quantity, like numbers, *precede* the noun, as do the interrogatives **¿cuánto/a?** and **¿cuántos/as?**

Hay **muchas** sillas y **dos** escritorios.
There are many chairs and two desks.

¿**Cuánto** dinero necesitas?
How much money do you need?

*Adjectives that end in **-dor, -ón, -án**, and **-ín** also have four forms: **trabajador, trabajador*a*, trabajador*es*, trabajador*as***.

OJO **Otro/a** by itself means *another* or *other.* The indefinite article is never used with **otro/a**.	Busco **otro** coche *I'm looking for another car.*
B. Adjectives that describe the qualities of a noun and distinguish it from others generally *follow* the noun. Adjectives of nationality are included in this category.	un perro **bueno** un dependiente **trabajador** una joven **delgada** y **morena** un joven **español**
C. The adjectives **bueno** and **malo** may precede or follow the noun they modify. When they precede a masculine singular noun, they shorten to **buen** and **mal**, respectively. [Práctica C]	un **buen** perro / un perro **bueno** una **buena** perra / una perra **buena** un **mal** día / un día **malo** una **mala** noche / una noche **mala**
D. The adjective **grande** may also precede or follow the noun. When it precedes a singular noun—masculine or feminine—it shortens to **gran** and means *great* or *impressive.* When it follows the noun, it means *large* or *big.* [Conversación]	Nueva York es una ciudad **grande**. *New York is a large city.* Nueva York es una **gran** ciudad. *New York is a great (impressive) city.*

FORMS OF *this/these*

A. The demonstrative adjective *this/these* has four forms in Spanish.* Learn to recognize them when you see them.	est**e** hijo — *this son* est**a** hija — *this daughter* est**os** hijos — *these sons* est**as** hijas — *these daughters*
B. You have already seen the neuter demonstrative **esto**. It refers to something that is as yet unidentified.	**¿Qué es esto?** *What is this?*

Práctica

A. La familia de José Miguel. For each item, choose the adjectives that can complete the statement logically.

1. El tío Miguel es _____. (trabajador/alto/nueva/grande/fea/amable)
2. Los abuelos son _____. (rubio/antipático/inteligentes/viejos/religiosos/sinceras)
3. Su madre es _____. (rubio/elegante/sentimental/buenas/simpática)
4. Las primas son _____. (solteras/morenas/lógica/bajos/mala)

*You will learn all forms of the Spanish demonstrative adjectives (*this, that, these, those*) in Grammar Section 8.

Answers A
1. *trabajador, alto, grande, amable* 2. *inteligentes, viejos, religiosos* 3. *elegante, sentimental, simpática* 4. *solteras, morenas*

Preliminary exercise A
Have students describe the following things. Cue students with questions and adjectives. 1. *¿Su famila?* → (*No*) *Es una familia grande.* (*interesante, importante, amable, intelectual*) 2. *¿Los perros?* → (*No*) *Son valientes.* (*fiel, impaciente, inteligente, importante*) 3. *¿Su universidad?* → (*No*) *Es nueva.* (*viejo, grande, pequeño, bueno, famoso, malo*)

Suggestion A
Have students correct the form of adjectives when inappropriate forms are provided.

PASO 3

CAPÍTULO 2

National Standards: Communication
Have students interview each other to determine at least 3 adjectives that best describe the interviewees. Have them report their findings about their classmates.

Vocabulario útil

Here are some adjectives to use in this section. You should be able to guess the meaning of some of them.

agresivo/a	¿ ?	**chistoso/a**	amusing	**sensible**	sensitive
amistoso/a	friendly	**comprensivo/a**	understanding	**suficiente**	¿ ?
animado/a	lively	**difícil**	difficult	**tolerante**	¿ ?
atrevido/a	daring	**encantador(a)**	delightful	**travieso/a**	mischievous
cariñoso/a	affectionate	**fácil**	easy		

Suggestion B
Have students correct statements given or provide their own.

Follow-up B
Have students describe family and family members: *Mi familia* (*no*) *es... Mi padre/madre* (*no*) *es... Mi ¿ ?* (*no*) *es... Mi gato/perro* (*no*) *es...*

Follow-up C
- Have students respond *cierto* or *falso:* **1.** *A Diego no le gusta estudiar.* **2.** *Diego es de Sudamérica.* **3.** *Le gustan los deportes.* **4.** *No habla español porque es norteamericano.*
- Have students change *Diego* to *Dolores* and change the text when possible to describe her as being the opposite of Diego. Then, change the subject of the paragraph to *Diego y Dolores.* ¡**OJO**! Help students make changes they do not yet know how to make, for example, *le gustan* → *les gustan* and *tiene* → *tienen.*

Extension D
Name famous people (imagine that they are all alive). Have students tell what language they speak and what their nationality is or where they are from. Examples: *Pablo Picasso, Napoleón, Antonio Banderas, Beethoven, Ricky Martin, Marc Anthony, Maria Callas y Renata Tebaldi, Pancho Villa, Juan y Eva Perón.*

Suggestions: Conversación
- Encourage students to give simple explanations using *porque* and *por eso.*
- Reenter or introduce expressions such as *¿Ah, sí? ¿De veras?* and so on, and encourage students to use them in their reactions.

B. **Hablando** (*Speaking*) **de la universidad.** Tell what you think about aspects of your university by telling whether you agree (**Estoy de acuerdo**.) or disagree (**No estoy de acuerdo**.) with the statements. If you don't have an opinion, say **No tengo opinión**.

1. Hay suficientes actividades sociales.
2. Los profesores son excelentes.
3. Las residencias son buenas.
4. Hay suficientes gimnasios.
5. Hay suficientes zonas verdes.
6. La cafetería es buena.
7. En la librería, los precios son bajos.
8. Los bibliotecarios son cooperativos.

C. **¡Dolores es igual!** Cambie Diego → Dolores.

Diego es un buen estudiante. Es listo y trabajador y estudia mucho. Es estadounidense de origen mexicano, y por eso habla español. Desea ser profesor de antropología. Diego es moreno, guapo y atlético. Le gustan las fiestas grandes y tiene buenos amigos en la universidad. Tiene parientes estadounidenses y mexicanos.

D. **Nacionalidades.** Tell what nationality the following people could be and where they might live: **Portugal, Alemania, China, Inglaterra, España, Francia, Italia**.

1. Monique habla francés; es francesa y vive (*she lives*) en Francia.
2. José habla español; es español y vive en España.
3. Greta y Hans hablan alemán; son alemanes y viven en Alemania.
4. Gilberto habla portugués; es portugués y vive en Portugal.
5. Gina y Sofía hablan italiano; son italianas y viven en Italia.
6. Winston habla inglés; es inglés y vive en Inglaterra.
7. Hai (*m.*) y Han (*m.*) hablan chino; son chinos y viven en China.

Conversación

Asociaciones: With several classmates, how many names can you associate with the following phrases? To introduce your suggestions, you can say **Creo que** (_____ **es un gran hombre**). To express agreement or disagreement, use (**No**) **Estoy de acuerdo**.

1. un mal restaurante
2. un buen programa de televisión
3. una gran mujer, un gran hombre
4. un buen libro, un libro horrible

¿Recuerda Ud.?

The personal endings used with **-ar** verbs share some characteristics of those used with **-er** and **-ir** verbs, which you will learn in the next section. Review the endings of **-ar** verbs by telling which subject pronoun(s) you associate with each of these endings.

1. -amos 2. -as 3. -áis 4. -an 5. -o 6. -a

W. Multimedia: Internet (Grammar Section 7)
Have students look up the website for *Universidad Autónoma Nacional de México.* Assign specific topics to different students or groups, for example, campus information, classes offered. Then have a class discussion comparing *UNAM* to your university or other universities in the United States and Canada.

7 Expressing Actions • Present Tense of *-er* and *-ir* Verbs; More about Subject Pronouns

Diego se presenta.

Hola. Me llamo Diego González. Soy estudiante de UCLA, pero este año *asisto* a la Universidad Nacional Autónoma de México. *Vivo* con mi tía Matilde en la Ciudad de México. *Como* pizza con frecuencia y *bebo* cerveza en las fiestas. Me gusta la ropa de moda; por eso *recibo* varios catálogos. *Leo* muchos libros de antropología para mi especialización. También *escribo* muchas cartas a mi familia. *Creo* que una educación universitaria es muy importante. Por eso estudio y *aprendo* mucho. ¡Pero *comprendo* también que es muy importante estar con los amigos y con la familia!

¿Es Diego un estudiante típico? ¿Cómo es Ud.? Adapte las oraciones de Diego a su conveniencia.

VERBS THAT END IN *-er* AND *-ir*

A. The present tense of **-er** and **-ir** verbs is formed by adding personal endings to the stem of the verb (the infinitive minus its **-er**/**-ir** ending). The personal endings for **-er** and **-ir** verbs are the same except for the first and second person plural.

comer (*to eat*)		**vivir** (*to live*)	
com**o**	com**emos**	viv**o**	viv**imos**
com**es**	com**éis**	viv**es**	viv**ís**
com**e**	com**en**	viv**e**	viv**en**

Diego introduces himself. Hello. My name is Diego González. I'm a student at UCLA, but this year I attend the Universidad Nacional Autónoma de México. I live with my aunt Matilde in Mexico City. I eat pizza frequently and I drink beer at parties. I like the latest fashions; that's why I receive various catalogues. I read lots of anthropology books for my major. I also write a lot of letters to my family. I think that a university education is very important. That's why I study and learn a lot. But I also understand that it's very important to be with friends and family!

B. Some frequently used **-er** and **-ir** verbs in this chapter include those on the right.

-er verbs		*-ir* verbs	
aprender	to learn	**abrir**	to open
beber	to drink	**asistir (a)**	to attend, go to (*a class, function*)
comer	to eat	**escribir**	to write
comprender	to understand	**recibir**	to receive
creer (en)	to think, believe (in)	**vivir**	to live
deber (+ *inf.*)	should, must, ought to (*do something*)		
leer	to read		
vender	to sell		

OJO Remember that the Spanish present tense has a number of present tense equivalents in English and can also be used to express future meaning.

como = *I eat, I am eating, I will eat*

USE AND OMISSION OF SUBJECT PRONOUNS

In English, a verb must have an expressed subject (a noun or pronoun): ***she*** *says,* ***the train*** *arrives*. In Spanish, however, as you have probably noticed, an expressed subject is not required. Verbs are accompanied by a subject pronoun only for clarification, emphasis, or contrast.

- *Clarification:* When the context does not make the subject clear, the subject pronoun is expressed. This happens most frequently with third person singular and plural verb forms.

  Ud./él/ella vende
  Uds./ellos/ellas venden

- *Emphasis:* Subject pronouns are used in Spanish to emphasize the subject when in English you would stress it with your voice.

  —¿Quién debe pagar?
  —¡**Tú** debes pagar!
  Who should pay?
  You *should pay!*

- *Contrast:* Contrast is a special case of emphasis. Subject pronouns are used to contrast the actions of two individuals or groups.

  Ellos leen mucho; **nosotros** leemos poco.
  They *read a lot;* ***we*** *read little.*

Preliminary exercises A
- Have students give the corresponding forms. ***yo:*** *aprender, vender, comprender, escribir,* ***tú:*** *comer, leer, beber, vivir* ***Ud./él/ella:*** *beber, creer, abrir, recibir* ***nosotros:*** *comprender, deber, asistir, vivir* ***vosotros:*** *deber, vener, aprender, abrir* ***Uds./ellos/ellas:*** *creer, leer, comer, escribir*
- Do a transformation activity: *Ud./tú* → *yo.* *¿Come Ud.?* → *Sí, como. ¿Comen Uds.?* → *Sí, comemos.*
- Have students state new sentences based on cues.

Preliminary exercise A
- Have students state new sentences based on cues.

En la sala de clase
1. *Yo asisto a clase todos los días.* (*tú, nosotros, Ud., todos los estu diantes, Carlos, vosotros*) 2. *Aprendes español en clase, ¿verdad?* (*nosotros, yo, Ud., la estudiante francesa, Uds., vosotros*) (continue

Práctica

A. En la clase de español

Paso 1. Read the following statements and tell whether they are true for your classroom environment. If any statement is not true for you or your class, make it negative or change it in another way to make it correct.

MODELO: Bebo café en clase. → Sí, bebo café en clase. (No, no bebo café en clase. Bebo café en casa.)

En una fiesta de Navidad **(Christmas)**
1. *Todos comen y beben.* (*yo, los tíos, tú, Uds., la prima y yo, Ud., vosotras*) 2. *Los niños reciben regalos.* (*papá, tú, nosotras, los hijos de Juan, Alicia, los nietos, vosotros*)

1. Debo estudiar más para esta clase.
2. Leo todas las partes de las lecciones.
3. Comprendo bien cuando mi profesor profesor(a) habla.
4. Asisto al laboratorio con frecuencia.
5. Debemos abrir más los libros en clase.
6. Escribimos mucho en esta clase.
7. Aprendemos a hablar español en esta clase.*
8. Vendemos nuestros libros al final del año (*year*).

Paso 2. Now turn to the person next to you and rephrase each sentence, using **tú** forms of the verbs. Your partner will indicate whether the sentences are true for him or her.

MODELO: Debes estudiar más para esta clase, ¿verdad (*right*)? →
Sí, debo estudiar más.
(No, no debo estudiar más.)
(No, debo estudiar más para la clase de matemáticas.)

B. Diego habla de su padre. Complete este párrafo con la forma correcta de los verbos entre paréntesis.

Mi padre (vender[1]) coches y trabaja mucho. Mis hermanos y yo (aprender[2]) mucho de papá. Según mi padre, los jóvenes (deber[3]) (asistir[4]) a clase todos los días, porque es su[a] obligación. Papá también (creer[5]) que no es necesario mirar la televisión por la noche. Es más interesante (leer[6]) el periódico[b] o un buen libro. Por eso nosotros (leer[7]) o (escribir[8]) por la noche y no miramos la televisión mucho. Yo admiro mucho a[†] mi papá y (creer[9]) que él (comprender[10]) la importancia de la educación.

[a]*their* [b]*newspaper*

C. Un sábado (*Saturday*) **en Sevilla.** Using all the cues given, form complete sentences about Manolo's narration about a certain Saturday at home with his family. Make any changes and add words when necessary. When the subject pronoun is in parentheses, do not use it in the sentence.

1. yo / leer / periódico
2. mi hija, Marta / mirar / televisión
3. también / (ella) escribir / composición
4. mi esposa, Lola / abrir / y / leer / cartas
5. ¡hoy / (nosotros) recibir / carta / tío Ricardo!
6. (él) ser de / España / pero / ahora / vivir / México
7. ¡ay! / ser / dos / de / tarde
8. ¡(nosotros) / deber / comer / ahora!

Extension A
Paso 1: 9. *Recibo muchos paquetes de mi familia.* **10.** *Como en* ______ (place) *por la noche.* **11.** *Vivo con mi familia este semestre/trimestre.* **12.** *Mi profesor(a) cree que yo debo estar en clase con más frecuencia.* **13.** *Debo aprender a leer más rápido.*

Follow-up A
Paso 2: Ask students about their partner's answers; they will use third person singular verbs.

Suggestions B
- Model pronunciation of each infinitive in paragraph. Use *yo* form of each in a brief simple sentence about yourself; then in *Ud.* and *Uds.* questions to students.
- Have students scan paragraph for meaning before attempting to do items. After individual items are done, have a volunteer read entire paragraph.

Point out B
Explain to students that the verb *asistir* is a false cognate.

Answers B
1. *vende* **2.** *aprendemos* **3.** *deben* **4.** *asistir* **5.** *cree* **6.** *leer* **7.** *leemos* **8.** *escribimos* **9.** *creo* **10.** *comprende*

Reciclado C
Review interrogative words from *Primeros pasos.* Give students an interrogative word for which they provide a full question.

Follow-up C
¿Quién lee el periódico? ¿Quién mira la televisión? ¿Quién abre y lee cartas? ¿Por qué reciben cartas del tío Ricardo? ¿De dónde es el tío Ricardo? ¿A qué hora come la familia de Manolo?

Note:* **aprender + **a** + infinitive = to learn how to (*do something*)
[†]Note the use of **a** here. In this context, the word **a** has no equivalent in English. It is used in Spanish before a direct object that is a specific person. You will learn more about this use of **a** in **Capítulo 6.** Until then, the exercises and activities in *¿Qué tal?* will indicate when to use it.

PASO 3

Note: Nota comunicativa
Use *casi nunca* and *nunca* at the beginning of a sentence only.

Conversación

Extension: Conversación
Have students add 3 original items before doing *Paso 2.*

NOTA COMUNICATIVA

Reciclado: Nota comunicativa
Todos los días and *con frecuencia* were presented in *Capítulo 1.*

Telling How Frequently You Do Things

Use the following words and phrases to tell how often you perform an activity. Some of them will already be familiar to you.

todos los días, siempre	every day, always	**una vez a la semana**	once a week
con frecuencia	frequently	**casi nunca**	almost never
a veces	at times	**nunca**	never

Hablo con mis amigos **todos los días.** Hablo con mis padres **una vez a la semana. Casi nunca** hablo con mis abuelos. Y **nunca** hablo con mis tíos que viven en Italia.

For now, use the expressions **casi nunca** and **nunca** only at the beginning of a sentence. You will learn more about how to use them in Grammar 18.

Follow-up: Conversación
- Have students interview their partner to obtain more specific information about items in *Paso 2.* Examples: *¿Cuál es tu pizzería favorita? ¿Qué recibes por correo, cartas o revistas?* and so on. Remind students to use *tu(s).*
- Have students prepare brief *informe oral* about their partner or about similarities and differences between themselves and their partner, using all the information they have learned about him/her.

¿Con qué frecuencia?

Paso 1. How frequently do you do the following things?

	CON FRECUENCIA	A VECES	CASI NUNCA	NUNCA
1. Asisto al laboratorio de lenguas (o uso las cintas [*tapes*]).	☐	☐	☐	☐
2. Recibo cartas.	☐	☐	☐	☐
3. Escribo poemas.	☐	☐	☐	☐
4. Leo novelas románticas.	☐	☐	☐	☐
5. Como en una pizzería.	☐	☐	☐	☐
6. Recibo y leo catálogos.	☐	☐	☐	☐
7. Aprendo palabras nuevas en español.	☐	☐	☐	☐
8. Asisto a todas mis clases.	☐	☐	☐	☐
9. Compro regalos para los amigos.	☐	☐	☐	☐
10. Vendo los libros al final del semestre/trimestre.	☐	☐	☐	☐

Paso 2. Now compare your answers with those of a classmate. Then answer the following questions. (*Note:* **los/las dos** = *both* [*of us*]; **ninguno/a** = *neither*)

	YO	MI COMPAÑERO/A	LOS/LAS DOS	NINGUNO/A
1. ¿Quién es muy estudioso/a?	☐	☐	☐	☐
2. ¿Quién come mucha pizza?	☐	☐	☐	☐
3. ¿Quién compra muchas cosas?	☐	☐	☐	☐
4. ¿Quién es muy romántico/a?	☐	☐	☐	☐
5. ¿Quién recibe mucho (*a lot*) por correo (*by mail*)?	☐	☐	☐	☐

Suggestion: En los Estados Unidos y el Canadá...
Encourage students to search the Internet for more information about the Sheen family. Have them write a brief description of each family member in Spanish, using adjectives listed in this chapter and cognates presented in *Primeros pasos.*

En los Estados Unidos y el Canadá...

Los Sheen, una familia de actores

Two generations of Sheens have made names for themselves in film and television. Martin Sheen, the father, was born Ramón Estévez in Dayton, Ohio (1940), to a Spanish father and an Irish mother. Martin explains that he felt he needed to change his Hispanic name in order to successfully pursue an acting career in the 1950s. In his heart, however, he says he is still Ramón. Martin's acting career spans several decades and includes important movies such as *Apocalypse Now.* Most recently, he stars as a U.S. president in the television series "The West Wing," which won several 2001 Emmy awards, including Best Drama Series.

Charlie Sheen, Martin Sheen y Emilio Estevez

Martin and his wife of more than 40 years, Janet Sheen, have four children—Emilio (1962), Ramón (1963), Carlos (1965), and Renée (1967)—all of whom have pursued acting careers. Emilio, who uses his father's original last name, Estévez, and Carlos, who is known as Charlie Sheen, are the most famous actors of the Sheen children.

UN POCO DE TODO

¿Existe la familia hispánica típica? Complete the following paragraphs about families. Give the correct form of the words in parentheses, as suggested by the context.

Muchas personas (creer[1]) que (todo[2]) las familias (hispánico[3]) son (grande[4]). Pero el concepto de la familia (ser[5]) diferente ahora, sobre todo[a] en las ciudades (grande[6]).

(Ser[7]) cierto que la familia rural (típico[8]) es grande, pero es así[b] en casi (todo[9]) las sociedades rurales del mundo.[c] Muchos hijos (trabajar[10]) la tierra[d] con sus padres. Por eso es bueno y (necesario[11]) tener muchos niños.

Pero en los grandes centros (urbano[12]) las familias con sólo dos o tres hijos (ser[13]) más comunes. Es difícil[e] tener (mucho[14]) hijos en una sociedad (industrializado[15]). Y cuando los padres (trabajar[16]) fuera de[f] casa, ellos (pagar[17]) mucho para cuidar a[g] los niños. Esto pasa especialmente en las familias de la clase media.[h]

Pero es realmente difícil (hablar[18]) de una familia (hispánico[19]) típica. ¿Hay una familia (norteamericano[20]) típica?

[a]sobre... *above all* [b]es... *that's the way it is* [c]*world* [d]*land* [e]*difficult* [f]fuera... *outside of the* [g]cuidar... *care for* [h]*middle*

Comprensión: ¿Cierto o falso? Corrija las oraciones falsas.

F **1.** Todas las familias hispánicas son iguales.
C **2.** Las familias rurales son grandes en casi todas partes del mundo.
C **3.** Las familias rurales necesitan muchos niños.
C **4.** Por lo general (*Generally*), las familias urbanas son más pequeñas.

Suggestion
Have students work in small groups to rewrite the paragraph to describe the "typical" view of U.S. or Canadian families. Compare paragraphs of different groups. In what ways are they similar? How are they different? Can students explain what accounts for their differences and similarities?

In the *Capítulo 2* segment of "Chapter-by-Chapter Supplementary Materials" in the IM, you will find a chapter-culminating activity. You can use this activity to consolidate and review the vocabulary and grammar skills students have acquired.

Answers
1. *creen* **2.** *todas* **3.** *hispánicas* **4.** *grandes* **5.** *es* **6.** *grandes* **7.** *Es* **8.** *típica* **9.** *todas* **10.** *trabajan* **11.** *necesario* **12.** *urbanos* **13.** *son* **14.** *muchos* **15.** *industrializada* **16.** *trabajan* **17.** *pagan* **18.** *hablar* **19.** *hispánica* **20.** *norteamericana*

Answers: Comprensión
1. *F: Es difícil hablar de una familia hispánica típica.* **2.** *C* **3.** *C* **4.** *C*

PASO 4 Un paso más

Paso 4: Un paso más
Optional section

See IM for suggestions and follow-up activities for this video segment.

Suggestion: En contexto
Ask the following questions to check comprehension: **1.** *¿A qué hora debe llegar Sabina al parque?* **2.** *¿Por qué no está Sabina en el parque?* **3.** *¿Cómo es Sabina?*

VIDEOTECA: En contexto

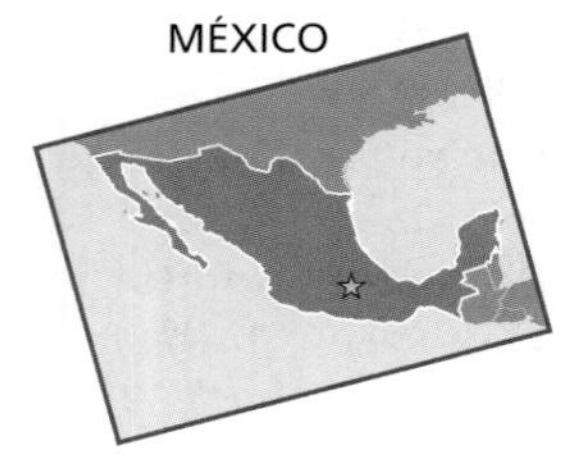

FUNCTION
Describing people

Cultura en contexto
La familia extendida

In Spanish-speaking countries, a first cousin is often called **primo hermano / prima hermana**. This is because they are children of siblings. The expression illustrates the close relationship among extended family members, that is, cousins, aunts, uncles, and so forth. Family members frequently live close to one another, which facilitates close-knit relationships.

Point out
Roberto and Martín are meeting Sabina in the park. Parks can be very centrally located in Hispanic cities, and they are places where people of all ages can be seen. Ask students: *¿Hay un parque como* (like) *este en su pueblo? Generalmente, ¿cómo son los parques de este país?*

In this video segment, Roberto and Martín are walking in the park, looking for Roberto's cousin Sabina. As you watch the segment, pay particular attention to the words the characters use to describe Sabina. How does Roberto describe her? Is this accurate?

Suggestion A
Have students describe themselves, as if they were describing themselves to someone who cannot see them.

A. Lluvia de ideas

- What words do you use most often to describe people physically? Do you generally describe their height or weight? Their eye and hair color? Other qualities?
- If you are arranging to meet someone you don't know in a public place, how do you describe yourself? What do you do to make sure that the two of you recognize each other? Do you wear a flower in your lapel? Do you identify yourself in some other way?

B. Dictado

Here is the first part of this segment's dialogue. Fill in the missing portions of Roberto's dialogue.

ROBERTO: No entiendo.[a] Ya ___son___[1] las tres. Mi prima Sabina ___debe___[2] estar aquí.
MARTÍN: No, todavía no[b] son las tres. ___Es___[3] temprano. Yo tengo las tres menos cinco.
ROBERTO: Ah, bueno.
MARTÍN: ¿Cómo es tu prima?
ROBERTO: Es una chica ___joven___;[4] tiene 16 años.
MARTÍN: Mira… la chica allí es joven. ¿Es Sabina?
ROBERTO: No, no es ___ella___.[5] Esa chica es ___rubia___.[6] Sabina es morena.
MARTÍN: Ajá.

[a]comprendo [b]todavía… *not yet*

C. Un diálogo original

Paso 1. With a classmate, reenact the situation between Roberto and Martín.

Paso 2. Then, imagine that you and a different classmate are looking for someone during a crowded party at your school. These are the roles:

E1: You are looking for a friend that you are supposed to meet at the party.
E2: You don't know the person that **Estudiante 1** is looking for. You ask questions about that person's appearance, to help find him or her.

PASO FINAL

A CONVERSAR

La familia y los amigos

Paso 1. Using the verbs and adjectives you have learned, write five sentences describing what your family members and friends do or what they are like.

MODELO: Mi padre trabaja mucho. Mi amigo John es perezoso.

Paso 2. Work with a partner to find out which of your family members and friends do the same thing or fit the same description. Use **¿Quién de tu familia... ?** (*Who in your family . . . ?*) and **¿Cuál de tus amigos... ?** (*Which of your friends . . . ?*) to get the information. If your answer to a question is *no one* or *none*, use **Nadie en mi familia es...** (*No one in my family is . . .*) or **Ninguno de mis amigos es...** (*Not one of my friends is . . .*).

MODELOS: E1: Mi padre trabaja mucho. ¿Quién de tu familia trabaja mucho?
E2: Mi tía Anita trabaja mucho. (OR: Nadie en mi familia trabaja mucho.) Pero mi amigo John es perezoso. ¿Cuál de tus amigos es perezoso?
E1: Mi amiga Raquel es perezosa. (OR: Ninguno de mis amigos es perezoso.)

Paso 3. Ask follow-up questions about information you learned.

MODELO: E1: ¿Dónde trabaja tu tía Anita?
E2: Trabaja en un hospital.

Paso 4. Compare notes with the rest of the class. Talk about your family and friends and what you learned about your partner's family and friends.

MODELO: La tía de Jorge, Anita, trabaja en un hospital. Ella trabaja mucho...

Suggestion: Paso 4
Tally or have a student tally the information on the board to make generalizations about the families and friends of the class.

Follow-up: A conversar
Have students ask additional questions about the people described: *¿Es doctora tu tía Anita? ¿Trabaja por la noche o por el día?*, and so on.

En resumen

GRAMÁTICA

To review the grammar points presented in this chapter, refer to the indicated grammar presentations. You'll find further practice of these structures in the Workbook/Laboratory Manual, on the CD-ROM, and on the website.

4. Present Tense of *ser;* Summary of Uses

Can you conjugate and use the irregular verb **ser** in the present tense?

5. Possessive Adjectives (Unstressed)

You should be able to recognize and use the possessive adjectives **mi, tu, su, nuestro**, and **vuestro**.

6. Adjectives: Gender, Number, and Position

You should know how to modify adjectives such as **alto, inteligente, español**, and **inglés** to agree with the nouns they describe, as well as where to place an adjective.

7. Present Tense of *-er* and *-ir* Verbs; More about Subject Pronouns

Can you conjugate verbs such as **comer** and **escribir** in the present tense? Do you know how to use subject pronouns and when to omit them?

VOCABULARIO

Los verbos

abrir	to open
aprender	to learn
asistir (a)	to attend, go to (*a class, function*)
beber	to drink
comer	to eat
comprender	to understand
creer (en)	to think, believe (in)
deber (+ *inf.*)	should, must, ought to (*do something*)
escribir	to write
leer	to read
llegar	to arrive
mirar	to look at, watch
mirar la televisión	to watch television
recibir	to receive
ser (*irreg.*)	to be
vender	to sell
vivir	to live

La familia y los parientes

el/la abuelo/a	grandfather/grandmother
los abuelos	grandparents
el/la esposo/a	husband/wife
el/la hermano/a	brother/sister
el/la hijo/a	son/daughter
los hijos	children
la madre (mamá)	mother (mom)
el/la nieto/a	grandson/granddaughter
el/la niño/a	small child; boy/girl
el padre (papá)	father (dad)
los padres	parents
el/la primo/a	cousin
el/la sobrino/a	niece/nephew
el/la tío/a	uncle/aunt

Las mascotas

el gato	cat
el pájaro	bird
el perro	dog

Suggestions: Vocabulario
- Have students make and exchange word puzzles.
- Play *hangman,* using family words and adjectives.
- Have student group adjectives in different ways (opposites, negative/positive).

Suggestions: Vocabulario

- Have students list adjectives that they associate with different nationalities. Encourage them to discuss whether or not these associations are stereotypical.
- To practice possessive adjectives, ask students questions about their family and possessions: *Su padre, ¿tiene coche? ¿Cuántos años tiene su coche? ¿Cuántos teléfonos hay en su casa? en la casa de sus padres?,* and so on.

Otros sustantivos

la carta	letter
la casa	house, home
la ciudad	city
el coche	car
el estado	state
el/la médico/a	(medical) doctor
el país	country
el periódico	newspaper
el regalo	present, gift
la revista	magazine

Los adjetivos

alto/a	tall
amable	kind; nice
antipático/a	unpleasant
bajo/a	short (*in height*)
bonito/a	pretty
buen, bueno/a	good
casado/a	married
corto/a	short (*in length*)
delgado/a	thin, slender
este/a	this
estos/as	these
feo/a	ugly
fiel	faithful
gordo/a	fat
gran, grande	large, big; great
guapo/a	handsome; good-looking
inteligente	intelligent
joven	young
largo/a	long
listo/a	smart; clever
mal, malo/a	bad
moreno/a	brunet(te)
mucho/a	a lot
muchos/as	many
necesario/a	necessary
nuevo/a	new
otro/a	other, another
pequeño/a	small
perezoso/a	lazy
pobre	poor
posible	possible
rico/a	rich
rubio/a	blond(e)
simpático/a	nice; likeable
soltero/a	single (*not married*)
todo/a	all; every
tonto/a	silly, foolish
trabajador(a)	hardworking
viejo/a	old

Los adjetivos de nacionalidad

alemán/alemana, español(a), francés/francesa, inglés/inglesa, mexicano/a, norteamericano/a

Los adjetivos posesivos

mi(s)	my
tu(s)	your (*fam. sing.*)
nuestro/a(s)	our
vuestro/a(s)	your (*fam. pl. Sp.*)
su(s)	his, hers, its, your (*form. sing.*); their, your (*form. pl.*)

Los números

treinta, cuarenta, cincuenta, sesenta, setenta, ochenta, noventa, cien (ciento)

¿Con qué frecuencia... ?

a veces	sometimes, at times
casi nunca	almost never
con frecuencia	frequently
nunca	never
siempre	always
una vez a la semana	once a week

Palabras adicionales

bueno...	well . . .
¿de dónde es Ud.?	where are you from?
¿de quién?	whose?
del	of the, from the
(no) estoy de acuerdo	I (don't) agree
para	(intended) for; in order to
¿por qué?	why?
porque	because
que	that; who
según	according to
si	if
tener (*irreg.*)... **años**	to be . . . years old

CAPÍTULO 3

De compras

Suggestion: Chapter Opening photo
Point out the chapter opening photo and have students talk about their own shopping experiences and ideas about shopping in Hispanic countries. Encourage them to describe the people in the photo.

Resources
You and your students may find the following *¿Qué tal?* supplements helpful as you teach this chapter:

For the Instructor
- *Instructor's Manual and Resource Kit*, "Chapter-by-Chapter" Supplementary Materials
- Testing Program
- Overhead Transparencies 22–27
- Video (VHS or CD)
- *¿Qué tal?* Online Learning Center Website
- Audioscript
- Instructor's Resource CD

For Students
- Workbook/Laboratory Manual and Audio Program or Electronic Workbook/ Laboratory Manual
- Video on CD
- Interactive CD-ROM
- *¿Qué tal?* Online Learning Center Website
- Listening Comprehension Audio CD
- McGraw-Hill Electronic Language Tutor (MHELT)

◀ Estas personas van de compras (*are going shopping*) en el Metrocentro, un centro comercial en Managua, Nicaragua.

VOCABULARIO

- Shopping and clothing
- Numbers over 100
- Colors

GRAMÁTICA

8 Demonstrative Adjectives
9 **Tener, venir, preferir, querer,** and **poder**; Some Idioms with **tener**
10 **Ir; ir** + **a** + Infinitive; The Contraction **al**

CULTURA

- **Enfoque cultural:** Nicaragua
- **Nota cultural:** Clothing in the Hispanic World
- **En los Estados Unidos y el Canadá:** Los hispanos en el mundo de la moda (*fashion*)
- **Cultura en contexto:** Hispanic Currencies

Multimedia

You will learn more about shopping for clothes in the **En contexto** video segment.

Review vocabulary and grammar and practice language skills with the interactive CD-ROM.

Get connected to the Spanish-speaking world with the *¿Qué tal?* Online Learning Center: **www.mhhe.com/quetal**.

Vocabulario PASO 1

❖ Transparencies 22–23

De… *Shopping: Clothing*

De compras: La ropa°

Multimedia: Audio
Students can listen to and practice this chapter's vocabulary on their Listening Comprehension Audio CD.

Los verbos

comprar	to buy
llevar	to wear; to carry; to take
regatear	to haggle, bargain
usar	to wear; to use
vender	to sell
venden de todo	they sell (have) everything

Los lugares

el almacén	department store
el centro	downtown
el centro comercial	shopping mall
el mercado	market(place)
la tienda	shop, store

¿Cuánto cuesta?

la ganga	bargain
el precio	price
el precio fijo	fixed (set) price
las rebajas	sales
barato/a	inexpensive
caro/a	expensive

Otras expresiones útiles

un par de (zapatos, medias,…)	a pair of (shoes, stockings, . . .)
es de (lana, algodón, seda)†	it is made of (wool, cotton, silk)
¡Es de última moda!	It's the latest style!

¿Qué más?

la bolsa	purse
las botas	boots
la cartera	wallet
las sandalias	sandals
el traje	suit
el traje de baño	swimsuit
el vestido	dress
los zapatos de tenis	tennis shoes

*The influx of North American goods to Latin America and Spain has affected common language. *Jeans* is one example of an English word that is commonly used in Spanish-speaking countries.
†Note another use of **ser** + **de**: to tell what material something is made of.

Paso 1: Vocabulario
See detailed supplementary materials and exercises for this section and a model for vocabulary presentation and other material in the *Capítulo 3 Paso 1: Vocabulario* section of "Chapter-by-Chapter Supplementary Materials," IM.

PASO 1

Extension A
Have students give appropriate clothing (*ropa apropiada*): *¿Para los yuppies? ¿los cantantes* country-western*? ¿los líderes militares? ¿los detectives? ¿los personajes* (characters) *bíblicos?*

❖ **Transparency 24**

Conversación

A. La ropa. ¿Qué ropa llevan estas personas?

Follow-up A
Ask: *De estas personas, ¿quién trabaja hoy? ¿Quién va a* (is going to) *una fiesta? ¿Quién no trabaja en este momento?*

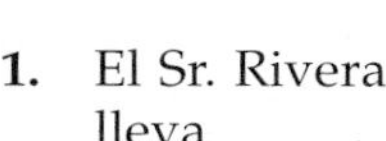

1. El Sr. Rivera lleva ______.
2. La Srta. Alonso lleva ______. El perro lleva ______.
3. Sara lleva ______.
4. Alfredo lleva ______. Necesita comprar ______.

Follow-up B
Have students answer the following questions: **1.** *¿Dónde compra Ud. la ropa generalmente, en una tienda o en un almacén?* **2.** *En esta ciudad, ¿hay tiendas o mercados donde regateen los clientes? ¿donde haya buenas rebajas?* **3.** *¿Lleva Ud. ___ hoy?* **4.** *¿Necesita Ud. comprar ropa nueva? ¿Qué necesita comprar? ¿Qué tipo de ropa compra con más frecuencia?* **5.** *Imagine que Ud. es un profesor conservador / un estudiante típico / el presidente / un famoso artista de Hollywood. ¿Qué lleva hoy?* **6.** *Por lo general, ¿le gusta llevar ropa elegante o ropa vieja?*

B. Asociaciones. Complete las oraciones lógicamente.

1. Un ___almacén___ es una tienda grande.
2. No es posible ___regatear___ cuando hay precios fijos.
3. En la librería, ___venden___ de todo: libros, cuadernos, lápices, cintas (*tapes*). Hay grandes ___rebajas___ ahora y todo es muy barato.
4. Siempre hay *boutiques* en los ___centros comerciales___.
5. El ___centro___ de una ciudad es la parte céntrica.
6. Estos artículos de ropa no son para hombres: ___Answers will vary.___.
7. Estos artículos de ropa son para hombres y mujeres: ___Answers will vary.___.
8. La ropa de ___seda___ (*material*) es muy elegante.
9. La ropa de ___algodón___ es muy práctica.

Vocabulario útil

Use the preposition **para** followed by an infinitive to express *in order to.*

Para llegar al centro, tomo el autobús número 16.
(In order) To get downtown, I take the number 16 bus.

C. ¿Qué lleva Ud.? Para hablar de Ud. y de la ropa, complete estas oraciones lógicamente.

1. Para ir (*go*) a la universidad, me gusta usar ______.
2. Para ir a las fiestas con los amigos, me gusta usar ______.
3. Para pasar un día en la playa (*beach*), me gusta llevar ______.
4. Cuando estoy en casa todo el día, llevo ______.
5. Nunca uso ______.
6. ______ es un artículo de ropa absolutamente necesario.

Suggestion: Nota cultural

Poll students to find out what they typically wear to classes. Then ask those who work in office environments how they are expected to dress there. What are the tendencies of those in the class, to dress more formally or more casually?

NOTA CULTURAL

Clothing in the Hispanic World

In Hispanic countries, people tend to dress more formally than do people in this country. As a rule, Hispanics consider neatness and care for one's appearance to be very important.

In the business world, women wear dressy pants, skirts, or dresses, and many wear high-heeled shoes. Men generally dress in trousers, shirts, and ties. Jeans, T-shirts, and tennis shoes are considered inappropriate in traditional business environments. Students at some business schools, like ESAN (**Escuela de administración de negocios**) in Peru, are even required to wear formal business attire to attend classes as if they were already working at a company. Shorts and sweatpants are considered very casual and are reserved almost exclusively for use at home, for a day at the beach, or for sports.

Young adults generally dress casually in social situations, and as in other countries, are often concerned with dressing according to current styles. As a rule, what is considered stylish in this country is also in style in Europe and Latin America.

Ropa diseñada por (*designed by*) la famosa venezolana Carolina Herrera

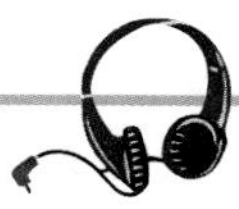

¿De qué color es?

Here are colors and other helpful phrases you can use to describe clothing and other objects.

amarillo/a	yellow
anaranjado/a	orange
azul	blue
blanco/a	white
gris	gray
morado/a	purple
negro/a	black
pardo/a	brown
rojo/a	red
rosado/a	pink
verde	green

National Standards: Connections

Gonzalo Endara Crow was born in Bucay, Ecuador, in 1936 and died in 1996. He was interested in popular art and was inspired by the artisans of his native country. In his work, one can see the bright colors and naïve approach present in Ecuador's pottery and textiles.

¿Cuántos colores hay en este cuadro (*painting*) de Gonzalo Endara Crow? ¿Cuáles son?

Después de (After) *la noche*, por Gonzalo Endara Crow (ecuatoriano)

Otras frases útiles

de cuadros	plaid
de lunares	polka-dotted
de rayas	striped

OJO

Note that some colors only have one form for masculine and feminine nouns.

el traje **azul**, la camisa **azul**

❖ Transparency 25

Note A
Point out that the adjective *alerta* is used to modify both masculine and feminine nouns.

Expansion A
Have students describe differences between these department stores: J.C. Penney's, Saks Fifth Avenue, Macy's, and K-Mart.

Follow-up A
Dictate the following items for students to write down: **1.** *una camisa negra* **2.** *un impermeable viejo* **3.** *medias blancas* **4.** *una falda de cuadros* **5.** *una camisa de rayas* **6.** (colors of your university) **7.** *una camisa o chaqueta verde militar*, and so on. After the dictation, ask students which items from the dictation they associate with the following: **1.** *un detective famoso de la televisión* **2.** *una persona que se llama Scottie McTavish* **3.** *un cantante* (country-western) **4.** *un estudiante de* (university) **5.** *un grupo de beisbolistas* **6.** *un prisionero* **7.** *Fidel Castro*

Suggestion B
Have students bring a copy of their favorite painting (or choose one in *¿Qué tal?*) and explain colors and clothing (if any) they see in it. Have them explain why they like the painting.

Conversación

A. ¿Escaparates idénticos? These showcase windows are almost alike . . . but not quite! Can you find at least eight differences between them? In Spanish, activities like this one are often called **¡Ojo alerta!** (*Eagle eye!*).

MODELO: En el dibujo A hay ____, pero en el dibujo B hay ____.

A.

B.

B. ¿De qué color es?

Paso 1. Tell the color of things in your classroom, especially the clothing your classmates are wearing.

MODELO: El bolígrafo de Anita es amarillo. Roberto lleva calcetines azules, una camisa de cuadros morados y azules, *jeans*…

Paso 2. Now describe what someone in the class is wearing, without revealing his or her name. Using your clues, can your classmates guess whom you are describing?

C. Asociaciones. ¿Qué colores asocia Ud. con… ?

1. el dinero
2. la una de la mañana
3. una mañana bonita
4. una mañana fea
5. el demonio
6. los Estados Unidos
7. una jirafa
8. un pingüino
9. un limón
10. una naranja
11. un elefante
12. las flores (*flowers*)

Más allá del° número 100

Más... *Beyond the*

Continúe la secuencia:

noventa y nueve, cien, ciento uno,...
mil, dos mil,...
un millón, dos millones,...

100	cien, ciento	500	quinientos/as	1.000*	mil
101	ciento uno/una	600	seiscientos/as	2.000	dos mil
200	doscientos/as	700	setecientos/as	1.000.000	un millón
300	trescientos/as	800	ochocientos/as	2.000.000	dos millones
400	cuatrocientos/as	900	novecientos/as		

- **Ciento** is used in combination with numbers from 1 to 99 to express the numbers 101 through 199: **ciento uno, ciento dos, ciento setenta y nueve**, and so on. **Cien** is used in counting and before numbers greater than 100: **cien mil, cien millones**.
- When the numbers 200 through 900 modify a noun, they must agree in gender: **cuatrocientas niñas, doscientas dos casas**.
- **Mil** means *one thousand* or *a thousand*. It does not have a plural form in counting, but **millón** does. When used with a noun, **millón** (**dos millones**, and so on) must be followed by **de**.

3.000 habitantes	tres mil habitantes
14.000.000 **de** habitantes	catorce millones de habitantes

- Note how years are expressed in Spanish.

1899	mil ochocientos noventa y nueve
2002	dos mil dos

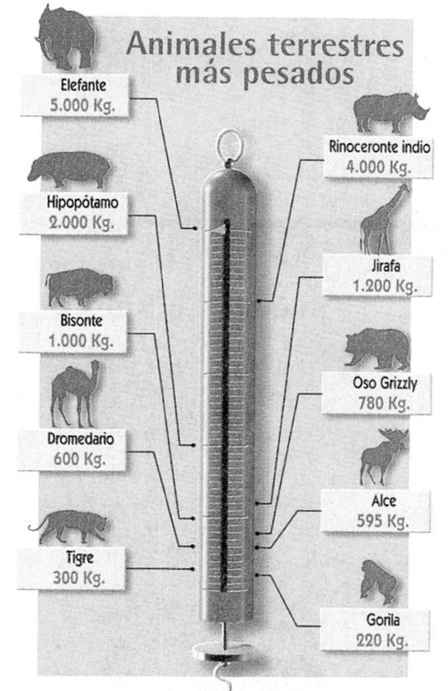

De los animales terrestres, el elefante, con sus 5.000 kilos de peso medio entre todas sus especies, es sin duda el mamífero más pesado. El hipopótamo y el rinoceronte son los siguientes en la lista, y el hombre, ni aparece.

Conversación

A. ¿Cuánto pesan? (*How much do they weigh?*) Mire el gráfico que acompaña (*to accompany*) la presentación del vocabulario. ¿Cuánto pesan los animales en kilos? **¡OJO!** Use el artículo masculino para todos los nombres, menos para (*except for*) los nombres que terminan (*that end*) en **-a**.

B. ¿Cuánto es? Diga los precios.

el dólar (los Estados Unidos, el Canadá, Puerto Rico), el nuevo peso (México), el bolívar (Venezuela), el euro† (España), el quetzal (Guatemala)

1. 750 euros	**4.** 670 bolívares	**7.** 836 bolívares
2. $100	**5.** $1.000.000	**8.** 101 euros
3. 5.710 quetzales	**6.** 528 nuevos pesos	**9.** $4.000.000,00

Preliminary exercises A
- Dictate numbers in Spanish as students write digits: **1.** *100, 50, 60* **2.** *400, 600, 800* **3.** *2.000, 1.000.000, 50.000* **4.** *150, 500, 1.500* **5.** *660, 960, 760*
- Write numbers on board and model them. Then have students say them. **1.** *2, 12, 20, 200* **2.** *3, 13, 30, 300* **3.** *4, 14, 40, 400,* and so on.

Note A
To convert kilograms to pounds, use the following formula: *kilogram × 2.2 = lbs.)*

Follow-up A
Have students give the weight of the following things: **1.** *su perro/gato* **2.** *su mochila* **3.** *su coche* **4.** *su libro de español* **5.** *el animal terrestre más grande del mundo*

*In many parts of the Spanish-speaking world, a period in numerals is used where English uses a comma, and a comma is used to indicate the decimal where English uses a period: **$10,45; 65,9%**.
†As of January 1, 2002, the **euro** became the official monetary unit of Spain and 11 other European countries.

Paso 2: Gramática
See detailed supplementary materials for these grammar sections in IM.

¿Recuerda Ud.?

You have already used the forms of **este** (*this*), one of the Spanish demonstrative adjectives. Review them by describing objects near you and the clothes you are wearing.

MODELO: Esta camisa es de rayas. Estos lápices son amarillos.

8 Pointing Out People and Things • Demonstrative Adjectives

Suéteres a buenos precios

VENDEDOR: *Estos* suéteres de aquí cuestan 150 pesos y *ese* suéter en su mano cuesta 250 pesos.
SUSANA: ¿Por qué es más caro *este*?
VENDEDOR: Porque *esos* son de pura lana virgen, de excelente calidad.
SUSANA: ¿Y *aquellos* suéteres de rayas?
VENDEDOR: *Aquellos* cuestan cien pesos solamente; son acrílicos.

¿Quién habla, Susana, Jorge o el vendedor?

1. Me gustan estos suéteres de rayas, y sólo cuestan cien pesos.
2. Señores, miren (*look at*) estos suéteres rojos. Cuestan 150 pesos.
3. Voy a (*I am going*) comprar este suéter. Me gusta la ropa de lana.
4. Este suéter acrílico es más barato que aquel suéter de lana.

Singular			Plural		
this	este libro	esta mesa	*these*	estos libros	estas mesas
that	ese libro	esa mesa	*those*	esos libros	esas mesas
	aquel libro (allí)	aquella mesa (allí)		aquellos libros (allí)	aquellas mesas (allí)

Sweaters at good prices SALESMAN: These sweaters here cost 150 pesos and that sweater in your hand costs 250 pesos. SUSANA: Why is this one more expensive? SALESMAN: Because those are of pure virgin wool, of excellent quality. SUSANA: What about those striped sweaters over there? SALESMAN: Those cost only one hundred; they are acrylic.

OJO **est*e*** *but* **est*os*, es*e*** *but* **es*os*** (no **o** in the masculine singular forms)

Demonstrative adjectives (**los adjetivos demostrativos**) are used to point out or indicate a specific noun or nouns. In Spanish, demonstrative adjectives precede the nouns they modify. They also agree in number and gender with the nouns.

est**e** cuaderno	*this notebook*
es**a** cas**a**	*that house*
aquell**os** chic**os**	*those boys (over there)*

- There are two ways to say *that/those* in Spanish. Forms of **ese** refer to nouns that are not close to the speaker in space or in time. Forms of **aquel** are used to refer to nouns that are even farther away.

Este niño es mi hijo. **Ese** joven es mi hijo también. Y **aquel** señor allí es mi esposo.
This boy is my son. That young man is also my son. And that man over there is my husband.

- To express English *this one* (*that one*), just drop the noun.

este coche y **ese**
this car and that one

aquella casa y **esta***
that house (over there) and this one

- Use the neuter demonstratives **esto, eso**, and **aquello** to refer to as yet unidentified objects or to a whole idea, concept, or situation.

¿Qué es **esto**?
What is this?

Eso es todo.
That's it. That's all.

¡**Aquello** es terrible!
That's terrible!

Preliminary exercise A
Have students respond: **1.** *Dé el plural de* (point to or hold up objects)*: este lápiz, este libro, este bolígrafo, esta mesa, esta bolsa, esta carta.* **2.** *Dé el singular de* (point to or hold up objects)*: estos libros, estos bolígrafos*, and so on. **3.** *Dé el plural de* (point to articles of clothing worn by students)*: ese zapato, ese traje, ese abrigo, esa chaqueta, esa falda, esa camisa*, and so on. Expand to practice with other objects and articles of clothing in the classroom.

Práctica

A. Comparaciones

Paso 1. Restate the sentences, changing forms of **este** to **ese** and adding **también**, following the model.

MODELO: Este abrigo es muy grande. →
Ese abrigo también es muy grande.

1. Esta falda es muy pequeña.
2. Estos pantalones son muy largos.
3. Este libro es muy bueno.
4. Estas corbatas son muy feas.

Answers A
Paso 1: **1.** *Esa falda...* **2.** *Esos pantalones...* **3.** *Ese libro...* **4.** *Esas corbatas... Paso 2:* **1.** *Aquella* **2.** *Aquellos* **3.** *Aquel* **4.** *Aquellas*

Follow-up A
Have students point out things in class using demonstratives. Students must repeat appropriate form of demonstrative to doublecheck comprehension, for example, *Esa ventana es grande. → ¿Esta/Esa/Aquella ventana? → Sí, esa.*

Reciclado A
Ask personalized questions regarding items in classroom. Use possessive as well as demonstrative adjectives. Have students respond with correct statements: *¿Es ese mi lápiz, ____? → No, este es el lápiz de ____. ¿Son estos libros de los estudiantes de filosofía? → No, son nuestros libros.* Emphasize the *de* + noun in case of ambiguity.

---

*Some Spanish speakers prefer to use accents on these forms: **este coche y ése, aquella casa y ésta**. However, it is acceptable in modern Spanish, per the **Real Academia Española** in Madrid, to omit the accent on these forms when context makes the meaning clear and no ambiguity is possible. To learn more about these forms, consult Appendix 2, Using Adjectives as Nouns.

Variation B
Have students provide cues similar to those given in items 1–5 to other students, who then react appropriately.

Paso 2. Now change the forms of **este** to **aquel**.

MODELO: Este abrigo es muy grande. →
Aquel abrigo también es muy grande.

B. Situaciones. Find an appropriate response for each situation.

Posibilidades: ¡Eso es un desastre!, ¿Qué es esto?, ¡Eso es magnífico!, ¡Eso es terrible!

1. Aquí hay un regalo para Ud.
2. Ocurre un accidente en la cafetería: Ud. tiene tomate en su camisa favorita.
3. No hay clases mañana.
4. La matrícula cuesta más este semestre/trimestre.
5. Ud. tiene una A en su examen de español.

Suggestion: Conversación
Ask the following questions. **1.** *¿Qué va a hacer Ud. esta noche? ¿Y este fin de semana?* **2.** *¿Cómo es esta universidad? ¿Cómo es esta clase? Y este libro, ¿cómo es?* **3.** *¿Cómo es esta ciudad? ¿Y este estado?* **4.** *¿Cómo se llama el decano* (dean) *de esta facultad? ¿el rector* (president) *de esta universidad? ¿el presidente / primer ministro de este país?* **5.** *¿Cuántos estados hay en este país?* **6.** *¿Tiene Ud. muchos exámenes esta semana? ¿Tiene que estudiar mucho esta noche?*

❖ **Transparency 26**

Conversación

Una tarde en un patio mexicano

Paso 1. ¿A qué parte del dibujo se refieren las siguientes oraciones? Habla la mujer de los zapatos verdes.

Answers: Conversación
1. 3 **2.** 1 **3.** 2 **4.** 3

1. Aquella mujer es de Cuernavaca.
2. Estas plantas son un regalo de un amigo chileno.
3. Ese pájaro habla inglés y español.
4. Aquel joven es un primo de Taxco.

Paso 2. Ahora, con un compañero/una compañera, imagine que Uds. son otras personas en el dibujo e inventen oraciones sobre el dibujo.

9 Expressing Actions and States • *Tener, venir, preferir, querer,* and *poder;* Some Idioms with *tener*

Una gorra para José Miguel, después de mirar en tres tiendas

ELISA: ¿Qué gorra *prefieres*, José Miguel?
JOSÉ MIGUEL: *Prefiero* la gris.
ELISA: ¡Pero ya *tienes* una gris, y es casi idéntica!
JOSÉ MIGUEL: Pues, no *quiero* esas otras gorras. *¿Podemos* mirar en la tienda anterior otra vez?
ELISA: ¿Otra vez? Bueno, si realmente insistes…

Comprensión: ¿Sí o no?

1. José Miguel quiere comprar una corbata.
2. Él prefiere la gorra azul.
3. No puede decidir entre las gorras.
4. Parece que (*It seems that*) Elisa tiene mucha paciencia.

tener (*to have*)	**venir** (*to come*)	**preferir** (*to prefer*)	**querer** (*to want*)	**poder** (*to be able, can*)
tengo	vengo	prefiero	quiero	puedo
tienes	vienes	prefieres	quieres	puedes
tiene	viene	prefiere	quiere	puede
tenemos	venimos	preferimos	queremos	podemos
tenéis	venís	preferís	queréis	podéis
tienen	vienen	prefieren	quieren	pueden

- The **yo** forms of **tener** and **venir** are irregular.
- In other forms of **tener, venir, preferir,** and **querer,** when the stem vowel **e** is stressed, it becomes **ie**.
- Similarly, the stem vowel **o** in **poder** becomes **ue** when stressed. In vocabulary lists these changes are shown in parentheses after the infinitive: **poder (ue)**. You will learn more verbs of this type in Grammar 12.

Irregularities:
tener: yo tengo, tú tienes (e → ie)…
venir: yo vengo, tú vienes (e → ie)…
preferir, querer: (e → ie)
poder: (o → ue)

OJO **Nosotros** and **vosotros** forms for these verbs do not have irregular changes.

A cap for José Miguel, after looking in three stores ELISA: Which cap do you prefer, José Miguel? JOSÉ MIGUEL: I prefer the gray one. ELISA: But you already have a gray one, and it's almost identical! JOSÉ MIGUEL: Well, I don't want those other caps. Can we look in the previous store again? ELISA: Again? Well, if you really insist . . .

SOME IDIOMS WITH *tener*

A. Many ideas expressed in English with the verb *to be* are expressed in Spanish with *idioms* (**los modismos**) using **tener**. You have already used one **tener** idiom: **tener... años**. At the right are some additional ones. Note that they describe a condition or state that a person can experience.

OJO: Idiomatic expressions are often different from one language to another. For example, in English, *to pull Mary's leg* usually means *to tease her*, not *to grab her leg and pull it*. In Spanish, *to pull Mary's leg* is **tomarle el pelo a Mary** (literally, *to take hold of Mary's hair*).

tener miedo (de)	to be afraid (of)
tener prisa	to be in a hurry
(no) tener razón	to be right (wrong)
tener sueño	to be sleepy

Preliminary exercises A

- Have students imagine that it is exam week and the following situations take place. Have them give new sentences based on cues: **1.** *Sara tiene muchos exámenes.* (*Pepe, nosotros, Alicia y Carlos, yo, tú, vosotras*) **2.** *Ramón viene a la biblioteca todas las noches. Prefiere estudiar aquí.* (*yo, los estudiantes, tú, Uds., nosotras, vosotros*) **3.** *Silvia quiere estudiar más, pero no puede.* (*yo, ella, nosotros, todos, tú, vosotros*)
- Have students answer questions based on cues: **1.** *¿Qué tiene Ud. que hacer* (to do) *esta noche?* → *Tengo que llegar a casa temprano.* (*asistir a una clase a las siete, aprender unas palabras en español, estudiar el Capítulo 3, leer toda la noche, hablar con un amigo, ¿ ?*) **2.** *Pero, ¿qué tiene ganas de hacer?* → *Tengo ganas de descansar.* (*abrir una botella de vino, mirar la televisión, comer en un buen restaurante, ¡no estudiar más!, ¿ ?*)

B. Other **tener** idioms include **tener ganas de** (*to feel like*) and **tener que** (*to have to*). The infinitive is always used after these two idiomatic expressions.

OJO: Note that the English translation of one of these examples results in a verb ending in *-ing*, not the infinitive.

Tengo ganas de **comer**.
I feel like eating.

¿No tiene Ud. que **leer** este capítulo?
Don't you have to read this chapter?

Follow-up: Nota comunicativa

- Ask: *¿Cuál es el antónimo de* mucho/a(s)?
- Have students give sentences using *poco/a(s)*.

adverb = a word that modifies a verb, adjective, or another adverb

NOTA COMUNICATIVA

Using *mucho* and *poco*

In the first chapters of *¿Qué tal?*, you have used the words **mucho** and **poco** as both adjectives and adverbs. *Adverbs* (**Los adverbios**) are words that modify verbs, adjectives, or other adverbs: ***quickly***, ***very*** *smart*, ***very*** *quickly*. In Spanish and in English, adverbs are invariable in form. However, in Spanish adjectives agree in number and gender with the word they modify.

ADVERB

Rosario estudia **mucho** hoy.	*Rosario is studying a lot today.*
Julio come **poco**.	*Julio doesn't eat much.*

ADJECTIVE

Rosario tiene **mucha** ropa. Sobre todo tiene **muchos** zapatos.	*Rosario has a lot of clothes. She especially has a lot of shoes.*
Julio come **poca** carne. Come **pocos** postres.	*Julio doesn't eat much meat. He eats few desserts.*

Práctica

A. ¡Sara tiene mucha tarea (*homework*)**!**

Paso 1. Haga oraciones con las palabras indicadas. Añada (*Add*) palabras si es necesario.

1. Sara / tener / muchos exámenes
2. (ella) venir / a / universidad / todos los días
3. hoy / trabajar / hasta (*until*) / nueve / de / noche
4. preferir / estudiar / en/ biblioteca
5. querer / leer / más / pero / no poder
6. por eso / regresar / a / casa
7. tener / ganas de / leer / más
8. pero / unos amigos / venir a mirar / televisión
9. Sara / decidir / mirar / televisión / con ellos

Paso 2. Now retell the same sequence of events, first as if they had happened to you, using **yo** as the subject of all but sentence number 8, then as if they had happened to you and your roommate, using **nosotros/as**.

B. Situaciones. Expand the situations described in these sentences by using an appropriate idiom with **tener**. There is often more than one possible answer.

MODELO: Tengo un examen mañana. Por eso... → Por eso tengo que estudiar mucho.

1. ¿Cuántos años? ¿Cuarenta? No, yo...
2. Un perro grande y feo vive en esa casa. Por eso yo...
3. ¿Ya son las tres de la mañana? Ah, por eso...
4. No, dos y dos no son cinco. Son cuatro. Tú...
5. Tengo que estar en el centro a las tres. Ya (*Already*) son las tres menos cuarto. Yo...
6. Cuando hay un terremoto (*earthquake*), todos...
7. ¿Los exámenes de la clase de español? ¡Esos son siempre muy fáciles! Yo no...
8. Sí, la capital de la Argentina es Buenos Aires. Tú...

Preliminary exercises B

- Dictate the following sentences: **1.** *Tienen prisa y miedo.* **2.** *Tiene toda la razón.* **3.** *Nunca tiene razón.* **4.** *No tienen ganas de estudiar.* **5.** *Tenemos que trabajar.*
- Have students give expressions they associate with the following: **1.** *el cliente* **2.** *los tres cochinitos* (draw a pig face or tail on the board) **3.** *el conejo blanco* (draw rabbit ears on the board)

Conversación

A. Estereotipos. Draw some conclusions about Isabel based on the following scene. Think about things that she has, needs to or has to do or buy, likes, and so on. When you have finished, compare your predictions with those of others in the class. Did you all reach the same conclusions?

Suggestion A

Coach students to help them invent a situation for or a story about the drawing. Caution them to stay within limits of language they know. Offer brief model sentences: *Isabel no estudia mucho.*

Follow-up A
Ask the following questions: *¿Es Ud. como Isabel? ¿Qué problemas tienen Isabel y Ud. en común? ¿Cómo es su cuarto? ¿Vive Ud. solo/a?*

❖ **Transparency 27**

Palabras útiles: los aretes (*earrings*), el juguete (*toy*), hablar por teléfono, los muebles (*furniture*), el sofá, tener alergia a (*to be allergic to*)

Suggestion B
Have students add two or three options of their own invention.

Follow-up B
Have selected students report back information they have learned. You may wish to help them organize their presentations.

B. Entrevista: Más preferencias. With a classmate, explore preferences in a number of areas by asking and answering questions based on the following cues. Form your questions with expressions like these:

¿Prefieres... o ... ?
¿Te gusta más (*infinitive*) o (*infinitive*)?

If you have no preference, express that by saying **No tengo preferencia**. Be prepared to report some of your findings to the class. If you both agree, you will express this by saying **Preferimos...** or **No tenemos preferencia**. If you do not agree, give the preferences of both persons: **Yo prefiero..., pero Cecilia prefiere...**

1. Los animales: ¿los gatos siameses o los persas? ¿los perros pastores alemanes o los perros de lanas (*poodles*)?
2. El color de la ropa informal: ¿el color negro o el blanco? ¿el rojo o el azul?
3. La ropa informal: ¿las camisas de algodón o las de seda? ¿los *jeans* de algodón o los pantalones de lana?
4. La ropa de mujeres: ¿las faldas largas o las minifaldas? ¿los pantalones largos o los pantalones cortos?
5. La ropa de hombres: ¿las camisas de cuadros o las de rayas? ¿las camisas de un solo (*single*) color? ¿chaqueta y pantalón o un traje formal?
6. Las actividades en casa: ¿mirar la televisión o leer una novela? ¿escribir cartas o hablar con unos amigos?

Enfoque *cultural*

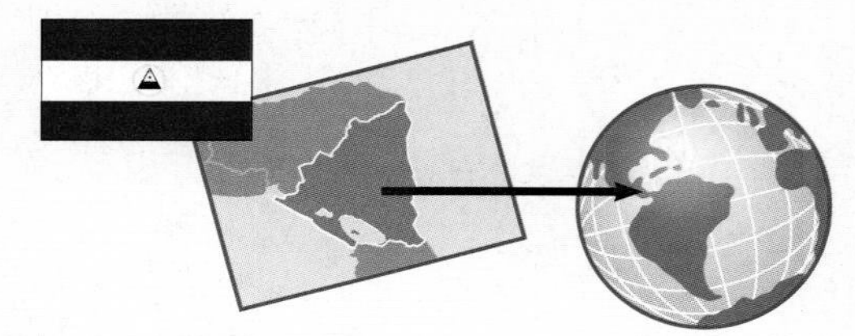

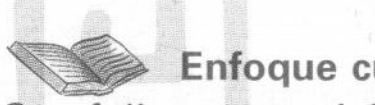

Enfoque cultural
See follow-up activities for this section in chapter-by-chapter materials in the IM.

Nicaragua

Datos esenciales

Nombre oficial: República de Nicaragua

Capital: Managua

Población: 4.000.000 de habitantes

Moneda: el córdoba

Idiomas: el español (oficial), el misquito, el sumo*

Suggestion: Enfoque cultural
You might wish to offer students additional information on subjects such as the following: Nicaraguan poets Rubén Darío and Ernesto Cardenal; the Nicaraguan sign language (developed almost entirely by children); the Nicaraguan civil war; the history of the United Fruit Company in Nicaragua; and so on.

Nota histórica

Cristóbal Colón llegó[a] a las costas de Nicaragua en 1502, pero la región no fue colonizada[b] hasta[c] 1524.

Nicaragua tiene una historia turbulenta por las luchas[d] entre las fuerzas conservadoras y las fuerzas liberales. La lucha se complicó[e] por la intervención de los Estados Unidos en la política del país. En 1990 terminó[f] una época[g] difícil de dictadura y lucha: hubo[h] una revolución y un movimiento en contra de la revolución. Esta lucha fue entre los sandinistas (revolucionarios marxistas) y los «contras» (antirrevolucionarios).

[a]*arrived* [b]no... *was not colonized* [c]*until* [d]*struggles* [e]se... *was complicated* [f]*ended* [g]*time* [h]*there was*

¡Fíjese!

- En 1856, un norteamericano, William Walker, se declaró[a] presidente de Nicaragua. Dos años después, fue derrotado por[b] los nicaragüenses, liberales y conservadores que se unieron[c] para expulsarlo[d] del país.

Violeta Barrios de Chamorro

- El Lago de Nicaragua es el lago más grande de Centroamérica. Hay más de 300 islas en el lago. En «las Isletas», hay pequeñas comunidades agrícolas[e] y, en algunas,[f] casas de personas ricas.
- Violeta Barrios de Chamorro fue[g] presidenta de Nicaragua de 1990 a 1997. Fue la primera[h] presidenta en Centroamérica. En 2001, Enrique Bolaños Geyer fue elegido[i] presidente.

[a]se... *declared himself* [b]fue... *he was defeated by* [c]se... *joined together* [d]*expel him* [e]*agricultural* [f]*some* [g]*was* [h]*first* [i]fue... *was elected*

Capítulo 3 of the video to accompany *¿Qué tal?* contains cultural footage of Nicaragua.

Visit the *¿Qué tal?* website at www.mhhe.com/quetal.

*En la costa oeste (*west coast*) de Nicaragua, también se habla un dialecto criollo (*creole*) que está basado en el inglés.

PASO 3 Gramática

Paso 3: Gramática
See detailed supplementary materials for this grammar section in IM.

10 Expressing Destination and Future Actions • *Ir; ir + a +* Infinitive; The Contraction *al*

¿Qué *va a* hacer Ud. este fin de semana?

- ¿*Va a ir al* centro? — Sí, *voy a ir al* centro.
- ¿*Va a ir* de compras? — No, no *voy a ir* de compras.
- ¿*Va a* hablar con sus amigos? — Sí, *voy a* hablar con mis amigos.
- ¿*Va a* estudiar español? — ¡Claro que sí!

Si quiere añadir (*add*) otras actividades a la lista, use la frase **También voy a** + *infinitive.*

Ir is the irregular Spanish verb used to express *to go.*

ir (*to go*)	
voy	**vamos**
vas	**vais**
va	**van**

The first person plural of **ir, vamos** (*we go, are going, do go*), is also used to express *let's go.*

Vamos a clase ahora mismo.
Let's go to class right now.

Ir + **a** + infinitive is used to describe actions or events in the near future.

Van a venir a la fiesta esta noche.
They're going to come to the party tonight.

Voy a ir de compras esta tarde.
I'm going to go shopping this afternoon.

THE CONTRACTION *al*

In **Capítulo 2** you learned about the contraction **del** (**de** + **el** ⟶ **del**). The only other contraction in Spanish is **al** (**a** + **el** ⟶ **al**). **¡OJO!** Both **del** and **al** are obligatory contractions.

a + **el** ⟶ **al**

Voy **al** centro comercial.
I'm going to the mall.

Vamos **a la** tienda.
I'm going to the store.

Preliminary exercises A
- Have students indicate the subject: *van, voy, va, vas, vamos, vais.*
- Have students give Spanish equivalents: **1.** I'm going to the market. **2.** He's going to class. **3.** My mother is going to teach Spanish. **4.** You are going to read. **5.** We are going to be sleepy. **6.** You and Mrs. Robinson are going to eat.

Práctica

A. ¿Adónde van de compras? Haga oraciones completas usando **ir**. Recuerde: **a** + **el** = **al**.

MODELO: Marta / el centro ⟶ Marta *va al* centro.

1. Ud. / una *boutique*
2. Francisco / el almacén Goya

Answers A
1. *Ud. va a...* **2.** *Francisco va al...* **3.** *Jorge y Carlos van al...* **4.** *Vas a...* **5.** *Vamos a...* **6.** *Voy a...*

3. Jorge y Carlos / el centro comercial
4. tú / un mercado
5. nosotros / una tienda pequeña
6. yo / ¿ ?

B. ¡Vamos de compras en Sevilla! Describa el día, desde el punto de vista (*from the point of view*) de Lola Benítez. Use **ir** + **a** + el infinitivo.

MODELO: Manolo compra un regalo para su madre. →
Manolo *va a comprar* un regalo para su madre.

1. Llegamos al centro a las diez de la mañana.
2. La niña quiere comer algo (*something*).
3. Compro unos chocolates para Marta.
4. Manolo busca una blusa de seda.
5. No compras esta blusa de rayas, ¿verdad? (*right?*)
6. Buscamos algo más barato ¿no? (*right?, OK?*)
7. ¿Vas de compras mañana también?

Conversación

A. ¿Adónde vas si… ? ¿Cuántas oraciones puede hacer Ud.?

Me gusta {
leer novelas.
ir de compras —y ¡no regateo!
buscar gangas y regatear.
hablar con mis amigos.
comer en restaurantes elegantes.
mirar programas de detectives.
} Por eso voy a ____.

B. Entrevista: El fin de semana

Paso 1. Interview a classmate about his or her plans for the weekend. Try to personalize the interview by asking additional questions. For example, if your partner is going to read a novel, ask questions like **¿Qué novela?** or **¿Quién es el autor?**

¿Sí o no? ¿Vas a… ?

1. ir de compras
2. leer una novela
3. asistir a un concierto
4. estudiar para un examen
5. ir a una fiesta
6. escribir una carta
7. ir a bailar
8. escribir los ejercicios para la clase de español
9. practicar un deporte (*sport*)
10. mirar mucho la televisión

Paso 2. En general, ¿es muy activo/a su compañero/a? ¿O prefiere la tranquilidad? En el **Paso 1**, los números pares (2, 4, 6,…) son actividades más o menos pasivas o tranquilas. Los números impares (1, 3, 5,…) representan actividades más activas. ¿Cómo es su compañero/a?

Note B
Students may need extra help with item 7. *¿Vas a ir de… ?*

Variation B
Personalize sequence, having students do all items with *yo* forms; then change details as necessary.

Answers B
1. *Vamos a llegar…* **2.** *va a querer…* **3.** *Voy a comprar…* **4.** *va a buscar…* **5.** *No vas a comprar…* **6.** *Vamos a buscar…* **7.** *¿Vas a ir… ?*

Follow-up B
Make statements that are true for students right now, varying information according to individuals in your class. Using follow-up question, students will tell what they will do in the future. **1.** *Este semestre/trimestre Ud. toma clases muy fáciles. ¿Y el próximo semestre/trimestre?* **2.** *Ud. vive ahora en la residencia. ¿Y el próximo semestre/trimestre?* **3.** *Ahora ____ es el presidente / primer ministro. ¿Y en cuatro años?* **4.** *Ud. lleva ropa muy vieja hoy. ¿Y mañana?* **5.** *Ud. tiene problemas económicos ahora. ¿Y en cinco años?* **6.** *Este año Ud. escucha música rap. ¿Y en diez años?*

Suggestion A
Do as a conversational exchange between you and the students, or have students work in pairs to ask and answer questions: *¿Adónde vas si te gusta… ?* → *Voy a…*

Suggestion B
Have students add their own preference to the questions. Answers in *Paso 2* can be reported back, with students using *nosotros* form whenever possible.

Follow-up B
Ask the following questions: *¿Cuál es su actividad favorita? ¿y su autor favorito (autora favorita)? ¿Cuántas horas de televisión mira por semana? ¿Con qué frecuencia escribe a sus padres / a sus amigos / a otras personas?*

Suggestion: En los Estados Unidos y el Canadá...
Have students search the Internet for non-profit organizations that target Hispanic causes. Ask them to identify prominent Hispanics in the world of film, TV, music, sports, and politics who donate time and money to these causes.

En los Estados Unidos y el Canadá...

Los hispanos en el mundo de la moda

Christy Turlington

Christy Turlington is one of many Hispanic celebrities in the U.S. world of fashion. Born in San Francisco, California (1969), to a Salvadoran mother, Turlington has been a household name since the 1990s. During her career as a supermodel, she became an activist for and benefactor of several causes, including breast cancer and animal rights. Furthermore, after being diagnosed with early-stage emphysema and subsequently quitting smoking, Christy became the spokesperson for a government anti-tobacco campaign.

Multimedia: Internet
Have students imagine that they are fashion critics. Have them write a short paragraph describing the fashion for next season. Provide vocabulary on the board to facilitate the paragraph: *invierno* = winter; *verano* = summer. Students should include colors, fabrics, and styles. Suggest the following phrase to get started: *La moda para la próxima temporada* (season) *va a tener... / usar...*

UN POCO DE TODO

Pero, ¿no se puede (*can't one*) **regatear?** Complete the following paragraph with the correct form of the words in parentheses, as suggested by the context. When two possibilities are given in parentheses, select the correct word.

En (los/las[1]) ciudades hispánicas, hay una (grande[2]) variedad de tiendas para (ir[3]) de compras. Hay almacenes, centros comerciales y *boutiques* (elegante[4]), como en (los/las[5]) Estados Unidos, donde los precios son siempre (fijo[6]).

También hay tiendas (pequeño[7]) que venden un solo[a] producto. Por ejemplo,[b] en una zapatería sólo hay zapatos. En español el sufijo **-ería** se usa[c] para (formar[8]) el nombre de la tienda. ¿Dónde (creer[9]) Ud. que venden papel y (otro[10]) artículos de escritorio? ¿A qué tienda (ir[11]) a ir Ud. a comprar fruta?

Si Ud. (poder[12]) pagar el precio que piden,[d] (deber[13]) comprar los recuerdos[e] en (los/las[14]) almacenes o *boutiques*. Pero si (tener[15]) ganas o necesidad de regatear, tiene (de/que[16]) ir a un mercado: un conjunto[f] de tiendas o locales[g] donde el ambiente[h] es más (informal[17]) que[i] en los (grande[18]) almacenes. Ud. no (deber[19]) pagar el primer[j] precio que menciona el vendedor.[k] ¡Casi siempre va (a/de[20]) ser muy alto!

[a]*single* [b]Por... *For example* [c]se... *is used* [d]*they ask* [e]*souvenirs* [f]*group* [g]*stalls* [h]*atmosphere* [i]*than* [j]*first* [k]*seller*

Comprensión: ¿Cierto o falso? Corrija las oraciones falsas.

1. En el mundo hispánico, todas las tiendas son similares.
2. Uno puede regatear en un almacén hispánico.
3. Es posible comprar limones en una papelería.
4. En un mercado, el vendedor siempre ofrece un precio bajo al principio (*beginning*).

Answers
1. *las* 2. *gran* 3. *ir* 4. *elegantes* 5. *los* 6. *fijos* 7. *pequeñas* 8. *formar* 9. *cree* 10. *otros* 11. *va* 12. *puede* 13. *debe* 14. *los* 15. *tiene* 16. *que* 17. *informal* 18. *grandes* 19. *debe* 20. *a*

Follow-up: Un poco de todo
- Have students give names of stores: *La tienda donde se venden zapatos se llama...* → *una zapatería; fruta* → *frutería; carne* (meat) → *carnicería; papel* → *papelería; pan* (bread) → *panadería; perfume* → *perfumería; ¿y animales?* ¡OJO! → *tienda de animales*
- Have students write similar paragraphs, comparing shopping experiences in different towns and cities, or in different kinds of stores and shopping areas.

In the *Capítulo 3* segment of "Chapter-by-Chapter Supplementary Materials" in the IM, you will find a chapter-culminating activity. You can use this activity to consolidate and review the vocabulary and grammar skills students have acquired.

Un paso más PASO 4

Paso 4: Un paso más
Optional section

See IM for suggestions and follow-up activities to accompany this video segment.

VIDEOTECA: En contexto

In this video segment, which takes place in Costa Rica, Mariela bargains with a street vendor for a very special item. As you watch this segment, pay particular attention to the words that the salesperson uses to convince Mariela to buy. Do they both agree on prices? Who "wins"?

A. Lluvia de ideas

- ¿Hay mercados al aire libre en su ciudad? ¿Qué venden? ¿Compra Ud. en ellos con frecuencia?
- En este país, ¿son normales los precios fijos? ¿Hay alguna (*any*) ocasión en que Ud. regatea?

B. Dictado

Here is the first part of this segment's dialogue. Fill in the missing portions of the dialogue.

MARIELA: Buenos días, señora. ¿ __De__[1] qué son las chaquetas?
VENDEDORA: Las chaquetas __son__[2] de pura __lana__.[3] Son muy bonitas, ¿__verdad__[4]?
MARIELA: Sí, son bonitas. ¿__Cuánto__[5] cuestan?
VENDEDORA: __Cuestan__[6] 5.000 colones. Son muy buenas chaquetas.
MARIELA: No estoy segura... Es __mucho__.[7]
VENDEDORA: Pero ¡el precio es una __ganga__![8] Son realmente buenas.
MARIELA: Sí, Ud. tiene __razón__.[9] Son chaquetas muy bonitas, pero de todos modos son un __poco__[10] caras.

C. Un diálogo original

Paso 1. Con un compañero/una compañera, dramatice la escena de Mariela con la vendedora.

Paso 2. Imagine que Ud. y su compañero/a están de compras en casa de una persona que va a mudarse (*move*).

E1: You want to buy some old clothes that are for sale. You want a cheaper price because you want to buy several items.
E2: You are selling household items. You are willing to lower your prices, but not too much. Your items are high-quality.

FUNCTION
Shopping for clothes

Cultura en contexto
Hispanic Currencies

Due to emerging political and commercial alliances, some currencies in the Spanish-speaking world are changing.

- While the **colón** continues to be the currency in Costa Rica, the U.S. dollar replaced the **sucre** in Ecuador in 2000 and the **colón** in El Salvador in 2001.
- In January 2002, the **euro** replaced the currencies of 11 of the 14 European Union member states, including the Spanish **peseta**.

Follow-up A
Ask students the following questions: *¿Cree Ud. que es posible regatear por Internet? ¿En qué tipo de comercio se puede regatear?*

Follow-up B
Check comprehension: *¿De qué son las chaquetas que mira Mariela? ¿Cuánto paga Mariela por la chaqueta que compra? ¿Para quién es la chaqueta? ¿De dónde es la vendedora?*

En resumen

GRAMÁTICA

To review the grammar points presented in this chapter, refer to the indicated grammar presentations. You'll find further practice of these structures in the Workbook/Laboratory Manual, on the CD-ROM, and on the website.

8. Demonstrative Adjectives

Do you know the forms for **este, ese,** and **aquel**? Do you know the differences in meaning?

9. *Tener, venir, preferir, querer,* and *poder;* Some Idioms with *tener*

You should be able to conjugate the verbs **tener, venir, preferir, querer**, and **poder** in the present tense. Do you know how to use expressions like **tengo ganas de, tenemos miedo**, and **tienes razón**?

10. *Ir; ir + a +* Infinitive; The Contraction *al*

You should know the forms of **ir** and how to express *going to do (something)*. You should also know when to use the contraction **al**.

VOCABULARIO

Los verbos

ir (*irreg.*) to go
ir a + *inf.* to be going to (*do something*)
ir de compras to go shopping
llevar to wear; to carry; to take
poder (ue) to be able, can
preferir (ie) to prefer
querer (ie) to want
regatear to haggle, bargain
tener (*irreg.*) to have
usar to wear; to use
venir (*irreg.*) to come

Repaso: comprar, vender

La ropa

el abrigo coat
los aretes earrings
la blusa blouse
la bolsa purse
la bota boot
los calcetines socks
la camisa shirt
la camiseta T-shirt
la cartera wallet
la chaqueta jacket
el cinturón belt
la corbata tie
la falda skirt
el impermeable raincoat
los *jeans* jeans
las medias stockings
los pantalones pants
el par pair
el reloj watch
la ropa interior underwear
la sandalia sandal
el sombrero hat
el suéter sweater
el traje suit
el traje de baño swimsuit
el vestido dress
el zapato (de tenis) (tennis) shoe

Suggestions: Vocabulario

- Bring or have students bring magazine clippings with images of people wearing a variety of clothes and colors. Hold up one image and allow students 20 seconds to look at it. Then put it away and have them jot down in Spanish as many things about the picture as they can remember. You might place a volunteer at board to write his or her version, and use that as a starting point to remember what they saw.

Los colores

amarillo/a	yellow
anaranjado/a	orange
azul	blue
blanco/a	white
gris	gray
morado/a	purple
negro/a	black
pardo/a	brown
rojo/a	red
rosado/a	pink
verde	green

De compras

de cuadros	plaid
de lunares	polka-dotted
de rayas	striped
de última moda	the latest style
la ganga	bargain
el precio (fijo)	(fixed) price
las rebajas	sales, reductions
¿cuánto cuesta?	how much does it cost?
¿cuánto es?	how much is it?

Los materiales

es de...	it is made of . . .
algodón (*m.*)	cotton
lana	wool
seda	silk

Los lugares

el almacén	department store
el centro	downtown
el centro comercial	shopping mall
el mercado	market(place)
la tienda	shop, store

Otros sustantivos

la cinta	tape
el ejercicio	exercise
el examen	exam, test

Los adjetivos

barato/a	inexpensive
caro/a	expensive
poco/a	little

Los números

doscientos/as, trescientos/as, cuatrocientos/as, quinientos/as, seiscientos/as, setecientos/as, ochocientos/as, novecientos/as, mil, un millón (de)

Repaso: cien(to)

Formas demostrativas

aquel, aquella, aquellos/as	that, those (over there)
ese/a, esos/as	that, those
esto, eso, aquello	this, that, that (over there)

Repaso: este/a, estos/as

Palabras adicionales

¿adónde?	where (to)?
al	to the
algo	something
allí	(over) there
de todo	everything
tener...	
ganas de + *inf.*	to feel like (*doing something*)
miedo (de)	to be afraid (of)
prisa	to be in a hurry
que + *inf.*	to have to (*do something*)
razón	to be right
sueño	to be sleepy
no tener razón	to be wrong
¿no?, ¿verdad?	right?, don't they (you, etc.)?

- Give students 5 minutes to write short paragraph that uses as many words from the vocabulary as possible. Find out who used the most words. Have volunteers read their paragraphs.
- Have a "number bee" competition. Give contestants increasingly complicated numbers in digit form, and have them tell the number in Spanish. Continue until you have one number bee champion.
- Use the *tener* expressions to ask absurd questions. Have students respond with corrections. For example, *¿Tienes miedo de los zapatos? No, pero tengo miedo de no tener razón cuando hablo español.*

Suggestions: Chapter Opening photo

- Point out the chapter opening photo. Have students talk about the places where they and their families live and about their ideas about housing in Hispanic countries.
- Have students imagine and describe the home in the photo. *¿Cómo cree Ud. que es la casa?* Encourage them to give as many adjectives as they can. Help them along by using word pairs: *moderno/ antiguo, bonito/feo, caro/barato, elegante/ simple, de buen gusto/de mal gusto,* and so on.

CAPÍTULO 4

En casa

Resources

You and your students may find the following *¿Qué tal?* supplements helpful as you teach this chapter:

For the Instructor

- *Instructor's Manual and Resource Kit,* "Chapter-by-Chapter" Supplementary Materials
- Testing Program (*continues below*)

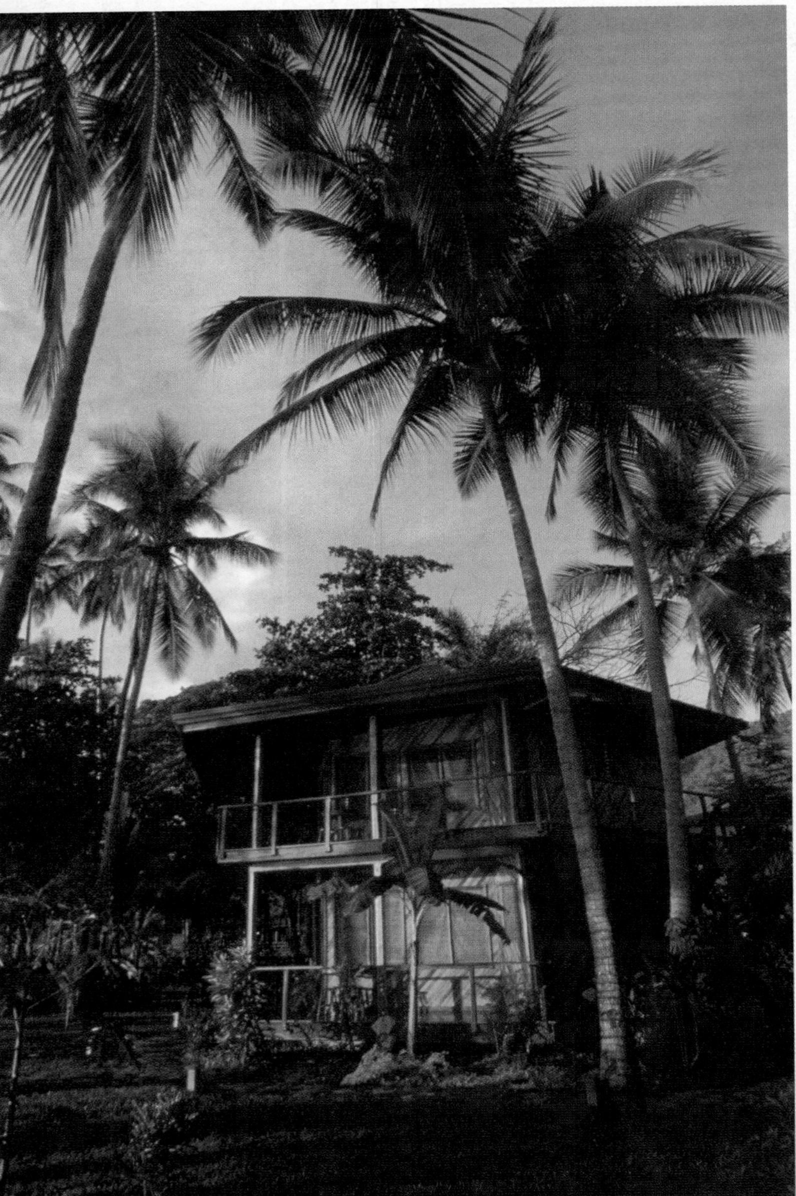

VOCABULARIO

- Days of the week
- Furniture, rooms, and parts of the house
- Prepositions

GRAMÁTICA

11 **Hacer, oír, poner, salir, traer,** and **ver**

12 Present Tense of Stem-Changing Verbs

13 Reflexive Pronouns

CULTURA

- **Enfoque cultural:** Costa Rica
- **Nota cultural:** Houses in the Hispanic World
- **En los Estados Unidos y el Canadá:** Vicente Wolf
- **Cultura en contexto:** Living with Parents

Multimedia

You will learn more about searching for an apartment in the **En contexto** video segment.

Review vocabulary and grammar and practice language skills with the interactive CD-ROM.

Get connected to the Spanish-speaking world with the *¿Qué tal?* Online Learning Center: **www.mhhe.com/ quetal**.

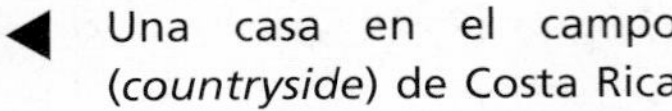

◀ Una casa en el campo (*countryside*) de Costa Rica

- Overhead Transparencies 28–32
- Video (VHS or CD)
- *¿Qué tal?* Online Learning Center Website
- Audioscript
- Instructor's Resource CD

For Students

- Workbook/Laboratory Manual and Audio Program or Electronic Workbook/ Laboratory Manual
- Video on CD
- Interactive CD-ROM
- *¿Qué tal?* Online Learning Center Website
- Listening Comprehension Audio CD
- McGraw-Hill Electronic Language Tutor (MHELT)

Vocabulario PASO 1

Paso 1: Vocabulario
See detailed supplementary materials and exercises for this section and a model for vocabulary presentation and other material in the *Capítulo 4 Vocabulario: Preparación* section of "Chapter-by-Chapter Supplementary Materials," IM.

Multimedia: Audio
Students can listen to and practice this chapter's vocabulary on their Listening Comprehension Audio CD.

¿Qué día es hoy?

lunes	Monday
martes	Tuesday
miércoles	Wednesday
jueves	Thursday
viernes	Friday
sábado	Saturday
domingo	Sunday
el lunes, el martes...	on Monday, on Tuesday . . .
los lunes, los martes...	on Mondays, on Tuesdays . . .
Hoy (Mañana) es viernes.	Today (Tomorrow) is Friday.
Ayer fue miércoles.	Yesterday was Wednesday.
el fin de semana	(on) the weekend
pasado mañana	the day after tomorrow
el próximo (martes, miércoles,...)	next (Tuesday, Wednesday, . . .)
la semana que viene	next week

agosto

lunes 14
martes 15
miércoles 16
jueves 17
viernes 18
sábado 19
domingo 20

OJO

- Except for **el sábado / los sábados** and **el domingo / los domingos**, all the days of the week use the same form for the plural as they do for the singular.
- The definite articles are used to express *on* with the days of the week.
- The days are not capitalized in Spanish.
- In Spanish-speaking countries, the week usually starts with **lunes**.

Note A
Stress the use in item 1 of *ayer,* which students should understand in context. *Fue* and other forms of the preterite are introduced in *Capítulo 7*.

Reciclado A
Remind students of the meaning of *de la mañana* (*tarde, noche*) and contrast it with *por la mañana* (*tarde, noche*).

Conversación

A. Preguntas

1. ¿Qué día es hoy? ¿Qué día es mañana? Si hoy es sábado, ¿qué día es mañana? Si hoy es jueves, ¿qué día es mañana? ¿Qué día fue ayer?
2. ¿Qué días de la semana tenemos clase? ¿Qué días no?
3. ¿Estudia Ud. mucho durante (*during*) el fin de semana? ¿y los domingos por la noche?
4. ¿Qué le gusta hacer (*to do*) los viernes por la tarde? ¿Le gusta salir (*to go out*) con los amigos los sábados por la noche?

Follow-up A
Dictate the following sentences. Then have students respond *sí* or *no* to each. **1.** *Los viernes por la tarde hay muy pocas personas en la biblioteca, ¿verdad?* **2.** *Por lo general, los lunes son días fenomenales, ¿no?* **3.** *Los días del fin de semana son martes y miércoles, ¿no?* **4.** *Muchas personas no tienen que trabajar los sábados, ¿verdad?*

National Standards: Communication
Have students work in pairs to describe and compare their weekly schedules with their partner's.

B. Mi semana. Indique una cosa que Ud. quiere, puede o tiene que hacer cada (*each*) día de esta semana.

MODELO: El lunes tengo que (puedo, quiero) ir al laboratorio de lenguas.

Palabras útiles: dormir (*to sleep*) hasta muy tarde, jugar (*to play*) al tenis (al golf, al vólibol, al…), ir al cine (*movies*), ir al bar (al parque, al museo, a…)

❖ **Transparencias 28–30**

Los muebles,° los cuartos y otras partes de la casa

Los… *Furniture*

el jardín	yard
la pared	wall
el patio	patio; yard
la piscina	swimming pool
la alfombra	rug
el escritorio	desk
el estante	bookshelf
los platos	dishes; plates
la silla	chair

Note: This is the first group of words you will learn for talking about where you live and the things found in your house or apartment. You will learn additional vocabulary for those topics in **Capítulos 9, 12,** and **14**.

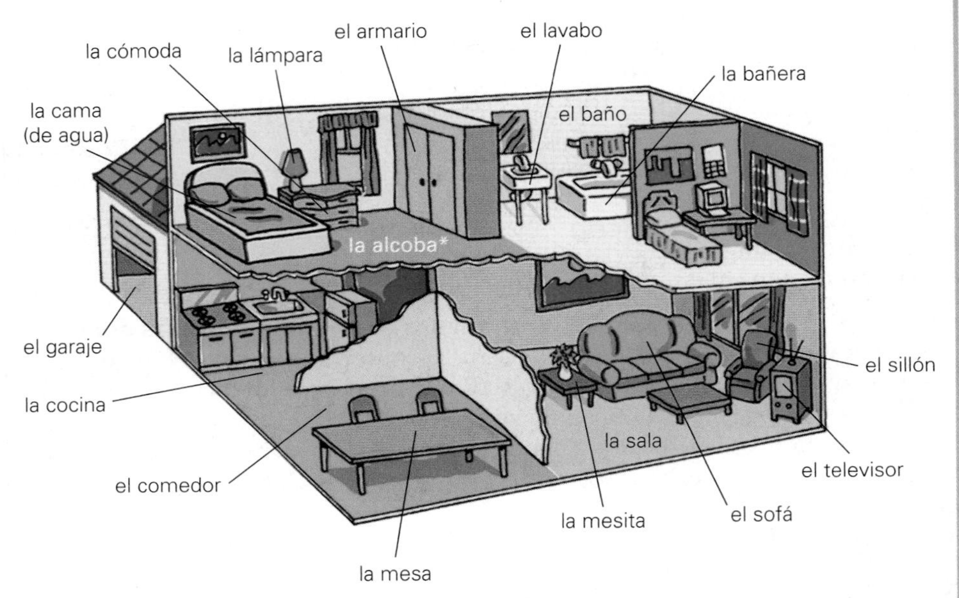

Answers A
1. *garaje: coche y bicicleta* 2. *sala: televisor, sillón, mesita, lámpara, cuadro* 3. *dormitorio: cama, cómoda, armario, alfombra* 4. *baño: lavabo* 5. *cocina: platos* 6. *comedor: mesa, sillas* 7. *jardín*

Conversación

A. ¿Qué hay en esta casa? Identifique las partes de esta casa y diga lo que hay en cada cuarto. ¿Qué hay en el patio? ¿Hay una piscina? ¿O solamente hay plantas?

*Other frequently used words for *bedroom* include **el dormitorio** and **la habitación**.

Suggestion A
Have students draw a sketch of their home similar to the one in the textbook. Then have them describe their homes and indicate what they like to do in each room. If students live in a dorm, have them sketch their family's home.

B. Asociaciones

Paso 1. ¿Qué muebles o partes de la casa asocia Ud. con las siguientes actividades?

1. estudiar para un examen
2. dormir la siesta (*taking a nap*) por la tarde
3. pasar una noche en casa con la familia
4. celebrar con una comida (*meal*) especial
5. tomar el sol (*sunbathing*)
6. hablar de temas (*topics*) serios con los amigos (padres, hijos)

Paso 2. Ahora compare sus asociaciones con las (*those*) de otros estudiantes. ¿Tienen todos las mismas costumbres (*customs*)?

Suggestion B
Do as a pair activity, then have partners report each other's answers to the class.

Note B
More than 1 answer is possible for many of these items. Encourage students to give several answers and to explain their reasons.

Reciclado: Preposiciones
Review telling time. Write times on board: 9:15 A.M., 12, 1:10 P.M., 7:45 P.M., 3:30 A.M. Then ask students: *¿Cómo se dice... ?* Encourage them to ask partners for specific times of day when they provide answers.

¿Cuándo? • Preposiciones

Note: Preposiciones
The concept of the infinitive following prepositions was seen in *Capítulo 3: para +* infinitive.

Prepositions express relationships in time and space.

The book is *on* the table.

The homework is *for* tomorrow.

Some common prepositions you have already used include **a, con, de, en, para**, and **por**.

Here are some prepositions that express time relationships.

antes de	*before*	**durante**	*during*
después de	*after*	**hasta**	*until*

The infinitive is the only verb form that can follow a preposition.

¿Adónde vas **después de estudiar**?
Where are you going after studying (after you study)?

Conversación

A. ¿Antes o después? Complete las oraciones lógicamente, con **antes de** o **después de**.

1. Voy a la clase de español __después de__ preparar la lección.
2. Por lo general, prefiero estudiar __antes de / después de__ mirar un poco la televisión.
3. Los viernes siempre descanso (*I rest*) __antes de__ salir para una fiesta.
4. Me gusta investigar un tema __antes de__ escribir una composición.
5. Prefiero comer fuera (*to eat out*) __antes de / después de__ ir al cine.
6. Tengo que estudiar mucho __antes de__ tomar un examen.

Follow-up B
Use information in this activity to create descriptive table of students' habits. Have students characterize themselves as a class (*¿trabajadores? ¿estudiosos?*).

B. Preguntas

1. ¿Estudia Ud. durante su programa favorito de televisión? ¿Qué más hace (*do you do*) cuando estudia?
2. ¿Habla por teléfono antes o después de estudiar? ¿Dónde habla por teléfono, en la sala o en su cuarto?
3. ¿Hasta qué hora estudia, generalmente? ¿Estudia hasta dormirse (*you fall asleep*)?
4. ¿Lee durante las conferencias (*lectures*) en una clase? ¿Lee la lección antes o después de la explicación (*explanation*) del profesor / de la profesora?
5. ¿Trabaja durante las vacaciones? ¿Cuántas horas? ¿Trabaja por la noche hasta muy tarde?

Suggestion: Nota cultural
Describe some Hispanic homes you know.

NOTA CULTURAL

Houses in the Hispanic World

There is no such thing as a typical Hispanic house. Often, the style of housing depends on geographic location. For example, in hot regions, such as southern Spain, many houses are built around a central interior patio. These patios are filled with plants, and some even have a fountain.

The population in Hispanic countries tends to be centered in urban areas. Due to population density in cities, many people live in apartments, like people in larger cities in this country. Here are some more details about Hispanic houses.

- While the Spanish word **hogar** literally means *home*, the word **casa** is often used to mean *home*.

    Voy a casa. *I'm going home.* Estoy en casa. *I'm at home.*

- In Spain, people use the word **piso** or **apartamento** to refer to an apartment; in some Hispanic countries, the word **departamento** is used.
- In big Latin American cities and in more modern homes, a small front yard with ornamental plants and/or small trees is called **un jardín**. Except in rural areas and small towns, a large backyard is uncommon because the lots where houses are built are rather small. If a house has a back area, it is generally referred to as **el patio**. This area, usually paved, adjoins the house and is commonly enclosed by the walls of neighboring buildings.

Un patio interior en Sevilla, España

 **Paso 2: Gramática**
See detailed supplementary materials for these grammar sections in IM.

11 Expressing Actions • *Hacer, oír, poner, salir, traer,* and *ver*

Los jóvenes de hoy

«¡Estos muchachos sólo quieren *salir*! No *ponen* sus cosas en orden en su cuarto… Los jóvenes de hoy día no *hacen* nada bien; no son responsables… ¡Hasta quieren *traer* muchachas a su cuarto!»

¿Son estos comentarios típicos de las personas mayores (*adults*) de su país?
¿Cree Ud. que tienen razón?
¿Tienen los jóvenes algunos (*any*) estereotipos sobre (*about*) las personas mayores?

hacer (*to do; to make*)		**oír** (*to hear*)		**poner** (*to put; to place*)		**salir** (*to leave; to go out*)		**traer** (*to bring*)		**ver** (*to see*)	
hago	hacemos	oigo	oímos	pongo	ponemos	salgo	salimos	traigo	traemos	veo	vemos
haces	hacéis	oyes	oís	pones	ponéis	sales	salís	traes	traéis	ves	veis
hace	hacen	oye	oyen	pone	ponen	sale	salen	trae	traen	ve	ven

- **hacer**

Some common idioms with **hacer** are **hacer ejercicio** (*to exercise*), **hacer un viaje** (*to take a trip*), and **hacer una pregunta** (*to ask a question*).

¿Por qué no **haces** los ejercicios?
Why aren't you doing the exercises?

Quieren **hacer un viaje** al Perú.
They want to take a trip to Peru.

Los niños siempre **hacen muchas preguntas**.
Children always ask a lot of questions.

- **oír**

The command forms of **oír—oye (tú), oiga (Ud.)**, and **oigan (Uds.)**—are used to attract someone's attention in the same way that English uses *Listen!* or *Hey!*

No **oigo** bien por el ruido.
I can't hear well because of the noise.

Oye, Juan, ¿vas a la fiesta?
Hey, Juan, are you going to the party?

¡Oigan! ¡Silencio, por favor!
Listen! Silence, please!

Today's young people These boys only want to go out! They don't put things in order in their rooms . . . Today's young people don't do anything right; they are not responsible people . . . They even want to bring girls to their rooms!

• **poner**	Siempre **pongo** leche y mucho azúcar en el café. *I always put milk and a lot of sugar in my coffee.*
Many Spanish speakers use **poner** with appliances to express *to turn on.*	Voy a **poner** el televisor. *I'm going to turn on the TV.*
• **salir**	**Salen de** la clase ahora. *They're leaving class now.*
Note that **salir** is always followed by **de** to express leaving a place. **Salir con** can mean *to go out with, to date.*	**Salgo con** el hermano de Cecilia. *I'm going out with Cecilia's brother.*
Use **salir para** to indicate destination.	**Salimos para** la sierra pasado mañana. *We're leaving for the mountains the day after tomorrow.*
• **traer**	¿Por qué no **traes** la radio a la cocina? *Why don't you bring the radio to the kitchen?*
• **ver**	No **veo** bien sin mis lentes de contacto. *I can't see well without my contact lenses.*

Preliminary exercises: Práctica
- Have students give corresponding *yo* form to *Ud.* forms: *hace, trae, pone, oye, sale, ve.*
- Have students give corresponding subject pronouns: *hago, hacemos, pongo, pone, pones, oye, oyes, sale, sales, salgo, traéis, traemos, traigo, traes.*

Follow-up: Práctica
Have students give Spanish equivalents: **1.** *I'm going to turn on the TV. I want to turn on the radio.* **2.** *She's going out with her boyfriend. He wants to go out with Margarita.* **3.** *She's leaving for Rome tomorrow. I'm leaving for Bogotá on Friday.* **4.** *We have to take a trip. They should ask a question.*

Práctica

Cosas rutinarias

Paso 1. ¿Cierto o falso?

1. Hago ejercicio en el gimnasio con frecuencia.
2. Siempre veo la televisión por la noche.
3. Nunca salgo con mis primos por la noche.
4. Siempre hago los ejercicios para la clase de español.
5. Salgo para clase a las ocho de la mañana.
6. Nunca pongo la ropa en la cómoda o en el armario.
7. Siempre traigo todos los libros necesarios a clase.
8. Siempre oigo todo lo que dice (*says*) el profesor / la profesora de español.

Paso 2. Now rephrase each sentence in **Paso 1** as a question and interview a classmate. Use the **tú** form of the verb.

Conversación

A. Consecuencias lógicas. Con un compañero / una compañera, indique una acción lógica para cada situación, usando (*using*) las siguientes frases.

Frases útiles: poner el televisor / el estéreo, oír al profesor / a la profesora,* salir con/de/para… , hacer un viaje / una pregunta, traer el libro a clase, ver mi programa favorito.

1. Me gusta esquiar en las montañas. Por eso…
2. En la clase de español usamos este libro todos los días. Por eso…
3. Mis compañeros de cuarto hacen mucho ruido en la sala. Por eso…
4. El televisor no funciona. Por eso no…
5. Hay mucho ruido en la clase. Por eso no…
6. Estoy en la biblioteca y ¡no puedo estudiar más! Por eso…
7. Queremos bailar y necesitamos música. Por eso…
8. No comprendo la lección. Por eso…

B. Preguntas

1. ¿Qué pone Ud. en el armario? ¿en la cómoda? ¿Qué pone en su mochila o bolsa todos los días para ir a clase? Generalmente, ¿qué más trae a clase?
2. ¿Qué quiere hacer esta noche (*tonight*)? ¿Qué necesita hacer? ¿Qué va a hacer? ¿Va a salir con sus amigos (con su familia)? ¿Adónde van?
3. ¿A qué hora sale Ud. de la clase de español? ¿de las otras clases? ¿A veces sale tarde de clase? ¿Por qué?
4. ¿Oye Ud. las noticias (*news*) todos los días? ¿Pone Ud. la radio o el televisor para oír las noticias? ¿Y para oír música? ¿Qué programa ve en la televisión todas las semanas?

Reciclado A
Have students review clothing. Write on board: *La ropa. Voy a hacer un viaje y en mi maleta voy a poner…* Divide class in small groups and have them take turns adding an item to list of clothing they will pack. Each student must name all items previously mentioned by others before adding his or her own.

¿Recuerda Ud.?

The change in the stem vowels of **querer** and **poder** (**e** and **o**, respectively) follows the same pattern as that of the verbs presented in the next section. Review the forms of **querer** and **poder** before beginning that section.

querer: **e** → ¿ ?	qu _____ ro	queremos
	qu _____ res	queréis
	qu _____ re	qu _____ ren
poder: **o** → ¿ ?	p _____ do	podemos
	p _____ des	podéis
	p _____ de	p _____ den

*Remember that the word **a** is necessary in front of a human direct object. You will study this usage of **a** in **Capítulo 6**. For now, you can answer following the pattern of this **frase útil**.

12 Expressing Actions • Present Tense of Stem-Changing Verbs

¡Nunca más!

ALICIA: ¡No *vuelvo* a comprar en la papelería Franco!
ARMANDO: Yo también *empiezo* a cansarme de esa tienda. Nunca *tienen* los materiales que les *pido*.
ALICIA: ¿No *piensas* que los precios son muy caros? Yo creo que siempre *perdemos* dinero cuando compramos allí.
ARMANDO: Te *entiendo* perfectamente. Los precios son horribles. Como la papelería está tan cerca de la facultad, ¡*piensan* que *pueden* pedir mucho dinero por todo!

¿Quién piensa que…

1. los precios de la papelería son muy caros?
2. la papelería no tiene muchas cosas necesarias?
3. pueden pedir mucho dinero porque la papelería está muy cerca de la facultad?
4. los estudiantes pierden dinero cuando compran en la papelería Franco?

National Standards: Community
Specialized shops are much more common in Hispanic countries than they are in this country. Some of them include *zapaterías* and *papelerías*. More names for specialized stores can be found in *Capítulo 6* when foods are introduced.

Reciclado
Review *querer* and *poder*, pointing out the diphthongization of the stem vowel in stressed positions, except for the *nosotros* and *vosotros* forms.

e → ie **pensar (ie)** (*to think*)		**o (u) → ue** **volver (ue)** (*to return*)		**e → i** **pedir (i)** (*to ask for; to order*)	
pienso	pensamos	vuelvo	volvemos	pido	pedimos
piensas	pensáis	vuelves	volvéis	pides	pedís
piensa	piensan	vuelve	vuelven	pide	piden

A: You have already learned five *stem-changing verbs* (**los verbos que cambian el radical**): **querer, preferir, tener, venir,** and **poder**. In these verbs the stem vowels **e** and **o** become **ie** and **ue**, respectively, in stressed syllables. The stem vowels are stressed in all present tense forms except **nosotros** and **vosotros**. All three classes of stem-changing verbs follow this regular pattern in the present tense. In vocabulary lists, the stem change will always be shown in parentheses after the infinitive: **volver (ue)**.

Stem vowel changes:

e → ie
e → i
o → ue

Nosotros and **vosotros** forms do not have a stem vowel change.

Never again! ALICIA: I'm not going to shop at Franco's stationery store again! ARMANDO: I'm also beginning to get fed up with that store. They never have the things I ask them for. ALICIA: Don't you think that the prices are very expensive? I think that we always lose money when we buy there. ARMANDO: I understand you perfectly. The prices are awful. Since the stationery store is so close to the campus, they think that they can ask a lot of money for everything!

B: Some stem-changing verbs practiced in this chapter include the following.

e → ie		o (u) → ue		e → i	
cerrar (ie)	*to close*	almorzar (ue)	*to have lunch*	pedir (i)	*to ask for; to order*
empezar (ie)	*to begin*	dormir (ue)	*to sleep*	servir (i)	*to serve*
entender (ie)	*to understand*	jugar (ue)*	*to play* (a game, sport)		
pensar (ie)	*to think*				
perder (ie)	*to lose; to miss* (a function)	volver (ue)	*to return* (to a place)		

- When used with an infinitive, **empezar** is followed by **a**.

Uds. **empiezan a hablar** muy bien el español.
You're beginning to speak Spanish very well.

- When used with an infinitive, **volver** is also followed by **a**. The phrase then means *to do (something) again.*

¿Cuándo **vuelves a jugar** al tenis?
When are you going to play tennis again?

- When followed directly by an infinitive, **pensar** means *to intend, plan to.*

¿Cuándo **piensas contestar** la carta?
When do you intend to answer the letter?

The phrase **pensar en** can be used to express *to think about.*

—¿**En** qué **piensas**?
What are you thinking about?

—**Pienso en** la tarea para la clase de física.
I'm thinking about the homework for physics class.

❖ **Transparency 32** may be used with many of the verbs presented in this grammar section, along with prepositions from *Paso 1: Vocabulario,* this chapter.

Práctica

A. ¿Dónde están Diego y Antonio? Tell in what part of Antonio's apartment the following things are happening. More than one answer may be possible.

MODELO: Diego y Antonio empiezan la tarea. → Están en la alcoba.

1. Antonio sirve el desayuno (*breakfast*).
2. Antonio cierra la revista y pone el televisor.
3. Los dos almuerzan con un compañero de la universidad.
4. Los dos juegan al ajedrez (*chess*), y Diego pierde.
5. Diego piensa en las cosas que tiene que hacer hoy.

Preliminary exercises A

- Have students give correct form of each verb for subject given.
  yo: *cerrar, empezar, entender, almorzar, pedir*
  tú: *pensar, preferir, jugar, dormir*
  Ud./él/ella: *perder, empezar, volver, servir*
  nosotros: *empezar, preferir, jugar, volver*
  vosotros: *pensar, cerrar, entender, dormir, servir*
  Uds./ellos/ellas: *preferir, almorzar, jugar, pedir*
- Have students give new sentences based on subject cues: **1.** *Sara y Anita almuerzan en el patio.* (*Ud., nuestros hijos, nosotros, tú, yo, vosotros*) **2.** *Felipe pide un refresco.* (*yo, nosotros, ellos, Lisa, tú, vosotros*) **3.** *Yo prefiero descansar en la playa* (beach). (*Sergio, nosotros, Ana, ellas, tú, vosotras*) **4.** *Yo pierdo muchas cosas.* (*ellos, yo, Fernando, tú, los niños, vosotros*) **5.** *Los González vuelven de su viaje el sábado.* (*yo, nosotras, mis primas, Manuel, tú, vosotros*)

*__Jugar__ is the only **u** → **ue** stem-changing verb in Spanish. **Jugar** is often followed by **al** when used with the name of a sport: **Juego *al* tenis**. Some Spanish speakers, however, omit the **al**.

6. Antonio vuelve a casa después de las clases.
7. Antonio duerme la siesta.
8. Diego pide una pizza por teléfono.

B. Una tarde típica en casa. ¿Cuáles son las actividades de todos? Haga oraciones completas con una palabra o frase de cada grupo. Use sólo los nombres que son apropiados para Ud.

yo		almorzar	descansar, dormir
mi padre/madre		volver	en un sillón cómodo (*comfortable*) / en el patio
mi esposo/a		preferir	toda la tarde
los niños		perder	su pelota (*ball*)
mi amigo/a ____ y yo	(no)	pensar	muchos refrescos (*soft drinks*)
el perro/gato		jugar	tarde / temprano a casa
mi compañero/a		pedir	afuera (*outside*)
		dormir	la siesta
		¿ ?	en el patio / en la piscina
			al golf (tenis, vólibol…)
			las películas (*movies*) viejas/recientes
			¿ ?

Notes C

- *Paella* is a typical dish from the Mediterranean coast of Spain (Valencia), made with saffron rice and a variety of ingredients. It can contain shrimp, prawns, mussels, clams, squid, as well as chicken or pork. *Paella* is a favorite dish for tourists, and it can be found in restaurants all over Spain. Many other areas of Spain as well as other Spanish-speaking countries have their own versions of *paella.*
- Point out the use of the third person plural form of the verb as an impersonal form in item 5.

Follow-up C

Ask students the following questions to check comprehension and personalize information: **1.** *¿Qué pide la familia primero* (first)*? ¿Por qué piden tacos después? ¿Qué hacen después de almorzar? ¿Por qué? ¿Qué quieren hacer también? ¿Por qué?* **2.** *¿A Ud. le gusta la paella? ¿y los tacos? ¿Qué prefiere, los tacos o la paella?*

Suggestion: Conversación

Have students work in small groups and use *tú* forms for items 2–3.

C. Hoy queremos comer paella

Paso 1. Using the following cues as a guide, tell about the visit of Ismael's family to a restaurant that specializes in Hispanic cuisine. Use **ellos** as the subject except where otherwise indicated.

1. familia / de / Ismael / tener ganas / comer / paella
2. volver / a / su / restaurante / favorito
3. pensar / que / paella / de / restaurante / ser / estupendo
4. pedir / paella / para / seis / persona
5. pero / hoy / sólo / servir / menú (*m.*) / mexicano
6. por eso / pedir / tacos / y / guacamole (*m.*)

Paso 2. Now retell the story as if it were your family, using **nosotros** as the subject, except in item 5, where you will use **ellos**.

Conversación

Preguntas

1. ¿A qué hora cierran la biblioteca? ¿A qué hora cierran la cafetería? Y durante la época de los exámenes finales, ¿a qué hora cierran?
2. ¿A qué hora almuerza Ud., por lo general? ¿Dónde le gusta almorzar? ¿Con quién? ¿Dónde piensa Ud. almorzar hoy? ¿mañana?
3. ¿Es Ud. un poco olvidadizo/a? Es decir (*That is*), ¿pierde las cosas con frecuencia? ¿Qué cosa pierde Ud.? ¿El dinero? ¿su cuaderno? ¿su mochila? ¿sus llaves (*keys*)?

Enfoque *cultural*

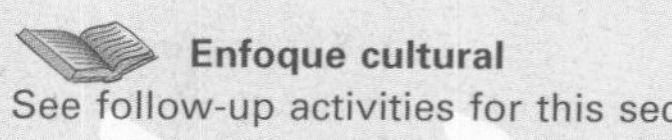

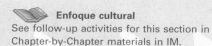

Enfoque cultural
See follow-up activities for this section in Chapter-by-Chapter materials in IM.

Costa Rica

Datos esenciales

Nombre oficial: República de Costa Rica

Capital: San José

Población: 3.534.174 de habitantes

Moneda: el colón

Idioma oficial: el español

¡Fíjese!

El ecoturismo es importante para la economía de Costa Rica y para la preservación de la biodiversidad y la belleza[a] natural que existe en el país. El ecoturismo tiene como propósito[b] controlar la entrada[c] de turistas en regiones protegidas[d] y, a la vez,[e] obtener fondos[f] para continuar con la protección de las regiones naturales. Aproximadamente un treinta por ciento (%) del territorio costarricense está cubierto de selvas o bosques.[g] En total, más de un cuarto[h] del territorio del país ha sido destinado[i] para la preservación.

[a]*beauty* [b]*purpose* [c]*entrance* [d]*protected* [e]a... *at the same time* [f]*funds* [g]está... *is covered with jungles or forests* [h]*fourth* [i]ha... *has been set aside*

Conozca a...
Óscar Arias Sánchez

Óscar Arias Sánchez (1941–), presidente de Costa Rica de 1986 a 1990, asistió a[a] la Universidad de Costa Rica, a Boston University y a otras universidades en Inglaterra.[b] En 1987, Arias recibió[c] el Premio Nóbel de la Paz[d] por sus esfuerzos[e] por aliviar las tensiones entre el gobierno sandinista de Nicaragua y los Estados Unidos. El acuerdo de paz[f] de Arias se firmó[g] en 1986. Desde 1990, se encarga de[h] la Fundación Arias para la paz y el progreso humano.

Óscar Arias Sánchez

[a]asistió... *attended* [b]*England* [c]*received* [d]Premio... *Nobel Peace Prize* [e]*efforts* [f]acuerdo... *peace agreement* [g]se... *was signed* [h]se... *he has been running*

Multimedia: Internet
Have students look up additional information about Costa Rica's history, government, people, culture, geography, tourism, and media on the Internet. Encourage them to look for the CIA World Factbook online and phone books for Costa Rica. You might assign specific topics and have students give brief oral reports about Costa Rica.

Capítulo 4 of the video to accompany *¿Qué tal?* contains cultural footage of Costa Rica.

Visit the *¿Qué tal?* website at www.mhhe.com/quetal.

Paso 3: Gramática
See detailed supplementary materials for these grammar sections in IM.

13 Expressing -self/selves • Reflexive Pronouns

❖ Transparency 31

La rutina diaria de Diego

1. 

2. 

3. 

4. 

5. 

6. 

Follow-up: Reflexive Pronouns
Have students respond *cierto* or *falso:* **1.** *Me despierto temprano.* **2.** *Me levanto a las 6.* **3.** *El sábado me levanto a las 7.* **4.** *Prefiero bañarme por la mañana.* **5.** *Me gusta acostarme a las 10.* **6.** *El sábado me acuesto a las 12.*

7. 

Me despierto a las siete y media y *me levanto* en seguida (1). Primero, *me ducho* (2) y luego *me cepillo* los dientes (3). *Me peino* (4), *me pongo* la bata (5) y voy al cuarto a *vestirme* (6). Por fin, salgo para mis clases (7). No tomo nada antes de salir para la universidad porque, por lo general, ¡tengo prisa!

¿Cómo es la rutina diaria de Ud.?

1. Yo me levanto a las ______.
2. Me ducho por la (mañana/noche).
3. Me visto en (el baño/mi cuarto).
4. Me peino (antes de/después de) vestirme.
5. Antes de salir para las clases, (tomo/no tomo) el desayuno.

Diego's daily routine I wake up at seven-thirty and I get up right away. First, I take a shower and then I brush my teeth. I comb my hair, I put on my robe, and I go to my room to get dressed. Finally, I leave for my classes. I don't eat or drink anything before leaving for the university because I'm generally in a hurry!

USES OF REFLEXIVE PRONOUNS

bañarse (*to take a bath*)

(yo)	**me** baño	*I take a bath*	(nosotros)	**nos** bañamos	*we take baths*
(tú)	**te** bañas	*you take a bath*	(vosotros)	**os** bañáis	*you take baths*
(Ud.)	**se** baña	*you take a bath*	(Uds.)	**se** bañan	*you take baths*
(él)		*he takes a bath*	(ellos)		*they take baths*
(ella)		*she takes a bath*	(ellas)		*they take baths*

Suggestion: Reflexive Pronouns
Contrast *I bathe the kids* with *I bathe (myself)* (*I take a bath*). In the first sentence, the subject and object are different; in the second, they are the same person (object pronoun reflects subject).

Suggestion
Refer students to the vocabulary list to see the *-se* at the end of reflexive verbs.

A. The pronoun **se** at the end of an infinitive indicates that the verb is used reflexively. The reflexive pronoun in Spanish reflects the subject doing something to or for himself, herself, or itself. When the verb is conjugated, the reflexive pronoun that corresponds to the subject must be used.

Many English verbs that describe parts of one's daily routine—to get up, to take a bath, and so on—are expressed in Spanish with a reflexive construction.

Reflexive Pronouns

me	myself
te	yourself (*fam., sing.*)
se	himself, herself, itself; yourself (*form. sing.*)
nos	ourselves
os	yourselves (*fam. pl. Sp.*)
se	themselves; yourselves (*form. pl.*)

me baño = I take a bath (bathe myself)

B. Here are some reflexive verbs you will find useful as you talk about daily routines. Note that some of these verbs are also stem-changing.

acostarse (ue)	to go to bed	**levantarse**	to get up; to stand up
afeitarse	to shave	**ponerse**	to put on (*clothing*)
bañarse	to take a bath	**quitarse**	to take off (*clothing*)
despertarse (ie)	to wake up	**sentarse (ie)**	to sit down
divertirse (ie)	to have a good time, enjoy oneself	**vestirse (i)**	to get dressed
dormirse (ue)	to fall asleep		
ducharse	to take a shower		

Note also the verb **llamarse** (*to be called*), which you have been using since **Primeros pasos**.

Me llamo_____. ¿Cómo se llama Ud.?

All of these verbs can also be used nonreflexively, often with a different meaning. Some examples of this appear at the right:

dormir = to sleep **dormirse** = to fall asleep
poner = to put, place **ponerse** = to put on

OJO After **ponerse** and **quitarse**, the definite article, not the possessive as in English, is used with articles of clothing.

Se pone **el** abrigo.
He's putting on his coat.

Se quitan **el** sombrero.
They're taking off their hats.

[Práctica A–B]

PLACEMENT OF REFLEXIVE PRONOUNS

Reflexive pronouns are placed before a conjugated verb but after the word **no** in a negative sentence: **No *se* bañan.** They may either precede the conjugated verb or be attached to an infinitive.

Me tengo que levantar temprano.
Tengo que levantar**me** temprano.
I have to get up early.

[Práctica B]

Preliminary exercises: Reflexive Pronouns

- Have students give corresponding subject pronoun: *te, me, nos, os.* Ask what subject pronouns correspond to reflexive pronoun *se.*
- Have students give *yo* form: *bañarse, levantarse, ducharse, vestirse, ponerse, despertarse, dormirse, acostarse.*
- Read sentences and have students tell whether they are reflexive or not: **1.** *María se despierta a las 8 de la mañana.* **2.** *María acuesta a los niños a las 9 de la noche.* **3.** *Se quita la ropa.* **4.** *Baña a los niños.* **5.** *María se sienta.* **6.** *Sienta a los niños.* **7.** *Levanta a los niños a las 7.* **8.** *Todos se divierten.*

Follow-up A
Ask students: *¿Tiene Ud. una rutina diferente los sábados? ¿Qué día prefiere? ¿Por qué?*

Variation A
Have students correct the sentences to express what they actually do.

Suggestion B
Have students make up routines for some typical characters: *los estudiantes típicos de esta universidad, su compañero/a de cuarto,* and so on.

Práctica

A. Su rutina diaria. ¿Hace Ud. lo mismo (*the same thing*) todos los días? Conteste con **sí** o **no**.

	LOS LUNES		LOS SÁBADOS	
	SÍ	NO	SÍ	NO
1. Me levanto antes de las ocho.	☐	☐	☐	☐
2. Siempre me baño o me ducho.	☐	☐	☐	☐
3. Siempre me afeito.	☐	☐	☐	☐
4. Me pongo un traje / un vestido / una falda.	☐	☐	☐	☐
5. Me quito los zapatos después de llegar a casa.	☐	☐	☐	☐
6. Me acuesto antes de las once de la noche.	☐	☐	☐	☐

B. La rutina diaria

Note B
Point out the use of the preposition + infinitive.

Paso 1. ¿Qué acostumbran hacer Ud. y las otras personas de su casa? Conteste usando las siguientes indicaciones. Use el sujeto pronominal cuando sea (*whenever it is*) necesario.

MODELO: yo / despertarse / a las ¿ ? → Me despierto a las seis de la mañana.

1. yo / levantarse / a las ¿ ?
2. ¿ ? / levantarse / más tarde
3. ¿ ? / ducharse / por la mañana

Follow-up B
Have students use the verbs and situations from **Paso 2** to describe a typical day in the life of their husband, wife, best friend, parents, children, and so on.

4. por costumbre / ¿ ? / no bañarse / por la noche
5. yo / vestirse / antes de ¿ ?
6. ¿ ? / vestirse / después de ¿ ?
7. por la noche / ¿ ? / acostarse / temprano
8. yo / acostarse / a las ¿ ?
9. por lo general / ¿ ? / (no) acostarse / más tarde que (*than*) yo

Paso 2. En su casa, ¿quién… ?

1. se levanta primero
2. se acuesta primero
3. no se baña por la mañana
4. se viste antes de tomar el desayuno

Note: En los Estados Unidos y el Canadá…
One of the most famous Latin American artists in the U.S. is the Mexican architect and designer Luis Barragán. His original designs are inspired by old Mexican colonial convents, monasteries, and haciendas. A Pritzker Architecture Prize Laureate, Barragán is best known in the U.S. for his houses, especially since the New York publication of *Casa mexicana,* a photography art book that focuses completely on Barragán's designs.

En los Estados Unidos y el Canadá…

Vicente Wolf

As a boy in Cuba, designer Vicente Wolf spent hours in architects' studios and at construction sites. The visits he paid to museums in Havana when he was a teenager awakened his love for art. The experience of being a Cuban refugee who moved to Miami at age 14 and was forced to begin a new life in a foreign country also drove him in his determination to succeed.

Una sala decorada por Vicente Wolf

Wolf never formally studied interior design but rather learned it on the job. When he was 18, he moved from Miami to New York and found work at the Design and Decoration Building in Manhattan. He successfully completed several commissions and then became a business associate of the Spanish designer Robert Patino, a partnership that lasted for sixteen years.

Currently, Wolf runs his own business and lectures at the Parsons School of Design. He believes that it is important for Hispanics to hear about the success that other Hispanic immigrants have had in this country, with the hope that it will instill in them the desire to succeed as he has done.

Conversación

Hábitos. ¿Dónde hace Ud. lo siguiente? Indique el cuarto o la parte de la casa donde Ud. hace cada actividad. Debe indicar también los muebles y otras cosas que usa.

MODELO: estudiar →
Cuando estudio, prefiero estar (por lo general estoy) en la alcoba. Uso el escritorio, una silla, los libros y la computadora.

1. estudiar
2. dormir la siesta
3. quitarse los zapatos
4. bañarse o ducharse
5. despertarse
6. tomar el desayuno
7. sentarse a almorzar
8. vestirse
9. divertirse
10. acostarse

Suggestions
- Remind students to use the appropriate reflexive pronouns with infinitives, for example, *Tengo que levantarme, Queremos divertirnos*, and so on.
- Emphasize that when two verbs work together, the reflexive object pronouns can be placed before the conjugated verb or after and attached to the infinitive. Students will learn more about object pronoun placement in *Capítulos 6, 7,* and *8*.

UN POCO DE TODO

De compras y amistades (*friendships*). Complete the following paragraphs with the correct forms of the words in parentheses, as suggested by the context. When two possibilities are given in parentheses, select the correct word. In addition to reviewing vocabulary from previous chapters, these paragraphs ask you to choose between **ser** and **estar** in several situations that you should already know well. You will learn more about **ser** and **estar** in **Capítulo 5**.

(Me/Mi[1]) gusta ir de (comprar/compras[2]) con mi amiga Margarita cuando ella tiene (gangas/ganas[3]) de acompañarme.[a] (Este/Esta[4]) fin de semana, necesito (buscar[5]) unos regalos para los hijos (de el / del[6]) Sr. Suárez. Él (trabajar[7]) con mi madre en el hospital. (Mi[8]) padres (ser/estar[9]) muy buenos amigos de los Suárez, aunque[b] no (ser/estar[10]) siempre de acuerdo con sus opiniones (político[11]). La familia Suárez (venir[12]) a (nuestro[13]) casa con frecuencia.

Este mes[c] todos los niños de los Suárez (celebrar[14]) su cumpleaños.[d] Por (ese/eso[15]) tengo que (ir[16]) de compras antes (de/en[17]) su visita. La hija mayor,[e] Ana, (ser/estar[18]) una chica muy simpática que (asistir[19]) a la secundaria. (*Yo:* Querer[20]) comprarle[f] un vestido de cuadros o de (rayos/rayas[21]). Ya tiene (tres/trece[22]) años y (empezar[23]) a tener interés en (vestirse[24]) con más elegancia. (Su[25]) hermanos son muy jóvenes todavía —casi siempre (llevar[26]) camisetas y pantalones cortos. Por eso no (*yo:* ir[27]) a comprarles[g] ropa. Creo que (*ellos:* divertirse[28]) más con los juguetes.[h]

Más tarde, por teléfono

—¿Diga?[i]
—Margarita, ¿eres tú?
—Sí, chica. ¿Qué hay?[j] ¿Cómo (*tú:* ser/estar[29])?
—Muy bien. Oye, ¿qué (hacer[30]) ahora?
—(*Yo:* Leer[31]) una novela para la clase de literatura (inglés[32]). ¿Por qué?
—¿Qué te parece si[k] (*nosotros:* ir[33]) al centro? Hay (mucho[34]) gangas en las tiendas (este[35]) días y tengo que comprar unos regalos.
—¡(Encantado[36])! Voy a (ponerse[37]) el abrigo y (salir[38]) de casa en unos minutos.

[a]*going with me* [b]*although* [c]*month* [d]*birthday* [e]*oldest* [f]*to buy her* [g]*buy them* [h]*toys* [i]*Hello?* (on the telephone, Spain) [j]¿Qué... *What's up?* [k]¿Qué... *What if . . . ?*

Suggestion
Dictate the following note from Margarita to her roommate: *Querida Susana: Espero que puedas encontrar esta nota. Me voy de compras con María. No puedo leer más esta novela aburrida. Además hay rebajas buenas en el centro. Voy a traer pan y papel higiénico. Hasta luego, Margarita.* Encourage students to guess spelling by sound, even if they do not know the meaning. To follow up, have students read dictation and guess meaning of new words.

Follow-up A
Ask students: **1.** *¿Cómo se llaman los mejores amigos de sus padres? ¿Se reúnen con frecuencia? ¿Ud. es amigo de los hijos?* **2.** *¿Compra regalos con frecuencia? ¿Para quién? ¿Le gusta ir de compras? ¿Va solo/a o con alguien?*

In the *Capítulo 4* segment of "Chapter-by-Chapter Supplementary Materials" in the IM, you will find a chapter-culminating activity. You can use this activity to consolidate and review the vocabulary and grammer skills students have acquired.

Answers
1. *Me* **2.** *compras* **3.** *ganas* **4.** *Este* **5.** *buscar* **6.** *del* **7.** *trabaja* **8.** *Mis* **9.** *son* **10.** *están* **11.** *políticas* **12.** *viene* **13.** *nuestra* **14.** *celebran* **15.** *eso* **16.** *ir* **17.** *de* **18.** *es* **19.** *asiste* **20.** *Quiero* **21.** *rayas* **22.** *trece* **23.** *empieza* **24.** *vestirse* **25.** *Sus* **26.** *llevan* **27.** *voy* **28.** *se divierten* **29.** *estás* **30.** *haces* **31.** *Leo* **32.** *inglesa* **33.** *vamos* **34.** *muchas* **35.** *estos* **36.** *Encantada* **37.** *ponerme* **38.** *salir*

Paso 4: Un paso más
Optional section

See IM for suggestions and follow-up activities to accompany the video segment.

VIDEOTECA: En contexto

In this video segment, Juan Carlos, the Peruvian student, talks to a real estate agent about an apartment. As you watch the segment, pay particular attention to the questions that the agent asks and to Juan Carlos' answers. What kind of apartment does Juan Carlos want? What rooms would he like?

FUNCTION

Searching for an apartment

Extension A

Ask students questions to check comprehension and personalize information:

1. *¿Dónde viven, generalmente, los estudiantes de primer* (pantomime) *año de esta universidad? ¿Y los estudiantes graduados?*
2. *Por lo general, ¿cree Ud. que los estudiantes universitarios (los estudiantes que están en la universidad) de su país viven independientemente o con sus familias? ¿Cree Ud. que eso es similar a los estudiantes universitarios de países hispánicos?*

A. Lluvia de ideas

- ¿Vive Ud. en un apartamento o en una casa? ¿Con quién vive? ¿Le gusta a Ud. su vivienda (*home*)? ¿Por qué?
- ¿Cambia Ud. de vivienda con frecuencia? ¿Qué hace para buscar una nueva vivienda? ¿Usa los servicios de un(a) agente de inmobiliaria (*real estate agent*)?
- ¿Piensa cambiar de vivienda en un futuro próximo (*in the near future*)? ¿Qué tipo de vivienda va a buscar?

B. Dictado

Here is part of this segment's dialogue. Fill in the missing portions of the dialogue.

JUAN CARLOS: Prefiero vivir en un apartamento cerca del[a] centro.
AGENTE: ¿Qué tipo de apartamento ___prefiere___[1]? Tenemos muchísimos[b]...
JUAN CARLOS: No ___quiero___[2] nada grande. Prefiero un ___apartamento___[3] con un dormitorio.
AGENTE: Muy bien. ¿Y qué más quiere?
JUAN CARLOS: Bueno... No necesito mucho. Prefiero un apartamento con ___sala___,[4] una ___ducha___[5] en el baño y una ___cocina___[6] con lavaplatos.
AGENTE: No hay problema. ___Tenemos___[7] muchísimos ___apartamentos___[8] así.

[a]cerca... *near the* [b]*lots*

Cultura en contexto
Living with Parents

In both Latin America and Spain, many young people live with their parents until they are ready to settle down and have families of their own. College students who study away from home tend to live with relatives or in apartments shared with nonfamily members. Unlike U.S. and Canadian college students, Hispanic students, particularly women, are less likely to live on their own.

PASO 1 Vocabulario

Paso 1: Vocabulario
See detailed supplementary materials and exercises for this section and a model for vocabulary presentation and other material in "Teaching Techniques" for the *Capítulo 5 Paso 1: Vocabulario* section of "Chapter-by-Chapter Supplementary Materials," IM.

¿Qué tiempo hace hoy?°

°¿Qué... *What's the weather like today?*

❖ **Transparency 33**

Hace frío.

Hace calor.

Hace viento.

Hace sol.

Está (muy) nublado.

Llueve.

Nieva.

Hay mucha/poca contaminación.

Hace (mucho) frío (calor, viento, sol). It's (very) cold (hot, windy, sunny).
Hace fresco. It's cool.
Hace (muy) buen/mal tiempo. It's (very) good/bad weather. The weather is (very) good/bad.

Pronunciation hint: Remember that, in most parts of the Spanish-speaking world, **ll** is pronounced exactly like **y: llueve**.

In Spanish, many weather conditions are expressed with **hace**. The adjective **mucho** is used with the nouns **frío, calor, viento,** and **sol** to express *very*.

Multimedia: Audio
Students can listen to and practice this chapter's vocabulary on their Listening Comprehension Audio CD.

Follow-up A
Ask students: **1.** *¿Dónde prefiere Ud. vivir, donde hace calor o donde hace fresco?* **2.** *¿Le gusta vivir donde llueve mucho? ¿donde nieva mucho?* **3.** *Describa la diferencia entre el clima de Michigan y el de Texas.* **4.** *¿Prefiere Ud. vivir en un lugar con cuatro estaciones o con solamente una?* **5.** *¿En qué partes de este país hay solamente una estación?*

Multimedia: Internet
Have students search for a weather site in Spanish and bring a printout from it to class. Have students identify the weather expressions they are learning and others they may recognize, for example, *temperatura.*

Conversación

A. El tiempo y la ropa. Diga qué tiempo hace, según la ropa de cada persona.

1. San Diego: María lleva pantalones cortos y una camiseta.
2. Madison: Juan lleva suéter, pero no lleva chaqueta.
3. Toronto: Roberto lleva suéter y chaqueta.
4. San Miguel de Allende: Ramón lleva impermeable y botas y también tiene paraguas (*umbrella*).
5. Buenos Aires: Todos llevan abrigo, botas y sombrero.

B. Consejos (*Advice*) **para Joaquín.** Joaquín es de Valencia, España. El clima (*climate*) allí es mediterráneo: Hace mucho sol y las temperaturas son moderadas. No hay mucha contaminación.

Paso 1. Joaquín tiene una lista de lugares que desea visitar en los Estados Unidos. Ayúdelo (*Help him*) con información sobre el clima.

1. Seattle, Washington
2. Los Ángeles, California
3. Phoenix, Arizona
4. Nueva Orleans, Louisiana
5. Buffalo, Nueva York

Paso 2. Es obvio que la lista de Joaquín no está completa. ¿Qué otros tres lugares cree Ud. que debe visitar? ¿Qué clima hace allí?

C. El tiempo y las actividades. Haga oraciones completas, indicando una actividad apropiada para cada situación.

cuando llueve	me quedo (*I stay*) en cama/casa
cuando hace buen tiempo	juego al basquetbol/vólibol con mis amigos
cuando hace calor	almuerzo afuera (*outside*) / en el parque
cuando hace frío	me divierto en el parque / en la playa (*beach*) con mis amigos
cuando nieva	no salgo de casa
cuando hay mucha contaminación	vuelvo a casa y trabajo o estudio

NOTA COMUNICATIVA

More *tener* Idioms

Several other conditions expressed in Spanish with **tener** idioms—not with *to be*, as in English—include the following.

tener (mucho) calor	to be (very) warm, hot
tener (mucho) frío	to be (very) cold

These expressions are used to describe people or animals only. To be comfortable—neither hot nor cold—is expressed with **estar bien**.

D. ¿Tienen frío o calor? ¿Están bien? Describe the following weather conditions and tell how the people pictured are feeling.

Suggestion B

Have students work in groups to prepare descriptions of a particular city/state, identifying weather and type of clothing that is appropriate. Have each group read its description to class, which then guesses city described. If students cannot guess immediately (which is likely), allow 5 *sí/no* questions.

Follow-up B

Ask students: *¿Llueve mucho en Inglaterra? ¿en el desierto Sahara? ¿Nieva mucho en el Brasil? ¿en Minnesota? ¿Hace mucho frío en Siberia? ¿en el Ecuador? ¿Hace mucho sol en la Florida? ¿en España? ¿Hace calor en Panamá? ¿en Alaska?*

Suggestions C

- Ask students if the following activities are typical on their campus when it's bad weather: **1.** *Cuando llueve, juegan al basquetbol en el gimnasio.* **2.** *Cuando nieva, pasan la tarde en la sala de la residencia estudiantil* (translate). **3.** *Cuando nieva, hacen hombres de nieve.* **4.** *Cuando llueve, no salen de la residencia.* **5.** *Cuando llueve, duermen todo el día.*
- Ask students if they do the following things when it is hot: *Cuando hace calor...* **1.** *¿bebe Ud. agua, refrescos o cerveza? ¿o jugo de fruta?* **2.** *¿prefiere estar en casa o afuera?* **3.** *¿prefiere estar en el parque o en la playa?* **4.** *¿juega al tenis* (*al golf*, and so on) *o duerme?*

Suggestions: Nota comunicativa

- Point out that with *tener* + noun expressions, *very* is expressed with *mucho/a*: *tener mucho frío/calor; tener muchas ganas.*
- Point out that *tener* means *to feel* in these idioms.

Preliminary exercise D

Before beginning activity ask students: **1.** *¿Qué tiempo hace hoy?* **2.** *Imagine que hoy es un día fatal. ¿Qué tiempo hace hoy?* **3.** *Hoy es un día estupendo. ¿Qué tiempo hace hoy?*

❖ **Transparency 34**

PASO 1

❖ Transparency 35

Los meses y las estaciones° del año

°seasons

septiembre, octubre, noviembre — el otoño

diciembre, enero, febrero — el invierno

marzo, abril, mayo — la primavera

junio, julio, agosto — el verano

enero						
	1	2	3	4	5	6
7	8	9	10	11	12	13
14	15	16	17	18	19	20
21	22	23	24	25	26	27
28	29	30	31			

abril						
1	2	3	4	5	6	7
8	9	10	11	12	13	14
15	16	17	18	19	20	21
22	23	24	25	26	27	28
29	30					

febrero						
				1	2	3
4	5	6	7	8	9	10
11	12	13	14	15	16	17
18	19	20	21	22	23	24
25	26	27	28			

mayo						
		1	2	3	4	5
6	7	8	9	10	11	12
13	14	15	16	17	18	19
20	21	22	23	24	25	26
27	28	29	30	31		

marzo						
				1	2	3
4	5	6	7	8	9	10
11	12	13	14	15	16	17
18	19	20	21	22	23	24
25	26	27	28	29	30	31

junio						
					1	2
3	4	5	6	7	8	9
10	11	12	13	14	15	16
17	18	19	20	21	22	23
24	25	26	27	28	29	30

¿Cuál es la fecha de hoy?	What is today's date?
(Hoy) Es el primero de abril.	(Today) It is the first of April.
(Hoy) Es el cinco de febrero.	(Today) It is the fifth of February.

- The ordinal number **primero** is used to express the first day of the month. Cardinal numbers (**dos, tres**, and so on) are used for other days.
- The definite article **el** is used before the date. However, when the day of the week is expressed, **el** is omitted: **Hoy es jueves, tres de octubre**.
- As you know, **mil** is used to express the year after 999.

1950 mil novecientos cincuenta   2003 dos mil tres

Reciclado: Los meses...
Review numbers and years: *¿En qué año estamos? ¿En qué año nació Ud.? ¿En qué año nació su padre (madre, abuela,* and so on*)? ¿En qué año piensa graduarse?*

Note B
Some important Hispanic holidays are not generally celebrated in the U.S. or Canada, for example, *el Día de los Reyes Magos (6 de enero)*. Some holidays that are celebrated in the U.S. and Canada are also celebrated in the Spanish-speaking world but on different dates, for example, *el Día del Padre* and *el Día de la Madre*.

Conversación

A. El mes de noviembre. Mire este calendario para el mes de noviembre. ¿Qué día de la semana es el 12 (1, 20, 16, 11, 4, 29) de noviembre?

Noviembre

L	M	M	J	V	S	D
1	2	3	4	5	6	7
8	9	10	11	12	13	14
15	16	17	18	19	20	21
22	23	24	25	26	27	28
29	30					

B. Fechas

Paso 1. Exprese estas fechas en español. ¿En qué estación caen (*do they fall*)?

1. March 7
2. August 24
3. December 1
4. June 5
5. 9-19-1997
6. 5-28-1842
7. 1-31-1660
8. 7-4-1776

Follow-up B
¿En qué año... ? 1. *la Declaración de la Independencia* (1776) **2.** *el asesinato* (pantomime) *de John F. Kennedy, padre* (1963) **3.** *Cristóbal Colón* (write on board) *llega a América* (1492) **4.** *la novela famosa de George Orwell* (1984) **5.** *este año* (Answers will vary.)

Paso 2. ¿Cuándo se celebran?

1. el Día de la Raza (*Columbus Day*)
2. el Día del Año Nuevo
3. el Día de los Enamorados (de San Valentín)
4. el Día de la Independencia de los Estados Unidos
5. el Día de los Inocentes (*Fools*), en los Estados Unidos
6. la Navidad (*Christmas*)
7. su cumpleaños (*birthday*)

OJO
Note that the word **se** before a verb changes the verb's meaning slightly. **¿Cuándo se celebran?** = *When are they celebrated?* You will see this construction throughout *¿Qué tal?*

Extension B
- Ask students what holidays they associate with the following: **1.** *desfiles* (parades) **2.** *tomar/beber champán* **3.** *mandar* (to send) *tarjetas, chocolates, flores* **4.** *barbacoas y picnics en el parque, fuegos artificiales* (fireworks) **5.** *bromas* (jokes) **6.** *un árbol decorado, regalos*
- Have students tell what activities they do for different holidays.

C. ¡Feliz (*Happy*) cumpleaños!

Paso 1. Entreviste a un compañero / una compañera de clase acerca de (*about*) su cumpleaños. Use las siguientes preguntas.

1. ¿Cuál es la fecha de tu cumpleaños?
2. ¿En qué estación es?
3. Generalmente, ¿qué tiempo hace en tu ciudad el día de tu cumpleaños?
4. ¿Cómo celebras tu cumpleaños? (por lo menos tres actividades)
5. ¿Con quién(es) prefieres celebrar tu cumpleaños?

Paso 2. Su profesor(a) o un(a) estudiante va a escribir en la pizarra los nombres de los meses del año. Luego cada estudiante va a escribir la fecha de su cumpleaños en la columna apropiada. ¿En qué mes son la mayoría de los cumpleaños de los estudiantes de la clase? ¿Qué signo del horóscopo tienen?

Los signos: Aries, Tauro, Géminis, Cáncer, Leo, Virgo, Libra, Escorpión, Sagitario, Capricornio, Acuario, Piscis

Note C
Point out the difference between *la fecha de cumpleaños* and *la fecha de nacimiento.*

WW. Multimedia: Internet
Have students who are interested look for the Colombian newspaper, *El tiempo,* on the Internet to find their horoscope in Spanish.

Suggestion: Las preposiciones
Have students work in small groups to compose similar paragraphs that help locate their city and their university.

¿Dónde está? • Las preposiciones

¿Dónde está España? Está *en* la Península Ibérica, *al lado de* Portugal. *Al norte* está Francia, y el continente de Africa está *al sur. Al oeste* está el Océano Atlántico y *al este* está el Mar Mediterráneo. La capital de España es Madrid. *Cerca de* la Península Ibérica están las Islas Baleares, que son parte de España. Las Islas Canarias, también parte de España, están *al oeste de* África. Gibraltar está *entre* España y África. No es parte de España. Pertenece (*It belongs*) a Inglaterra.

cerca de	close to	**delante de**	in front of
lejos de	far from	**detrás de**	behind
encima de	on top of	**a la izquierda de**	to the left of
debajo de	below	**a la derecha de**	to the right of
al lado de	alongside of		
entre	between, among		

al este / oeste / norte / sur de to the east / west / north / south of

In Spanish, the pronouns that serve as objects of prepositions are identical in form to the subject pronouns, except for **mí** and **ti**.

Julio está delante de **mí**.	*Julio is in front of me.*
María está detrás de **ti**.	*María is behind you.*
Me siento a la izquierda de **ella**.	*I sit on her left.*

OJO Note that **mí** has a written accent, but **ti** does not. This is to distinguish the object of a preposition (**mí**) from the possessive adjective (**mi**).

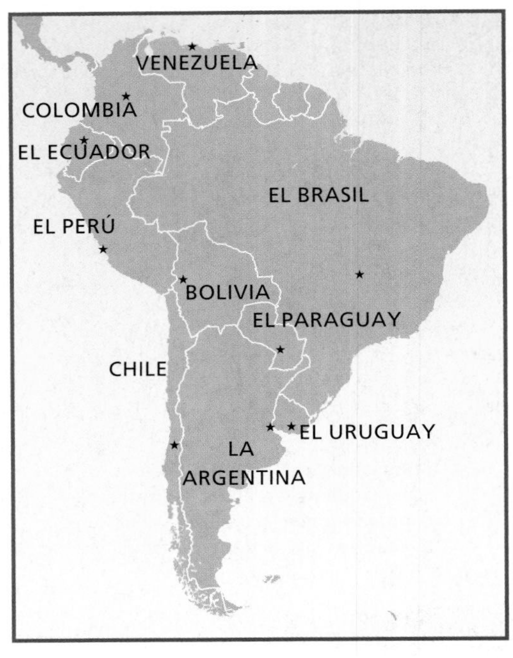

Suggestion A
Model a description: *Este país está al sur de los Estados Unidos. También está cerca de Panamá. Pero está lejos de la Argentina. ¿Cómo se llama?*

Conversación

A. ¿De qué país se habla?

Paso 1. Escuche la descripción que da (*gives*) su profesor(a) de un país de Sudamérica. ¿Puede Ud. identificar el país?

Paso 2. Ahora describa un país de Sudamérica. Sus compañeros de clase van a identificarlo. Siga el modelo, usando (*using*) todas las frases que sean (*are*) apropiadas.

MODELO: Este país está al norte/sur/este/oeste de _____. También está cerca de _____. Pero está lejos de _____. Está entre _____ y _____. ¿Cómo se llama?

Paso 3. Ahora trate de (*try to*) emparejar los nombres de estas capitales de Sudamérica con sus países.

MODELO: _____ es la capital de _____.

Capitales: Brasilia, Buenos Aires, Bogotá, La Paz, Santiago, Asunción, Quito, Caracas, Montevideo, Lima

B. ¿De dónde es Ud.? Give as much information as you can about the location of your hometown or state, or about the country you are from. You should also tell what the weather is like there.

MODELO: Soy del pueblo (de la ciudad) de _____. Está cerca de la ciudad de _____. En verano hace _____. En invierno _____. (No) Llueve mucho en primavera.

NOTA CULTURAL

El Niño

Most people have heard of **El Niño**, a weather phenomenon that is often associated with devastating climatic events. But why is it called **El Niño**?

The name **El Niño** dates from the end of the nineteenth century, when Peruvian fishermen noticed the periodic appearance of an abnormally warm ocean current off the coast of Peru. This warm current made its appearance around Christmas time. The name **El Niño** is a reference to the Christ Child, or **El Niño Jesús**, who for Christians also arrived at Christmas. At the time the name only referred to the current. Nowadays, it is used to refer to the meteorological phenomenon as a whole. Torrential rains, flooding, and landslides can occur from the southwestern United States to Peru, whereas in Australia, Indonesia, and southeast Africa, the opposite may happen: severe droughts and the potential for destructive fires.

Destrucción en California causada por (*caused by*) El Niño

 **Paso 2: Gramática**

See detailed supplementary materials for these grammar sections in IM.

14 ¿Qué están haciendo? • Present Progressive: *estar* + *-ndo*

¿Qué están haciendo en Quito, Ecuador?

José Miguel juega al tenis y levanta pesas con frecuencia. Ahora no *está jugando al tenis*. Tampoco *está levantando* pesas. ¿Qué *está haciendo? Está* _____.

Elisa es periodista. Por eso escribe mucho y habla mucho por teléfono. Pero ahora, no *está escribiendo*. Tampoco *está hablando* por teléfono. ¿Qué *está haciendo? Está* _____.

¿Y Ud.? ¿Qué está haciendo Ud. en este momento?

1. ¿Está estudiando en casa? ¿en clase? ¿en la cafetería?
2. ¿Está leyendo? ¿Está mirando la tele al mismo (*same*) tiempo?
3. ¿Está escuchando al profesor / a la profesora?

USES OF THE PROGRESSIVE

In Spanish, you can use special verb forms to describe an action in progress—that is, something actually happening at the time it is being described. These Spanish forms, called **el progresivo**, correspond in form to the English *progressive: I am walking, we are driving, she is studying*. But their use is not identical. Compare the Spanish and English verb forms in the sentences at the right.

In Spanish, the present progressive is used primarily to describe an action that is actually *in progress*, as in the first example. The simple Spanish present is used in other cases where English would use the present progressive: to tell what is going to happen (the second sentence), and to tell what someone is doing over a period of time but not necessarily at this very moment (the third sentence).

1. Ramón **está comiendo** ahora mismo.
   Ramón is eating right now.
2. **Compramos** la casa mañana.
   We're buying the house tomorrow.
3. Adelaida **estudia** química este semestre.
   Adelaida is studying chemistry this semester.

Aquí está el otro lado de la conversación… pero las respuestas no están en orden. Ponga las respuestas en el orden apropiado.

a. 5 Es muy moderno. Me gusta mucho.
b. 9 Sí, pero vive en Nueva York ahora.
c. 4 Son las once y media.
d. 1 Hola, querido (*dear*). ¿Qué tal?
e. 8 Es el Sr. Cortina.
f. 6 Pues, todavía (*still*) tengo que trabajar.
g. 11 Sí, hasta pronto.
h. 3 Estoy en Nueva York.
i. 2 Un poco cansada, pero estoy bien.
j. 10 Pues, hace buen tiempo, pero está un poco nublado.
k. 7 Con un señor de Computec, una nueva compañía de computadoras.

Suggestions: *Ser* and *estar*
- Review uses of *ser* and *estar*.
- Have students give additional examples of each use listed, where possible.
- Have students explain why *ser* and *estar* are used each time in minidialogue.
- Point out that *ser* is used to tell where an event takes place, for example, *El baile (La fiesta, La reunión) es en la calle Goya.* This use is presented in *Capítulo 8*.
- Have students reenact conversation as if they were talking on the phone, sitting back-to-back, if possible. Emphasize that they don't have to memorize conversation on the phone between the 2 spouses.

Summary of the Uses of *ser*

• To *identify* people and things	Ella **es doctora.**
• To express *nationality;* with **de** to express *origin*	**Son cubanos. Son de** La Habana.
• With **de** to tell of what *material* something is made	Este bolígrafo **es de plástico.**
• With **para** to tell *for whom something is intended*	El regalo **es para Sara.**
• To tell *time*	**Son las once. Es la una y media.**
• With **de** to express *possession*	**Es de** Carlota.
• With *adjectives* that describe *basic, inherent characteristics*	Ramona **es inteligente.**
• To form many *generalizations*	**Es necesario** llegar temprano **Es importante** estudiar.

Summary of the Uses of *estar*

• To tell *location*	El libro **está en la mesa.**
• To describe *health*	**Estoy** muy **bien**, gracias.
• With *adjectives* that describe *conditions*	**Estoy** muy **ocupada.**
• In a number of *fixed expressions*	**(No) Estoy de acuerdo. Está bien.**
• With *present participles* to form the *progressive tense*	**Estoy estudiando** ahora mismo.

Ser AND *estar* WITH ADJECTIVES

A. **Ser** is used with adjectives that describe the fundamental qualities of a person, place, or thing.

Esa mujer es muy **baja**.
That woman is very short.

Sus calcetines son **morados**.
His socks are purple.

Este sillón es **cómodo**.
This armchair is comfortable.

Sus padres son **cariñosos**.
Their parents are affectionate people.

B. **Estar** is used with adjectives to express conditions or observations that are true at a given moment but that do not describe inherent qualities of the noun. The following adjectives are generally used with **estar**.

abierto/a	open	**limpio/a**	clean
aburrido/a	bored	**loco/a**	crazy
alegre	happy	**nervioso/a**	nervous
cansado/a	tired	**ocupado/a**	busy
cerrado/a	closed	**ordenado/a**	neat
congelado/a	frozen; very cold	**preocupado/a**	worried
contento/a	content, happy	**seguro/a**	sure, certain
desordenado/a	messy	**sucio/a**	dirty
enfermo/a	sick	**triste**	sad
furioso/a	furious, angry		

C. Many adjectives can be used with either **ser** or **estar**, depending on what the speaker intends to communicate. In general, when *to be* implies *looks, feels,* or *appears,* **estar** is used. Compare the following pairs of sentences.

Daniel **es** guapo.
Daniel is handsome. (*He is a handsome person.*)

Daniel **está** muy guapo esta noche.
Daniel looks very nice (*handsome*) *tonight.*

—¿Cómo **es** Amalia?
—**Es** simpática.
What is Amalia like (*as a person*)?
She's nice.

—Cómo **está** Amalia?
—**Está** enferma todavía.
How is Amalia (*feeling*)?
She's still sick.

❖ **Transparency 37**
Transparency 37 includes additional help with *ser* and *estar.*

Preliminary exercises: *Ser* and *estar*
- Have students tell whether *ser* or *estar* is required: **1.** She is a very pretty woman. **2.** María is very pretty tonight. **3.** I'm nervous because of the test. **4.** We are in class now. **5.** These students are from the U.S. **6.** It's 2:00. **7.** This is my mom.
- Have students form sentences based on the cues, for example, *¿El vestido? (muy elegante)* → *El vestido es muy elegante.* **1.** *¿John? (norteamericano)* **2.** *¿Mi escritorio? (desordenado)* **3.** *¿Los Hernández* (The Hernández family)*? (ocupados)* **4.** *¿Yo? (muy bien)* **5.** *¿Su abuelo? (muy viejo)* **6.** *¿El problema? (difícil)* **7.** *¿María? (de acuerdo con nosotros)?* **8.** *¿Mis hijos? (simpáticos y buenos)* **9.** *¿La tienda? (abierta ahora)*
- Ask for basic information: *¿Qué es? ¿Quién es? ¿Dónde está? ¿Cómo es? ¿Tiene una computadora? ¿Dónde está? ¿Le gusta?*

PASO 3 Gramática

CAPÍTULO 5

Paso 3: Gramática

See detailed supplementary materials for these grammar sections in IM.

16 Describing • Comparisons

Dos ciudades

México, D.F. (Distrito Federal)

Ricardo hace comparaciones entre la Ciudad de México, o el D.F. (Distrito Federal), y Sevilla.

«De verdad, me gustan las dos ciudades.

- La Ciudad de México es *más* grande *que* Sevilla.
- Tiene *más* edificios altos *que* Sevilla.
- En el D.F. no hace *tanto* calor *como* en Sevilla.

Pero…

- Sevilla es *tan* bonita *como* la Ciudad de México.
- No tiene *tantos* habitantes *como* el D.F.
- Sin embargo, los sevillanos son *tan* simpáticos *como* los mexicanos.

En total, ¡me gusta Sevilla *tanto como* la Ciudad de México!»

Ahora, hable Ud. de su ciudad o pueblo.

Mi ciudad/pueblo…

- (no) es tan grande como Chicago
- es más/menos cosmopolita que Quebec

Me gusta _____ (nombre de mi ciudad/pueblo)

- más que _____ (nombre de otra ciudad)
- menos que _____ (nombre de otra ciudad)
- tanto como _____ (nombre de otra ciudad)

El barrio de Santa Cruz, Sevilla, España

Follow-up: Comparisons

Have students compare their university with another: *¿Cuál es más grande? ¿Es tan cara su universidad como _____ (la otra)? Los estudiantes de esta universidad, ¿estudian tanto como los estudiantes de la otra (universidad)?*

Two Cities Ricardo makes comparisons between Mexico City, or D.F. (Federal District), and Seville. Really, I like both cities.

- Mexico City is bigger than Seville.
- It has more tall buildings than Seville.
- It is not as hot in Mexico City as it is in Seville.

But…

- Seville is as beautiful as Mexico City.
- It doesn't have as many inhabitants as Mexico City.
- Nevertheless, the people from Seville are as nice as those from Mexico City.

All told, I like Seville as much as Mexico City!

WWW Multimedia: Internet

Have students search Internet for more information on attractions and tourism in Mexico City or Seville. You might assign specific topics and have students give brief oral presentations based on their findings.

	Unequal Comparisons	Equal Comparisons
With Adjectives or Adverbs	más/menos ____ que	tan ____ como
With Nouns	más/menos ____ que	tanto/a/os/as ____ como
With Verbs	____ más/menos que	____ tanto como

COMPARISON OF ADJECTIVES

EQUAL COMPARISONS

tan + *adjective* + como
(*as*) (*as*)

Enrique es **tan** trabajador **como** Amalia.
Enrique is as hardworking as Amalia.

In English the *comparative* (**el comparativo**) is formed by using the adverbs *more* or *less* (***more** intelligent*, ***less** important*), or by adding *-er* at the end of the adjective (*tall**er**, smart**er***).

Suggestions: Comparisons
- Point out plural forms of irregular comparisons.
- Explain that *más grande* and *más pequeño* refer to size. *Mayor* and *menor* generally refer to age.

UNEQUAL COMPARISONS (REGULAR)

más + *adjective* + que
(*more*) (*than*)

Alicia es **más** perezosa **que** Marta.
Alicia is lazier than Marta.

menos + *adjective* + que
(*less*) (*than*)

Julio es **menos** listo **que** Jaime.
Julio is not as bright as Jaime.

UNEQUAL COMPARATIVES WITH IRREGULAR FORMS

bueno/a → mejor

Estos coches son **buenos,** pero esos son **mejores**.
These cars are good, but those are better.

malo/a → peor

Mi lámpara es **peor que** esta.
My lamp is worse than this one.

mayor (*older*)

Mi hermana es **mayor que** yo.
My sister is older than I (am).

menor (*younger*)

Mis primos son **menores que** yo.
My cousins are younger than I (am).

❖ Transparency 40

Conversación

A. La familia de Amalia y Sancho Jordán

Paso 1. Mire la siguiente foto e identifique a los miembros de esta familia. Luego compárelos (*compare them*) con otro pariente. **¡OJO!** Amalia tiene dos hermanos y un sobrino.

MODELO: Amalia es la hermana de Sancho. Ella es menor que Sancho, pero es más alta que él.

Paso 2. Su familia. Now compare the members of your own family, making ten comparative statements.

MODELO: Mi hermana Mary es mayor que yo, pero yo soy más alto/a que ella.

Paso 3. Now read your sentences from **Paso 2** to a classmate, who should not take notes on them. Ask him or her questions about your comparisons and see if he or she remembers the details of your family.

MODELO: ¿Qué miembro de mi familia es mayor que yo?

Suggestion A
Have students bring family picture and introduce and compare members as in *Conversación A.*

Follow-up B
- Have students use items as guide to ask a partner about the same information. As follow-up homework, have students write comparison of their activities with their partner's.
- Have students report findings to class. Tally answers and end activity with some generalizations provided by students, for example, *Por lo general, nos acostamos más tarde en el verano que en el invierno...*

B. La rutina diaria... en invierno y en verano

Paso 1. ¿Es diferente nuestra rutina diaria en las diferentes estaciones? Complete las siguientes oraciones sobre su rutina.

Palabras útiles: el gimnasio, el parque, afuera

	EN INVIERNO...	EN VERANO...
1.	me levanto a ____ (hora)	me levanto a ____
2.	almuerzo en ____	almuerzo en ____
3.	me divierto con mis amigos en ____	me divierto con mis amigos en ____
4.	estudio ____ horas todos los días	(no) estudio ____ horas todos los días
5.	estoy / me quedo en ____ (lugar) por la noche	estoy / me quedo en ____ por la noche
6.	me acuesto a ____	me acuesto a ____

Paso 2. Ahora compare sus actividades en invierno y en verano, según el modelo.

MODELO: En invierno me levanto más temprano/tarde que en verano.
(En invierno me levanto a la misma hora que en verano.)
(En invierno me levanto tan temprano como en verano.)

UN POCO DE TODO

A. ¿Qué están haciendo? Diga qué están haciendo las siguientes personas, usando una palabra o frase de cada columna y la forma progresiva. Si Ud. no sabe (*know*) exactamente qué están haciendo esas personas, ¡use su imaginación!

yo	jugar (al)	fútbol/basquetbol
mi mejor amigo/a	dormir(se)	un libro / una novela
mis padres	leer	la radio
los Bills de Buffalo / los Bulls de Chicago	descansar	a los estudiantes / a sus consejeros
el presidente / la presidenta de la universidad	viajar	un informe
el presidente de los Estados Unidos	escuchar	ejercicio físico
el profesor / la profesora de español	trabajar	¿ ?
—— (un compañero / una compañera de la clase de español que está ausente hoy)	practicar	
	hacer	
	¿ ?	
mi consejero/a		

Suggestion A
Encourage students to be creative and to use verbs and phrases other than those on the list.

B. Dos hemisferios. Complete the following paragraphs with the correct forms of the words in parentheses, as suggested by the context. When two possibilities are given in parentheses, select the correct word.

Hay (mucho[1]) diferencias entre el clima del hemisferio norte y el del hemisferio sur. Cuando (ser/estar[2]) invierno en este país, por ejemplo, (ser/estar[3]) verano en la Argentina, en Bolivia, en Chile… Cuando yo (salir[4]) para la universidad en enero, con frecuencia tengo que (llevar[5]) abrigo y botas. En (los/las[6]) países del hemisferio sur, un estudiante (poder[7]) asistir (a/de[8]) clases en enero llevando sólo pantalones (corto[9]), camiseta y sandalias. En muchas partes de este país, (antes de / durante[10]) las vacaciones en diciembre, casi siempre (hacer[11]) frío y a veces (nevar[12]). En (grande[13]) parte de Sudamérica, al otro lado del ecuador, hace calor y (muy/mucho[14]) sol durante (ese[15]) mes. A veces en enero hay fotos, en los periódicos, de personas que (tomar[16]) el sol y nadan[a] en las playas sudamericanas.

Tengo un amigo que (ir[17]) a (hacer/tomar[18]) un viaje a Buenos Aires. Él me dice[b] que allí la Navidad[c] (ser/estar[19]) una fiesta de verano y que todos (llevar[20]) ropa como la que[d] llevamos nosotros en julio. Parece[e] increíble, ¿verdad?

[a]*are swimming* [b]Él… *He tells me* [c]*Christmas* [d]la… *that which* [e]*It seems*

Follow-up B
To personalize the information ask students: *¿Le gustaría pasar la Navidad en Sudamérica? ¿Por qué? ¿Qué asocia Ud. con la Navidad? ¿Qué hizo el año pasado?*

Extension B
To review *ser, estar,* and *tener* phrases used in this chapter, have students ask and answer questions about figures in Transparency 38.

Answers B
1. *muchas* **2.** *es* **3.** *es* **4.** *salgo* **5.** *llevar* **6.** *los* **7.** *puede* **8.** *a* **9.** *cortos* **10.** *durante* **11.** *hace* **12.** *nieva* **13.** *gran* **14.** *mucho* **15.** *ese* **16.** *toman* **17.** *va* **18.** *hacer* **19.** *es* **20.** *llevan*

Comprensión: ¿Probable o improbable?

1. Los estudiantes argentinos van a la playa en julio.
2. Muchas personas sudamericanas hacen viajes de vacaciones en enero.
3. Hace frío en Santiago (Chile) en diciembre.

In the *Capítulo 5* section of "Chapter-by-Chapter Supplementary Materials" in the IM, you will find a chapter-culminating activity. You can use this activity to consolidate and review the vocabulary and grammar skills students have acquired.

PASO 4 Un paso más

Paso 4: Un paso más
Optional section

See IM for suggestions and follow-up activities to accompany the video segment.

VIDEOTECA: En contexto

FUNCTION:

Discussing travel plans

In this video segment, Roberto visits a travel agent to find out about vacation options. What kind of a vacation would Roberto prefer? What suggestions does the agent make?

A. Lluvia de ideas

- ¿Le gusta a Ud. hacer viajes? ¿Con quién? ¿Adónde le gusta ir? ¿En qué estación del año prefiere ir?
- Imagine Ud. que una persona quiere visitar su ciudad o su estado. ¿En qué estación debe ir? ¿Qué se puede hacer allí?

B. Dictado

Here is part of this segment's dialogue. Fill in the missing portions of the dialogue.

ROBERTO: ¿Es caro el Caribe?

AGENTE: Depende de la ___estación___.[1] En el invierno, cuesta más. En el ___verano___,[2] es más barato.

ROBERTO: Claro. ¿Y qué ___tiempo___[3] hace en el Caribe durante el verano?

AGENTE: En julio y ___agosto___,[4] por ejemplo, hace ___calor___.[5] Y llueve mucho también. ___Llueve___[6] casi todos los días.

ROBERTO: ¿Y qué tiempo ___hace___[7] durante el ___invierno___?[8]

AGENTE: Hace más fresco, y no llueve ___tanto___.[9]

ROBERTO: ¿Tiene alguna otra recomendación?

AGENTE: El país de Belice tiene lugares maravillosos para bucear.[a] Pero no es una ___isla___.[10]

ROBERTO: ¡Belice! ¡Qué buena idea!

[a]*scuba dive*

C. Un diálogo original

Paso 1. Con un compañero/una compañera, dramatice la escena de Roberto con la agente.

Paso 2. Imagine que Ud. y su compañero/a desean hacer un viaje juntos (*together*). Pero primero deben decidir adónde quieren ir.

E1: You like warm weather and exotic places. You don't have money to go to Europe.

E2: You like both eco-tourism (**ecoturismo**) as well as visiting important cities. You'd like to go to Europe, but will consider other options.

Cultura en contexto *Belize*

Belize, formerly known as British Honduras, has many beautiful beaches and coral reefs that attract an increasing number of tourists, particularly those interested in world-class scuba diving. Belize (in Spanish, **Belice**) was once part of Guatemala, though under British occupation at the time. Due to the influence of this British occupation, Belize is the only Central American country whose official language is English.

Follow-up B
To check comprehension ask students: *¿Qué desea hacer Roberto en sus vacaciones? ¿Qué lugar recomienda la agente? ¿Hay islas allí? ¿En qué época es más barato ir?*

WW. Multimedia: Internet
In small groups, have students prepare travel brochure for a vacation spot in a Spanish-speaking country. Direct them to Internet to do research and find resources. Have them present their brochures to class.

PASO FINAL

A LEER

Estrategia: Forming a General Idea about Content

Before starting a reading, it is a good idea to try to form a general sense of the content. The more you know about the reading before you begin to read, the easier it will seem to you. Here are some things you can do to prepare yourself for reading. You have already applied some of these strategies to the readings thus far in *¿Qué tal?*

1. Make sure you understand the title. Think about what it suggests to you and what you already know about the topic. Do the same with any subtitles in the reading.
2. Look at the drawings, photos, or other visual clues that accompany the reading. What do they indicate about the content?
3. Read the comprehension questions before starting to read the selection. They will direct you to the kind of information you should be looking for.

You should be able to determine the general message of the reading if you apply the preceding strategies.

- **The title.** The reading, "**Todos juntos en los trópicos**," contains a key word in the title: **trópicos**. It is a cognate. Can you guess what it means?
- **The art.** The reading is accompanied by a photograph and caption. What additional information do these tell you about the reading?
- **The comprehension questions.** Scan the questions in **Comprensión**. What additional clues do they give you about the content of the passage?

Suggestion: A leer
Do *Estrategia* in class the day you assign reading as homework for the next class period. Note that the strategy is applied point by point to reading.
Stress that this reading is authentic, with a few words changed to accommodate beginning students. If students can do comprehension activities, they have understood enough. Emphasize importance of this accomplishment at this stage of their language-learning.

WWW. Multimedia: Internet
After students have completed *A leer* have them search Internet for websites in Spanish about the Amazon and other rainforests (*selvas tropicales*) in Latin America. Encourage them to team up with a native speaker. Then, have them write a list of new words that they recognize as cognates, using reading strategies that they have learned so far. Encourage them to compare their lists with other classmates.

Sobre la lectura... This reading is taken from the magazine *Muy interesante,* which generally contains articles about popular science and related topics. Remember that knowing the source of a passage can also help you formulate hypotheses about the reading before you begin to read.

Todos juntos en los trópicos

Los trópicos son las regiones biológicamente más diversas del planeta y cuentan con[a] el triple de especies que en cualquier otra zona. Pero, ¿por qué? Los biólogos no han sido capaces[b] de dar una respuesta unívoca.[c] Es más, las diferentes teorías que se han propuesto[d] tienen todos sus puntos débiles.[e]

En resumen, existen tres razones expuestas para esta riqueza.[f] La primera teoría fue diseñada[g] hace 20 años[h] por Michael Rosenzweigh, de Arizona. Según él, en los trópicos hay más especies, sencillamente[i] porque se cuenta con más espacio geográfico habitable.

[a]cuentan... tienen [b]no... *have not been able* [c]respuesta... *unambiguous answer* [d]que... *that have been proposed* [e]puntos... *weak points* [f]expuestas... *given for this wealth* [g]fue... *was outlined* [h]hace... *20 years ago* [i]*simply*

No hay una teoría única para explicar la exuberancia natural que se produce en los trópicos.

La segunda es de los últimos años 80 y fue diseñada por George Stevens, de Nuevo México: las especies tropicales son esclavas[j] de sus condiciones térmicas;[k] por eso no pueden colonizar nuevos territorios menos cálidos[l] y se concentran como un gueto[m] en el trópico.

La tercera es una teoría histórica y explica que los trópicos fueron[n] las áreas de la Tierra que escaparon al efecto destructor del aumento[o] de las regiones heladas[p] durante las glaciaciones.

Ninguna de las tres ha sido confirmada.[q] ■

[j]*slaves* [k]*thermal* [l]*hot* [m]*ghetto* [n]*were* [o]*increase* [p]*frozen* [q]ha... *has been confirmed*

Suggestion: A escribir
Have several students read their essays. Ask the entire class 2–3 comprehension questions after each description, to encourage students to listen to one another.

Variations: A escribir
- Have students write 1–2 paragraphs on climate where they live. They can start *Vivo en un pueblo (una ciudad) cerca del mar (cerca de las montañas / en el desierto)...* They should mention weather during all seasons, and what students do because of weather.
- Bring weather map from a Hispanic country (from newspapers online). Have students study it and then prepare short meteorological report (*Informe del tiempo*).

Extension: A escribir
After students have searched Internet for websites that talk about rainforests in Latin America, have them answer following questions in Spanish. Then have them rewrite this information in 1–2 brief paragraphs. **1.** *¿Qué países de Latinoamérica tienen selvas tropicales?* **2.** *¿Cómo se llaman estas selvas?* **3.** *¿Cómo se llaman los grupos indígenas que viven en estas selvas?* **4.** *¿Qué tiempo hace en las selvas tropicales? ¿Hace buen tiempo? ¿Llueve mucho?*

Comprensión

A. ¿Se menciona o no? ¿Cuáles de los siguientes temas se mencionan en la lectura?

	SÍ	NO
1. Información sobre la gente (*people*) indígena de los trópicos.	☐	☐
2. Teorías que explican (*explain*) la biodiversidad de los trópicos.	☐	☐
3. Información sobre la deforestación de los trópicos.	☐	☐
4. Teorías que explican la climatología de los trópicos.	☐	☐

B. Resumen (*Summary*). En inglés, escriba un breve resumen de las tres teorías presentadas en la lectura. Compare su resumen con el de otro estudiante. ¿Cuál de las teorías parece más factible (*feasible*)?

A ESCRIBIR

La biodiversidad local. La lectura comenta la gran biodiversidad de los trópicos, y propone teorías que explican este fenómeno. ¿Cómo es la biodiversidad en la región donde Ud. vive? ¿Hay muchos animales y plantas indígenas? ¿Cuál es la relación entre el clima de la región y la flora y la fauna? Escriba un breve ensayo (*essay*) que comente cómo es el clima donde Ud. vive y qué animales y plantas habitan la zona. (Consulte un diccionario bilingüe si es necesario.)

En resumen

GRAMÁTICA

To review the grammar points presented in this chapter, refer to the indicated grammar presentations. You'll find further practice of these structures in the Workbook/Laboratory Manual, on the CD-ROM, and on the website.

14. Present Progressive: *estar* + *-ndo*

Do you know how to form the present progressive? When is this structure used in Spanish?

15. Summary of the Uses of *ser* and *estar*

You should know whether to use **ser** or **estar** in the following situations: to describe inherent qualities, to describe health and physical conditions, to express time, to form the present progressive.

16. Comparisons

Do you know how to compare things and people?

VOCABULARIO

Los verbos

celebrar	to celebrate
pasar	to spend (*time*); to happen
quedarse	to stay, remain (*in a place*)

¿Qué tiempo hace?

está (muy) nublado	it's (very) cloudy, overcast
hace...	it's . . .
buen/mal tiempo	good/bad weather
calor	hot
fresco	cool
frío	cold
sol	sunny
viento	windy
hay (mucha) contaminación	there's (lots of) pollution
llover (ue)	to rain
llueve	it's raining
nevar (ie)	to snow
nieva	it's snowing

Los meses del año

enero, febrero, marzo, abril, mayo, junio, julio, agosto, septiembre, octubre, noviembre, diciembre

Las estaciones del año

la primavera	spring
el verano	summer
el otoño	fall, autumn
el invierno	winter

Los lugares

la capital	capital city
la isla	island
el parque	park
la playa	beach

Otros sustantivos

el clima	climate
el cumpleaños	birthday

Suggestions: Vocabulario

- Divide class into 2 teams. Call out a month and have representatives from each team take turns mentioning a word or phrase related to that month. Other members of the team can offer suggestions, if their representative falters. When all related terms have been suggested, call out another month.
- Play charades in Spanish, using nouns adjectives, and comparisons from the *Vocabulario* list.
- Using a map or a globe, have students compare geographical locations. Prompt them with questions like *¿Qué ciudad está más al norte, Nueva York o Quito?* and have them answer in full sentences.
- Place common classroom item in different places in classroom (behind the door, underneath a desk, and so on) and have students describe location.

la fecha	date (*calendar*)
el/la novio/a	boyfriend/girlfriend
la respuesta	answer

Los adjetivos

abierto/a	open
aburrido/a	bored
alegre	happy
cansado/a	tired
cariñoso/a	affectionate
cerrado/a	closed
congelado/a	frozen; very cold
contento/a	content, happy
desordenado/a	messy
difícil	hard, difficult
enfermo/a	sick
fácil	easy
furioso/a	furious, angry
limpio/a	clean
loco/a	crazy
nervioso/a	nervous
ocupado/a	busy
ordenado/a	neat
preocupado/a	worried
querido/a	dear
seguro/a	sure, certain
sucio/a	dirty
triste	sad

Las comparaciones

más/menos… que	more/less . . . than
tan… como	as . . . as
tanto/a(s)… como	as much/many . . . as
tanto como	as much as
mayor	older
mejor	better; best
menor	younger
peor	worse

Las preposiciones

a la derecha de	to the right of
a la izquierda de	to the left of
al lado de	alongside of
cerca de	close to
debajo de	below
delante de	in front of
detrás de	behind
encima de	on top of
entre	between, among
lejos de	far from

Los puntos cardinales

el norte, el sur, el este, el oeste

Palabras adicionales

afuera	outdoors
¿Cuál es la fecha de hoy?	What's today's date?
esta noche	tonight
estar (*irreg.*) **bien**	to be comfortable (*temperature*)
mí (*obj. of prep.*)	me
el primero de	the first of (*month*)
siguiente	following
tener (*irreg.*) **(mucho) calor**	to be (very) warm, hot
tener (*irreg.*) **(mucho) frío**	to be (very) cold
ti (*obj. of prep.*)	you
todavía	still

CAPÍTULO 6

¿Qué le gusta comer?

Suggestion: Chapter Opening photo

Point out the chapter opening photo. Have students talk about the food in the photo. Ask whether everything is available in markets in this country and/or is familiar to them. Invite them to share their ideas about Hispanic foods. Encourage them to consider where residents of Panama shop for food. They can verify their responses on the Internet.

Resources

You and your students may find the following *¿Qué tal?* supplements helpful as you teach this chapter:

For the Instructor

- *Instructor's Manual and Resource Kit,* "Chapter-by-Chapter" Supplementary Materials
- Testing Program
- Overhead Transparencies 41–45
- Video (VHS or CD)
- *¿Qué tal?* Online Learning Center Website
- Audioscript
- Instructor's Resource CD

For Students

- Workbook/Laboratory Manual and Audio Program or Electronic Workbook/Laboratory Manual
- Video on CD
- Interactive CD-ROM
- *¿Qué tal?* Online Learning Center Website
- Listening Comprehension Audio CD
- McGraw-Hill Electronic Language Tutor (MHELT)

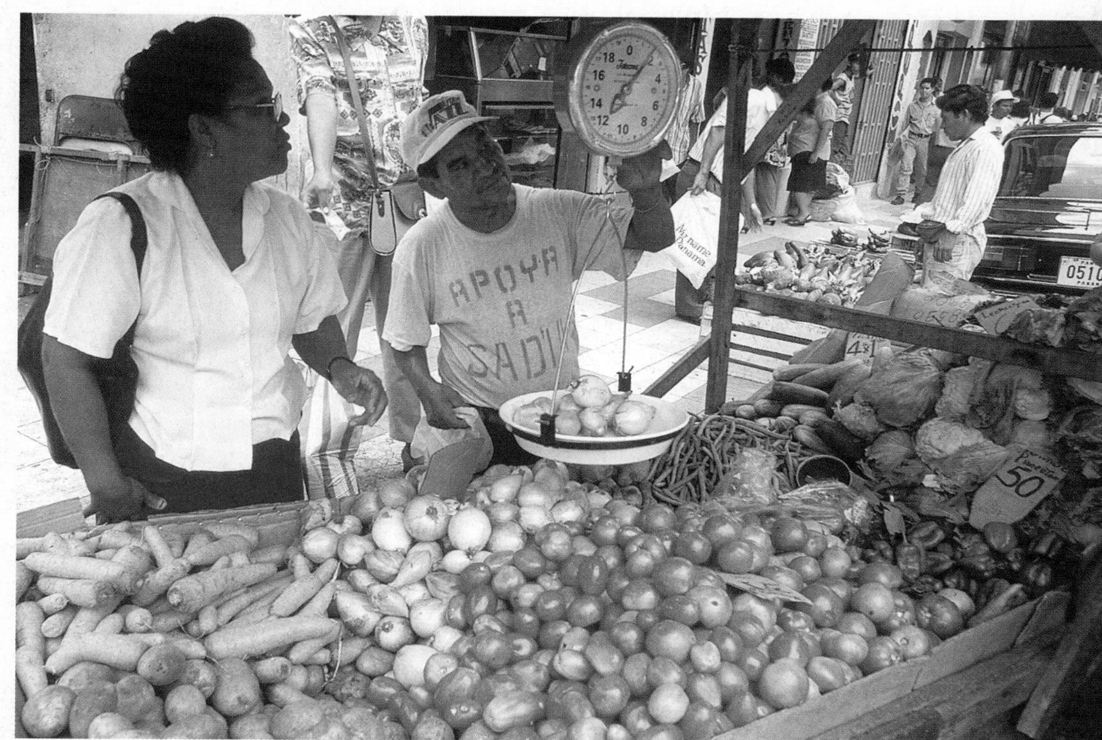

Esta señora compra cebollas (*onions*) en un mercado en Panamá. ▶

VOCABULARIO

- Food and eating in restaurants
- **Saber** and **conocer**; Personal **a**

GRAMÁTICA

17 Direct Object Pronouns
18 Indefinite and Negative Words
19 Formal Commands

CULTURA

- **Enfoque cultural:** Panamá
- **Nota cultural:** Foods in the Spanish-Speaking World
- **En los Estados Unidos y el Canadá:** Goya Foods, Inc.
- **Cultura en contexto:** El mercado

Multimedia

You will learn about shopping for food in the **En contexto** video segment.

Review vocabulary and grammar and practice language skills with the interactive CD-ROM.

Get connected to the Spanish-speaking world with the *¿Qué tal?* Online Learning Center: **www.mhhe.com/quetal**.

PASO 1 Vocabulario

Paso 1: Vocabulario
See detailed supplementary materials and exercises for this section and a model for vocabulary presentation and other material in the *Capítulo 6 Paso 1: Vocabulario* section of "Chapter-by-Chapter Supplementary Materials," IM.

La comida

Multimedia: Audio
Students can listen to and practice this chapter's vocabulary on their Listening Comprehension Audio CD.

❖ Transparencias 41–44

Las comidas

el desayuno → desayunar
breakfast → to have (eat) breakfast

el almuerzo → almorzar (ue)
lunch → to have (eat) lunch

la cena → cenar
dinner → to have (eat) dinner, supper

Otras bebidas

el refresco soft drink
el té tea
el vino blanco white wine

Otras verduras

el champiñón mushroom
los espárragos asparagus
los frijoles beans

---

*The noun **agua** (*water*) is feminine, but the masculine articles are used with it in the singular: ***el agua***. This occurs with all feminine nouns that begin with a stressed **a** sound, for example, ***el* (*un*) ama de casa** (*homemaker*).

Heritage speakers
Algunos mexicanos y mexicoamericanos dicen *guajolote* en vez de *pavo*. Pregúnteles a los hispanohablantes de la clase qué otras variaciones usan para referirse a la comida.

Otras frutas

la banana banana
la naranja orange

Otras carnes

el bistec steak
la chuleta (de cerdo) (pork) chop
la hamburguesa hamburger
el jamón ham
el pavo turkey
la salchicha sausage; hot dog

Otros pescados y mariscos

el atún tuna
los camarones shrimp
la langosta lobster
el salmón salmon

Otros postres

el flan (baked) custard
la galleta cookie
el helado ice cream

Otras comidas

el arroz rice
el huevo egg
el queso cheese
el sándwich sandwich
el yogur yogurt

Conversación

A. ¿Qué quiere tomar? Match the following descriptions of meals with these categories: **un menú ligero** (*light*) **para una dieta, una comida rápida, una cena elegante, un desayuno estilo norteamericano**.

1. una sopa fría, langosta, espárragos, una ensalada de lechuga y tomate, todo con vino blanco y, para terminar, un pastel
2. jugo de fruta, huevos con jamón, pan tostado y café
3. pollo asado, arroz, arvejas, agua mineral y, para terminar, una manzana
4. una hamburguesa con patatas fritas, un refresco y un helado

B. Definiciones. ¿Qué es?

1. un plato de lechuga y tomate
2. una bebida alcohólica blanca o roja
3. un líquido caliente (*hot*) que se toma* con cuchara (*spoon*)
4. una verdura anaranjada
5. la carne típica para la barbacoa en este país
6. una comida muy común en la China y en el Japón
7. la comida favorita de los ratones
8. una verdura frita que se come con las hamburguesas
9. una fruta roja o verde
10. una fruta amarilla de las zonas tropicales

*Placing **se** before a verb form can change its English equivalent slightly: **usa** (*he/she/it uses*) → **se usa** (*is used*).

Reciclado: Vocabulario

- Review names of colors. Have students tell what foods or drinks they associate with: *negro, blanco, amarillo, verde, rojo, anaranjado.* On first day of vocabulary presentation, allow students to have books open.
- Recycle place names. Have students tell what foods or drinks they associate with: *Francia, Inglaterra, México, China, Centroamérica, Colombia, San Francisco.*

Follow-up A
Have students give alternative menus for types of meals listed in directions.

Variation B
Do activity once, according to directions. Then, with books closed, give names of food items and have students give corresponding definitions, following model of items in *Conversación B.*

Note B
The *se* + verb structure is not stressed for active use in *¿Qué tal?*

Answers B
1. *una ensalada* 2. *el vino* 3. *la sopa* 4. *una zanahoria* 5. *la hamburguesa* 6. *el arroz* 7. *el queso* 8. *las patatas* 9. *la manzana* 10. *la banana*

PASO 2

Suggestion: Nota comunicativa
Do a series of actions, then state in Spanish what you have just done, for example, write your name on board, then erase it, turn lights off or on, open and close a book, sit down, stand up, and so on.

Note: Nota comunicativa
Remind students that they have already learned the preposition + infinitive structure.

NOTA COMUNICATIVA

Talking about What You Have Just Done

To talk about what you have *just* done, use the phrase **acabar** + **de** with an infinitive.

Acabo de almorzar con Beto.	*I just had lunch with Beto.*
Acabas de celebrar tu cumpleaños, ¿verdad?	*You just celebrated your birthday, didn't you?*

Note that the infinitive follows **de**. As you already know, the infinitive is the only verb form that can follow a preposition in Spanish.

Preliminary exercise D
Have students answer questions using *acabar de*, for example, *¿Quiere comer?* → *Acabo de comer.* **1.** *ver la televisión* **2.** *leer* **3.** *ir al centro* **4.** *desayunar* **5.** *almorzar* **6.** *cenar*

Suggestion D
Have students tell what they have just done before leaving these places: *¿Qué acaba de hacer Ud. cuando sale de... ?* **1.** *¿un mercado?* **2.** *¿una discoteca?* **3.** *¿un restaurante?* **4.** *¿una librería?* **5.** *¿el laboratorio de lenguas?* **6.** *¿una clase de literatura inglesa?* **7.** *¿un bar?*

Variation D
Have students work in groups of 2–3 to make suggestions to each other. Students respond by saying they have just done it: *¿Quiere Ud. comer?* → *No, acabo de comer. ¿Quiere Ud. mirar la televisión?* → *No, acabo de mirar la televisión.*

D. ¡Acabo de hacerlo! Imagine that a friend is pressuring you to do the following things. With a classmate, tell him or her that you just did each one, using either of the forms in the model.

MODELO: E1: ¿Por qué no estudias la lección? →
E2: Acabo de estudiar*la*. (*La* acabo de estudiar.)

1. ¿Por qué no escribes las composiciones para tus clases?
2. ¿Vas a comprar el periódico hoy?
3. ¿Por qué no pagas los cafés?
4. ¿Vas a preparar la comida para la fiesta?
5. ¿Puedes pedir la cuenta?
6. ¿Tienes hambre? ¿Por qué no comes los tacos que preparé (*I made*)?

Conversación

Una encuesta sobre la comida. Hágales (*Ask*) preguntas a sus compañeros de clase para saber si toman las comidas o bebidas indicadas y con qué frecuencia. Deben explicar también por qué toman o *no* toman cierta cosa.

MODELO: la carne → E1: ¿Comes carne?
E2: No *la* como casi nunca porque tiene mucho colesterol.

Palabras útiles: la cafeína, las calorías, el colesterol, la grasa (*fat*)

Frases útiles: estar a dieta, ser alérgico/a a, ser bueno/a para la salud (*health*), me pone (*it makes me*) nervioso/a, lo/la/los/las detesto

1. la carne
2. los mariscos
3. el yogur
4. la pizza
5. las hamburguesas
6. el pollo
7. el café
8. los dulces (*sweets; candy*)
9. el alcohol
10. el atún
11. los espárragos
12. el hígado (*liver*)

18 Expressing Negation • Indefinite and Negative Words

En la cocina de Diego y Antonio

DIEGO: Quiero comer *algo*, pero *no* hay *nada* de comer en esta casa. Y no tengo ganas de ir de compras. Y además, ¡*no* tengo *ni* un centavo!

ANTONIO: ¡Ay! *Siempre* eres así. Tú *nunca* tienes ganas de ir de compras. Y lo del dinero… ¡esa es otra historia!

¿Quién… ?

1. tiene hambre
2. nunca tiene dinero
3. critica a su amigo
4. no quiere ir de compras

A. Here is a list of the most common indefinite and negative words in Spanish. You have been using many of them since the first chapters of *¿Qué tal?*

Follow-up: Indefinite...
To personalize information and to check comprehension, ask: **1.** *¿Tienen Uds. ganas de comer algo ahora mismo? ¿Qué?* **2.** *¿Quién no tiene dinero nunca?* **3.** *¿A alguien le gusta ir de compras para comprar comida?* **4.** *¿A quién nunca le gusta ir de compras?*

algo	something, anything	**nada**	nothing, not anything
alguien	someone, anyone	**nadie**	no one, nobody, not anybody
algún (alguno/a/os/as)	some, any	**ningún (ninguno/a)**	no, none, not any
siempre	always	**nunca, jamás**	never
también	also	**tampoco**	neither, not either

Pronunciation hint: Pronounce the ***d*** in ***nada*** and ***nadie*** as a fricative, that is, like a *th* sound: ***na đa, na đie***.

Point out
Ch. 6 of the Workbook/Laboratory Manual offers pronunciation practice for the letter *d*.

B. Pay particular attention to the following aspects of using negative words.

- When a negative word comes after the main verb, Spanish requires that another negative word—usually **no**—be placed before the verb. When a negative word precedes the verb, **no** is not used.

¿**No** estudia **nadie**?
¿**Nadie** estudia? } *Isn't anyone studying?*

No estás en clase **nunca**.
Nunca estás en clase. } *You're never in class.*

No quieren cenar aquí **tampoco**.
Tampoco quieren cenar aquí. } *They don't want to have dinner here, either.*

In Diego and Antonio's kitchen DIEGO: I want to eat something, but there's nothing to eat in this house. And I don't feel like going shopping. And furthermore, I don't have a cent! ANTONIO: Ah! You're always like that. You never feel like going shopping. And that bit about the money . . . , that's another story!

Preliminary exercise A
Say the following words and have students respond with the corresponding opposite: *algo, alguien, alguno, siempre, también, nada, nadie, ninguno, nunca, tampoco.*

Extension A
En casa... 7. *Quiero escuchar algo en la radio.* 8. *Siempre me gusta escuchar música popular.* 9. *Hay algunas ideas fascinantes en este libro.* 10. *Tengo algunos libros muy interesantes.*

- The adjectives **alguno** and **ninguno** shorten to **algún** and **ningún,** respectively, before a masculine singular noun—just as **uno** shortens to **un, bueno** to **buen,** and **malo** to **mal**. The plural forms **ningunos** and **ningunas** are rarely used.

—¿Hay **algunos** recados para mí hoy?
—Lo siento, pero hoy no hay **ningún** recado para Ud.
Are there any messages for me today?
I'm sorry, but there are no messages for you today. (There is not a single message for you today.)

Follow-up A
Have students give the negative: 1. *Hay algo interesante en el menú.* 2. *Tienen algunos platos típicos.* 3. *El profesor cena allí también.* 4. *Mis amigos siempre almuerzan allí.* 5. *Preparan algo especial para grupos grandes.* 6. *Siempre hacen platos nuevos.* 7. *Y también sirven paella, mi plato favorito.*

Extension B
Using several books, set up a similar pattern with *¿Hay algunos libros en el suelo* (floor)*?* → *Sí, hay algunos. / No, no hay ninguno.* Expand activity by using other classroom objects and student possessions at hand.

❖ Transparency 45

Práctica

A. Manolo está de mal humor (*in a bad mood*)**.** Hoy Manolo tiene una actitud muy negativa. ¿Qué opina Manolo de las afirmaciones de su esposa Lola?

MODELO: LOLA: Tengo algunos estudiantes excelentes este año.
MANOLO: Pues, yo no tengo ningún estudiante excelente este año.

1. Hay muchas clases interesantes en el departamento.
2. Me gusta tomar café con mis estudiantes con frecuencia.
3. Hay algunas personas buenas en la administración.
4. También hay un candidato bueno para el puesto (*position*) de rector.
5. Hay muchas personas inteligentes en la universidad.

B. ¿Qué pasa esta noche en casa? Tell whether the following statements about what is happening at this house are true (**cierto**) or false (**falso**). Then create as many additional sentences as you can about what is happening, following the model of the sentences.

1. No hay nadie en el baño.
2. En la cocina, alguien está preparando la cena.
3. No hay ninguna persona en el patio.
4. Hay algo en la mesa del comedor.
5. Algunos amigos se están divirtiendo en la sala.
6. Hay algunos platos en la mesa del comedor.
7. No hay ningún niño en la casa.

Conversación

Preguntas

1. ¿Vamos a... ? ¿vivir en la luna (*moon*) algún día? ¿viajar (*to travel*) a otros planetas? ¿vivir allí algún día? ¿establecer contacto con seres (*beings*) de otros planetas algún día?
2. ¿Algunos de los estudiantes de esta universidad son de países extranjeros? ¿De dónde son? ¿Algunos de sus amigos son de habla española (*Spanish-speaking*)? ¿De dónde son?

Extension: Conversación
3. *¿Hay algo más importante que el dinero? ¿que la amistad? ¿que el amor?* 4. *En la clase, ¿hay alguien más inteligente que el profesor / la profesora? ¿más estudioso/a que Ud.? ¿más rico/a que Ud.?* 5. *La perfección es una meta* (goal) *imposible, ¿verdad? ¿Hay alguna clase perfecta en esta universidad? ¿Hay alguna residencia perfecta? ¿una familia perfecta?*

Enfoque *cultural*

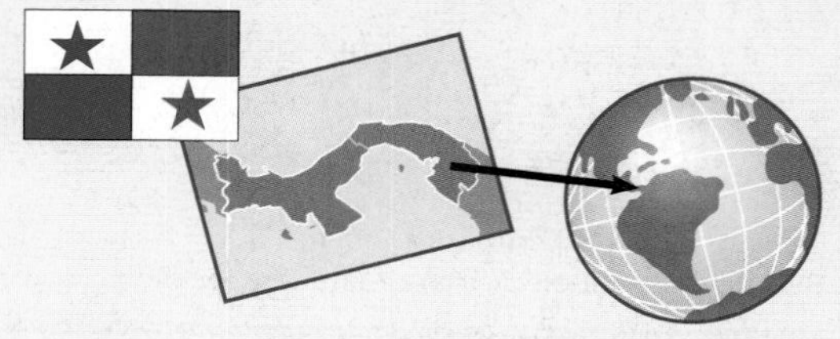

Panamá

Enfoque cultural
See follow-up activities for this section in chapter-by-chapter materials in IM.

Datos esenciales

Nombre oficial: República de Panamá

Capital: Ciudad de Panamá

Población: 2.778.526 de habitantes

Moneda: el balboa (también se usa el dólar estadounidense)

Idioma oficial: el español

Conozca... el Canal de Panamá

El Canal de Panamá, construido a través del[a] istmo entre los dos continentes americanos, comunica los océanos Atlántico y Pacífico. Mide[b] aproximadamente 80 kilómetros (50 millas) de largo, 12,5 metros (41 pies[c]) de ancho[d] y 200 metros (más de 63 pies) de profundidad. Su construcción facilita la comunicación marítima entre las costas este y oeste de los continentes. Antes de la existencia del canal, los barcos tenían que darle la vuelta a[e] América del Sur para ir de una costa a otra. Hoy, el viaje por el Canal de Panamá toma aproximadamente ocho horas, pues[f] es necesario pasar por un número de esclusas.[g]

La idea de construir un canal a través del istmo data de 1534, cuando el emperador español Carlos V (Quinto) la propone. Más tarde, en 1881, el ingeniero francés Fernando de Lesseps también va a sugerir un proyecto similar. Pero el canal no se construye hasta el siglo XX, por los Estados Unidos. Esto ocasiona[h] la presencia de los Estados Unidos en la vida de Panamá. Como resultado, hay un uso extendido del inglés en el país, se usa el dólar y ha habido[i] una gran intervención en la política del país.

Una esclusa del Canal de Panamá

El canal se inaugura en 1914 y es administrado por los Estados Unidos hasta 1999. Desde el primero de enero del año 2000, la República de Panamá está a cargo de[j] su gran canal.

[a]construido... *built across the* [b]*It measures* [c]*feet* [d]de... *in width* [e]tenían... *had to go around* [f]*because* [g]*canal locks* [h]*brings about* [i]ha... *there has been* [j]a... *in control of*

¡Fíjese!

- **Panamá** es una palabra indígena que significa «tierra de muchos peces[a]».
- La Carretera[b] Panamericana, el sistema de carreteras que va de Alaska al Panamá, se interrumpe[c] en la densa e[d] impenetrable selva[e] panameña de Darién. Para llegar a Sudamérica es necesario tomar un barco[f] hasta Colombia, donde continúa la carretera.
- La Sra. Mireya Moscoso ganó[g] las elecciones presidenciales de 1998. La viuda[h] de otro presidente, doña Mireya es la primera mujer panameña en asumir el cargo.[i]

[a]*fish* [b]*Highway* [c]se... *breaks off, is interrupted* [d]y [e]*jungle* [f]*boat* [g]*won* [h]*widow* [i]*post*

Capítulo 6 of the video to accompany *¿Qué tal?* contains cultural footage of Panama.

Visit the *¿Qué tal?* website at www.mhhe.com/quetal.

Notes

- Vasco Núñez de Balboa explored the Isthmus of Panama in 1513 and discovered that it was only a short distance from the Atlantic Ocean to the Pacific Ocean. He founded the first European settlements on the north coast.
- Gold from Peru traveled across Panama during Spanish colonial times, as did prospectors headed for the California gold fields in 1849.
- General Manuel Noriega ousted the Panamanian president in 1985 and became acting head of government. After Noriega was indicted for drug activities and other illegal acts, the U.S. Army invaded Panama and brought Noriega to Miami for trial. He was convicted in 1992.

PASO 3 Gramática

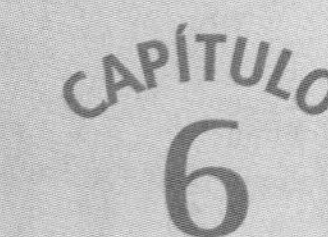

Paso 3: Gramática
See detailed supplementary materials for these grammar sections in IM.

19 Influencing Others • Formal Commands

Receta para guacamole

El guacamole

Ingredientes:
1 aguacate[a]
1 diente de ajo,[b] prensado[c]
1 tomate
jugo de un limón
sal
un poco de cilantro fresco[d]

Cómo se prepara
Corte el aguacate y el tomate en trozos[e] pequeños. *Añada* el jugo del limón, el ajo, el cilantro y la sal a su gusto. *Mezcle* bien todos los ingredientes y *sírvalo* con tortillas fritas de maíz.[f]

En español, los mandatos se usan con frecuencia en las recetas. Estos verbos se usan en forma de mandato en esta receta. ¿Puede encontrarlos?

añadir	to add
cortar	to cut
mezclar	to mix
servir (i, i)	to serve

[a]*avocado* [b]diente… *clove of garlic* [c]*crushed* [d]*fresh* [e]*pieces* [f]*corn*

Suggestion: Formal Commands
Help students formulate recipes for simple foods such as a salad or a sandwich.

FORMAL COMMAND FORMS

In *¿Qué tal?* you have seen commands throughout the direction lines of exercises: **haga, complete, conteste**, and so on.

Commands (imperatives) are verb forms used to tell someone to do something. In Spanish, *formal commands* (**los mandatos formales**) are used with people whom you address as **Ud.** or **Uds.** Here are some of the basic forms.

	hablar	**comer**	**escribir**	**volver**	**decir**
Ud.	habl**e**	com**a**	escrib**a**	vuelv**a**	dig**a**
Uds.	habl**en**	com**an**	escrib**an**	vuelv**an**	dig**an**
English	*speak*	*eat*	*write*	*come back*	*tell*

A. Almost all formal commands are based on the **yo** form of the present tense. Replace the **-o** with **-e** or **-en** for **-ar** verbs; replace the **-o** with **-a** or **-an** for **-er** and **-ir** verbs.

hablo → habl**e**
como → com**a**
escribo → escrib**a**

B. Formal commands of stem-changing verbs will show the stem change.

p**ie**nse Ud.
v**ue**lva Ud.
p**i**da Ud.

C. Verbs ending in **-car, -gar**, and **-zar** have a spelling change to preserve the **-c-, -g-**, and **-z-** sounds.	c → qu g → gu z → c	buscar: bus**que** Ud. pagar: pa**gue** Ud. empezar: empie**ce** Ud.
D. The **Ud./Uds.** commands for verbs that have irregular **yo** forms will reflect the irregularity.	conocer decir* (*to say, tell*) hacer oír poner salir tener traer venir ver	→ **conozca** Ud. → **diga** Ud. → **haga** Ud. → **oiga** Ud. → **ponga** Ud. → **salga** Ud. → **tenga** Ud. → **traiga** Ud. → **venga** Ud. → **vea** Ud.
E. A few verbs have irregular **Ud./Uds.** command forms.	dar* (*to give*) estar ir saber ser	→ **dé** Ud. → **esté** Ud. → **vaya** Ud. → **sepa** Ud. → **sea** Ud.

POSITION OF PRONOUNS WITH FORMAL COMMANDS

• Direct object pronouns and reflexive pronouns must follow affirmative commands and be attached to them. In order to maintain the original stress of the verb form, an accent mark is added to the stressed vowel if the original command has two or more syllables.	Léa**lo** Ud. Siénte**se,** por favor.	*Read it.* *Sit down, please.*
• Direct object and reflexive pronouns must precede negative commands.	**No lo** lea Ud. **No se** siente.	*Don't read it.* *Don't sit down.*

Práctica

A. Profesor(a) por un día. Imagine que Ud. es el profesor / la profesora hoy. ¿Qué mandatos debe dar a la clase?

MODELOS: hablar español → Hablen Uds. español.
hablar inglés → No hablen Uds. inglés.

1. llegar a tiempo
2. leer la lección
3. escribir una composición
4. abrir los libros
5. estar en clase mañana
6. traer los libros a clase
7. estudiar los verbos nuevos
8. ¿ ?

Preliminary exercises: Formal Commands
- Have students give singular formal command: *ir, comer, bailar, estar, ser, volver, levantarse.*
- Have students give plural formal command: *saber, conocer, tener, esperar, jugar, dormir, acostarse.*
- Ask students: *¿Dónde se pone el pronombre de complemento directo* ***lo****, delante o detrás de estos verbos? no coma, mire, estudie, no compren, no paguen, haga.*

*__Decir__ and **dar** are used primarily with indirect objects. Both of these verbs and indirect object pronouns will be formally introduced in **Capítulo 7**.

Suggestion A
Have students offer commands about what you should or should not do in class. Remind them to add *por favor* for politeness, and perhaps a begging tone to convince you to be nice to them.

Note B
The verbs on which commands should be based are indicated in *italics*.

Variation B
Have students give advice to *los Sres. Rossi*.

Note B, C
Not all Hispanics have Spanish last names. In Argentina, for example, a large percentage of the population is of Italian origin and has Italian last names, as in *Prácticas B* and *C*.

Preliminary exercises C
- Have students give negative command for each affirmative command: **1.** *Cómprelo.* **2.** *Estúdielas.* **3.** *Mírelo.* **4.** *Llámeme.* **5.** *Apréndalo.* **6.** *Escríbame.*
- Have students give affirmative command for each negative command: **1.** *No lo coma.* **2.** *No lo lea.* **3.** *No lo haga.* **4.** *No lo sirva.* **5.** *No lo traiga.*

Preliminary exercises D
- Have students give negative command for each affirmative command: **1.** *Acuéstese.* **2.** *Aféitese.* **3.** *Lávese.* **4.** *Siéntese.*
- Have students give affirmative command for each negative command: **1.** *No se bañe.* **2.** *No se levante.* **3.** *No se quite los zapatos.* **4.** *No se ponga la chaqueta.*

B. ¡Pobre Sr. Rossi!

Paso 1. El Sr. Rossi no se siente (*feel*) bien. Lea la descripción que él da de algunas de sus actividades.

«*Trabajo* muchísimo[a] —¡me gusta trabajar! En la oficina, *soy* impaciente y *critico* bastante[b] a los otros. En mi vida personal, a veces *soy* un poco impulsivo. *Fumo* bastante y también *bebo* cerveza y otras bebidas alcohólicas, a veces sin moderación… *Almuerzo* y *ceno* fuerte, y casi nunca *desayuno*. Por la noche, con frecuencia *salgo* con los amigos —me gusta ir a las discotecas— y *vuelvo* tarde a casa.»

[a]*a whole lot* [b]*a good deal*

Paso 2. ¿Qué *no* debe hacer el Sr. Rossi para estar mejor? Aconséjele (*Advise him*) sobre lo que (*what*) no debe hacer. Use los verbos indicados o cualquier (*any*) otro, según los modelos.

MODELOS: Trabajo → Sr. Rossi, no trabaje tanto.
soy → Sr. Rossi, no sea tan impaciente.

C. Situaciones. El Sr. Rossi quiere adelgazar (*to lose weight*). ¿Debe o no debe comer o beber las siguientes cosas? Con otro/a estudiante, haga y conteste preguntas según los modelos:

MODELOS: ensalada → E1: ¿Ensalada?
E2: Cómala.
postres → E1: ¿Postres?
E2: No los coma.

1. alcohol (*m.*)
2. verduras
3. pan
4. dulces
5. leche
6. hamburguesas con queso
7. frutas
8. refrescos dietéticos
9. pollo
10. carne
11. pizza
12. jugo de fruta

D. ¡Estoy harto de Uds. dos! (*I'm fed up with you two!*) Imagine que Ud. acaba de volver de clase y la casa es un desastre. Está enojado/a y empieza a gritarles (*yell*) mandatos a sus compañeros de casa sobre su apariencia física y sus hábitos.

MODELO: afeitarse → ¡Aféitense!

1. despertarse más temprano
2. levantarse más temprano
3. bañarse más
4. quitarse esa ropa sucia
5. ponerse ropa limpia
6. vestirse mejor
7. estudiar más
8. no divertirse todas las noches con los amigos
9. ir más a la biblioteca
10. no acostarse tan tarde
11. ayudar con los quehaceres
12. ¿ ?

Note: Nota comunicativa
This introduction to the subjunctive will familiarize students with its forms and uses. At this point, students will only be expected to passively recognize forms and understand why/how they are used. More detailed explanations of and subsequent practice with the subjunctive are provided in *Capítulo 12*. From this point on, however, instructor's annotations may use subjunctive so that students receive meaningful input.

NOTA COMUNICATIVA

El subjuntivo

Except for the command form, all verb forms that you have learned thus far in *¿Qué tal?* have been part of what is called the *indicative mood* (**el modo indicativo**). In both English and Spanish, the indicative is used to state facts and to ask questions. It objectively expresses most real-world actions or states of being.

Both English and Spanish have another verb system called the *subjunctive mood* (**el modo subjuntivo**). The **Ud./Uds.** command forms that you have just learned are part of the subjunctive system. You will not use the subjunctive actively until it is introduced (in **Capítulo 12**). But from this point on in *¿Qué tal?* you will see the subjunctive used where it is natural to use it. What follows is a brief introduction to the subjunctive that will make it easy for you to recognize it when you see it.

Here are some examples of the forms of the subjunctive. The **Ud./Uds.** forms (identical to the **Ud./Uds.** command forms) are highlighted.

hablar		**comer**		**servir**		**salir**	
hable	hablemos	coma	comamos	sirva	sirvamos	salga	salgamos
hables	habléis	comas	comáis	sirvas	sirváis	salgas	salgáis
hable	hablen	coma	coman	sirva	sirvan	salga	salgan

The subjunctive is used to express more subjective or conceptualized states, in contrast to the indicative, which reports facts, information that is objectively true. Here are just a few of the situations in which the subjunctive is used in Spanish.

- to express what the speaker wants others to do (I want you to . . .)
- to express emotional reactions (I'm glad that . . .)
- to express probability or uncertainty (it's likely that . . .)

E. El cumpleaños de María. Fíjese en (*Notice*) los verbos subrayados (*underlined*). Diga por qué razón están subrayados. (Use la lista de la **Nota comunicativa**.)

En el parque

RAÚL: Como hoy es tu cumpleaños, quiero invitarte a cenar. ¿En qué restaurante quieres que cenemos?
MARÍA: Prefiero que tú me[a] prepares una de tus espléndidas cenas.
RAÚL: ¡Con mucho gusto!

En casa de María

MADRE: (*Hablando por teléfono.*) No, lo siento,[b] pero María no está en casa.
LUISA: ¿Es posible que esté en la biblioteca?
MADRE: No. Sé que ella y Raúl están cenando en casa de él.
LUISA: Ah, sí. Bueno, ¿puede pedirle a ella que llame a Luisa cuando regrese?
MADRE: Sí, cómo no,[c] Luisa. Adiós.
LUISA: Hasta luego.

[a]*for me* [b]lo... *I'm sorry* [c]cómo... *of course*

Suggestions: Nota comunicativa
- Conjugate present subjunctive of *bailar* and *comer* on board. Start with *Quiero que (tú/él/ella...*). Point out that if the subject of both clauses is the same, the second verb is often used in the infinitive.
- Point out that subjunctive also occurs in English, though not as much: *God bless you, I wish I were rich, We hope that he may be able to come,* and so on.

Preliminary exercises E
- Have students tell whether these verbs are *yo* subjunctive or *yo* indicative: *cene, cena; vaya, va; hago, haga; pido, pida; lleve, llevo; me visto, me vista.*
- Have students complete sentence with correct *Uds.* forms of subjunctive of verbs: *Yo deseo que Uds... estudiar, bailar, comprarme regalos, hacerme feliz, llegar a tiempo a clase, divertirse.*

Note E
This activity deals with recognition of forms and conceptualization of the subjunctive only.

Follow-up E
Ask students *sí/no* questions. **1.** *¿María quiere ir a un restaurante? ¿Quiere cocinar?* **2.** *Y Raúl, ¿quiere hacer algo por María? ¿Quiere María que Raúl haga algo por ella?* **3.** *¿Quiere María que Raúl la invite a un restaurante? ¿Quiere que él cocine para ella?* **4.** *La amiga de María, ¿quiere hablar con la madre de María? ¿Sabe la amiga dónde está María? Y la madre, ¿sabe dónde está María?* **5.** *La amiga, ¿quiere ir a casa de Raúl para hablar con María? ¿Quiere que María la llame?* **6.** *¿Quiere la amiga que María la llame durante la cena con Raúl? ¿cuando María vuelva a casa?*

Suggestions: En los Estados Unidos y el Canadá...

- Check comprehension with *¿cierto o falso?* statements: **1.** *La familia Unanue es originalmente de México.* **2.** *La compañía Goya siempre tuvo* (had) *el nombre «Goya».* **3.** *Los productos Goya sólo son productos de la cocina de España.* **4.** *Los propietarios de Goya en la actualidad no son hispanos.* Also ask: *¿Cuál es uno de los grandes honores de la compañía Goya?*

En los Estados Unidos y el Canadá...*

Necesita Tenerlos

Goya Foods, Inc.

En Norteamérica muchos conocen la marca Goya: hay **frijoles, arroz, condimentos, bebidas, café, productos de coco,**[a] **jugos de frutas tropicales** y muchos productos más que son fundamentales para **las cocinas caribeña, mexicana, centroamericana y sudamericana.**

En los años 30 Prudencio Unanue, **un emigrante vasco** de una región del norte de España, funda[b] la compañía Goya. Unanue y **su esposa puertorriqueña** llegan a Nueva York en 1916 y fundan Unanue Inc. en Manhattan en 1935, una compañía especializada en **importaciones de productos españoles** como **olivas, aceite de oliva**[c] **y sardinas enlatadas.**[d] En 1936 la compañía recibe el nombre de Goya. Desde 1974 la oficina principal está en Nueva Jersey. Hoy tiene **centros de procesamiento y distribución** en diversos estados, además de Puerto Rico, la República Dominicana y España.

La compañía Goya está todavía en manos de[e] la familia Unanue: los hijos de Prudencio, Joseph y Frank, y seis miembros de **la tercera**[f] **generación**. Goya es la primera compañía propiedad de hispanos representada en el Museo Nacional de Historia Americana del Instituto Smithsonian, en Washington, D.C., donde hay una colección de sus anuncios y envases.[g]

[a]*coconut* [b]*founds* [c]aceite... *olive oil* [d]*canned* [e]está... *still belongs to* [f]*third* [g]anuncios... *ads and containers*

- Ask students which Latin American and Spanish dishes they have tried. Have them list ingredients they know that are used in Spain and some Latin American countries. Supplement that list if necessary. Ask: *¿Qué ingredientes tiene la paella? ¿Qué ingredientes llevan las enchiladas? ¿Quién conoce el choclo* (maíz) *del Perú?*
- Ask students if they know or buy the Goya brand.
- Have students visit a grocery store that sells Hispanic food to find Goya products and learn what they are for. Have them find other brands of Hispanic foods. Students can also find the Goya website on the Internet.

Follow-up: Conversación

- Have students respond with affirmative and negative commands: **1.** *Estoy cansado.* **2.** *Tengo sed.* **3.** *Tengo hambre.* **4.** *No puedo dormir.* **5.** *No entiendo el ejercicio.* **6.** *Necesito más dinero.* **7.** *Mis padres quieren saber cómo estoy.* **8.** *No puedo encontrar mi libro de español.*

Conversación

En la oficina del consejero. Imagine that you are a guidance counselor. Students consult you with all kinds of questions, some trivial and some important. Offer advice to them in the form of affirmative or negative commands. How many different commands can you invent for each situation?

1. EVELIA: No me gusta tomar clases por la mañana. Siempre estoy muy cansada durante esas clases y además a esa hora tengo hambre. Pienso constantemente en el almuerzo... y no puedo concentrarme en las explicaciones.
2. FABIÁN: En mi clase de cálculo, ¡no entiendo nada! No puedo hacer los ejercicios y durante la clase tengo miedo de hacer preguntas, porque no quiero parecer (*seem*) tonto.
3. FAUSTO: Fui (*I went*) a México el verano pasado y me gustó (*I liked it*) mucho. Quiero volver a México este verano. Ahora que lo conozco mejor, quiero ir en mi coche y no en autobús como el verano pasado. Desgraciadamente (*Unfortunately*) no tengo dinero para hacer el viaje.

*From this point on in *¿Qué tal?*, the **En los Estados Unidos y el Canadá...** sections will be written in Spanish. Important words will be in boldface type. Scanning those words before you begin to read will help you get the gist of the passage.

- Have students write commands they would like to give to: **1.** *el presidente / el primer ministro* **2.** *los candidatos* **3.** *Jay Leno, David Letterman* (or any other television personality) **4.** *sus amigos* **5.** *el profesor / la profesora*

UN POCO DE TODO

A. ¿Qué hace Roberto los martes?

Paso 1. Describa la rutina de Roberto, haciendo oraciones según las indicaciones.

1. martes / Roberto / nunca / salir / apartamento / antes de / doce
2. esperar / su amigo Samuel / en / parada (*bus stop*) del autobús
3. (ellos) llegar / universidad / a / una
4. (ellos) buscar / su amiga Ceci / en / cafetería
5. a / dos / todos / tener / clase / de / sicología
6. siempre / (ellos) oír / conferencias (*lectures*) / interesante / y / hacer / alguno / pregunta
7. a / cinco / Samuel y Roberto / volver / esperar / autobús
8. Roberto / preparar / cena / y / luego / mirar / televisión

B. La forma de comer. Complete the following paragraphs with the correct form of the words in parentheses, as suggested by the context. When two possibilities are given, select the correct word.

La forma de comer diferencia a las personas. Aquí habla Pilar Fuentes, una española que (vivir[1]) en California con dos estudiantes (norteamericano[2]).

«Yo creo que las costumbres[a] de mis compañeros son un poco (extraño[3]). Generalmente, (por/para[4]) la mañana, mi compañero Peter (desayunar[5]) dos huevos fritos, y un vaso[b] de leche (frío[6]). También él (preparar[7]) pan tostado sin mantequilla. A la una (almorzar[8]) en la universidad. (Comprar[9]) comida china en uno de (ese[10]) restaurantes pequeños que hay en el *campus*. Por (el/la[11]) tarde, (comer[12]) su cena típica: (un/una[13]) pizza grande y un plato de helado de pistacho con chocolate.

Carol, la otra compañera, es muy diferente. Siempre (ser/estar[14]) a dieta. Además cree que su manera de comer (es/estar[15]) muy natural. (*Ella:* Desayunar[16]) café negro. Para el almuerzo, ella (preparar[17]) un sándwich de pan integral[c] y también (unos/unas[18]) zanahorias y una naranja. Su cena (ser[19]) sencilla:[d] arroz integral y verduras. Parece que ella quiere compensar[e] las calorías de los dulces que (*ella*: comer[20]) para la merienda[f]… »

[a]*customs* [b]*glass* [c]*whole grain* [d]*simple* [e]*make up for* [f]*snack*

Comprensión: ¿Probable o improbable?

1. Pilar cree que la forma de comer de sus compañeros es muy normal.
2. Peter sabe cocinar muy bien.
3. Carol nunca tiene ganas de comer un bistec.
4. Carol es vegetariana.

Follow-up A
Have students narrate their routine on a given day of the week. This can be done in pairs or directed by questions.

Variation B
Have students imagine that a foreigner in this country asks them about certain foods and where he/she can find them in your area. Have students give as much information as possible. **1.** *una tortilla española* **2.** *una langosta* **3.** *una hamburguesa* **4.** *unas chuletas* **5.** *pizza* **6.** *arándanos* (blueberries)

Suggestion B
Ask students: **1.** *¿Prefiere Ud. cenar en casa o en la cafetería estudiantil?* **2.** *¿Hay días que no almuerza / cena? ¿Por qué?* **3.** *¿Prefiere Ud. una hamburguesa o un bistec?* **4.** *¿Qué / Dónde come Ud. cuando tiene mucha prisa / mucho dinero / poco dinero?* **5.** *¿Qué bebida prefiere por la mañana / noche?* **6.** *¿Qué le gusta comer como merienda?*

In the *Capítulo 6* segment of "Chapter-by-Chapter Supplementary Materials" in the IM, you will find a chapter-culminating activity. You can use this activity to consolidate and review the vocabulary and grammar skills students have acquired.

PASO 4 Un paso más

CAPÍTULO 6

Paso 4: Un paso más
Optional section

See IM for suggestions and follow-up activities to accompany the video segment.

VIDEOTECA: En contexto

FUNCTION:
Shopping for food

Cultura en contexto
El mercado

En Latinoamérica y España, muchas personas todavía compran verduras, fruta, carne y pescado en los mercados del barrio donde viven. Aunque cada vez más[a] hay grandes supermercados con comidas congeladas[b] y enlatadas,[c] los mercados locales todavía son importantes centros económicos y sociales.

[a]cada... *more and more* [b]*frozen* [c]*canned*

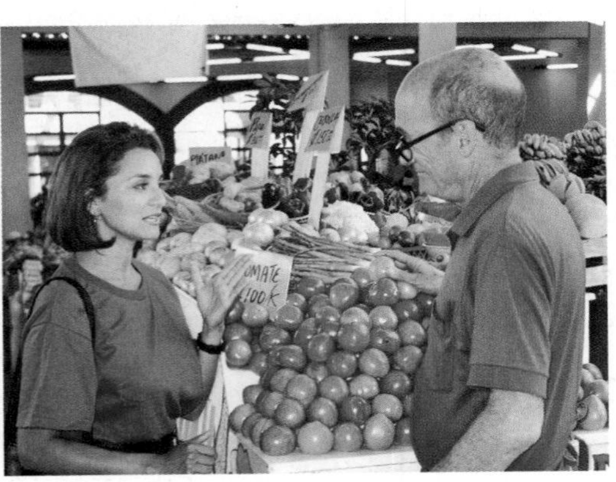

In this video segment, Mariela shops for produce. As you watch the segment, pay particular attention to the information Mariela gives about the meal she's planning. What does the vendor tell her about the produce?

COSTA RICA

A. Lluvia de ideas

- ¿A Ud. le gusta cocinar? ¿Qué sabe preparar? ¿Cuál es su especialidad?
- Cuando hay una ocasión especial, ¿le gusta celebrar en un restaurante o prefiere cocinar algo en casa? ¿Tiene algunas recetas para días importantes?
- ¿Hace Ud. la compra con frecuencia? Por lo general, ¿a qué tiendas va a comprar comida? ¿Compra muchos alimentos precocinados (*precooked foods*)?

B. Dictado. Aquí está una parte del diálogo entre Mariela y el vendedor, que aparece en la sección de vídeo de este capítulo. Complete el diálogo con las palabras o frases que faltan.

SR. VALDERRAMA: Hola, Srta. Castillo. ¿Qué le doy[a] hoy?
MARIELA: Voy a __preparar__[1] una cena deliciosa, Sr. Valderrama... Es la primera vez que los padres de mi novio vienen a __cenar__.[2] ¡Pienso causar una gran impresión!
SR. VALDERRAMA: ¿Qué va a preparar? ¿Tal vez[b] un buen __pescado__[3] frito con __arroz__[4]?
MARIELA: No, a mi novio no le gusta el pescado frito.
SR. VALDERRAMA: ¿Le gustan los __camarones__[5] a su novio?
MARIELA: Sí, le gustan muchísimo.[c]
SR. VALDERRAMA: Entonces, de primer __plato__,[6] prepare un ceviche de camarones.

[a]le... *can I give you* [b]Tal... *Perhaps* [c]*very much*

Note A
Frozen food in Spanish is *comida congelada;* homemade food is *comida casera.*

Follow-up A
After completing *Lluvia de ideas* activity, ask students: *¿Quién cocina mejor, Ud. o su compañero/a de casa (esposo/a, madre/padre)? ¿Qué días asocia Ud. con una buena comida?*

Suggestion B
To check comprehension ask: **1.** *¿Para quién va a cocinar Mariela?* **2.** *¿Qué no le gusta comer al novio de Mariela?* **3.** *¿Qué otros platos sugiere el Sr. Valderrama?* **4.** *¿Qué cantidades de verdura compra Mariela?*

C. Un diálogo original

Paso 1. Con un compañero / una compañera dramatice el diálogo entre Mariela y el Sr. Valderrama.

Paso 2. Imagine que Ud. y su compañero/a desean preparar una comida especial para celebrar la visita de sus padres. Hagan un menú y una lista de la comida que deben comprar para hacer la cena.

PASO FINAL

A CONVERSAR

El menú del día

Paso 1. En grupos de tres o cuatro estudiantes, lean el siguiente menú del restaurante El toro bravo. Basándose en el menú, ¿qué tipo de restaurante es? ¿Creen que es un restaurante con un ambiente elegante y caro o un restaurante con un ambiente relajado y precios módicos (*moderate*)? El menú que Uds. leen es el menú del día, es decir, las especialidades del día. En su opinión, ¿qué otras cosas sirven en este restaurante?

Restaurante 'El toro bravo'
Menú del día: €12,60

De entrada:

Ensalada mixta
(lechuga, tomate, zanahoria, cebolla y aceitunas[a] verdes con salsa vinagreta)

Sopa de cebolla con queso fundido[b]

Espárragos con jamón serrano[c]

De plato principal:

Paella de mariscos
(arroz, camarones, almejas,[d] pescado, salchicha)

Pollo asado con patatas al horno

Verduras asadas con cous-cous
(pimiento verde, cebolla, berenjena,[e] broculí, champiñones)

De postre:

Ensalada de frutas
(fresas,[f] melón, manzana, naranja)

Flan

Varios helados

[a]*olives* [b]*melted* [c]*jamón... a type of cured Spanish ham* [d]*clams* [e]*eggplant* [f]*strawberries*

Point out: Menu
On January 1, 2002, the *euro* replaced the *peseta* as the standard monetary denomination for Spain. Eleven other European Union member countries also adopted the common currency on that date. At the time of publication, 1 *euro* equaled approximately 160 *pesetas*. The price in this menu is read as *doce euros sesenta* (*céntimos* [*Sp.*]).

Paso 2. Ahora, imaginen que Uds. están en el restaurante. Uno/a de Uds. es camarero/a y los demás (*the rest*) son clientes que desean cenar. Antes de improvisar una escena, revisen las expresiones a continuación y piensen en el tipo de personaje que va a representar (un camarero difícil o un camarero simpático, una clienta exigente (*demanding*) o una clienta paciente, etcétera).

Clientes	Camarero/a
¿Qué recomienda (de plato principal / de postre)? ¿Qué hay en (la sopa de cebolla)? Quiero (la paella de mariscos), por favor. Para mí, (los espárragos), por favor. ¿Hay (tomates) en (la ensalada mixta)? Por favor, preparen (los espárragos) sin (jamón).	¿Qué les* traigo (hoy / de beber)? ¿Ya saben lo que (*what*) desean tomar? ¿Y qué quiere de (entrada / plato principal / postre)? ¿Y para Ud.? Lo siento mucho, no hay más (flan) hoy. Le(s)* recomiendo (la sopa de cebolla). La especialidad de la casa es (la paella). Lo siento, no podemos preparar (los espárragos) sin (jamón). Muy bien, le* preparamos (los espárragos) sin (jamón).

Follow-up
Have the waiters move to a different group of clients and begin a new role-play.

Paso 3. Improvisen una escena entre los clientes y el camarero / la camarera. La escena debe incluir saludos, preguntas y respuestas sobre los platos, recomendaciones y sugerencias, el orden. Después de practicar la escena, represéntenla para la clase.

***Le** and **les** are *indirect object pronouns*. Their equivalents in English are *you* (*sing.*) and *you* (*pl.*), respectively. You will learn more about indirect object pronouns in **Capítulo 7**. For now, you can just use them in the phrases indicated.

En resumen

GRAMÁTICA

To review the grammar points presented in this chapter, refer to the indicated grammar presentations. You'll find further practice of these structures in the Workbook/Laboratory Manual, on the CD-ROM, and on the website.

17. Direct Object Pronouns

Do you know how to avoid repetition by using direct object pronouns?

18. Indefinite and Negative Words

Do you know how to use the double negative in Spanish?

19. Formal Commands

You should know how to use commands to order in restaurants and to have someone do something for you.

VOCABULARIO

Los verbos

acabar de + *inf.* — to have just (*done something*)
ayudar — to help
cenar — to have (eat) dinner
cocinar — to cook
conocer — to know, be acquainted with
desayunar — to have (eat) breakfast
esperar — to wait (for); to expect
invitar — to invite
llamar — to call
preguntar — to ask a question
preparar — to prepare
saber (*irreg.*) — to know;
  saber + *inf.* — to know how to (*do something*)

Repaso: almorzar (ue)

La comida

el arroz — rice
las arvejas — peas
el atún — tuna
el bistec — steak
los camarones — shrimp
la carne — meat
los cereales — cereal
el champiñón — mushroom
la chuleta (de cerdo) — (pork) chop
los dulces — sweets; candy
los espárragos — asparagus
el flan — (baked) custard
los frijoles — beans
la galleta — cookie
el helado — ice cream
el huevo — egg
el jamón — ham
la langosta — lobster
la lechuga — lettuce
la mantequilla — butter
la manzana — apple
los mariscos — shellfish
la naranja — orange
el pan — bread
  el pan tostado — toast
el pastel — cake; pie
la patata (frita) — (French fried) potato
el pavo — turkey
el pescado — fish
el pollo (asado) — (roast) chicken

el postre	dessert
el queso	cheese
la salchicha	sausage; hot dog
la sopa	soup
las verduras	vegetables
la zanahoria	carrot

Las bebidas

el agua (mineral)	(mineral) water
el jugo (de fruta)	(fruit) juice
la leche	milk
el refresco	soft drink
el té	tea
el vino (blanco, tinto)	(white, red) wine

Repaso: el café, la cerveza

Los cognados

la banana, la ensalada, la fruta, la hamburguesa, el salmón, el sándwich, el tomate, el yogur

Las comidas

el almuerzo	lunch
la cena	dinner, supper

Repaso: el desayuno

En un restaurante

el/la camarero/a	waiter/waitress
la cuenta	check, bill
el menú	menu
el plato	dish; course

Otros sustantivos

el consejo	(piece of) advice
el detalle	detail
el/la dueño/a	owner
la tarjeta de crédito	credit card

Los adjetivos

fresco/a	fresh
frito/a	fried
fuerte	heavy (*meal, food*); strong
ligero/a	light, not heavy
rápido/a	fast

Palabras indefinidas y negativas

alguien	someone, anyone
algún (alguno/a/os/as)	some, any
jamás	never
nada	nothing, not anything
nadie	no one, nobody, not anybody
ningún (ninguno/a)	no, none, not any
tampoco	neither, not either

Repaso: algo, nunca, siempre, también

Palabras adicionales

tener (*irreg.*) **(mucha) hambre**	to be (very) hungry
tener (*irreg.*) **(mucha) sed**	to be (very) thirsty

Suggestions: Vocabulario

- Have students respond *cierto* or *falso:* **1.** *El bistec viene del cerdo.* **2.** *El bistec es más caro que la hamburguesa.* **3.** *Son populares los sándwiches de jamón.*
- Ask students: *¿Cuál es correcto?* **1.** *En Nebraska, ¿sirven mucho el bistec o muchos mariscos frescos?* **2.** *¿Cuál es más barata, la hamburguesa o la langosta?* **3.** *¿Se usa* Shake 'n' Bake *con los mariscos o con el pollo?*
- Have students work in small groups to write up menu for tonight's meal. To compare menus, have a member of each group read their menu. The class should vote on most appealing menu.
- Remind students that *conocer* is irregular in the *yo* form: *conozco.*
- Have students write brief reviews of restaurants based on recent visits. Encourage them to use negative and indefinite words.

De vacaciones

Suggestion: Chapter Opening photo
Point out the chapter opening photo. Have students describe the scene. Have them talk about ruins or historical areas they have visited. Encourage them to describe things they saw and liked.

Resources
You and your students may find the following *¿Qué tal?* supplements helpful as you teach this chapter:

For the Instructor
- *Instructor's Manual and Resource Kit,* "Chapter-by-Chapter" Supplementary Materials
- Testing Program
- Overhead Transparencies 46–50
- Video (VHS or CD)
- *¿Qué tal?* Online Learning Center Website
- Audioscript
- Instructor's Resource CD

For Students
- Workbook/Laboratory Manual and Audio Program or Electronic Workbook/Laboratory Manual
- Video on CD
- Interactive CD-ROM
- *¿Qué tal?* Online Learning Center Website
- Listening Comprehension Audio CD
- McGraw-Hill Electronic Language Tutor (MHELT)

Muchas personas visitan las fascinantes ruinas mayas de Copán cuando van de vacaciones en Honduras. ▶

VOCABULARIO

- Vacation and travel

GRAMÁTICA

20 Indirect Object Pronouns; **Dar** and **decir**
21 **Gustar**
22 Preterite of Regular Verbs and of **dar, hacer, ir,** and **ser**

CULTURA

- **Enfoque cultural:** Honduras y El Salvador
- **Nota cultural:** Vacaciones en el mundo hispánico
- **En los Estados Unidos y el Canadá:** Ellen Ochoa, una viajera espacial
- **Cultura en contexto:** El AVE

Multimedia

You will learn about purchasing a train ticket in the **En contexto** video segment.

Review vocabulary and grammar and practice language skills with the interactive CD-ROM.

WWW. Get connected to the Spanish-speaking world with the *¿Qué tal?* Online Learning Center: **www.mhhe.com/quetal**.

PASO 1 Vocabulario

Paso 1: Vocabulario

See detailed supplementary materials and exercises for this section and a model for vocabulary presentation and other material in the *Capítulo 7 Paso 1: Vocabulario* section of "Chapter-by-Chapter Supplementary Materials," in the IM.

¡Buen viaje!°

°¡Buen… *Have a good trip*!

Multimedia: Audio

Students can listen to and practice this chapter's vocabulary on their Listening Comprehension Audio CD.

❖ **Transparency 46**

Ir en avión

el aeropuerto airport
el/la asistente de vuelo flight attendant
la sala de espera waiting room
la sección de (no) fumar (non)smoking section
el vuelo flight

Ir en tren/autobús/barco

el barco boat, ship
la cabina cabin (*in a ship*)
la estación station
  de autobuses bus
  del tren train
el maletero porter
el puerto port

De viaje

la agencia de viajes travel agency
el/la agente de viajes travel agent
el asiento seat
el billete/el boleto/el pasaje* ticket
  de ida one way
  de ida y vuelta round-trip
la demora delay
el equipaje baggage, luggage
la llegada arrival
el/la pasajero/a passenger
la salida departure

bajar (de) to get down (from, off of)
estar atrasado/a to be late
facturar el equipaje to check one's bags
guardar (un puesto) to save (a place)
hacer (*irreg.*) **cola** to stand in line
hacer (*irreg.*) **escalas/paradas** to make stops
hacer (*irreg.*) **la(s) maleta(s)** to pack one's suitcase(s)
hacer (*irreg.*) **un viaje** to take a trip
ir (*irreg.*) **/ estar** (*irreg.*) **de vacaciones** to go/be on vacation
sacar fotos to take photos
subir (a) to go up; to get on (*a vehicle*)
viajar to travel

De vacaciones

hacer (*irreg.*) ***camping*** to go camping
nadar to swim
tomar el sol to sunbathe

la camioneta station wagon
el camping campground
el mar sea
las montañas mountains
el océano ocean
la playa beach
la tienda (de campaña) tent

---

*Throughout Spanish America, **el boleto** is the word used for a *ticket for travel*. **El billete** is commonly used in Spain. **El pasaje** is used throughout the Spanish-speaking world. The words **la entrada** and **la localidad** are used to refer to tickets for movies, plays, or similar functions.

Follow-up A
Have students imagine they are traveling with children and need to give them commands for each circumstance represented in activity. **Modelo:** f: Suban al taxi. Siéntense., and so on.

Conversación

A. Un viaje en avión. Imagine que Ud. va a hacer un viaje en avión. El vuelo sale a las siete de la mañana. Usando los números del 1 al 9, indique en qué orden van a pasar las siguientes cosas.

a. __8__ Subo al avión.
b. __5__ Voy a la sala de espera.
c. __3__ Hago cola para comprar el boleto de ida y vuelta y facturar el equipaje.
d. __2__ Llego al aeropuerto a tiempo (*on time*) y bajo del taxi.
e. __7__ Por fin se anuncia la salida del vuelo.
f. __1__ Estoy atrasado/a. Salgo para el aeropuerto en taxi.
g. __9__ La asistente me indica el asiento.
h. __4__ Pido asiento en la sección de no fumar.
i. __6__ Hay demora. Por eso todos tenemos que esperar el vuelo allí antes de subir al avión.

B. En el aeropuerto. ¿Cuántas cosas y acciones puede Ud. identificar o describir en este dibujo?

Preliminary exercise B
Read descriptions and have students identify person described: *Gregorio, vicepresidente de la IBM,* or *Harry, típico estudiante universitario.* **1.** *Siempre viaja en clase turística porque es más económico.* **2.** *No le importan nada las demoras; no tiene prisa.* **3.** *Nunca hace cola para comprar el boleto porque su secretaria le arregla todo el viaje.* **4.** *Cuando viaja en avión, es porque está de vacaciones.* **5.** *Por lo general prefiere viajar en tren porque es más económico.* **6.** *Muchas veces no lleva equipaje porque hace viajes de un solo día.* **7.** *Siempre que viaja, lleva traje y corbata.*

❖ **Transparency 47**

NOTA CULTURAL

Vacaciones en el mundo hispánico

Cuando los habitantes de países hispanohablantes **van de vacaciones**, ¿adónde van? Si quieren **viajar al extranjero**, generalmente viajan a Europa o a los Estados Unidos. Entre **los destinos**[a] **preferidos** de los Estados Unidos están California, Nueva York, Texas y Florida.

Las playas nacionales e internacionales son una atracción común para las vacaciones también. Como a todo el mundo, a los hispanos les gusta disfrutar del[b] **sol**, del **clima tropical** y de las **playas**. Todos los países latinoamericanos que se encuentran en el Caribe ofrecen playas hermosas[c] y actividades como **bucear**[d] y **montar en tabla de vela**.[e]

De noche en South Beach, Miami

Esquiar es otra actividad popular para las vacaciones. Durante junio, julio y agosto, los meses del invierno en el hemisferio sur, **las montañas** de Chile y la Argentina son destinos muy populares.

[a]*destinations* [b]disfrutar de = *to enjoy* [c]*beautiful* [d]*scuba diving; snorkling* [e]montar... *windsurfing*

Suggestions: Nota cultural
- Describe some of the places in the Hispanic world you have been to or know well. Then ask students the names of the places they have been.
- Ask students which places mentioned in the *Nota cultural* they would like to visit and why.

Extension C

3. *¿Cómo reacciona Ud. cuando hay una demora de 30 minutos? ¿Está furioso/a? ¿irritado/a? ¿indiferente? ¿Y cuando hay una demora de una hora?*

C. Preguntas

1. Por lo general, ¿cuándo toma Ud. sus vacaciones? ¿En invierno? ¿en verano? En las vacaciones, ¿le gusta viajar o prefiere no salir de su ciudad? ¿Le gusta ir de vacaciones con su familia? ¿Prefiere ir solo/a (*alone*), con un amigo/una amiga o con un grupo de personas?
2. De los medios de transporte ilustrados en **¡Buen viaje!** (página 174), ¿cuáles conoce Ud. por experiencia? De estos medios de transporte, ¿cuál es el más rápido? ¿el más económico? ¿Cuáles hacen más escalas o hacen paradas con más frecuencia? ¿Cómo prefiere Ud. viajar?

Notes: Nota comunicativa

- Passive *se* has been presented for passive recognition and used frequently in listening comprehension activities and reading passages.
- This *Nota* does not emphasize difference between personal *you / they,* which refers to specific persons, vs. impersonal *you / they,* which is nonspecific. You may want to point out the difference.

Suggestions: Nota comunicativa

- Have students state ideas in Spanish: **1.** You study a lot here. **2.** You don't talk in the library. **3.** You wear a suit in the office. **4.** You bargain at the market.
- To practice impersonal *se* ask: **1.** *¿Qué lengua se habla en Francia? ¿en México? ¿en el Brasil? ¿en Alemania? ¿en Inglaterra? ¿en los EE.UU.?* **2.** *¿Cuáles son las diferentes maneras de viajar?* (*Se viaja en... avión, coche, tren, autobús, bicicleta.*)

NOTA COMUNICATIVA

Other Uses of *se* (For Recognition)

It is likely that you have often seen and heard the phrase shown in the photo that accompanies this box: **Se habla español.** (*Spanish is spoken* [*here*]). Here are some additional examples of this use of **se** with Spanish verbs. Note how the meaning of the verb changes slightly.

Se venden billetes aquí.	*Tickets are sold here.*
Aquí no **se fuma**.	*You don't* (*One doesn't*) *smoke here. Smoking is forbidden here.*

Be alert to this use of **se** when you see it, because it will occur with some frequency in readings and in direction lines in *¿Qué tal?* The activities in this text will not require you to use this grammar point on your own, however.

Nueva York

Extension D

9. *Se hacen las camas.* **10.** *Se pide información sobre los viajes* **11.** *No se fuma.* **12.** *Se hace cola.*

Suggestions D

Have students tell what is and is not done in certain places: *¿Qué se hace y no se hace en... la biblioteca?* → *En la biblioteca, se estudia, pero no se habla.* **1.** *¿en una clase de idiomas?* **2.** *¿en un mercado al aire libre?* **3.** *¿en un avión?* **4.** *¿en una discoteca?* **5.** *¿en una tienda de ropa?* **6.** *¿en una fiesta?* **7.** *¿en la cafetería?*

D. ¿Dónde se hace esto? Indique el lugar (o los lugares) donde se hacen las siguientes actividades.

Lugares: en casa, en la agencia de viajes, en el aeropuerto, en el avión, en la playa

1. Se factura el equipaje.
2. Se hacen las maletas.
3. Se compran los pasajes.
4. Se hace una reservación.
5. Se espera en la sala de espera.
6. Se pide un cóctel.
7. Se mira una película.
8. Se nada y se toma el sol.

Paso 2: Gramática
See detailed supplementary materials for these grammar sections in IM.

20 Expressing *to whom or for whom* • Indirect Object Pronouns; *Dar* and *decir*

Prueba: ¿Cómo son sus relaciones con otros?

¿Con qué frecuencia hace Ud. las siguientes actividades, con mucha frecuencia, a veces o nunca?

1. *Les* escribo mensajes electrónicos (*e-mail*) a mis amigos.
2. *Les* escribo cartas a mis padres (hijos).
3. *Les* doy (*I give*) consejos a mis amigos.
4. *Les* doy consejos a mis padres (hijos).
5. *Les* digo (*I tell*) la verdad a mis amigos.
6. *Les* digo la verdad a mis padres (hijos).
7. *Les* pido dinero a mis amigos.
8. *Les* pido dinero a mis padres (hijos).

La siguiente parte de la prueba le va a mostrar (*show*) si hay reciprocidad en sus relaciones con sus amigos y con sus padres (hijos). Conteste con: **con mucha frecuencia, a veces** o **nunca**.

1. Mis amigos me escriben mensajes electrónicos.
2. Mis padres (hijos) me escriben cartas.
3. Mis amigos me dan consejos.
4. Mis padres (hijos) me dan consejos.
5. Mis amigos me dicen sus problemas.
6. Mis padres (hijos) me dicen sus problemas.
7. Mis amigos me piden dinero.
8. Mis padres (hijos) me piden dinero.

Follow-Up: Indirect Object Pronouns
After completing the *Prueba,* ask the following question to introduce the concept of indirect objects: *¿Qué palabras en cada oración indican las personas afectadas por las acciones de los verbos?* Emphasize the meaning of indirect object pronouns: *me* = to me, *le* = to him/her/you (*form. sing.*), *les* = to them/you (*form. pl.*).

¿Qué le dicen a Ud. sus respuestas? ¿Cómo son sus relaciones con otros?

INDIRECT OBJECT PRONOUNS

me	to/for me	**nos**	to/for us
te	to/for you (*fam. sing.*)	**os**	to/for you (*fam. pl.*)
le	to/for you (*form. sing.*), him, her, it	**les**	to/for you (*form. pl.*), them

OJO Note that indirect object pronouns have the same form as direct object pronouns, except in the third person: **le, les**.

A. Indirect object nouns and pronouns are the second recipient of the action of the verb. They usually answer the questions *to whom?* or *for whom?* in relation to the verb. The word *to* is frequently omitted in English.

Indicate the direct and indirect objects in the following sentences.

1. I'm giving her the present tomorrow.
2. Could you tell me the answer now?
3. El profesor nos va a hacer algunas preguntas.
4. ¿No me compras una revista ahora?

B. Like direct object pronouns, *indirect object pronouns* (**los pronombres del complemento indirecto**) are placed immediately before a conjugated verb. They may also be attached to an infinitive or a present participle.

No, no **te** presto el coche.
No, I won't lend you the car.

Voy a guardar**te** el asiento.
Te voy a guardar el asiento.
I'll save your seat for you.

Le estoy escribiendo una carta **a Marisol**.
Estoy escribiéndo**le** una carta **a Marisol**.
I'm writing Marisol a letter.

C. Since **le** and **les** have several different equivalents, their meaning is often clarified or emphasized with the preposition **a** followed by a pronoun (object of a preposition).

Voy a mandar**le** un telegrama **a Ud.** (**a él, a ella**).
I'm going to send you (him, her) a telegram.

Les hago una comida **a Uds.** (**a ellos, a ellas**).
I'm making you (them) a meal.

D. It is common for a Spanish sentence to contain both the indirect object noun and the indirect object pronoun, especially with third person forms.

Vamos a decir**le** la verdad **a Juan**.
Let's tell Juan the truth.

¿**Les** guardo los asientos **a Jorge y Marta**?
Shall I save the seats for Jorge and Marta?

E. As with direct object pronouns, indirect object pronouns are attached to the affirmative command form and precede the negative command form.

Sírva**nos** un café, por favor.
Serve us some coffee, please.

No me dé su número de teléfono ahora.
Don't give me your phone number now.

F. Here are some verbs frequently used with indirect objects.

dar (*irreg.*)	to give	**pedir (i, i)**	to ask for
decir (*irreg.*)	to say; to tell	**preguntar**	to ask (*a question*)
escribir	to write	**prestar**	to lend
explicar	to explain	**prometer**	to promise
hablar	to speak	**recomendar (ie)**	to recommend
mandar	to send	**regalar**	to give (*as a gift*)
ofrecer (ofrezco)	to offer	**servir (i, i)**	to serve

Dar AND decir

dar (*to give*)		decir (*to say; to tell*)	
doy	damos	digo	decimos
das	dais	dices	decís
da	dan	dice	dicen

- **Dar** and **decir** are almost always used with indirect object pronouns in Spanish.

¿Cuándo **me das** el dinero?
When will you give me the money?

¿Por qué no **le dice** Ud. la verdad, señor?
Why don't you tell him/her the truth, sir?

OJO In Spanish it is necessary to distinguish between the verbs **dar** (*to give*) and **regalar** (*to give as a gift*). Also, do not confuse **decir** (*to say* or *to tell*) with **hablar** (*to speak*).

- **Dar** and **decir** also have irregular formal command forms. There is a written accent on **dé** to distinguish it from the preposition **de**.

Formal commands of **dar** and **decir**:

dar → **dé, den**
decir → **diga, digan**

Práctica

A. De vuelta a Honduras

Paso 1. Your friends the Padillas, from Honduras, need help arranging for and getting on their flight back home. Explain how you will help them, using the cues as a guide.

MODELO: confirmar el vuelo → Les confirmo el vuelo.

1. llamar un taxi
2. bajar (*to carry down*) las maletas
3. guardar el equipaje
4. facturar el equipaje
5. guardar el puesto en la cola
6. guardar el asiento en la sala de espera
7. comprar una revista
8. por fin decir adiós

Paso 2. Now explain the same sequence of actions as if you were talking about your friend Guillermo: ***Le* confirmo el vuelo**.

Paso 3. Finally, tell your friend Marisol how you will help her: ***Te* confirmo el vuelo**.

Preliminary exercises: Indirect Object Pronouns

- Use chain drill to practice indirect object pronouns: **1.** *Les escribo tarjetas postales a mis padres* (*a ti, a Ud., a Andrés, a Uds., a Alicia, a vosotros*) **2.** *Ahora le compro un regalo a Jorge.* (*a Sergio, a ti, a Eva, a Uds., a Martín y Rosa, a vosotros*) **3.** *El conductor le dice la hora de la llegada* (*yo, ellos, tú, nosotros, Uds.*) **4.** *Juan le da el billete, ¿verdad?* (*tú, nosotros, yo, Uds., ellas*)
- Act out question/answer series with students: *¿Ud. me da el libro? ¿Ud. nos da el dinero* (student standing with you)? *¿Uds. me dicen siempre la verdad? ¿la hora? ¿las respuestas correctas? ¿Yo les digo siempre la fecha de los exámenes? ¿la tarea* (homework) *para mañana? ¿cosas interesantes sobre la cultura hispánica?*
- Have students answer: *En la clase de español, ¿quién le... a Ud.?* (*explicar la gramática, hacer preguntas, dar exámenes, prestar un papel, dar las respuestas durante un examen*) Encourage students to answer in complete sentences. Model first answer. *La profesora me explica la gramática.* As students answer, avoid overt correction; instead, repeat all answers, including corrections when necessary.

Follow-up B
Follow up with these questions: **1.** *¿A quién le manda Ud. flores? ¿Quién le manda flores a Ud.?* **2.** *¿A quién le escribe Ud. cartas? ¿Qué tipo de cartas escribe Ud.? ¿cartas políticas? ¿amistosas? ¿románticas? ¿Quién le escribe cartas a Ud.?* **3.** *¿Les va a comprar algo a sus padres/hijos este año? ¿a su mejor amigo/a? ¿a su profesor(a)?*

B. ¿Qué hacen estas personas? Complete las siguientes oraciones con un verbo lógico y un pronombre de complemento indirecto.

MODELO: El vicepresidente *le ofrece* consejos al presidente.

Verbos posibles: dar, ofrecer, prestar, prometer, servir

1. Romeo le da flores a Julieta.
2. Snoopy le da besos (*kisses*) a Lucy... ¡Y a ella no le gusta!
3. Eva le ofrece una manzana a Adán.
4. Ann Landers les ofrece consejos a sus lectores (*readers*).
5. Los bancos les prestan dinero a las personas que quieren comprar una casa.
6. Los asistentes de vuelo les sirven bebidas a los pasajeros.
7. George Washington le promete a su padre decir la verdad.

C. ¿Qué va a pasar? Dé varias respuestas.

Palabras útiles: medicinas, Santa Claus, tarjetas navideñas (*Christmas cards*), flores, juguetes (*toys*)

1. Su amiga Elena está en el hospital con un ataque de apendicitis. Todos le mandan... Le escriben... Las enfermeras (*nurses*) le dan... De comer, le sirven...
2. Es Navidad. Los niños les prometen a sus padres... Les piden... También le escriben... Le piden... Los padres les mandan... a sus amigos. Les regalan...
3. Hay una demora y el avión no despega (*takes off*) a tiempo. Un asistente de vuelo nos sirve... Otra asistente de vuelo nos ofrece... El piloto nos dice...
4. Mi coche no funciona hoy. Mi amigo me presta... Mis padres me preguntan... Luego me dan...
5. Es la última (*last*) semana de clases y hay exámenes finales la próxima semana. En la clase de computación, todos le preguntan al profesor... El profesor les explica a los estudiantes...

Follow-up D
Ask questions about the story and have students answer as if they were Benjamín.

D. En un restaurante. Imagine that your four-year-old cousin Benjamín has never eaten in a restaurant before. Explain to him what will happen, filling in the blanks with the appropriate indirect object pronoun.

Primero el camarero nos[1] indica una mesa desocupada.[a] Luego tú le[2] pides el menú al camarero. También le[3] haces preguntas sobre los platos y las especialidades de la casa y le[4] dices tus preferencias. El camarero nos[5] trae la comida. Por fin tu papá le[6] pide la cuenta al camarero. Si tú quieres pagar, le[7] pides dinero a tu papá y le[8] das el dinero al camarero.

[a]*vacant*

Conversación

Entrevista: ¿Quién… ? Whom do you associate with the below actions? Working with a partner, ask and answer questions to find out information about each topic.

MODELO: darle consejos →
E1: ¿A quién le das consejos?
E2: Con frecuencia le doy consejos a mi compañero de cuarto. ¡Él los necesita!
E1: ¿Quién te da consejos a ti?
E2: Mis abuelos me dan muchos consejos.

1. darle consejos
2. pedirle ayuda con los estudios
3. mandarle flores
4. decirle secretos
5. hacerle favores
6. escribirle tarjetas postales (*postcards*)
7. ofrecerle bebidas

Suggestions: Conversación

- Ask questions based on cues before assigning activity to pairs: *¿A quién le da consejos? ¿De quién acepta consejos? ¿A quién le pide ayuda con el español? ¿A quién le da ayuda?* and so on.
- Have students report to class at least 2 interesting things they learned about their partner.
- Have students pass around small object (ball, toy, book, pen). As they do it, have them provide a sentence about what they did or about what they are about to do. Their sentences should include both direct and indirect objects, for example: *Voy a darle la pelota a Jim. / Le doy la pelota a Jim.* Other useful verbs that you might write on board are *tirar, pasar, llevar.*

¿Recuerda Ud.?

Note: Gustar
Students have been using the *gustar* construction since *Primeros pasos.*

You have already used forms of **gustar** to express your likes and dislikes (**Primeros pasos**). Review what you know by answering the following questions. Then, changing their form as needed, use them to interview your instructor:

1. ¿Te gusta el café (el vino, el té,…)?
2. ¿Te gusta jugar al béisbol (al golf, al vólibol, al…)?
3. ¿Te gusta viajar en avión (fumar, viajar en tren,…)?
4. ¿Qué te gusta más, estudiar o ir a fiestas (trabajar o descansar, cocinar o comer)?

Follow-Up: Gustar
After discussing the ad, ask: **1.** *A las personas de los Estados Unidos/del Canadá, ¿les gusta ir a la playa? ¿Qué playas les gusta visitar? ¿Les gusta viajar en avión?* **2.** *Y a Ud., ¿le gustan más las playas o las montañas? ¿Adónde le gustaría viajar este verano?*

21 Expressing Likes and Dislikes • *Gustar*

Los chilenos viajeros

Según el anuncio, a muchos chilenos les gusta viajar a otros países. Lea el anuncio y luego indique si las oraciones son ciertas o falsas.

MEDIO MILLON DE CHILENOS
DE VACACIONES 2003 AL EXTRANJERO
Y USTED... NO SE QUEDE SIN VIAJAR
¡ RESERVE AHORA MISMO !
El próximo verano '03, con el bajo valor del dólar, muchas personas desearán viajar, los cupos disponibles se agotarán rapidamente. ¡Asegure sus vacaciones! Elija ahora cualquiera de nuestros fantásticos programas.
MIAMI - ORLANDO - BAHAMAS - MÉXICO - CANCÚN
ACAPULCO - IXTAPA - COSTA RICA - RIO - SALVADOR
PLAYA TAMBOR - PUNTA CANA - LA HABANA
VARADERO - GUATEMALA - SUDÁFRICA
Infórmese sobre nuestro SUPER CRÉDITO PREFERENCIAL
Economy Tour
Santa Magdalena 94, Providencia
☎ 2334429 - 2331774 - 2314252
2328294 - 2318608 - 2334862
Fax: 2334428

1. A los chilenos les gusta viajar sólo en este hemisferio.
2. A los chilenos les gustan mucho las playas.
3. Sólo les gusta viajar en países de habla española.
4. No les gustaría el precio del viaje.

Y a Ud., ¿le gusta viajar? ¿Le gustan los viajes en avión? ¿Cuál de estos lugares le gustaría visitar?

Heritage speakers
En algunos dialectos del español el verbo *gustar* puede tener conotaciones románticas cuando se usa en la primera y segunda personas del singular (*yo* y *tú*). *¿Te gusto?* (Do you like me? / Are you attracted to me?) *Sí, me gustas mucho.* (Yes, I like you. / Yes, I am attracted to you.)

CONSTRUCTIONS WITH *gustar*

Spanish	Literal Equivalent	English Phrasing
Me gusta la playa.	The beach is pleasing to me.	*I like the beach.*
No le gustan sus cursos.	His courses are not pleasing to him.	*He doesn't like his courses.*
Nos gusta leer.	Reading is pleasing to us.	*We like to read.*

You have been using the verb **gustar** since the beginning of *¿Qué tal?* to express likes and dislikes. However, **gustar** does not literally mean *to like*, but rather *to be pleasing*.

Me gusta viajar.
Traveling is pleasing to me. (*I like traveling.*)

A. **Gustar** is always used with an indirect object pronoun: Someone or something is pleasing *to* someone else. The verb must agree with the subject of the sentence—that is, the person or thing that is pleasing.

Me **gusta** la comida mexicana.
Mexican food is pleasing to me. (*I like Mexican food.*)

Me **gustan** los viajes aventureros.
Adventurous trips are pleasing to me. (*I like adventurous trips.*)

B. A phrase with **a** + a *noun* or *pronoun* is often used for clarification or emphasis. This prepositional phrase usually appears before the indirect object pronoun, but it can also appear after the verb.

Note that an infinitive is viewed as a singular subject in Spanish.

OJO The indirect object pronoun *must* be used with **gustar** even when the prepositional phrase **a** + *noun* or *pronoun* is used.

CLARIFICATION

¿Le gusta **a Ud.** viajar?
Do you like to travel?

A David no le gustan los aviones.
David doesn't like airplanes.

EMPHASIS

A mí me gusta viajar en avión, pero **a mi esposo** le gusta viajar en coche.
I *like to travel by plane, but* ***my husband*** *likes to travel by car.*

WOULD LIKE/WOULDN'T LIKE

What one *would* or *would not* like to do is expressed with the form **gustaría*** + *infinitive* and the appropriate indirect objects.

A mí me gustaría viajar a Colombia.
I would like to travel to Colombia.

Nos gustaría hacer *camping* este verano.
We would like to go camping this summer.

*This is one of the forms of the conditional of **gustar**. You will study all of the forms of the conditional in Grammar Section 45.

Práctica

A. Gustos y preferencias

Paso 1. Using the models as a guide, tell whether or not you like the following.

MODELOS: ¿el café? → (No) Me gusta el café.
¿los pasteles? → (No) Me gustan los pasteles.

1. ¿el vino?
2. ¿los niños pequeños?
3. ¿la música clásica?
4. ¿Ricky Martin?
5. ¿el invierno?
6. ¿hacer cola?
7. ¿el chocolate?
8. ¿las películas de terror?
9. ¿las clases que empiezan a las ocho de la mañana?
10. ¿cocinar?
11. ¿la gramática?
12. ¿las clases de este semestre/trimestre?
13. ¿los vuelos con muchas escalas?
14. ¿bailar en las discotecas?

Paso 2. Now share your reactions with a classmate. He or she will respond with one of the following reactions. How do your likes and dislikes compare?

REACCIONES

A mí también.	*So do I.*	Pues a mí, sí.	*Well, I do.*
A mí tampoco.	*Neither do I.*	Pues a mí, no.	*Well, I don't.*

B. ¿Adónde vamos este verano?

Paso 1. The members of the Soto family all prefer different vacation activities and, of course, would like to go to different places this summer. Imagine that you are one of the Sotos and describe the family's various preferences, following the model.

MODELO: padre/nadar: ir a la playa →
A mi padre le gusta nadar. Le gustaría ir a la playa.

1. padre/el oceano: ir a la playa
2. hermanos pequeños/nadar también: ir a la playa
3. hermano Ernesto/hacer *camping*: ir a las montañas
4. abuelos/descansar: quedarse en casa
5. madre/la tranquilidad: visitar un pueblecito (*small town*) en la costa
6. hermana Elena/discotecas: pasar las vacaciones en una ciudad grande
7. mí/¿ ?

Paso 2. Now, remembering what you have learned about the vacation preferences of your imaginary family, answer the following questions.

1. ¿A quién le gustaría ir a Nueva York?
2. ¿A quién le gustaría viajar a Acapulco?
3. ¿Quién no quiere salir de casa?
4. ¿A quién le gustaría ir a Cabo San Lucas?
5. ¿Quién quiere ir a Colorado?

Preliminary exercises: Gustar

- To make sure *gustar* construction is clearly understood, have students give Spanish for the following sentences, then have them give literal equivalents in English of Spanish construction, for example, I like the car. → *Me gusta el coche* → The car is pleasing to me. **1.** We / He / You / I like(s) the car. **2.** I / We / She / They like(s) to read. **3.** She likes the soup / chicken / coffee. **4.** He likes tomatoes / tacos / movies / to go to the movies. (¡OJO! Use the definite articles.)
- Have students give Spanish equivalents to stress redundancy of indirect object pronoun and noun: **1.** My father likes to travel. **2.** My mother likes trains. **3.** The boys like the beach. **4.** María likes to ski.

Suggestion A

Paso 2. Model exchanges of several kinds for students:

—Me gusta el café.
—A mí también.
—Pues a mí, no.

—No me gusta el café.
—A mí tampoco.
—Pues a mí, sí.

Extension A

Paso 2. Have students add 2–3 things that they like or dislike to the list in *Paso 1.* Then partners can respond in a similar manner as before.

Note B

These sentences require the redundant use of the indirect object pronoun and noun.

Extension B

Paso 1. *8. ti/(no)/los sitios que prefiere la familia Soto: visitar a la familia* **9.** *el perro/(no)/quedarse en casa: ir con la familia* **10.** *la tía Ramona/las visitas de la familia: recibirlos en su casa*

Paso 2. *6. ¿Quién quiere recibir a la familia en su casa?*

❖ **Transparency 48**
This transparency can be used as a springboard for talking about what someone else likes.

Conversación

A. ¿Conoce bien a sus compañeros de clase? Piense en una persona de la clase que Ud. conoce. En su opinión, ¿a esa persona le gustan o no las siguientes cosas? Apunte: **Sí, le gusta(n)** o **No, no le gusta(n)**. Luego, entreviste a su compañero/a para verificar sus respuestas.

1. la música clásica
2. el color negro
3. viajar en coche
4. la comida mexicana
5. tener clases por la mañana
6. estudiar otras lenguas
7. las películas trágicas
8. las casas viejas

Note: Nota comunicativa
Odiar is not like *gustar:* (*Yo*) *Odio el café* / (*A mí*) *Me gusta el café.*

Suggestion: Nota comunicativa
Ask students to list favorite and least favorite things and categorize them as *Cosas que odio, cosas que no me gustan, cosas que me interesan, cosas que me gustan mucho, cosas que me encantan.* Then ask them to compare their lists with those of a partner (for example, *A mí me encanta la música rock, pero Juan la odia.*

NOTA COMUNICATIVA

More about Expressing Likes and Dislikes

Here are some ways to express intense likes and dislikes.

Me gusta mucho/muchísimo.	*I like it a lot/a whole lot.*
No me gusta (para) nada.	*I don't like it at all.*

To express *love* and *hate* in reference to likes and dislikes, you can use **encantar** and **odiar**.

- **Encantar** is used just like **gustar**.

  Les encanta viajar, ¿verdad? — *You love traveling, right?*

- **Odiar,** on the other hand, functions like a transitive verb (one that can take a direct object).

  Mi madre **odia** viajar sola. — *My mother hates traveling alone.*

To express interest in something, use **interesar**. This verb is also used like **gustar** and **encantar**.

Me interesa la comida salvadoreña. — *I'm interested in Salvadorian food.*

Suggestion B
Use *me molesta(n)* instead of *odio.*

Follow-up B
Have students describe likes and dislikes of various family members on different topics. In addition to *gustar,* encourage students to use *encantar, interesar, molestar, odiar,* and *preferir.*

B. ¿Qué te gusta? ¿Qué odias? Almost every situation has aspects that one likes or dislikes, even hates. Pick at least two of the following situations and tell what you like or don't like about them. Add as many details as you can, using **me gustaría** when possible.

MODELO: en la playa →
Me gusta mucho el agua, pero no me gusta el sol. Por eso no me gusta pasar todo el día en la playa. Me encanta nadar pero odio la arena. Me gustaría más ir a nadar en una piscina.

Situaciones: en un avión, en el coche, en un autobús, en un tren, en una discoteca, en una fiesta, en la biblioteca, en clase, en casa con mis padres/hijos, en casa con mis amigos, en una cafetería, en la playa

Enfoque *cultural*

Enfoque cultural
See follow-up activities for this section in chapter-by-chapter materials in IM.

Honduras y El Salvador

Datos esenciales

Honduras

- Nombre oficial: República de Honduras
- Capital: Tegucigalpa
- Población: 6.000.000 de habitantes
- Moneda: el lempira
- Idioma oficial: el español

El Salvador

- Nombre oficial: República de El Salvador
- Capital: San Salvador
- Población: 6.000.000 de habitantes
- Moneda: el dólar
- Idioma oficial: el español

¡Fíjese!

- El centro ceremonial maya de Copán, en Honduras, es hoy un parque nacional que contiene una colección de ruinas mayas superadas[a] sólo por las ruinas de Tikal en Guatemala.
- La moneda de Honduras, el lempira, lleva el nombre de un cacique[b] indígena que luchó contra[c] los españoles.
- El nombre indígena de la capital de Honduras, Tegucigalpa, significa «cerros de plata».[d] Honduras recibe su nombre español por la profundidad[e] de sus aguas costeras.[f] El nombre indígena de El Salvador es Cuzcatlán, que significa «tierra de joyas[g] y cosas preciosas».
- Las erupciones del Volcán de Izalco en El Salvador son constantes entre los años 1770 y 1966, por casi dos siglos.[h] Este volcán se conoce con el nombre de «el faro[i] del Pacífico», porque está encendido[j] por muchos años y sirve de[k] guía a los navegantes.

[a]*exceeded (in quality)* [b]*chief* [c]luchó... *fought against* [d]cerros... *silver hills* [e]*depth* [f]*coastal* [g]*jewels*

[h]*centuries* [i]*lighthouse* [j]*lit up* [k]sirve de... *serves as a*

El Volcán de Izalco, El Salvador

Conozca... al Arzobispo[a] Óscar Arnulfo Romero

El 24 de marzo de 1980 un héroe de El Salvador es asesinado mientras oficia una misa.[b] En vida,[c] el arzobispo Óscar Arnulfo Romero (1917–1980) es la conciencia de su país. Critica a los líderes políticos por su violencia e injusticia, y trabaja para mejorar[d] las condiciones económicas y sociales del país. Por eso, es nominado para el premio Nóbel de la Paz[e] en 1979.

[a]*Archbishop* [b]oficiaba... *he celebrates a Mass* [c]*life* [d]*improve* [e]premio... *Nobel Peace Prize*

Capítulo 7 of the video to accompany *¿Qué tal?* contains cultural footage about Honduras and El Salvador.

Visit the *¿Qué tal?* website at www.mhhe.com/quétal.

PASO 3 Gramática

Paso 3: Gramática
See detailed supplementary materials for these grammar sections in IM.

22 Talking about the Past (1) • Preterite of Regular Verbs and of *dar, hacer, ir,* and *ser*

Elisa habla de su viaje a Puerto Rico

«Recientemente *fui* a Puerto Rico para escribir un artículo sobre ese país. *Hice* el viaje en avión. El vuelo *fue* largo, pues el avión *hizo* escala en Miami. *Pasé* una semana entera en la isla. *Hablé* con muchas personas de la industria turística y *visité* los lugares más interesantes de Puerto Rico. También *comí* mucha comida típica de la isla. Además, *tomé* el sol en las preciosas playas puertorriqueñas y *nadé* en el mar Caribe. Me *divertí* mucho. ¡Mi viaje *fue* casi como unas vacaciones!»

Comprensión: ¿Cierto o falso?

1. Elisa fue a Puerto Rico para pasar sus vacaciones.
2. El avión hizo escala en los Estados Unidos.
3. Elisa no visitó ningún lugar importante de Puerto Rico.
4. Elisa también pasó tiempo cerca del océano.

Follow-up: Preterite
Follow up narration by having students respond to the following questions, using direct object pronouns: *Elisa Velasco, ¿visitó lugares interesantes en Puerto Rico? ¿Entrevistó* (write on board) *a muchas personas? ¿Comió comida típica? ¿Visitó las playas puertorriqueñas? ¿Hizo el viaje en avión? ¿Pasó la semana en Puerto Rico? ¿Tomó el sol en las playas?*

In previous chapters of *¿Qué tal?,* you have talked about a number of your activities, but always in the present tense. In this section, you will begin to work with the forms of the preterite, one of the tenses that will allow you to talk about the past. To talk about all aspects of the past in Spanish, you need to know how to use two *simple tenses* (tenses formed without an auxiliary or "helping" verb): the preterite and the imperfect. In this chapter, you will learn the regular forms of the preterite and those of four irregular verbs: **dar, hacer, ir,** and **ser**. In this chapter and in **Capítulos 8, 9, 10,** and **11,** you will learn more about preterite forms and their uses as well as about the imperfect and the ways in which it is used alone and with the preterite.

The *preterite* **(el pretérito)** has several equivalents in English. For example, **hablé** can mean *I spoke* or *I did speak.* The preterite is used to report finished, completed actions or states of being in the past. If the action or state of being is viewed as completed—no matter how long it lasted or took to complete—it will be expressed with the preterite.

Elisa talks about her trip to Puerto Rico. Recently I went to Puerto Rico to write an article about that country. I made the trip by plane. The flight was long because the plane made a stop in Miami. I spent a whole week on the island. I spoke with many people in the tourist industry and I visited the most interesting places in Puerto Rico. I also ate lots of typical food from the island. Furthermore, I sunbathed on the beautiful Puerto Rican beaches and swam in the Caribbean Sea. I had lots of fun. My trip was almost like a vacation!

PASO 3

❖ **Transparency 49**
This transparency includes additional practice items you may wish to present to your students.

PRETERITE OF REGULAR VERBS

hablar		comer		vivir	
habl**é**	*I spoke (did speak)*	com**í**	*I ate (did eat)*	viv**í**	*I lived (did live)*
habl**aste**	*you spoke*	com**iste**	*you ate*	viv**iste**	*you lived*
habl**ó**	*you/he/she spoke*	com**ió**	*you/he/she ate*	viv**ió**	*you/he/she lived*
habl**amos**	*we spoke*	com**imos**	*we ate*	viv**imos**	*we lived*
habl**asteis**	*you spoke*	com**isteis**	*you ate*	viv**isteis**	*you lived*
habl**aron**	*you/they spoke*	com**ieron**	*you/they ate*	viv**ieron**	*you/they lived*

- Note that the **nosotros** forms of regular preterites are the same as the present tense forms for **-ar** and **-ir** verbs. Context usually helps determine meaning.

  Hoy **hablamos** con la profesora Benítez.
  Today we're speaking with Professor Benítez.

  Ayer **hablamos** con el director de la facultad.
  Yesterday we spoke with the head of the department.

- Note the accent marks on the first and third person singular of the preterite tense. These accent marks are dropped in the conjugation of **ver: vi, vio**.

  ver: v**i**, viste, v**io**, vimos, visteis, vieron

- Verbs that end in **-car, -gar**, and **-zar** show a spelling change in the first person singular (*yo*) of the preterite. (This is the same change you have already learned to make in present subjunctive forms.)

  -car → qu buscar: bus**qué**, buscaste,...
  -gar → gu pagar: pa**gué**, pagaste,...
  -zar → c empezar: empe**cé**, empezaste,...

- **-Ar** and **-er** stem-changing verbs show no stem change in the preterite.
  -Ir stem-changing verbs do show a change.*

  despertar (ie): **desperté, despertaste,**...
  volver (ue): **volví, volviste,**...

- An unstressed **-i-** between two vowels becomes **-y-**.

  creer: creyó, creyeron leer: leyó, leyeron

IRREGULAR PRETERITE FORMS

dar		hacer		ir/ser	
di	dimos	hice	hicimos	fui	fuimos
diste	disteis	hiciste	hicisteis	fuiste	fuisteis
dio	dieron	hizo	hicieron	fue	fueron

*You will practice the preterite of most stem-changing verbs in **Capítulo 8**.

- The preterite endings for **dar** are the same as those used for regular **-er/-ir** verbs in the preterite, except that the accent marks are dropped.

- **Hizo** is spelled with a **z** to keep the [s] sound of the infinitive.

hic- + -o → hizo

- **Ir** and **ser** have identical forms in the preterite. Context will make the meaning clear.

Fui a la playa el verano pasado.
I went to the beach last summer.

Fui agente de viajes.
I was a travel agent.

Preliminary exercises: Preterite
- Use rapid-response drill before beginning activities: *Ud.* → *yo, Uds.* → *nosotros.* MODELO: *¿Llamó Ud.?* → *Sí, llamé, ¿Estudió? ¿Trabajó? ¿Habló? ¿Escuchó? ¿Terminó? ¿Mandó? ¿Bajó? ¿Cantó? ¿Bailó? ¿Comió? ¿Bebió? ¿Abrió? ¿Asistió? ¿Escribió? ¿Preguntaron? ¿Contestaron? ¿Bajaron? ¿Mandaron? ¿Escucharon? ¿Miraron? ¿Bebieron? ¿Comieron? ¿Comprendieron? ¿Vivieron? ¿Recibieron?*
- Use chain drill before beginning activities: **1.** *Pepe estudió hasta muy tarde.* (*yo, Uds. tú, Graciela, nosotros, vosotros*) **2.** *Tú escribiste todos los ejercicios.* (*Rodrigo, yo, nosotras, ellas, Uds., vosotros*) **3.** *Julio fue al laboratorio.* (*yo, Paula, tú, nosotros, Estela y Clara, vosotras*) **4.** *Ana hizo los experimentos.* (*yo, nosotros, Uds., tú, Adolfo*)

Variation A
Have students work in pairs and report each other's actions to the class.

Práctica

A. ¿Qué hizo Ud. el verano pasado? Indique las oraciones que son ciertas para Ud., contestando con **sí** o **no**.

El verano pasado…

1. tomé una clase en la universidad
2. asistí a un concierto
3. trabajé mucho
4. hice *camping* con algunos amigos / mi familia
5. viví con mis padres / mis hijos
6. me quedé en este pueblo / esta ciudad
7. fui a una playa
8. hice una excursión a otro país
9. fui a muchas fiestas
10. no hice nada especial

B. El día de tres compañeras

Paso 1. Teresa, Evangelina y Liliana comparten (*share*) un apartamento en un edificio viejo. Ayer Teresa y Evangelina fueron a la universidad mientras Liliana se quedó en casa. Describa lo que (*what*) hicieron, según la perspectiva de cada una.

Suggestion B
Reenter items using *tú* as the subject when appropriate.

TERESA Y EVANGELINA

1. (nosotras) salir / de / apartamento / a / nueve
2. llegar / biblioteca / a / diez
3. estudiar / toda la mañana / para / examen
4. escribir / muchos ejercicios
5. almorzar / con / amigos / en / cafetería
6. ir / a / laboratorio / a / una
7. hacer / todos los experimentos / de / manual (*m.*)
8. tomar / examen / a / cuatro
9. ¡examen / ser / horrible!
10. regresar / a casa / después de / examen
11. ayudar / Liliana / a / preparar / cena
12. cenar / todas juntas / a / siete

LILIANA

1. (yo) quedarse / en casa / todo el día
2. ver / televisión / por / mañana
3. llamar / mi / padres / a / once
4. tomar / café / con / vecinos (*neighbors*)
5. estudiar / para / examen / de / historia / y / escribir / composición / para / clase / sociología
6. ir / a / garaje / para / dejar / muebles / viejo / allí
7. ir / a / supermercado / y / comprar / comida
8. empezar / a / preparar / cena / a / cinco

Paso 2. ¿Quién lo dijo (*said*), Evangelina o Liliana?

1. Mis compañeras no pasaron mucho tiempo en casa hoy.
2. ¡El examen fue desastroso!
3. Estudié mucho hoy.
4. Me gustó mucho el programa de «Oprah» hoy.
5. ¿Saben? Hablé con mis padres hoy y…

Paso 3. Ahora vuelva a contar (*tell*) cómo fue el día de Liliana, pero desde el punto de vista de sus compañeras de cuarto. Luego diga cómo fue el día de Teresa y Evangelina según Liliana.

Follow-up B
Ask: *¿Cómo fue su día ayer?* Then have students work in pairs to describe what they did yesterday.

En los Estados Unidos y el Canadá...

Ellen Ochoa, una viajera espacial

La Dra. Ellen L. Ochoa, de California (1958–), es **la primera mujer hispana astronauta** de los Estados Unidos; trabaja en la NASA desde 1990. Se graduó con un **doctorado**[a] en **ingeniería eléctrica** de la Universidad de Stanford. Pasó más de 700 horas viajando en el espacio, y su próxima misión está programada para el año 2002. Entre[b] sus muchos honores está el de ser[c] miembro de la Comisión Presidencial para la Celebración de Mujeres en la Historia Americana.

Ellen Ochoa

La Dra. Ochoa no es la única persona hispana en la NASA. Hay otros **cinco astronautas hispanos** en misiones espaciales: el argentino Frank Caldeiro, el costarricense[d] Franklin Chang-Díaz, los españoles Pedro Duque y Michael López-Alegría y el peruano Carlos Noriega.

[a]*Ph.D.* [b]*Among* [c]*el… that of being* [d]*Costa Rican*

Suggestion: En los Estados Unidos y el Canadá…
Have students visit NASA's website for more information about the astronauts.

Conversación

NOTA COMUNICATIVA

Putting Events in Sequence

You can use the following phrases to put past events into a simple sequence in Spanish. You will learn additional words and phrases of this kind as you learn more about the past tenses.

Primero…	First . . .
Luego… y…	Then . . . and . . .
Después… y…	Afterward . . . and . . .
Finalmente (Por fin)…	Finally . . .

PASO 3

Note A
This is the first of several narration sequences that appears in this text. Use the drawing to give input with preterite and imperfect (even though students have not learned imperfect yet). After introducing the imperfect (*Capítulo 9*), come back to this drawing and exploit its narrative potential.

Suggestions A

- Read the following whole paragraph out loud. Then repeat, phrase by phrase. Have students retell story line by line. *Anoche Julián volvió a casa a las siete. Preparó la comida y cenó rápidamente. Estudió para su examen de filosofía hasta las ocho y después habló por teléfono con una compañera de clase. Y a las nueve en punto llegaron sus padres.*
- Ask students about well-known people. Have them use their imagination and make up necessary details: *¿Qué hicieron estas personas ayer?* (*Madonna, el presidente, Julia Roberts, Emeril, el profesor / la profesora*) Write actions on board to support their responses: *dar un discurso* (speech), *ensayar* (rehearse), *cocinar, cantar, enseñar, no hacer nada.*
- Have students tell about daily lives of people. They should tell if his/her life is very different from theirs on a daily basis. Have students invent as many details as possible and try to include trivial details: **1.** *un actor famoso / una actriz famosa* **2.** *la reina de Inglaterra, Isabel II* **3.** *los empleados de la Casa Blanca* **4.** *un(a) atleta profesional* **5.** *un bebé de dos años*

Answers A
a. *hicieron* **b.** *regresó* **c.** *volvió* **d.** *fueron* **e.** *llegaron* **f.** *llamó* **g.** *no les gustó* **h.** *comió* **i.** *se duchó y se afeitó* **j.** *entraron* **k.** *fue* **l.** *decidieron*

Variation B
Have students work in small groups to ask each other questions using *tú* forms.

Follow-up B

- For the next class, have students write down **1.** 1–2 unusual things they did in the past. **2.** 1–2 unusual things they did *not* do. Have students read their statements in class as others tell whether they think statements are *cierto* or *falso*.
- Have students write questions about personal habits and life events they can then use to interview classmates. Write verbs on board to give them ideas: *despertarse, regresar, pagar, enamorarse* (to fall in love), *sacar una nota* (grade).

A. El sábado por la tarde... The following drawings depict what Julián did last Saturday night. Match the phrases below with the individual drawings in the sequence. Then narrate what Julián did, using verbs in the preterite. Use as many of the words and phrases from the preceding **Nota comunicativa** as possible.

❖ Transparency 50

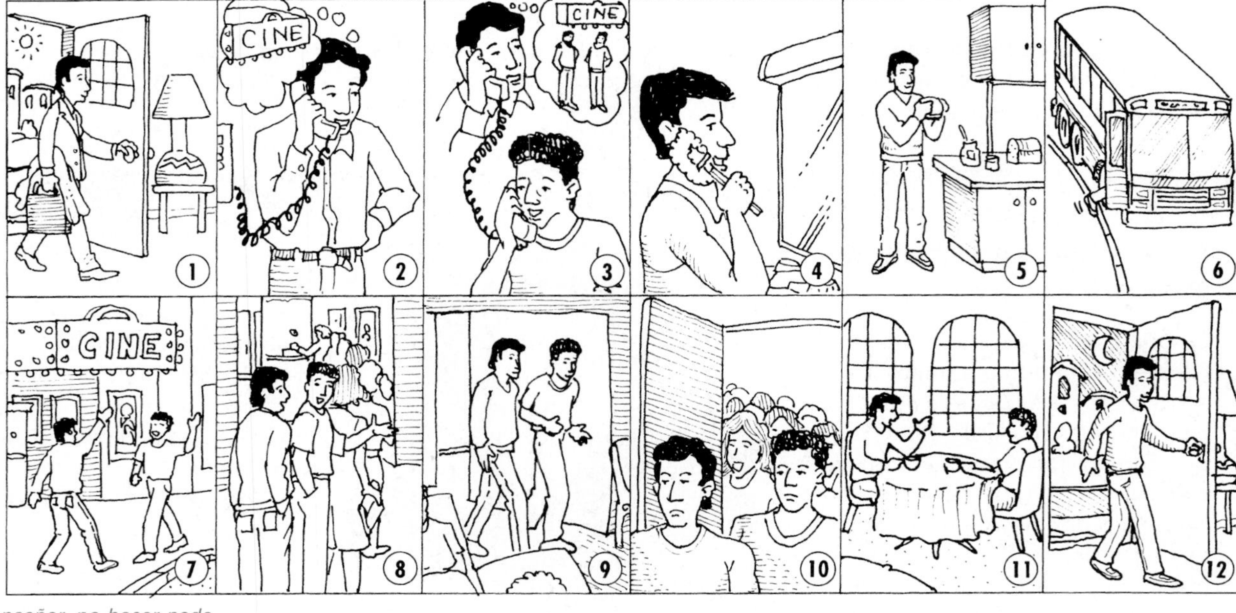

a. ___8___ hacer cola para comprar las entradas (*tickets*)
b. ___12___ regresar tarde a casa
c. ___1___ volver a casa después de trabajar
d. ___11___ ir a un café a tomar algo
e. ___7___ llegar al cine al mismo tiempo
f. ___2___ llamar a un amigo
g. ___10___ no gustarles la película
h. ___5___ comer rápidamente
i. ___4___ ducharse y afeitarse
j. ___9___ entrar en el cine
k. ___6___ ir al cine en autobús
l. ___3___ decidir encontrarse (*to meet up*) en el cine

B. Preguntas o/a s/a o/u

1. ¿Qué le(s) dio Ud. a su mejor amigo/a (su esposo/a, su novio/a, sus hijos) para su cumpleaños el año pasado? ¿Qué le regaló a Ud. esa persona para su cumpleaños? ¿Alguien le mandó a Ud. flores el año pasado? ¿Le mandó Ud. flores a alguien?
2. ¿Dónde y a qué hora comió Ud. ayer? ¿Con quién(es) comió? ¿Le gustaron todos los platos que comió? Si comió fuera, ¿quién pagó?
3. ¿Cuándo decidió Ud. estudiar español? ¿Cuándo lo empezó a estudiar? ¿Va a seguir con el español el semestre/trimestre que viene?
4. ¿Qué hizo Ud. ayer? ¿Adónde fue? ¿Con quién(es)? ¿Ayudó a alguien a hacer algo? ¿Lo/La llamó alguien? ¿Llamó Ud. a alguien?

UN POCO DE TODO

A. Preguntas: La última vez. Conteste las siguientes preguntas. Añada (*Add*) más información si puede.

MODELO: La última vez que Ud. fue a una fiesta, ¿le llevó un regalo al anfitrión (*host*)? → Sí, le llevé flores / una botella de vino. (No, no le llevé nada.)

La última vez que Ud...

1. hizo un viaje, ¿le mandó una tarjeta postal a un amigo / a una amiga?
2. tomó el autobús / el metro, ¿le ofreció su asiento a una persona mayor?
3. vio a su profesor(a) de español en público, ¿le habló en español?
4. comió en un restaurante, ¿le recomendó un plato a su compañero/a?
5. entró en un edificio, ¿le abrió la puerta a otra persona?

Suggestion A
Have students complete activity in pairs, then report to class at least 2 interesting things they learned about their partner.

Reciclado A
Recycle family and food words. Have students say the following sentences in Spanish. **1.** My father likes vegetables, but he doesn't like cheese **2.** My mother likes milk, but she doesn't like apple juice. **3.** My grandparents like eggs, but they don't like meat. **4.** I like everything (*todo*), but my siblings don't like anything!

B. Recomendaciones para las vacaciones. Complete the following vacation suggestion with the correct form of the words in parentheses, as suggested by the context. When two possibilities are given in parentheses, select the correct word.

(Les/Los[1]) quiero decir (algo/nada[2]) sobre (el/la[3]) ciudad de Machu Picchu. ¿Ya (lo/la[4]) (saber/conocer[5]) Uds.? (Ser/Estar[6]) situada en los Andes, a unos ochenta kilómetros[a] de la ciudad de Cuzco, Perú. Machu Picchu es conocida[b] como (el/la[7]) ciudad escondida[c] de los incas. Se dice que (ser/estar[8]) una de las manifestaciones (más/tan[9]) importantes de la arquitectura incaica. Era[d] refugio y a la vez[e] ciudad de vacaciones de los reyes[f] (incaico[10]).

Uds. deben (visitarlo/visitarla[11]). (Le/Les[12]) gustariá porque (ser/estar[13]) un sitio inolvidable.[g] Es mejor (ir/van[14]) a Machu Picchu en primavera o verano —son las (mejor[15]) estaciones para visitar este lugar. Pero es necesario (comprar/compran[16]) los boletos con anticipación,[h] porque (mucho[17]) turistas de todos los (país[18]) del mundo visitan este sitio extraordinario. ¡(*Yo:* Saber/Conocer[19]) que a Uds. (los/les[20]) va a gustar el viaje!

[a]ochenta... 50 millas [b]*known* [c]*hidden* [d]*It was* [e]a... *at the same time* [f]*kings* [g]*unforgettable* [h]con... *ahead of time*

Comprensión: ¿Cierto a falso? Conteste según la descripción.

1. Machu Picchu está en Chile.
2. Fue un lugar importante en el pasado.
3. Todavía es una atracción turística de gran interés.
4. Sólo los turistas latinoamericanos conocen Machu Picchu.

Suggestion B
Read the following sentences and have students indicate whether they are *cierto* or *falso.* Keep in mind that students have only been introduced to the concept of subjunctive for recognition. **1.** *Sus padres (hijos) quieren que Ud. vaya de vacaciones este año.* **2.** *Su mejor amigo/a no desea que Ud. viaje en avión.* **3.** *Es bueno que muchas personas pasen sus vacaciones en lugares exóticos.* **4.** *Es malo que (no) haya muchos turistas que vienen a esta ciudad.*

Answers B
1. *Les* **2.** *algo* **3.** *la* **4.** *la* **5.** *conocen* **6.** *Está* **7.** *la* **8.** *es* **9.** *más* **10.** *incaicos* **11.** *visitarla* **12.** *Les* **13.** *es* **14.** *ir* **15.** *mejores* **16.** *comprar* **17.** *muchos* **18.** *países* **19.** *Sé* **20.** *les*

In the *Capítulo 7* segment of "Chapter-by-Chapter Supplementary Materials" in the IM, you will find a chapter-culminating activity. You can use this activity to consolidate and review the vocabulary and grammar skills students have acquired.

PASO 1 Vocabulario

CAPÍTULO 8

 **Paso 1: Vocabulario**
See detailed supplementary materials and exercises for this section and a model for vocabulary presentation and other material in the *Capítulo 8 Paso 1: Vocabulario* section of "Chapter-by-Chapter Supplementary Materials," IM.

❖ **Transparency 51**

Los días festivos y las fiestas

Multimedia: Audio
Students can listen to and practice this chapter's vocabulary on their Listening Comprehension audio CD.

Magda cumple años hoy. Sus amigos le hacen una fiesta de sorpresa y le regalan algo especial.

la sorpresa	surprise
celebrar	to celebrate
dar (*irreg.*)/**hacer** (*irreg.*) **una fiesta**	to give/have a party
divertirse (ie, i)	to have a good time
faltar	to be absent, lacking
gastar dinero	to spend money
pasarlo bien/mal	to have a good/bad time
reunirse (me reúno) (con)	to get together (with)
ser (*irreg.*) + **en** + *place*	to take place at (*place*)
—¿**Dónde es** la fiesta?	*Where is the party?*
—(**Es**) **En** casa de Julio.	*(It's) At Julio's house.*

Vocabulario útil*

el Día de Año Nuevo	New Year's Day
el Día de los Reyes Magos	Day of the Magi (Three Kings)
el Día de San Valentín (de los Enamorados)	Valentine's Day

*All of the items on this list are not considered active vocabulary for this chapter. Just learn the holidays and celebrations that are relevant to you.

el Día de San Patricio	Saint Patrick's Day
la Pascua (de los hebreos)	Passover
la Pascua (Florida)	Easter
las vacaciones de primavera	spring break
el Cinco de Mayo	Cinco de Mayo (*Mexican awareness celebration in some parts of the U.S.*)
el Día del Canadá	Canada Day (July 1)
el Cuatro de Julio (el Día de la Independencia [estadounidense])	Independence Day (*U.S.*)
el Día de la Raza	Columbus Day (*Hispanic awareness day in some parts of the U.S.*)
el Día de todos los Santos	All Saints' Day (November 1)
el Día de los Muertos	Day of the Dead (November 2)
el Día de Acción de Gracias	Thanksgiving
la Fiesta de las Luces	Hanukkah
la Nochebuena	Christmas Eve
la Navidad	Christmas
la Noche Vieja	New Year's Eve
el cumpleaños	birthday
el día del santo	saint's day (*the saint for whom one is named*)
la quinceañera	young woman's fifteenth birthday party

Conversación

A. Definiciones. ¿Qué palabra o frase corresponde a estas definiciones?

1. el día en que se celebra el nacimiento (*birth*) de Jesús
2. algo que alguien no sabe o no espera
3. algo de comer y algo de beber que se sirve en las fiestas (dos respuestas)
4. el día en que algunos hispanos visitan el cementerio para honrar la memoria de los difuntos (*deceased*)
5. la fiesta en que se celebra el hecho (*fact*) de que una muchacha cumple quince años
6. el día en que todo el mundo (*everybody*) debe llevar ropa verde
7. la noche en que se celebra el final del año
8. palabra que se dice para mostrar una reacción muy favorable, por ejemplo, cuando un amigo cumple años

Heritage speakers

- Pídales a los estudiantes hispanohablantes que hablen acerca de los días de fiesta que se celebran en sus hogares, entre sus amigos o en sus vecindarios. Si algunos de ellos han participado en las fiestas patronales de un pueblo, anímelos a describirlas.
- Pídales a los hispanohablantes que describan la manera en que su familia celebra las fiestas nacionales de su país de origen. Pregúnteles, por ejemplo, cómo celebran la Nochebuena, qué caracteriza el Día de los Reyes Magos, adónde van con sus parientes el Día de los Muertos. Si la fiesta se suele celebrar de un modo parecido al de los Estados Unidos o el Canadá (como, por ejemplo, la Navidad), pregúnteles qué opinan con respecto a las diferencias entre cómo se celebra el día en las dos culturas. Pregúnteles, por ejemplo: *¿Opinan Uds. que la celebración de la Navidad es más religiosa entre los hispanos? ¿En cuál de las celebraciones tiene más influencia el comercio? ¿Qué hacen los latinoamericanos el día de las Pascuas? ¿Se celebra la Fiesta de las Luces de la misma manera en su país?*

Suggestion A
Have students give definitions of holidays not already defined in list.

PASO 1

CAPÍTULO 8

NOTA CULTURAL

☼ **Heritage speakers**
Pregúnteles a sus estudiantes hispanohablantes si saben cuándo es su día del santo, y si se celebra en casa.

Celebraciones

En la vida de uno hay muchas ocasiones para dar fiestas. Claro que todos los años hay que celebrar **el cumpleaños**. Pero en partes del mundo hispánico se celebra también **el día del santo**. En el calendario religioso católico cada día corresponde al nombre de un santo. Si Ud. se llama Juan, por ejemplo, su santo es San Juan Bautista y el día de su santo es el 24 de junio. En muchas ocasiones este día se celebra igual que el día de su cumpleaños.

Para las señoritas, la fiesta de los quince años, **la quinceañera**, es una de las más importantes, porque desde esa edad a la muchacha se le considera ya[a] mujer.

[a]*already*

Una quinceañera mexicana

Notes: Nota cultural

- Not all Hispanic countries celebrate the *quinceañera* to the same degree or in the same manner. In Puerto Rico, for example, the elaborate celebration of the fifteenth birthday is often a matter of social or economic standing. Called a *debut,* the celebration for a middle- or upper-class teenager is held in a hotel or hall and as many as several hundred friends and relatives may attend.
- In more traditional Mexican families, the girl celebrating her *quinceañera* is serenaded by a *mariachi* band in front of her house the night before her 15th birthday. The next day, the girl has a party at her house. The men and boys take turns dancing with the girl. The first dance is traditionally a waltz that she dances with her father.

Follow-up B
Have students describe holidays in brief paragraphs. Then have them read paragraphs to class without identifying the holiday.

National Standards: Comparisons

- The *día del santo* is more important in some areas of the Hispanic world than others. Also, the importance of celebrations will vary from family to family.
- *La quinceañera* is not celebrated in Spain.
- Have students compare the *quinceañera* celebration with the concept of the "sweet sixteen" birthday.

B. Hablando de fiestas

Paso 1. ¿Es su opinión de las siguientes fiestas positiva, negativa o neutra?

1. el Cuatro de Julio
2. el Día de Acción de Gracias
3. el Día de San Patricio
4. la Noche Vieja
5. el Día de la Raza
6. el Día de los Enamorados

Paso 2. Ahora compare sus respuestas con las (*those*) de sus compañeros de clase. ¿Coinciden todos en su opinión de algunas fiestas?

Paso 3. Ahora piense en su fiesta favorita. Puede ser una de la lista del **Paso 1** o una del **Vocabulario útil** de las páginas 198–199. Piense en cómo celebra Ud. esa fiesta, para explicárselo (*explain it*) luego a un compañero / una compañera de clase. Debe pensar en lo siguiente:

- los preparativos que Ud. hace de antemano (*beforehand*)
- la ropa especial que lleva
- las comidas o bebidas especiales que compra o prepara
- el lugar donde se celebra
- los adornos especiales que hay

Vocabulario útil

el árbol	tree	**la fiesta del barrio**	neighborhood (block) party
el corazón	heart		
la corona	wreath	**los fuegos artificiales**	fireworks
el desfile	parade	**el globo**	balloon

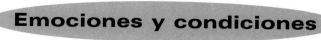

❖ Transparency 52

Emociones y condiciones

David está contento. **Se ríe**.

David **llora** porque **se siente triste**.

David **se pone feliz** otra vez y **sonríe**.

discutir (sobre) (con)	to argue (about) (with)
enfermar(se)	to get sick
enojar(se) (con)	to get mad (at)
llorar	to cry
olvidar(se) de	to forget about
ponerse + *adj.*	to become, get + *adjective*
portarse bien/mal	to behave well/poorly
quejarse (de)	to complain (about)
recordar (ue)	to remember
reír(se) (i, i) (de)	to laugh (about)
sentir(se) (ie, i)	to feel
sonreír(se) (i, i)	to smile

NOTA COMUNICATIVA

Being Emphatic

To emphasize the quality described by an adjective or an adverb, speakers of Spanish often add **-ísimo/a/os/as** to it, adding the idea *extremely* (*exceptionally; very, very; super*) to the quality. You have already used one emphatic form of this type: **Me gusta muchísimo**.

Estos entremeses son **dificilísimos** de preparar.	*These hors d'œuvres are very hard to prepare.*
Durante la época navideña, los niños son **buenísimos**.	*At Christmastime, the kids are extremely good.*

- If the adjective ends in a consonant, **-ísimo** is added to the singular form: **difícil** → **dificilísimo** (drop any accents on the word stem).
- If the adjective ends in a vowel, the final vowel is dropped before adding **-ísimo: bueno** → **buenísimo**.
- Spelling changes occur when the final consonant of an adjective is **c**, **g**, or **z: riq*u*ísimo, larg*u*ísimo, feli*c*ísimo**.

Suggestions: Nota comunicativa

- Emphasize change in stress and written accent in *fácil* → *facilísimo* and *difícil* → *dificilísimo*. Remind students to drop final vowel of adjectives that end in a vowel: *triste* → *tristísimo*.
- Emphasize and model spelling changes: *c* → *qu*, *g* → *gu*, *z* → *c*. Ask students where they have seen these changes before (preterite and formal commands).
- Ask students: **1.** *¿Es Ud. perezosísimo/a?* **2.** *¿Hay una persona rica en su familia? ¿Quién es? ¿Es una persona riquísima? ¿alta? ¿altísima? ¿interesante? ¿interesantísima? ¿simpática? ¿simpatiquísima?*

Conversación

Suggestions A
- Do as listening comprehension only.
- Offer optional vocabulary: *de buen/mal humor, impaciente.*

Extension A
7. Llueve todo el día **8.** *Ud. no sabe la respuesta, pero el profesor le pide que hable.* **9.** *Ud. sabe la respuesta y levanta la mano, pero el profesor no le presta atención.* **10.** *Ud. quiere bañarse y no hay agua caliente.* **11.** *Ud. está solo/a en casa y oye un ruido.* **12.** *Ud. le pide a alguien que no fume, pero la persona sigue fumando.*

Suggestion B
Have students write a description of a negative aspect of a holiday, for them in particular or for people in general, for example, *La Navidad es una fiesta demasiado comercializada. No me gusta el Día de Acción de Gracias… ¡porque no me gusta comer ni pavo ni calabaza!* The descriptions should be anonymous (assign numbers to students to track work). Have students hand in their ideas. Redistribute descriptions to other students, and have them write responses to negative aspect of holiday in form of advice or recommendations for having a better time or improving situation. Return complaint and advice to original author of negative description. Alternatively, read negative descriptions to class, and have students give advice orally.

A. Reacciones. ¿Cómo reacciona o cómo se pone Ud. en estas situaciones? Use estos adjetivos o cualquier otro, y también los verbos que describen las reacciones emocionales. No se olvide de usar las formas enfáticas cuando sea (*whenever it is*) apropiado.

serio/a	feliz/triste	avergonzado/a (*embarrassed*)
nervioso/a	furioso/a	contento/a

1. Es Navidad y alguien le hace a Ud. un regalo carísimo.
2. Es su cumpleaños y sus padres/hijos no le regalaron nada.
3. Ud. da una fiesta en su casa pero los invitados no se divierten. Nadie ríe ni sonríe.
4. Hay un examen importante hoy, pero Ud. no estudió anoche.
5. Ud. acaba de terminar un examen difícil/fácil y cree que lo hizo bien/mal.
6. En un examen de química, Ud. no puede recorder una fórmula muy importante.

B. ¿Son buenos todos los días festivos? Los días festivos pueden ser difíciles para muchas personas. Para Ud., ¿son ciertas o falsas las siguientes oraciones? Cambie las oraciones falsas para que sean (*so that they are*) ciertas. Luego compare sus respuestas con las de sus compañeros de clase.

EN LAS FIESTAS DE FAMILIA

1. Toda o casi toda mi familia, incluyendo a mis tíos, primos, abuelos, etcétera, se reúne por lo menos (*at least*) una vez al año.
2. Las fiestas de familia me gustan muchísimo.
3. Hay un pariente que siempre se queja de algo.
4. Uno de mis parientes siempre me hace preguntas indiscretas.
5. Alguien siempre bebe/come demasiado y luego se enferma.
6. A todos les gustan los regalos que reciben.
7. Todos lo pasan bien en las fiestas de familia.

LOS DÍAS FESTIVOS EN GENERAL

8. La Navidad / La Fiesta de las Luces es esencialmente una excusa para gastar dinero.
9. La época de fiestas en noviembre y diciembre es triste y deprimente (*depressing*) para mí.
10. Sólo las personas que practican una religión deben tener vacaciones en los días de fiestas religiosas.
11. Las vacaciones de primavera son para divertirse muchísimo. De hecho (*In fact*), son las mejores vacaciones del año.
12. Debería haber (*There should be*) más días festivos… por lo menos uno al mes.

Paso 2: Gramática
See detailed supplementary materials for these grammar sections in IM.

23 Talking about the Past (2) • Irregular Preterites

La fiesta de la Noche Vieja

❖ Transparency 53

Conteste las siguientes preguntas sobre esta fiesta.

1. ¿Quién *estuvo* hablando por teléfono?
2. ¿Quién *dio* la fiesta?
3. ¿Quién no *pudo* ir a la fiesta?
4. ¿Quién *puso* su copa de champán en el televisor?
5. ¿Quién *hizo* mucho ruido?
6. ¿Quiénes *tuvieron* que salir temprano?
7. ¿Quiénes no *quisieron* beber más?
8. ¿Quiénes *vinieron* con sus niñas?
9. ¿Quiénes le *trajeron* un regalo al anfitrión (*host*)?

Y Ud., *¿estuvo* alguna vez en una fiesta como esta? ¿*Tuvo* que salir temprano o se quedó hasta después de la medianoche (*midnight*)? ¿Le *trajo* algo al anfitrión / a la anfitriona?

Variation: Irregular Preterites
To follow up, have students think of the last party they or their family hosted and answer the questions.

- You have already learned the irregular preterite forms of **dar, hacer, ir,** and **ser**. The following verbs are also irregular in the preterite. Note that the first and third person singular endings, which are the only irregular ones, are unstressed, in contrast to the stressed endings of regular preterite forms.

estar	
estuve	**estuvimos**
estuviste	**estuvisteis**
estuvo	**estuvieron**

Preliminary exercises: Irregular Preterites
- Have students give the infinitive: *¿Cuál es el infinitivo de... ? ¿quise? ¿estuve? ¿vine? ¿tuve? ¿puse? ¿pude? ¿supe? ¿dije? ¿traje?*
- Have students give the subject (*yo, tú, Ud.*): *¿Cuál es el sujeto de... ? ¿vino? ¿tuviste? ¿tuvo? ¿pudo? ¿supo? ¿estuvo? ¿trajiste? ¿dijo? ¿puse? ¿dije? ¿supiste? ¿puso? ¿quise? ¿vino? ¿estuviste?*
- Have students give preterite: **yo**: *estar, poder, poner;* **tú**: *querer, saber, tener;* **Ud.**: *decir, traer, estar;* **nosotros**: *poder, poner, saber;* **Uds.**: *tener, decir, traer.*

estar: **estuv-**
poder: **pud-**
poner: **pus-**
querer: **quis-**
saber: **sup-**
tener: **tuv-**
venir: **vin-**

} **-e**, -iste, **-o**, -imos, -isteis, -ieron

- When the preterite verb stem ends in **-j-**, the **-i-** of the third person plural ending is omitted: **dijeron, trajeron**.

decir: **dij-**
traer: **traj-**

} -e, -iste, -o, -imos, -isteis, **-eron**

- Have students tell if the forms are present indicative or preterite: *dice, dije, decimos, dijimos, estamos, estuvimos, puede, podemos, pudimos, pude, ponemos, pusimos, tuve, tenemos, traigo, trajo, traemos, trajimos, vinimos, venimos, vinieron.*

• The preterite of **hay** (**haber**) is **hubo** (*there was/were*).	**Hubo** un accidente ayer en el centro. *There was an accident yesterday downtown.*
• Several of the following Spanish verbs have an English equivalent in the preterite tense that is different from that of the infinitive.	

	Infinitive Meaning	Preterite Meaning
saber	to know (*facts, information*) Ya lo sé. *I already know it.*	to find out Lo **supe** ayer. *I found it out* (*learned it*) *yesterday.*
conocer	to know (*be familiar with*) people, places Ya la conozco. *I already know her.*	to meet (*for the first time*) La **conocí** ayer. *I met her yesterday.*
querer	to want Quiero hacerlo hoy. *I want to do it today.*	to try **Quise** hacerlo ayer. *I tried to do it yesterday.*
no querer	not to want No quiero hacerlo hoy. *I don't want to do it today.*	to refuse **No quise** hacerlo anteayer. *I refused to do it the day before yesterday.*
poder	to be able Puedo leerlo *I can* (*am able to*) *read it.*	to succeed (*in doing something*) **Pude** leerlo ayer. *I could* (*and did*) *read it yesterday.*
no poder	not to be able, capable No puedo leerlo. *I can't* (*am not able to*) *read it.*	to fail (*in doing something*) **No pude** leerlo anteayer. *I couldn't* (*did not*) *read it the day before yesterday.*

Preliminary exercise A
Ask students: **1.** *¿Tuvo Ud. una entrevista ayer? ¿un examen? ¿una cita con el dentista?* **2.** *¿Estuvo Ud. en España el verano pasado? ¿en México? ¿en Florida?* **3.** *¿Ud. se puso rojo/a ayer? ¿Por qué razón?* **4.** *¿Quién no pudo dormir bien anoche? ¿Le ocurre esto con frecuencia?* **5.** *¿Quién dijo una mentira ayer? ¿A quién?* **6.** *¿Quién vino temprano hoy a clase? ¿Quién no vino a clase ayer?*

Práctica

A. La última Noche Vieja. Piense en lo que Ud. hizo la Noche Vieja del año pasado e indique si las siguientes oraciones son ciertas o falsas para Ud.

1. Fui a una fiesta en casa de un amigo / una amiga.
2. Di una fiesta en mi casa.
3. No estuve con mis amigos, sino (*but rather*) con la familia.
4. Quise ir a una fiesta, pero no pude.
5. No pude encontrar (*find*) el lugar de la fiesta.

6. Les dije «¡Feliz Año Nuevo!» a muchas personas.
7. No le dije «¡Feliz Año Nuevo!» a nadie.
8. Conocí a algunas personas nuevas.
9. Tuve que preparar la comida de esa noche.
10. Me puse ropa elegante esa noche.
11. Pude quedarme despierto/a (*awake*) hasta la medianoche.
12. No quise bailar.

Follow-up A
Have students add one action that they did and one that they didn't do.

B. Una Nochebuena en casa de los Ramírez. Describa lo que pasó en casa de los Ramírez, haciendo el papel (*playing the role*) de uno de los hijos. Haga oraciones en el pretérito según las indicaciones, usando el sujeto pronominal cuando sea necesario.

1. todos / estar / en casa / abuelos / antes de / nueve
2. (nosotros) poner / mucho / regalos / debajo / árbol
3. tíos y primos / venir / con / comida y bebidas
4. yo / tener / que / ayudar / a / preparar / comida
5. haber / cena / especial / para / todos
6. más tarde / alguno / amigos / venir / a / cantar / villancicos (*carols*)
7. niños / ir / a / alcoba / a / diez y / acostarse
8. niños / querer / dormir / pero / no / poder
9. a / medianoche / todos / decir / «¡Feliz Navidad!»
10. al día siguiente / todos / decir / que / fiesta / estar / estupendo

Extension B
Have students tell what happened on Christmas Day at the Ramírez house, inventing more details.

Variations B
- Have students use activity items as a guide for describing their own Christmas (or other holiday) celebrations.
- Dictate sentences but have students transform the verbs to preterite as they take dictation: **1.** *El nieto de Ana viene a visitarnos. El niño se porta muy bien. Está en casa una hora; luego dice adiós y se va.* **2.** *Los Sres. Torres hacen la cena y ponen la mesa a las seis. Luego tienen que lavar los platos* (pantomime the action). *No pueden ir al cine hasta muy tarde.* **3.** *Quiero estudiar pero no puedo porque mi amigo Octavio viene a casa con un amigo ecuatoriano. Tengo que ver las fotos que trae.*

Conversación

A. Un viaje inolvidable. Piense en un viaje inolvidable (malo o bueno) de su vida. Con un compañero / una compañera, haga y conteste las siguientes preguntas sobre sus viajes.

1. ¿Adónde fue de viaje? ¿Con quién(es) fue?
2. ¿Cuánto tiempo estuvo allí? ¿Dónde se alojó (*did you stay*)?
3. ¿Conoció a alguien allí? ¿Le gustó conocer a esa(s) persona(s)?
4. ¿Qué cosas hizo durante el viaje? ¿Qué no pudo hacer?
5. ¿Compró algún recuerdo (*souvenir*)? ¿Para quién?

Suggestion A
Assign first as homework, then have students complete activity together in class.

B. Preguntas

1. ¿En qué mes conoció Ud. al profesor / a la profesora de español? ¿A quién(es) más conoció ese mismo (*same*) día? ¿Tuvo Ud. que hablar español el primer día de clase?
2. El año pasado, ¿dónde pasó Ud. la Nochebuena? ¿el Día de Acción de Gracias? ¿Dónde estuvo durante las vacaciones de primavera? ¿Dónde piensa Ud. estar este año en estas ocasiones?
3. ¿Alguien le dio a Ud. una fiesta de cumpleaños este año? ¿Fue una fiesta sorpresa? ¿Dónde fue? ¿Qué le trajeron sus amigos? ¿Qué le regalaron sus parientes? ¿Alguien le hizo un pastel?

Follow-up B
- Ask students the following question after completing item **1**: *Ahora que Ud. conoce bien al profesor / a la profesora, ¿cree que ese día representó una clase típica?*
- Follow-up item **3**: *¿Le hizo Ud. una fiesta de cumpleaños a algún amigo o pariente?* (Encourage use of object pronouns.) *¿Quién preparó la comida? ¿Dio la fiesta en su casa o en casa de otra persona? ¿Puso Ud. adornos* (decorations)*? ¿Invitó a sus amigos? ¿Preparó una sangría? ¿Qué bebieron sus invitados? ¿Lo pasaron bien todos?*

PASO 2

CAPÍTULO 8

❖ **Transparency 54**
You may wish to use this transparency for additional grammar practice.

24 Talking about the Past (3) • Preterite of Stem-Changing Verbs

La quinceañera de Lupe Carrasco

Imagine los detalles de la fiesta de Lupe cuando cumplió quince años.

1. Lupe *se vistió* con
   - ☐ un vestido blanco muy elegante.
   - ☐ una camiseta y unos *jeans*.
   - ☐ el vestido de novia[a] de su abuela.
2. Cortando el pastel de cumpleaños, Lupe
   - ☐ *empezó* a llorar.
   - ☐ *rió* mucho.
   - ☐ *sonrió* para una foto.
3. Lupe *pidió* un deseo[b] al cortar el pastel. Ella
   - ☐ les dijo a todos su deseo.
   - ☐ *prefirió* guardarlo en secreto.
4. En la fiesta *sirvieron*
   - ☐ champán y otras bebidas alcohólicas.
   - ☐ refrescos.
   - ☐ sólo té y café.
5. Todos *se divirtieron* mucho en la fiesta. Los invitados *se despidieron*[c] a la(s)_____.

[a]vestido... *wedding gown* [b]*wish* [c]se... *said good-bye*

Follow-up: Preterite Y Ud., ¿recuerda qué hizo cuando cumplió quince años? ¿*Pidió* muchos regalos? ¿*Se divirtió*? ¿Cómo *se sintió*?

Follow up the sentences about Lupe's *quinceañera* with questions about the party: *¿A qué hora llegaron / se fueron los invitados? ¿Con quién bailó Lupe?* and so on.

A. As you learned in **Capítulo 7**, the **-ar** and **-er** stem-changing verbs have no stem change in the preterite (or in the present participle).

recordar (ue): rec**o**rdé, rec**o**rdaste, rec**o**rdó, rec**o**rdamos, rec**o**rdasteis, rec**o**rdaron; rec**o**rdando

perder (ie): p**e**rdí, p**e**rdiste, p**e**rdió, p**e**rdimos, p**e**rdisteis, p**e**rdieron; p**e**rdiendo

B. The **-ir** stem-changing verbs do have a stem change in the preterite, but only in the third person singular and plural, where the stem vowels **e** and **o** change to **i** and **u**, respectively. This is the same change that occurs in the present participle of **-ir** stem-changing verbs.

pedir (i, i)		dormir (ue, u)	
pedí	pedimos	dormí	dormimos
pediste	pedisteis	dormiste	dormisteis
p**i**dió	p**i**dieron	d**u**rmió	d**u**rmieron
p**i**diendo		d**u**rmiendo	

C. Here are some **-ir** stem-changing verbs. You already know or have seen many of them. The reflexive meaning, if different from the non-reflexive meaning, is in parentheses.

OJO

Note the simplification:
ri-ió → rió; ri-ieron → rieron
son-ri-ió → sonrió
son-ri-ieron → sonrieron

conseguir (i, i)	to get, obtain	**pedir (i, i)**	to ask for; to order
conseguir + *inf.*	to succeed in (*doing something*)	**preferir (ie, i)**	to prefer
despedirse (i, i) (de)	to say good-bye (to), take leave (of)	**reír(se) (i, i)**	to laugh
divertir(se) (ie, i)	to entertain (to have a good time)	**sentir(se) (ie, i)**	to feel
dormir(se) (ue, u)	to sleep (to fall asleep)	**servir (i, i)**	to serve
morir(se) (ue, u)	to die	**sonreír(se) (i, i)**	to smile
		sugerir (ie, i)	to suggest
		vestir(se) (ie, i)	to dress (to get dressed)

Práctica

A. ¿Quién lo hizo? ¿Ocurrieron algunas de estas co
pasada? Conteste con el nombre de la persona a
hizo, conteste con **Nadie...**

1. _____ se vistió de una manera muy elegante.
2. _____ se vistió de una manera rara (*strange*).
3. _____ se durmió en clase.
4. _____ se sintió muy contento/a.
5. _____ se divirtió muchísimo, riendo y sonriendo.
6. ___
7. ___
8. ___
9. ___

B. Historias breves. Cuente las siguientes histori
Luego continúelas, si puede.

1. **Un día típico:** Rosa (acostarse) temprano y (dormirse) en seguida. (Dormir) bien y (despertarse) temprano. (Vestirse) y (salir) para la universidad. En el autobús (ver) a su amigo José y los dos (sonreír). A las nueve _____.
2. **Dos noches diferentes:** Yo (vestirse), (ir) a una fiesta, (divertirse) mucho y (volver) tarde a casa. Mi compañero de cuarto (decidir) quedarse en casa y (ver) la televisión toda la noche. No (divertirse) nada. (Perder) una fiesta excelente y lo (sentir) mucho. Yo _____.

Conversación

La fiesta de disfraz (*Costume party*). Use the following sentences as a guide for telling about a childhood or more recent costume party, if appropriate.

1. ¿De qué se vistió?
2. ¿Cómo se sintió?
3. ¿Fue de casa en casa?
4. ¿Qué les dijo y qué les pidió a los vecinos (*neighbors*)?
5. ¿Qué le dieron?
6. ¿Se rieron los vecinos cuando lo/la vieron?
7. ¿Consiguió muchos dulces?
8. ¿También asistió a una fiesta?
9. ¿Qué sirvieron en la fiesta?
10. ¿Se divirtió mucho?

Preterite
the third person
of the following verbs:
orir, dormirse **2.** (*i, i*)
dir **3.** (*ie, i*) *preferir,*
ertirse, sugerir
ractice preterite: *Todos*
l ayer. **1.** *Dormimos*
yo, todos, Irma, tú, Ud.,
cordaste traer los
osotros, Ud., ellos,
perdió las llaves (keys)
racio y Estela, yo, Ud.,
nos mariscos pero no
out of them). (*yo,*
vosotros) **5.** *Todos se*
Nati. (*nosotros, Esteban,*
s)

Have students add statements about other topics: *¿Pasó algo muy interesante en la clase? ¿y en el país?*

Suggestion B
Have students read through each sequence before beginning activity.

Answers B
1. *se sentó, vino, pidió, recordó, pidió, sirvió, quiso, dijo, pedí, contestó* **2.** *se acostó, se durmió, Durmió, se despertó, Se vistió, salió, vio, sonrieron* **3.** *me vestí, fui, me divertí, volví, decidió, vio, se divirtió, Perdió, sintió*

Suggestion: Conversación
Have students ask you questions first as a model for the interviews.

Follow-up: Conversación
Have students decide who wore: *el disfraz más cómico/espantoso* (frightening)/ *original.*

Enfoque cultural

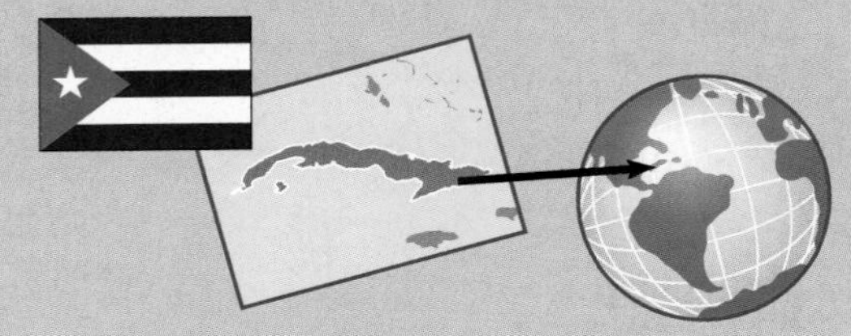

Enfoque cultural
See follow-up activities for this section in chapter-by-chapter materials in IM.

Cuba

☼ **Heritage speakers**
Invite a un(a) estudiante hispanohablante a leer en voz alta el poema de Guillén.

Datos esenciales

Nombre oficial: República de Cuba

Capital: La Habana

Población: 11.000.000 de habitantes

Moneda: el peso cubano

Idioma oficial: el español

¡Fíjese!

- Cuba obtuvo[a] su independencia de España en 1898, tras[b] la guerra de Cuba.[c] Los Estados Unidos ayudó a Cuba en esta guerra.
- Hay una distancia de 145 kilómetros (90 millas) entre Florida y Cuba.
- Después de la revolución socialista cubana en 1959, hubo un éxodo de cubanos a los Estados Unidos. La mayor parte de ellos se estableció en Florida, con la esperanza[d] de volver muy pronto a su isla. Pero empezó el milenio y todavía[e] Fidel Castro, el primer líder de la revolución, gobierna a Cuba.
- El régimen de Castro ha reducido[f] el analfabetismo[g] a menos de 5 por ciento y ha reformado el sistema educativo con resultados admirables. Pero la situación económica del país es difícil. Con la caída[h] de la Unión Soviética, Cuba perdió fondos de apoyo[i] indispensables. El embargo económico de los Estados Unidos afectó las condiciones de vida[j] de los cubanos, pero últimamente se exploran las posibilidades de exportación e importación entre los Estados Unidos y Cuba.

[a]*obtained* [b]*after* [c]guerra... *Spanish-American War* [d]*hope* [e]*still*
[f]ha... *has reduced* [g]*illiteracy* [h]*fall* [i]fondos... *economic assistance*
[j]condiciones... *living conditions*

Conozca a... Nicolás Guillén

Nicolás Guillén (1902–1989), poeta cubano de origen africano y europeo, es quizás[a] el poeta que mejor refleja la influencia africana en la cultura hispana. El lenguaje, los mitos[b] y las leyendas afrocubanos aparecen en su obra. Sus temas incluyen la injusticia social y una crítica al colonialismo. El siguiente fragmento de un poema de Guillén es representativo de su obra. Después de leerlo, piense: ¿Quiénes son los hombres del poema? ¿Cuál es su condición de vida? ¿Por qué es la sangre[c] «un mar inmenso»?

Nicolás Guillén

[a]*perhaps* [b]*myths* [c]*blood*

Poema con niños

La sangre es un mar inmenso
que baña todas las playas...
sobre sangre van los hombres
navegando[a] en sus barcazas:[b]
reman, que reman,[c] que reman
¡nunca de remar descansan!
Al negro[d] de negra piel
la sangre el cuerpo le baña;
la misma sangre, corriendo,[e]
hierve[f] bajo carne[g] blanca.

[a]*sailing* [b]*boats* [c]reman... *rowing and rowing* [d]persona negra
[e]*flowing* [f]*boils* [g]*flesh*

Capítulo 8 of the video to accompany *¿Qué tal?* contains cultural footage about Cuba.

Visit the *¿Qué tal?* website at www.mhhe.com/quetal.

Suggestion
Write the following names and topics on separate slips of paper, repeating each 3–4 times depending on size of your class: José Martí, Elián González, The Buena Vista Social Club, Iván Hernández, Fidel Castro, *la Bahía de Guantánamo*, Radio Martí, Fulgencio Batista, *los marielitos*, the USS Maine, and Theodore Roosevelt. Have each student pick a slip. Ask students to investigate significance of the name on their slip to Cuban history. In another class period, work with students to construct a time line of modern Cuban history.

Paso 3: Gramática
See detailed supplementary materials for these grammar sections in IM.

25 Expressing Direct and Indirect Objects Together • Double Object Pronouns

¡ES MUY LINDO!...¿ME LO PRESTÁS?

¡PEATONA![a]

[a] *Pedestrian!*

Susanita es una amiga de Mafalda. A veces se porta muy mal y es un poco egocéntrica. ¿Conoce Ud. a personas como Susanita? ¿Le han pasado (*have happened*) las siguientes cosas a Ud.?

		SÍ	NO
1.	Una vez le presté un libro a alguien y no me lo devolvió (*returned*).	☐	☐
2.	Le pedí una bebida al camarero en un restaurante y no me la trajo.	☐	☐
3.	Pedí algunos regalos específicos para mi cumpleaños, pero nadie me los regaló.	☐	☐
4.	Les mostré fotos a unas personas, y las doblaron (*they bent them*).	☐	☐

ORDER OF PRONOUNS

When both an indirect and a direct object pronoun are used in a sentence, the indirect object pronoun (**I**) precedes the direct (**D**): **ID**. Note that nothing comes between the two pronouns. The position of double object pronouns with respect to the verb is the same as that of single object pronouns.

—¿Tienes el trofeo?
Do you have the trophy?

—Sí, acaban de dár**melo**.
Yes, they just gave it to me.

—Mamá, ¿está listo el almuerzo?
Mom, is lunch ready?

—**Te lo** preparo ahora mismo.
I'll get it ready for you right now.

Suggestions: Double Object Pronouns
- Treat *Grammar 25* as a topic for passive recognition or, at best, for partial control.
- Ask questions about the cartoon: **1.** *¿Quién tiene triciclo?* **2.** *¿Qué le pide Susanita a Mafalda?* **3.** *¿Mafalda le presta el triciclo a Susanita?* (Rephrase the answer: *Es verdad. Mafalda se lo presta.*) **4.** *Susanita debe darle las gracias a Mafalda, ¿verdad?* (Rephrase the answer: *Es verdad. Susanita debe dárselas.*) **5.** *¿Qué le dice Susanita a Mafalda?*
- Have students identify direct objects (verb + what/whom) and indirect objects (to/for whom) in the cartoon.

Le(s) → *se*

A. When both the indirect and the direct object pronouns begin with the letter **l**, the indirect object pronoun always changes to **se**. The direct object pronoun does not change.

Le compra unos zapatos.	*He's buying her some shoes.*
Se los compra.	*He's buying them for her.*
Les mandamos la blusa.	*We'll send you the blouse.*
Se la mandamos.	*We'll send it to you.*

B. Since **se** can stand for **le** (*to/for you* [*sing.*], *him, her*) or **les** (*to/for you* [*pl.*], *them*), it is often necessary to clarify its meaning by using **a** plus the pronoun objects of prepositions.

Se lo escribo (**a Uds., a ellos, a ellas...**).
I'll write it to (*you, them . . .*).

Se las doy (**a Ud., a él, a ella...**).
I'll give them to (*you, him, her . . .*).

Práctica

A. Lo que se oye en casa. ¿A qué se refieren las siguientes oraciones? ¿unas fotos, la sal, unos billetes de avión para Guadalajara, la fiesta, el televisor, los discos compactos de Enrique Iglesias? Fíjese en (*Note*) los pronombres y en el sentido (*meaning*) de la oración.

1. No **lo** prendan (*switch on*). Es mejor que los niños lean o que jueguen.
2. ¿Me **la** pasas? Gracias.
3. Tengo muchas ganas de comprárme**los** todos. Me encanta esa música.
4. ¿Por qué no se **las** mandas a los abuelos? Les van a gustar muchísimo.
5. Tengo que reservárte**los** hoy mismo, porque se va a terminar (*expire*) la oferta especial de Aeroméxico.
6. Yo se **la** organicé a Lupe para su cumpleaños. Antonio y Diego le hicieron un pastel.

B. En el aeropuerto. Cambie los sustantivos a pronombres para evitar (*avoid*) la repetición.

1. ¿La hora de la salida? Acaban de decirnos la hora de la salida.
2. ¿El horario? Sí, léeme el horario, por favor.
3. ¿Los boletos? No, no tiene que darle los boletos aquí.
4. ¿El equipaje? Claro que le guardo el equipaje.
5. ¿Los pasajes? Acabo de comprarte los pasajes.
6. ¿El puesto? No te preocupes. Te puedo guardar el puesto.
7. ¿La clase turística? Sí, les recomiendo la clase turística, señores.
8. ¿La cena? La asistente de vuelo nos va a servir la cena en el avión.

Conversación

A. Regalos especiales. The drawings in **Grupo I** show the presents that a number of people have just received. They were sent by the people in **Grupo II**. Can you match the presents with the sender? Make as many logical guesses as you can. Then compare your matches with those of a partner.

MODELO: ¿Quién le regaló (mandó) a Maritere _____?
¿Quién les regaló (mandó) a Carlos y Juanita _____?
Se lo/la/los/las regaló (mandó) _____.

Preliminary exercises A
- Ask students which of the following sentences could refer to *el dinero* (*sí* or *no*): **1.** *¿Me lo prestas?* **2.** *Voy a dársela.* **3.** *Te lo mando mañana.*
- Ask students which of the following sentences could refer to *las recomendaciones* (*sí* or *no*): **1.** *Te los doy, si quieres.* **2.** *¿Cuándo se las pediste?* **3.** *Sí, quiero que me las traiga ahora.*

Note A
Students need not produce double object pronouns in this activity.

Suggestion A
Have students use emphatic prepositional phrase *me* → *a mí* with indirect object pronouns.

Answers A
1. *el televisor* **2.** *la sal* **3.** *los discos compactos de Enrique Iglesias* **4.** *unas fotos* **5.** *unos billetes de avión para Guadalajara* **6.** *la fiesta*

Follow-up A
Have students convert all the sentences to commands.

Suggestions A
- Have students guess occasion for those gifts.
- Suggest the following answers: **A.** *las flores de Estela: Se las mandó su mejor amiga, la Sra. Santana.* **B.** *los billetes de Carlos y Juanita: Se los regaló su nieto Jorge.* **C.** *la fiesta de Rigoberto. Se la preparó su madre.* **D.** *la computadora de Maritere: Se la regaló su hermano Raúl.*

Suggestion B
Start activity by assigning pairs to practice giving definitions. Have students explain what gifts were (without naming them) while classmates try to guess correct item. Name of object can be given in English. Task is to practice circumlocution.

❖ Transparency 55

GRUPO I

GRUPO II

B. ¿Quién le regaló eso?

Paso 1. Haga una lista de los cinco mejores regalos que Ud. ha recibido (*have received*) en su vida. Si no sabe cómo decir algo, pregúnteselo a su profesor(a).

Paso 2. Ahora déle a un compañero / una compañera su lista. Él/Ella le va a preguntar: **¿Quién te regaló _____?** Use pronombres en su respuesta. **¡OJO!** Fíjese en (*Note*) estas formas plurales (**ellos**): **regalaron, dieron, mandaron**.

MODELO: E1: ¿Quién te regaló los aretes?
E2: Mis padres me los regalaron.

Follow-up B
As a composition assignment, students describe history of their favorite gift (or their partner's): who gave it to them, why, when, and so on.

Suggestion: En los Estados Unidos y el Canadá…
- Point out that César Chávez is profiled in the *Enfoque cultural* of *Capítulo 1*. To learn more about the holiday and Chávez, have students look for websites that feature Chávez.
- Have students find out more about Senator Polanco's agenda, as well as other Hispanic government leaders.

En los Estados Unidos y el Canadá…

El día de César Chávez

Desde el año 2000, el líder sindical[a] mexicoamericano César Chávez (1927–1993) tiene **un día festivo** en su honor en el estado de **California**. El lunes o el viernes alrededor del[b] 31 de marzo, los colegios y otros organismos[c] pueden cerrar para **honrar**[d] a Chávez y el movimiento en defensa de los **trabajadores agrícolas**[e] que él defendió.

César Chávez

El senador Richard Polanco fue el autor de la legislación que estableció **el día de César Chávez.** Polanco es un senador demócrata en el senado de California desde 1994 y representa al distrito de Los Ángeles. Desde 2000, Polanco es el Líder de la Mayoría en el Senado.

«[César Chávez] debe ser **honrado** porque su trabajo formó la América en la que hoy vivimos. Su vida nos dio a todos **el coraje**[g] y **la esperanza**[h] de que podemos hacer una diferencia. En su vida, nos enseñó que es importante **llevar una vida moral y responsable.**»

[a]*union* [b]alrededor… *around the* [c]*institutions* [d]*honor* [e]trabajadores… *farm workers* [f]fue… *was signed* [g]*courage* [h]*hope*

PASO FINAL

A CONVERSAR

¿Cómo celebraron los días festivos?

Paso 1. En una hoja de papel aparte, prepare un cuadro como el siguiente. Primero, escoja cuatro de los días festivos de la lista en las páginas 198–199. Luego escríbalos en el cuadro. Deje espacios en blanco para escribir el nombre de una persona y sus respuestas breves a tres preguntas.

MODELO:

día festivo:	el Día de San Patricio	la Noche Vieja	el cumpleaños	el Cinco de Mayo
persona:				
actividades:				

Suggestion
Remind students that there are expressions and verbs throughout the chapter that they may wish to use in their questions and responses, not only those in the end-of-chapter list. For example, the lists on pages 199 and 200 include many appropriate words.

Follow-up
Ask students how they themselves spent the holidays on their charts: *¿Qué hizo Ud.* (name of holiday)*? ¿Recibió regalos? ¿Le regaló algo a otra persona? ¿Hizo una fiesta? ¿Sirvió algún plato especial?*, and so on.

Paso 2. Apunte tres preguntas que Ud. puede hacerles a sus compañeros sobre cómo celebraron los días festivos el año pasado.

MODELO: El año pasado, ¿qué hiciste en la Noche Vieja? ¿Te reuniste con amigos en algún lugar especial? ¿Lo pasaste bien o mal?

Paso 3. Formen parejas para hacer y contestar las tres preguntas sobre el primer día festivo en el cuadro. Después de hacer y contestar esas tres preguntas, formen parejas con otras personas para hacer y contestar las preguntas del siguiente día festivo. En total, van a formar cuatro parejas diferentes para hacer y contestar las preguntas sobre los cuatro días festivos. Escriban los nombres de sus compañeros y sus respuestas debajo del día festivo correspondiente para recorder con quiénes hablaron y qué dijeron.

MODELO: la Noche Vieja →
Felipe: Salió con su novia. Se reunieron con unos amigos en un bar. Lo pasaron muy bien.

Paso 4. Escoja uno de los días festivos y cuéntele a la clase cómo lo celebró la persona que contestó sus preguntas.

En resumen

GRAMÁTICA

To review the grammar points presented in this chapter, refer to the indicated grammar presentations. You'll find further practice of these structures in the Workbook/Laboratory Manual, on the CD-ROM, and on the website.

23. Irregular Preterites

Do you know how to conjugate verbs that are irregular in the preterite? How does the preterite change the meaning of **saber, conocer, querer,** and **poder**?

24. Preterite of Stem-Changing Verbs

You should know the stem-changing patterns in the preterite for **-ir** verbs like **pedir, sentir,** and **dormir**.

25. Double Object Pronouns

Do you know in which order the direct and indirect object pronouns occur when they are used together in Spanish? You should also know where to place the pronouns and when an accent is required on the verb form.

VOCABULARIO

Los verbos

conseguir (i, i)	to get, obtain
conseguir + *inf.*	to succeed in (*doing something*)
despedirse (i, i) (de)	to say good-bye (to), take leave (of)
discutir (sobre) (con)	to argue (about) (with)
encontrar (ue)	to find
enfermarse	to get sick
enojarse (con)	to get angry (at)
gastar	to spend (*money*)
llorar	to cry
morir(se) (ue, u)	to die
olvidarse (de)	to forget (about)
ponerse (*irreg.*) + *adj.*	to become, get + *adjective*
portarse	to behave
quejarse (de)	to complain (about)
reaccionar	to react
recordar (ue)	to remember
reír(se) (i, i)	to laugh
sentirse (ie, i)	to feel
sonreír(se) (i, i)	to smile
sugerir (ie, i)	to suggest

Los días festivos y las fiestas

el anfitrión / la anfitriona	host, hostess
el chiste	joke
el deseo	wish
los entremeses	hors d'œuvres
el/la invitado/a	guest
el pastel de cumpleaños	birthday cake
los refrescos	refreshments
la sorpresa	surprise
cumplir años	to have a birthday
dar (*irreg.*) **/ hacer** (*irreg.*) **una fiesta**	to give/have a party
faltar	to be absent, lacking
pasarlo bien/mal	to have a good/bad time
reunirse (me reúno) (con)	to get together (with)

Repaso: celebrar, el cumpleaños, el dinero, divertirse (ie, i), regalar

Los sustantivos

la emoción	emotion
el hecho	event
la medianoche	midnight
la noticia	piece of news

Los adjetivos

avergonzado/a	embarrassed
feliz (*pl.* **felices**)	happy
raro/a	strange

Suggestions: Vocabulario

- Give a series of situations or problems and have students react quickly by expressing how they would feel. For example: *examen difícil* → *Me pongo nervioso. chiste cómico* → *Me río.*
- Play a game of word associations with words from *Vocabulario.* Continue round-robin associations for at least 10 turns for each word. For example, *entremeses* → *sándwiches* → *fiestas* → *cumpleaños,* and so on.
- Ask students: *¿En qué días festivos mandamos tarjetas?* **1.** *¿la Navidad?* **2.** *¿el Cuatro de Julio?* **3.** *¿el Día de San Valentín?* **4.** *¿el cumpleaños? ¿Qué colores asociamos con estos días festivos?* **5.** *la Pascua Florida* **6.** *la Navidad* **7.** *el Cuatro de Julio* **8.** *el Día de San Patricio*
- Have students respond *probable* or *improbable:* **1.** *Ud. se siente triste si los amigos se olvidan del cumpleaños.* **2.** *Ud. se ríe si su novio/a sale con otra persona.* **3.** *El profesor se enoja si los estudiantes se portan bien.*

Palabras adicionales

¡felicitaciones!	congratulations!
ser (*irreg.*) **en** + *place*	to take place in/at (*place*)
ya	already

Algunos días festivos

la Navidad, la Nochebuena, la Noche Vieja, la Pascua (Florida)

El tiempo libre

Suggestion: Chapter Opening photo
Point out the chapter opening photo. Encourage students to describe the people in the photo. What are they doing? Ask students to compare this image to any stereotypes they may have held about Colombia. What day of the week do they think it is? Have them talk about the things they do in their free time and their ideas about how people from different countries spend their free time.

Resources
You and your students may find the following *¿Qué tal?* supplements helpful as you teach this chapter:

For the Instructor

- *Instructor's Manual and Resource Kit,* "Chapter-by-Chapter" Supplementary Materials
- Testing Program
- Overhead Transparencies 56–62
- Video (VHS or CD)
- *¿Qué tal?* Online Learning Center Website
- Audioscript
- Instructor's Resource CD

For Students

- Workbook/Laboratory Manual and Audio Program or Electronic Workbook/ Laboratory Manual
- Video on CD
- Interactive CD-ROM
- *¿Qué tal?* Online Learning Center Website
- Listening Comprehension Audio CD
- McGraw-Hill Electronic Language Tutor (MHELT)

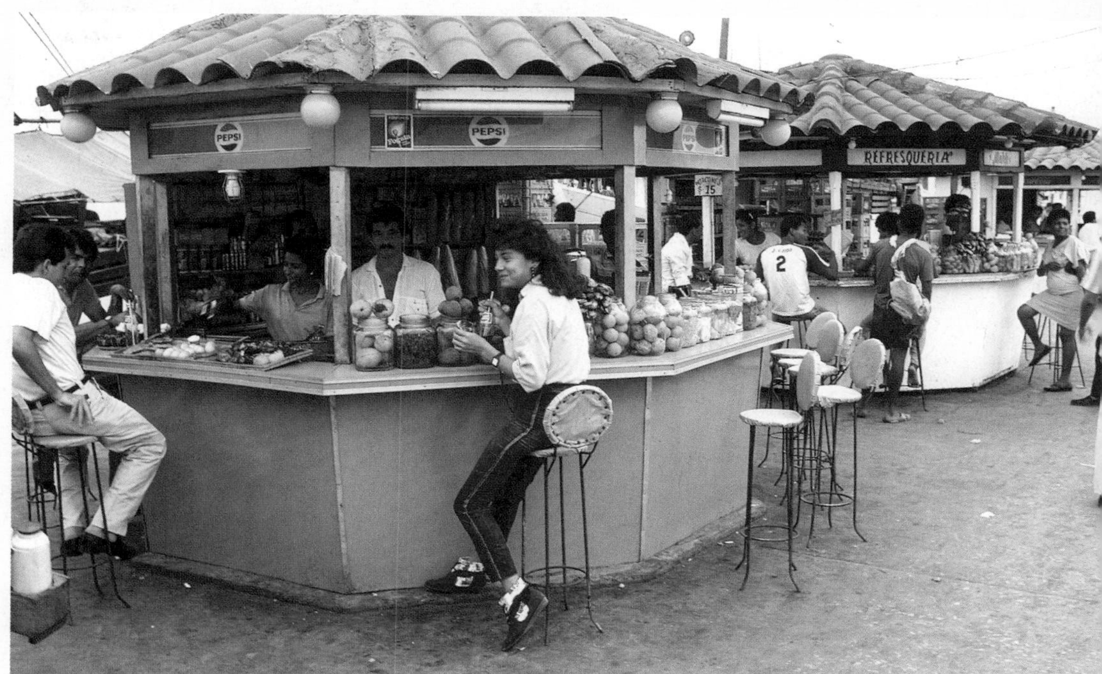

Esta señorita lo pasa bien tomando un refresco en Cartagena, Colombia. ▶

VOCABULARIO

- Pastimes, fun activities, and hobbies
- Household chores

GRAMÁTICA

26 Imperfect of Regular and Irregular Verbs
27 Superlatives
28 Summary of Interrogative Words

CULTURA

- **Enfoque cultural:** Colombia
- **Nota cultural:** El fútbol y el béisbol
- **En los Estados Unidos y el Canadá:** La impresionante variedad de la música hispana
- **Cultura en contexto:** El voseo

Multimedia

You will learn more about making plans in the **En contexto** video segment.

Review vocabulary and grammar and practice language skills with the interactive CD-ROM.

WWW. Get connected to the Spanish-speaking world with the *¿Qué tal?* Online Learning Center: **www.mhhe.com/quetal**.

PASO 1 Vocabulario

Paso 1: Vocabulario
See detailed supplementary materials and exercises for this section and a model for vocabulary presentation and other material in the *Capítulo 9 Paso 1: Vocabulario* section of "Chapter-by-Chapter Supplementary Materials," IM.

Pasatiempos... *Pastimes, fun activities, and hobbies*

Pasatiempos, diversiones y aficiones°

❖ **Transparencias 56–58** provide examples and practice of *pasatiempos*.

Multimedia: Audio
Students can listen to and practice this chapter's vocabulary on their Listening Comprehension Audio CD.

Note: Vocabulario
Point out that a popular Hispanic table game, especially for men, is *dominó*. Men gather at their homes, in parks, or at clubs to play. In Miami's Little Havana, *el parque Máximo Gómez* on *la calle Ocho* is also known as Domino Park. Cuban and other Hispanics from the community gather daily in this park to play dominoes and chess.

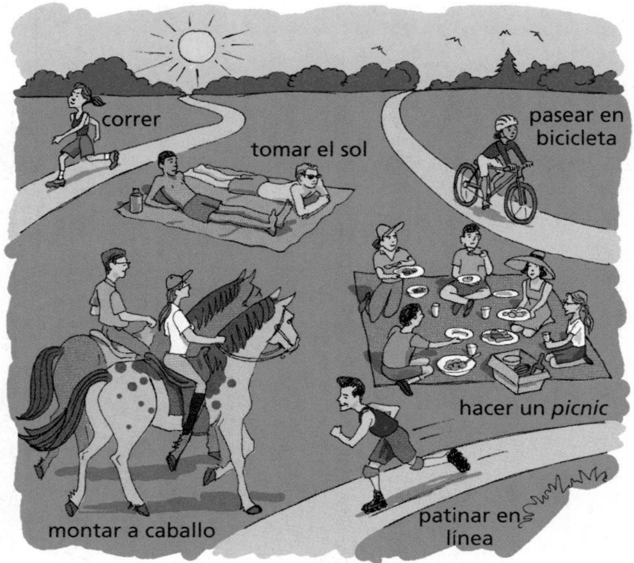

Heritage speakers
- En algunos dialectos del español, se dice *aficionado de* en vez de *aficionado a*. Pregúnteles a los hispanohablantes de la clase cuál de las dos expresiones prefieren.
- En algunos dialectos del español del suroeste de los Estados Unidos y del Caribe, se dice *jugar béisbol* en vez de *jugar al béisbol*. Se omite la preposición *a* después de *jugar* con frecuencia en el habla popular.

Los pasatiempos

los ratos libres	spare (free) time
dar (*irreg.*) / **hacer** (*irreg.*) **una fiesta**	to give a party
dar (*irreg.*) **un paseo**	to take a walk
hacer (*irreg.*) ***camping***	to go camping
hacer (*irreg.*) **planes para** + *inf.*	to make plans to (*do something*)
ir (*irreg.*)...	to go . . .
al cine / a ver una película	to the movies / to see a movie
a una discoteca / a un bar	to a disco / to a bar
al teatro / a un concierto	to the theater / to a concert
jugar (ue) a las cartas / al ajedrez	to play cards/chess
visitar un museo	to visit a museum
aburrirse	to get bored
ser (*irreg.*) **divertido/a, aburrido/a**	to be fun, boring

Los deportes

el ciclismo	bicycling
esquiar (esquío)	to ski
el fútbol	soccer
el fútbol americano	football
nadar	to swim
la natación	swimming
patinar	to skate

Otros deportes: el basquetbol, el béisbol, el golf, el hockey, el tenis, el vólibol

entrenar	to practice, train
ganar	to win
jugar (ue) al + *sport*	to play (*a sport*)
perder (ie)	to lose
practicar	to participate (*in a sport*)
ser aficionado/a (a)	to be a fan (of)

Suggestions A
- Have students write down answers, then compare. Do any answers predominate?
- Have students name activities they associate with: **1.** *el estadio* **2.** *el campo* **3.** *el gimnasio* **4.** *la piscina* **5.** *el cine* **6.** *el teatro*
- Assign *Paso 1* as written homework. Then compare answers in class.

PASO 1

Conversación

A. ¿Cómo pasan estas personas su tiempo libre?

Paso 1. ¿Qué cree Ud. que hacen las siguientes personas para divertirse en un sábado típico? Use su imaginación pero manténgase (*keep yourself*) entre los límites de lo posible.

1. una persona rica que vive en Nueva York
2. un grupo de buenos amigos que trabajan en una fábrica (*factory*) de Detroit
3. un matrimonio joven con poco dinero y dos niños pequeños

Paso 2. ¿Cómo se divierten los jóvenes españoles?

Este recorte (*clipping*) de una revista eapañola indica el tiempo medio (*average*) que los jóvenes españoles dedican a sus aficiones. ¿Puede explicar en español lo que significan los términos **Tomar copas** y **prensa**? ¿A qué tipos de «juegos» cree Ud. que se refiere el recorte?

Paso 3. Indique el número de minutos que Ud. les dedica a estas aficiones cada día. ¿Qué diferencia hay entre Ud. y los jóvenes españoles?

- For *Pasos 2* and *3,* have students interview at least six classmates, making a list of the answers. Have them share results and then compare them to the results for Spaniards.

TIEMPO QUE DEDICAN A SUS AFICIONES

(Media de minutos diarios)

Ver la televisión	120
Tomar copas	60
Pasear	22
Leer libros	15
Escuchar música	15
Oír la radio	8
Hacer deporte	9
Practicar *hobbies*	8
Leer la prensa	6
«Juegos»	4

NOTA CULTURAL

El fútbol y el béisbol

Sin duda,[a] el deporte más popular en el mundo hispánico es **el fútbol.*** El campeonato mundial de fútbol, conocido como **la Copa Mundial**, es el evento deportivo más popular del mundo. Este **torneo internacional** ocurre cada cuatro años y tiene más **espectadores** que cualquier[b] otro evento deportivo. Por ejemplo, en 1998, 1.7 billones de televidentes miraron la Copa Mundial mientras 800 millones miraron el *Super Bowl* de los Estados Unidos. Como es un deporte tan popular, en todas las ciudades hispanas hay muchos **campos**[c] **de fútbol**. Los niños y los adultos van a jugar siempre que pueden.[d]

Un partido de la Copa Mundial entre el Brasil y Honduras

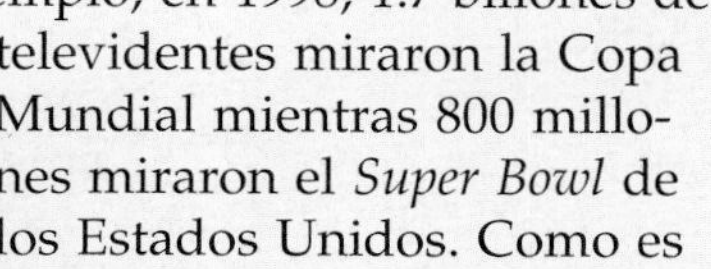

El béisbol también es muy popular, sobre todo en el Caribe. Hay muchos hispanos en **las ligas profesionales** de los Estados Unidos. Por ejemplo, el gran **jugador** de los Chicago Cubs, Sammy Sosa, es de la República Dominicana. El puertorriqueño Roberto Clemente fue el primer hispano elegido al *Baseball Hall of Fame* en 1973.

Sammy Sosa es de la República Dominicana.

[a]*doubt* [b]*any* [c]*fields* [d]siempre... *whenever they can*

*Remember that **fútbol** is *soccer*, not U.S.-style *football.*

Suggestion: Nota cultural
Ask how many students like and play soccer. Then have those people explain to their classmates what makes soccer, in their opinion, a fun sport. Discuss as a class why soccer is less popular in the U.S. and Canada than in Latin America and Europe.

Note B
This is a review of comparisons.

Extension B
5. *Los estudiantes universitarios tienen tanto tiempo libre como los estudiantes de la escuela secundario.* 6. *El ajedrez es muy interesante.*

Reciclado
Recycle house vocabulary with the following question: *¿Qué quehaceres domésticos asocia Ud. con... ? ¿la alcoba? ¿la cocina? ¿la sala? ¿el garaje? ¿el baño?*

❖ **Transparency 59**

B. ¿Cierto o falso? Corrija (*Correct*) las oraciones falsas según su opinión.

1. Ver una película en vídeo es más aburrido que ir al cine.
2. Lo paso mejor con mi familia que con mis amigos.
3. Las actividades educativas me gustan más que las deportivas.
4. Odio el béisbol tanto como el fútbol.

Trabajando en casa

Algunos aparatos domésticos

Heritage speakers
Pídales a sus estudiantes hispanohablantes que compartan otras palabras o variaciones que usan para describir aparatos y quehaceres domésticos.

Los quehaceres domésticos°

Los... *Household chores*

barrer (el piso)	to sweep (the floor)	**pasar la aspiradora**	to vacuum
dejar (en...)	to leave behind (in [*a place*])	**pintar (las paredes)**	to paint (the walls)
hacer (*irreg.*) **la cama**	to make the bed	**planchar la ropa**	to iron clothing
lavar (las ventanas, los platos, la ropa)	to wash (the windows, the dishes, the clothes)	**poner** (*irreg.*) **la mesa**	to set the table
limpiar la casa (entera)	to clean the (whole) house	**quitar la mesa**	to clear the table
		sacar la basura	to take out the trash
		sacudir los muebles	to dust the furniture

Suggestions A
- Have students complete sentence with correct activity, based on subject: 1. *La secadora sirve para _____ la ropa.* 2. *La plancha sirve para _____ la ropa.* 3. *En la cocina se puede _____.* 4. *La lavadora sirve para _____ la ropa.*
- Ask: 1. *¿Ud. hace la cama todos los días? ¿En qué ocasiones no la hace? Si tiene prisa por la mañana, ¿hace la cama o la deja sin hacer? Cuando visita la casa de su familia, ¿su mamá le hace la cama?* 2. *¿Cuándo limpia Ud. la casa, durante el fin de semana? ¿La limpia entera o limpia sólo una parte? ¿Alguien lo/la ayuda a limpiarla?* 3. *¿Qué prefiere Ud., sacudir los muebles o pasar la aspiradora? ¿lavar la ropa o barrer el piso? ¿quitar la mesa o lavar los platos?... Yo odio* (fill in what you dislike). *¿Quién también odia _____? ¿Quién lo hace en casa de Ud.?*

Conversación

A. Los quehaceres. ¿En qué cuarto o parte de la casa se hacen las siguientes actividades? Hay más de una respuesta en muchos casos.

1. Se hace la cama en _____.
2. Se saca la basura de _____ y se deja en _____.
3. Se sacuden los muebles de _____.
4. Uno se baña en _____. Pero es mejor que uno bañe al perro en _____.
5. Se barre el piso de _____.
6. Se pasa la aspiradora en _____.
7. Se lava y se seca la ropa en _____. La ropa se plancha en _____.
8. Se usa la cafetera en _____.

NOTA COMUNICATIVA

Talking about Obligation

You already know several ways to express the obligation to carry out particular activities.

Tengo que **Necesito** **Debo**	barrer el piso.	*I have to* *I need to* *I should*	*sweep the floor.*

Of the three alternatives, **tener que** + *infinitive* expresses the strongest sense of obligation.

The concept *to be someone's turn or responsibility* (to do something) is expressed in Spanish with the verb **tocar** plus an indirect object.

—¿**A quién le toca** lavar los platos esta noche? — *Whose turn is it to wash the dishes tonight?*

—**A mí me toca** solamente sacar la basura. Creo que **a papá le toca** lavar los platos. — *I only have to take out the garbage. I think it's Dad's turn to wash the dishes.*

B. Los fines de semana: ¿Tiempo libre o quehaceres?

Paso 1. Marque las actividades típicas para Ud. durante los fines de semana.

- ☐ barrer el piso
- ☐ lavar la ropa
- ☐ hacer deporte/ejercicio
- ☐ limpiar la casa
- ☐ ir de compras al supermercado
- ☐ ir de compras al centro comercial
- ☐ hacer las tareas y estudiar
- ☐ dar fiestas
- ☐ salir a bailar con amigos
- ☐ ¿ ?

Paso 2. Usando la información del **Paso 1**, describa un fin de semana típico. También incluya información sobre las cosas que *no* hace. Para Ud., ¿cuándo empieza el fin de semana? ¿El viernes? ¿El sábado? Finalmente, apunte las cosas que tiene que hacer este fin de semana.

MODELO: Normalmente, los fines de semana yo descanso y salgo con amigos. El viernes, casi siempre... Pero este fin de semana tengo que limpiar la casa porque mis padres vienen a visitarme. Necesito barrer el piso...

Paso 3. Ahora, hable con un compañero / una compañera para comparar sus fines de semanas típicos y sus planes para el próximo fin de semana. Apunte lo que dice su compañero/a para compartir la información con la clase.

Reciclado
Have students give commands to imaginary maid in the following circumstances: *¿Qué mandatos le va a dar a la criada en las siguientes circunstancias?* **1.** *Ud. tiene hambre.* **2.** *La comida está preparada y Ud. quiere sentarse a la mesa a comer.* **3.** *La sala está muy oscura porque entra muy poca luz* (light). **4.** *Ud. quiere que la casa esté bien arreglada* (in good shape) *porque vienen a visitarlo/la esta noche algunos amigos muy importantes de su esposo/a.*

Suggestion: Nota comunicativa
Model and review first 3, then introduce the expression *tocarle* to express the concept *to be someone's turn* or *responsibility to do something.* The structure for *tocar* is similar to the *gustar* construction.

Suggestion B
Assign *Paso 1* as homework and have students come prepared with 10 questions for *Paso 2.* After pair work, have students write a comparison of 1–2 paragraphs.

Optional B
Write *A principios del siglo XX* on board, then have students modify statements to reflect how life was at the beginning of the 20th century. *¿Cómo era la vida a principios del siglo XX? Por ejemplo, ahora casi todos los bebés nacen* (are born) *en un hospital, pero al principio del siglo XX casi todos los bebés nacían en casa.* **1.** *Ahora muchas personas viven en apartamentos.* **2.** *Hoy día se come con mucha frecuencia en restaurantes.* **3.** *Muchísimas mujeres trabajan fuera de casa.* **4.** *Muchas personas miran la tele y los vídeos.* **5.** *Ahora hay muchas máquinas y aparatos y por eso hacemos menos trabajo físico.* **6.** *Muchas parejas viven juntas sin estar casados.*

Follow-up B
Ask students how they spend their weekends in the following situations: *¿Cómo pasa Ud. el fin de semana cuando... ?* **1.** *¿llueve?* **2.** *¿no tiene mucho dinero?* **3.** *¿tiene ganas de hacer algo «cultural»?* **4.** *¿hace calor y sol?* **5.** *¿desea divertirse con sus amigos?* **6.** *¿quiere hacer un poco de ejercicio?* **7.** *¿prefiere estar solo/a?* **8.** *¿quiere hacer algo «productivo» en casa?*

Paso 2: Gramática
See detailed supplementary materials for these grammar sections in IM.

26 Descriptions and Habitual Actions in the Past • Imperfect of Regular and Irregular Verbs

Los aztecas

«Los aztecas construyeron grandes pirámides para sus dioses. En lo alto de cada pirámide *había* un templo donde *tenían* lugar las ceremonias y *se ofrecían* los sacrificios. Las pirámides *tenían* muchísimos escalones, y *era* necesario subirlos todos para llegar a los templos.

Cerca de muchas pirámides *había* un terreno como el de una cancha de basquetbol. Allí *se celebraban* partidos que *eran* parte de una ceremonia. Los participantes *jugaban* con una pelota de goma dura, que sólo *podían* mover con las caderas y las rodillas... »

Comprensión: ¿Cierto o falso?

1. Los aztecas creían en un solo dios.
2. Las pirámides aztecas tenían una función religiosa.
3. Los aztecas practicaban un deporte similar al basquetbol.

❖ Transparency 60
Transparency 60 provides examples of uses of the imperfect.

Follow-up: Imperfect
Ask students the following questions to follow up the *minidiálogo: Cuando Ud. era pequeño/a...* **1.** *¿creía en Santa Claus?* **2.** *¿iba a ceremonias religiosas con su familia?* **3.** *¿jugaba a algún deporte con sus padres? ¿con sus hermanos?* **4.** *¿siempre hacía sus quehaceres?*

Suggestion: Imperfect
Ask students what modern sports are related or similar to this Aztec sport: *¿Con qué deportes modernos se puede relacionar el antiguo deporte azteca?*

You have already learned to use the *preterite* (**el pretérito**) to express events in the past. The *imperfect* (**el imperfecto**) is the second simple past tense in Spanish. In contrast to the preterite, which is used when you view actions or states of being as finished or completed, the imperfect tense is used when you view past actions or states of being as habitual or as "in progress." The imperfect is also used for describing the past.

The imperfect has several English equivalents. For example, **hablaba**, the first person singular of **hablar**, can mean *I spoke, I was speaking, I used to speak*, or *I would speak* (when *would* implies a repeated action). Most of these English equivalents indicate that the action was still in progress or was habitual, except for *I spoke*, which can correspond to either the preterite or the imperfect.

WWW. Multimedia: Internet
Have students search Internet for more information on ancient Aztec civilization as well as information on other ancient Latin American civilizations. Encourage them to look for images of cities, for information about rituals, and the famous Aztec calendar. You might assign specific topics and have students develop brief oral presentations based on their findings.

The Aztecs. "The Aztecs constructed large pyramids for their gods. At the top of each pyramid there was a temple where ceremonies took place and sacrifices were offered. The pyramids had many, many steps, and it was necessary to climb them all in order to get to the temples.

"Close to many pyramids there was an area of land like that of a basketball court. Ceremonial matches were celebrated there. The participants played with a ball made of hard rubber that they could only move with their hips and knees . . ."

FORMS OF THE IMPERFECT

hablar		comer		vivir	
habl**aba**	habl**ábamos**	com**ía**	com**íamos**	viv**ía**	viv**íamos**
habl**abas**	habl**abais**	com**ías**	com**íais**	viv**ías**	viv**íais**
habl**aba**	habl**aban**	com**ía**	com**ían**	viv**ía**	viv**ían**

- Stem-changing verbs do not show a change in the imperfect. The imperfect of **hay** is **había** (*there was, there were, there used to be*).

Pronunciation Hint: The pronunciation of a **b** between vowels, such as in the imperfect ending **-aba**, is pronounced as a fricative [ß] sound.

In the other imperfect forms, it is important not to pronounce the ending **-ía** as a diphthong, but to pronounce the **i** and the **a** in separate syllables (the accent mark over the **í** helps remind you of this).

Imperfect of stem-changing verbs = no change

almorzar (ue) → almorzaba
perder (ie) → perdía
pedir (i, i) → pedía

Imperfect of **hay** = **había**

- Only three verbs are irregular in the imperfect: **ir, ser,** and **ver**.

ir		ser		ver	
iba	íbamos	era	éramos	veía	veíamos
ibas	ibais	eras	erais	veías	veíais
iba	iban	era	eran	veía	veían

USES OF THE IMPERFECT

Note the following uses of the imperfect. If you have a clear sense of when and where the imperfect is used, understanding where the preterite is used will be easier. When talking about the past, the preterite *is* used when the imperfect *isn't*. That is an oversimplification of the uses of these two past tenses, but at the same time it is a general rule of thumb that will help you out at first.

The imperfect has the following uses.

- To describe *repeated habitual actions* in the past

Siempre **nos quedábamos** en aquel hotel.
We always stayed (used to stay, would stay) at that hotel.

Todos los veranos **iban** a la costa.
Every summer they went (used to go, would go) to the coast.

Preliminary exercises: Imperfect

- Use rapid response drill to practice forms: *Dé el imperfecto:* ***yo:*** *cerrar, escuchar, mirar, querer, asistir, recibir;* ***tú:*** *pensar, visitar, entrar, tener, vivir, pedir;* ***Ud./él/ella:*** *preguntar, comprar, enseñar, volver, abrir, servir;* ***nosotros:*** *jugar, bailar, tomar, aprender, preferir, venir;* ***Uds./ellos/ellas:*** *trabajar, ganar, creer, divertir, ser.*
- Use chain drill to practice imperfect forms: ***En la escuela primaria...*** **1.** *Tina estudiaba y jugaba mucho.* (*yo, Uds., tú, nosotros, Julio, vosotros*) **2.** *Todos bebían leche y dormían la siesta.* (*Tina, tú, nosotros, Alicia, yo, vosotros*) ***¿Qué hacían Uds. anoche a las doce?*** **1.** *Ceci veía un programa interesante.* (*tú, yo, Uds., Pablo, ellas, vosotros*) **2.** *Mis padres iban a acostarse.* (*tú, yo, nosotros, Hernando, ellas, vosotros*) **3.** *Yo (no) estaba ____.* (*leer, mirar la televisión, escribir una carta, dormir, llorar, comer, ¿ ?*)

• To describe an *action that was in progress* (*when something else happened*)	**Pedía** la cena. *She was ordering dinner.* **Buscaba** el coche. *He was looking for the car.*
• To describe two *simultaneous past actions in progress*, with **mientras**	Tú **leías mientras** Juan **escribía** la carta. *You were reading while Juan was writing the letter.*
• To describe ongoing *physical, mental*, or *emotional states* in the past	**Estaban** muy distraídos. *They were very distracted.* La **quería** muchísimo. *He loved her a lot.*
• To tell *time* in the past and to *express age* with **tener** OJO Just as in the present, the singular form of the verb **ser** is used with one o'clock, the plural form from two o'clock on.	**Era** la una. / **Eran** las dos. *It was one o'clock. / It was two o'clock.* **Tenía** 18 años. *She was 18 years old.*
• To form a *past progressive:* imperfect of **estar** + *present participle** Note that the simple imperfect—**cenábamos, estudiabas**—could also be used in the example sentences to express the ongoing actions. The use of the progressive emphasizes that the action was actually in progress.	**Estábamos cenando** a las diez. *We were having dinner at ten.* ¿No **estabas estudiando**? *Weren't you studying?*

Práctica

Extension A
Have students add 2–3 original sentences about their childhood.

Follow-up A
Poll students to see which descriptions were true for them.

A. Mi niñez (*childhood*). Indique si las siguientes oraciones eran ciertas o falsas para Ud. cuando tenía 10 años. Luego, corrija las oraciones falsas.

MODELO: 2. Es falso. Me acostaba a las diez, no a las nueve.

1. Estaba en cuarto (*fourth*) grado.
2. Me acostaba a las nueve todas las noches.
3. Los sábados me levantaba temprano para mirar los dibujos animados.
4. Mis padres me pagaban por los quehaceres que hacía: cortar el césped (*cutting the grass*), lavar los platos…
5. Me gustaba acompañar a mi madre/padre al supermercado.
6. Pegaba (*I hit*) a mi hermano/a con frecuencia.
7. Tocaba un instrumento musical en la orquesta de la escuela.
8. Mis héroes eran personajes de las tiras cómicas (*comic strip characters*) como Superman y Wonder Woman.

*A progressive tense can also be formed with the preterite of **estar**: ***Estuvieron*** **cenando hasta las doce**. The use of the progressive with the preterite of **estar**, however, is relatively infrequent, and it will not be practiced in *¿Qué tal?*

B. Cuando Tina era niña... Describa la vida de Tina cuando era muy joven, haciendo oraciones según las indicaciones.

La vida de Tina era muy diferente cuando tenía 6 años.

1. todos los días / asistir / a / escuela primaria
2. por / mañana / aprender / a / leer / y / escribir / en / pizarra
3. a / diez / beber / leche / y / dormir / un poco
4. ir / a / casa / para / almorzar / y / regresar / a / escuela
5. estudiar / geografía / y / hacer / dibujos
6. jugar / con / compañeros / en / patio / de / escuela
7. camino de (*on the way*) casa / comprar / dulces / y / se los / comer
8. frecuentemente / pasar / por / casa / de / abuelos
9. cenar / con / padres / y / ayudar / a / lavar / platos
10. mirar / tele / un rato / y / acostarse / a / ocho

Suggestion B
Ask students: *¿Qué cosas no hacía Ud. que Tina sí hacía? ¿Qué cosas no hacía Tina que Ud. sí hacía?*

Extension B
Have students describe Tina and her sister: *Describa a Tina y a su hermanita Mariana.*

❖ **Transparency 61**

Suggestion C
Give students dictation but have them write verbs in imperfect tense. **1.** *Olga va a la universidad todos los días. Siempre asiste a sus clases. Hace muchas preguntas porque es inteligente. Sus profesores están contentos con ella.* **2.** *Yo trabajo en una oficina. Mi jefe* (boss)*, que se llama Ángel, nos hace trabajar mucho. Siempre almorzamos juntos en el mismo restaurante y a veces jugamos al basquetbol por la tarde.* **3.** *Vivo en Sacramento. Siempre llueve mucho en invierno y en primavera, pero me gusta mucho el clima. Además* (Besides)*, las montañas están cerca y puedo esquiar.*

C. El trabajo de niñera (*baby-sitter*). El trabajo de niñera puede ser muy pesado (*difficult*), pero cuando los niños son traviesos (*mischievous*), también puede ser peligroso (*dangerous*). ¿Qué estaba pasando cuando la niñera perdió por fin la paciencia? Describa todas las acciones que pueda, usando **estaba(n)** + **-ndo**.

Palabras útiles: ladrar (*to bark*), pelear (*to fight*), sonar (ue)* (*to ring; to sound*)

Conversación

¡Qué cambio! Una entrevista. Hágale las siguientes preguntas a un compañero / una compañera de clase. Él/Ella va a pensar en las costumbres que tenía a los 14 años, es decir, cuando estaba en el noveno (*ninth*) o décimo (*tenth*) grado.

1. ¿Qué te gustaba comer? ¿Y ahora?
2. ¿Qué programa de televisión no te perdías (*missed*) nunca? ¿Y ahora?
3. ¿Qué te gustaba leer? ¿Y ahora?
4. ¿Qué hacías los sábados por la noche? ¿Y ahora?
5. ¿Qué deportes te gustaba practicar? ¿Y ahora?
6. ¿Con quién discutías mucho? ¿Y ahora?
7. ¿A quién te gustaba molestar (*annoy*)? ¿Y ahora?

Follow-up: Conversación
Complete sentences to model an answer, then elicit sentences from students with a follow-up question: **1.** *En otra época siempre me gustaba ______. No me gustaba nada ______.* (*En otra época siempre me gustaba comer fuera. No me gustaba nada cocinar. ¿A Ud. le gusta cocinar ahora? ¿Le gustaba en otra época?*) **2.** *Siempre veía* (programa de televisión), *pero ahora prefiero ver ______.* **3.** *De niño/a, siempre leía ______, pero ahora leo ______.*

*Although **sonar** is a stem-changing verb (**o** → **ue**), remember that the stem of present participles does not change with these verbs (**sonando**).

Suggestion: *¡El número uno!*
Ask students what Hispanic artists have contributed to the rise in popularity of a *latino* sound in pop music. Have them identify the artists pictured here: Enrique Iglesias (one of Julio Iglesias' sons), Jennifer López, Ricky Martin. Which artist do they prefer and why? The following Hispanic artists have also had a major impact on music in the English-speaking countries: Pablo Casals, Gloria Estefan, Julio Iglesias, Tito Puente, Carlos Santana, and Jon Secada.

¿Recuerda Ud.?

Before you move on to the next Grammar Section, review comparisons, which were introduced in **Capítulo 5**. How would you say the following in Spanish?

1. I work as much as you do.
2. I work more/less than you do.
3. Bill Gates has more money than I have.
4. My housemate has fewer things than I do.
5. I have as many friends as you do.
6. My computer is worse/better than this one.

27 Expressing Extremes • Superlatives

Follow-up: Superlatives
After reviewing *¡El número uno!*, have students give superlatives in other categories: *la comida, los quehaceres domésticos, las marcas* (brand names) *de ropa, las tiendas.*

¡El número uno!

Jennifer López

Ricky Martin

¿Está Ud. de acuerdo con las opiniones expresadas en estas oraciones?

1. Jennifer López es la mujer más bella (*beautiful*) del mundo.
2. Enrique Iglesias es el mejor cantante (*singer*) de su familia.
3. Ricky Martin es el puertorriqueño más conocido (*well-known*) hoy día (*nowadays*).

WWW. Multimedia: Internet
Have students search Internet for information on Hispanic musicians. Encourage them to look for music clips, as well as official websites for artist or for his or her fan club.

The *superlative* (**el superlativo**) is formed in English by adding *-est* to adjectives or by using expressions such as *the most* and *the least* with the adjective. In Spanish, this concept is expressed in the same way as the comparative but is always accompanied by the definite article. In this construction **mejor** and **peor** tend to precede the noun; other adjectives follow. *In* or *at* is expressed with **de**.

OJO The superlative forms **-ísimo/a/os/as** cannot be used with this type of superlative construction.

el/la/los/las + *noun* + **más/menos** + *adjective* + **de**

David es **el estudiante más inteligente de** la clase.
David is the most intelligent student in the class.

el/la/los/las + **mejor/peor** + *noun* + **de**

Son **los mejores doctores de** aquel hospital.
They are the best doctors at that hospital.

Preliminary exercise A
Complete with relevant information, then have students respond to each statement *cierto* or *falso*: **1.** ______ *es la persona más alta / baja / joven de la clase.* **2.** *Los perros / gatos son los animales más fieles / cariñosos.* **3.** *El* ______ *es el mejor / peor coche del mundo.* **4.** ______ *es el mejor periódico de esta ciudad.* **5.** *Los exámenes de* ______ *son los más difíciles / fáciles (de todos).* **6.** ______ *es el actor más guapo (de todos).* **7.** ______ *es la actriz más guapa (de todas).* **8.** *Uds. son los estudiantes más trabajadores / amables / perezosos / simpáticos de la universidad.*

Práctica

A. **¿Está Ud. de acuerdo o no?** Indique si Ud. está de acuerdo o no con las siguientes oraciones. Para cada una que no refleje su opinión, invente otra.

MODELO: 4. No estoy de acuerdo. Creo que el día festivo más divertido del año es el Cuatro de Julio.

1. El descubrimiento (*discovery*) científico más importante del siglo XX fue la vacuna (*vaccine*) contra la poliomielitis.
2. La persona más influyente (*influential*) del mundo es el presidente de los Estados Unidos.
3. El problema más serio del mundo es la deforestación de la región del Amazonas.
4. El día festivo más divertido del año es la Noche Vieja.
5. La mejor novela del mundo es *Don Quijote de la Mancha*.

B. **Superlativos.** Expand the information in these sentences according to the model. Then, if you can, restate each sentence with true information at the beginning.

MODELO: Es una estudiante muy *trabajadora*. (la clase) →
Es la estudiante *más trabajadora de la clase*. →
Carlota es la estudiante más trabajadora de la clase.

1. Es un día festivo muy divertido. (el año)
2. Es una clase muy interesante. (todas mis clases)
3. Es una persona muy inteligente. (todos mis amigos)
4. Es una ciudad muy grande. (los Estados Unidos / el Canadá)
5. Es una montaña muy alta. (el mundo)

Extension B
6. *El Presidente Reagan fue un presidente viejo.* **7.** *El Presidente Kennedy fue un presidente joven.* **8.** *Rip Van Winkle fue un hombre perezoso.* **9.** *El chihuahua es un perro pequeño.*

Suggestion B
Have students imagine that Rodolfo, a big exaggerator, visits their house during the Christmas holidays. Have them invent things he might say: *¿Qué va a decir Rodolfo sobre los siguientes aspectos del día de Navidad en su casa?* **1.** *¿su árbol de Navidad?* (*grande, elegante*) **2.** *¿los platos?* (*ricos, muchos*) **3.** *¿Sus hermanitos?* (*felices*) **4.** *¿los regalos?* (*caros, bonitos, muchos*)

Conversación

Entrevista. With another student, ask and answer questions based on the following phrases. Then report your opinions to the class.

1. la persona más guapa del mundo
2. la noticia más seria de esta semana
3. un libro interesantísimo y otro pesadísimo (*very boring*)
4. el mejor restaurante de la ciudad y el peor
5. el cuarto más importante de la casa y el menos importante
6. un plato riquísimo y otro malísimo
7. un programa de televisión interesantísimo y otro pesadísimo
8. un lugar tranquilísimo, otro animadísimo y otro peligrosísimo
9. la canción (*song*) más bonita del año y la más fea
10. la mejor película del año y la peor

Note: Conversación
This activity integrates superlative and absolute superlative forms.

Follow-up: Conversación
Have students work in small groups to describe the following, using superlatives: **1.** Alaska **2.** Rhode Island **3.** John F. Kennedy **4.** *el monte Everest* **5.** *el río Amazonas* **6.** *esta universidad* **7.** *la comida de la residencia / cafetería estudiantil.* Suggest additional items about people, places, and things on campus that students like to discuss.

Enfoque *cultural*

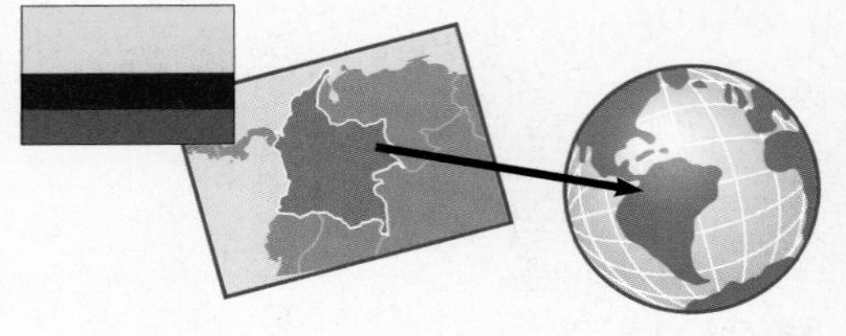

Colombia

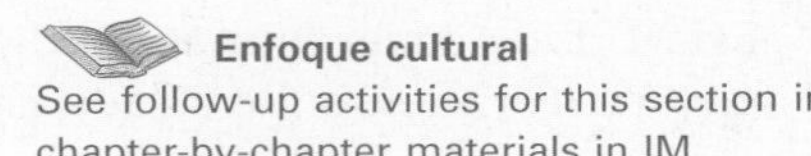

Enfoque cultural
See follow-up activities for this section in chapter-by-chapter materials in IM.

Datos esenciales

Nombre oficial: República de Colombia

Capital: Santafé de Bogotá (Bogotá)

Población: 36.000.000 de habitantes

Moneda: el peso

Idioma oficial: el español

Conozca a... Gabriel García Márquez

El escritor latinoamericano más leído en el mundo entero es el colombiano Gabriel García Márquez, ganador[a] del Premio Nóbel de Literatura en 1982. Su novela *Cien años de soledad* se considera una de las novelas más importantes del siglo XX en cualquier lengua. La novela narra la historia de la familia Buendía durante varias generaciones. En ella García Márquez usa una técnica literaria llamada *realismo mágico:* una mezcla[b] de elementos reales y fantásticos en la narración.

Además de ser novelista, García Márquez es un respetado periodista y columnista que escribe para los periódicos más importantes de la lengua castellana.[c]

[a] *recipient* [b] *combination* [c] lengua... *Castilian (Spanish) language*

¡Fíjese!

- Colombia obtuvo su independencia de España en 1819, bajo la dirección de Simón Bolívar. Bolívar fue declarado el primer presidente de la independiente República de la Gran Colombia.

Estatuas de piedra, de San Agustín

- Colombia produce más oro que cualquier[a] otro país sudamericano y tiene los yacimientos[b] de platino más grandes del mundo. Las esmeraldas también son un producto minero importante.
- Aunque el café es reconocido[c] como el producto agrícola principal de exportación de Colombia, en los años noventa lo sobrepasó[d] el petróleo como primer producto de exportación.
- Aproximadamente un 14 por ciento de la población colombiana es de origen africano.
- Las misteriosas estatuas de piedra de San Agustín fueron creadas por una cultura indígena de la cual[e] se sabe muy poco. Se cree que las estatuas son del siglo VI antes de Cristo. Una de las estatuas representa un pájaro con una serpiente en el pico,[f] imagen muy similar a la de una leyenda azteca.

[a] *any* [b] *deposits* [c] *recognized* [d] *surpassed* [e] de... *of which* [f] *beak*

Capítulo 9 of the video to accompany *¿Qué tal?* contains cultural footage of Colombia.

Visit the *¿Qué tal?* website at www.mhhe.com/quetal.

 **Paso 3: Gramática**
See detailed supplementary materials for these grammar sections in IM.

28 Getting Information • Summary of Interrogative Words

Este es un anuncio de un restaurante de Connecticut.

1. ¿Cómo se llama el restaurante?
2. ¿En qué ciudad de Connecticut está?
3. ¿Cuáles son las especialidades de este restaurante?

¿Cuántas preguntas más puede Ud. hacer sobre este restaurante, basándose en el anuncio?

El Pavo real
RESTAURANTE • CLUB DE BAILE
32 Garvey St., New Haven, CT
El lugar más amplio y más lujoso de CT.
Comida Colombiana
con Especialidad en Mariscos
Venga y deléitese con nuestros sabrosos platos
ABIERTO TODOS LOS DÍAS DESDE LAS 11:30 A.M. - 2:00 A.M
VIERNES, 6 DE OCTUBRE
• PRESENTANDO LA SENSACIÓN DEL MERENGUE •
ORQUESTA MALA FE
CANTANDO TODOS SUS ÉXITOS

 **Reciclado: Interrogatives**
Remind students that *ser en + place* is used to express *to take place at (place)*. Model the expression in communicative exchanges with a student: *¿Dónde es su primera clase los lunes? ¿Dónde es el partido de fútbol?*

¿Cómo?	How?	**¿Dónde?**	Where?
¿Cuándo?	When?	**¿De dónde?**	From where?
¿A qué hora?	At what time?	**¿Adónde?**	Where (to)?
¿Qué?	What? Which?	**¿Cuánto/a?**	How much?
¿Cuál(es)?	What? Which one(s)?	**¿Cuántos/as?**	How many?
¿Por qué?	Why?	**¿Quién(es)?**	Who?
		¿De quién(es)?	Whose?

You have been using interrogative words to ask questions and get information since the beginning of *¿Qué tal?* The preceding chart shows all of the interrogatives you have learned so far. Be sure that you know what they mean and how they are used. If you are not certain, the index and end-of-book vocabularies will help you find where they are first introduced. Only the specific uses of **¿qué?** and **¿cuál?** represent new information.

USING *¿qué?* AND *¿cuál?*

- **¿Qué?** asks for a definition or an explanation.

¿Qué es esto?
What is this?

¿Qué quieres?
What do you want?

¿Qué tocas?
What (instrument) do you play?

- **¿Qué?** can be directly followed by a noun.

¿Qué traje necesitas?
What (Which) suit do you need?

¿Qué playa te gusta más?
What (Which) beach do you like most?

¿Qué instrumento musical tocas?
What (Which) musical instrument do you play?

- **¿Cuál(es)?** expresses *what?* or *which?* in all other cases.

OJO

The **¿cuál(es)?** + *noun* structure is not used by most speakers of Spanish: ***¿Cuál* de los dos libros quieres?** (*Which of the two books do you want?*) BUT ***¿Qué* libro quieres?** (*Which [What] book do you want?*)

¿Cuál es la clase más grande?
What (Which) is the biggest class?

¿Cuáles son tus actrices favoritas?
What (Which) are your favorite actresses?

¿Cuál es la capital del Uruguay?
What is the capital of Uruguay?

¿Cuál es tu teléfono?
What is your phone number?

Preliminary Exercises: Interrogatives
- Ask students whether the following questions require *¿qué?* or *¿cuál?* in Spanish: **1.** What is an aardvark? **2.** What is the capital of Bolivia? **3.** What are the colors of the U.S. flag? **4.** What's that?
- Ask students: **1.** *¿Cuál es la capital de ______?* **2.** *¿Cuál es su teléfono?* **3.** *¿Qué es esto?* (indicate an object or use a visual) **4.** *¿Qué es un elefante? ¿un restaurante? ¿una discoteca? ¿Qué son las sandalias?*

Suggestion: Conversación
Think of or have a student think of a famous person. Have the class try to identify the person by asking questions using interrogative words. Students may not repeat interrogative words during a single round of guessing.

Follow-up: Conversación
Ask students the following questions to summarize findings: **1.** *¿Nacieron varias personas de la clase en la misma ciudad?* **2.** *¿En quiénes confían más Uds.?* **3.** *¿Cuál es la tienda más popular entre los estudiantes de esta clase?* **4.** *¿Quién tiene un examen pronto* (soon)*?*

Variation: Conversación
Have students work in pairs to interview each other about how they generally spend their free time. Give them steps to prepare and conduct their interviews.
Paso 1. *En preparación para la entrevista, haga una lista de ocho a diez preguntas básicas que necesita hacerle a su compañero/a. Estas preguntas van a servir de base para otras preguntas, según las respuestas de su compañero/a.*
Paso 2. *Haga la entrevista. Apunte* (Jot down) *las respuestas de su compañero/a. Hágale todas las preguntas que pueda.*
Paso 3. *Ponga en orden los apuntes de la entrevista y comparta con la clase algunos de los datos que aprendió en su entrevista.*

Práctica

¿Qué o cuál(es)?

1. ¿__Qué__ es esto? —Un lavaplatos.
2. ¿__Qué__ son los Juegos Olímpicos? —Son un conjunto de competiciones deportivas.
3. ¿__Cuál__ es el quehacer que más te gusta? —Lavar los platos.
4. ¿__Qué__ bicicleta vas a usar? —La de mi hermana.
5. ¿__Cuáles__ son los cines más modernos? —Los del centro.
6. ¿__Qué__ vídeo debo sacar? —El nuevo de Robert Rodríguez.
7. ¿__Qué__ es una cafetera? —Es un aparato que se usa para preparar el café.
8. ¿__Cuál__ es Rivaldo? —En la foto, es el hombre a la izquierda de la pelota.

Conversación

Datos (*Information*) **personales.** Forme preguntas para averiguar (*find out*) datos de un compañero / una compañera. Puede usar más de una palabra interrogativa para conseguir la información. (Debe usar las formas de **tú**.)

MODELO: su dirección → ¿Cuál es tu dirección? (¿Dónde vives?)

1. su teléfono
2. su dirección
3. su cumpleaños
4. la ciudad en que nació (*you were born*) naciste
5. su número de seguro (*security*) social
6. la persona en que más confía (*you trust*)
7. su tienda favorita
8. la fecha de su próximo examen

Suggestions: En los Estados Unidos y el Canadá...

- Have students research salsa on Internet and report to class. Many websites have general as well as specific (artists) information, including calendars of performances.
- Bring some salsa to class, maybe offer a dance lesson.
- Mention to students that salsa can be the musical vehicle for serious social commentaries, such as the songs by Rubén Blades and Juan Luis Guerra.

En los Estados Unidos y el Canadá...

La impresionante variedad de la música latina

Es difícil hablar de «música latina» porque hay una inmensa **variedad**. La música de España y de toda Latinoamérica cuenta con[a] **diversos orígenes** que luego **se mezclan.**[b] La música de los españoles y portugueses llegó al Nuevo Mundo, pero pronto se mezcló con fuertes **tradiciones indígenas.** Cuando los conquistadores trajeron **esclavos**[c] **africanos** al Nuevo Mundo, estos trajeron consigo[d] sus propias tradiciones musicales, que influyeron en varios tipos de música que hoy consideramos música hispana.

Tito Puente

La salsa es una de las formas musicales hispanas más reconocidas. La salsa es una mezcla de **ritmos afrocaribeños**, y fue creada en Nueva York por músicos hispanos en los años sesenta y setenta del siglo XX. La salsa es muy variada, pero siempre tiene una característica clara: es muy **bailable**. Uno de los nombres más asociados con la salsa es Tito Puente (1923–2000), el famoso **percusionista**. **Carlos Santana** grabó su versión de la composición de Puente, «Oye ¿cómo va?» e introdujo a Puente y un estilo de música hispana no sólo a una nueva generación, sino también al público no hispano.

[a]cuenta... *contains* [b]se... *are combined* [c]*slaves* [d]*with them*

UN POCO DE TODO

Los fines de semana. Complete the following paragraphs with the correct form of the words in parentheses, as suggested by the context. When two possibilities are given in parentheses, select the correct word. *P* and *I* stand for preterite and imperfect, respectively.

Los fines de semana son como las burbujas[a] de oxígeno del calendario. Para muchos, son (los/las[1]) días más especiales. Casi todos los niños (esperar[2]) el sábado y el domingo con ansiedad. Quieren ir (a el / al[3]) parque, o a ver una película o mirar los dibujos animados toda la mañana.

También para los mayores los fines de semana son días diferentes. Hay novios que sólo (poder[4]) verse[b] los sábados y los domingos. (Otro[5]) personas tienen (de/que[6]) hacer visitas o las compras o limpiar la casa. Algunas necesitan (dormir[7]) porque no (dormir: *P*[8]) lo suficiente[c] durante la semana. Hay gente que no (querer[9]) hacer (nada/nunca[10]) y gente que espera hacer todo lo que no (hacer: *P*[11]) durante la semana.

En el mundo moderno, parece[d] que (hay/son[12]) cosas que sólo se pueden hacer los fines de semana, porque (*nosotros:* estar/ser[13]) muy ocupados durante la semana y no podemos hacer (ese[14]) cosas.

¿Qué le (gustar[15]) a Ud. hacer los fines de semana? ¿Qué (preferir: *I*[16]) hacer cuando era más joven?

[a]*bubbles* [b]*see each other* [c]lo... *enough* [d]*it seems*

❖ **Transparency 62**
This transparency provides practice review with preterite.

In the *Capítulo 9* segment of "Chapter-by-Chapter Supplementary Materials" in the IM, you will find a chapter-culminating activity. You can use this activity to consolidate and review the vocabulary and grammar skills students have acquired.

Answers: Un poco de todo
1. *los* **2.** *esperan* **3.** *al* **4.** *pueden* **5.** *Otras* **6.** *que* **7.** *dormir* **8.** *durmieron* **9.** *quiere* **10.** *nada* **11.** *hizo* **12.** *hay* **13.** *estamos* **14.** *esas* **15.** *gusta* **16.** *prefería*

PASO 4 Un paso más

Paso 4: Un paso más
Optional section

See IM for suggestions and follow-up activities to accompany the video segment.

VIDEOTECA: En contexto

FUNCTION

Making plans with a friend

Follow-up A
Ask students what they would like to do this weekend that they will not be able to do: *¿Qué le gustaría hacer este fin de semana pero que no va a poder hacerlo?* Have them explain why they won't be able to do it.

Suggestion
Remind students that *costarricense* means *una persona de Costa Rica.* Another, more popular, expression to refer to people of Costa Rica is *ticos.*

Cultura en contexto
El voseo

Vos, un pronombre personal como **Ud.** y **tú**, tiene origen en el español antiguo. Su eso se llama **el voseo** y se usa en circunstancias de gran familiaridad social en ciertas partes del mundo hispanohablante. Los costarricenses, en particular, usan **vos** y sus formas verbales en vez de **tú**.

Follow-up B
To check comprehension, ask: *¿Qué piensa Mariela de ir al cine? ¿Qué piensan de ir al teatro? ¿Qué deciden hacer al final* (at last)*?*

Heritage speakers
Pregúnteles a los hispanohablantes de la clase si usan o si han oído usar las formas de *vos.*

In this video segment, Mariela and Amalia are trying to make plans for the weekend. As you watch the segment, pay particular attention to the friends' use of language variants that are common in Costa Rica, words such as **tenés, salís, vos**, and **sos**. Can you tell what the traditional Spanish meanings of these words are?

A. Lluvia de ideas

- ¿Qué tipo de actividades prefiere Ud. hacer los fines de semana? ¿Con quién las hace? ¿Hay alguna actividad que Ud. haga todos los fines de semana, sin falta (*without fail*)?
- ¿Cómo se entera (*do you find out*) de los eventos en que puede participar? ¿Consulta Ud. algún periódico en particular?

B. Dictado

A continuación está la primera parte del diálogo entre Mariela y Amalia. Complétela con las palabras o frases que faltan.

MARIELA: Quiero hacer algo interesante este fin de semana. ¿Vos tenés __planes__[1] para mañana?

AMALIA: No, no __tengo__[2] planes. Soy muy aburrida, nunca salgo de mi casa. ¿Por qué? ¿Querés hacer algo juntas?

MARIELA: Me encantaría. ¿__Qué__[3] querés hacer?

AMALIA: ¿Ir al __cine__[4]? ¿Hay alguna película __interesante__[5]?

MARIELA: A ver… la verdad que no. No me interesan para nada estas __películas__.[6] Pero podemos ir al __teatro__.[7]

C. Un diálogo original

Paso 1. Con un compañero / una compañera, dramatice la escena entre Amalia y Mariela.

Paso 2. **Planes para este fin de semana.** Dos amigos/as hacen planes para este domingo.

E1: Ud. desea salir el domingo, porque el sábado por la noche le toca trabajar y no va a poder hacer nada interesante. Afortunadamente (*Luckily*), tiene la mañana del lunes libre (*free*) para estudiar o descansar.

E2: Ud. tiene ganas de salir el domingo. El único obstáculo es que tiene bastante tarea y su primera clase es a las 8 de la mañana el lunes.

PASO FINAL

A LEER

Estrategia: Recognizing Derivative Adjectives

In previous chapters you learned to recognize cognates, word endings, and new words that are related to familiar words. In this chapter you will learn about derivative adjectives, a large group of adjectives derived from verbs. These adjectives end in **-ado** or **-ido**. You can often guess their meaning if you know the related verb. For example: **conocer** (*to know*) → **conocido** (*known, famous*); **preparar** (*to prepare*) → **preparado** (*prepared*).

In the following reading there are many **-do** adjectives. Try to guess their meaning from context. You might also notice past participle forms (**-do**) in conjunction with a verb form you don't recognize, such as **ha comentado** (*has commented*). You will study this form, known as the present perfect, in a later chapter of this text. For now, simply learn to recognize it.

Suggestions: A leer
- Do the *Estrategia* as an in-class activity the day before you cover the reading.
- Work with students to decode underlined words, and have students write sentences using them.

Sobre la lectura... Este artículo apareció en la revista *Quo,* una publicación española que trata temas populares, como la tecnología, la salud, las relaciones entre los sexos y los sitios turísticos. La lectura, un fragmento del artículo original, relata el interés creciente (*growing*) en los parques de atracciones (*amusement parks*) en España.

El sitio de mi recreo

La proliferación de parques temáticos y de museos interactivos revela que la concepción del ocio[a] y de vacaciones está cambiando. «Damos una oferta complementaria al sol y la playa. Ahora llegan turistas de toda España, cuando normalmente este no sería[b] un destino turístico», afirma José María Brugués, de Port Aventura, un parque temático en Tarragona.

Ante el éxito[c] de Port Aventura, España intenta ponerse a la altura de[d] mercados como los de los Estados Unidos, Francia o Gran Bretaña. Ya existen más de cincuenta proyectos de parques temáticos en España, entre ellos, en San Martín de la Vega (Madrid) dedicado al cine, un proyecto en el que está involucrada[e] la Warner Brothers.

Julián Rodríguez Luna, consejero delegado del Grupo Parque en España, comenta la popularidad creciente de estas nuevas atracciones. Según él, nuestra sociedad disfruta[f] cada vez más de tiempo libre, y por ello tiende[g] a buscar más opciones de ocio. Los parques, ya sean de atracciones, acuáticos o zoos, son una buena elección. Están configurados para que se puedan disfrutar[h] de una forma participativa, porque fuera del hogar[i] buscamos un ocio activo. Los jóvenes suelen buscar el riesgo[j] y las emociones fuertes, mien-

[a]*leisure time* [b]no... *would not be* [c]*success* [d]ponerse... *compete on the same level as* [e]*involved* [f]*enjoys* [g]*tends, is inclined to* [h]para... *to be enjoyed* [i]fuera... *outside the home* [j]*risk*

tras que las familias buscan tranquilidad y pasar un buen rato con los niños.

Aparte de las novedades[k] en parques temáticos y de atracciones, la tecnología también ha llegado[l] a los museos. Al contrario de lo que se podría pensar,[m] los museos de siempre no morirán,[n] aunque muchos de ellos están comenzando a reciclarse. Algunos ya han adaptado varias salas para convertirlas en interactivas. Lo que le interesa al público es tocar y que los museos sean divertidos y lúdicos.[o] ■

[k]*novelties* [l]ha... *has arrived* [m]Al... *Contrary to what one might believe* [n]no... *will not die* [o]*entertaining*

Un parque de atracciones en Barcelona, España

Comprensión

A. Selección múltiple. Escoja la respuesta correcta según la lectura.

1. ¿Cómo se explica el número creciente de parques temáticos en España?
   - **a.** El gobierno (*government*) español desea atraer (*attract*) a más turistas internacionales.
   - **b.** A los españoles no les gustan los museos.
   - **c.** La gente tiene más tiempo libre y busca diversiones interactivas.
2. ¿Qué buscan los jóvenes cuando van a los parques?
   - **a.** un sitio romántico
   - **b.** un sitio sin adultos
   - **c.** un sitio que ofrece riesgos

B. Palabras relacionadas. ¿De qué verbos se derivan los siguientes adjetivos?

1. involucrada __________
2. dedicado __________
3. configurados __________
4. divertidos __________

A ESCRIBIR

Atracciones locales. Para muchas personas, ir a un parque temático es una buena diversión. Pero hay otras atracciones también. ¿Qué atracciones locales hay donde Ud. vive? Imagine que Ud. está en un comité universitario para reclutar (*recruit*) a nuevos estudiantes. A Ud. le toca escribir un ensayo de 250 palabras que describe todas las atracciones que ofrecen la universidad y la ciudad. El título del ensayo es: «Atracciones y diversiones para estudiantes de la Universidad».

En resumen

GRAMÁTICA

To review the grammar points presented in this chapter, refer to the indicated grammar presentations. You'll find further practice of these structures in the Workbook/Laboratory Manual, on the CD-ROM, and on the website.

26. Imperfect of Regular and Irregular Verbs

You should know the imperfect forms of all verbs. What are the three irregular imperfect verbs?

27. Superlatives

Do you know how to express that something is the best or the most?

28. Summary of Interrogative Words

You should know how to form questions and which question words to use in Spanish.

VOCABULARIO

Los verbos

aburrirse — to get bored
dejar (en) — to leave (behind) (in, at)
pegar — to hit
pelear — to fight
sonar (ue) — to ring; to sound

Los pasatiempos, las diversiones y las aficiones

los ratos libres — spare (free) time

dar (*irreg.*) **un paseo** — to take a walk
hacer (*irreg.*) **un *picnic*** — to have a picnic
hacer (*irreg.*) **planes para** + *inf.* — to make plans to (*do something*)
ir (*irreg.*)... — to go . . .
al cine / a ver una película — to the movies/to see a movie
a una discoteca / a un bar — to a disco/to a bar
al teatro / a un concierto — to the theater/to a concert
jugar (ue) a las cartas / al ajedrez — to play cards/chess
ser (*irreg.*) **divertido/a** — to be fun
visitar un museo — to visit a museum

Repaso: aburrido/a, dar (*irreg.*) **/ hacer** (*irreg.*) **una fiesta, hacer *camping,* jugar (ue) (al), pasarlo bien/mal, tomar el sol**

Los deportes

el/la aficionado/a (a) — fan (of)
el ciclismo — bicycling
el fútbol — soccer
el fútbol americano — football
el/la jugador(a) — player
la natación — swimming

Otros deportes: el basquetbol, el béisbol, el golf, el hockey, el tenis, el vólibol

correr — to run; to jog
entrenar — to practice, train
esquiar (esquío) — to ski
ganar — to win
montar a caballo — to ride a horse
pasear en bicicleta — to ride a bicycle

patinar	to skate
patinar en linea	to rollerblade
ser aficionado/a (a)	to be a fan (of)

Repaso: nadar, perder (ie), practicar

Algunos aparatos domésticos

la aspiradora	vacuum cleaner
la cafetera	coffeepot
el congelador	freezer
la estufa	stove
el horno de microondas	microwave oven
la lavadora	washing machine
el lavaplatos	dishwasher
el refrigerador	refrigerator
la secadora	clothes dryer
la tostadora	toaster

Algunos quehaceres domésticos

barrer (el piso)	to sweep (the floor)
hacer (*irreg.*) **la cama**	to make the bed
lavar (las ventanas, los platos, la ropa)	to wash (the windows, the dishes, the clothes)
limpiar la casa (entera)	to clean the (whole) house
pasar la aspiradora	to vacuum
pintar (las paredes)	to paint (the walls)
planchar la ropa	to iron clothing
poner (*irreg.*) **la mesa**	to set the table
quitar la mesa	to clear the table
sacar la basura	to take out the trash
sacudir los muebles	to dust the furniture

Otros sustantivos

la costumbre	custom, habit
la época	era, time (*period*)
la escuela	school
el grado	grade, year (*in school*)
el/la niñero/a	baby-sitter
la niñez	childhood

Adjetivos

deportivo/a	sports-loving
pesado/a	boring; difficult

Palabras adicionales

de joven	as a youth
de niño/a	as a child
mientras	while
tocarle a uno	to be someone's turn

Suggestions: Vocabulario

- Bring or have students bring clippings that illustrate items and activities from the *Vocabulario.* Use these to review (have students describe, play word games, and so on).
- Have students respond *cierto* or *falso*: **1.** *El béisbol requiere la participación de varias personas.* **2.** *El ejercicio es importante para la salud mental.* **3.** *Para una persona que le gusta estar entre mucha gente, la natación es el deporte favorito.*
- Have students answer: **1.** *¿Dónde se puede escuchar música, en un concierto o en un museo?* **2.** *¿Cuál es una actividad cultural, hacer* camping *o ir al teatro?* **3.** *¿Dónde se puede ver a su actor favorito, en un bar o en el cine?*
- Have students make single statements about something they used to do when they were younger (*de joven / de niño/a*). Have them make their statements in round-robin, without repeating anything someone else has already said.
- Have students describe 3–4 activities that they think someone famous used to do as a child without naming the person. The class should try to guess identity.

La salud

Suggestions: Chapter Opening photo

- Point out the chapter opening photo. Have students discuss their ideas about exercise and health. Encourage them to describe the people in the photo. Do they look healthy? Are they concerned about their health and fitness?
- Ask students the following personal questions: *¿Hace Ud. ejercicio con frecuencia? ¿Qué hace? ¿Va a un gimnasio o hace deporte al aire libre? ¿Hizo Ud. ejercicio ayer? ¿Cuándo fue la última vez que hizo ejercicio?*

Resources

You and your students may find the following *¿Qué tal?* supplements helpful as you teach this chapter:

For the Instructor

- *Instructor's Manual and Resource Kit,* "Chapter-by-Chapter" Supplementary Materials
- Testing Program
- Overhead Transparencies 63–66
- Video (VHS or CD)
- *¿Qué tal?* Online Learning Center Website
- Audioscript
- Instructor's Resource CD

VOCABULARIO

- Health and well-being
- At the doctor's office

GRAMÁTICA

29 Using the Preterite and the Imperfect

30 Reciprocal Actions and Reflexive Pronouns

CULTURA

- **Enfoque cultural:** Venezuela
- **Nota cultural:** La medicina en los países hispanos
- **En los Estados Unidos y el Canadá:** Edward James Olmos: Actor y activista de la comunidad
- **Cultura en contexto:** En la farmacia

Multimedia

You will learn about describing an illness in the **En contexto** video segment.

Review vocabulary and grammar and practice language skills with the interactive CD-ROM.

Get connected to the Spanish-speaking world with the *¿Qué tal?* Online Learning Center: **www.mhhe.com/quetal**.

For Students

- Workbook/Laboratory Manual and Audio Program or Electronic Workbook/Laboratory Manual
- Video on CD
- Interactive CD-ROM
- *¿Qué tal?* Online Learning Center Website
- Listening Comprehension Audio CD
- McGraw-Hill Electronic Language Tutor (MHELT)

Caminar y pasear en bicicleta son buenas formas de ejercicio (*exercise*). Estas personas pasean por el Museo de los Niños en Caracas, Venezuela. ▶

PASO 1 Vocabulario

CAPÍTULO 10

Paso 1: Vocabulario
See detailed supplementary materials and exercises for this section and a model for vocabulary presentation and other material in the *Capítulo 10 Paso 1: Vocabulario* section of "Chapter-by-Chapter Supplementary Materials," IM.

La salud y el bienestar°

°La… *Health and well-being*

❖ **Transparencias 63–64**
Transparency 64 has additional vocabulary you may wish to present to your students.

El cuerpo humano

Multimedia: Audio
Students can listen to and practice this chapter's vocabulary on their Listening Comprehension Audio CD.

108-503

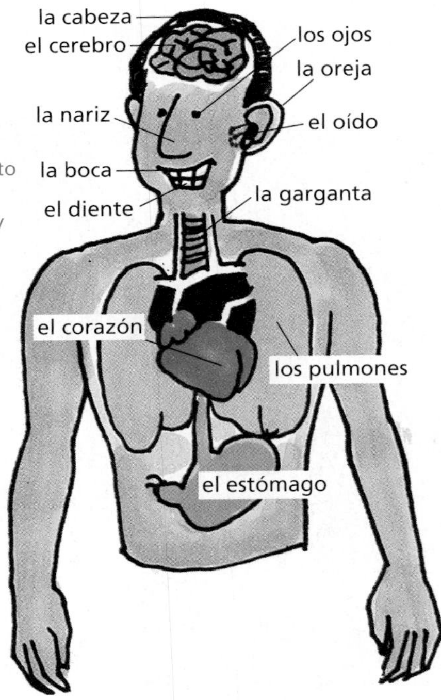

Para cuidar de la salud

caminar	to walk
comer equilibradamente	to eat well-balanced meals
correr	to run; to jog
cuidarse	to take care of oneself
dejar de + *inf.*	to stop (*doing something*)
dormir (ue, u) lo suficiente	to sleep enough
hacer (*irreg.*) **ejercicio**	to exercise; to get exercise
hacer (*irreg.*) **ejercicios aeróbicos**	to do aerobics
llevar gafas / lentes de contacto	to wear glasses / contact lenses
llevar una vida sana/tranquila	to lead a healthy / calm life
practicar deportes	to practice, play sports

A-1y2-108-503

Conversación

Preliminary exercise A
Have students respond *cierto* or *falso:* **1.** *Comemos con los pulmones.* **2.** *Respiramos con la nariz.* **3.** *La comida pasa por la boca y la garganta antes de llegar al estómago.* **4.** *Se usan los ojos para ver.* **5.** *Se come bien en las cafeterías de esta universidad.* **6.** *Los estudiantes siempre se cuidan bien y duermen lo suficiente.* **7.** *Alguien que lleva una vida sana fuma mucho y toma mucho café.* **8.** *Las personas mayores no deben hacer ejercicio.* **9.** *Los cigarrillos afectan principalmente los pulmones de la persona que los fuma.* **10.** *Si una persona no ve bien, lo único que puede hacer es llevar gafas.*

A. Asociaciones

Paso 1. ¿Qué partes del cuerpo humano asocia Ud. con las siguientes palabras? A veces hay más de una respuesta posible.

1. un ataque **2.** comer **3.** cantar **4.** las gafas **5.** pensar **6.** la digestión **7.** el amor **8.** fumar **9.** la música **10.** el perfume

Paso 2. ¿Qué palabras asocia Ud. con las siguientes partes del cuerpo?

1. los ojos **2.** los dientes **3.** la boca **4.** el oído **5.** el estómago

B. Hablando de la salud

Paso 1. ¿Qué significan, para Ud., las siguientes oraciones?

MODELO: Se debe comer equilibradamente. →
Eso quiere decir (*means*) que es necesario comer muchas verduras, que…

Palabras y frases útiles: Eso quiere decir… , Esto significa que… , También…

1. Se debe dormir lo suficiente todas las noches.
2. Hay que hacer ejercicio.
3. Es necesario llevar una vida tranquila.
4. En general, uno debe cuidarse mucho.

Paso 2. ¿Lleva una vida sana? Dígale a un compañero / una compañera cómo vive, usando las frases del **Paso 1** y del **Vocabulario**.

MODELO: Creo que llevo una vida sana porque como equilibradamente: No como muchos dulces, excepto en los días festivos como la Navidad… Además (*Moreover*) duermo por lo menos (*at least*) ocho horas por día.

Paso 3. Ahora cambie su narración para describir lo que hacía de niño/a. ¿Qué hacía y qué *no* hacía Ud.? Debe organizar las ideas lógicamente.

MODELO: De niño, no llevaba una vida muy sana. Comía muchos dulces. También odiaba las frutas y verduras…

Suggestion B
Use these items to discuss the lifestyle of citizens in this country and people in industrialized countries: *¿Llevamos una vida sana?*

Extension B
- Have students name and discuss other aspects of our preoccupation with health.
- Ask students the following question: *¿Hay personas que se preocupen demasiado por la salud? Describa a estas personas.*

WWW. Multimedia: Internet
Students can find diet and nutrition guidelines online that can serve as a springboard for the discussion of their food habits. UNAM includes a page on the subject at their Website. There are also pages online with health and fitness tests such as the longevity test. Encourage students to find these pages.

En el consultorio°

°*doctor's office*

98,6 grados Fahrenheit

37,0 grados centígrados

el/la enfermero/a nurse
el/la farmacéutico/a pharmacist
el/la médico/a physician
el/la paciente patient

congestionado/a congested, stuffed-up
mareado/a dizzy; nauseated

el antibiótico antibiotic
el jarabe (cough) syrup
la pastilla pill
la receta prescription
el resfriado cold
la tos cough

doler (ue)* to hurt, ache
enfermarse to get sick
guardar cama to stay in bed
internarse (en) to check in (*to a hospital*)
ponerle (*irreg.*) **una inyección** to give (someone) a shot

resfriarse to get/catch a cold
respirar to breathe
sacar to extract
  sacar la lengua to stick out one's tongue
  sacar una muela to extract a tooth
tener (*irreg.*) **dolor (de cabeza, estómago, muela)** to have a (head, stomach, tooth) ache
tener (*irreg.*) **fiebre** to have a fever
tomar(le) la temperatura to take someone's temperature
toser to cough

— Pero ¿cómo quiere que le opere,[a] si no tiene Ud. nada?
— Mejor, doctor. Así la operación le será[b] más fácil…

[a]cómo… *why do you want me to operate on you* [b]*will be*

*Doler is used like gustar: Me duel*e* la cabeza. Me duel*en* los ojos.

Conversación

Preliminary exercise A
Have students give the word for each: **1.** *Es un sinónimo de «ponerse enfermo».* **2.** *Es un líquido que se toma contra la tos.* **3.** *Esto se hace con un termómetro.* **4.** *No se puede hacer esto sin los pulmones.* **5.** *Es el papelito que nos da el médico cuando nos manda a la farmacia.*

Suggestion A
Have students tell whether or not the statements are *cierto* or *falso* for them based on their last dental visit: **1.** *Me examinó los dientes.* **2.** *Me limpió los dientes.* **3.** *Me puso una inyección.* **4.** *Me sacó un diente.* **5.** *Me empastó* (he/she filled) *un diente.* **6.** *Me sacó unos rayos X.* **7.** *Me hizo muchas preguntas.* **8.** *Me preguntó si uso hilo dental* (dental floss) *con regularidad.*

A. Estudio de palabras. Complete las siguientes oraciones con una palabra de la misma (*same*) familia que la palabra en letras cursivas (*italics*).

1. Si me *resfrío*, tengo _____.
2. La *respiración* ocurre cuando alguien _____.
3. Si me _____, estoy *enfermo/a*. Un(a) _____ me toma la temperatura.
4. Cuando alguien *tose*, se oye una _____.
5. Si me *duele* el estómago, tengo un _____ de estómago.

NOTA CULTURAL

La medicina en los países hispanos

Como regla general, los hispanos **consultan** sobre sus **problemas de salud** no sólo con los médicos sino también[a] con **otros profesionales**. Por ejemplo, ya que[b] muchas medicinas se venden sin receta, se puede pedirle al farmacéutico / a la farmacéutica recomendaciones sobre **medicinas apropiadas** para tratar alguna **enfermedad**. Los farmacéuticos son profesionales con un **entrenamiento** riguroso en la universidad. Están al tanto[c] de los adelantos[d] en **farmacología**. En algunos países, la gente también consulta con los **practicantes** que son profesionales que poseen, por lo menos, tres años de entrenamiento médico y que están facultados[e] para poner inyecciones y aplicar ciertos tratamientos a los pacientes.

En los países hispanos, solamente algunas farmacias están abiertas[f] por la noche y durante los fines de semana. Cada semana diferentes farmacias se alternan para operar en tales[g] horarios. La gente se refiere a ellas como **farmacias de turno** o **de guardia**. Generalmente, los periódicos y los noticieros de radio y televisión locales publican los nombres y las direcciones de las farmacias de turno. Así la gente sabe adónde ir a comprar sus medicinas. En algunas ciudades, las farmacias de turno encienden[h] una luz roja al lado de la entrada para indicar que están atendiendo al público.

[a]sino… *but also* [b]ya… *since* [c]al… *up-to-date* [d]*advances* [e]*authorized* [f]*open* [g]*such* [h]*turn on*

Follow-up B

Read the following statements and have students respond *cierto* or *falso:* 1. *Si la persona sentada a mi lado empieza a toser, me quedo donde estoy.* 2. *Me pongo nervioso/a en el consultorio del médico.* 3. *Cuando tengo que ir al médico porque estoy enfermo/a, me siento mejor antes de ver al médico en el consultorio.* 4. *Cuando tengo un resfriado, nunca tomo pastillas ni jarabes ni antibióticos.* 5. *Mente sana en cuerpo sano.* 6. *Odio ir al dentista.* 7. *Si no hago ejercicio todos los días, empiezo a sentirme nervioso/a.*

B. Situaciones. Describa Ud. la situación de estas personas. ¿Dónde y con quiénes están? ¿Qué síntomas tienen? ¿Qué van a hacer?

1. Anamari está muy bien de salud. Nunca le duele(n) ______. Nunca tiene ______. Siempre ______. Más tarde, ella va a ______.
2. Martín tiene ______. Debe ______. El dentista va a ______. Después, Martín va a ______.
3. A Inés le duele(n) ______. Tiene ______. El médico y la enfermera van a ______. Luego, Inés tiene que ______.

1.

2.

3.

❖ **Transparency 65**

Suggestions: Nota comunicativa

- If you have worked with nominalization, present the *lo* + adjective structure as part of that system.
- Point out that students have already learned one expression that involves nominalization with *lo: lo suficiente.*
- Have students express these phrases in Spanish: the important thing / part, the bad thing / part, the interesting thing / part. Model these expressions in communicative exchanges with students: *¿Qué es lo importante de hacer ejercicio? ¿Qué es lo malo de ir al consultorio?*

Preliminary exercise C

Have students nominalize adjectives with *lo.* Encourage them to use them in model sentences: *importante* → *lo importante* → *Lo importante en esta clase es practicar.* 1. *divertido* 2. *peor* 3. *interesante* 4. *curioso* 5. *necesario* 6. *bueno*

NOTA COMUNICATIVA

The Good News... The Bad News...

To describe general qualities or characteristics of something, use **lo** with the masculine singular form of an adjective.

lo bueno / lo malo lo más importante lo mejor / lo peor
lo mismo

This structure has a number of English equivalents, especially in colloquial speech.

lo bueno = the good thing/part/news, what's good

Suggestions C

- Have students express ideas about more important things of life: *Lo más importante de la vida (no) es/son ____. (las clases, la libertad, las vacaciones, la salud, los amigos, la familia, ¿ ?)* Point out that *son* anticipates a plural noun.
- Have students work in pairs to give each other good and bad news for each of the following situations, for example, *en el restaurante* → *Lo bueno es que la comida es excelente. Lo malo son los precios.* 1. *en la clase de español* 2. *en la oficina de la profesora / en esta universidad* 3. *en el aeropuerto* 4. *en el consultorio del médico / dentista* 5. *en casa / durante un viaje* 6. *en el trabajo o durante una entrevista.*

C. Ventajas y desventajas (*Advantages and disadvantages*). Casi todas las cosas tienen un aspecto bueno y otro malo.

Paso 1. ¿Qué es lo bueno y lo malo (o lo peor y lo mejor) de las siguientes situaciones?

1. tener un resfriado
2. ir a una universidad cerca/lejos del hogar familiar (*family home*)
3. tener hijos cuando uno es joven (entre 20 y 25 años)
4. ser muy rico/a
5. ir al consultorio médico / del dentista

Paso 2. Compare sus respuestas con las de sus compañeros. ¿Dijeron algo que Ud. no consideró?

PASO 2 Gramática

CAPÍTULO 10

Paso 2: Gramática
See detailed supplementary materials for this grammar section in IM.

¿Recuerda Ud.?

Throughout the last chapters of *¿Qué tal?*, beginning with **Capítulo 7**, you have been using first the preterite and then the imperfect in appropriate contexts. Do you remember which tense you used to do each of the following?

1. to tell what you did yesterday
2. to tell what you used to do when you were in grade school
3. to explain the situation or condition that caused you to do something
4. to tell what someone did as the result of a situation
5. to talk about the way things used to be
6. to describe an action that was in progress

If you understand those uses of the preterite and the imperfect, the following summary of their uses will not contain much that is new information for you.

108 - 503

29 Narrating in the Past • Using the Preterite and the Imperfect

En el consultorio de la Dra. Méndez

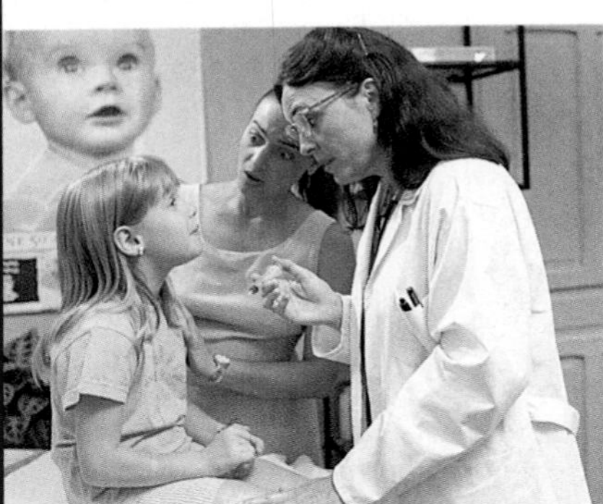

DRA. MÉNDEZ: ¿Cuándo *empezó* a sentirse mal su hija?
LOLA: Ayer por la tarde. *Estaba* congestionada, *tosía* mucho y *se quejaba* de que le *dolían* el cuerpo y la cabeza.
DRA. MÉNDEZ: ¿Y le *notó* algo de fiebre?
LOLA: Sí. Por la noche le *tomé* la temperatura y *tenía* treinta y ocho grados.
DRA. MÉNDEZ: A ver... Tal vez necesito ponerle una inyección...
MARTA: Eh... bueno... ¡Creo que ahora me encuentro un poco mejor!

In the preceding dialogue, locate all of the verbs that do the following.

1. indicate actions (or lack of action)
2. indicate conditions or descriptions

Note: Preterite/Imperfect
This section contrasts the uses of the preterite and the imperfect and provides practice in deciding which tense to use. Students have been using these tenses in controlled activities in *Capítulos 7–9*.

In Dr. Méndez's office DR. MÉNDEZ: When did your daughter begin to feel bad? LOLA: Yesterday afternoon. She was stuffed up, she coughed a lot, and she complained that her body and head were hurting. DR. MÉNDEZ: And did you note any fever? LOLA: Yes. At night I took her temperature and it was thirty-eight degrees. DR. MÉNDEZ: Let's see . . . Perhaps I'll need to give her a shot . . . MARTA: Um . . . well . . . I think I feel a little bit better now! . . .

Follow-Up: Preterite/Imperfect
After reviewing *minidiálogo*, check comprehension: *¿Quién estaba enferma? ¿Qué síntomas tenía? ¿Por qué se sintió mejor rápidamente?*

PASO 2

When speaking about the past in English, you choose different past tense forms to use, depending on the context: *I wrote letters, I was writing letters, I used to write letters*, and so on. Similarly, you can use either the preterite or the imperfect in many Spanish sentences, depending on the meaning you wish to convey. Often the question is: How do you view the action or state of being?

Note: Preterite/Imperfect
The beginning of an action is usually expressed with the preterite: *Empezó a llover. Comenzaron el ejercicio.* An example of an exception is: *Isabel empezaba el ejercicio cuando su hermano entró.*

A. Use the preterite to…

- tell about the beginning or the end of a past action

El sábado pasado, el partido de fútbol **empezó** a la una. **Terminó** a las cuatro.
Last Saturday, the soccer game began at one. It ended at four.

Use the imperfect to…

- talk about the habitual nature of an action (something you always did)

Había un partido todos los sábados. Muchas personas **jugaban** todas las semanas.
There was a game every Saturday. Many people played every week.

B. Use the preterite to…

- express an action that is viewed as completed

El partido **duró** tres horas. **Ganaron** Los Lobos, de Villalegre.
The game lasted three hours. The Lobos of Villalegre won.

Use the imperfect to…

- tell what was happening when another action took place and tell about simultaneous events (with **mientras** = *while*)

Yo no vi el final del partido. **Estaba** en la cocina cuando **terminó**.
I didn't see the end of the game. I was in the kitchen when it ended.

Mientras mi amigo **veía** el vídeo, **hablaba** con su novia.
While my friend was watching the video, he was talking with his girlfriend.

C. Use the preterite to…

- express a series of completed actions

Durante el partido, los jugadores **corrieron, saltaron y gritaron**.
During the game, the players ran, jumped, and shouted.

Suggestions: Preterite/Imperfect
- Model the difference in meaning of *pensó* (he thought, it occurred to him) and *pensaba* (he was of the opinion, planned/intended to). Use *creer* forms in a similar contrast.
- Offer additional examples: *Carlos fue al médico ayer. / Carlos siempre iba al médico cuando se resfriaba. Juanita estuvo* (became) *nerviosa. / Juanita estaba* (was) *nerviosa.*

Use the imperfect to...

- give background details of many kinds: time, location, weather, mood, age, physical and mental characteristics

Llovía un poco durante el partido. Todos los jugadores **eran** jóvenes; **tenían** 17 ó 18 años.* ¡Y todos **esperaban** ganar!
It rained a little bit during the game. All the players were young; they were 17 or 18 years old. And all of them hoped to win!

D. Certain words and expressions are frequently associated with the preterite, others with the imperfect.

Suggestions: Preterite/Imperfect

- Model cue words associated with preterite and imperfect in exchanges with students. Discuss how words relate to concepts of preterite and imperfect.
- Point out that *dos veces, tres veces,* and so on are associated with the preterite, not the imperfect, because they refer to completed past actions. Model and contrast these expressions with *todos los días,* for example, *Fui al consultorio del médico tres veces este mes. Tenía un dolor de cabeza todos los días al levantarme.*

Some words often associated with the preterite are:

ayer, anteayer, anoche
una vez (*once*), dos veces (*twice*),...
el año pasado, el lunes pasado,...
de repente (*suddenly*)

Some words often associated with the imperfect are:

todos los días, todos los lunes,...
siempre, frecuentemente
mientras
de niño/a, de joven

Some English equivalents also associated with the imperfect are:

was ____ *-ing, were* ____ *-ing* (in English) *used to, would* (when *would* implies *used to* in English)

OJO These words do not *automatically* cue either tense, however. The most important consideration is the meaning that the speaker wishes to convey.

Ayer cenamos temprano.
Yesterday we had dinner early.

Ayer cenábamos cuando Juan llamó.
Yesterday we were having dinner when Juan called.

De niño jugaba al fútbol.
He played soccer as a child.

De niño empezó a jugar al fútbol.
He began to play soccer as a child.

E. Remember that, when used in the preterite, **saber, conocer, querer**, and **poder** have English equivalents different from the infinitives (see **Capítulo 8**). The English equivalents of these verbs in the imperfect do not differ from the infinitive meanings.

Suggestion: Preterite/Imperfect
Model sentences with preterite and imperfect of *saber, conocer, poder,* and *querer* and have students explain differences in meaning.

*Between digits, the word **o** (*or*) carries an accent to distinguish it from the digit 0.

F. The preterite and the imperfect frequently occur in the same sentence. In the first sentence the imperfect tells what was happening when another action—conveyed by the preterite—broke the continuity of the ongoing activity. In the second sentence, the preterite reports the action that took place because of a condition, described by the imperfect, that was in progress or in existence at that time.

Miguel **estudiaba** cuando **sonó** el teléfono.
Miguel was studying when the phone rang.

Olivia **comió** tanto porque **tenía** mucha hambre.
Olivia ate so much because she was very hungry.

G. The preterite and imperfect are also used together in the presentation of an event. The preterite narrates the action while the imperfect sets the stage, describes the conditions that caused the action, or emphasizes the continuing nature of a particular action.

Práctica

A. En el consultorio. What did your doctor do the last time you had an appointment with him or her? Assume that you had the following conditions and match them with the appropriate procedure.

CONDICIONES: (YO)...	ACCIONES: El médico...
1. __c__ tenía mucho calor y temblaba.	a. me hizo muchas preguntas.
2. __f__ me dolía la garganta.	b. me puso una inyección.
3. __g__ tenía un poco de congestión en el pecho (*chest*).	c. me tomó la temperatura.
4. __e__ creía que estaba anémico/a.	d. me auscultó (*listened to*) los pulmones y el corazón.
5. __a__ no sabía lo que tenía.	e. me analizó la sangre (*blood*).
6. __b__ necesitaba medicinas.	f. me hizo sacar la lengua.
7. __d__ sólo necesitaba un chequeo rutinario.	g. me hizo toser.

B. Pequeñas historias. Complete the brief paragraphs on the following page with the appropriate phrases from the list. Before you begin, it is a good idea to look at the drawing that accompanies each paragraph and to scan through the complete paragraph to get the gist of it, even though you may not understand everything the first time you read it.

Preliminary exercise A
Have students tell if each sentence would require preterite or imperfect in Spanish, and why: **1.** She used to eat eggs every day. **2.** I ate breakfast, brushed my teeth, and left for the university. **3.** He was tall and blond. **4.** She was playing the piano. **5.** They begin to sing. **6.** Thomas was playing tennis while I was studying. **7.** It was three o'clock. **8.** The car was yellow and black.

Note A
This activity helps students link conditions (imperfect) with actions (preterite) in logical sentence pairs. Even though students do not have to create forms themselves, they are working with preterite / imperfect contrast.

Variation A
This activity can be done in question/answer format. Have students form questions based on *ACCIONES*. Other students should answer beginning *CONDICIONES* with *Sí, porque...*

Suggestion B
Have students explain why they choose preterite or imperfect.

Extension B
Have students change subject in first paragraph to *Jorge y Alicia.*

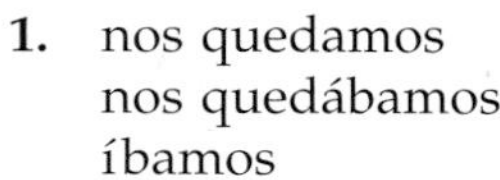

1. nos quedamos / nos quedábamos / íbamos / nos gustó / nuestra familia decidió / vivíamos

Cuando éramos niños, Jorge y yo ___vivíamos___[1] en la Argentina. Siempre ___íbamos___[2] a la playa, a Mar del Plata, para pasar la Navidad. Allí casi siempre ___nos quedábamos___[3] en el Hotel Fénix. Un año, ___nuestra familia decidió___[4] quedarse en otro hotel, el Continental. No ___nos gustó___[5] tanto como el Fénix y por eso, al año siguiente, ___nos quedamos___[6] en el Fénix otra vez.

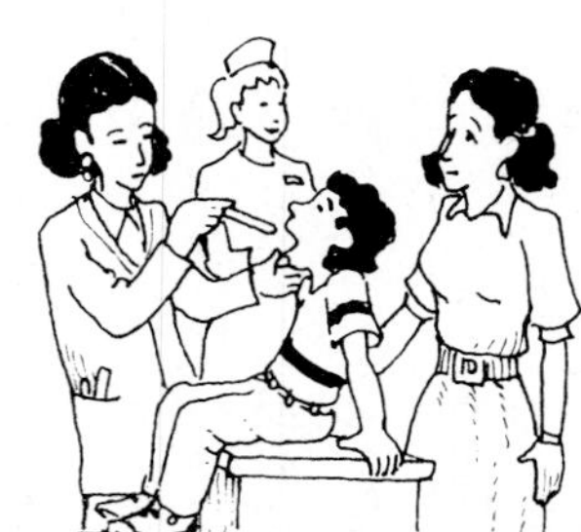

2. examinó / intentaba[a] tomarle / estaba / esperaba / puso / llegó / dio / se sintió

El niño tosía mientras que la enfermera ___intentaba tomarle___[1] la temperatura. La madre del niño ___esperaba___[2] pacientemente. Por fin ___llegó___[3] la médica. Le ___examinó___[4] la garganta al niño, le ___puso___[5] una inyección y le ___dio___[6] a su madre una receta para un jarabe. La madre todavía ___estaba___[7] muy preocupada, pero inmediatamente después que la médica le habló, ___se sintió___[8] más tranquila.

[a]*tried to*

Answers C
1. *estaba* 2. *entró* 3. *preguntó* 4. *quería* 5. *dijo* 6. *sentía* 7. salieron 8. Vieron 9. se rieron 10. hacía 11. entraron 12. tomaron 13. Eran 14. regresaron 15. se acostó 16. estaba 17. empezó

C. Rubén y Soledad

Paso 1. Read the following paragraph at least once to familiarize yourself with the sequence of events, and look at the drawing. Then reread the paragraph, giving the proper form of the verbs in parentheses in the preterite or the imperfect, according to the needs of each sentence and the context of the paragraph as a whole.

Rubén (estar[1]) estudiando cuando Soledad (entrar[2]) en el cuarto. Le (preguntar[3]) a Rubén si (querer[4]) ir al cine con ella. Rubén le (decir[5]) que sí porque se (sentir[6]) un poco aburrido con sus estudios. Los dos (salir[7]) en seguida[a] para el cine. (Ver[8]) una película cómica y (reírse[9]) mucho. Luego, como (hacer[10]) frío, (entrar[11]) en su café favorito, El Gato Negro, y (tomar[12]) un chocolate. (Ser[13]) las dos de la mañana cuando por fin (regresar[14]) a casa. Soledad (acostarse[15]) inmediatamente porque (estar[16]) cansada, pero Rubén (empezar[17]) a estudiar otra vez.

[a]en… *right away*

Paso 2. Now answer the following questions based on the paragraph about Rubén and Soledad. **¡OJO!** A question is not always answered in the same tense as that in which it is asked.

1. ¿Qué hacía Rubén cuando Soledad entró?
2. ¿Qué le preguntó Soledad a Rubén?
3. ¿Por qué dijo Rubén que sí?
4. ¿Les gustó la película? ¿Por qué?
5. ¿Qué hicieron cuando llegaron a casa?

Suggestions C
- Do *Pasos 1* and *2* as a whole-class narration with students taking turns to complete the story.
- Have students work in pairs to tell each other a story about themselves: the happiest / saddest / most embarrassing moment of their lives, how they met their best friend / spouse / boyfriend / girlfriend, and so on. Encourage students to ask their partner for details and to offer help if their partner needs it.

WWW Multimedia: Internet
Have students print out images from the Internet to bring to class. Working in groups of 3–4 students, each group writes an imaginary story about the image using preterite and imperfect.

Conversación

A. El primer día. Dé Ud. sus impresiones del primer día de su primera clase universitaria. Use estas preguntas como guía.

1. ¿Cuál fue la primera clase? ¿A qué hora era la clase y dónde era?
2. ¿Vino a clase con alguien? ¿Ya tenía su libro de texto o lo compró después?
3. ¿Qué hizo Ud. después de entrar en la sala de clase? ¿Qué hacía el profesor / la profesora?
4. ¿A quién conoció Ud. aquel día? ¿Ya conocía a algunos miembros de la clase? ¿A quiénes?
5. ¿Aprendió Ud. mucho durante la clase? ¿Ya sabía algo de esa materia?
6. ¿Le gustó el profesor / la profesora? ¿Por qué sí o por qué no? ¿Cómo era?
7. ¿Cómo se sentía durante la clase? ¿nervioso/a? ¿aburrido/a? ¿cómodo/a?
8. ¿Les dio tarea el profesor / la profesora? ¿Pudo Ud. hacerla fácilmente?
9. ¿Su primera impresión de la clase y del profesor / de la profesora, ¿fue válida o cambió con el tiempo? ¿Por qué?

B. Unas preguntas sobre el pasado

Paso 1. Con un compañero / una compañera, haga y conteste las siguientes preguntas.

¿Cuántos años tenías cuando… ?

1. aprendiste a pasear en bicicleta
2. hiciste tu primer viaje en avión
3. tuviste tu primera cita
4. empezaste a afeitarte
5. conseguiste tu licencia de manejar (*driver's license*)
6. abriste una cuenta corriente (*checking account*)
7. dejaste de crecer (*grow*)

¿Cuántos años tenías cuando tus padres… ?

8. te dejaron cruzar la calle solo/a
9. te permitieron ir de compras a solas
10. te dejaron acostarte después de las nueve
11. te dejaron quedarte en casa sin niñero/a
12. te permitieron usar la estufa
13. te dejaron ver una película «R»
14. te dejaron conseguir un trabajo

Paso 2. Ahora, en grupos de cuatro, comparen sus respuestas. ¿Son muy diferentes las respuestas que dieron? ¿Quién del grupo tiene los padres más estrictos? ¿los menos estrictos?

Follow-up A

- Have students write short paragraphs about their first day at the university (or a similar topic). Have them narrate their story in the past, using preterite and imperfect. Collect and choose the best 2–3 narrations, edit them, and develop activities based on them (on overhead transparencies or reproduced copies). The preceding paragraphs in *Prácticas C* and *D* are based on actual student paragraphs.
- Have students give oral presentations using questions as a guide.

Extension A

10. *¿Qué hora era cuando llegó Ud. a la universidad? ¿Por qué llegó a esa hora? ¿Qué ropa llevaba?* **11.** *¿Cuántos estudiantes había en la clase? ¿Qué hacían cuando Ud. entró?* **12.** *¿Sabían todos más que Ud.? ¿Habló Ud. durante la clase? ¿Le hizo algunas preguntas al profesor / a la profesora?* **13.** *¿Ya sabía Ud. el nombre del profesor / de la profesora? ¿Sabía qué tipo de profesor(a) era?* **14.** *¿Tenía ganas de regresar a clase o quería dejarla?*

Suggestions B

- Have students add 3 questions of their own to each list.
- Tell students to imagine that you are a detective who has to write a report about the theft of a rare book that disappeared from the university library yesterday. You need to know exactly where they were and what they were doing from ______ to ______ yesterday.

Enfoque *cultural*

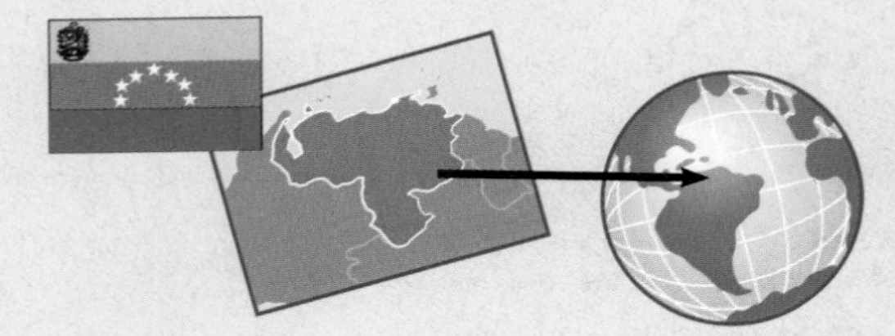

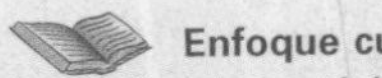

Enfoque cultural
See follow-up activities for this section in chapter-by-chapter materials in IM.

Venezuela

Datos esenciales

Nombre oficial: República de Venezuela

Capital: Caracas

Población: 21.000.000 de habitantes

Moneda: el bolívar

Idiomas: el español (oficial), varios idiomas indígenas

¡Fíjese!

Por su variedad de climas, Venezuela le ofrece al turista atracciones diversas. El clima venezolano varía entre el clima templado de las regiones andinas y el clima tropical de los llanos[a] y la costa. De hecho, el clima es agradable la mayor parte del año. Entre las atracciones turísticas hay lo siguiente:

- las hermosas[b] playas tropicales de la Isla Margarita y la costa caribeña
- la famosa catarata[c] Salto Ángel que, siendo dieciséis veces más alta que las cataratas del Niágara, es considerada la más alta del mundo
- la belleza[d] colonial de Ciudad Bolívar y Coro
- la progresiva y cosmopolita ciudad de Caracas y las majestuosas montañas andinas

[a]*plains* [b]*beautiful* [c]*waterfall* [d]*beauty*

Conozca a... Simón Bolívar

Simón Bolívar (1783–1830) nació en Caracas. La fecha de su cumpleaños, el 24 de julio, es hoy día una fiesta nacional en Venezuela. Bolívar, llamado «el Libertador», ocupa un puesto[a] importante tanto en la historia de Venezuela como en la historia de Colombia, el Perú, el Ecuador y Bolivia por ser el personaje principal en las luchas[b] por la independencia de estos países. Bolívar, influenciado por las ideas de Jean Jacques Rousseau[c] y por la lucha de las colonias estadounidenses contra Inglaterra en el siglo XVIII, soñaba con[d] una América hispánica unida, sueño que nunca vio realizado.[e]

[a]*position* [b]*struggles* [c]*French writer and philosopher* (1712–1778) *whose ideas helped spark the French Revolution* [d]soñaba... *dreamed about* [e]*achieved*

Salto Ángel

Capítulo 10 of the video to accompany *¿Qué tal?* contains cultural footage about Venezuela.

Visit the *¿Qué tal?* website at www.mhhe.com/quetal.

Multimedia: Internet
Have students look for the *Biblioteca Virtual* on the Internet. Here they can learn more about *Simón Bolívar* and other Latin American heroes and historical moments.

Paso 3: Gramática

See detailed supplementary materials for this grammar section in IM.

108 - 5 '03

30 Expressing *each other* • Reciprocal Actions with Reflexive Pronouns

—¿Tú crees que cada vez que nos encontramos tenemos que *saludarnos dándonos* la mano?[a]

[a]*hand*

1. ¿Dónde *se encuentran* los dos pulpos?
2. ¿Cómo *se saludan* (*do they greet each other*)?
3. ¿*Se conocen?* ¿Cómo se sabe?

Follow-up: Reciprocal Actions . . .
Ask questions to expand use of art: *Si los pulpos siguen conversando, ¿qué van a decir? ¿Cómo termina la conversación?*

The plural reflexive pronouns, **nos, os,** and **se**, can be used to express *reciprocal actions* (**las acciones recíprocas**). Reciprocal actions are usually expressed in English with *each other* or *one another*.

Nos queremos.

Nos queremos.	*We love each other.*
¿**Os** ayudáis?	*Do you help one another?*
Se miran.	*They're looking at each other.*

Práctica

A. Buenos amigos. Indique las oraciones que describen lo que hacen Ud. y un buen amigo / una buena amiga para mantener su amistad (*friendship*).

1. ☐ Nos vemos con frecuencia.
2. ☐ Nos conocemos muy bien. No hay secretos entre nosotros.
3. ☐ Nos respetamos mucho.
4. ☐ Nos ayudamos con cualquier (*any*) problema.
5. ☐ Nos escribimos cuando no estamos en la misma ciudad.
6. ☐ Nos hablamos por teléfono con frecuencia.
7. ☐ Nos decimos la verdad siempre, sea esta (*be it*) bonita o fea.
8. ☐ Cuando estamos muy ocupados, no importa si no nos hablamos por mucho tiempo.

B. ¿Qué se hacen? Describa las relaciones familiares o sociales en la siguiente página, haciendo oraciones completas con una palabra o frase de cada grupo.

Preliminary exercises A

- Ask students how to express in Spanish: **1.** We help each other. (you, they) **2.** We love each other. (you, they) **3.** We write to each other. (you, they)
- Have students restate as reciprocal actions: **1.** *Estela me mira a mí. Yo miro a Estela.* **2.** *Eduardo habla con Pepita. Pepita habla con Eduardo.* **3.** *El padre necesita a su hijo. El hijo necesita a su padre.* **4.** *Tomás me conoce a mí. Yo conozco a Tomás.* **5.** *Tú le escribes a Luisa. Luisa te escribe a ti.* **6.** *La profesora escucha a los estudiantes. Los estudiantes escuchan a la profesora.* **7.** *Ud. quiere a su esposo. Su esposo la quiere también a Ud.* **8.** *Jorge le da la mano a Mario. Mario le da la mano a Jorge.*

Suggestion A
Have students repeat items using *ellos* as subject, then *vosotros*.

Suggestion B
Provide cues for students to construct story about *La triste historia de amor de Orlando y Patricia.* Have students narrate story in preterite. **1.** *verse en clase* **2.** *mirarse* **3.** *saludarse* **4.** *empezar a llamarse por teléfono* **5.** *escribirse durante las vacaciones* **6.** *ayudarse con sus problemas* **7.** casarse (translate) **8.** *no llevarse bien* (translate) **9.** *separarse* **10.** *divorciarse*

Follow-up B
To personalize the construction, ask: *Ud. y sus amigos/as, ¿se llaman por teléfono? ¿se ven frecuentemente? ¿se ayudan? ¿se escriben? ¿se mandan regalos? ¿ ?*

Suggestions: En los Estados Unidos y el Canadá...
- Have students describe movie and TV roles Olmos has portrayed.
- Have students watch *American Me* or *Stand and Deliver* and prepare a report on it.
- Have students name other actor-activists and community leaders of Hispanic origin (César Chávez, *Enfoque cultural* in *Capítulo 1;* Martin Sheen, *En los Estados Unidos y el Canadá... , Capítulo 2;* state Sen. Richard Polanco, *En los Estados Unidos y el Canadá... , Capítulo 8*).

los buenos amigos los parientes los esposos los padres y los niños los amigos que no viven en la misma ciudad los profesores y los estudiantes los compañeros de cuarto/casa	(no)	verse con frecuencia quererse, respetarse ayudarse (con los problemas económicos o los problemas personales) hablarse (todos los días, con frecuencia, sinceramente) llamarse por teléfono (con frecuencia), escribirse mirarse (en la clase, con cariño [*affection*]) necesitarse conocerse bien saludarse, darse la mano

Conversación

Preguntas

1. ¿Con qué frecuencia se ven Ud. y su novio/a (esposo/a, mejor amigo/a)? ¿Cuánto tiempo hace que se conocen? ¿Con qué frecuencia se dan regalos? ¿se escriben? ¿se telefonean?
2. ¿Con qué frecuencia se ven Ud. y sus abuelos/primos? ¿Por qué se ven Uds. tan poco (tanto)? ¿Cómo se mantienen en contacto? En la sociedad norteamericana, ¿los parientes se ven con frecuencia? En su opinión, ¿es esto común entre los hispanos?

En los Estados Unidos y el Canadá...

Edward James Olmos: Actor y activista de la comunidad

El conocido **actor** de origen mexicano, Edward James Olmos (Los Ángeles, 1947), tiene en su historia profesional papeles inolvidables[a] como el de Jaime Escalante en *Stand and Deliver*, y el de policía en la famosa película cultista[b] *Blade Runner*. Además es un reconocido[c] **productor** y fue **director** y **guionista**[d] de la película *American Me*, sobre las pandillas[e] de Los Ángeles. Ha recibido los premios[f] Golden Globe y un Emmy.

Edward James Olmos

Pero el Sr. Olmos no es sólo un artista sino también un destacado[g] líder de la comunidad latina en los Estados Unidos. Su **trabajo humanitario** y **comunitario** demuestra[h] un profundo compromiso[i] a favor de **la juventud** y **la salud** y contra la violencia de las pandillas y el racismo. Entre los muchos cargos que ha desempeñado[j] están los de embajador[k] de los Estados Unidos en UNICEF, portavoz[l] nacional de la Fundación Juvenil contra la Diabetes, de la Fundación Alerta contra el **SIDA**[m] y del Registro de Votantes, además de ser miembro de varios comités que van desde hospitales para niños al Concejo Nacional de Adopción.

[a]papeles... *unforgettable roles* [b]*cult* [c]*well-known* [d]*scriptwriter* [e]*gangs* [f]Ha... *He has received the awards* [g]*distinguished* [h]*shows* [i]*commitment* [j]Entre... *Among the many positions he has held* [k]*ambassador* [l]*spokesperson* [m]Fundación... *AIDS Awareness Foundation*

UN POCO DE TODO

A. Lo mejor de estar enfermo

Paso 1. Form complete sentences using the words in the order given. Conjugate the verbs in the preterite or the imperfect and add or change words as needed. Use subject pronouns only when needed.

1. cuando / yo / ser / niño, / pensar / que / lo mejor / de / estar enfermo / ser / guardar cama
2. lo peor / ser / que / con frecuencia / (yo) resfriarse / durante / vacaciones
3. una vez / (yo) ponerme / muy / enfermo / durante / Navidad
4. mi / madre / llamar / a / médico / en / quien / tener / confianza
5. Dr. Matamoros / venir / casa / y / darme / antibiótico / porque / tener / mucho / fiebre
6. ser / cuatro / mañana / cuando / por fin / (yo) empezar / respirar / sin dificultad
7. desgraciadamente (*unfortunately*) / día / de / Navidad / (yo) tener / tomar / jarabe / y / no / gustar / nada / sabor (*taste, m.*)
8. lo bueno / de / este / enfermedad / ser / que / mi / padre / tener / dejar / fumar / mientras / yo / estar / enfermo

Paso 2. Now tell the story again from the point of view of the mother of the sick person. The first sentence is done for you.

MODELO: **1.** cuando / yo / ser / niño, / pensar / que / lo mejor / de / estar enfermo / ser / guardar cama → Cuando mi hijo era niño, pensaba que lo mejor de estar enfermo era guardar cama.

B. Caperucita Roja

Paso 1. Retell this familiar story, based on the drawings, sentences, and cues that accompany each drawing, using the imperfect or preterite of the verbs in parentheses. Add as many details as you can, using the **Vocabulario útil** box in the margin. Using context, try to guess the meaning of words that are glossed with ¿ ?

1. Érase una vez[a] una niña hermosa que (llamarse[1]) Caperucita Roja. Todos los animales del bosque[b] (ser[2]) sus amigos y Caperucita Roja los (querer[3]) mucho.
2. Un día su mamá le (decir[4]): —Lleva en seguida esta jarrita de miel[c] a casa de tu abuelita. Ten cuidado[d] con el lobo[e] feroz.

[a]¿ ? [b]¿ ? [c]jarrita... *jar of honey* [d]Ten... *Be careful* [e]¿ ?

Follow-up A
Have students change the story to accommodate authentic information about their childhood.

Follow-up B
Have students tell about an accident they had or were involved in.

Notes B
- This retelling of the Little Red Riding Hood story is an authentic version from Spain. You and the students may be familiar with other versions of the story. Encourage the students to provide additional details.
- *Había una vez, Había una vez y dos son tres,* and *Érase una vez* are traditional beginnings for tales. Some traditional endings include: *Y vivieron felices y comieron perdices: Y colorín, colorado, este cuento se ha acabado.*

Vocabulario útil

abalanzarse sobre	to pounce on
avisar	to warn
dispararle	to shoot at someone/something
esconderse	to hide
enterarse de	to find out about
huir (huyó)	to flee
saltar	to jump

1

2

❖ Transparency 66

Follow-up B

Have students retell the story in their own words in Spanish.

Variation B

Have students invent a new tale together in round-robin. The story can begin on one side of the room and "travel" from student to student. Each student says one sentence. Remind them to use the preterite and imperfect in the narration. Avoid direct correction. Repeat each sentence students say, rephrasing as necessary to correct errors.

(3)

(4)

(5)

(6)
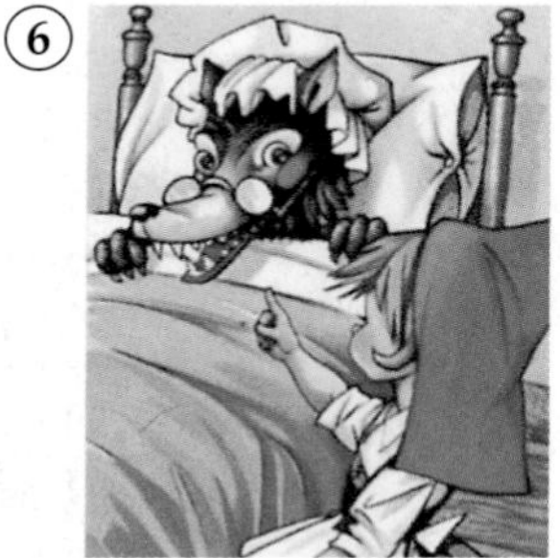

(7)

(8)

(9)

(10)

3. En el bosque, el lobo (salir[5]) a hablar con la niña. Le (preguntar[6]): —¿Adónde vas, Caperucita? Esta le (contestar[7]) dulcemente:[f] —Voy a casa de mi abuelita.
4. —Pues, si vas por este sendero,[g] vas a llegar antes, (decir[8]) el malvado[h] lobo. Él (irse[9]) por otro camino más corto.

[f]*sweetly* [g]*path* [h]¿ ?

5. El lobo (llegar[10]) primero a la casa de la abuelita y (entrar[11]) silenciosamente. La abuelita (tener[12]) mucho miedo. (*Ella:* Saltar[13]) de la cama y (correr[14]) a esconderse.
6. Caperucita Roja (llegar[15]) por fin a la casa de la abuelita. (*Ella:* Encontrar[16]) a su «abuelita», que (estar[17]) en la cama. Le (decir[18]): —¡Qué dientes tan largos tienes! —¡Son para comerte mejor!— (decir[19]) su «abuelita».
7. Una ardilla[i] del bosque (enterarse[20]) del peligro. Por eso (avisar[21]) a un cazador.[j]
8. El lobo (saltar[22]) de la cama y (abalanzarse[23]) sobre Caperucita. Ella (salir[24]) de la casa corriendo y pidiendo socorro[k] desesperadamente.

[i]¿ ? [j]¿ ? [k]*help*

9. El cazador (ver[25]) lo que (ocurrir[26]). (*Él:* Dispararle[27]) al lobo y le (hacer[28]) huir.
10. Caperucita (regresar[29]) a la casa de su abuelita. La (abrazar: *ella*[30]) y le (prometer[31]) escuchar siempre los consejos de su mamá.

Paso 2. Hay varias versiones del cuento de Caperucita Roja. La que Ud. acaba de leer termina felizmente, pero otras no. Con otros dos compañeros, vuelvan a contar la historia, empezando por el dibujo número 7. Inventen un diálogo más largo entre Caperucita y el lobo y cambien por completo el final del cuento.

WWW. Multimedia: Internet

Have students look for online versions of *Caperucita Roja* in Spanish. They can also find the following stories in Spanish on the Internet: *La Cenicienta, Peter Pan, Simbad el marino. Los tres cerditos, Blancanieves, El flautista de Hamelín*, and *Merlín el mago.*

Más vocabulario útil

atacar	to attack	**matar**	to kill
comérselo/la	to eat something up		

In the *Capítulo 10* segment of "Chapter-by-Chapter Supplementary Materials" in the IM, you will find a chapter-culminating activity. You can use this activity to consolidate and review the vocabulary and grammar skills students have acquired.

Paso 4: Un paso más
Optional section

 See IM for suggestions and follow-up activities to accompany the video segment.

VIDEOTECA: En contexto

In this video segment, Juan Carlos talks to the pharmacist about medication to ease his cold. What cold medications do you prefer? Do you believe that any medication can cure a cold?

Follow-up A
Ask: *¿Consulta Ud. algunas veces a los farmacéuticos en vez de ir al médico? ¿Para qué tipo de enfermedades?*

A. Lluvia de ideas

- ¿Se enferma Ud. a menudo? ¿De qué se enferma?
- ¿Va Ud. inmediatamente al consultorio médico cuando se siente mal o prefiere esperar a ver si se pone (*you get*) mejor/peor? ¿Por qué?
- En este episodio, el farmacéutico le dice a Juan Carlos que dormir es una de las mejores medicinas. ¿Qué hace Ud. para sentirse mejor?

Suggestion B
To check comprehension, ask: **1.** *Hay una palabra en el diálogo que puede ser sinónimo de «muy». ¿Cuál es?* **2.** *¿Qué le pasa a Juan Carlos? ¿Por qué va a la farmacia?*

B. Dictado

A continuación está la primera parte del diálogo entre Juan Carlos y el farmacéutico. Complétela con las palabras o frases que faltan.

FARMACÉUTICO: Buenas tardes, Juan Carlos. ¿__Cómo__[1] estás hoy? ¿__Mejor__?[2]
JUAN CARLOS: Pues, me __duele__[3] mucho la __garganta__[4] y estoy bien __resfriado__.[5]
FARMACÉUTICO: ¿Fuiste a ver al __médico__[6]?
JUAN CARLOS: Sí, tuve una consulta esta mañana.
FARMACÉUTICO: ¿Y qué te dijo?
JUAN CARLOS: Tengo una infección respiratoria. Me dio una __receta__[7] para un __antibiótico__.[8]

FUNCTION

Describing an illness

C. Un diálogo original

Paso 1. Con un compañero / una compañera, dramatice la escena entre Juan Carlos y el farmacéutico.

Paso 2. Consejos de sus padres. Imagine que Ud. y su compañero son miembros de una familia. Tengan la siguiente conversación.

E1: Ud. está bien resfriado/a. Hable con su mamá/papá u otro pariente para preguntarle lo que debe hacer Ud. para curarse. Por ejemplo, Ud. puede decirles que no sabe si debe ir al médico o no.

E2: Ud. es la mamá / el papá u otro pariente de su compañero/a y le dice lo que debe hacer para cuidarse cuando está enfermo/a. No se olvide de preguntarle por todos los síntomas posibles antes de dar sus consejos (*advice*).

Cultura en contexto *En la farmacia*

En muchas farmacias de Latinoamérica y España los productos están detrás del mostrador[a] y los clientes tienen que pedírselos al farmacéutico / a la farmacéutica. Incluso[b] pastillas como la aspirina no están al alcance[c] del cliente.

[a]*counter* [b]*Even* [c]al... *within reach*

PASO FINAL

A CONVERSAR

Note: A conversar
Remind students that the relationship between a pharmacist and a customer is generally a formal one. The pharmacist is considered a highly qualified medical professional who takes his or her responsibilities very seriously. This should be reflected in the language of the improvisation.

Suggestion: A conversar
Have students practice their scenes several times, then have volunteers present to the class.

En la farmacia

Como Ud. leyó en la **Nota cultural** de este capítulo, en muchos países hispanos la gente puede consultar a un farmacéutico / una farmacéutica en vez de ir al médico. La persona enferma describe sus síntomas y el farmacéutico / la farmacéutica o (*either*) le receta un medicamento apropiado o (*or*) le manda a ver al médico.

Paso 1. En una hoja de papel aparte, prepare un cuadro como el siguiente. En su cuadro, escriba los síntomas y los posibles tratamientos para las enfermedades en los espacios en blanco.

enfermedad	una infección de garganta	un resfriado	una migraña
síntomas			
tratamientos			

Paso 2. Con un compañero / una compañera, prepare una escena entre una persona enferma y un farmacéutico / una farmacéutica. Escojan el papel que quieren hacer e improvisen una escena basándose en los cuadros del **Paso 1**. Su escena debe incluir saludos, una descripción de los síntomas, las recomendaciones médicas y una despedida.

MODELO: E1: Buenos días, Sr. Maldonado.
E2: Buenos días, Sra. Velázquez. ¿En qué le puedo servir?
E1: Me siento muy mal hoy. No sé qué me pasa.
E2: ¿Qué síntomas tiene?…

Paso 3. Cambien papeles e improvisen la escena otra vez.

En resumen

GRAMÁTICA

To review the grammar points presented in this chapter, refer to the indicated grammar presentations. You'll find further practice of these structures in the Workbook/Laboratory Manual, on the CD-ROM, and on the website.

29. Using the Preterite and the Imperfect

Do you know which tense to use to express habitual or repeated actions? Which tense should be used to express the beginning or end of an action?

30. Reciprocal Actions and Reflexive Pronouns

Which reflexive pronouns are used in reciprocal constructions? How can you distinguish a reciprocal from a reflexive action?

VOCABULARIO

Los verbos

encontrarse (ue) (con) — to meet (*someone somewhere*)
saludarse — to greet each other

La salud y el bienestar

caminar — to walk
cuidarse — to take care of oneself
dejar de + *inf.* — to stop (*doing something*)
doler (ue) — to hurt, ache
encontrarse (ue) — to be, feel
examinar — to examine
guardar cama — to stay in bed
hacer (*irreg.*) **ejercicios aeróbicos** — to do aerobics
internarse (en) — to check in (*to a hospital*)
llevar una vida sana/tranquila — to lead a healthy/calm life
ponerle (*irreg.*) **una inyección** — to give (someone) a shot, injection
resfriarse (me resfrío) — to get/catch a cold
respirar — to breathe
sacar — to extract
  sacar la lengua — to stick out one's tongue
  sacar una muela — to extract a tooth
tener (*irreg.*) **dolor de** — to have a pain in
tomarle la temperatura — to take someone's temperature
toser — to cough

Repaso: comer, correr, dormir (ue, u), enfermarse, hacer (*irreg.*) **ejercicio, practicar deportes**

Algunas partes del cuerpo humano

la boca — mouth
la cabeza — head
el cerebro — brain
el corazón — heart
el diente — tooth
el estómago — stomach
la garganta — throat
la nariz — nose
el oído — inner ear
el ojo — eye
la oreja — outer ear
los pulmones — lungs
la sangre — blood

Las enfermedades y los tratamientos

el antibiótico — antibiotic
el chequeo — checkup
el consultorio — (medical) office
el dolor (de) — pain, ache (in)

la farmacia	pharmacy
la fiebre	fever
las gafas	glasses
el jarabe	(cough) syrup
los lentes de contacto	contact lenses
la medicina	medicine
el/la paciente	patient
la pastilla	pill
la receta	prescription
el resfriado	cold
la sala de emergencias/ urgencia	emergency room
la salud	health
el síntoma	symptom
la temperatura	temperature
la tos	cough

El personal médico

el/la dentista	dentist
el/la enfermero/a	nurse
el/la farmacéutico/a	pharmacist

Repaso: el/la médico/a

Suggestions: Vocabulario

- Describe absurd creatures and have students draw them, for example, *Era una criatura inmensa. Tenía tres piernas y un brazo. En la cabeza tenía una oreja que extendía de la frente...*
- Ask: **1.** *¿Con qué órgano o parte del cuerpo se asocian estas cosas? la comida, la música, el oxígeno, las películas, el amor, el cálculo* **2.** *¿Se refiere a la médica o al paciente? Examina los ojos. Tiene fiebre. Saca la lengua. Escribe recetas. Le duele la garganta. Recomienda un jarabe.*
- Ask: **1.** *Una persona come hamburguesas y toma Coca-Cola todo el tiempo. ¿Come bien o come mal?* **2.** *Si se tiene problemas del corazón, ¿se debe caminar o correr para hacer ejercicio?* **3.** *Si se duerme siete horas y media cada noche, ¿duerme lo suficiente o necesita dormir más?* (*lo suficiente*)

Los sustantivos

la desventaja	disadvantage
la ventaja	advantage

Los adjetivos

congestionado/a	congested
mareado/a	dizzy; nauseated
mismo/a	same

Palabras adicionales

de repente	suddenly
dos veces	twice
equilibradamente	in a balanced way
eso quiere decir...	that means . . .
lo bueno / lo malo	the good thing, news / the bad thing, news
lo suficiente	enough
por lo menos	at least
una vez	once

Presiones de la vida moderna

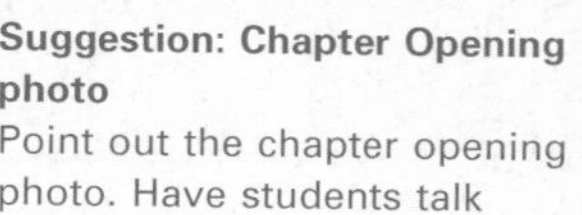

Suggestion: Chapter Opening photo
Point out the chapter opening photo. Have students talk about the campus and students in photo. Where are they going? How do they feel? Have them discuss their own situations as students, and their ideas about handling school-related stress. Encourage them to describe stress and accidents they have had.

Resources
You and your students may find the following *¿Qué tal?* supplements helpful as you teach this chapter:
For the Instructor
- *Instructor's Manual and Resource Kit,* "Chapter-by-Chapter" Supplementary Materials
- Testing Program
- Overhead Transparencies 67–68
- Video (VHS or CD)
- *¿Qué tal?* Online Learning Center Website
- Audioscript
- Instructor's Resource CD

VOCABULARIO

- Pressures of student life
- Accidents and clumsiness
- How things are done: Adverbs

GRAMÁTICA

31 Another Use of **se**
32 A Summary of the Uses of **por** and **para**

CULTURA

- **Enfoque cultural:** Puerto Rico
- **Nota cultural:** Palabras y frases para momentos difíciles
- **En los Estados Unidos y el Canadá:** Ricky Martin
- **Cultura en contexto:** El bar: Un pasatiempo social

Multimedia

You will learn about asking for and giving directions in the **En contexto** video segment.

Review vocabulary and grammar and practice language skills with the interactive CD-ROM.

WWW. Get connected to the Spanish-speaking world with the *¿Qué tal?* Online Learning Center: **www.mhhe.com/quetal**.

Students
rkbook/Laboratory Manual and Audio
gram or Electronic Workbook/
oratory Manual
eo on CD
eractive CD-ROM
ué tal? Online Learning Center Website
ening Comprehension Audio CD
Graw-Hill Electronic Language Tutor (MHELT)

Caminar es buena manera de aliviar (*to relieve*) el estrés. Estas estudiantes caminan en el campus de la Universidad de Puerto Rico en Río Piedras. ▶

PASO 1 Vocabulario

Paso 1: Vocabulario
See detailed supplementary materials and exercises for this section and a model for vocabulary presentation and other material in the *Capítulo 11 Paso 1: Vocabulario* section of "Chapter-by-Chapter Supplementary Materials," IM.

Las presiones de la vida estudiantil

Multimedia: Audio
Students can listen to and practice this chapter's vocabulary on their Listening Comprehension Audio CD.

Agenda:° del 1 al 7 de febrero

°*Appointment calendar*

1° al 7° de febrero

lunes, 1 de febrero
ir a la biblioteca (sacar libros para historia de arte)
informe oral de sociología

martes, 2 de febrero
examen de química

miércoles, 3 de febrero
recoger[a] nuevo permiso de estacionamiento

jueves, 4 de febrero
fecha límite para entregar informe[b] escrito para historia del arte

viernes, 5 de febrero
prueba[c] de español

sábado, 6 de febrero
hacer llave para apartamento
fiesta de cumpleaños para Rosa

domingo, 7 de febrero

[a]*pick up* [b]*report* [c]*test*

acordarse (ue) (de)	to remember
entregar	to turn, hand in
estacionar	to park
llegar a tiempo/tarde	to arrive early/late
pedir (i, i) disculpas	to apologize
Discúlpeme.	Pardon me. / I'm sorry.
¡Lo siento (mucho)!	Pardon me! / I'm (very) sorry!
Perdón.	Pardon me. / I'm sorry.
recoger	to collect; to pick up
sacar	to take out
sacar buenas/malas notas	to get good/bad grades
ser (*irreg.*) **flexible**	to be flexible
sufrir	to suffer
sufrir (muchas) presiones	to be under (a lot of) pressure

Otros sustantivos

el calendario	calendar
el despertador	alarm clock
la llave	key
la calificación	grade
el estrés	stress
el examen	exam
la (falta de) flexibilidad	(lack of) flexibility
la fecha límite	deadline
el horario	schedule
el informe (oral/escrito)	(oral/written) report
la prueba	quiz; test
la tarjeta de identificación	identification card
el trabajo	job, work; report, (piece of) work
de tiempo completo/parcial	full/part time

National Standards: Communication
Have a round table discussion in groups of 6 or more students on the stresses students suffer, strategies to avoid stress, and ways to alleviate stress. Have students pinpoint major causes of stress. As you study *Capítulo 11,* have the groups organize their ideas and create a pamphlet in Spanish that could be used to distribute to university students. The pamphlets can be presented as you finish the chapter.

Conversación

A. Asociaciones

Paso 1. ¿Qué palabras asocia Ud. con estos verbos? Pueden ser sustantivos, antónimos o sinónimos.

1. estacionar
2. recoger
3. acordarse
4. entregar
5. sacar

Paso 2. ¿Qué palabras y/o situaciones asocia Ud. con los siguientes sustantivos?

1. el calendario
2. el despertador
3. las calificaciones
4. el estrés
5. la fecha límite
6. el horario
7. los informes
8. la llave
9. la tarjeta identificación

B. Situaciones. La lista de la izquierda consta de (*consists of*) preguntas o comentarios hechos por varias personas. La otra incluye las respuestas de otras personas. Decida qué respuesta corresponde a cada comentario. Luego invente un contexto para cada diálogo. ¿Dónde están las personas que hablan? ¿En casa? ¿en una oficina? ¿en clase?

1. —Anoche no me acordé de poner el despertador.
2. —No puede estacionar el coche aquí. No tiene permiso de estacionamiento para esta zona.
3. —¿Sacaste una buena nota en la prueba?
4. —Ramiro no tiene buen aspecto (*doesn't look right*). Creo que algo le causa mucho estrés.
5. —Aquí tiene mi trabajo escrito sobre el Mercado Común.

a. —Pues estoy cansado de buscar estacionamiento por todo el *campus*. Lo voy a dejar aquí.
b. —¿Lo olvidaste otra vez? ¿A qué hora llegaste a la oficina?
c. —Pero la fecha límite era ayer. Es la última vez que acepto un informe suyo (*of yours*) tarde.
d. —Muy buena, pero no la esperaba. No tuve tiempo de estudiar.
e. —Es porque tiene un trabajo de tiempo completo, y también toma tres cursos este semestre.

Extension A
Have students give all the antonyms and synonyms they know for the following words: **1.** *abrir* **2.** *perder* **3.** *estar feliz* **4.** *llegar a tiempo* **5.** *ser flexible* **6.** *la tranquilidad.*

Variation A
Use a game format to get synonyms and antonyms. Divide the class into teams. Allow teams to work on each word for only one minute; the team with the most associations wins the round.

Preliminary exercise B
Have students answer: *¿Qué palabras o expresiones asocia Ud. con estos verbos?* **1.** *estacionar* **2.** *recoger* **3.** *acordarse* **4.** *entregar* **5.** *sacar ¿Qué palabras y/o situaciones asocia Ud. con estos sustantivos?* **1.** *el calendario* **2.** *el despertador* **3.** *las calificaciones* **4.** *el estrés* **5.** *la fecha límite* **6.** *el horario* **7.** *los informes* **8.** *las llaves* **9.** *la tarjeta de identificación*

Answers B
1. b **2.** a **3.** d **4.** e **5.** c

Suggestion B
Have students give possible reactions. Compare answers and vote on most original ones: *¿Cómo se debe o se puede reaccionar en estas situaciones?* **1.** *Son las seis de la mañana. Ud. oye el despertador pero todavía tiene sueño.* **2.** *Ud. quiere despedirse, pero la persona con quien está hablando quiere hablar más.* **3.** *Ud. está en Buenos Aires. Pierde su cartera y con ella todo su dinero y el pasaporte.* **4.** *Su vecino dejó su coche delante de su garaje y ahora Ud. no puede sacar su coche.* **5.** *Ud. sufre muchas presiones a causa de los exámenes finales.*

PASO 1

Heritage speakers
Muchos hispanohablantes dicen *Casi me caigo* o *Por poco me caigo;* usan el presente para expresar *I almost fell* (el pasado).

❖Transparencias 67, 68

¡La profesora Martínez se levantó con el pie izquierdo!°

°con... *on the wrong side of the bed*

Le duele la cabeza.

Se dio contra el escritorio. Se cayó y se lastimó la pierna.

«Fue sin querer. Estaba distraída».

Accidentes

caerse	to fall down
darse (*irreg.*) **en/con/contra**	to hit (a part of one's body)/to run into/bump against
Se dio en el pie.	She bumped her foot.
Se dio con la silla.	She ran into the chair.
Se dio contra la puerta.	She bumped against the door.
doler (ue)	to hurt, ache
equivocarse	to be wrong, make a mistake
hacerse (*irreg.*) **daño**	to hurt oneself
lastimarse	to injure oneself
pegar	to hit, strike
pegarse en/con/contra	to run, bump into
romper	to break
Fue sin querer.	It was unintentional.
distraído/a	absentminded
torpe	clumsy

Reciclado: ¡La profesora... !

- Recycle clothing vocabulary: *¿Qué parte del cuerpo asocia Ud. con... ?* **1.** *el reloj* **2.** *los pantalones* **3.** *el sombrero* **4.** *la camisa* **5.** *los zapatos* **6.** *los guantes.*
- Recycle subjunctive. This activity is designed for recognition of forms and conceptualization. Have students respond *cierto* or *falso.* **1.** *Si una persona se da con la cabeza contra una puerta, es lógico que le duela.* **2.** *Si una persona sufre muchas presiones, es posible que también tenga más accidentes.* **3.** *Es cierto que todos trabajamos mal cuando estamos bajo muchas presiones.* **4.** *Es probable que la vida moderna cause más problemas que beneficios.* **5.** *Es bueno que una persona tome aspirinas cuando le duele el estómago.*

Conversación

A. Posibilidades. ¿Qué puede Ud. hacer o decir —o qué le puede pasar— en cada situación?

1. A Ud. le duele mucho la cabeza.
2. Ud. le pega a otra persona sin querer.
3. Ud. se olvida del nombre de otra persona.
4. Ud. está muy distraído/a y no mira por dónde camina.
5. Ud. se lastima la mano (el pie).

NOTA CULTURAL

Palabras y frases para momentos difíciles

Hay muchas expresiones para ocasiones de mala suerte[a] o de presión. Varían mucho de región en región y de país en país. Estas son algunas de las más comunes.

Para expresar dolor, sorpresa o compasión

¡Ay!	*Ah! Ouch!*	¿Qué le vamos a hacer?	*What can you do?*
¡Uy!	*Oops! Oh!*	¡No me digas!	*You're kidding! (You don't say!)*
¡No puede ser!	*That can't be!*		

Para dar ánimo[b]

¡Venga!	*Come on!*	¡No es para tanto!	*It's not so bad!*
¡Órale! (*Méx.*)	*Come on!*	¡Anímate!	*Cheer up!*

[a]*luck* [b]Para... *To cheer*

B. Accidentes y tropiezos (*mishaps*)

Paso 1. ¿Le han pasado a Ud. alguna vez las siguientes cosas? Complete las oraciones con información verdadera para Ud. Si nunca le pasó nada de esto, invente una situación que podría haber ocurrido (*could have happened*).

1. Me caí por las escaleras (*stairs*) y ____.
2. No me acordé de hacer la tarea para la clase de ____.
3. Me equivoqué cuando ____.
4. El despertador sonó, pero ____.
5. No pude encontrar ____.
6. Me di con ____ y me lastimé ____.
7. Pasó la fecha límite para entregar un informe y ____.
8. Caminaba un poco distraído/a y ____.

Paso 2. Ahora usando las oraciones del **Paso 1** como guía, pregúntele a un compañero / una compañera cómo le fue ayer. También puede preguntarle si le pasaron desastres adicionales.

MODELO: ¿Te caíste por las escaleras ayer? ¿Te hiciste daño?

Talking about How Things Are Done: Adverbs

- You already know some of the most common Spanish *adverbs* (**los adverbios**). Note that the form of adverbs is invariable.

bien	mucho	pronto	siempre
mal	poco	a tiempo	nunca
mejor	más	tarde	sólo
peor	menos	temprano	muy

- Adverbs that end in *-ly* in English usually end in **-mente** in Spanish. The suffix **-mente** is added to the feminine singular form of adjectives. Adverbs ending in **-mente** have two stresses: one on the adjective stem and the other on **-men**. The stress on the adjective stem is the stronger of the two.

Adjective	Adverb	English
rápido	**rápidamente**	*rapidly*
fácil	**fácilmente**	*easily*
valiente	**valientemente**	*bravely*

- In Spanish, adverbs modifying a verb are placed as close to the verb as possible. When they modify adjectives or adverbs, they are placed directly before them.

Hablan **estupendamente** el español.
They speak Spanish marvelously.

Ese libro es **poco** interesante.*
That book is not very interesting.

Vamos a llegar **muy tarde**.
We're going to arrive very late.

Preliminary exercise A
Have students give corresponding adverb (rapid response): **1.** *práctico* **2.** *especial* **3.** *perfecto* **4.** *triste* **5.** *alegre* **6.** *felíz* **7.** *final* **8.** *típico* **9.** *personal* **10.** *rápido* **11.** *leal* **12.** *elegante* **13.** *cariñoso* **14.** *tranquilo* **15.** *directo*

Conversación

Follow-up A
Have students tell what actions they associate with the following adverbs. Have them create sentences about themselves. *¿Qué acción personal asocia Ud. con los siguientes adverbios?* **1.** *infrecuentemente* **2.** *lentamente* **3.** *tristemente* **4.** *felizmente* **5.** *fielmente* **6.** *fabulosamente*

Follow-up B
- Have students complete sentences. Model your own answer for each sentence, then follow up with a question: *Yo ______ rápidamente, pero no ______ rápidamente,* → *Yo leo rápidamente, pero no escribo rápidamente. ¿Y Ud.? ¿Qué hace rápidamente?* **1.** *Yo ______ rápidamente. pero no ______ rápidamente.* **2.** *Yo siempre ______ tranquilamente.* **3.** *Yo ______ mejor que mis padres.* **4.** *Yo ______ peor que mi mejor amigo/a.*

A. ¡Seamos (*Let's be*) **lógicos!** Complete estas oraciones lógicamente con adverbios basados en los siguientes adjetivos: **constante, directo, fácil, inmediato, paciente, posible, puntual, rápido, total, tranquilo**.

1. La familia está esperando _____ en la cola.
2. Hay examen mañana y tengo que empezar a estudiar _____.
3. ¿Las enchiladas? Se preparan _____.
4. ¿Qué pasa? Estoy _____ confundido/a (*confused*).
5. Cuando mira la tele, mi hermanito cambia el canal _____.
6. Es necesario que las clases empiecen _____.

B. Entrevista. Con un compañero / una compañera, haga y conteste las siguientes preguntas.

1. ¿Qué haces rápidamente?
2. ¿Qué te toca hacer inmediatamente?
3. ¿Qué hiciste (comiste,...) solamente una vez que te gustó muchísimo?
4. ¿Qué haces tú fácilmente que es difícil para otras personas?

*Note that in Spanish one equivalent of *not very + adjective* is **poco** + *adjective*.

- Ask: **1.** *¿Habla Ud. solamente en español en esta clase?* **2.** *¿Llega Ud. puntualmente a todas sus clases?* **3.** *En la librería, ¿espera Ud. pacientemente en cola cuando compra libros?* **4.** *Cuando recibe correo electrónico de un amigo / una amiga, ¿le responde inmediatamente?*

Paso 2: Gramática
See detailed supplementary materials for this grammar section in IM.

31 Expressing Unplanned or Unexpected Events • Another Use of *se*

Note: Another Use of *se*
Aim for partial control. This can include a few fixed or memorized sentences, such as, *se me olvidó, se me perdió,* and so on.

Un día fatal

A Diego *se le cayó* la taza de café.

También *se le perdió* la cartera.

A Antonio *se le olvidaron* sus libros y su trabajo cuando fue a clase.

También *se le perdieron* las llaves de su apartamento.

¿Le pasaron a Ud. las mismas cosas —o cosas parecidas (*similar*)— esta semana? Conteste, completando las oraciones.

1. (Se me perdieron / No se me perdieron) las llaves de mi coche/casa.
2. (Se me olvidó / No se me olvidó) una reunión importante.
3. (Se me cayó / No se me cayó) una taza de café.
4. (Se me rompió / No se me rompió) un objeto de mucho valor (*value*) sentimental.

Extension: Another use of *se*
Provide additional situations for *Un día fatal*: **5.** (*No*) *Se me acabó el dinero cuando estaba de vacaciones.* **6.** (*No*) *Se me olvidó hacer una tarea importante.* **7.** (*No*) *Se me perdieron unos apuntes de clase.* **8.** (*No*) *Se me rompió el brazo.*

A. Unplanned or unexpected events (*I dropped . . . , We lost . . . , You forgot . . .*) are frequently expressed in Spanish with **se** and a third person form of the verb. In this structure, the occurrence is viewed as happening *to* someone—the unwitting recipient of the action. Thus the victim is indicated by an indirect object pronoun, often clarified by **a** + *noun* or *pronoun*. In such sentences, the subject (the thing that is dropped, broken, forgotten, and so on) usually follows the verb.

Se le olvidaron las llaves.
He forgot the keys. (*The keys were forgotten by him.*)

(*a* + Noun or Pronoun)	*se*	Indirect Object Pronoun	Verb	Subject
(A mí)	Se	me	cayó	la taza de café.
¿(A ti)	Se	te	perdió	la cartera?
A Antonio	se	le	olvidaron	los apuntes.

The verb agrees with the grammatical subject of the Spanish sentence (**la taza, la cartera, los apuntes**), not with the indirect object pronoun. **No** immediately precedes **se**.

A Antonio ***no se*** **le olvidaron los apuntes.**
Antonio didn't forget his notes.

B. Here are some verbs frequently used in this construction.

Note: Although all indirect object pronouns can be used in this construction, this section will focus on the singular of first, second, and third persons (**se me... , se te... , se le...**).

acabar	to finish; to run out of
caer	to fall
olvidar	to forget
perder (ie)	to lose
quedar	to remain, be left
romper	to break

Práctica

Preliminary exercises A

- Ask students what indirect object pronoun they hear: **1.** *Se me olvidó el bolígrafo.* **2.** *Se le rompieron los platos.* **3.** *Se nos cayeron las flores.* **4.** *Se te acabó la gasolina.* **5.** *Se nos quedaron en casa los boletos.*
- Dictate: **1.** *Se me cayeron las llaves.* **2.** *Se nos rompieron los vasos.* **3.** *A Pepe se le rompió el despertador.* **4.** *A María se le olvidaron las aspirinas.* Follow-up dictation with questions to check comprehension or by having students provide the English equivalents.
- Do chain drill to practice structure. *¡Qué distraídos estuvimos todos ayer! Dé oraciones nuevas según las indicaciones:* **1.** *A Pablo se le olvidó la cartera.* (*mí, nosotros, Inés, ti, los chicos, vosotros*) **2.** *¿Se te perdieron las llaves otra vez?* (*Ernesto, Uds. niña, mí, vosotros*) **3.** *María fue la más distraída de todos. Se le olvidó / olvidaron...* (*tomar el desayuno, las gafas, estudiar para el examen, los cheques, venir a clase*)
- Have students give Spanish equivalents: **1.** I dropped the glasses / plate / books. **2.** Robert lost the book / keys / alarm clock.

A. ¡Qué mala memoria! Hortensia sufre muchas presiones en su vida. Por eso cuando se fue de vacaciones al Perú, estaba tan distraída que se le olvidó hacer muchas cosas importantes antes de salir. Empareje (*Match*) los lapsos de Hortensia con las consecuencias.

LAPSOS

1. _____ Se le olvidó cerrar la puerta de su casa.
2. _____ Se le olvidó pagar sus cuentas.
3. _____ Se le olvidó pedirle a alguien que cuidara a (*to take care of*) su perro.
4. _____ Se le olvidó cancelar el periódico.
5. _____ Se le olvidó pedirle permiso a su jefa (*boss*).
6. _____ Se le olvidó llevar el pasaporte.
7. _____ Se le olvidó hacer reserva en un hotel.

CONSECUENCIAS

a. Va a perder el trabajo.
b. No la van a dejar entrar en el Perú.
c. Le van a suspender el servicio de la luz (*electricity*) y de gas... ¡y cancelar sus tarjetas de crédito!
d. Alguien le va a robar el televisor.
e. ¡«King» se va a morir!
f. No va a tener dónde alojarse (*to stay*).
g. Todos van a saber que no está en casa.

B. ¡Desastres por todas partes (*everywhere*)**!**

Paso 1. ¿Es Ud. una persona distraída o torpe? Indique las oraciones que se apliquen (*apply*) a Ud. Puede cambiar algunos de los detalles de las oraciones si es necesario.

1. ☐ Con frecuencia se me caen los libros (los platos,…).
2. ☐ Se me pierden constantemente las llaves (los calcetines,…).
3. ☐ A menudo (*Often*) se me olvida apagar la computadora (la luz,…).
4. ☐ Siempre se me rompen las gafas (las lámparas,…).
5. ☐ De vez en cuando se me quedan los libros (los cuadernos,…) en la clase.
6. ☐ Se me olvida fácilmente mi horario (el teléfono de algún amigo,…).

Paso 2. ¿Es Ud. igual ahora que cuando era más joven? Complete cada oración del **Paso 1** para describir cómo era de niño/a. No se olvide de usar el imperfecto en sus oraciones.

MODELO: De niño/a, (no) se me caían los libros con frecuencia.

Paso 3. Ahora compare sus respuestas con las de un compañero / una compañera. ¿Quién es más distraído/a o torpe ahora? ¿Quién lo era de niño/a?

Follow-up B
Paso 2. Ask students: *¿Qué más le pasaba a Ud.? ¿Qué ha cambiado?* Have students give sentences with actions that used to happen to them but do not happen to them anymore: *Antes se me perdían las gafas. Ahora se me pierden los suéteres.*

En los Estados Unidos y el Canadá…

Ricky Martin

Enrique Martín Morales es el puertorriqueño que todo el mundo[a] conoce como **Ricky Martin.** Nació el día de Nochebuena, 1971, en San Juan, Puerto Rico. Desde niño sabía que quería ser artista. En 1984, cuando tenía solamente 12 años, se presentó a un *casting call* para sustituir a un miembro del famoso grupo juvenil **Menudo,** y ¡ganó el puesto! Se quedó con Menudo hasta 1989, y desde entonces no sólo ha sido[b] cantante sino[c] también actor. Desempeñó un papel[d] en una telenovela en México y otro en el programa norteamericano «**General Hospital**» en 1994.

Ricky Martin

Al talentoso Ricky Martin le gusta todo tipo de música y puede cantar con igual[e] facilidad en inglés como en español. Aunque[f] el español es su lengua materna y siempre cantará[g] en español, le gusta la posibilidad de comunicarse con el público norteamericano también. A finales del siglo XX[h] tuvo un tremendo éxito en los Estados Unidos y en el resto del mundo con su álbum «**Livin' La Vida Loca**» y la canción del mismo nombre. Los hispanos no se sorprendieron; ya lo conocían muy bien.

[a]todo… *everybody* [b]ha… *has he been* [c]*but* [d]Desempeñó… *He played a part* [e]*the same* [f]*Although* [g]*he will sing* [h]A… *At the end of the twentieth century*

Suggestion: En los Estados Unidos y el Canadá…

- To check comprehension, ask: **1.** *¿Cuál es el nombre de nacimiento* (birth) *de Ricky?* **2.** *¿Cuándo y dónde nació? ¿En qué grupo cantó desde los 12 a los 17 años? ¿Qué otra actividad artística se puede asociar con Ricky?*
- Play some songs in Spanish by Ricky Martin in class. You might prepare a fill-in-the-blank worksheet from lyrics for students to complete as they listen.

Multimedia: Internet
Have students search the Internet for the official website and other sites about Ricky Martin with photos, music clips, and biographical information.

Suggestions: Conversación

- Have volunteers answer: *¿Recuerda Ud. alguno de los días más desastrosos de su vida? ¿Qué le pasó?*
- Have students work in groups to discuss their most recent *día fatal*.

Conversación

A. Pablo tuvo un día fatal

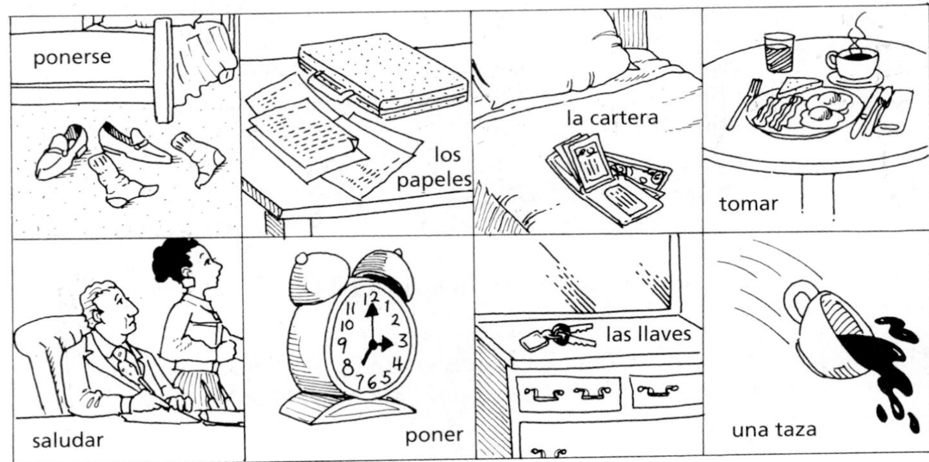

Paso 1. Lea la siguiente descripción de lo que le pasó a Pablo ayer. Va a usar los números entre paréntesis en el **Paso 2**.

Pablo no se levantó a las siete, como lo hace generalmente. Se levantó tarde, a las ocho. (1) Se vistió rápidamente y salió de casa descalzo.[a] (2) Entró en el garaje pero no pudo abrir la puerta del coche. (3) Por eso tuvo que llegar a la oficina en autobús, pero cuando quiso pagarle al conductor, no tenía dinero. (4) Por eso tuvo que llegar a pie.

Cuando Pablo por fin entró a la oficina, su jefa se ofendió porque Pablo la trató descortésmente. (5) Su primer cliente se enojó porque Pablo no tenía toda la información necesaria para resolver su caso. (6)

Para las diez de la mañana, Pablo tenía muchísima hambre. (7) Por eso fue a la cafetería a comer algo. Se sentó con el vicepresidente de la compañía. Muy pronto este[b] se levantó furioso de la mesa. (8) Dijo que su chaqueta estaba arruinada. ¡Pablo ya no podía más! También se levantó y regresó a casa.

[a]*barefoot* [b]*the latter*

Paso 2. Ahora, con un compañero / una compañera, haga y conteste preguntas para explicar por qué Pablo lo pasó tan mal ayer. La primera persona debe hacer una pregunta. La segunda persona debe contestar, usando las sugerencias en los dibujos. El número uno ya está hecho (*done*).

MODELO: (1) →
E1: ¿Por qué se levantó tarde Pablo?
E2: Porque se le olvidó poner el despertador.

Frases útiles: Se le olvidó/olvidaron… , Se le perdió/perdieron… , Se le cayó/cayeron… , Se le quedó/quedaron…

NOTA COMUNICATIVA

Telling How Long Something Has Been Happening / How Long Ago Something Happened

- In Spanish, the phrase **hace** + *period of time* + **que** + *present tense* is used to express an action that has been going on over a period of time and is still going on.

  —**¿Cuánto tiempo hace que** vives en esta residencia?
  How long have you been living in this dorm?

  —**Dos meses.**
  (For) Two months.

- To say how long *ago* something happened, use the same **hace… que** construction but with the preterite tense instead of the present. Notice also the omission of **que** when the **hace** phrase does not come at the beginning of the sentence.

  Hace tres años **que fui** a Bogotá.
  I went to Bogotá three years ago.

  Fui a Cancún **hace** un mes.
  I went to Cancún a month ago.

B. ¿Quién… ?

¿Quién hace qué? Haga oraciones completas emparejando (*matching*) las personas con las acciones correspondientes.

MODELO: hace mucho tiempo que / profesor(a) / enseñar español → Hace mucho tiempo que el profesor / la profesora enseña español.

Hace mucho/poco tiempo que…

Gloria Estefan
Sammy Sosa
Antonio Banderas
los «Teletubbies»
John Grisham
el rector / la rectora (*president*) de la universidad
el profesor / la profesora de español
un compañero / una compañera de clase

hacen programs para niños
canta en español
habla español
vive en esta ciudad
escribe novelas
juega al béisbol
trabaja en esta universidad
trabaja en Hollywood
¿ ?

Preliminary exercises B

- Have students give appropriate formal commands: *¿Qué sugerencias tiene Ud. para estas personas?* **1.** *Hace una semana que Juan no abre su libro de español y tiene un examen mañana.* **2.** *Hace dos días que Amanda no come. Está a dieta.* **3.** *Sara tiene un fuerte dolor de cabeza y hace doce horas que tomó la última aspirina.* **4.** *Hace un mes que Raúl llamó a sus padres la última vez.*
- Have students form sentences, for example, *Julio / trabajar / una hora* → *Hace una hora que Julio trabaja.* You can put cues on transparency or on board, or they can be dictated. **1.** *yo / descansar / una hora* **2.** *tú / cocinar / media hora* **3.** *Jaime / estudiar / dos horas* **4.** *nosotros / leer / hora y media* **5.** *niños / escribir cartas / dos horas* **6.** *Tina / hablar por teléfono / veinte minutos*
- Have students tell how long ago they did the following things: **1.** you were born (*nacer: nací*) **2.** you moved (*mudarse*) to this town **3.** you met your best friend **4.** you handed in your last major paper

Suggestions B

- Give names of famous people and have students provide sentences following pattern from activity. *Gabriel García Márquez, el Presidente ______. Oprah Winfrey, Mariah Carey,* and so on.
- Have students tell what they feel like doing in the following situations: *¿Qué tienen ganas de hacer en las siguientes situaciones?* **1.** *Están en casa. Hace tres horas que escriben ejercicios de español.* **2.** *Hace dos meses que viven en la residencia y siempre hay mucho ruido.* **3.** *Hace diez años que tienen un coche viejo que no funciona bien.* **4.** *Están en una discoteca. Hace media hora que bailan.*

Enfoque cultural

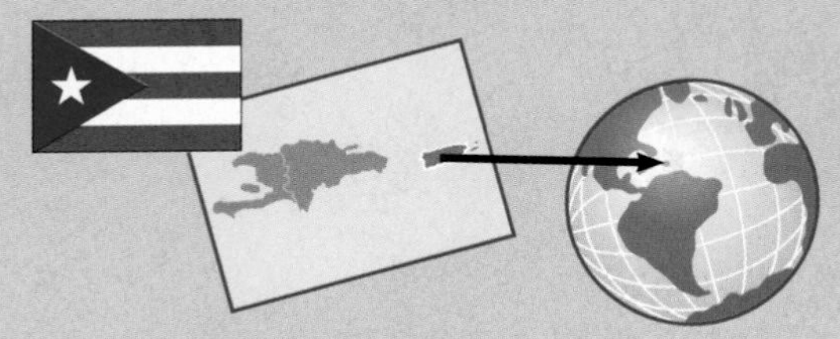

Puerto Rico

Enfoque cultural
See follow-up activities for this section in chapter-by-chapter materials in IM.

Datos esenciales

Nombre oficial: Estado Libre Asociado[a] de Puerto Rico

Capital: San Juan

Población: 4.000.000 de habitantes

Moneda: el dólar estadounidense

Idiomas oficiales: el español y el inglés

[a]Estado... *Free Associated State*

Una calle en el viejo San Juan

¡Fíjese!

- Puerto Rico ha estado relacionado[a] políticamente con los Estados Unidos desde la Guerra hispano-norteamericana de 1898, año en que España perdió las ultimas colonias de su imperio. En 1952, Puerto Rico se convirtió en Estado Libre Asociado. Bajo[b] este sistema de gobierno, los puertorriqueños son ciudadanos[c] estadounidenses. Sin embargo,[d] los que viven en la isla no pueden votar por el presidente de los Estados Unidos y deben servir en el ejército[e] de ese país en caso de guerra.

[a]ha... *has been associated* [b]*Under* [c]*citizens* [d]Sin... *However* [e]*army*

- Otro nombre de Puerto Rico es Borinquen y los puertorriqueños se conocen también como boricuas. Estas palabras originaron en el lenguaje de los indios taínos. Los taínos llegaron a la isla en el siglo[f] XIII pero su cultura casi desapareció con la llegada de los españoles en 1493.
- El Parque Nacional del Yunque, ubicado[g] en una montaña de 1.065 metros de altura que está al noreste de la isla, es pequeño cuando se compara a otros bosques[h] nacionales, pero es el único bosque tropical del sistema de Bosques nacionales de los Estados Unidos.

[f]*century* [g]*located* [h]*forests*

Conozca a... Alonso Ramírez

En 1690 se publica en México la primera novela del Nuevo Mundo, *Infortunios[a] de Alonso Ramírez.* Aunque esta obra[b] se atribuyó al mexicano Carlos Sigüenza y Góngora, hoy se cree que el verdadero[c] autor fue el mismo Alonso Ramírez del título. También se cree que la obra no es ficticia, sino autobiográfica: la vida de un puertorriqueño que se cría[d] en la isla, viaja a México y tiene aventuras en muchas partes del Mar Pacífico. Sus aventuras incluyen batallas contra piratas, una estadía[e] en una isla desierta y muchos otros eventos interesantísimos. Es una novela que vale la pena[f] leer.

[a]*Misfortunes* [b]*work* [c]*real* [d]se... *is brought up* [e]*stay* [f]que... *that is worth the trouble*

Capítulo 11 of the video to accompany *¿Qué tal?* contains cultural footage of Puerto Rico.

Visit the *¿Qué tal?* website at www.mhhe.com/quetal.

Paso 3: Gramática
See detailed supplementary materials for this grammar section in IM.

Note: ***Por* and *para***
Students already know the most important uses of these prepositions.

32 *¿Por o para?* • A Summary of Their Uses

108 - A'03

¿Qué se representa?

a.

b.

c.

d.

Empareje cada dibujo con la oración que le corresponde.

1. _____ Le da mil pesos *para* las revistas.
2. _____ Le da mil pesos *por* las revistas.
3. _____ Van *por* las montañas.
4. _____ Van *para* las montañas.

You have been using the prepositions **por** and **para** throughout your study of Spanish. Although most of the information in this section will be a review, you will also learn some new uses of **por** and **para**.

POR

The preposition **por** has the following English equivalents.

• *by, by means of*	Vamos **por** avión (tren, barco,...). *We're going by plane (train, ship, . . .).* Nos hablamos **por** teléfono mañana. *We'll talk by (on the) phone tomorrow.*
• *through, along*	Me gusta pasear **por** el parque y **por** la playa. *I like to stroll through the park and along the beach.*
• *during, in* (time of day)	Trabajo **por** la mañana. *I work in the morning.*
• *because of, due to*	Estoy nervioso **por** la entrevista. *I'm nervous because of the interview.*
• *for = in exchange for*	Piden 1.000 dólares **por** el coche. *They're asking $1,000 for the car.* Gracias **por** todo. *Thanks for everything.*

- *for = for the sake of, on behalf of*

Lo hago **por** ti.
I'm doing it for you (for your sake).

- *for = duration* (often omitted)

Vivieron allí (**por**) un año.
They lived there for a year.

Por is also used in a number of fixed expressions.

por Dios	for heaven's sake
por ejemplo	for example
por eso	that's why
por favor	please
por fin	finally
por lo general	generally, in general
por lo menos	at least
por primera/última vez	for the first/last time
por si acaso	just in case
¡por supuesto!	of course!
por todas partes	everywhere

PARA

Although **para** has many English equivalents, including *for,* it always has the underlying purpose of referring to a goal or destination.

- *in order to* + infinitive

Regresaron pronto **para** estudiar.
They returned soon (in order) to study.

Estudian **para** conseguir un buen trabajo.
They're studying (in order) to get a good job.

- *for = destined for, to be given to*

Todo esto es **para** ti.
All this is for you.

Le di un libro **para** su hijo.
I gave her a book for her son.

- *for = by* (deadline, specified future time)

Para mañana, estudien **por** y **para**.
*For tomorrow, study **por** and **para**.*

La composición es **para** el lunes.
The composition is for Monday.

- *for = toward, in the direction of*

Salió **para** el Ecuador ayer.
She left for Ecuador yesterday.

• *for = to be used for*	El dinero es **para** la matrícula. *The money is for tuition.*
OJO Compare the example at the right to **un vaso de agua** = *a glass (full) of water.*	Es un vaso **para** agua. *It's a water glass.*
• *for = as compared with others, in relation to others.*	**Para** mí, el español es fácil. *For me, Spanish is easy.* **Para** (ser) extranjera, habla muy bien el inglés. *For (being) a foreigner, she speaks English very well.*
• *for = in the employ of*	Trabajan **para** el gobierno. *They work for the government.*

Preliminary exercise: Práctica
Have students respond *por* or *para* to indicate the correct prepositions: **1.** We stayed for 3 days. **2.** We drove through the park. **3.** The report is for Monday. **4.** They left for Alaska. **5.** The money is for his mom. **6.** Math is hard for me. **7.** We canceled the trip for 2 reasons. **8.** This class is for advanced students.

Práctica

¿Por o para? Complete los siguientes diálogos y oraciones con **por** o **para**.

1. Los señores Arana salieron ___para___ el Perú ayer. Van ___por___ avión, claro, pero luego piensan viajar en coche ___por___ todo el país. Van a estar allí ___por___ dos meses. Va a ser una experiencia extraordinaria ___para___ toda la familia.
2. Mi prima Graciela quiere estudiar ___para___ (ser) doctora. ___Por___ eso trabaja ___para___ un médico ___por___ la mañana; tiene clases ___por___ la tarde.
3. —¿ ___Por___ qué están Uds. aquí todavía? Yo pensaba que iban a dar un paseo ___por___ el parque.
   —Íbamos a hacerlo, pero no fuimos ___por___ la nieve.
4. Este cuadro fue pintado (*was painted*) por Picasso ___para___ expresar los desastres de la guerra (*war*). ___Para___ muchos críticos de arte, es la obra maestra de este artista.
5. La «Asociación Todo ___Por___ Ellos» trabaja ___para___ las personas mayores, ___para___ ayudarlos cuando lo necesitan. ¿Trabaja Ud. ___Para___ alguna asociación de voluntarios? ¿Qué hizo ___para___ inscribirse (*sign-up*)?

ASOCIACION
TODO
POR
ELLOS
Trabajamos por las personas mayores que están solas y con escasos recursos económicos
AYÚDANOS, NO ES POSIBLE SIN TI
Para más información llama al teléfono 907 98 91 15, de 18.00 a 20.00 h. tardes, martes y viernes
CAJAMADRID, SUC. 1028
C/C 6000854579
TODO POR ELLOS es una asociación no gubernamental inscrita en el Registro de Asociaciones del Ministerio del Interior con el número 160.589

Suggestions: Práctica
- Have students give reason for each use of *por* or *para*. Expand items with personal questions.
- To personalize the structures, ask: **1.** *¿Para qué (profesión) estudia Ud.?* **2.** *¿Para qué compañía trabaja Ud. (su padre / madre, su esposo/a)?* **3.** *Para Ud., ¿son más difíciles los exámenes escritos o los orales? ¿los exámenes de matemáticas o los de historia?* **4.** *¿Tiene Ud. mucho que hacer para mañana? ¿mucho que leer? ¿mucho que escribir?* **5.** *¿Tiene Ud. que comprar algo esta noche? ¿o para su casa / apartamento / cuarto? ¿algo para un amigo? ¿algo para la familia?*
- For item **5**, ask: *¿Qué se puede hacer por las personas mayores?*

Conversación

Entrevista. Hágale preguntas a su profesor(a) para saber la siguiente información.

1. la tarea para mañana y para la semana que viene
2. lo que hay que estudiar para el próximo examen
3. si para él/ella son interesantes o aburridas las ciencias
4. la opinión que tiene de la pronunciación de Uds., para ser principiantes
5. qué debe hacer Ud. para mejorar su pronunciación del español

UN POCO DE TODO

Answers: Un poco de todo
1. *nuestra* 2. *disfruta* 3. *anteriores* 4. *Por* 5. *está* 6. *tenemos* 7. *muy* 8. *eran* 9. *para* 10. *estar* 11. *que* 12. *es* 13. *Para* 14. *esto* 15. *todas* 16. *deben* 17. *para* 18. *sufren* 19. *ponerse* 20. *esta* 21. *sentarnos* 22. *establecer* 23. *para*

Follow-up: Un poco de todo
Ask: **1.** *¿Para qué tipos de enfermedades hay vacunas?* (*la polio, la hepatitis, el sarampión* [measles], *¿ ?*) **2.** *¿Qué tareas es necesario hacer casi a diario en una casa donde hay niños pequeños? ¿Tiene Ud. experiencia personal en ese aspecto?* **3.** *¿Qué actividades y aficiones son buenas para «poner un poco de calma» en nuestra vida? ¿Cuáles prefiere Ud. para aliviar el estrés?*

In the *Capítulo 11* segment of "Chapter-by-Chapter Supplementary Materials" in the IM, you will find a chapter-culminating activity. You can use this activity to consolidate and review the vocabulary and grammar skills students have acquired.

Presiones de la vida moderna. Complete the following paragraphs with the correct form of the words in parentheses—for verbs, the present, preterite, or imperfect—as suggested by the context. When two possibilities are given in parentheses, select the correct word.

Es cierto que (nuestro[1]) generación (disfrutar[2]) de[a] muchas ventajas comparada con las generaciones (anterior[3]). (Por/Para[4]) ejemplo, la medicina (está/es[5]) muy avanzada: Desde hace[b] muchas décadas (*nosotros:* tener[6]) vacunas[c] (muy/mucho[7]) buenas contra enfermedades que antes (ser[8]) mortales. Además, hoy es más fácil (por/para[9]) los amigos y familiares (ser/estar[10]) en contacto, gracias a los avances tecnológicos.

Sin embargo,[d] nuestra vida es también más complicada (que/de[11]) antes. Ahora (ser[12]) necesario trabajar más. (Por/Para[13]) dar una idea de (este/esto[14]), piense en (todo[15]) las madres que tienen un trabajo de tiempo completo y que también (deber[16]) cuidar a sus niños. O piense en las personas que tienen teléfono en el coche (por/para[17]) hacer negocios en la carretera.[e] Por eso, muchas personas (sufrir[18]) de estrés. Y cuando se sufre de estrés, es mucho más posible (ponerse/ponerte[19]) enfermo y tener accidentes.

¿Es toda (este[20]) actividad necesaria? Quizás[f] todos necesitamos (sentarse/sentarnos[21]) a pensar un poco, y (establecer[22]) un poco de calma en nuestra vida. Los avances científicos deben ser una ayuda (por/para[23]) nosotros, no una fuente[g] de más problemas, ¿verdad?

[a]disfrutar... *to enjoy* [b]Desde... *For* [c]*vaccinations* [d]Sin... *Nevertheless* [e]*highway* [f]*Perhaps* [g]*source*

Comprensión. Escoja la respuesta más apropiada.

1. Hoy día nuestra vida es (más/menos) complicada que hace un siglo.
2. (Es posible / No es posible) controlar el estrés.
3. Por los avances tecnológicos y científicos, hoy día es posible estar en (más/menos) contacto con nuestra familia.

Un paso más PASO 4

Paso 4: Un paso más
Optional section

See IM for suggestions and follow-up activities to accompany the video segment.

Follow-up A
Have students answer questions about these gender stereotypes: *¿los hombres o las mujeres? ¿Quiénes saben leer un mapa / conducir / estacionar mejor? Normalmente, ¿quiénes les piden direcciones a otras personas si se pierden? ¿Quiénes tienen menos accidentes?*

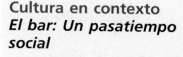

VIDEOTECA: En contexto

In this video segment, Roberto gets lost and asks a passerby for directions. As you watch the segment, pay particular attention to the questions that Roberto asks to get directions, and to the man's responses. Where is Roberto trying to go? What landmarks does the man suggest he look for?

FUNCTION
Asking for and giving directions

A. Lluvia de ideas

- ¿Tiene Ud. un buen sentido de orientación o se pierde con frecuencia? ¿Puede Ud. leer un mapa con facilidad?
- ¿Qué hace Ud. cuando se pierde? ¿Busca la dirección en un mapa? ¿Le pregunta a alguien? ¿Camina hasta encontrar el lugar?

B. Dictado. A continuación está parte del diálogo entre Roberto y el hombre en la calle. Complétela con las palabras o frases que faltan.

ROBERTO: Esto es imposible… estoy __totalmente__[1] perdido. Esta es la calle Milagros. __Acabo__[2] de venir de la calle Ibáñez. ¡El bar debe estar __cerca__[3]! No lo __entiendo__.[4] Disculpe, señor…

SEÑOR: ¿Sí?

ROBERTO: Perdone la molestia… pero estoy __perdido__.[5] Busco el bar La copa alegre. ¿Lo __conoce__[6] Ud.?

SEÑOR: […] Ah, sí. __Conozco__[7] el bar. Mire, es muy fácil llegar. No queda[a] __lejos__.[8] ¿Ve Ud. el teléfono? Esa es la calle Martín Gómez. Doble a la derecha en esa calle. Luego __camine__[9] dos cuadras y doble a la __izquierda__[10] en la avenida Flores.

[a]No... *It is not located*

Suggestion B
To check comprehension, ask **1.** *En el diálogo aparece varias veces la forma* ***queda*** *(****quedar****). ¿Qué otro verbo puede sustituir* ***queda*** *en el diálogo?* **2.** *¿Qué verbo se usa para expresar* to turn? **3.** *Haga una lista de las palabras que se pueden usar para hablar del tráfico en una ciudad.* **4.** *¿Se acuerda Ud. de las instruciones que le dio el señor a Roberto para llegar al bar La copa alegre?*

Cultura en contexto
El bar: Un pasatiempo social

En los países hispanohablantes, es un pasatiempo común ir a un bar para tomar una cerveza, una copa de vino, un refresco o un café. Muchos bares también sirven comida. En España, los bares son famosos por sus tapas, diversos platos de porciones pequeñas. El propósito[a] de reunirse en bares no es emborracharse,[b] sino pasar tiempo con amigos y participar en discusiones y conversaciones interesantes. Es raro ver a una persona tomada[c] en un bar y se considera de muy mala educación[d] emborracharse en público.

[a]*purpose* [b]*to get drunk* [c]*drunk* [d]*se… it is considered very bad manners*

C. Un diálogo original

Paso 1. Con un compañero / una compañera, dramatice la escena entre Roberto y el hombre en la calle.

Paso 2. Perdidos en el *campus*

Imagine que Ud. y un compañero / una compañera son las siguientes personas que tienen una conversación.

E1: Ud. está visitando el *campus* de su universidad por primera vez y ahora está perdido/a. Pare (*Stop*) a una persona en la calle y pregúntele cómo llegar a la biblioteca principal. No se olvide de ser muy amable.

E2: Ud. es una persona que no conoce el *campus* y necesita instrucciones para llegar a la biblioteca.

PASO FINAL

A LEER

Suggestions: A leer

- Review previous *Estrategias* as a class. Have students rank them in order of helpfulness or importance.
- Have students work in small groups to create original titles in Spanish for each section of article. Compare titles and have class vote on best one for each passage.

Repaso de estrategias: Guessing the Content of a Passage

In previous reading sections, you have learned several different strategies to improve your comprehension of a text. Whenever you can, it's a good idea to utilize as many of these strategies as possible. Of course, this may not always be possible. For example, in the short passages that follow, there is only one visual item that accompanies the text. What else can you rely on to make predictions about the content? One strategy is to identify the source of the passages (see **Sobre la lectura** below). You should also consider the focus of the current chapter. And, of course, the title often reveals a great deal about the content of a passage. Considering all of these sources of information, what do you think these readings will be about?

1. vacation spots in the Spanish-speaking world
2. health-related issues associated with our modern way of life
3. fashion trends in Mexico
4. decorating ideas for your home

If you picked number 2, you were right. The following short passages discuss some of the negative effects that modern life can have on our health.

Sobre la lectura... Esta lectura fue recopilada (*compiled*) de varios ejemplares (*issues*) de la revista española *GeoMundo*. Como Ud. ya sabe (Capítulo 7), el contenido de esta revista es muy similar al de *National Geographic*.

La vida moderna: ¿Saludable o no?

Pasaje 1

La Organización Mundial de la Salud ha determinado[a] que las diez regiones del mundo con mayor incidencia de casos de cáncer en la piel[b] son: Australia, Noruega, Suiza, Dinamarca, Suecia, Escocia, Finlandia, la región francesa de Calvados, Polonia e Italia. En Australia cerca de 40 de cada 100.000 personas desarrollan melanomas malignos, debido[c] principalmente, afirman los especialistas, al origen inglés de su población. La piel de los ingleses evolucionó bajo cielos nublados, pero los descendientes australianos de los ingleses viven bajo los intensos rayos solares subtropicales.

Actualmente la piel bronceada impresiona a la gente ignorante, y el riesgo de sufrir de cáncer en la piel se ha incrementado[d] por la contaminación y la falta de información. Lo mejor: si es Ud. de piel clara, descanse en la playa debajo de una sombrilla.

Pasaje 2

Más del 8% de 15 millones de europeos que trabajan con ordenadores[e] ocho (o seis) horas del día padecen[f] de males oculares por la «fatiga de la pantalla»[g] y los campos[h] magnéticos y electrostáticos producidos por esas máquinas. Han aparecido[i] en París especialistas médicos del «mal[j] del ordenador» que están trabajando rápidamente para encontrar alivio de este mal sufrido por muchos.

Pasaje 3

¿Son los dolores de cabeza, los vahídos[k] y las náuseas los únicos inconvenientes de la inadecuada ventilación en las cabinas de los aviones? Aparentemente no.

Los asistentes de vuelo y muchos viajeros frecuentes se quejan de que a menudo[l] se enferman de gripe[m] después de los vuelos largos. La pobre calidad del aire también puede complicar la bronquitis, el asma, el enfisema y las alergias de los pasajeros. La baja humedad requerida en los aviones agrava estos problemas secando las membranas mucosas y disminuyendo[n] las defensas contra infecciones.

Lo más inquietante[o] es que la pobre ventilación y los asientos estrechamente apiñados[p] pueden conducir a[q] la transmisión de serias enfermedades.

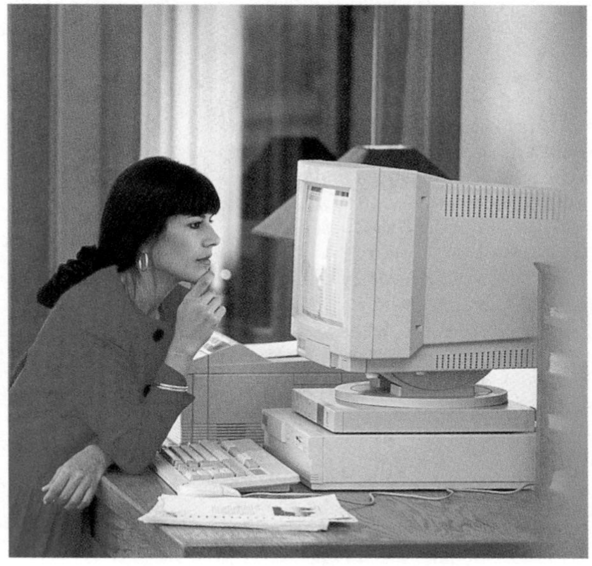

Esta española puede padecer del «mal del ordenador».

[a]ha… *has determined* [b]*skin* [c]*due* [d]se… *has increased* [e]computadoras [f]sufren [g]*screen* [h]*fields* [i]Han… *Have appeared* [j]*sickness* [k]los… *dizziness* [l]a… *often* [m]*flu* [n]*diminishing* [o]*worrisome* [p]estrechamente… *tightly arranged together* [q]conducir… *lead to*

Suggestion: Comprensión
Give students these additional *Comprensión* items: **1.** *Según el artículo, algunos australianos tienen cáncer de piel porque:* **a.** *les impresiona la piel bronceada* **b.** *son de origen inglés* **c.** *no tienen suficiente información* (b) **2.** *En París, los especialistas desean:* **a.** *evitar la «fatiga de la pantalla»* **b.** *controlar los campos magnéticos y electrostáticos* **c.** *curar el estrés de los ojos* (c) **3.** *Según el artículo, la falta de ventilación en los aviones puede causar:* **a.** *dolores de cabeza y humedad* **b.** *gripe y claustrofobia* **c.** *vahídos y problemas de asma* (c) **4.** *El artículo sugiere que:* **a.** *la vida moderna no es saludable* **b.** *la gente pasa demasiado tiempo bajo el sol y en los aviones* **c.** *la gente tiene poca información* (a)

Follow-up: Comprensión
Ask students how many hours on average they spend in front of a computer screen, and what physical effects this behavior has on them (for example, eye strain, back pain, and so on).

Variation: A escribir
Based on the *A leer* format, have students write 2 or more *pasajes* on health in modern life. Some topics for compositions: *el estrés en los conductores de automóviles, los problemas de comunicación y los teléfonos celulares, las presiones de tiempo en las grandes ciudades, las enfermedades respiratorias en las áreas contaminadas.*

Follow-up B
List on board each item students named as biggest source of pressure for students. Group similar, though not identical, items under an inclusive category. Which was named most often? Have groups debate to defend different sources.

Comprensión

A. ¿A qué pasaje se refiere? A continuación se presentan tres títulos. En su opinión, ¿qué título mejor le corresponde a cada pasaje de la lectura?

a. _____ Las enfermedades de viaje comienzan en el aire.
b. _____ Los peligros del sol
c. _____ Ojos cansados en el lugar de trabajo

B. Problemas. De los siguientes problemas asociados con el sol, el ordenador y el avión, ¿cuáles *no* se mencionan en la lectura? Indique los problemas no mencionados.

EL SOL

1. el cáncer en la piel
2. los problemas oculares
3. la deshidratación

EL ORDENADOR

1. los problemas con los músculos de las manos
2. los problemas oculares
3. los dolores de cabeza

EL AVIÓN

1. las náuseas
2. los problemas respiratorios
3. el insomnio

A ESCRIBIR

A. Resúmenes breves. Ahora en uno o dos oraciones, resuma (*summarize*) cada uno de los tres pasajes de la lectura. Debe incluir la información más importante de cada uno.

B. El estrés y los estudiantes. Aunque las presiones de la vida moderna nos afectan a todos, sin duda (*doubt*) tienen un impacto tremendo en los estudiantes universitarios. Escríbale una carta al editor del periódico local comentando lo que Ud. cree que es la mayor presión para los estudiantes en su universidad. En la carta, debe identificar la causa de la presión, las consecuencias que tiene y algunas soluciones posibles para combatirla.

Puede comenzar su carta así:

Estimado editor: / Estimada editora: …

En resumen

GRAMÁTICA

To review the grammar points presented in this chapter, refer to the indicated grammar presentations. You'll find further practice of these structures in the Workbook/Laboratory Manual, on the CD-ROM, and on the website.

31. Another Use of *se*

Do you know how to use **se** to express unplanned or unexpected events?

32. A Summary of the Uses of *por* and *para*

Do you know the difference between **por** and **para** and when to use one or the other?

VOCABULARIO

Los verbos

acabar	to finish; to run out of
acordarse (ue) (de)	to remember
caer (*irreg.*)	to fall
caerse	to fall down
entregar	to turn, hand in
equivocarse	to be wrong, make a mistake
estacionar	to park
quedar	to remain, be left
recoger	to collect; to pick up
romper	to break
sacar	to take out; to get
ser (*irreg.*) **flexible**	to be flexible
sufrir	to suffer
(muchas) presiones	to be under (a lot of) pressure

Repaso: caminar, doler (ue), llegar a tiempo/tarde olvidarse de

Accidentes

darse (*irreg.*) **con**	to run, bump into
hacerse (*irreg.*) **daño**	to hurt oneself
lastimarse	to injure oneself
levantarse con el pie izquierdo	to get up on the wrong side of the bed
pedir (i, i) disculpas	to apologize
pegarse en/contra	to run/bump into
Discúlpeme.	Pardon me. / I'm sorry.
Fue sin querer.	It was unintentional.
¡Lo siento (mucho)!	Pardon me! / I'm (very) sorry!
¡Qué mala suerte!	What bad luck!

Repaso: perdón

Presiones de la vida estudiantil

la calificación	grade
el estrés	stress
la fecha límite	deadline
la (falta de) flexibilidad	(lack of) flexibility
el horario	schedule
el informe (oral/escrito)	(oral/written) report
la nota	grade
la prueba	quiz; test
la tarjeta de identificación	identification card
el trabajo	job, work; report, (piece of) work
de tiempo completo/parcial	full time/part time

Repaso: el examen

Más partes del cuerpo

el brazo	arm
el dedo (de la mano)	finger
el dedo del pie	toe
la pierna	leg

Repaso: la cabeza

Los adjetivos

distraído/a	absentminded
escrito/a	written
flexible	flexible
torpe	clumsy
universitario	(of the) university

Otros sustantivos

el calendario	calendar
el despertador	alarm clock
la llave	key
la luz	light, electricity

Palabras adicionales

hace + *time*	(*time*) ago
hace + *time* + **que...** + *present*	it's been (*time*) since . . .
por Dios	for heaven's sake
por ejemplo	for example
por lo menos	at least
por primera/ última vez	for the first/last time
por si acaso	just in case
por supuesto	of course
por todas partes	everywhere

Repaso: por eso, por favor, por fin, por lo general, por lo menos

Suggestions: Vocabulario

- Remind students that the plural of *luz* is *luces*.
- Have students use vocabulary words to narrate a round-robin *un día fatal*. As a class, they can establish subject (an individual, real or imaginary). Each student gives a sentence that describes subject's terrible day.
- Have students complete sentences, such as: **1.** *Por primera vez en mi vida, yo...* **2.** *Por supuesto, yo...* **3.** *Por si acaso hay...* **4.** *En esta clase, por lo menos...* Encourage them to be creative and humorous in their responses. Have them compose new sentences that use *Palabras adicionales*.

CAPÍTULO 12

La calidad de la vida

Suggestion: Chapter Opening photo
Point out the chapter opening photo. Ask students what technology they see represented. Was it important/advanced at the time? Have them name/describe other early technological advances. How does technology affect daily life? Encourage them to try to compare their situation with those of people of early civilizations.

Resources
You and your students may find the following *¿Qué tal?* supplements helpful as you teach this chapter:

For the Instructor
- *Instructor's Manual and Resource Kit,* "Chapter-by-Chapter" Supplementary Materials
- Testing Program
- Overhead Transparencies 69–72
- Video (VHS or CD)
- *¿Qué tal?* Online Learning Center Website
- Audioscript
- Instructor's Resource CD

For Students
- Workbook/Laboratory Manual and Audio Program or Electronic Workbook/ Laboratory Manual
- Video on CD
- Interactive CD-ROM
- *¿Qué tal?* Online Learning Center Website
- Listening Comprehension Audio CD
- McGraw-Hill Electronic Language Tutor (MHELT)

No toda la tecnología es nueva. La tecnología de los incas, quienes construyeron el famoso centro de Machu Picchu, era muy avanzada para su tiempo. ▶

VOCABULARIO

- Things we have, need, and want
- Housing

GRAMÁTICA

33 **Tú** Commands
34 Present Subjunctive: An Introduction
35 Use of the Subjunctive: Influence

CULTURA

- **Enfoque cultural:** el Perú
- **Nota cultural:** Los nombres de los pisos de un edificio
- **En los Estados Unidos y el Canadá:** Las computadoras y la comunidad hispana
- **Cultura en contexto:** El léxico (Las palabras) de la nueva tecnología

Multimedia

You will learn about giving instructions in the **En contexto** video segment.

Review vocabulary and grammar and practice language skills with the interactive CD-ROM.

Get connected to the Spanish-speaking world with the *¿Qué tal?* Online Learning Center: **www.mhhe.com/quetal**.

PASO 1 Vocabulario

CAPÍTULO 12

Paso 1: Vocabulario
See detailed supplementary materials and exercises for this section and a model for vocabulary presentation and other material in the *Capítulo 12 Paso 1: Vocabulario* "Chapter-by-Chapter Supplementary Materials," IM.

Tengo... Necesito... Quiero...

Los vehículos

la bicicleta (de montaña)	(mountain) bike
el carro / el coche (descapotable)	(convertible) car
el monopatín	skateboard
la moto(cicleta)	motorcycle, moped
los patines	roller skates

La electrónica

el contestador automático	answering machine
el correo electrónico	e-mail
el disco duro	hard drive
la impresora	printer
el ordenador (*Spain*)	computer
el ratón	mouse
la red	net
navegar la red	to surf the net
el teléfono (celular, de coche)	(cellular, car) phone

Cognados

el CD-ROM, la computadora, el disco compacto, el disco de computadora, el fax, la memoria, el módem

Verbos útiles

cambiar (de canal, de cuarto, de ropa...)	to change (channels, rooms, clothing)
conseguir (i, i)	to get, obtain
copiar / hacer copia	to copy
fallar	to "crash" (*a computer*)
funcionar	to work, function (*machines*)
grabar	to record, to tape
guardar	to keep, to save (*documents*)

❖ **Transparency 69**

Multimedia: Audio
Students can listen to and practice this chapter's vocabulary on their Listening Comprehension Audio CD.

imprimir	to print	**Para poder gastar**	
manejar	to drive; to operate (*a machine*)	**el aumento**	raise
obtener (*irreg.*)	to get, obtain	**el/la jefe/a**	boss
sacar fotos	to take photos	**el sueldo**	salary

Conversación

A. Ud. y los aparatos

Paso 1. ¿Qué se usa en estas situaciones?

1. para mandar inmediatamente copias de documentos no originales
2. para grabar un programa de televisión
3. para cambiar el programa de la tele sin levantarse del sillón
4. para recibir llamadas telefónicas cuando no estamos en casa
5. para escuchar música mientras hacemos ejercicio

Paso 2. Con un compañero / una compañera, piense en cuatro situaciones similares a las del **Paso 1**. La otra persona debe identificar el aparato.

Paso 3. Para Ud., ¿son ciertas o falsas las siguientes oraciones?

1. Soy una persona que tiene habilidad mecánica. Es decir, entiendo cómo funcionan los aparatos.
2. Aprendí con facilidad a usar la computadora.
3. No me puedo imaginar la vida sin los aparatos electrónicos modernos.
4. Me interesa saber qué vehículo maneja una persona, porque el vehículo es una expresión de la personalidad.
5. Una vez me falló la computadora y perdí unos documentos y archivos (*files*) muy importantes.
6. Uso la videocasetera para ver películas, pero no sé grabar.
7. Me gusta navegar la red porque siempre encuentro lo que busco.

B. ¿Qué vehículos… ? ¿Qué vehículo deben tener y usar las siguientes personas?

1. una persona joven no convencional y que vive en Sevilla, una ciudad grande en el sur de España
2. una persona joven que vive en Key West, una isla soleada e informal en el sur de Florida
3. una familia con tres hijos
4. un estudiante de artes liberales que vive en el *campus*
5. unos chicos que viven en Venice Beach, California, y que pasan gran parte de su tiempo libre en la playa y en el *boardwalk*
6. un matrimonio jubilado (*retired*) que vive en Nueva Inglaterra

Reciclado: Vocabulario
Review words students have already learned: *el coche = el carro, el tren, el autobús, el avión, el barco.*

Preliminary exercise A
Ask: *¿Qué aparatos asocia Ud. con los siguientes verbos?* **1.** *hablar* **2.** *mirar* **3.** *trabajar* **4.** *viajar* **5.** *escuchar* **6.** *bailar* **7.** *cantar*

Suggestions A
- **Paso 3.** Have students interview each other and present their partner's profile and/or a comparison of answers.
- Have students write paragraph about what they have in their rooms or homes, what they need, and what they would like to have some day. Then have students work in groups to read and compare items.

Answers A, Paso 1
1. *el* fax **2.** *la videocasetera* **3.** *el control remoto* **4.** *el contestador automático* **5.** *el walkman*

Follow-up B
Have students work together to make list of *ventajas* and *desventajas* of each type of vehicle presented in text.

Follow-up C
Have students share opinions as you tally answers on board. As whole class, try to explain why certain things are (or are not) a necessity, and why there are inconsistent answers for some items (if there are).

❖ **Transparency 70**
Transparency 70 offers practice and additional vocabulary.

Notes: Vocabulario
- Ordinal numbers are formally presented in *Capítulo 13*. You may need to help students with ordinals as they talk about where they live.
- Point out that *suburbio* is a false cognate. It means "slums." *Afueras* is used to refer to suburbs.

C. ¿Necesidad o lujo (*luxury*)?

Paso 1. ¿Considera Ud. que las siguientes posesiones son un lujo o una necesidad de la vida moderna? Indique si Ud. tiene este aparato o vehículo. Dé tres cosas más que Ud. considera necesarias en la vida moderna.

MODELO: un televisor → Para mí, un televisor es una necesidad. Tengo uno. (No tengo uno ahora.)

1. un contestador automático
2. una videocasetera
3. el equipo estereofónico
4. una computadora
5. un coche
6. una bicicleta
7. un *walkman* (una grabadora)
8. el aviso de llamada, la llamada en espera (*call-waiting*)
9. la línea de teléfono
10. el televisor de pantalla (*screen*) grande

Paso 2. Para terminar, entreviste a un compañero / una compañera para saber si está de acuerdo con Ud. y si tiene las mismas posesiones.

MODELO: el televisor → E1: ¿El televisor?
E2: Yo lo considero un lujo y por eso no tengo uno.

La vivienda°

°La... *Housing*

La comunidad

el apartamento*	apartment
el barrio / la vecindad	neighborhood
la casa	house
el cuarto	room
el/la dueño/a	owner; landlord, landlady
el/la inquilino/a	tenant; renter
el/la portero/a	building manager, doorperson
la residencia	residence
el/la vecino/a	neighbor

El área

las afueras	outskirts, suburbs
la avenida	avenue
la calle	street
el campo	countryside
la casa (el bloque) de apartamentos	apartment building
el centro	(downtown) shopping area
la dirección	address
la planta	floor
la planta baja	first (ground) floor
el piso	floor (of a building)
el (primer, segundo) piso	(first, second [*Sp.*: second, third]) floor
la vista	view

Los gastos

el alquiler	rent
alquilar	to rent
el gas	gas; heat
la luz (*pl.* **luces**)	light; electricity

*__El apartamento__ is used throughout Latin America and the Caribbean. **El departamento** is used in Mexico, Peru, and other Latin American countries, but **el piso** is the word most commonly used in Spain.

Suggestion: Nota cultural
Emphasize the expression and meaning of *la planta baja.* Review the *Nota cultural* on floors, using familiar buildings as examples.

NOTA CULTURAL

Los nombres de los pisos de un edificio

En la mayoría de los dialectos del inglés, las frases *ground floor* y *first floor* tienen el mismo significado. En español, hay dos modos de expresar estos conceptos. Aunque ha habido[a] cambios al lenguaje debido a[b] la influencia norteamericana, **la planta baja** es el equivalente más común de *ground floor*, mientras que **el primer piso** se refiere al *second floor* de los anglohablantes.[c] También en español, el segundo piso se refiere al *third floor*, etcétera.

[a]ha... *there have been* [b]debido... *due to* [c]*English speakers*

Conversación

Follow-up A
Paso 1. Have students explain which ad appeals to them the most and why.

Follow-up A
Paso 2. Have students tally their answers on board, then have class discussion about similarities and differences.

A. A buscar vivienda

Paso 1. Lea los tres anuncios de viviendas en el Perú y conteste las siguientes preguntas.

1. ¿Qué tipo de vivienda se vende en cada anuncio? ¿Son para comprar o alquilar?
2. ¿Cuántos dormitorios tiene cada vivienda?
3. ¿Cree Ud. que estas viviendas son para familias con mucho o poco dinero?

Paso 2. Con un compañero / una compañera, hable sobre el tipo de vivienda que prefiere.

1. Como estudiante universitario, ¿prefiere vivir en el *campus* o fuera del *campus*? ¿en una residencia o en una casa o apartamento de alquiler con otras personas?
2. ¿Prefiere Ud. vivir en la planta baja o en los pisos más altos?
3. ¿Prefiere que el alquiler incluya (*include*) todos los gastos o prefiere pagar la luz y el gas por separado?
4. Si pudiera (*If you could*) escoger, ¿qué le gustaría más, tener un apartamento pequeño en un barrio elegante del centro o una casa grande en las afueras?
5. ¿Qué tipo de vecinos le gusta tener?

Variation B
Play Jeopardy. Give or have students give definition. Class (or teams) should respond with corresponding question: *Es un lugar donde viven muchos estudiantes.* → *¿Qué es una residencia?*

B. Definiciones. Dé las definiciones de las siguientes palabras.

MODELO: la residencia →
Es un lugar donde viven muchos estudiantes. Por lo general está situada en el *campus* universitario.

Frases útiles: Es una persona que... Es un lugar donde... Es una cosa que...

1. el inquilino
2. el centro
3. el alquiler
4. el portero
5. la vecina
6. la dueña
7. la dirección
8. las afueras

1.
CUZCO
Alquilo casa. Barrio residencial. Semi-amueblada[a] con teléfono. Informes Teléf. Cuzco: 084-226752. Lima: 774153 (horario 2 a 5 p.m.)

2.
DEPARTAMENTOS MONTERRICO
Finos departamentos de 3 dormitorios, 3½ baños, sala de estar,[b] 1 ó 2 cocheras,[c] acabados de primera,[d] verlos todos los días en: Domingo de la Presa 165, espalda cuadra 12 Av. Primavera.

3.
CHACARILLA DEL ESTANQUE
Departamentos exclusivos, diseño especial, 3 dormitorios, comedor de diario, área de servicio, totalmente equipados. Desde $41.500. Buenas facilidades.
Av. Buena Vista N° 230
(a 2 Cdras. de Velasco Aslete)
Tels. 458107 – 357743

[a]*Partially furnished* [b]sala... *living room; sitting room* [c]1 ó 2... *one- or two-car garage* [d]acabados... *first-class finishing details*

Multimedia: Internet
Have students search the Internet for the online newspaper, *Perú al día,* for rental ads to print out and bring to class.

PASO 2 Gramática

Paso 2: Gramática
See detailed supplementary materials for these grammar sections in IM.

¿Recuerda Ud.?

In Grammar Section 18 you learned about **Ud.** and **Uds.** commands. Remember that object pronouns (direct, indirect, reflexive) must follow and be attached to affirmative commands; they must precede negative commands.

AFFIRMATIVE:	Háblele Ud.	Duérmase.	Dígaselo Ud.
NEGATIVE:	No le hable Ud.	No se duerma.	No se lo diga Ud.

¿Cómo se dice en español?

1. Bring me the book. (**Uds.**)
2. Don't give it to her. (**Uds.**)
3. Sit here, please. (**Ud.**)
4. Don't sit in that chair! (**Ud.**)
5. Tell them the truth. (**Uds.**)
6. Tell it to them now! (**Uds.**)
7. Never tell it to her. (**Uds.**)
8. Take care of yourself. (**Ud.**)
9. Lead a healthy life. (**Ud.**)
10. Listen to me. (**Ud.**)

Suggestions
- Have students give the infinitive forms of verbs in grammar presentation.
- Have students who heard each phrase as a teenager explain why their mother (or father) said that. *¿Te dijo tu madre eso una sola vez o te lo decía con frecuencia? ¿Por qué?*
- Use as continuing practice of preterite vs. imperfect.

33 Influencing Others • *Tú* Commands

¡Marta, tu cuarto es un desastre!

«¡Marta, qué desordenado está tu cuarto! Por favor, *arréglalo* antes de jugar con tus amigos. *Guarda* la ropa limpia en tu armario, *pon* la ropa sucia en el cesto, *haz* la cama, *recoge* los libros del piso y *ordénalos* en los estantes... Y no *dejes* los zapatos por todas partes... ¡Es muy peligroso!»

¿Quién diría (*would say*) lo siguiente, Marta o Manolo, su padre?

1. No te enojes... Ya voy a arreglarlo todo.
2. Hazlo inmediatamente... ¡antes de salir a jugar!
3. Dime, ¿por qué tengo que hacerlo ahora mismo?
4. La próxima vez, ¡no dejes tu cuarto en tales condiciones!

Informal commands (**los mandatos informales**) are used with persons whom you would address as **tú**.

Marta, your room is a disaster! "Marta, what a messy room you have! Please straighten it up before you go out to play with your friends. Put your clean clothes away in the closet, put your dirty clothes in the hamper, make your bed, pick your books up from the floor and arrange them on the shelves... And don't leave your shoes lying around everywhere... It's very dangerous!"

Note
If you have been using *tú* commands all along, start by having students list ones they know.

❖ Transparency 71
Transparency 71 provides examples of *tú* commands.

Preliminary exercise

Have students respond to statements with negative commands. Write example on board, then give additional statements: *No quiero cantarlo.* → *Pues, no lo cantes. No quiero comprarlo / mirarlo / leerlo / beberlo / escribirlo / decidirlo.*

NEGATIVE *tú* COMMANDS

-ar verbs		*-er/-ir* verbs	
No hables.	Don't speak.	**No comas.**	Don't eat.
No cantes.	Don't sing.	**No escribas.**	Don't write.
No juegues.	Don't play.	**No pidas.**	Don't order.

A. Like **Ud.** commands (Grammar Section 18), the negative **tú** commands are expressed using the "opposite vowel": **no hable Ud., no hables (tú).** The pronoun **tú** is used only for emphasis.

No cantes **tú** tan fuerte.
*Don't **you** sing so loudly.*

B. As with negative **Ud.** commands, object pronouns—direct, indirect, and reflexive—precede negative **tú** commands.

No lo mires.
Don't look at him.

No les escribas.
Don't write to them.

No te levantes.
Don't get up.

AFFIRMATIVE *tú* COMMANDS

-ar verbs		*-er/-ir* verbs	
Habla.	*Speak.*	**Come.**	*Eat.*
Canta.	*Sing.*	**Escribe.**	*Write.*
Juega.	*Play.*	**Pide.**	*Order.*

A. Unlike the other command forms you have learned, most affirmative **tú** commands have the same form as the third person singular of the present indicative.* Some verbs have irregular affirmative **tú** command forms.

decir:	**di**	salir:	**sal**
hacer:	**haz**	ser:	**sé**
ir:	**ve**	tener:	**ten**
poner:	**pon**	venir:	**ven**

Spelling Hint: One-syllable words, like the affirmative **tú** commands of some verbs (**decir, ir, tener,...**) do not need an accent mark: **di, ve, ten,...** Exceptions to this rule are those forms that could be mistaken for other words, like the command of **ser** (**sé**), which could be mistaken for the pronoun **se**.

Sé puntual pero **ten** cuidado.
Be there on time, but be careful.

*As you know, there are two different *moods* in Spanish: the *indicative mood* (the one you have been working with, which is used to state facts and ask questions) and the *subjunctive mood* (which is used to express more subjective actions or states). Beginning with Grammar Section 34, you will learn more about the subjunctive mood.

Suggestions: *Tú* commands
- Present *vosotros* commands. Affirmative forms are based on infinitive— **-d** replaces- **-r** ending: *comer* → *comed.* Negative forms use the present subjunctive: *no comáis.*
- Model and practice the *vosotros/as* commands for the students, especially if you are a Spaniard, if you use *vosotros/as* forms, and/or if your students are likely to study in Spain.

OJO The affirmative **tú** commands for **ir** and **ver** are identical: **ve**. Context will clarify meaning.

¡**Ve** esa película!
See that movie!

Ve a casa ahora mismo.
Go home right now.

B. As with affirmative **Ud.** commands, object and reflexive pronouns follow affirmative **tú** commands and are attached to them. Accent marks are necessary except when a single pronoun is added to a one-syllable command.

Dile la verdad.
Tell him the truth.

Léela, por favor.
Read it, please.

Póntelos.
Put them on.

Práctica

Suggestion A
Have students search the Internet for 5 extra *refranes* to share with the class.

A. Refranes para todo. Los refranes son frases populares que expresan consejos para todo tipo de situaciones en la vida. Empareje cada refrán en la columna a la izquierda con una explicación a la derecha. Si conoce algún equivalente en inglés, ¡délo!

1. __f__ Agua que no has de (vas a) beber, déjala correr.
2. __a__ Haz bien y no mires a quién.
3. __c__ Dondequiera que fueres (*you go*), haz lo que vieres (*you see*).
4. __b__ En martes, ni te cases (*get married*) ni te embarques (*set sail*).
5. __e__ Antes de que te cases (*get married*), mira bien lo que haces.
6. __d__ A caballo (*horse*) regalado no le mires el diente.

a. Sé una buena persona con todo el mundo, sin excepción.
b. El martes es un día de mala suerte: no hagas nada importante ese día.
c. Aprende las costumbres de otras personas y actúa a su manera cuando estés (*you are*) en su casa o en su país.
d. Da las gracias y no busques los defectos de un regalo.
e. Piensa bien antes de casarte en cómo va a cambiar tu vida.
f. Si no vas a hacer aprecio de alguien, deja a esa persona.

B. Julita, la mal educada

Paso 1. Los señores Villarreal no están contentos con el comportamiento de su hija Julita. Continúe los comentarios de ellos con mandatos informales lógicos según cada situación. Siga los modelos.

MODELOS: *Hablaste* demasiado ayer. → No *hables* tanto hoy, por favor.
Dejaste tu ropa en el suelo anoche. → No la *dejes* allí hoy, por favor.

1. También *dejaste* tus libros en el suelo.
2. ¿Por qué *regresaste* tarde a casa hoy después de las clases?
3. ¿Por qué *vas* al parque todas las tardes?
4. No es bueno que *mires* la televisión constantemente. ¿Y por qué quieres *ver* todos esos programas de detectives?
5. ¿Por qué le *dices* mentiras a tu papá?
6. Siempre *te olvidas* de sacar la basura, que es la única tarea que tienes que hacer.
7. Ay, hija, no te comprendemos. ¡*Eres* tan insolente!

Paso 2. La pobre Julita también escucha muchos mandatos de su maestra en clase. Invente Ud. esos mandatos según las indicaciones.

1. llegar / a / escuela / puntualmente
2. quitarse / abrigo / y / sentarse
3. sacar / libro de matemáticas / y / abrirlo / en / página diez
4. leer / nuevo / palabras / y / aprenderlas / para mañana
5. venir / aquí / a / hablar conmigo / sobre / este / composición

Follow-up B

- Have students give commands that Julita would like to give to others.
- Ask students: *¿Qué mandatos oye Ud. con frecuencia? ¿Qué mandatos da Ud. y a quién se los da?*

Conversación

A. Situaciones. ¿Qué consejos les daría (*would you give*) a las siguientes personas si fueran (*if they were*) sus amigos? Déles a todos consejos en forma de mandatos informales.

1. A Celia le encanta ir al cine, especialmente los viernes por la noche. Pero a su novio no le gusta salir mucho los viernes. Él siempre está muy cansado después de una larga semana de trabajo. Celia, en cambio (*on the other hand*), tiene mucha energía.
2. Nati tiene 19 años. El próximo año quiere vivir en un apartamento con cuatro amigos. Para ella es una situación ideal: un apartamento económico en un barrio estudiantil y unos buenos amigos (dos de ellos son hombres). Pero los padres de Nati son muy tradicionales y no les va a gustar la situación.
3. Mariana es una *yuppi*. Gana muchísimo dinero pero trabaja demasiado. Nunca tiene tiempo para nada. Duerme poco y bebe muchísimo café para seguir despierta (*awake*). No come bien y jamás hace ejercicio. Acaba de comprarse un teléfono celular para poder trabajar mientras maneja a la oficina.

Variation A

Have students write letter to columnist for popular magazine for their age group. Have them present serious or complex problems in their letters. Have students complete letters as homework, then have them read their letters to class so that others can offer advice using *tú* commands.

Suggestions B
- Have students complete this activity in groups of 3, then discuss the results with class.
- Have students write down, in infinitive form, 5 activities that can be performed in class, for example, *Apagar las luces.* Then have class select 5 people (or have 5 students volunteer) to carry out commands. The other students form commands based on the phrases they have written and give them to 1 of the selected students or volunteers, who, in turn, tries to do what he/she is told.

Variation B
Have students make up informal commands for the following situations:
1. *para cuando sale para una entrevista para un trabajo* **2.** *para cuando conoce a los padres de un nuevo amigo / una nueva amiga* **3.** *para cuando su amigo/a quiere comprar un nuevo estéreo* **4.** *para un(a) estudiante de primer año* (freshman) *en esta universidad.*

B. Entre compañeros de casa. En su opinión, ¿cuáles son los cinco mandatos que se oyen con más frecuencia en su casa (apartamento, residencia)? Piense no sólo en los mandatos que Ud. escucha sino (*but*) también en los que Ud. les da a los demás (*others*).

Frases útiles: poner la tele, sacar la basura, apagar la computadora, prestarme dinero, contestar el teléfono, no hacer ruido, lavar los platos, ¿ ?

Frase útil: no seas… impaciente, así, pesado/a (*a pain*), precipitado/a (*hasty*), loco, impulsivo/a, bobo/a (*dumb*)

34 Expressing Subjective Actions or States • Present Subjunctive: An Introduction

Una decisión importante

JOSÉ MIGUEL: Quiero comprar una computadora, pero no sé cuál. *No creo que sea* una decisión fácil de tomar.

GUSTAVO: Pues, yo sé bastante de computadoras. Te puedo hacer algunas recomendaciones.

JOSÉ MIGUEL: Bueno, te escucho.

GUSTAVO: Primero, *es buena idea que sepas* para qué quieres una computadora. ¿Quieres navegar por el *Internet*? Entonces, *te sugiero que busques* una computadora con módem y con memoria suficiente para hacerlo. Luego, *quiero que hables* con otras personas que ya manejan computadoras. Y por último, *te aconsejo que vayas* a varias tiendas para comparar precios.

JOSÉ MIGUEL: Bueno, *me alegro de que sepas* tanto de computadoras. ¡Ahora *quiero que vayas* conmigo a las tiendas!

Comprensión: ¿Cierto, falso o no lo dice?

1. José Miguel quiere que Gustavo le compre una computadora.
2. Gustavo le recomienda a José Miguel que aprenda algo sobre computadoras antes de comprarse una.
3. Gustavo no cree que José Miguel tenga suficiente dinero.
4. José Miguel se alegra de que Gustavo esté tan informado sobre computadoras.

An important decision JOSÉ MIGUEL: I want to buy a computer, but I don't know which one. I don't think it's an easy decision to make. GUSTAVO: Well, I know quite a bit about computers. I can give you some recommendations. JOSÉ MIGUEL: OK, I'm listening. GUSTAVO: First, it's a good idea for you to know why you want a computer. Do you want to get on the Internet? Then I suggest that you look for a computer with a modem and enough memory to do it. Then I want you to talk with other people who already work with computers. And finally, I suggest you go to various stores to compare prices. JOSÉ MIGUEL: Well, I'm glad you know so much about computers. Now I want you to go to the stores with me!

Suggestions: Present Subjunctive
Have students pick out subjunctive and subjunctive cues in the *minidiálogo.* Ask what the cues have in common (asking someone to do something).

Follow-up: Present Subjunctive
Ask: *En el diálogo, ¿quién quiere comprar una computadora? ¿Quién sabe mucho de computadoras? ¿Quién le da consejos a quién? ¿Sugiere Gustavo que José Miguel compre una computadora inmediatamente?*

PRESENT SUBJUNCTIVE: AN INTRODUCTION

A. Except for command forms, all the verb forms you have learned so far in *¿Qué tal?* are part of the *indicative mood* (**el modo indicativo**). In both English and Spanish, the indicative is used to state facts and to ask questions; it objectively expresses actions or states of being that are considered true by the speaker.

INDICATIVE:

¿Puedes venir a la fiesta?
Can you come to the party?

Prefiero llegar temprano a casa.
I prefer getting home early.

B. Both English and Spanish have another verb system called the *subjunctive mood* (**el modo subjuntivo**). The subjunctive is used to express more subjective or conceptualized actions or states. These include things that the speaker wants to happen or wants others to do, events to which the speaker reacts emotionally, things that are as yet unknown, and so on.

SUBJUNCTIVE:

Espero que **puedas** venir a la fiesta.
I hope (that) you can come to the party.

Prefiero que **llegues** temprano a casa.
I prefer that you be home early.

C. Sentences in English and Spanish may be simple or complex. A simple sentence is one that contains a single verb.

Complex sentences are comprised of two or more *clauses* (**las cláusulas**). There are two types of clauses: main (independent) clause and subordinate (dependent) clause. *Independent clauses* (**las cláusulas principales**) contain a complete thought and can stand alone. *Dependent clauses* (**las cláusulas subordinadas**) contain an incomplete thought and cannot stand alone. Dependent clauses require an independent clause to form a complete sentence.

Note in the indicative example above that when there is no change of subject in the sentence, the infinitive is used in the subordinate clause.

However, when the two subjects of a complex sentence are different, the subjunctive is often used in the subordinate clause in Spanish. Note that subordinate clauses are linked by the conjunction **que**, which is never optional (as it is in English).

Quiero pan.
I want bread.

INDICATIVE

MAIN CLAUSE	SUBORDINATE CLAUSE
Quiero *I want*	comprar pan. *to buy bread.*

SUBJUNCTIVE

MAIN CLAUSE	SUBORDINATE CLAUSE	
Quiere *She wants*	**que** (*for*)	compres pan. *you to buy bread.*
Espero *I hope*	**que** (*that*)	me visites pronto. *you visit me soon.*
¿Dudas *Do you doubt*	**que** (*that*)	puedan venir? *they can come?*

D. Three of the most common uses of the subjunctive are to express influence, emotion, and doubt or denial. These are signaled in the previous examples by the verb forms **quiere, espero**, and **dudas**.

FORMS OF THE PRESENT SUBJUNCTIVE

You already know that many Spanish command forms are part of the subjunctive. The **Ud./Uds.** command forms are shaded in the box that follows. What you have already learned about forming **Ud.** and **Uds.** commands will help you learn the forms of the present subjunctive.

	hablar	**comer**	**escribir**	**volver**	**decir**
Singular	hable	coma	escriba	vuelva	diga
	hables	comas	escribas	vuelvas	digas
	hable	coma	escriba	vuelva	diga
Plural	hablemos	comamos	escribamos	volvamos	digamos
	habléis	comáis	escribáis	volváis	digáis
	hablen	coman	escriban	vuelvan	digan

A. The personal endings of the present subjunctive are added to the first person singular of the present indicative minus its **-o** ending. **-Ar** verbs add endings with **-e**, and **-er/-ir** verbs add endings with **-a**.

-ar → -e
-er/-ir → -a

present tense **yo** stem = present subjunctive stem

B. Verbs ending in **-car, -gar,** and **-zar** have a spelling change in all persons of the present subjunctive, in order to preserve the **-c-, -g-,** and **-z-** sounds.

-car: c → qu
-gar: g → gu
-zar: z → c

buscar: bus**qu**e, bus**qu**es,...
pagar: pa**gu**e, pa**gu**es,...
empezar: empie**c**e, empie**c**es,...

C. Verbs with irregular **yo** forms show the irregularity in all persons of the present subjunctive.

conocer:	**conozca,...**	salir:	**salga,...**
decir:	**diga,...**	tener:	**tenga,...**
hacer:	**haga,...**	traer:	**traiga,...**
oír:	**oiga,...**	venir:	**venga,...**
poner:	**ponga,...**	ver:	**vea,...**

D. A few verbs have irregular present subjunctive forms.

dar:	**dé, des, dé, demos, deis, den**
estar:	**esté,...**
haber (hay):	**haya**
ir:	**vaya,...**
saber:	**sepa,...**
ser:	**sea,...**

E. **-Ar** and **-er** stem-changing verbs follow the stem-changing pattern of the present indicative.

pensar (ie): pi**e**nse, pi**e**nses, pi**e**nse, pensemos, penséis, pi**e**nsen
poder (ue): p**ue**da, p**ue**das, p**ue**da, podamos, podáis, p**ue**dan

F. **-Ir** stem-changing verbs show a stem change in the four forms that have a change in the present indicative. In addition, however, they show a second stem change in the **nosotros** and **vosotros** forms, similar to the present progressive tense.

-ir stem-changing verbs (**nosotros** and **vosotros**):
o → u
e → i

dormir (ue, u): duerma, duermas, duerma, d**u**rmamos, d**u**rmáis, duerman
pedir (i, i): pida, pidas, pida, p**i**damos, p**i**dáis, pidan
preferir (ie, i): prefiera, prefieras, prefiera, pref**i**ramos, pref**i**ráis, prefieran

Práctica

Su trabajo actual (*current*). Complete las oraciones de modo (*in such a way*) que se refieran a su situación laboral actual. (Siempre hay más de una respuesta posible.) Si Ud. no trabaja ahora, no importa. ¡Invéntese una respuesta!

1. El jefe / La jefa quiere que _____.
2. También espera que _____.
3. Y duda que _____.
4. Prohíbe (*He/She forbids*) _____.
5. En el trabajo, es importante que _____.
6. Yo espero que _____.

a. a veces trabajemos los fines de semana
b. todos lleguemos a tiempo
c. hablemos por teléfono con los amigos
d. me den un aumento de sueldo
e. nos paguen más a todos
f. no usemos el fax para asuntos (*matters*) personales
g. me den un trabajo de tiempo completo algún día
h. no perdamos mucho tiempo charlando (*chatting*) con los demás
i. fumemos en la oficina
j. ¿ ?

Preliminary exercises: Práctica
Have students tell whether each verb is in the present indicative or present subjunctive: ***-ar:*** *baile, cena, lleguemos, pago, recuerde, hablemos, miramos, buscan, te olvides;* ***-er/-ir:*** *aprende, aprenda, lea, leemos, escribamos, coma, asisten, recibo, beban, digo, pongamos, traigan, sabe, sepan.*
Use chain drill to practice subjunctive forms: *Dé oraciones nuevas según las indicaciones.* **1.** *En clase: El profesor no quiere que Uds. fumen.* (*yo, nosotros, tú, los estudiantes, Lupe, vosotros*) **2.** *En casa, el día antes de la fiesta, es necesario que alguien llame a nuestros amigos.* (*comprar los refrescos, buscar los discos compactos, invitar a María, traer la comida*)

Variation: Práctica
Change context to *los estudiantes de la clase de español.* Have students make all other necessary changes, keeping main clause verbs.

Follow-up: Conversación
Have students tell what advice their family and friends give them on a regular basis, for example, *Mis padres recomiendan que yo consiga trabajo en la librería.*

Conversación

Consejos para comprar y usar la tecnología de multimedia. Complete el siguiente párrafo según su opinión y sus conocimientos (*knowledge*). En el primer espacio en blanco, use el subjuntivo del verbo entre paréntesis. Luego, compare sus respuestas con las de algunos compañeros para ver si están de acuerdo. ¿Quién sabe más del tema en la clase?

Recomiendo que…

MODELO: _____ (encontrar) _____ para ayudarlo/la a montar (*set up*) la computadora porque… → *encuentre un experto* para ayudarlo/la a montar la computadora porque *es muy difícil*.

1. __vaya__ (ir) a _________ para comprar la computadora porque…
2. __compre__ (comprar) _________ [marca y modelo de computadora] porque…
3. __mire__ (mirar) las revistas especializadas, como _________ [nombre de revista] porque…
4. no __pague__ (pagar) más de $ _________ porque…
5. no __use__ (usar) el *software* _________ [marca o tipo] porque…
6. __se asegure__ (asegurarse [*to make sure*]) de que la computadora tenga _________ porque…
7. __ponga__ (poner) la computadora en _________ [lugar] porque…

Suggestions: En los Estados Unidos y el Canadá…
- Point out that *el computador* is used in some parts of Latin America; *el ordenador* is used in Spain.
- The article mentioned in this box comes from the newspaper *La opinión*. Have students find the *La opinión* website and read the main page (*la portada*) for the day.
- Have students discuss the importance of owning personal computers. *¿Por qué es importante que las familias tengan una computadora personal? ¿Cómo contribuye una computadora al desarrollo personal?*

En los Estados Unidos y el Canadá…

Las computadoras y la comunidad hispana

Según un estudio demográfico del año 2000, alrededor del 37 por ciento de las familias hispanas de Los Ángeles, Nueva York, Miami, Chicago y Houston (las cinco ciudades de los Estados Unidos con mayor población hispana) posee[a] una **computadora personal**. Se calcula que hay computadoras en más de un millón y medio de **hogares**[b] hispanos en los Estados Unidos.

El acceso de los hispanos a las computadoras y al Internet es un factor importante para su desarrollo[c] personal. Las computadoras y el Internet son herramientas[d] necesarias para **la educación, el trabajo, la comunicación** y sobre todo para **la información.** Casi todos los periódicos principales de los países hispanos se publican ahora en el Internet. A través de las publicaciones ciberespaciales, los hispanos pueden **informarse**. Leen sus noticias en español, y, es más,[e] pueden leer las noticias de su país o ciudad natal. También pueden participar en comunicaciones con **la comunidad hispana** del Internet.

En Chicago, Illinois

[a]*owns* [b]*homes* [c]*development* [d]*tools* [e]es… *furthermore*

Enfoque *cultural*

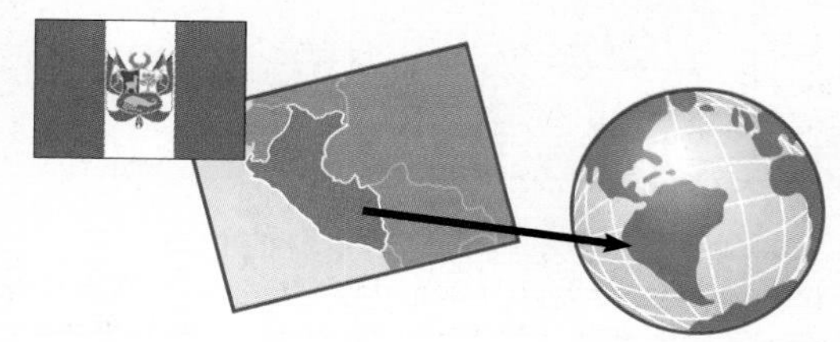

Enfoque cultural
See follow-up activities for this section in chapter-by-chapter materials in IM.

el Perú

Datos esenciales

Nombre oficial: República del Perú

Capital: Lima

Población: 24.000.000 de habitantes

Moneda: el nuevo sol

Idiomas oficiales: el español, el quechua, el aimara

Conozca... la cultura de los incas

Cuando los españoles llegaron al Perú en 1532, los incas ya dominaban una gran zona de Sudamérica, desde Colombia hasta Chile, y desde el Pacífico hasta las selvas[a] del este. A partir del siglo[b] XIII, muchos otros pueblos indígenas de la inmensa región vivían bajo[c] el dominio de los incas. La capital del imperio era Cuzco.

La palabra *inca* significa *rey* o *príncipe*[d] en quechua, lengua que todavía se habla en el Perú. Bajo su inca, el pueblo tenía un gobierno de poder absoluto y un sistema burocrático y social muy complejo.

Cuzco, Perú

El imperio inca se destacó[e] por la arquitectura, la ingeniería[f] y las técnicas de cultivo. También estableció un sistema de correo y un censo de la población. Tras la conquista[g] de los incas por los españoles Pizarro y Almagro, el Perú y su capital Lima, fundada por Pizarro en 1535, se convierten en un centro fundamental de las colonias españolas en América.

[a]*jungles* [b]A... *Beginning in the (thirteenth) century* [c]*under* [d]rey... *king or prince* [e]se... *distinguished itself* [f]*engineering* [g]Tras... *After the conquest*

¡Fíjese!

- El Lago Titicaca, que queda entre Bolivia y el Perú, es el lago más grande de Sudamérica y es la ruta de transporte principal entre estos dos países.
- Cientos de años antes de la llegada[a] de los españoles, la agricultura de los indígenas del Perú ya era muy sofisticada. Hace más de 2.000 años, los indígenas ya construían[b] terrazas para sembrar en las faldas[c] de los Andes. Muchas de estas terrazas se usan todavía.
- Uno de los cultivos[d] más importantes de los incas es la papa,[e] que originó en la región cerca del Lago Titicaca. La papa es una de las pocas plantas que puede subsistir[f] en altitudes de más de 13.000 pies y en regiones frías y áridas.

[a]*arrival* [b]ya... *were already building* [c]para... *so that they could plant on the slopes* [d]*crops* [e]*potato* [f]*survive*

Capítulo 12 of the video to accompany *¿Qué tal?* contains cultural footage of Peru.

Visit the *¿Qué tal?* website at www.mhhe.com/quetal.

Multimedia: Internet
Have students search the Internet for more information about Peru's government, educational system, geography, and economy. Remind them to look for the CIA World Factbook online. They can also search for the *Red científica peruana* online. This site, available in English and Spanish, contains information about Peru and links to cultural, economic, and tourist information.

 **Paso 3: Gramática**

See detailed supplementary materials for this grammar section in IM.

35 Expressing Desires and Requests • Use of the Subjunctive: Influence

Escoja la oración que describa cada dibujo.

1.

1. ____
   - **a.** Quiero repasar las formas del subjuntivo.
   - **b.** Quiero que nosotros repasemos juntos las formas del subjuntivo.

2.

2. ____
   - **a.** Insisto en hablar con Jorge.
   - **b.** Insisto en que tú hables con Jorge.

3.

3. ____
   - **a.** Es necesario arreglar esta habitación.
   - **b.** Es necesario que tú arregles esta habitación.

Follow-up: Subjunctive: Influence

Ask students the following questions about pairs of sentences that introduce this section: *¿Qué diferencia hay entre el significado de una oración y el significado de otra en cada par de oraciones? ¿Cuál es la diferencia lingüística?*

❖ **Transparency 72**

A. So far, you have learned to identify the subjunctive by the features listed at the right.

The subjunctive

- appears in a subordinate (dependent) clause.
- has a different subject from the one in the main (independent) clause.
- is preceded by **que**.

B. In addition, the use of the subjunctive is associated with the presence of a number of concepts or conditions that trigger the use of it in the dependent clause. The concept of influence is one trigger for the subjunctive in a dependent clause. When the speaker wants something to happen, he or she tries to influence the behavior of others, as in these sentences.

The verb in the main clause is, of course, in the indicative, because it is a fact that the subject of the sentence wants something. The subjunctive occurs in the dependent clause.

MAIN (INDEPENDENT) CLAUSE		SUBORDINATE (DEPENDENT) CLAUSE
Yo **quiero**	**que**	tú **pagues** la cuenta.
I want		*you to pay the bill.*
La profesora **prefiere**	**que**	los estudiantes no **lleguen** tarde.
The professor prefers	*that*	*the students don't arrive late.*

	STRONG	SOFT
C. **Querer** and **preferir** are not the only verbs that can express the main subject's desire to influence what someone else thinks or does. There are many other verbs of influence, some very strong and direct, some very soft and polite.	insistir en mandar permitir (*to permit*) prohibir (prohíbo)	desear pedir (i, i) recomendar (ie) sugerir (ie, i)
D. An impersonal generalization of influence or volition can also be the main clause that triggers the subjunctive. Some examples of this appear at the right.	Es necesario que… Es urgente que…	Es importante que… Es mejor que…

Práctica

A. En la tienda de aparatos electrónicos. Imagine que Ud. y un amigo / una amiga están en una tienda de aparatos electrónicos. Ud. quiere comprarse un estéreo pero no sabe cuál; por eso su amigo/a lo/la acompaña. ¿Quién dice las siguientes oraciones, Ud., su amigo/a o el vendedor (*salesperson*)?

1. Prefiero que busques un estéreo en varias tiendas; así puedes comparar precios.
2. Quiero que el estéreo tenga disco compacto con control remoto.
3. Recomiendo que no le digas cuánto dinero quieres gastar.
4. Insisto en que Ud. vea este modelo. ¡Es lo último!
5. Prefiero que me muestre otro modelo más barato.
6. Es mejor que vaya a buscar en otra tienda. No tengo tanto dinero.
7. Quiero que lo sepa: Este estéreo es el mejor de todos.

Preliminary exercise A
Have students express in Spanish: **1.** It's important to do it. **2.** It's important for Alice to do it. **3.** It's necessary to leave now. **4.** It's necessary that we leave now.

Follow-up A
Have students give formal commands for these situations. If it is a request, encourage them to use *por favor* and an appropriate tone.

B. Expectativas de la educación

Paso 1. ¿Qué expectativas de la educación tienen los profesores, los estudiantes y los padres de los estudiantes? Forme oraciones según las indicaciones y añada (*add*) palabras cuando sea necesario.

1. todos / profesores / querer / que / estudiantes / llegar / clase / a tiempo
2. profesor(a) de / español / preferir / que / (nosotros) ir / con frecuencia / laboratorio de lenguas
3. profesores / prohibir / que / estudiantes / traer / comida / y / bebida / clase
4. padres / de / estudiantes / desear / que / hijos / asistir a / clases
5. estudiantes / pedir / que / profesores / no dar / mucho / trabajo
6. también / (ellos) querer / que / haber / más vacaciones
7. padres / insistir en / que / hijos / sacar / buenas / notas

Paso 2. Y Ud., ¿qué quiere que hagan los profesores? Invente tres oraciones más para indicar sus deseos.

Suggestions A

- Point out that some recommendations may be direct commands. A combination of these with suggestions using subjunctive is typical for advice.
- Have students decide between *tú* and *Ud.* for each of the 3 cases. Remind them to think of the issue of formal vs. informal when they get to *Paso 2.*
- **Paso 1.** Have students work in small groups or pairs, and then share their findings with the class.

Suggestion A

Paso 2. Assign as written homework for next class.

Follow-up B

Have students share and compare sentences. Write inclusive categories on board that can be used to tally answers. Ask students if they see any patterns.

Conversación

A. Hablan los expertos en tecnología. Imagine que Ud. y sus compañeros de clase son un equipo (*team*) de expertos en problemas relacionados con la tecnología y que juntos (*together*) tienen un programa de radio.

Paso 1. Como miembro del equipo, lea las preguntas que les han mandado (*have sent*) los radioyentes (*radio audience*) por correo electrónico y déles una solución. Es bueno incluir frases como «Le recomiendo/sugiero que… », «Es importante/necesario/urgente que… »

1. Soy una joven de 20 años y soy extremadamente tímida. Por eso no me gusta salir. Prefiero asumir otra personalidad al conectarme en la red. Así estoy feliz por horas. Mi madre dice que esto no es normal y me pide que deje de hacerlo. Ella insiste en que vaya a las discotecas como otros jóvenes de mi edad. ¿Qué piensan Uds.?
2. Mi marido es un hombre muy bueno y trabajador. Tiene un buen trabajo, y es una persona muy respetada en su compañía. El problema es que sólo piensa en *software* y multimedia. Pasa todo su tiempo libre delante de la computadora o leyendo catálogos y revistas sobre computadoras. Yo prefiero que él pase más tiempo conmigo. En realidad (*In fact*), estoy tan aburrida que estoy pensando en dejarlo. ¿Qué recomiendan que haga?
3. Mi jefe quiere que deje de usar mi máquina de escribir (*typewriter*) y empiece a usar una computadora. Pero, no quiero hacerlo: Siempre he hecho bien mi trabajo sin la «caja boba» (*stupid box*). Mi jefe dice que tengo que ponerme al día (*up-to-date*) y me sugiere que tome un curso de computadoras que él promete pagar. Yo no entiendo por qué tengo que cambiar. ¿Me aconsejan (*do you advise*) que hable con un abogado/una abogada (*lawyer*)?

Paso 2. Ahora piense en un problema que se relacione con la tecnología que sea similar a los del **Paso 1**, y escríbalo. El resto de la clase le va a hacer sugerencias de cómo resolverlo.

B. Entrevista

Paso 1. Complete las siguientes oraciones lógicamente… ¡y con sinceridad!

1. Mis padres (hijos, abuelos,…) insisten en que (yo) _____.
2. Mi mejor amigo/a (esposo/a, novio/a,…) desea que (yo) _____.
3. Prefiero que mis amigos _____.
4. No quiero que mis amigos _____.
5. Es urgente que (yo) _____.
6. Es necesario que mi mejor amigo/a (esposo/a, novio/a,…) _____.

Paso 2. Ahora entreviste a un compañero / una compañera para saber cómo él/ella completó las oraciones del **Paso 1**.

MODELO: ¿En qué insisten tus padres?

UN POCO DE TODO

¿Qué quiere o necesita Ud.? Here is a series of answers to that question. Complete them with the correct form of each word in parentheses. When two possibilities are given in parentheses, select the correct word. **¡OJO!** You will use the present indicative, present subjunctive, or preterite of the infinitives. And sometimes, the infinitive itself will be the appropriate form.

1. Deseo que (haber[1]) paz[a] en (mí/mi[2]) país. Y quiero que mi familia (estar[3]) bien. También deseo que no (haber[4]) hambre en el mundo y que los niños no (sufrir[5]). Para (mí/mi[6]), (*yo:* pedir[7]) muy poco.
2. ¡Yo no (saber[8]) por dónde empezar la lista! Necesitamos una casa (tan/más[9]) grande, camas nuevas para los niños (pocos/pequeños[10]), (un/una[11]) televisor... Pero primero tenemos que (comprar[12]) (un/—[13]) otro coche, porque el que[b] tenemos (dejar[14]) de funcionar la semana pasada. ¡Ay!
3. Es necesario que mi jefa me (dar[15]) un aumento de sueldo. Ya trabajo (muchísimo[16]) horas, pero no (*yo:* ganar[17]) lo suficiente. El cheque que recibo cada dos semanas apenas[c] (cubrir[18])[d] los gastos (al/del[19]) apartamento, como (el/la[20]) alquiler, la luz y el gas. Por lo menos la dueña del apartamento es (mucho/muy[21]) simpática y me (gusta/gustan[22]) mucho el barrio donde vivo.
4. ¡Huy! ¡Muchas cosas! Quiero (comprar[23]) (un/una[24]) sofá para la sala, una computadora y equipo estereofónico. Además, me gustaría (comprar[25]) unas pinturas, (un/una[26]) fax...
5. Yo quiero que mi papá me (llevar[27]) al circo. Mi amigo Enrique (ir[28]) la semana pasada y le (gustar[29]) mucho. También necesito (un/una[30]) bici. Y quiero que el bebé que va (a/de[31]) tener mi mamá (ser[32]) un hermanito. Si es una niña, es un rollo,[e] ¡porque no va a (querer[33]) jugar al basquetbol!

[a]*peace* [b]el... *the one that* [c]*barely* [d]*to cover* [e]*pain*

Comprensión: ¿Cierto o falso?

1. No hay ninguna persona con deseos humanitarios.
2. Es necesario que alguien compre un coche.
3. Una persona quiere que su compañía le pague más.
4. Es completamente necesario que uno de los entrevistados compre unas pinturas y equipo estereofónico.
5. Otro entrevistado quiere que el nuevo bebé de sus padres sea una niña.

Follow-Up: Un poco de todo

To check comprehension, ask: *¿Cuál de las siguientes personas habla en cada párrafo?* ¡OJO! *Hay una persona que no encaja* (fit). **1.** *Rafael, un niño que tiene seis años.* **2.** *un representante de la UNICEF* **3.** *el presidente de una compañía de importación y exportación* **4.** *un soldado* **5.** *una mujer que tiene cuatro hijos y sólo trabaja su esposo* **6.** *Javier, un joven que acaba de conseguir su primer trabajo*

Answers: Un poco de todo

1. *haya* **2.** *mi* **3.** *esté* **4.** *haya* **5.** *sufran* **6.** *mí* **7.** *pido* **8.** *sé* **9.** *más* **10.** *pequeños* **11.** *un* **12.** *comprar* **13.** — **14.** *dejó* **15.** *dé* **16.** *muchísimas* **17.** *gano* **18.** *cubre* **19.** *del* **20.** *el* **21.** *muy* **22.** *gusta* **23.** *comprar* **24.** *un* **25.** *comprar* **26.** *un* **27.** *lleve* **28.** *fue* **29.** *gustó* **30.** *una* **31.** *a* **32.** *sea* **33.** *querer*

In the *Capítulo 12* segment of "Chapter-by-Chapter Supplementary Materials" in the IM, you will find a chapter-culminating activity. You can use this activity to consolidate and review the vocabulary and grammar skills students have acquired.

PASO 4 Un paso más

Paso 4: Un paso más
Optional section

 See IM for suggestions and follow-up activities to accompany the video segment.

VIDEOTECA: En contexto

FUNCTION
Giving instructions

In this video segment, Mariela helps a student in the computer laboratory to use e-mail for sending a document. As you watch the segment, pay particular attention to the use of computer-related vocabulary. What do you think **adjuntar documento** means? And what about **dirección electrónica**?

A. Lluvia de ideas

- ¿A quién le pide ayuda Ud. cuando tiene problemas con los programas informáticos? Otras personas, ¿le piden ayuda a Ud.?
- ¿Dónde prefiere Ud. hacer las tareas universitarias, en casa o en un laboratorio de computadoras? ¿Por qué? **Extension A**

Ask: 1. *En su familia, ¿quién es la persona que sabe más de informática? ¿Saben mucho de este tema sus padres (hijos)?* 2. *¿Cree Ud. que es importante saber de informática para encontrar un buen trabajo hoy día? ¿Por qué?*

B. Dictado

A continuación están las instrucciones que Mariela le da al estudiante. Complete la explicación con las palabras o frases que faltan.

ESTUDIANTE: Es que no sé __manejar__[1] bien este programa.
MARIELA: A ver... ¿qué es lo que intenta hacer?
ESTUDIANTE: Quiero __mandar__[2] este documento por correo __electrónico__[3] a mi profesor, pero no __funciona__.[4]
MARIELA: Vamos a ver. Con __permiso__[5]...
ESTUDIANTE: ¿Quiere Ud. hacerlo?
MARIELA: No. Prefiero que Ud. lo haga. Así aprende mejor. Bien. Primero, abra su cuenta[a] de __correo__[6] electrónico. No, es mejor que no abra el __documento__.[7] Bien. Ahora sugiero que ponga primero la __dirección__[8] electrónica del profesor en ese espacio. Cuidado,[b] un error tipográfico y no funciona.

[a]*account* [b]*Careful*

C. Un diálogo original

Paso 1. Con un compañero / una compañera, dramatice la escena entre Mariela y el estudiante.

Paso 2. Ayudando a un compañero / una compañera. Imagine que Ud. y un compañero / una compañera tienen una conversación en el laboratorio de computadoras de su universidad.

Suggestion B
To check comprehension, ask: 1. *¿Qué tipo de programa no sabe manejar el estudiante?* 2. *¿Qué debe hacer primero el estudiante para mandar el documento electrónicamente?* 3. *¿Con qué le sugiere Mariela que tenga cuidado?*

Cultura en contexto
El léxico (Las palabras) de la nueva tecnología

Tan rápido como se desarrollan[a] nuevas tecnologías, se inventan nuevas palabras para expresarlas. Hasta ahora, las palabras que se usan en español vienen principalmente del inglés: «el Internet», «el software», «hacer click en» (*to click on*). Este nuevo vocabulario varía de país en país. Por ejemplo, en Latinoamérica, se dice «la computadora» o «el computador». En España se dice «el ordenador».

[a]se... *are developed*

E1: Ud. es un novato / una novata (*novice*) en eso de computadoras y no sabe llegar al sitio web de su clase de ____ (o no sabe conseguir su correo electrónico). Por eso le pide ayuda a alguien de la clase.

E2: Ud. es «un experto / una experta» en computadoras y ayuda a otro/a estudiante de la clase con los problemas que tiene.

PASO FINAL

A CONVERSAR

Extension: A conversar
Have students vote on the best scene and then on the best apartment overall, based on price, location, and amenities.

Buscando apartamento

Paso 1. Lea los avisos (*ads*) de los apartamentos para alquilar, y escoja el apartamento que Ud. prefiere.

1.
3 dorm. 1 baño.
Cerca del parque y centro comercial. Planta Baja. $900.

2.
Zona residencial excelente. 3 dorm. 2 baños. Garaje gratis. Sala grande. $1000.

3.
¡Cocina para gourmet!
2 dorm. 1 baño. Autobús. Amueblado. Portero. $825.

Paso 2. En grupos de tres, imaginen que necesitan alquilar un apartamento juntos. Indiquen dónde prefieren vivir y por qué. Traten de comenzar sus oraciones con frases como **Prefiero que… , Recomiendo que… , Es mejor que…** o **Es importante que…** Después, cada grupo debe escoger uno de los apartamentos.

MODELO: Recomiendo que alquilemos el apartamento número dos porque tiene una sala grande. También es mejor que haya dos baños.

Paso 3. Cada grupo debe inventar más información sobre el apartamento que escogió. La información puede incluir: dónde está el apartamento, cuánto es el alquiler, si se permiten animales, si está en una casa particular o en una casa de apartamentos, si se incluye la luz en el alquiler, etcétera.

MODELO: El alquiler es setecientos dólares al mes. La luz no está incluida.

Paso 4. Cada grupo debe improvisar una escena entre dos personas que buscan apartamento y el dueño / la dueña que lo alquila, basándose en los avisos y la información que inventaron.

MODELO: E1: ¿Dónde está el apartamento?
E2: Está en el centro, en una zona muy bonita.

En resumen

GRAMÁTICA

To review the grammar points presented in this chapter, refer to the indicated grammar presentations. You'll find further practice of these structures in the Workbook/Laboratory Manual, on the CD-ROM, and on the website.

33. *Tú* Commands

Do you know how to give orders to friends and children in Spanish? How do you tell them what not to do?

34. Present Subjunctive: An Introduction

Do you understand how to form the present subjunctive?

35. Use of the Subjunctive: Influence

You should be able to express that you want or need someone else to do something without giving a direct command.

VOCABULARIO

Los verbos

alegrarse (de)	to be happy (about)
arreglar	to straighten (up); to fix, repair
cambiar (de)	to change
copiar / hacer copia	to copy
dudar	to doubt
esperar	to hope
fallar	to "crash" (*a computer*)
funcionar	to work, function; to run (*machines*)
grabar	to record; to tape
guardar	to keep; to save (*documents*)
haber (*infinitive form of* **hay**)	(*there is, there are*)
imprimir	to print
mandar	to order
manejar	to drive; to operate (*a machine*)
obtener (*irreg.*)	to get, obtain
permitir	to permit, allow
prohibir	to prohibit, forbid

Repaso: conseguir (i, i), sacar fotos

Vehículos

la bicicleta (de montaña)	(mountain) bike
el carro (descapotable)	(convertible) car
el monopatín	skateboard
la moto(cicleta)	motorcycle, moped
los patines	roller skates

Repaso: el coche

La electrónica

el archivo	(computer) file
el canal	channel
el contestador automático	answering machine
el correo electrónico	e-mail
el disco duro	hard drive
el equipo estereofónico/ fotográfico	stereo/photography equipment
la grabadora	tape recorder/ player
la impresora	printer
el ordenador (*Sp.*)	computer
el ratón	mouse
la red	net
navegar la red	to surf the net

el teléfono celular / de coche	cellular/car phone
la videocasetera	video cassette recorder (VCR)

Repaso: la cinta, el televisor

Cognados: la cámara (de vídeo), el CD-ROM, la computadora, el control remoto, el disco compacto, el disco de computadora, el fax, la memoria, el módem, el radio (portátil) / la radio,* el *walkman*

Para poder gastar

el aumento	raise
el/la jefe/a	boss
el sueldo	salary

La vivienda

alquilar	to rent
las afueras	outskirts; suburbs
el alquiler	rent
el área (*but f.*)	area
la avenida	avenue
el barrio	neighborhood
la calle	street
el campo	countryside
el *campus*	(university) campus
la casa (el bloque) de apartamentos	apartment building
la comunidad	community
la dirección	address
el/la dueño/a	landlord, landlady
el gas	gas; heat
el/la inquilino/a	tenant; renter
el piso	floor (of a building)
la planta baja	ground floor
el/la portero/a	building manager; doorman
la vecindad	neighborhood
el/la vecino/a	neighbor
la vista	view

Repaso: el apartamento, la casa, el centro, el cuarto, la luz, la residencia

Otros sustantivos

el gasto	expense
el lujo	luxury

Palabras adicionales

los/las demás	others

Suggestions: Vocabulario

- Remind students: first-person singular of *prohibir* is *prohíbo,* of *conseguir* is *consigo,* and of *poner* is *pongo.*
- Give definitions or descriptions and have students name item, for example, *El dinero que uno recibe cada una o dos semanas por el trabajo que hace* → *el sueldo.*
- Divide students into 2 teams and have them play Password. Cues must be a single word in Spanish and must not be a variation of the answer (*grabar / grabadora*). Allow only 1 cue and attempt per turn.
- Bring or have students bring images of *Vocabulario* activities and items. Use these to elicit descriptions, ask/answer questions, and play games.
- Ask questions using words from *Vocabulario:* **1.** *Además del teléfono tradicional, ¿qué otros tipos de teléfono hay?* **2.** *Para mandar documentos, fotos, etcétera, ¿qué aparato resulta muy rápido?* **3.** *¿Qué se necesita para comunicarse por correo electrónico?*

***El radio** is the apparatus; **la radio** is the medium.

Resources

You and your students may find the following *¿Qué tal?* supplements helpful as you teach this chapter:

For the Instructor

- *Instructor's Manual and Resource Kit,* "Chapter-by-Chapter" Supplementary Materials
- Testing Program
- Overhead Transparencies 73–75
- Video (VHS or CD)
- *¿Qué tal?* Online Learning Center Website
- Audioscript
- Instructor's Resource CD

El arte y la cultura

For Students

- Workbook/Laboratory Manual and Audio Program or Electronic Workbook/ Laboratory Manual
- Video on CD
- Interactive CD-ROM
- *¿Qué tal?* Online Learning Center Website
- Listening Comprehension Audio CD
- McGraw-Hill Electronic Language Tutor (MHELT)

VOCABULARIO

- The arts
- Ranking things

Suggestion: Chapter Opening photo

Point out chapter opening photo. Have students describe the scene in the photo (sidewalk art vendors). Have them talk about art and how it is presented and sold. Ask if they know of areas where vendors or artists sell paintings on the street or in open-air markets. Ask what art they have or their family has at home. What kind of art is it? Where did they get it?

GRAMÁTICA

36 Use of the Subjunctive: Emotion

37 Use of the Subjunctive: Doubt and Denial

CULTURA

- **Enfoque cultural:** Bolivia y el Ecuador
- **Nota cultural:** Los toros
- **En los Estados Unidos y el Canadá:** Carlos Santana y la Fundación Milagro
- **Cultura en contexto:** El arte y las artesanías

Multimedia

You will learn about bargaining in the **En contexto** video segment.

Review vocabulary and grammar and practice language skills with the interactive CD-ROM.

WWW. Get connected to the Spanish-speaking world with the *¿Qué tal?* Online Learning Center: **www.mhhe.com/quetal**.

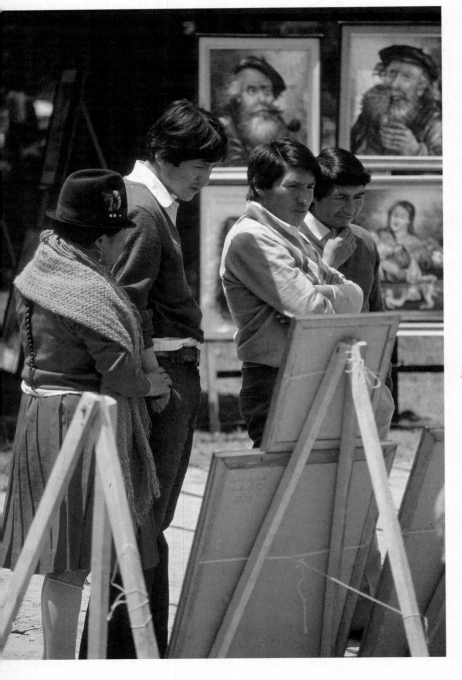

◀ Estos residentes de Quito, Ecuador, miran las obras de arte que se venden en el Parque de la Alameda.

Vocabulario PASO 1

Paso 1: Vocabulario

See detailed supplementary materials and exercises for this section and a model for vocabulary presentation and other material in the *Capítulo 13 Paso 1: Vocabulario* section of "Chapter-by-Chapter Supplementary Materials," IM.

Las artes*

❖ Transparency 73

En el teatro

La expresión artística

la arquitectura architecture
el baile / la danza dance
el cine film; movies
el drama drama
la escultura sculpture
la fotografía photography
la literatura literature
la música music
la ópera opera
la pintura painting

cantar to sing
crear to create
dibujar to draw
escribir to write
esculpir to sculpt
pintar to paint
tejer to weave

Otras personas

el/la aficionado/a fan
el/la arquitecto/a architect
el/la artista artist
el/la compositor(a) composer
el/la dramaturgo/a playwright
el/la escritor(a) writer
el/la escultor(a) sculptor
el/la pintora painter
el/la poeta poet

La tradición cultural

la artesanía arts and crafts
la cerámica pottery, ceramics
las ruinas ruins
los tejidos woven goods

Otras palabras útiles

la canción song
el cuadro / la pintura painting (*piece of art*) / painting (*piece of art; the art form*)
la obra (de arte) work (of art)
la obra maestra masterpiece

*The word **arte** is used with masculine articles and adjectives in the singular and with feminine ones when in the plural.

Guillermo es estudiante **del arte moderno**.
Me gustan mucho **las artes gráficas**.

Multimedia: Audio

Students can listen to and practice this chapter's vocabulary on their Listening Comprehension Audio CD.

Conversación

A. Obras de arte. ¿Qué tipo de arte representan las siguientes obras?

1. la catedral de Notre Dame y la de Santiago de Compostela
2. los murales de Diego Rivera
3. las estatuas griegas y romanas
4. *El lago de los Cisnes* (Swan Lake) y *El amor brujo* (Love, the Magician)
5. *El ciudadano Kane* y *El mago* (Wizard) *de Oz*
6. *La Bohème* y *La Traviata*
7. las ruinas aztecas y mayas
8. *Don Quijote* y *Cien años de soledad*

Answers A
1. *la arquitectura* 2. *la pintura* 3. *la escultura* 4. *el baile* 5. *el cine* 6. *la ópera* 7. *la arquitectura* 8. *la literatura*

B. ¿Qué hacen? Forme oraciones completas, emparejando palabras de cada columna. Luego, con dos o tres compañeros, dé nombres de artistas en cada categoría.

la compositora	escribe	novelas y poesía
la actriz	baila	canciones
el director	esculpe	en el ballet
el músico	toca	edificios y casas
el bailarín	interpreta	papeles (*roles*) en la televisión
el dramaturgo	diseña	guiones
la pintora	pinta	con actores
el escritor	mira	obras de teatro
la arquitecta	trabaja	cuadros
	dirige (*directs*)	instrumentos musicales
	compone (*composes*)	

Suggestion B
Do this as a contest. Have each group write their answers on board so that everyone can see what they came up with. Provide the following names after completing activity: ***el cine:*** *Robert Rodríguez, Pedro Almodóvar, Antonio Banderas, Luis Buñuel, Salma Hayek;* ***la literatura:*** *Isabel Allende, Laura Esquivel, Gabriel García Márquez, Octavio Paz, Carlos Fuentes;* ***la música:*** *Manuel de Falla, Pablo Casals, Gloria Estefan, Julio Iglesias, Tito Puente, Carlos Santana, Los Lobos, Ricky Martin, Jennifer López;* ***la pintura:*** *Frida Kahlo, Diego Rivera, José Clemente Orozco, Salvador Dalí, Pablo Picasso;* ***la arquitectura:*** *Antoni Gaudí.*

NOTA COMUNICATIVA

Más sobre los gustos y preferencias

Here are additional verbs to talk about what you like and don't like.

- The following two verbs are used like **gustar**.

aburrir	**Me aburre** el ballet moderno. *Modern ballet bores me.*
agradar	Pero **me agrada** el ballet folklórico. *But I like folkloric dances.*

- This verb functions as a transitive verb (takes a direct object).

apreciar	**Aprecio** mucho la arquitectura precolombina. *I really appreciate pre-Columbian architecture.*

Suggestions: Nota comunicativa
- Offer optional word: *atraer* → *Me atrae el ballet moderno.*
- Point out that *apreciar* is like *odiar.* They both require direct objects.

C. Preferencias personales

Paso 1. ¿Le gusta el arte? ¿Asiste a funciones culturales de vez en cuando o no asiste a esas funciones nunca? ¡Diga la verdad!

MODELO: asistir a los ballets clásicos →
Me gusta mucho asistir a los ballets clásicos.
(No me agrada para nada asistir a los ballets clásicos.)
(Me aburre asistir a los ballets clásicos. Prefiero ir a la ópera.)

Palabras útiles: gustar, apreciar, preferir, encantar, aburrir, agradar, interesar

1. ir a los museos de arte moderno
2. asistir a funciones teatrales
3. ver obras maestras en los museos grandes
4. escuchar a un(a) guía (*guide*) hablar en un museo
5. ir a conciertos de música clásica
6. asistir a lecturas de poesía en un café

Paso 2. Ahora entreviste a un compañero / una compañera para saber cuáles son sus preferencias con respecto a este tema.

MODELO: E1: ¿Te gusta ir a los museos de arte moderno?
E2: Sí, me gusta muchísimo. Voy siempre que puedo (*whenever I can*).

Follow-up C

- Have each student write another cultural cue on piece of paper. Collect all papers and write cultural cues on board so that students can answer them. Encourage both silly and serious cues.
- Ask: **1.** *¿Tiene Ud. talento artístico? ¿Para qué? ¿Qué le gusta crear? ¿Cuándo empezó a desarrollar* (develop) *esta actividad? ¿Tiene aspiraciones de dedicarse a esa actividad profesionalmente? ¿Cuáles son las ventajas y las desventajas de esa ocupación?* **2.** *Si Ud. cree que no posee ningún talento artístico en particular, ¿siente alguna atracción por el arte? ¿Qué tipo de arte en particular? ¿Por qué le gusta tanto?* **3.** *¿Le gusta ir a los mercados de artesanía? ¿Qué compra allí? Cuando va de viaje, ¿le interesa saber cuáles son los trajes y la música tradicionales del lugar que visita? ¿Colecciona Ud. obras de artesanía? ¿Qué colecciona?*

Heritage speakers

Pregúnteles a sus estudiantes hispanohablantes si han visto una corrida de toros. ¿Qué opinan? ¿Es un arte o un acto violento?

NOTA CULTURAL

Los toros

El toreo[a] es un espectáculo típicamente hispánico. Viene de una larga tradición histórica. De hecho, no se sabe exactamente cuándo surgió la primera **corrida de toros**,[b] pero hay evidencia histórica de corridas que data desde la Edad Media.

Para sus aficionados, el toreo es **un arte**, y **el torero** necesita mucho más que valor:[c] necesita destreza[d] técnica, gracia y mucha comprensión de **los toros**. Algunos creen que el toreo *no es* un arte, sino un espectáculo cruel y violento que causa la muerte[e] prematura e innecesaria de un animal valiente.

Sea cual sea la opinión que Ud. tiene[f] de las corridas de toros, las corridas son muy simbólicas para los aficionados. El toro es símbolo de fuerza,[g] coraje, bravura, independencia y belleza.[h] Si Ud. visita un país hispánico y tiene ganas de ver una corrida, es aconsejable que les pregunte a algunas personas nativas cuáles son las corridas que debe ver.

Una corrida de toros en Toledo, España

[a]El... *Bullfighting* [b]corrida... *bullfight* [c]*bravery* [d]*skill* [e]*death* [f]Sea... *Whatever your opinion may be* [g]*strength* [h]*beauty*

Multimedia: Internet
Have students search Internet for information about the history of bullfighting.

Ranking Things: Ordinals

primer(o/a)	first	**cuarto/a**	fourth	**sexto/a**	sixth	**noveno/a**	ninth
segundo/a	second	**quinto/a**	fifth	**séptimo/a**	seventh	**décimo/a**	tenth
tercer(o/a)	third			**octavo/a**	eighth		

- Ordinal numbers are adjectives and must agree in number and gender with the nouns they modify. Ordinals usually precede the noun: **la cuarta lección, el octavo ejercicio**.
- Like **bueno**, the ordinals **primero** and **tercero** shorten to **primer** and **tercer**, respectively, before masculine singular nouns: **el primer niño, el tercer mes**.
- Ordinal numbers are frequently abbreviated with superscript letters that show the adjective ending: **las 1as lecciones, el 1er grado, el 5° estudiante**.

Preliminary exercise: Ranking Things
Have students respond *cierto* or *falso:* **1.** *El* (*lunes*) *es el* (*primer*) *día de la semana.* (Vary days, creating some incorrect items.) **2.** (*Enero*) *es el* (*primer*) *mes del año.* (Vary months, creating some incorrect items.) **3.** *Bob es el* (*quinto*) *estudiante en esta fila.*

Suggestion A
Have students rank in order of importance to them the following characteristics in each category.
- ***Los cursos para el próximo semestre/trimestre:*** *la hora de la clase, el profesor / la profesora, la materia, la posibilidad de sacar una buena nota, el costo de los libros, si tiene laboratorio o no, el edificio donde se da la clase, el tamaño* (size) *de la clase.*
- ***La selección de un trabajo:*** *el sueldo, el prestigio de la compañía, la ciudad, la posibilidad de ascenso* (promotion), *la personalidad del jefe / de la jefa, las condiciones físicas de la oficina, si tiene una oficina privada o no.*

Conversación

A. Mis actividades favoritas

Paso 1. Piense en lo que le gusta hacer en su tiempo libre en cuanto a (*regarding*) actividades culturales. Luego ponga en el orden de su preferencia (del 1 al 10) las siguientes actividades.

_____ ir al cine
_____ ir a ver películas extranjeras o clásicas
_____ ir a museos
_____ asistir a conciertos de música clásica/rock
_____ leer poesía
_____ bailar en una discoteca
_____ ver programas de televisión
_____ ver obras teatrales
_____ leer una novela
_____ ¿ ?

Paso 2. Ahora cuéntele a un compañero / una compañera sus cinco actividades favoritas. Use números ordinales.

MODELO: Mi actividad favorita es ir a ver películas clásicas. Mi segunda actividad favorita es…

B. Preguntas

1. ¿Es Ud. estudiante de cuarto año?
2. ¿Es este su segundo semestre/trimestre de español?
3. ¿A qué hora es su primera clase los lunes? ¿y su segunda clase?
4. ¿Vive Ud. en una casa de apartamentos o en una residencia? ¿En qué piso vive? Si vive en una casa, ¿en qué piso está su alcoba?

Paso 2: Gramática
See detailed supplementary materials for this grammar section in IM.

36 Expressing Feelings • Use of the Subjunctive: Emotion

Diego y Lupe escuchan un grupo de mariachis

Note: Subjunctive: Emotion
There is more than one theory regarding origin of the word *mariachi*. Currently, the most favored theory is that the word has its origin in a Coca Indian word for music maker. The Coca were one of many indigenous groups that lived in parts of Mexico.

México, D.F.

DIEGO: Ay, ¡cómo me encanta esta música!
LUPE: *Me alegro de que te guste.*
DIEGO: Y yo *me alegro de que estemos* aquí. ¿Sabes el origen de la palabra **mariachi**?
LUPE: No… ¿Lo sabes tú?
DIEGO: Sí. Viene del siglo diecinueve, cuando los franceses ocuparon México. Ellos contrataban a grupos de músicos para tocar en las bodas. Y como los mexicanos no podían pronunciar bien la palabra francesa *mariage*, pues acabaron por decir **mariachi**. Y de allí viene el nombre de los grupos.
LUPE: ¡Qué fascinante! *Me sorprende que sepas* tantos datos interesantes de nuestra historia.
DIEGO: Pues, todo buen antropólogo debe saber un poco de historia también, ¿no?

Comprensión

1. Lupe se alegra de que _____.
2. Y Diego se alegra de que _____.
3. A Lupe le sorprende que _____.

Suggestion: Subjunctive: Emotion
Have students pick out subjunctive and subjunctive cues in *minidiálogo*. Ask: What do the cues have in common? (emotional responses)

MAIN (INDEPENDENT) CLAUSE		SUBORDINATE (DEPENDENT) CLAUSE
first subject + *indicative* (expression of emotion)	**que**	second subject + *subjunctive*

Follow-up: Subjunctive: Emotion
To check comprehension, ask: *¿Le sorprende a Ud. que la palabra* ***mariachi*** *venga del francés? ¿De qué cosas se alegra Ud.? ¿Qué le molesta que haga su compañero/a de cuarto / casa (esposo/a, etcétera)? ¿Qué le sorprende de la clase de español?*

A. Expressions of emotion are those in which speakers express their feelings: *I'm glad you're here; It's good that they can come.* Such expressions of emotion are followed by the subjunctive mood in the subordinate (dependent) clause.

Esperamos que Ud. **pueda** asistir.
We hope (that) you'll be able to come.

Tengo miedo de que mi abuelo **esté** muy enfermo.
I'm afraid (that) my grandfather is very ill.

Es una lástima que no **den** aumentos este año.
It's a shame they're not giving raises this year.

Diego and Lupe are listening to a mariachi group. DIEGO: Oh, how I love this music! LUPE: I'm glad you like it. DIEGO: And I'm glad we're here. Do you know the origin of the word **mariachi**? LUPE: No . . . Do you? DIEGO: Yes. It comes from the nineteenth century, when the French occupied Mexico. They used to hire musical groups to play at weddings. And because the Mexicans couldn't correctly pronounce the French word *mariage*, they ended up saying **mariachi**. And so that's where the name of the groups comes from. LUPE: How fascinating! I'm surprised you know so much interesting information about our history. DIEGO: Well, all good anthropologists should also know a little bit of history, shouldn't they?

WW. Multimedia: Internet
Have students search the Internet for music clips of *mariachi* music. If possible, bring tape or CD of *mariachi* performance to class.

B. Some common expressions of emotion are found in the list at the right.

alegrarse de	to be happy about
esperar	to hope
sentir (ie, i)	to regret; to feel sorry
temer	to fear
tener miedo (de)	to be afraid (of)

Some common expressions of emotion used with indirect object pronouns are in the second list at the right.

me (te, le,...) gusta que	I'm (you're, he's . . .) glad that
me (te, le,...) molesta que	it bothers me (you, him, . . .) that
me (te, le,...) sorprende que	it surprises me (you, him, . . .) that

C. When a new subject is introduced after a generalization of emotion, it is followed by the subjunctive in the subordinate (dependent) clause. Here are some general expressions of emotion.

es extraño	it's strange
es increíble	it's incredible
es mejor/bueno/malo	it's better/good/bad
es ridículo	it's ridiculous
es terrible	it's terrible
es una lástima	it's a shame
es urgente	it's urgent
¡qué extraño!	how strange!
¡qué lástima!	what a shame!

WWW. Multimedia: Internet
Have students search Internet for Spanish language newspapers (*El País, La Jornada,* and so on). Based on current news events, students should prepare 5 statements expressing their emotion and using subjunctive, for example: *Es increíble que haya tanto turismo en Costa Rica.*

Preliminary exercises A
- Use chain drill to practice forms: **1.** *Espero que tú sepas el número correcto.* (*Ud., ella, nosotros, Uds.*) **2.** *Los padres tienen miedo de que seamos malos estudiantes.* (*yo, tú, ellos, Elvira*) **3.** *Es una lástima que no podamos ir al museo.* (*yo, Uds. él, vosotras*)
- Have students express in Spanish: **1.** I'm afraid that they're not coming / that he can't do it. **2.** It surprises me that you can't do it / that he won't permit it.

Suggestion A
Have students express in Spanish: **1.** I'm sorry your daughter is sick. **2.** It's incredible that Johnny is already 12 years old! **3.** What a shame that Julio isn't feeling well! **4.** How strange that Jorge never calls you! **5.** I'm glad that you're going to get the painting for your grandmother.

Práctica

A. Opiniones sobre el cine

Paso 1. Indique si las siguientes oraciones son ciertas o falsas para Ud.

1. Me molesta que muchas películas sean tan violentas.
2. Es ridículo que algunos actores ganen tanto dinero.
3. Espero que salgan más actores asiáticos e hispánicos en las películas.
4. Temo que muchas actrices no desempeñen (*play*) papeles inteligentes.
5. Es increíble que gasten millones de dólares en hacer películas.
6. Me sorprende que Julia Roberts sea tan famosa.

Paso 2. Ahora invente oraciones sobre lo que Ud. quiere o no quiere que pase con respecto al cine. Use las oraciones del **Paso 1** como base.

MODELO: **1.** Quiero que las películas sean menos violentas.

Follow-up A
Have students give 2 opinions of their own. Use **Paso 1** as a model. Use **Paso 2** as a model for ensuing suggestions and wishes.

NOTA COMUNICATIVA

Expressing Wishes with *ojalá*

¡**Ojalá** que yo **gane** la lotería algún día!	*I hope I win the lottery some day!*

The word **ojalá** is invariable in form and means *I wish* or *I hope.* It is used with the subjunctive to express wishes or hopes. The use of **que** with it is optional.

¡**Ojalá (que) haya** paz en el mundo algún día!	*I hope (that) there will be peace in the world some day!*
Ojalá que no **pierdan** tu equipaje.	*I hope (that) they don't lose your luggage.*

Ojalá can also be used alone as an interjection in response to a question.

—¿Te va a ayudar Julio a estudiar para el examen?
—**¡Ojalá!**

Notes: Nota comunicativa

- **¡OJO!** *Ojalá* is invariable in form and always followed by subjunctive. *Ojalá* itself is not conjugated.
- *Ojalá* comes from Arabic expression *Allah (God) willing* or *may Allah want.* Point out that Arabs invaded Europe through and lived in what is today Spain and Portugal for 8 centuries (8th–15th). Their influence was great on the Iberian Peninsula; their language, especially, influenced Spanish vocabulary. Other commonly used Spanish words that come from Arabic include *el álgebra, el aceite, la almohada* (pillow).

B. Una excursión a la ópera. Imagine que Ud. y su amigo/a van a la ópera por primera vez en su vida. Piense en todas las expectativas que Ud. tiene y expréselas usando **ojalá**.

MODELO: las entradas / no costar mucho →
Ojalá que las entradas no cuesten mucho.

1. el escenario / ser / extravagante
2. haber / subtítulos / en inglés
3. el director (*conductor*) / estar / preparado
4. los cantantes / saber / sus papeles
5. nuestros asientos / no estar / lejos del escenario
6. (nosotros) llegar / a tiempo

Follow-up B

Ask: *¿A Ud. le interesa la ópera? ¿Le fascina, le aburre o no tiene opinión?*

❖ Transparency 74

Suggestion A
Show overhead transparency and have students close their books. Ask questions and have volunteers answer.

National Standards: Communication
Have students work in groups to react to each situation, and then resolve it by giving advice or making a request, for example, *Situación: Su profesor(a) de español les da muchos exámenes.* → *Reacción: (No) Me gusta eso. Quiero que nos dé más/menos exámenes. Solución: Profesor(a), dénos más/menos exámenes, por favor.* **1.** *Su profesor(a) les habla muy rápidamente en español.* **2.** *No hay asientos en la sección de no fumar y Ud. se sienta al lado de un señor que fuma mucho.* **3.** *Su vecino/a pone el estéreo por la mañana mientras Ud. trata de estudiar.* **4.** *Sus padres (amigos) siempre van de vacaciones al mismo sitio todos los veranos.*

Conversación

A. Situaciones. Las siguientes personas están pensando en otra persona o en algo que van a hacer. ¿Qué emociones sienten? ¿Qué temen? Conteste las preguntas según los dibujos.

①

②

③

1. Jorge piensa en su amiga Estela. ¿Por qué piensa en ella? ¿Dónde está? ¿Qué siente Jorge? ¿Qué espera? ¿Qué espera Estela? ¿Espera que la visiten los amigos? ¿que le manden algo?
2. Fausto quiere comer fuera esta noche. ¿Quiere que alguien lo acompañe? ¿Dónde espera que cenen? ¿Qué teme Fausto? ¿Qué le parecen (*seem*) los precios del restaurante?
3. ¿Dónde quiere pasar las vacaciones Mariana? ¿Espera que alguien la acompañe? ¿Dónde espera que pasen los días? ¿Qué teme Mariana? ¿Qué espera?

Suggestion B
Have students complete activity in groups of 4–6. Have 1 student act as secretary, taking notes on general reactions. Later he/she will summarize comments of his/her group with sentences like *Nuestro grupo piensa / opina / dice / no está de acuerdo en...* General results from all groups can serve as starting point for simple discussion or debate.

B. ¿Qué le molesta más? The following phrases describe aspects of university life. React to them, using phrases such as: **Me gusta que... , Me molesta que... , Es terrible que... , Es bueno/malo que... , Es una lástima que...**

1. Se pone mucho énfasis en los deportes.
2. Pagamos mucho/poco por la matrícula.
3. Se ofrecen muchos/pocos cursos en mi especialización (*major*).
4. Es necesario estudiar ciencias/lenguas para graduarse.
5. Hay muchos/pocos requisitos (*requirements*) para graduarse.
6. En general, hay muchas/pocas personas en las clases.

Enfoque *cultural*

Enfoque cultural
See follow-up activities for this section in chapter-by-chapter materials in IM.

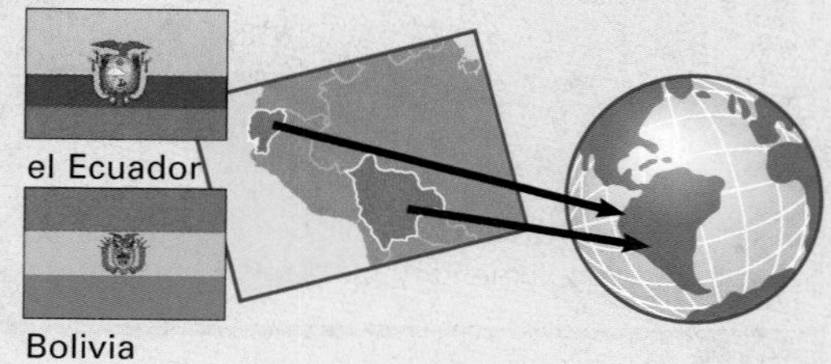

Bolivia y el Ecuador

Datos esenciales

Bolivia

Nombre oficial: República de Bolivia

Capital: La Paz (sede[a] del gobierno), Sucre (capital constitucional)

Población: 8.000.000 de habitantes

Moneda: el (peso) boliviano

Idiomas oficiales: el español, el quechua, el aimara

el Ecuador

Nombre oficial: República del Ecuador

Capital: Quito

Población: 11.000.000 de habitantes

Moneda: el sucre (el dolar)

Idiomas: el español (oficial), el quechua

[a]*seat*

¡Fíjese!

- Bolivia formó parte del antiguo imperio inca. Aproximadamente, el 55 por ciento de la población boliviana actual es de origen indígena.
- Bolivia fue nombrada[a] en honor a Simón Bolívar, quien luchó por la independencia del país.
- A 12.000 pies de altura, La Paz es la capital más alta del mundo.
- Las Islas Galápagos pertenecen[b] al Ecuador y son de origen volcánico. Fueron descubiertas[c] en 1535, por el español Berlanga. Berlanga las llamó las Islas Encantadas[d] porque las fuertes corrientes[e] marinas confundían a los navegantes[f] como si fuera por[g] acto de magia. Trescientos años más tarde, el biólogo Charles Darwin llegó a las islas. De sus investigaciones de las plantas y animales resultaron sus ideas sobre la evolución y su famoso libro, *El origen de las especies.* Darwin teorizó que los animales y las plantas cambian y se adaptan a su medio ambiente.[h]

[a]fue... *was named* [b]*belong* [c]Fueron... *They were discovered* [d]*Enchanted* [e]*currents* [f]*sailors* [g]como... *as if by* [h]medio... *environment*

Conozca a...

Oswaldo Guayasamín

Oswaldo Guayasamín (1919–1999) fue un pintor ecuatoriano cuyo[a] arte es un testimonio del sufrimiento[b] humano y de la vida difícil de los indios y los pobres de su país. Guayasamín se inspiró en los símbolos y motivos de los pueblos precolombinos y en el arte colonial del Ecuador.

[a]*whose* [b]*suffering*

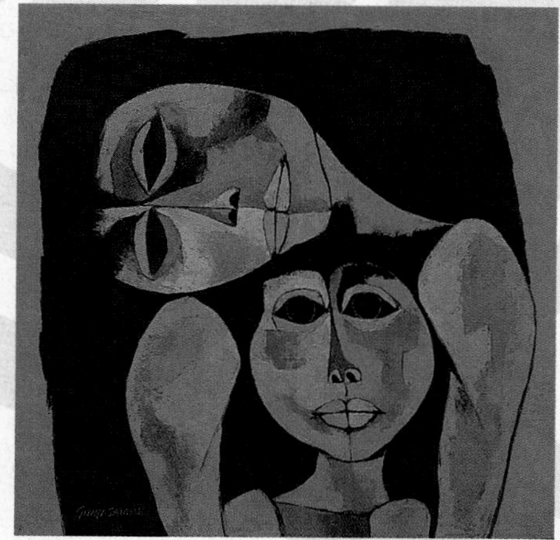

Madre y niño, por Oswaldo Guayasamín

Capítulo 13 of the video to accompany *¿Qué tal?* contains cultural footage of Bolivia and Ecuador.

Visit the *¿Qué tal?* website at www.mhhe.com/quetal.

PASO 3 Gramática

Paso 3: Gramática
See detailed supplementary materials for this grammar section in IM.

37 Expressing Uncertainty • Use of the Subjunctive: Doubt and Denial

Mire Ud. la siguiente pintura detenidamente (*carefully*) y luego complete las siguientes oraciones de acuerdo con su opinión.

Familia andina, por Héctor Poleo (venezolano)

Vocabulario útil	
la alegría	happiness
la esperanza	hope
el miedo	fear
la tristeza	sadness
los guardias	guardsmen

1. *Es posible que* los miembros de esta familia tengan (miedo/esperanza). Estoy seguro/a de que no tienen (miedo/esperanza).
2. Creo que los colores representan (la alegría / la tristeza). *Dudo que* representen (la alegría / la tristeza).
3. *Es probable que* los guardias estén (enojados/contentos). Estoy seguro/a de que no están (enojados/contentos).

Suggestion: Subjunctive: Doubt/Denial
Have students explain uses of subjunctive in sentences.

Follow-up: Subjunctive: Doubt/Denial
Show another painting and have students react to it with similar sentences.

MAIN (INDEPENDENT) CLAUSE		SUBORDINATE (DEPENDENT) CLAUSE
first subject + *indicative* (expression of doubt or denial)	**que**	second subject + *subjunctive*

A. Expressions of doubt and denial are those in which speakers express uncertainty or negation. Such expressions, however strong or weak, are followed by the subjunctive in the dependent clause in Spanish.

No creo que **sean** estudiantes.
I don't believe they're students.

Es imposible que ella **esté** con él.
It's impossible for her to be with him.

B. Some expressions of doubt and denial appear at the right. Not all Spanish expressions of doubt are given here. Remember that any expression of doubt is followed by the subjunctive in the dependent clause.

no creer	*to disbelieve*
dudar	*to doubt*
no estar seguro/a (de)	*to be unsure (of)*
negar (ie)	*to deny*

OJO: **Creer** and **estar seguro/a** are usually followed by the indicative in affirmative statements because they do not express doubt, denial, or negation. Compare these examples.

Estamos seguros de (Creemos) que el examen **es** hoy.
We're sure (We believe) that the exam is today.

No estamos seguros de (No creemos) que el examen **sea** hoy.
We're not sure (We don't believe) that the exam is today.

C. When a new subject is introduced after a generalization of doubt, the subjunctive is used in the dependent clause. Some generalizations of doubt and denial are included at the right.

es posible	it's possible
es imposible	it's impossible
es probable	it's probable (likely)
es improbable	it's improbable (unlikely)
no es cierto	it's not certain
no es seguro	it's not a sure thing
no es verdad	it's not true

OJO: Generalizations that express certainty are not followed by the subjunctive but by the indicative: **Es verdad que cocina bien.**

Práctica

Opiniones distintas. Imagine que Ud. y un amigo / una amiga están en un museo arqueológico. En este momento están mirando una figura. Desafortunadamente, no hay ningún letrero (*sign*) cerca de Uds. para indicar lo que representa la figura. Haga oraciones completas según las indicaciones. Añada (*Add*) palabras cuando sea necesario.

Habla Ud.:

1. creo / que / ser / figura / de / civilización / maya
2. es cierto / que / figura / estar / hecho (*made*) / de oro
3. es posible / que / representar / dios (*god*) / importante
4. no estoy seguro/a de / que / figura / estar / feliz / o / enojado

Habla su amigo/a:

5. no creo / que / ser / figura / de / civilización / maya
6. creo / que / ser / de / civilización / tolteca
7. estoy seguro/a de / que / estar / hecho / de bronce
8. creo / que / representar / víctima [*m.*] / de / sacrificio humano

Preliminary exercises: Práctica

- Have students tell whether the following sentences would require indicative or subjunctive in Spanish: **1.** I'm sure she's right. **2.** I doubt we'll get there on time. **3.** I don't think they know. **4.** It's impossible that he knows.
- Read sentences and have students respond *Es cierto que...* or *No es cierto que...*, using the subjunctive when necessary. **1.** *A la mayoría de la gente le gustan los museos.* **2.** *Todos mis amigos prefieren el teatro al cine.* **3.** *Conozco a muchas personas que son aficionadas a la arquitectura.* **4.** *En esta clase hay mucha gente con talento artístico.* **5.** *La expresión artística más popular entre los jóvenes es la música.* **6.** *Me encanta regalar objetos de cerámica.* **7.** *Voy a conciertos de música clásica con frecuencia.* **8.** El cascanueces (The Nutcracker) *es un ballet típico del mes de mayo.*

Note: Práctica
For *Práctica,* students can find information about Hispanic archeological museums in the encyclopedia or online. One of the most famous archeological museums of Latin America is *El Museo del Oro del Banco de la República de Colombia* in Bogotá, Colombia. The museum owns a magnificent collection of more than 33,000 pre-Hispanic pottery pieces from ancient Indian cultures that inhabited Colombia thousands of years ago. Students can find more information about *El Museo del Oro* and images of art housed there online.

PASO 3

Multimedia: Internet
Have students search the Internet for more of Pablo Picasso's works, including *Guernica.* The *Museo Nacional Centro de Arte Reina Sofía* in Madrid has its own website and features some of his works. Have students look up this museum and research its relationship to *Museo del Prado.*

UN POCO DE TODO

Guernica, por Pablo Picasso (español)

En el Museo de Arte Moderno Reina (*Queen*) **Sofía.** Imagine que Ud. y su amigo/a están en Madrid con un grupo turístico. Ahora están en el Museo de Arte Moderno Reina Sofía y el guía les habla sobre *Guernica,* el famoso cuadro del pintor español Pablo Picasso. Complete el siguiente diálogo con la forma correcta de los verbos entre paréntesis. Cuando se den dos posibilidades, escoja la palabra correcta.

Note: Un poco de todo
The *Museo Nacional Centro de Arte Reina Sofía* was declared a full-time national museum in 1992. The building this museum occupies was begun as a hospital in the mid 1700s, but was never completed. After surviving movements to have it demolished, the building was repaired, restored, and finished by several different architects. Before becoming a national museum, it was a cultural center called *Centro de Arte Reina Sofía,* in which temporary exhibits and events were held.

Answers: Un poco de todo
1. *Pasen* **2.** *dejen* **3.** *delante* **4.** *Es* **5.** *representa* **6.** *pintó* **7.** *de la* **8.** *durante* **9.** *estuvo* **10.** *se trasladó* **11.** *este* **12.** *sea* **13.** *es* **14.** *creo* **15.** *tengan* **16.** *ser* **17.** *sirve* **18.** *Por* **19.** *puede*

Follow-up: Un poco de todo
To personalize, ask: *¿Qué expresa para Ud. el cuadro de Guernica? ¿Por qué (no) le gusta? ¿Cree Ud. que el arte se debe usar para transmitir un mensaje o sólo para producir un placer estético?*

Reciclado: Un poco de todo
Reenter no-fault *se* expressions. Have students express in Spanish: **1.** It's incredible that Miguel is so clumsy. **2.** It's terrible that he breaks his glasses all the time. **3.** I think he loses his keys every week. **4.** I hope he doesn't run out of money this week!

GUÍA: (Pasar[1]) Uds. por aquí, por favor. También les pido que (dejar[2]) suficiente espacio para todos. Y bien, aquí estamos (delante/ detrás[3]) de *Guernica,* la obra maestra pintada por Picasso. (Ser[4]) obvio que el cuadro (representar[5]) los horrores de la guerra,[a] ¿no? En 1937 Picasso (pintar[6]) este cuadro como reacción al bombardeo[b] (del / de la[7]) ciudad de Guernica durante la Guerra Civil Española. Por razones políticas, (durante / encima de[8]) la dictadura[c] de Franco,[d] el cuadro (fue/estuvo[9]) muchos años en el Museo de Arte Moderno de Nueva York. Pero por deseo expreso del pintor, el cuadro (trasladarse[10])[e] a España después de la muerte de Franco…

UD.: Yo dudo que (este/esto[11]) cuadro (ser[12]) una obra maestra. Creo que no (ser[13]) nada bonito. ¡No hay colores en él!

SU AMIGO/A: Yo no (creer[14]) que todos los cuadros (tener[15]) que (ser[16]) bonitos. Para mí, la falta de color (servir[17]) para expresar el dolor y el desastre… (Por/Para[18]) eso uno (poder[19]) sentir el mensaje de la destrucción de la guerra en la pintura.

[a]*war* [b]*bombing* [c]*dictatorship* [d]Francisco Franco (1892–1975), dictador de España desde 1939 hasta su muerte [e]*to move*

Comprensión. ¿Quién pudo haber dicho (*could have said*) lo siguiente en el diálogo anterior: el guía, Ud. o su amigo/a?

1. Yo prefiero los cuadros en colores.
2. Ahora voy a mostrarles una obra maestra de la pintura española.
3. No me molesta que esta pintura esté pintada en blanco y negro.
4. Quiero que todos me sigan y que se pongan delante del cuadro.

In the *Capítulo 13* segment of "Chapter-by-Chapter Supplementary Materials" in the IM, you will find a chapter-culminating activity. You can use this activity to consolidate and review the vocabulary and grammar skills students have acquired.

Un paso más PASO 4

Paso 4: Un paso más
Optional section

See IM for suggestions and follow-up activities to accompany the video segment.

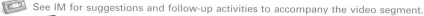

VIDEOTECA: En contexto

FUNCTION
Bargaining

Cultura en contexto
El arte y las artesanías

Los países hispanos han brindado al mundo[a] numerosos artistas importantes —tanto pintores como escritores, escultores y músicos. A la vez, los países hispanos son ricos en un arte menos formal: la artesanía, que es el arte folklórico del pueblo.

[a]han... *have given the world*

A. Lluvia de ideas

- ¿Qué tipo de artesanía se elabora (*is crafted*) en su estado o país? ¿Tiene Ud. algo hecho por artesanos locales?
- ¿Es común regatear en su país? ¿En qué tipo de negocio (*business*) se puede regatear? En su opinión, ¿sabe Ud. regatear bien? Dé un ejemplo.

B. Dictado

A continuación aparece un segmento del diálogo entre Juan Carlos y la vendedora de artesanías. Complete la explicación con las palabras o frases que faltan.

VENDEDORA: Todas mis __artesanías__[1] son muy buenas. ¿Quiere llevarse esa pieza? Le rebajo el __precio__[2] un poco, por ser mi __primera__[3] venta.

JUAN CARLOS: ¿En __cuánto__[4] me la deja? [...]

VENDEDORA: A ver... se __la__[5] dejo en 60 soles.

JUAN CARLOS: Ajá. [...] ¿Qué precio tiene esta máscara?

VENDEDORA: Pues, para Ud., nuestro joven viajero, le doy un precio especial. Si me compra la __cerámica__[6] y la máscara, sólo le pido 100 soles en total. Fíjese, ¡qué __ganga__[7]!

C. Un diálogo original

Con un compañero / una compañera, dramatice la siguiente situación.

E1: Ud. es un(a) estudiante de cuarto año, a punto de (*just about to*) graduarse. Como va a mudarse muy pronto, desea vender algunas cosas en una venta (*sale*) de garaje. Entre ellas hay tres cuadros que Ud. pintó en su clase de arte. Póngale un precio a cada uno y haga una lista de las características de sus «obras maestras».

E2: Ud. es un(a) estudiante de primer año y quiere decorar su cuarto en la residencia. Piensa comprar algunas cosas en la venta de garaje de otro estudiante. Se interesa especialmente en uno de los cuadros, pero el precio que tiene no le parece bueno.

Suggestion B
To check comprehension, ask: **1.** *¿Por qué sabe Juan Carlos tanto de la artesanía peruana?* **2.** *¿Cómo se llama la unidad monetaria del Perú?* **3.** *¿Cuánto va a pagar Juan Carlos por la máscara y la cerámica?*

National Standards: Communication
Have students bring a craft item that they own and give a brief presentation in Spanish to explain where and by whom it was made, how and when they obtained it, and why they do or do not like it.

PASO FINAL

A LEER

Repaso de estrategias: Guessing the Content of a Passage

Look at the photograph that accompanies the reading. Read the title of the passage also. Based on these clues, what do you think the article is going to be about? How do you know? What important information do the photo and the title provide? Remember to always look for these types of visual clues as a useful strategy to facilitate comprehension when reading in a second language (or even in your first language).

Suggestions: A leer

- Do the *Estrategia* in class and assign reading as homework for discussion next class meeting.
- Have students share predictions about the passage. Then ask what strategies they used to make predictions.

Sobre la lectura... Esta lectura es la adaptación de un artículo de la revista *GeoMundo*. Ud. ya leyó otro artículo de esta revista en el Capítulo 7. Recuerde que *GeoMundo* es como la revista *National Geographic* y que publica artículos sobre las ciencias, la geografía y otros temas similares.

Museo Virtual de Artes

Aprovechando las ventajas del ciberespacio, se creó el MUVA o Museo Virtual de Artes, sitio dedicado a divulgar el arte uruguayo y latinoamericano. Su directora es la historiadora de arte y curadora Alicia Haber. El sitio es recreativo, educativo y sin fines de lucro.[a]

La idea con que surgió este espacio es la de brindar[b] la sensación de estar en un museo real, pues debido a[c] las limitaciones originadas por la realidad socioeconómica de Uruguay, se ha visto impedida la construcción[d] de un museo nuevo. Cuatro arquitectos diseñaron un edificio con todos los adelantos,[e] la infraestructura técnica y las características edilicias[f] de un museo de primer nivel.[g] Existen innumerables museos en la supercarretera de la información, pero a diferencia de ellos, el MUVA no está construido como las páginas de un catálogo. Se trata de presentar arte uruguayo en el contexto más realista posible y brindarle al visitante la sensación de estar en un verdadero museo. Y no en cualquier museo, sino en una obra arquitectónica atractiva, cómoda, moderna y eficiente, con escaleras mecánicas, ascensor, sala de acceso con esculturas, varias salas con instalaciones, pisos encerados[h] y hasta un buen sistema de iluminación.

Este museo ya ha recibido[i] 32 premios internacionales desde que entró en línea el 20 de mayo de

Sitio Web del Museo Virtual de Artes

[a]sin... *not-for-profit* [b]ofrecer [c]pues... *because, due to* [d]se... *construction . . . has been impossible* [e]*latest advances (in architecture)* [f]*for preservation and inspection (of a public trust)* [g]*class* [h]pisos... *waxed floors* [i]ha... *has received*

Multimedia: Internet
Have students visit the MUVA website. Encourage them to visit the ground floor to get more information about the museum, the museum artists, and Uruguayan art in general. Ask them to visit the current expositions and encourage them to share their opinions on the art with the rest of the class.

1997. El más importante es *Best of the Web* (Lo Mejor de la Red), pero también se ha hecho acreedor[j] al *Best Virtual Exhibition* (Mejor Exhibición Virtual del Mundo) entre más de 155 museos en línea. Debido a sus peculiares características, ha sido filmado[k] en CNN Internacional, en la televisión brasileña y en muchos otros medios uruguayos e internacionales.

Se puede encontrar el MUVA en la dirección **http://www.diarioelpais.com/muva**. ■

[j]se... *it has been deemed worthy of inclusion* [k]ha... *it has been filmed*

Variation: A leer
Have students write 2 paragraphs about 1 of their favorite works of art (music, painting, movie, and so on). The first paragraph must include some historical background on work and its author. The second paragraph should explain why they are interested in that particular piece of work.

Comprensión

A. Preguntas. Conteste las siguientes preguntas.

1. ¿Qué tipo de museo es el MUVA?
2. ¿En qué país latinoamericano se creó el MUVA?
3. ¿Cuáles son algunos ejemplos del éxito de este museo?
4. ¿Cuál fue el objetivo de los diseñadores del MUVA?

B. Identificación. Identifique las conveniencias que le ofrece el MUVA al visitante, según el artículo.

1. ☐ diversas salas con exhibiciones
2. ☐ un tour guiado
3. ☐ un sistema de iluminación de alta calidad
4. ☐ diferentes maneras de navegar por el museo (ascensores, etcétera)
5. ☐ conversaciones con los artistas

A ESCRIBIR

La expresión artística. Muchas personas se expresan mediante el arte en sus varias formas. Es decir, el arte no se limita solamente a la pintura y la escultura. El arte puede tomar varias formas: la música, la escritura, el diseño de ropa o muebles, etcétera. ¿Qué «arte» usa Ud. para expresar su personalidad? Escriba un breve ensayo (*essay*) para explicar cómo Ud. se expresa por medio del arte. Ideas para considerar:

- el medio artístico (la música, etcétera)
- cómo el arte expresa sus emociones y personalidad
- si sus preferencias con respecto a la expresión artística están cambiando o si se mantienen estables

Cuando termine su ensayo, entrégueselo a su profesor(a). El profesor / La profesora lo va a presentar al resto de la clase para ver si puede adivinar quién es el autor / la autora.

En resumen

GRAMÁTICA

To review the grammar points presented in this chapter, refer to the indicated grammar presentations. You'll find further practice of these structures in the Workbook/Laboratory Manual, on the CD-ROM, and on the website.

36. Use of the Subjunctive: Emotion

You should know how and when to use the subjunctive in a dependent clause when the main clause of a sentence expresses emotion.

37. Use of the Subjunctive: Doubt and Denial

You should know how and when to use the subjunctive in a dependent clause when the main clause of a sentence expresses doubt or denial.

VOCABULARIO

Los verbos

aburrir	to bore
agradar	to please
apreciar	to appreciate
intentar	to try
negar (ie)	to deny
parecer	to seem
representar	to represent
sentir (ie, i)	to regret; to feel sorry
temer	to fear
tratar de + *inf.*	to try to (*do something*)

Repaso: alegrarse de, creer, dudar, esperar, gustar, tener (*irreg.*) **miedo de**

La expresión artística

la arquitectura	architecture
el arte (*but* **las artes** *pl.*)	art
el baile	dance
el ballet	ballet
la danza	dance
el drama	drama
la escultura	sculpture
la música	music
la ópera	opera
la pintura	painting (*general*)
el teatro	theater

Repaso: el cine, la fotografía, la literatura

crear	to create
desempeñar	to play, perform (*a part*)
dibujar	to draw
esculpir	to sculpt
tejer	to weave

Repaso: cantar, escribir, pintar

Los artistas

el actor / la actriz	actor, actress
el/la aficionado/a	fan
el/la arquitecto/a	architect
el/la artista	artist
el bailarín/la bailarina	dancer
el/la cantante	singer
el/la compositor(a)	composer
el/la director(a)	director
el/la dramaturgo/a	playwright
el/la escritor(a)	writer
el/la escultor(a)	sculptor
el/la músico	musician
el/la pintor(a)	painter
el/la poeta	poet

La tradición cultural

la artesanía	arts and crafts
la cerámica	pottery, ceramics
las ruinas	ruins
los tejidos	woven goods

Otros sustantivos

la canción	song
el cuadro / la pintura	painting (*piece of art*) / painting (*piece of art; the art form*)
el escenario	stage
el/la guía	guide
el guión	script
la obra (de arte)	work (of art)
la obra maestra	masterpiece
el papel	role

Repaso: el museo

Los adjetivos

clásico/a	classic(al)
folklórico/a	folkloric
moderno/a	modern

Los números ordinales

primer(o/a), segundo/a, tercer(o/a), cuarto/a, quinto/a, sexto/a, séptimo/a, octavo/a, noveno/a, décimo/a

Suggestions: Vocabulario

- Bring or have students bring images of fine and performing arts. Use images to elicit descriptions and ask/answer questions.
- Make statements about images displayed in class or about aspects of university life on your campus to which students can react with the following expressions: *No, no creo... , No, dudo que... , No, niego que...*
- Write expressions from *Palabras adicionales* on board. Make statements about people in class, university, state, or national events, or other people and events that students should know about. Have them respond to each statement using one of the expressions: *Muchos estudiantes estudian arte.* → *Me sorprende que tantos estudiantes estudien arte.*

Palabras adicionales

es extraño	it's strange
¡qué extraño!	how strange!
es...	it is . . .
cierto	certain
increíble	incredible
preferible	preferable
seguro	a sure thing
urgente	urgent
es una lástima	it's a shame
¡qué lástima!	what a shame!
hay que + *inf.*	it is necessary to (*do something*)
me (te, le,...) molesta	it bothers me (you, him, . . .)
me (te, le,...) sorprende	it surprises me (you, him, . . .)
ojalá (que)	I hope, wish (that)

CAPÍTULO 14

El medio ambiente

Suggestion: Chapter Opening photo
Point out chapter opening photo. Have students share their experiences with natural attractions such as waterfalls. Where are some of the major waterfalls located? Why do they attract tourists? What benefits besides tourism do waterfalls provide?

Resources
You and your students may find the following *¿Qué tal?* supplements helpful as you teach this chapter:

For the Instructor
- *Instructor's Manual and Resource Kit,* "Chapter-by-Chapter" Supplementary Materials
- Testing Program
- Overhead Transparencies 76–78
- Video (VHS or CD)
- *¿Qué tal?* Online Learning Center Website
- Audioscript
- Instructor's Resource CD

For Students
- Workbook/Laboratory Manual and Audio Program or Electronic Workbook/ Laboratory Manual
- Video on CD
- Interactive CD-ROM
- *¿Qué tal?* Online Learning Center Website
- Listening Comprehension Audio CD
- McGraw-Hill Electronic Language Tutor (MHELT)

◄ Las cataratas del Iguazú están entre las más grandes del mundo. Se encuentran en la región fronteriza (*border*) entre la Argentina, el Brasil y el Paraguay.

VOCABULARIO

- The environment
- Automobiles

GRAMÁTICA

38 Past Participle Used As an Adjective
39 Perfect Forms: Present Perfect Indicative and Present Perfect Subjunctive

CULTURA

- **Enfoque cultural:** la Argentina
- **Nota cultural:** Programas medioambientales
- **En los Estados Unidos y el Canadá:** Chi Chi Rodríguez
- **Cultura en contexto:** Los verificentros

Multimedia

You will learn about discussing car trouble in the **En contexto** video segment.

Review vocabulary and grammar and practice language skills with the interactive CD-ROM.

Get connected to the Spanish-speaking world with the *¿Qué tal?* Online Learning Center: **www.mhhe.com/quetal**.

Vocabulario PASO 1

Paso 1: Vocabulario

See detailed supplementary materials and exercises for this section and a model for vocabulary presentation and other material in the *Capítulo 14 Paso 1: Vocabularío* section of "Chapter-by-Chapter Supplementary Materials," IM.

El medio ambiente°

medio... *environment*

Multimedia: Audio
Students can listen to and practice this chapter's vocabulary on their Listening Comprehension Audio CD.

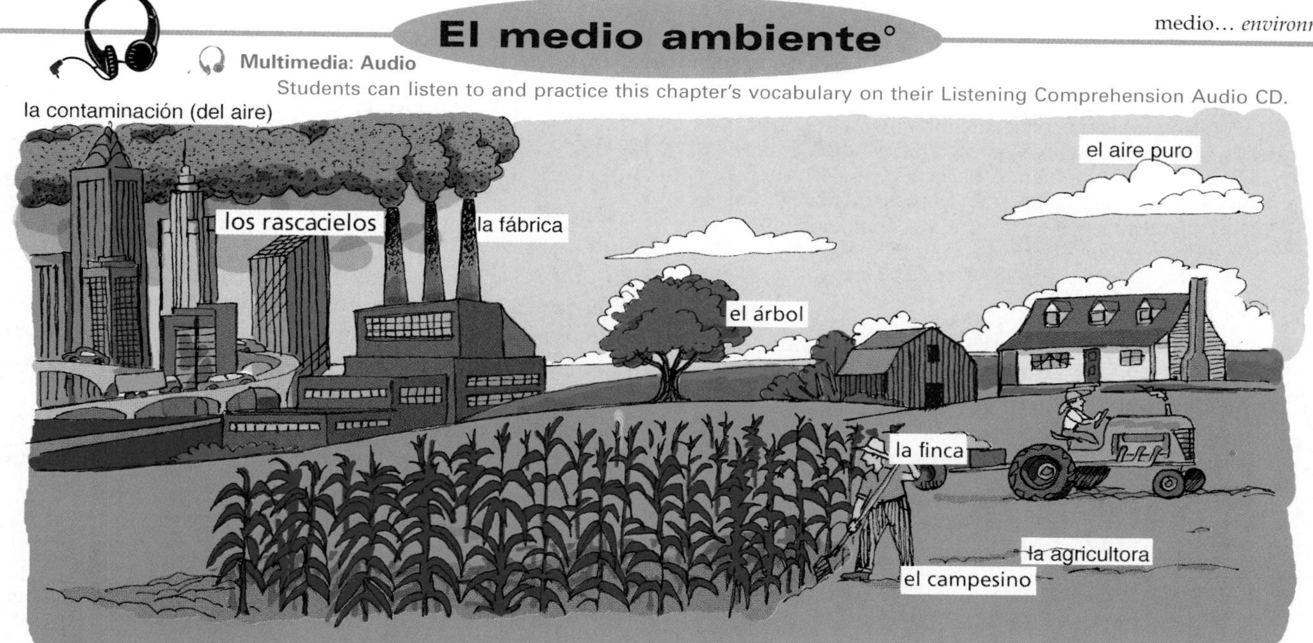

la capa de ozono	ozone layer
la energía	energy
eléctrica	electric
eólica	wind
hidráulica	hydraulic
nuclear	nuclear
solar	solar
la escasez	lack, shortage
la falta	lack, absence
el gobierno	government
la naturaleza	nature
la población	population
los recursos naturales	natural resources
acabar	to run out, use up completely
conservar	to save, conserve
construir*	to build
contaminar	to pollute
desarrollar	to develop
destruir*	to destroy
proteger	to protect

Más vocabulario

el aislamiento	isolation
el delito	crime
el ritmo (acelerado) de la vida	(fast) pace of life
los servicios públicos	public services
el transporte público	public transportation
la violencia	violence
bello/a	beautiful
denso/a	dense

National Standards: Communication
Divide the class into 3 groups. One will defend life in the city, another life in the country, and a third will prepare a list of questions to ask each group. Give students 10–15 minutes to prepare their arguments supporting their position and to prepare questions. The city and country groups should then give a simple opening statement, after which the third group will pose their first question. Provide specific time limits for the debating groups to answer, and allow time at the end for final arguments.

*Note the present indicative conjugation of **construir: construyo, construyes, construye, construímos, construís, construyen**. **Destruir** is conjugated like **construir**.

Suggestion A
Have students look through Spanish-language magazines and newspapers to locate ads with environmental statements or themes. Are there many? What kinds of messages do they convey?

Conversación

A. Un recurso natural importante

En ECOPETROL tenemos conciencia ambiental y social. Nuestra planeación incluye siempre los estudios de localización e impacto ambiental, buscando no perturbar la naturaleza y la vida de las poblaciones vecinas a nuestras futuras operaciones. En esta planeación el trabajo con la comunidad es indispensable.

Nuestro propósito: Una mejor convivencia

Paso 1. Lea este anuncio de una empresa (compañía) colombiana y conteste las preguntas.

1. ¿Qué tipo de negocio cree Ud. que es Ecopetrol? ¿Qué produce?
2. ¿Qué asuntos (*matters*) son de mayor interés para esta empresa? ¿El tránsito? ¿la deforestación? ¿las poblaciones humanas? ¿otros asuntos?
3. ¿Le parece que la foto que han elegido (*they have chosen*) para el anuncio es buena para la imagen de la empresa? ¿Por qué?
4. El sustantivo **convivencia** se relaciona con el verbo **vivir** y contiene la preposición **con**. ¿Qué cree Ud. que significa **convivencia**?
5. ¿Sabe Ud. cuáles son algunos de los países que producen lo mismo que Ecopetrol?

Paso 2. Diga a qué tipo de energía corresponde cada descripción.

1. Es la energía más usada en los hogares (*homes*).
2. Según los expertos, es la forma de energía más limpia; es decir, es la que menos contaminación produce.
3. Puede ser la forma de energía más eficiente, pero también la más peligrosa (*dangerous*).
4. Esta energía viene del viento; por eso sólo se puede desarrollar en lugares específicos.
5. Para producir esta forma de energía son necesarios los ríos y las cataratas.

Suggestions B

- Have students tally on board most important item for each student. In a second column, have them tally least important. Use this information to discuss general attitude of class toward issues.
- Create another chart on board to tally number of students for and against each item.

National Standards: Communication
Have students create pamphlets in Spanish on ways to educate the community to conserve energy and lessen environmental pollution. Have them first select an issue or plan to promote. They should select a format and images they would like to use (if any), come up with a slogan, and decide what information to include. Some topic suggestions: *la conservación de la energía, la contaminación del agua / aire, la promoción de energía alternativa, el transporte público, el reciclaje.* Have students share their completed pamphlets with their classmates.

B. Problemas del mundo en que vivimos. Comente las siguientes opiniones. Puede usar las siguientes expresiones para aclarar (*clarify*) su posición. **¡OJO!** Todas las expresiones requieren el uso del subjuntivo o del infinitivo.

Es / Me parece (*It seems to me*) fundamental / importantísimo / ridículo / ¿ ?
Me opongo a que (*I am against*)…
No creo que…

1. Para conservar energía debemos mantener bajo el termostato en el invierno y elevarlo en el verano.
2. Es mejor calentar las casas con estufas de leña (*wood stoves*) que con gas o electricidad.
3. Se debe crear más parques urbanos, estatales y nacionales.
4. La protección del medio ambiente no debe impedir la explotación de los recursos naturales.

National Standards: Communication
Have students interview their classmates to find out what they do to help conserve our natural resources. Students should then share findings. Write key words on board and remind students to try to use them in their interviews, for example, *reciclaje, apagar/prender las luces, caminar, andar en bicicleta.*

5. Para evitar la contaminación urbana, debemos limitar el uso de los coches y no usarlos algunos días de la semana, como se hace en otros países.
6. El gobierno debe poner multas (*fines*) muy graves a las compañías e individuos que causan la contaminación.
7. El desarrollo de las tecnologías promueve (*promotes*) el ritmo tan acelerado de nuestra vida.
8. Los países desarrollados están destruyendo los recursos naturales de los países más pobres.

C. **¿La ciudad o el campo?** De las siguientes oraciones, ¿cuáles corresponden a la ciudad? ¿al campo?

1. El aire es más puro y hay menos contaminación.
2. La naturaleza es más bella.
3. El ritmo de la vida es más acelerado.
4. Los delitos son más frecuentes.
5. Los servicios financieros y legales son más asequibles (*available*).
6. Hay pocos medios de transporte públicos.
7. La población es menos densa.
8. Hay escasez de viviendas (*housing*).

Follow-up C
- Ask students: **1.** *¿Hay mucha contaminación en esta ciudad? ¿En qué lugares hay mucha contaminación? ¿En dónde se encuentra aire puro?* **2.** *¿Cómo es el ritmo de vida en* (ciudad), *acelerado o lento? ¿Qué ritmo de vida prefiere Ud.? ¿Le gusta caminar por la ciudad durante la noche?* **3.** *¿Trata Ud. de conservar la energía? ¿Hay ahora una escasez de energía? Si una persona realmente quiere conservar energía, ¿qué puede hacer?* **4.** *¿Hay muchos delitos y crímenes en esta ciudad? ¿Qué lugares son famosos por la frecuencia de sus delitos? ¿Tiene Ud. miedo de visitar estos lugares?* **5.** *¿Va Ud. al campo con frecuencia? ¿Tiene su familia una finca en el campo? ¿La visita Ud.? ¿Cuándo? Descríbala. ¿Le gustaría vivir en una finca? ¿Cómo es el ritmo de vida en una finca típica?*
- Ask students: *¿Está de acuerdo o no?* **1.** *El sistema de transporte público es muy bueno.* **2.** *Hay muchos parques y zonas verdes.* **3.** *Ocurren muy pocos delitos.* **4.** *Hay poca contaminación.* **5.** *El ritmo de la vida es demasiado lento* (slow). **6.** *Hay demasiadas fábricas.* **7.** *La población es muy densa.* **8.** *No hay escasez de viviendas.*

NOTA CULTURAL

Programas medioambientales

Muchos países del mundo se encuentran en la posición de **equilibrar** la protección del **medio ambiente** con los objetivos del **desarrollo económico**. En muchos casos, **la explotación de recursos naturales** es la mayor fuente de ingreso[a] para la economía de un país. Los gobiernos latinoamericanos están conscientes de la necesidad de **proteger** el medio ambiente y de **conservar** los recursos naturales, y están haciendo lo posible por hacerlo. Los siguientes son algunos de los muchos programas **medioambientales** que se encuentran en los países hispanohablantes.

- En la Ciudad de México, existe un programa permanente de **restricción vehicular** que se llama **Hoy no circula**.[b] Los coches no deben **circular** un día por semana. El día está determinado por el último número de **la placa**.[c] El propósito de este programa es controlar **la emisión de contaminantes**. Programas semejantes a **Hoy no circula** existen también en otros países como Chile y la Argentina.
- En México, España y otros países existen programas de **separación de basura**. Se depositan materiales distintos en recipientes[d] de colores diferentes, desde **el papel** y **el cartón, el vidrio,**[e] **el metal** y **el plástico,** hasta **la materia orgánica** y **los desechos**[f] **sanitarios.**

Madrid, España

[a]fuente... *source of income* [b]Hoy... *Today [these] don't drive.* [c]*license plate* [d]*containers* [e]*glass* [f]*waste*

Los coches

En la gasolinera Gómez

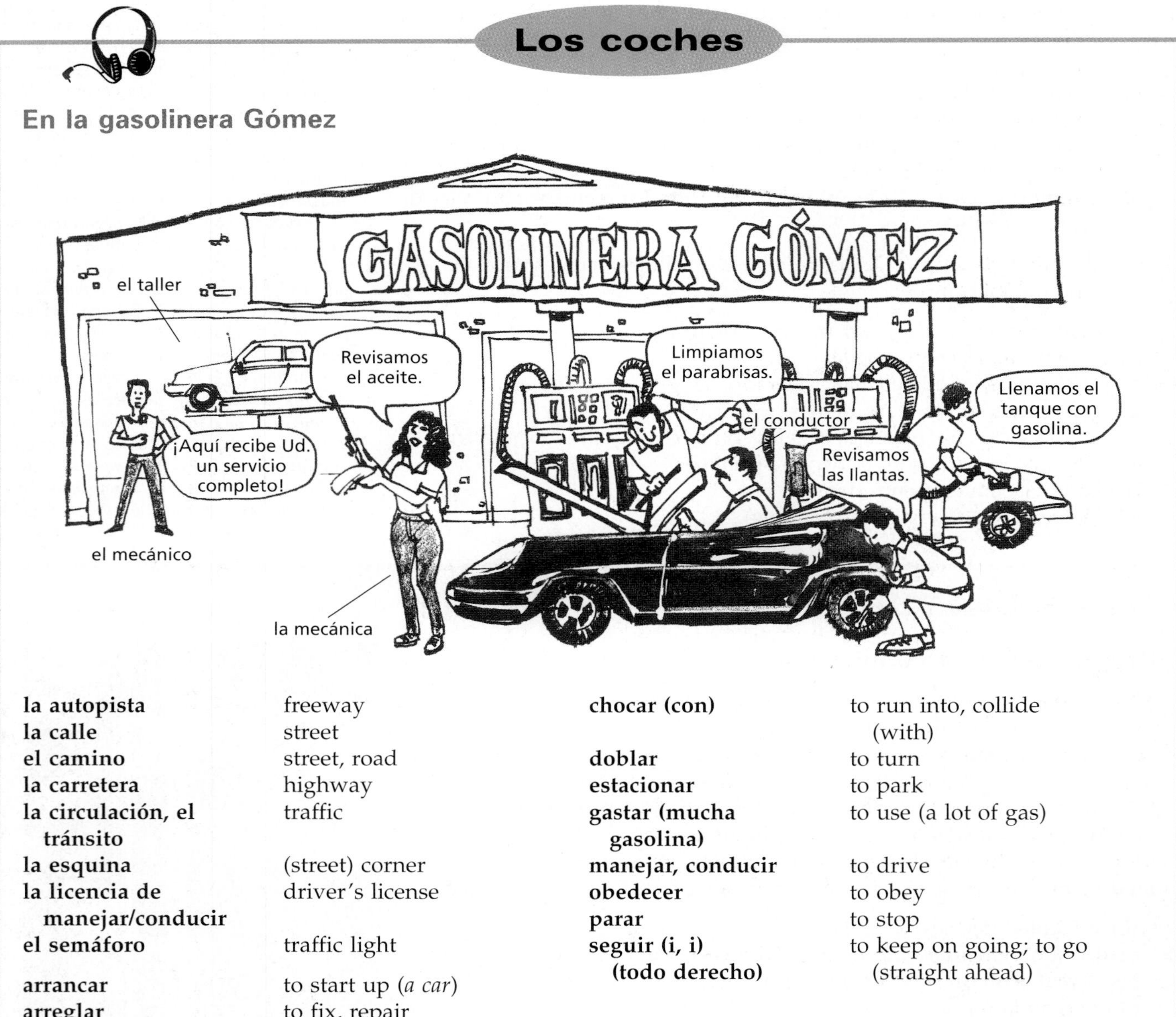
GASOLINERA GÓMEZ
el taller
Revisamos el aceite.
Limpiamos el parabrisas.
Llenamos el tanque con gasolina.
el conductor
¡Aquí recibe Ud. un servicio completo!
Revisamos las llantas.
el mecánico
la mecánica

la autopista	freeway	**chocar (con)**	to run into, collide (with)
la calle	street	**doblar**	to turn
el camino	street, road	**estacionar**	to park
la carretera	highway	**gastar (mucha gasolina)**	to use (a lot of gas)
la circulación, el tránsito	traffic	**manejar, conducir**	to drive
la esquina	(street) corner	**obedecer**	to obey
la licencia de manejar/conducir	driver's license	**parar**	to stop
el semáforo	traffic light	**seguir (i, i) (todo derecho)**	to keep on going; to go (straight ahead)
arrancar	to start up (*a car*)		
arreglar	to fix, repair		

❖ **Transparencias 76, 77**
Transparency 77 offers additional images and vocabulary.

Heritage speakers
En algunos países latinoamericanos, como Colombia por ejemplo, se dice *pase* en vez de *licencia de conducir*. Otro término usado principalmente en España es *el carnet de conducir*. También hay varios términos para expresar *to park: estacionar(se)*, *aparcar* (*Esp.*) y *parquear* (*Méx.*). Para referirse a *parking lot* o *parking place,* se puede decir *estacionamiento* o *parqueadero*. Pregúnteles a los hispanohablantes de la clase qué palabras usan y por qué.

Conversación

A. Definiciones

Paso 1. Busque Ud. la definición de las palabras de la columna de la derecha.

1. ____ Se pone en el tanque.
2. ____ Se llenan de aire.
3. ____ Lubrica el motor.
4. ____ Es necesaria para arrancar el motor.
5. ____ Cuando se llega a una esquina, hay que hacer esto o seguir todo derecho.
6. ____ No contiene aire suficiente y por eso es necesario cambiarla.
7. ____ Es un camino público ancho (*wide*) donde los coches circulan rápidamente.
8. ____ Se usan para parar el coche.
9. ____ El policía nos la pide cuando nos para en el camino.
10. ____ Allí se revisan y se arreglan los coches.

a. los frenos (*brakes*)
b. doblar
c. la carretera
d. la batería
e. el taller
f. una llanta desinflada (*flat*)
g. la gasolina
h. las llantas
i. el aceite
j. la licencia

Variation A
Have students work in pairs, one covering the first column and the other the second.

Paso 2. Ahora, siguiendo el modelo de las definiciones anteriores, ¿puede Ud. dar una definición de las siguientes palabras?

1. el semáforo
2. la circulación
3. estacionarse
4. gastar gasolina
5. la gasolinera
6. la autopista

B. Entrevista: Un conductor responsable

Paso 1. Entreviste a un compañero / una compañera de clase para determinar con qué frecuencia hace las siguientes cosas.

1. dejar la licencia en casa cuando va a manejar
2. acelerar (*to speed up*) cuando ve a un policía
3. manejar después de tomar bebidas alcohólicas
4. respetar o exceder el límite de velocidad
5. estacionar el coche donde dice «Prohibido estacionarse»
6. revisar el aceite y la batería
7. seguir todo derecho a toda velocidad cuando no sabe llegar a su destino
8. rebasar (*to pass*) tres carros a la vez (*at the same time*)

Paso 2. Ahora, con el mismo compañero / la misma compañera, hagan una lista de diez cosas que hace —o no hace— un conductor responsable. Pueden usar frases del **Paso 1**, si quieren.

Suggestions B
- Have students rank question items in order of importance.
- Ask: *¿Es símbolo de mucho prestigio social tener un Ferrari? ¿un Volkswagen? ¿un Hundai? ¿un BMW? ¿un Toyota? ¿una camioneta? ¿un pickup? ¿Cómo es el típico dueño / la típica dueña de cada uno de estos coches?*

PASO 2 Gramática

CAPÍTULO 14

Paso 2: Gramática
See detailed supplementary materials for this grammar section in IM.

38 Más descripciones • Past Participle Used As an Adjective

Algunos refranes y dichos en español

1. En boca *cerrada* no entran moscas.
2. Estoy tan *aburrido* como una ostra.
3. Cuando está *abierto* el cajón, el más *honrado* es ladrón.

Empareje estas oraciones con el refrán o dicho que explican.

1. Es posible que una persona honrada caiga en la tentación de hacer algo malo si la oportunidad se le presenta.
2. Hay que ser prudente. A veces es mejor no decir nada para evitar (*avoid*) problemas.
3. Las ostras ejemplifican el aburrimiento (*boredom*) porque llevan una vida tranquila… siempre igual.

Suggestion: Past Participle
Ask students what *cerrada, aburrido,* and *honrado* have in common. (→ = *do/a ending*)

Follow-up: Past Participle
- After reviewing *refranes,* ask: **1.** *A veces, ¿es mejor no decir nada? ¿Qué le puede pasar a uno cuando tiene la boca abierta?* **2.** *¿Llevan una vida muy interesante las ostras? ¿Por qué? ¿Sufren muchas presiones?* **3.** *¿Todos los que cometen delitos son criminales? ¿Es posible que una persona honrada llegue a cometer un crimen? ¿Cree que las personas sufrimos demasiadas tentaciones?*
- Have students give equivalent or similar English proverbs for Spanish *refranes.*

FORMS OF THE PAST PARTICIPLE

A. The past participle of most English verbs ends in *-ed:* for example, *to walk → walked; to close → closed.* Many English past participles, however, are irregular: *to sing → sung; to write → written.* In Spanish, the *past participle* (**el participio pasado**) is formed by adding **-ado** to the stem of **-ar** verbs, and **-ido** to the stem of **-er** and **-ir** verbs. An accent mark is used on the past participle of **-er/-ir** verbs with stems ending in **-a, -e,** or **-o.**

Pronunciation hint: Remember that the Spanish **d** between vowels, as found in past participle endings, is pronounced as the fricative [đ] (see **Pronunciación** in **Capítulo 6** of the Workbook/ Laboratory Manual).

hablar	comer	vivir
habl**ado** (*spoken*)	com**ido** (*eaten*)	viv**ido** (*lived*)

caer → **caído**	oír → **oído**
creer → **creído**	(son)reír → **(son)reído**
leer → **leído**	traer → **traído**

A few Spanish proverbs and sayings 1. Into a closed mouth no flies enter. 2. I am as bored as an oyster. 3. When the (cash) drawer is open, the most honest person is (can become) a thief.

B. The Spanish verbs at the right have irregular past participles.

abrir:	**abierto**	morir:	**muerto**
cubrir (*to cover*):	**cubierto**	poner:	**puesto**
decir:	**dicho**	resolver:	**resuelto**
descubrir:	**descubierto**	romper:	**roto**
escribir:	**escrito**	ver:	**visto**
hacer:	**hecho**	volver:	**vuelto**

THE PAST PARTICIPLE USED AS AN ADJECTIVE

A. In both English and Spanish, the past participle can be used as an adjective to modify a noun. Like other Spanish adjectives, the past participle must agree in number and gender with the noun modified.

Tengo una bolsa **hecha** en El Salvador.
I have a purse made in El Salvador.

El español es una de las lenguas **habladas** en los Estados Unidos y en el Canadá.
Spanish is one of the languages spoken in the United States and in Canada.

B. The past participle is frequently used with **estar** to describe conditions that are the result of a previous action.

La puerta **está abierta**.
The door is open.

Todos los lápices **estaban rotos**.
All the pencils were broken.

OJO English past participles often have the same form as the past tense: *I* ***closed*** *the book. The thief stood behind the* ***closed*** *door.* The Spanish past participle is never identical in form or use to a past tense.

Cerré la puerta. Ahora la puerta está **cerrada**.
I ***closed*** *the door. Now the door is* ***closed***.

Práctica

A. En este momento...

Paso 1. En este momento, ¿son ciertas o falsas las siguientes oraciones con relación a su sala de clase?

Palabras útiles: colgar (ue) (*to hang*), enchufar (*to plug in*), prender (*to turn on* [*lights or an appliance*])

1. La puerta está abierta
2. Las luces están apagadas.
3. Las ventanas están cerradas.
4. Algunos libros están abiertos.
5. Los estudiantes están sentados.
6. Hay algo escrito en la pizarra.
7. Una silla está rota.
8. Hay carteles y anuncios colgados en la pared.
9. Un aparato está enchufado.

Preliminary exercise A
Have students express in Spanish: *¿Cómo se dice en español?* **1.** money earned **2.** the lost luggage **3.** a repeated sentence **4.** the tired employee **5.** dead flies **6.** the broken cup

Suggestions A
- Point out that *prender* is a synonym of *encender* and *poner* in some contexts (to turn on, light).
- Have students invent additional sentences to describe classroom. Others respond *cierto* or *falso*. Write on board verbs that are useful for describing classroom.

Paso 2. Ahora describa el estado de las siguientes cosas en su casa (cuarto, apartamento).

1. las luces	**3.** el televisor	**5.** la puerta
2. la cama	**4.** las ventanas	**6.** las cortinas (*curtains*)

Variations B
- Point out that *de* is used to express *covered with snow: cubierta de nieve.*
- Have students give sentences with *tener* + past participle: *La carta no está escrita todavía.* → *Natalia no tiene la carta escrita todavía.*

B. Situaciones. ¿Cual es la situación en este momento? Conteste según el modelo.

MODELO: Natalia les tiene que *escribir* una carta a sus abuelos. →
La carta no está *escrita* todavía.

1. Los Sres. García deben *abrir* la tienda más temprano. ¡Ya son las nueve!
2. El gobernador quiere *cerrar* las fábricas que desperdician (*waste*) los recursos naturales de esta región.
3. Los niños esperan que la tierra se *cubra* de nieve para la Navidad.
4. Delia debe *poner* la mesa. Los invitados llegan a las nueve y ya son las ocho.
5. Claro está que la contaminación va a contribuir a la *destrucción* de la capa de ozono.
6. Es posible que los ingenieros *descubran* el error en la construcción del reactor nuclear.
7. Se debe *resolver* pronto el problema de la escasez de energía.

❖**Transparency 78**

Variation: Conversación
Have students use preterite and imperfect to create stories based on drawings. Ask questions to help them get started: *¿Por qué está preparada una familia y la otra no?*

Note: Conversación
Some possible answers: **1.** *En el dibujo A, el niño está dormido. En el dibujo B, la niña está despierta.* **2.** *En el dibujo A, la lámpara está apagada. En el dibujo B, la lámpara está encendida.* **3.** *En el dibujo A, las luces están encendidas. En el dibujo B, las luces están apagadas.* **4.** *En el dibujo A, las personas están sentadas en el sofá. En el dibujo B, tres personas están sentadas a la mesa.* **5.** *En el dibujo A, no hay comida en la mesa. En el dibujo B, hay comida en la mesa.* **6.** *En el dibujo A, el gato está despierto. En el dibujo B, el gato está dormido.*

Conversación

¡Ojo alerta! Hay por lo menos cinco cosas que difieren (*are different*) entre un dibujo y el otro. ¿Puede Ud. encontrarlas? Use participios pasados como adjetivos cuando pueda.

A.

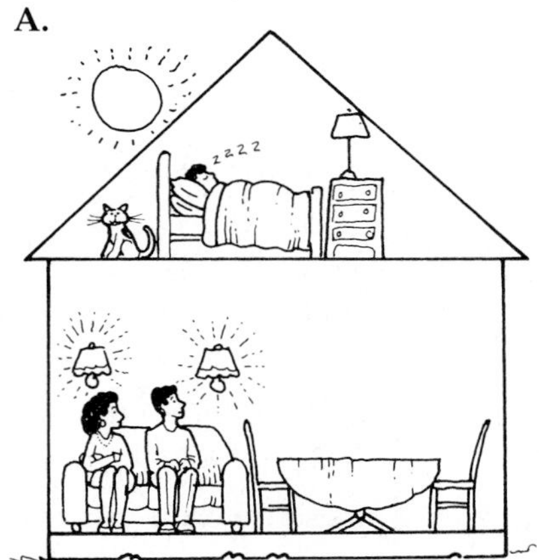

B.

Enfoque cultural

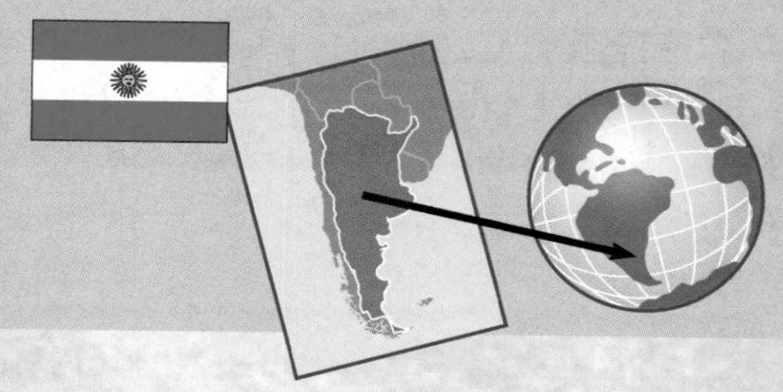

Enfoque cultural
See follow-up activities for this section in chapter-by-chapter materials in IM.

la Argentina

Datos esenciales

Nombre oficial: República Argentina

Capital: Buenos Aires

Población: 37.000.000 de habitantes

Moneda: el peso

Idioma oficial: el español

¡Fíjese!

- La inmigración de europeos en el siglo XIX tuvo un papel decisivo en la formación de la población de la Argentina (así como en la del Uruguay). En 1856 la población argentina era de 1.200.000 de habitantes; para 1930, 10.500.000 de extranjeros entraron en la Argentina por el puerto de Buenos Aires. La mitad[a] estaba formada por italianos, una tercera parte por españoles, y el resto estaba formado principalmente por alemanes y eslavos. Muchos de los que llegaron fueron trabajadores temporales que, más tarde o más temprano, regresaron a Europa. El resto, sin embargo,[b] se estableció permanentemente, porque el gobierno quería estimular la inmigración para poblar la Pampa. Pero muchos, acostumbrados a la vida urbana, se quedaron en Buenos Aires.
- Buenos Aires es una ciudad con una población de más de 10.000.000 de habitantes, lo cual supone[c] el 30 por ciento de la población del país. Es el centro cultural, comercial, industrial y financiero, así como el puerto principal de la Argentina. A las personas de Buenos Aires se les llama «porteños», derivado de «puerto».

[a]*half* [b]sin... *however* [c]lo... *which constitutes*

La Plaza de Mayo data de 1580, año de la fundación de Buenos Aires.

Conozca... el tango

El tango se originó en los barrios pobres de Buenos Aires a finales del siglo XIX. El tango se toca con los instrumentos de los inmigrantes: la guitarra española, el violín italiano y el típico bandoleón, una especie de acordeón alemán.

Los temas del tango muestran una dualidad. Por un lado, representan la agresividad machista,[a] que incluye dramas pasionales y peleas con cuchillos.[b] Por otro, simbolizan la nostalgia, la soledad[c] y el sentimiento de pérdida.[d] El intérprete de tangos más famoso fue el porteño Carlos Gardel (1887–1935).

[a]*male* [b]peleas... *knife fights* [c]*solitude* [d]*loss*

Capítulo 14 of the video to accompany *¿Qué tal?* contains cultural footage of Argentina.

WWW. Visit the *¿Qué tal?* website at www.mhhe.com/quetal.

PASO 3 Gramática

Paso 3: Gramática
See detailed supplementary materials for this grammar section in IM.

39 ¿Qué has hecho? • Perfect Forms: Present Perfect Indicative and Present Perfect Subjunctive

Una llanta desinflada

MANOLO: ¡Ay, qué mala suerte!
LOLA: ¿Qué pasa?
MANOLO: Parece que el coche tiene una llanta desinflada. Y como no hay ningún taller por aquí, tengo que cambiarla yo mismo.
LOLA: ¿*Has cambiado* una llanta alguna vez?
MANOLO: No. Siempre *he llevado* el coche a un taller cuando hay problemas.
LOLA: Pues, yo nunca *he cambiado* una llanta tampoco. Pero te puedo ayudar, si quieres.
MANOLO: Gracias. ¡Espero que la llanta de recambio no esté desinflada también!

¿Y Ud.? ¿Ha… ?

1. cambiado una llanta desinflada
2. revisado el aceite de su coche
3. arreglado otras cosas del coche
4. tenido un accidente con el coche
5. excedido el límite de velocidad en la autopista

Follow-up: Perfect Forms
Ask: **1.** *Si Ud. tiene una llanta desinflada, ¿le pide a alguien que lo/la ayude a cambiarla?* **2.** *¿Le dice Ud. al mecánico que le revise el aceite o lo hace Ud. mismo/a?* **3.** *¿Puede Ud. arreglar problemas del coche o necesita siempre que se lo haga un mecánico?*

PRESENT PERFECT INDICATIVE

he hablado	*I have spoken*	**hemos** hablado	*we have spoken*
has hablado	*you have spoken*	**habéis** hablado	*you (pl.) have spoken*
ha hablado	*you have spoken, he/she has spoken*	**han** hablado	*you (pl.) / they have spoken*

A flat tire MANOLO: Aw, what bad luck! LOLA: What's wrong? MANOLO: It seems the car has a flat tire. And, as there aren't any repair shops around here, I have to change it myself. LOLA: Have you ever changed a flat tire before? MANOLO: No. I've always taken the car to a repair shop when there are problems. LOLA: Well, I've never changed a tire either. But I can help you, if you want. MANOLO: Thanks. I hope that the spare tire isn't flat too!

A. In English, the present perfect is a compound tense consisting of the present tense form of the verb *to have* plus the past participle: *I have written, you have spoken*, and so on.

In the Spanish *present perfect* (**el presente perfecto**), the past participle is used with present tense forms of **haber**, the equivalent of English *to have* in this construction.

In general, the use of the Spanish present perfect parallels that of the English present perfect.

No **hemos estado** aquí antes.
We haven't been here before.

Me he divertido mucho.
I've had a very good time.

Ya le **han escrito** la carta.
They've already written her the letter.

OJO **Haber**, an auxiliary verb, is not interchangeable with **tener**.

B. The form of the past participle never changes with **haber**, regardless of the gender or number of the subject. The past participle always appears immediately after the appropriate form of **haber** and is never separated from it. Object pronouns and **no** are always placed directly before the form of **haber**.

[Práctica A]

Ella **ha cambiado** una llanta desinflada varias veces.
She's changed a flat tire several times.

Todavía **no le** han revisado el aceite al coche.
They still haven't checked the car's oil.

C. The present perfect form of **hay** is **ha habido** (*there has/have been*).

OJO Remember that **acabar** + **de** + *infinitive*—not the present perfect tense—is used to state that something *has just occurred*.

Ha habido un accidente.
There's been an accident.

Acabo de mandar la carta.
I've just mailed the letter.

PRESENT PERFECT SUBJUNCTIVE

The *present perfect subjunctive* (**el perfecto del subjuntivo**) is formed with the present subjunctive of **haber** plus the past participle. It is used to express *I have spoken* (*written*, and so on) when the subjunctive is required. Although its most frequent equivalent is *I have* plus the past participle, its exact equivalent in English depends on the context in which it occurs.

Note in the model sentences at the right that the English equivalent of the present perfect subjunctive can be expressed as a simple or as a compound tense: *did / have done; came / have come; built / have built.*

[Práctica B]

haya hablado	**hayamos** hablado
hayas hablado	**hayáis** hablado
haya hablado	**hayan** hablado

Es posible que lo **haya hecho**.
It's possible (that) he may have done (he did) it.

Me alegro de que **hayas venido**.
I'm glad (that) you have come (you came).

Es bueno que lo **hayan construido**.
It's good (that) they built (have built) it.

Reciclado: Perfect Forms
Students will often try to use present perfect indicative instead of *hace* + time + *que* construction, due to interference from English. For example, instead of *Hace un año que estudio español*, students might say *He estudiado español por un año*. Remind students regularly that Spanish speakers prefer *hacer* construction to express time passed. Reenter this construction by having them express the following ideas in Spanish. *¿Cómo se dice en español?* **1.** How long have you been at this university? / I have been here for two years. **2.** How long have you studied Spanish? / I have studied it for only one year. **3.** How long ago did you move to this town? / I moved here one year ago.

Preliminary exercises A

- Use rapid response drill to practice perfect tense forms. Have students give present perfect indicative for each cue. **1.** ***yo:*** *llegar, terminar, bañarse, acostarse* **2.** ***tú:*** *comer, prometer, romper, volver* **3.** ***Ud./él/ella:*** *asistir, insistir, sonreír, divertirse* **4.** ***nosotros:*** *abrir, decir, cubrir, descubrir* **5.** ***Uds./ellos/ellas:*** *escribir, poner, ver, hacer*
- Use chain drill to practice forms in sentences: *¿Qué hemos hecho hoy?* **1.** *José se ha preparado muy bien para la clase.* (*tú, el profesor, los estudiantes, Luis, Carmen y Pilar, vosotros*) **2.** *Yo he empezado la lección para hoy.* (*leer, escribir, estudiar, comprender, aprender*) **3.** *Lidia se ha despertado.* (*levantarse, bañarse, vestirse, desayunar, correr a la facultad, leer en la cafetería, reírse con los amigos, ir a su primera clase*)

Follow-up A

- To personalize, ask: **1.** *¿Qué ha hecho Ud. hoy? ¿Ha hablado con un amigo / una amiga? ¿Ha estudiado? ¿Ha comido?* **2.** *¿Qué ha hecho Ud. esta semana? ¿Ha ido a una fiesta? ¿Ha bailado? ¿Ha cantado? ¿Ha tomado Coca-Cola / cerveza / vino? ¿Ha visto una película?* **3.** *¿Ha escrito una carta este mes? ¿Ha visitado un museo? ¿Ha salido de la ciudad? ¿Se ha levantado antes de las seis? ¿antes de las cinco? ¿Por qué tan temprano?* **4.** *¿Ha depositado dinero en el banco? ¿Ha vendido / comprado algo?* Extend all of the questions with: *¿Qué más ha hecho Ud. hoy / esta semana / este mes?*

Preliminary exercises B

- Read and have students tell whether present perfect indicative or present perfect subjunctive is used: **1.** *Dice que ha hablado con ella.* **2.** *Es posible que haya hablado con ella.* **3.** *No, no han repetido las palabras.* **4.** *No creo que hayan repetido las palabras.* **5.** *Me alegro de que me hayas escrito.* **6.** *No vengas a menos que me hayas escrito antes.*
- Have students give subjunctive equivalents of *he hablado, he repetido, has comido, has manejado, ha mandado, ha venido, hemos podido, hemos alquilado, han comprendido, se han acostado.*

Follow-up B

Have students suggest other things that they think no one in class has ever done, for example, *No creo que nadie haya... ; Creo que nadie ha...*

Práctica

A. El coche de Carmina. Carmina acaba de comprarse un coche usado. Su papá es vendedor de autos en Los Ángeles. ¡Así que el coche fue una ganga! Describa lo que le ha pasado a Carmina, según el modelo.

MODELO: ir a la agencia de su padre → Ha ido a la agencia de su padre.

1. pedirle ayuda a su padre
2. hacer preguntas acerca de (*about*) los diferentes coches
3. ver uno bastante barato
4. revisar las llantas
5. conducirlo como prueba
6. regresar a la agencia
7. decidir comprarlo
8. comprarlo
9. volver a casa
10. llevar a sus amigas al cine esa noche

B. ¡No lo creo! ¿Tienen espíritu aventurero sus compañeros de clase? ¿Llevan una vida interesante? ¿O están tan aburridos como una ostra?

Paso 1. De cada par de oraciones, indique la que (*the one that*) expresa su opinión acerca de los estudiantes de esta clase.

Vocabulario útil: el paracaidismo (*skydiving*), escalar (*to climb*), hacer *autostop* (*to hitchhike*)

1. ☐ Creo que alguien en esta clase ha visto las pirámides de Egipto.
   ☐ Es dudoso que alguien haya visto las pirámides de Egipto.
2. ☐ Estoy seguro/a de que por lo menos uno de mis compañeros ha escalado una montaña alta.
   ☐ No creo que nadie haya escalado una montaña alta.
3. ☐ Creo que alguien ha viajado haciendo *autostop*.
   ☐ Dudo que alguien haya hecho *autostop* en un viaje.
4. ☐ Creo que alguien ha practicado el paracaidismo.
   ☐ Es improbable que alguien haya practicado el paracaidismo.
5. ☐ Estoy seguro/a de que alguien ha tomado el metro en Nueva York a medianoche (*midnight*).
   ☐ No creo que nadie haya tomado el metro neoyorquino a medianoche.

Paso 2. Ahora escuche mientras el profesor / la profesora pregunta si alguien ha hecho estas actividades. ¿Tenía Ud. razón en el **Paso 1**?

Conversación

A. Entrevista. Con un compañero / una compañera, haga y conteste preguntas con estos verbos. La persona que contesta debe decir la verdad.

MODELO: visitar México →
E1: ¿Has visitado México?

Follow-up A

¿Qué es posible que hayan hecho las siguientes personas? **1.** *Un hombre que lleva máscara sale corriendo de un banco, con una bolsa en la mano.* **2.** *Un joven está saliendo de una lavandería con un montón de ropa limpia.* **3.** *Un sábado de otoño, a las cuatro y media de la tarde, muchas personas están saliendo de un estadio.* **4.** *Unos turistas están hablando ansiosamente con un policía. La mujer no lleva bolsa.* **5.** *Una familia está saliendo de McDonald's.*

E2: Sí, he visitado México una vez. / No, no he visitado México nunca. / Sí, he visitado México durante las vacaciones de los últimos años.

1. comer paella
2. estar en Nueva York
3. manejar un Alfa Romeo
4. correr en un maratón
5. abrir hoy tu libro de español
6. escribir un poema
7. actuar en una obra teatral
8. ver un monumento histórico
9. conocer a una persona famosa
10. romperse la pierna alguna vez

B. **Dos dibujos, un punto de vista.** Un español hizo el dibujo de la derecha; un argentino, el de la izquierda. Pero los dos comentan el mismo tema.

Palabras útiles: el arado (*plow*), la deshumanización, la flor, la gente, la mecanización, la mula, el tractor

Suggestion B
Bring or have students bring additional pieces that make commentaries about modern life. The pieces can be in English or in Spanish. Use them to elicit discussion in Spanish.

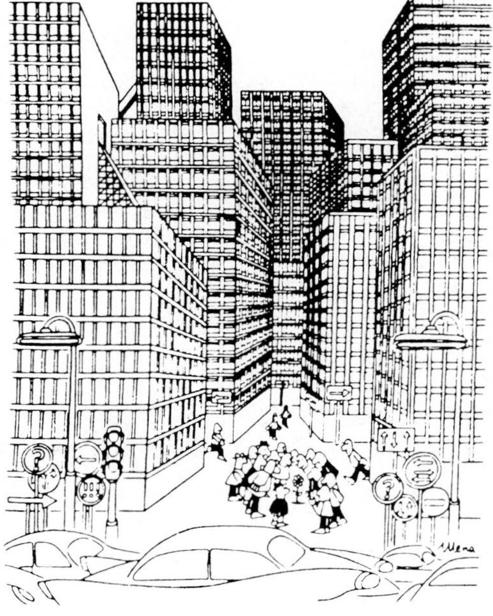

Paso 1. Conteste estas preguntas sobre el dibujo de la derecha.

1. Describa la ciudad que se ve en el dibujo.
2. ¿Qué ha descubierto la gente? ¿Por qué mira con tanto interés?
3. Para construir esta ciudad, ¿qué han hecho? ¿Qué han destruido?

Paso 2. Conteste estas preguntas sobre el dibujo de la izquierda.

1. ¿Qué se ha comprado el agricultor? ¿Qué ha vendido?
2. ¿Qué es «más moderno», según el otro agricultor?
3. ¿Qué desventaja tiene el tractor?

Paso 3. Ahora explique su reacción personal a estos dos dibujos. ¿Son chistosos (*funny*)? ¿serios?

Suggestion: Nota comunicativa
The past perfect is presented here and practiced in *Conversación D.* Use additional activities, such as the following, if you prefer to stress this tense. *Jaime es un acusón* (tattletale). *Siempre le dice a su madre las cosas que ha hecho Laura, su hermana mayor. ¿Qué le dijo a su madre ayer? Jaimito le dijo que Laura había dicho una mentira.* (*mirar la televisión toda la tarde, no estudiar, perder sus libros, romper un plato, faltar a clase, comer todo el pastel, pegarle. ¿ ?*)

NOTA COMUNICATIVA

Talking about What You Had Done

Use the past participle with the imperfect form of **haber** (**había, habías,...**) to talk about what you had—or had not—done before a given time in the past. This form is called the past perfect.

Antes de graduarme en la escuela secundaria, no **había estudiado** español. — *Before graduating from high school, I hadn't studied Spanish.*

Antes de 1985, siempre **habíamos vivido** en Kansas. — *Before 1985, we had always lived in Kansas.*

Follow-up D
- Have students describe what they had already done or not done by the time they turned 18 years old: *Antes de cumplir 18 años, ¿qué había hecho? ¿Qué no había hecho?*
- Have students complete logically using past perfect tense. **1.** *Antes de 1492 Cristóbal Colón no* ______. **2.** *Antes de 1938 la Segunda Guerra Mundial no* ______. **3.** *Antes de 1980 mis padres* (*no*) ______. **4.** *Antes de 1990 yo* (*no*) ______.
- Have students talk about things they had done or had not done before year 2000. *¿Qué cosas habían hecho, o no habían hecho, Uds. antes del año 2000?*

D. Entrevista. Use the cues to interview a classmate about his or her activities before coming to this campus. Begin your questions with **Dime...**

MODELO: algo / no haber aprendido a hacer antes del año pasado →
E1: Dime algo que no habías aprendido a hacer antes del año pasado.
E2: Pues... no había aprendido a nadar. Aprendí a nadar este año en mi clase de natación.

1. algo / no haber aprendido a hacer antes del año pasado
2. una materia / no haber estudiado antes del año pasado
3. el nombre de un deporte / haber practicado mucho
4. algo sobre un viaje / haber hecho varias veces
5. el nombre de un libro importante / no haber leído
6. una decisión / no haber tomado
7. ¿ ?

En los Estados Unidos y el Canadá...

Chi Chi Rodríguez

Juan «Chi Chi» Rodríguez nació en Río Piedras, Puerto Rico, en 1935. Se hizo[a] golfista profesional en 1960 y ha ganado ocho competiciones en la *PGA Tour* y veintidós en la *Senior Tour*. Rodríguez también se hizo popular por su arrolladora[b] personalidad y su fabulosa **precisión técnica** en el golf.

Chi Chi Rodríguez

En los años setenta, Bill Hayes, otro golfista profesional y además maestro y agente de un centro de detención juvenil, invitó a Rodríguez a dirigir un programa de golf para unos **jóvenes detenidos**.[c] Hayes y Rodríguez decidieron que el campo de golf sería[d] el lugar ideal para ayudar a estos y otros jóvenes en peligro de **fracasar**[e] en la escuela y en la vida. El golf, reconocido como[f] el deporte de las personas que **han tenido éxito**[g] en la vida, requiere **autocontrol, responsabilidad** y **respeto** para los demás. Rodríguez fundó *The Chi Chi Rodríguez Foundation* para los jóvenes del condado[h] de Pinellas, Florida. En la actualidad,[i] hay unos 500 jóvenes entre las edades de 5 y 17 años en el programa.

[a]Se... *He became* [b]*irresistible* [c]*incarcerated* [d]*would be* [e]en... *in danger of failing* [f]reconocido... *recognized as* [g]tenido... *succeeded* [h]*county* [i]En... *Currently*

Follow-up: En los Estados Unidos y el Canadá...
Have students name and/or research other organizations that help children in need and other famous Hispanics involved in humanitarian work. Remind them that they have already read about Carlos Santana in *Capítulo 13.*

UN POCO DE TODO

¡Qué descuidado (*careless*) **eres!** Complete the following paragraphs with the correct form of the words in parentheses, as suggested by the context. When two possibilities are given in parentheses, select the correct word. Begin with the present indicative. There are also command forms. Use the preterite or the imperfect of infinitives in italics.

En casa

RIGOBERTO: Me parece que debo (llevar / a llevar[1]) el coche (al / a la[2]) taller. Hace varios días que tiene una lucecita encendida.[a]

MARGARITA: (*Tú:* Ser/Estar[3]) muy descuidado con esas cosas. Un día vas a tener una sorpresa desagradable.

RIGOBERTO: Bueno, espero que el mecánico (tener[4]) tiempo (por/para[5]) arreglarlo. Hasta luego.

En el taller

MECÁNICO: Buenos días. ¿Qué desea?

RIGOBERTO: Pues, (mirar: *Ud.*[6]). ¿Ve Ud. (este[7]) luz roja que está encendida? ¿Qué puede ser?

MECÁNICO: Eso es (el/la[8]) aceite. ¿Hace mucho tiempo que no (lo/la[9]) cambia?

RIGOBERTO: La verdad es que no lo (*yo:* recordar[10]).

MECÁNICO: (Dejarme: *Ud.*[11]) revisarlo todo. (Volver: *Ud.*[12]) dentro de (un/una[13]) par de horas.

Más tarde

MECÁNICO: Ud. no (preocuparse[14]) mucho por el auto, ¿verdad? Todos los niveles (*estar*[15]) muy bajos. También le (*yo: poner*[16]) agua al depósito del limpiaparabrisas[b] y le (*cambiar*[17]) el filtro del aceite.

RIGOBERTO: ¿Eso (*ser*[18]) todo?

MECÁNICO: El coche casi no (*tener*[19]) aceite. Sinceramente, si Ud. (seguir[20]) manteniendo el auto así, algún día va a quemar[c] el motor.

RIGOBERTO: No me diga... [d]

MECÁNICO: Y otro consejo. (Cambiar: *Ud.*[21]) pronto las llantas. Hace tiempo que (*perder*[22]) la banda,[e] y eso (ser/estar[23]) peligroso.

[a]lucecita... *little light turned on* [b]¿ ? [c]*burn up* [d]No... *You don't say . . .* [e]*tread*

Comprensión: ¿Cierto o falso? Corrija las oraciones falsas.

1. Rigoberto se interesa mucho por su coche.
2. Su esposa sabe más de coches que él.
3. El mecánico trata a Rigoberto muy descortésmente.
4. El coche estaba en muy malas condiciones.
5. Rigoberto va a empezar a cuidar su coche.

Answers: Un poco de todo
1. *llevar* **2.** *al* **3.** *Eres* **4.** *tenga* **5.** *para* **6.** *mire* **7.** *esta* **8.** *el* **9.** *lo* **10.** *recuerdo* **11.** *Déjeme* **12.** *Vuelva* **13.** *un* **14.** *se preocupa* **15.** *estaban* **16.** *puse* **17.** *cambié* **18.** *fue* **19.** *tenía* **20.** *sigue* **21.** *Cambie* **22.** *perdió* **23.** *es*

Follow-up: Un poco de todo
- Ask the following questions: *¿Es Ud. como Rigoberto con su coche? ¿En algún otro aspecto?*
- Have students describe car / mechanic experiences they have had.

In the *Capítulo 14* segment of "Chapter-by-Chapter Supplementary Materials" in the IM, you will find a chapter-culminating activity. You can use this activity to consolidate and review the vocabulary and grammar skills students have acquired.

PASO 4 Un paso más

Paso 4: Un paso más
Optional section

See IM for suggestions and follow-up activities to accompany the video segment.

VIDEOTECA: En contexto

FUNCTION

Discussing car trouble

Cultura en contexto
Los verificentros

En México, como en los Estados Unidos, los coches tienen que pasar por una verificación que determina si el nivel[a] de contaminantes emitidos por el coche está dentro de los límites aceptables. Esta verificación se hace en lugares designados que se llaman **verificentros**. Como en otros países, esta es una de las medidas gubernamentales[b] para controlar la contaminación.

[a]*level* [b]medidas... *governmental measures*

In this video segment, Roberto talks to Miguel, his car mechanic, about the problems that he has been having with his car. As you watch the segment, pay particular attention to the problems that Roberto imagines his car has, as opposed to the real problem that Miguel discovers. Do you think Roberto is overreacting?

A. Lluvia de ideas

- ¿Tiene Ud. su propio coche? (Si no tiene uno, refiérase al coche de otra persona al contestar las siguientes preguntas.) ¿Cuándo lo compró? ¿De qué año es el modelo de su coche? ¿Está Ud. contento/a con el coche?
- ¿Sabe Ud. arreglar un coche? ¿Sabe Ud. algo de mecánica en general? ¿Cuáles son los problemas más típicos de un coche?

B. Dictado

A continuación aparece un fragmento del diálogo entre Roberto y Miguel, el mecánico. Complete la explicación con las palabras que faltan.

ROBERTO: ¡Este carro me tiene como loco, Miguel! ¡Es la ___tercera___[1] vez que lo arreglas este año!

MIGUEL: Sí, ya lo sé, Roberto. Primero arreglé los ___frenos___[2]... y ___luego___[3] fue la transmisión. ¿Y cómo están los frenos y la transmisión?

ROBERTO: ¡Los frenos y la transmisión están bien! ¡No ___sé___[4] qué pasa, este carro ___tonto___[5] simplemente no quiere ___arrancar___[6]!

MIGUEL: Cálmate, Roberto. Vamos a ver... ___Dime___,[7] viejo, ¿qué te pasa esta vez? ¿Por qué no arrancas, eh? ¿Qué tienes? ¿Qué necesitas?

ROBERTO: Lo que necesita este carro es ser ___reciclado___[8] para convertirlo en lata de aluminio.[a]

[a]lata... *tin can*

Follow-up B
To check comprehension, ask: **1.** *¿Cuántas veces ha arreglado Miguel el carro de Roberto este año?* **2.** *¿Ha tenido Roberto un buen día hoy? ¿Por qué?* **3.** *¿Es serio el problema del carro de Roberto?*

C. Un diálogo original

Paso 1. Con un compañero / una compañera, dramatice el diálogo entre Roberto y Miguel.

Paso 2. La compra de un carro. Con un compañero / una compañera, piense en un carro que Uds. podrían (*could*) comprar. Como no tienen mucho dinero, van a comprar un carro de segunda mano. Hagan una lista de todas las cosas que le deben preguntar al dueño antes de hacer la compra.

PASO FINAL

A CONVERSAR

¿Somos buenos o malos conductores?

Paso 1. Con un compañero / una compañera, haga y conteste preguntas basadas en el siguiente cuadro. Utilice el presente perfecto en sus preguntas y respuestas y marque el cuadro según las respuestas de su compañero/a. También añada (*add*) al cuadro otro problema relacionado con los coches.

MODELO: E1: ¿Has superado (*Have you exceeded*) el límite de velocidad recientemente?
E2: Sí, (*No, no*) he superado el límite de velocidad recientemente.

	sí	**no**
chocar con otro coche		
superar el límite de velocidad		
pasarse (*to run*) un semáforo en rojo		
desobedecerle a un policía		
¿ ?		

Paso 2. Ahora, entre todos, hablen de sus compañeros/as. En general, ¿son Uds. buenos o malos conductores? Deben marcar la información en un cuadro como el del Paso 1. Incluyan los problemas que añadieron al cuadro.

MODELOS: ¿Quiénes han chocado con otro coche recientemente? → Tom ha chocado con otro coche este mes.

Paso 3. Calculen el porcentaje de personas que contestaron **sí** a cada pregunta del Paso 1. Reaccionen a los porcentajes con las siguientes frases. **¡OJO!** Las frases requieren el uso del subjuntivo.

Es bueno / malo que…
Me alegra / No me alegra que…
Me sorprende que / No me sorprende que…

MODELO: Siete de veintiún estudiantes han superado recientemente el límite de velocidad. → El 33% de la clase ha superado recientemente el límite de velocidad.
E1: No me sorprende que el 33% de la clase haya superado el límite de velocidad.

Suggestion: A conversar, Paso 2
Have students draw chart and tally answers on board.

Follow-up: A conversar
Ask: *Según estos porcentajes, ¿son Uds. buenos o malos conductores? ¿Es importante obedecer las reglas de tránsito? ¿Cuál es peor, superar el límite de velocidad o desobedecerle a un policía? ¿Por qué? ¿Ha tenido alguien un accidente grave? ¿Qué le pasó?*

Variation: A conversar
If you teach in an area where most students do not drive but use bikes or public transportation, create a chart of pedestrian, cyclist, and passenger no-no's for this activity.

En resumen

GRAMÁTICA

To review the grammar points presented in this chapter, refer to the indicated grammar presentations. You'll find further practice of these structures in the Workbook/Laboratory Manual, on the CD-ROM, and on the website.

38. Past Participle Used As an Adjective

Do you know how to form past participles? You should remember that past participles that are used as adjectives agree with the noun they describe.

39. Perfect Forms: Present Perfect Indicative and Present Perfect Subjunctive

How do you express that you have done something? Do you know how to say that you're happy or sad that someone else did or has done something?

VOCABULARIO

El medio ambiente

acabar	to run out, use up completely
conservar	to save, conserve
construir	to build
contaminar	to pollute
cubrir	to cover
desarrollar	to develop
descubrir	to discover
desperdiciar	to waste
destruir	to destroy
evitar	to avoid
proteger	to protect
reciclar	to recycle
resolver (ue)	to solve, resolve
el aire	air
el bosque	forest
la capa de ozono	ozone layer
la energía	energy
eléctrica	electric
eólica	wind
hidráulica	hydraulic
nuclear	nuclear
solar	solar
la escasez	lack, shortage
la fábrica	factory
la falta	lack, absence
el gobierno	government
la naturaleza	nature
la población	population
los recursos naturales	natural resources

Repaso: la contaminación

¿La ciudad o el campo?

el/la agricultor(a)	farmer
el aislamiento	isolation
el árbol	tree
el/la campesino/a	farm worker; peasant
el delito	crime
la finca	farm
el rascacielos	skyscraper
el ritmo	rhythm, pace
el servicio	service
el transporte	(means of) transportation
la vida	life
la violencia	violence
la vivienda	housing

Hablando de coches

arrancar	to start (*a car*)
gastar	to use, expend

llenar	to fill (up)
revisar	to check
el aceite	oil
la batería	battery
la estación de gasolina	gas station
los frenos	brakes
la gasolina	gasoline
la gasolinera	gas station
la llanta (desinflada)	(flat) tire
el/la mecánico/a	mechanic
el nivel	level
el parabrisas	windshield
el taller	(repair) shop
el tanque	tank

Repaso: arreglar, limpiar

En el camino

chocar (con)	to run into, collide (with)
conducir	to drive
doblar	to turn
estacionar(se)	to park
obedecer	to obey
parar	to stop
seguir (i, i)	to continue

Suggestions: Vocabulario

- Bring or have students bring magazine clippings of images related to vocabulary words. Use images for quick comprehension checks (*¿Qué es eso?* → *Es una llanta desinflada.*) and as springboard for questions and short discussions.
- Remind students that *conducir* and *obedecer* are conjugated like *conocer,* with *-zc-* in first person singular: *conduzco, obedezco.* They should also remember spelling changes for *construir* (*y*), *destruir* (*y*), *proteger* (*j*), *arrancar* (*qu*), *chocar* (*qu*), and *seguir* (*g*).
- Have students regroup words under new categories, for example, *negativo* vs. *positivo* or *infraestructura* vs. *naturaleza* vs. *mecanismos.*
- Play word association game. Begin each round with 1 of the 5 adjectives. After each round write the first and last word on board.

la autopista	freeway
la calle	street
el camino	street, road
la carretera	highway
la circulación	traffic
el/la conductor(a)	driver
la esquina	(street) corner
la licencia de manejar/conducir	driver's license
el límite de velocidad	speed limit
el/la policía	police officer
el semáforo	traffic signal
el tránsito	traffic
todo derecho	straight ahead

Repaso: manejar

Los adjetivos

acelerado/a	fast, accelerated
bello/a	beautiful
denso/a	dense
público/a	public
puro/a	pure

La vida social y la vida afectiva

CAPÍTULO 15

Suggestion: Chapter Opening photo
Point out the chapter opening photo. Have students talk about the people in the photo. Encourage them to comment on their perceptions about the relationships between the different groups of people. Do they seem to them to resemble people they know in this country? In what ways? Have them share their ideas about relationships among people. For example, do relationships among students further or impede their education? Do older people fare better if they have a partner? Ask them to share any information they have about such relationships in Hispanic countries.

Resources
You and your students may find the following *¿Qué tal?* supplements helpful as you teach this chapter:
For the Instructor
- *Instructor's Manual and Resource Kit,* "Chapter-by-Chapter" Supplementary Materials
- Testing Program
- Overhead Transparencies 79–81
- Video (VHS or CD)
- *¿Qué tal?* Online Learning Center Website
- Audioscript
- Instructor's Resource CD

◀ Las relaciones sociales son importantes para todo el mundo. Estas personas están sentadas en los bancos de la Plaza de Armas en Punta Arenas, Chile.

VOCABULARIO

- Sentimental relationships
- Stages of life

GRAMÁTICA

40 Subjunctive after Nonexistent and Indefinite Antecedents

41 Subjunctive after Conjunctions of Contingency and Purpose

CULTURA

- **Enfoque cultural:** Chile
- **Nota cultural:** Relaciones en la vida social
- **En los Estados Unidos y el Canadá:** Isabel Allende
- **Cultura en contexto:** Lo social en el mundo de los negocios

Multimedia

You will learn about making an appointment in the **En contexto** video segment.

Review vocabulary and grammar and practice language skills with the interactive CD-ROM.

Get connected to the Spanish-speaking world with the *¿Qué tal?* Online Learning Center: **www.mhhe.com/quetal**.

For Students
- Workbook/Laboratory Manual and Audio Program or Electronic Workbook/Laboratory Manual
- Video or CD
- Interactive CD-ROM
- *¿Qué tal?* Online Learning Center Website
- Listening Comprehension Audio CD
- McGraw-Hill Electronic Language Tutor (MHELT)

Vocabulario PASO 1

 **Paso 1: Vocabulario**

See detailed supplementary materials and exercises for this section and a model for vocabulary presentation and other material in the *Capítulo 15 Paso 1: Vocabulario* section of "Chapter-by-Chapter Supplementary Materials," IM.

Las relaciones sentimentales

❖ **Transparencies 79, 80** Transparency 80 offers additional images and vocabulary.

Multimedia: Audio Students can listen to and practice this chapter's vocabulary on their Listening Comprehension Audio CD.

la amistad

la cita

el amor

el noviazgo

la luna de miel

el matrimonio

la boda

el divorcio

Más vocabulario

el/la amigo/a	friend	**amar**	to love
la esposa / la mujer	wife	**casarse (con)**	to marry
el esposo / el marido	husband	**divorciarse (de)**	to get divorced (from)
el/la novio/a	boyfriend/girlfriend; fiancé(e); groom/bride	**enamorarse (de)**	to fall in love (with)
la pareja	(married) couple; partner	**llevarse bien/mal (con)**	to get along well/poorly (with)
		pasar tiempo (con)	to spend time (with)
amistoso/a	friendly	**querer (ie)**	to love
cariñoso/a	affectionate	**romper (con)**	to break up (with)
casado/a*	married	**salir (con)**	to go out (with)
soltero/a*	single, not married	**separarse (de)**	to separate (from)

*In **Capítulo 2,** you began to use **ser casado/a**. **Estar casado/a** means *to be married;* **ser casado/a** means *to be a married person*. **Ser soltero/a** is used exclusively to describe an unmarried person.

PASO 1

CAPÍTULO 15

Preliminary exercises: Las relaciones sentimentales

- To check comprehension and reinforce meaning, ask: **1.** *¿Qué palabras asocia Ud. con la amistad? ¿el amor? ¿una boda? ¿la luna de miel? ¿el novio? ¿la esposa?* **2.** *¿Cómo es el novio / la novia ideal? ¿Es rubio/a o moreno/a? ¿joven o viejo/a? ¿alto/a o bajo/a? ¿guapo/a o feo/a? ¿trabajador(a) o perezoso/a? ¿romántico/a (cariñoso/a) o frío/a?*
- To personalize, ask: *¿Pasa Ud. mucho tiempo con sus amigos? ¿Qué hacen? ¿Siempre se llevan bien? ¿Sus amigos tienen los mismos intereses que Ud.? ¿Cree que un matrimonio debe tener intereses parecidos? ¿Es importante que los esposos sean amigos? ¿Cuál es la edad ideal para casarse?*

Answers: A

1. e **2.** c **3.** b **4.** d **5.** a

Follow-up A

Have students react to statements using *estoy de acuerdo* and *no estoy de acuerdo:* **1.** *El matrimonio (La luna de miel) es un concepto muy anticuado.* **2.** *Si el noviazgo es corto, el matrimonio va a ser corto también.* **3.** *Las mujeres son más románticas que los hombres.* **4.** *El noviazgo debe ser largo y formal.* **5.** *El matrimonio es una obligación social necesaria.*

Answers B

1. *esposo* **2.** *noviazgo* **3.** *cita* **4.** *boda* **5.** *cita* **6.** *amistad* **7.** *amor*

Extension B

8. Para algunas personas, el ______ es un concepto anticuado. Prefieren vivir juntos, sin casarse. (el matrimonio)
9. Algunas parejas modernas no quieren gastar su dinero en ______. (la luna de miel)
10. Algunas personas creen que es posible ______ a primera vista (at first sight). (amarse)

Suggestions: Nota cultural

- Provide some additional common terms of endearment such as *gordo/a* (Sp.) and *negro/a* (Venezuela). Remind students that terms like these have nothing to do with a person's weight or skin color.
- Point out that a common word to refer to a live-in significant other is *compañero/a.*

Conversación

A. Definiciones. Empareje las palabras con sus definiciones. Luego, para cada palabra definida, dé un verbo y el nombre de una persona asociada con esa relación social. Hay más de una respuesta posible en cada caso.

1. ______ el matrimonio
2. ______ el amor
3. ______ el divorcio
4. ______ la boda
5. ______ la amistad

a. Es una relación cariñosa entre dos personas. Se llevan bien y se hablan con frecuencia.
b. Es el posible resultado de un matrimonio, cuando los esposos no se llevan bien.
c. Es una relación sentimental, apasionada, muy especial, entre dos personas. Puede llevar al (*lead to*) matrimonio.
d. Es una ceremonia religiosa o civil en la que (*which*) la novia a veces lleva un vestido blanco.
e. Es una relación legal entre dos personas que viven juntas (*together*) y que a veces tienen hijos.

B. ¡Seamos lógicos! Complete las oraciones lógicamente.

1. Mi abuelo es el ________ de mi abuela.
2. Muchos novios tienen un largo ________ antes de la boda.
3. María y Julio tienen una ________ el viernes para comer en un restaurante. Luego van a bailar.
4. La ________ de Juan y Pati es el domingo a las dos de la tarde, en la iglesia (*church*) de San Martín.
5. En una ________, ¿quién debe pagar o comprar los boletos, el hombre o la mujer?
6. La ________ entre los ex esposos es imposible. No pueden ser amigos.
7. ¡El ________ es ciego (*blind*)!

NOTA CULTURAL

Relaciones en la vida social

Dos palabras españolas que no tienen equivalente exacto en inglés son **amigo** y **novio**. En el diagrama se indica cuándo es apropiado usar estas palabras para describir relaciones sociales en muchas culturas hispánicas y en la norteamericana.

friend *girlfriend/boyfriend* *fiancée/fiancé* *bride/groom*

amiga/amigo novia/novio

PASO 1

National Standards: Community

Have students work in groups to write 3 questions that they would ask someone about their concept of family and friends. Have groups share and "pool" questions. Encourage them to use these to interview people in community. They should try to include someone from each stage of life, people from both genders, and at least 1 or more persons, especially Hispanics, who are not from U.S. or Canada. Have them share their findings with their classmates, and use results to make generalizations about importance of family and friends to different genders, age groups, and nationalities.

Como en todas partes del mundo, los enamorados hispanos usan muchos términos de cariño: **mi amor, mi amorcito/a, mi vida, viejo/vieja, querido/querida, cielo, corazón**. Es también frecuente el uso afectuoso de las frases **mi hijo / mi hija** entre esposos y aun[a] entre buenos amigos.

[a]*even*

Etapas de la vida°

Etapas... *Stages of life*

el nacimiento	birth
la infancia	infancy
la niñez	childhood
la adolescencia	adolescence
la juventud	youth
la madurez	middle age
la vejez	old age
la muerte	death

nacer	to be born
crecer	to grow
morir (ue, u)	to die

Conversación

A. Etapas de la vida. Relacione las siguientes palabras y frases con las distintas etapas de la vida de una persona. **¡OJO!** Hay más de una posible relación en algunos casos.

1. el amor
2. los nietos
3. los juguetes (*toys*)
4. no poder comer sin ayuda
5. los hijos en la universidad
6. los granos (*pimples*)
7. la universidad
8. la boda

B. Una receta para unas buenas relaciones. En su opinión, ¿cuáles son los ingredientes necesarios para un buen matrimonio o una buena amistad?

Paso 1. Haga una lista de los cinco ingredientes más esenciales. Los ingredientes pueden expresarse con una palabra o una frase.

Paso 2. Compare su lista con las de otros tres estudiantes. ¿Coinciden en la selección de algunos ingredientes? Hablen de todos los ingredientes y hagan una lista de los cinco más importantes.

Paso 3. Ahora comparen los resultados de todos los grupos. ¿Han contestado todos más o menos de la misma manera?

Extension A

9. *dos coches y un perro* **10.** *pasarlo bien* **11.** *los amigos íntimos* **12.** *un coche con cuatro puertas*

Optional B

To personalize, ask: **1.** *¿Son importantes los amigos en su vida? ¿Quién es su mejor amigo/a? ¿Cuánto tiempo hace que lo/la conoce? ¿Crecieron Uds. juntos/as? Es decir, ¿se han conocido desde la niñez? ¿desde la adolescencia? ¿Por qué se lleva bien con esa persona?* **2.** *¿Quiere Ud. casarse algún día? (¿Ya se casó?) ¿Le gusta la idea de tener una boda grande? (¿Tuvo una boda grande?) ¿Piensa hacer un viaje de luna de miel? (¿Hizo un viaje de luna de miel?) ¿Adónde?* **3.** *¿Qué es lo bueno de estar casado? ¿y lo malo? ¿Qué es lo bueno de ser soltero? ¿y lo malo?* **4.** *¿En qué década del siglo* (century) *pasado nació Ud.? ¿Ha visto muchos cambios desde entonces? ¿Cuáles son? ¿Cómo piensa pasar su vejez? (Si Ud. ya es una persona madura, ¿cómo pasa su tiempo?)* **5.** *¿Ha sido Ud. afectado/a personalmente por la muerte de alguien? ¿Quién murió? ¿Cómo se sintió Ud.? ¿Tiene buenos recuerdos* (memories) *de esa persona? ¿Cuáles son?*

PASO 2 Gramática

Paso 2: Gramática
See detailed supplementary materials for this grammar section in IM.

40 ¿Hay alguien que... ? ¿Hay un lugar donde... ? • Subjunctive after Nonexistent and Indefinite Antecedents

❖ **Transparency 81**
Transparency 81 provides examples of this structure.

Un buen lunes

Mafalda *tiene un padre que la quiere, la protege y que pasa mucho tiempo* con ella. Por eso, Mafalda ve a su padre como *un hombre que ahora es más guapo* que cuando era joven. Todos los niños *necesitan padres que los quieran, los cuiden y que tengan tiempo* para pasar con ellos.

Suggestions: Subjunctive: Nonexistent/Indefinite

- Have students complete: **1.** *Mi padre/ madre es una persona que...* **2.** *Un padre / Una madre ideal es una persona que...*
- Ask: *Los lunes por la mañana, ¿Hay algo que lo/la haga feliz? ¿que lo/la haga sonreír? ¿Y los martes por la mañana? ¿los viernes por la mañana?* Help students with negative answers: *No, no hay nada que me haga sonreír.*

Comprensión

¿Quién lo dice o piensa, el padre de Mafalda u otro pasajero en el autobús?

1. No hay nadie en este autobús que sea más feliz que yo.
2. Tengo una hija que es una maravilla, ¿verdad?
3. Todos los lunes por la mañana trato de pensar en algo que me haga sonreír en camino al trabajo… pero casi nunca lo puedo hacer.

A. In English and Spanish, statements or questions that give or ask for information about a person, place, or thing often contain two clauses.

Each of the example sentences contains a main clause (*I have a car, Is there a house for sale*). In addition, each sentence also has a subordinate clause (*that gets good mileage, that is closer to the city*) that modifies a noun in the main clause: *car, house*. The noun (or pronoun) modified is called the *antecedent* (**el antecedente**) of the subordinate clause, and the clause itself is called an adjective clause because—like an adjective—it modifies a noun (or pronoun).

I have a **car** *that gets good mileage.*
Is there a **house for sale** *that is closer to the city?*

A good Monday Mafalda has a father who loves her, protects her, and spends a lot of time with her. That's why Mafalda sees her father as a man who is now more handsome than when he was young. All children need parents who love them, take care of them, and have time to spend with them.

B. Sometimes the antecedent of an adjective clause is something that, in the speaker's mind, does not exist or whose existence is indefinite or uncertain.

NONEXISTENT ANTECEDENT:

There is *nothing* that you can do.

INDEFINITE ANTECEDENT:

We need *a car* that will last us for years. (We don't have one yet.)

In these cases, the subjunctive must be used in the adjective (subordinate) clause in Spanish.

Note in the examples that adjective clauses that describe a place can be introduced with **donde...** as well as with **que...**

EXISTENT ANTECEDENT:

Hay algo aquí que me **interesa**.
There is something here that interests me.

NONEXISTENT ANTECEDENT

No veo nada que me **interese**.
I don't see anything that interests me.

DEFINITE ANTECEDENT:

Hay muchos restaurantes donde **sirven** comida mexicana auténtica.
There are a lot of restaurants where they serve authentic Mexican food.

INDEFINITE ANTECEDENT:

Buscamos un restaurante donde **sirvan** comida salvadoreña auténtica.
We're looking for a restaurant where they serve authentic Salvadoran food.

National Standards: Communication
Have students make lists of hypothetical situations, possessions, and so on for each other. Then have them use these to interview each other. List examples on board: *¿Hay alguien aquí que viva en una mansión? ¿sepa hablar otro idioma? ¿tenga un Mercedes u otro coche de lujo? ¿viaje a México todos los años? ¿quiera ser médico algún día?*

OJO The dependent adjective clause structure is often used in questions to find out about someone or something the speaker does not know much about. Note, however, that the indicative is used to answer the question if the antecedent is known to the person who answers.

INDEFINITE ANTECEDENT:

¿Hay algo aquí que te **guste**?
Is there anything here that you like?

DEFINITE ANTECEDENT:

Sí, **hay varias bolsas** que me **gustan**.
Yes, there are several purses that I like.

OJO The personal **a** is not used with direct object nouns that refer to hypothetical persons.* Compare the use of the indicative and the subjunctive in the sentences at the right.

NONEXISTENT ANTECEDENT:

Busco **un señor** que **sepa francés.**
I'm looking for a man who knows French.

EXISTENT ANTECEDENT:

Busco **al señor** que **sabe francés**.
I'm looking for the man who knows French.

---

*Remember that **alguien** and **nadie** always take the personal **a** when they are used as direct objects: **Busco a alguien que lo sepa. No veo a nadie que sea norteamericano.**

Práctica

Preliminary exercises A

- Read each English sentence and have students tell whether the antecedent is existent or nonexistent. Then read Spanish sentence. **1.** There's nothing here that I like. / *No hay nada aquí que me guste.* **2.** Here's something that you will like. / *Aquí hay algo que te va a gustar.* **3.** I don't know anyone who can do it. / *No conozco a nadie que lo pueda hacer.* **4.** I know many people who can do it. / *Conozco a muchas personas que lo pueden hacer.* **5.** There's no car that is economical. *No hay ningún coche que sea económico.*
- Read each English sentence and ask students whether the antecedent is definite or indefinite. Then read Spanish sentence. **1.** I have a book that is interesting. / *Tengo un libro que es interesante.* **2.** I want to buy a book that is interesting. / *Quiero comprar un libro que sea interesante.* **3.** I'm looking for a secretary who speaks Spanish. / *Busco un secretario que hable españo!.*

Extension A

- Ask students: *¿Tiene más parientes que hagan algo «especial»?*
- Give students 1 minute to form a question about some unusual activity they like, then have them ask if anyone else shares their hobby.

A. Hablando de gente que conocemos. En su familia, ¿hay personas que tengan las siguientes características? Indique la oración apropiada en cada par de oraciones.

	TENGO UN PARIENTE...	NO TENGO NINGÚN PARIENTE...
1.	☐ que habla alemán.	☐ que hable alemán.
2.	☐ que vive en el extranjero.	☐ que viva en el extranjero.
3.	☐ que es dueño de un restaurante.	☐ que sea dueño de un restaurante.
4.	☐ que sabe tocar el piano.	☐ que sepa tocar el piano.
5.	☐ que es médico/a.	☐ que sea médico/a.
6.	☐ que fuma.	☐ que fume.
7.	☐ que está divorciado/a.	☐ que esté divorciado/a.
8.	☐ que trabaja en la televisión.	☐ que trabaje en la televisión.
9.	☐ ¿ ?	☐ ¿ ?

B. Las preguntas de Carmen

Paso 1. Carmen acaba de llegar aquí de otro estado. Quiere saber algunas cosas sobre la universidad y la ciudad. Haga las preguntas de Carmen según el modelo.

MODELO: restaurantes / sirven comida latinoamericana →
¿Hay restaurantes que sirvan (donde se sirva) comida latinoamericana?

1. librerías / venden libros usados
2. tiendas / se puede comprar revistas de Latinoamérica
3. cafés cerca de la universidad / se reúnen muchos estudiantes
4. apartamentos cerca de la universidad / son buenos y baratos
5. cines / pasan (*they show*) películas en español
6. un gimnasio en la universidad / se juega al ráquetbol
7. parques / la gente corre o da paseos
8. museos / hacen exposiciones de arte latinoamericano

Paso 2. ¿Son ciertas o falsas las siguientes declaraciones?

1. A Carmen no le interesa la cultura hispánica.
2. Carmen es deportista.
3. Es posible que sea estudiante.
4. Este año piensa vivir con unos amigos de sus padres.

Paso 3. Ahora conteste las preguntas de Carmen con información verdadera sobre la ciudad donde Ud. vive y su universidad.

MODELO: ¿Hay restaurantes que sirvan comida latinoamericana? →
No, no hay ningún restaurante que sirva comida latinoamericana. / Sí, hay restaurantes que sirven comida latinoamericana.

Conversación

A. Una encuesta. Las habilidades o características de un grupo de personas pueden ser sorprendentes. ¿Qué sabe Ud. de los compañeros de su clase de español? Pregúnteles a los miembros de la clase si saben hacer lo siguiente o a quién le ocurre lo siguiente. Deben levantar la mano sólo los que puedan contestar afirmativamente. Luego la persona que hizo la pregunta debe hacer un comentario apropiado. Siga el modelo.

MODELO: hablar chino →
En esta clase, ¿hay alguien que hable chino? (*Nadie levanta la mano.*) No hay nadie que hable chino.

1. hablar ruso
2. saber tocar la viola
3. conocer a un actor / una actriz
4. saber preparar comida vietnamita
5. tener el cumpleaños hoy
6. escribir poemas
7. vivir en las afueras
8. ¿ ?

B. Entrevista

Paso 1. Con un compañero / una compañera, haga y conteste las siguientes preguntas.

1. ¿Hay alguien en tu vida que te quiera locamente (*madly*)?
2. ¿Hay algo que te importe más que los estudios universitarios?
3. ¿Con qué tipo de persona te gusta salir?
4. Para el semestre/trimestre que viene, ¿qué clases buscas? ¿una que empiece a las ocho de la mañana?
5. ¿Tienes algún amigo o alguna amiga de la escuela secundaria que esté casado/a? ¿que tenga hijos? ¿que esté divorciado/a?
6. **¡OJO!** Unas preguntas indiscretas: ¿Has conocido recientemente a alguien que te haya gustado mucho? ¿de quien te hayas enamorado? ¿Hay alguna persona de tu familia con quien te lleves muy mal? ¿o muy, muy bien?

Paso 2. Ahora, comparta los detalles interesantes con la clase.

MODELO: Bob dice que no hay nadie en su vida que lo quiera locamente, pero dice que ha conocido a alguien que le ha gustado mucho.

Suggestion B
Encourage students to use conversation-extending techniques to elicit more information.

Extension B
Write sentences on board. Have students supply their own details to form questions to use in an interview situation. **7.** *¿Tienes algún amigo que... ?* **8.** *¿Tienes alguna clase que... ?* **9.** *En mi opinión, no hay nada / nadie que...*

Enfoque *cultural*

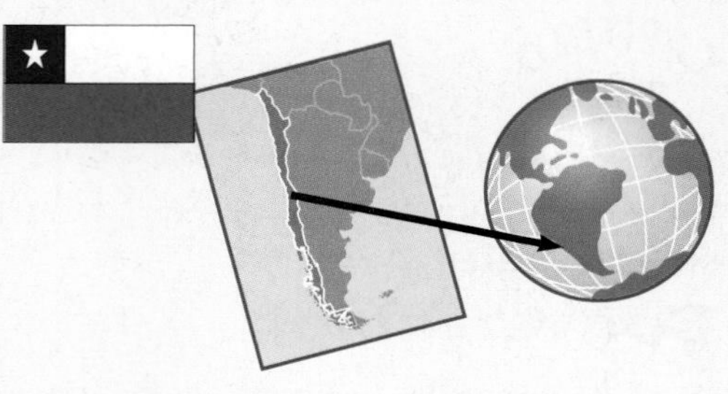

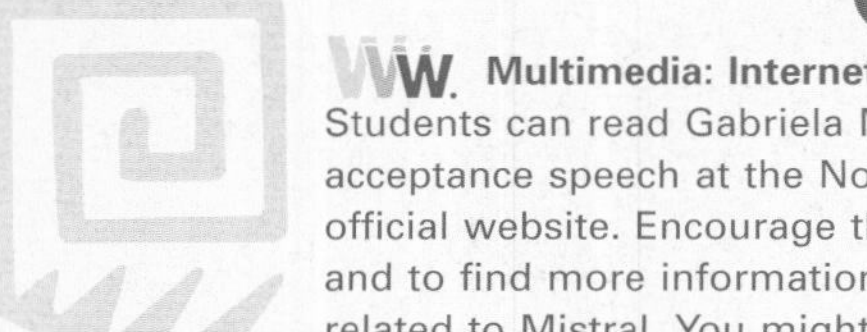

Multimedia: Internet
Students can read Gabriela Mistral's acceptance speech at the Nobel Foundation's official website. Encourage them to look for it, and to find more information and images related to Mistral. You might assign specific topics about Chile and Gabriela Mistral and have students give brief oral presentations on their findings.

Chile

Enfoque cultural
See follow-up activities for this section in chapter-by-chapter materials in IM.

Datos esenciales

Nombre oficial: República de Chile

Capital: Santiago

Población: 15.000.000 de habitantes

Moneda: el peso

Idiomas: el español (oficial), el mapuche, el quechua

Conozca a... Gabriela Mistral

La primera hispanoamericana en ganar el premio Nóbel de Literatura fue Gabriela Mistral (1889–1957). Maestra de escuela, además de poeta, fue una mujer que vivió tristes momentos en su vida (el abandono de su padre, el suicidio de su prometido[a] y su maternidad frustrada) que se ven reflejados en su poesía. El siguiente poema es uno de sus más conocidos.

[a]*fiancé*

Riqueza[a]

Tengo la dicha fiel[b]
y la dicha perdida:
la una como una rosa,
la otra como una espina.[c]
De lo que me robaron
no fui desposeída:[d]
tengo la dicha fiel
y la dicha perdida
y estoy rica de púrpura[e]
y de melancolía.
¡Ay, qué amada[f]
es la rosa
y qué amante[g] es la espina!
Como el noble contorno[h]
de las frutas mellizas[i]
tengo la dicha fiel
y la dicha perdida...

[a]*Wealth* [b]dicha... *constant happiness* [c]*thorn* [d]no... *I was not dispossessed* [e]*purple* [f]qué... *how beloved* [g]qué... *how loving* [h]*contour* [i]*twin*

¡Fíjese!

- El nombre de Chile se deriva de la palabra indígena *chilli* que significa «lugar donde termina la tierra».
- A través del largo y estrecho territorio de Chile, la geografía va de selva[a] a desierto, a fértil valle,[b] a zona de nieves perpetuas en el extremo sur.
- Chile tiene una de las economías más fuertes de Sudamérica. Es el mayor productor de cobre[c] del mundo, y tiene una importante industria vinícola.[d]

[a]*jungle* [b]*valley* [c]*copper* [d]*wine*

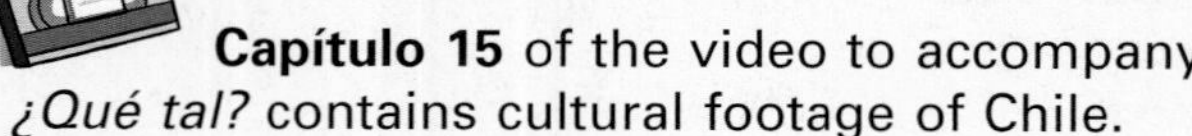

Capítulo 15 of the video to accompany *¿Qué tal?* contains cultural footage of Chile.

Visit the *¿Qué tal?* website at www.mhhe.com/quetal.

Un viñedo (*vineyard*) chileno, con los Andes al fondo (*in the background*)

Suggestions: Enfoque cultural
- Ask the following questions and accept any thoughtful answer that reflects an understanding of Mistral's imaginative process: **1.** *¿A qué creen que se refiere Mistral cuando habla de la «dicha fiel y la dicha perdida»?* (Answers will vary.) **2.** *¿Cómo es que a la hablante le puedan robar algo, sin que ella resulte «disposeída»?* (Answers will vary.) **3.** *¿Cómo se llama la forma retórica que explica «la rosa» y «la espina»* (*la metáfora*) **4.** *¿Qué representan la rosa y la espina?* (Answers will vary.) **5.** *¿Qué son «las frutas mellizas»?* (Answers will vary.)

 **Paso 3: Gramática**
See detailed supplementary materials for this grammar section in IM.

41 Lo hago para que tú... • Subjunctive after Conjunctions of Contingency and Purpose

Maneras de amar

¿A qué dibujo corresponde cada una de las siguientes oraciones? ¿Quién las dice?

Follow-up: Subjunctive: Contingency/Purpose
Ask: *¿Han estado Uds. en situaciones similares a las de los dibujos?* Encourage students to give details.

1. Aquí tienes la tarjeta de crédito, pero úsala sólo *en caso de que haya una emergencia*, ¿eh?
2. Escúchame bien. No vas a salir *antes de que termines* la tarea.
3. Quiero casarme contigo *para que estemos* siempre juntos *y no salgas más* con Raúl.

Comprensión

1. En el primer dibujo, es obvio que el chico _____. Es normal que la madre _____.
2. En el segundo dibujo está claro que la chica _____; por eso el padre se siente _____ (adjetivo).
3. En el tercer dibujo, creo que el chico _____. No estoy seguro/a de que la chica _____. Pienso que esta pareja es muy joven para _____.

A. When one action or condition is related to another—X will happen provided that Y occurs; we'll do Z unless A happens—a relationship of *contingency* is said to exist: one thing is contingent, or depends, on another.

The Spanish *conjunctions* (**las conjunciones**) at the right express relationships of contingency or purpose. The subjunctive always occurs in subordinate clauses introduced by these conjunctions.

a menos que	unless
antes (de) que	before
con tal (de) que	provided (that)
en caso de que	in case
para que	so that

B. Note that these conjunctions introduce subordinate clauses in which the events have not yet materialized; the events are conceptualized, not real-world, events.

Voy **con tal de que** ellos me **acompañen**.
I'm going, provided (that) they go with me.

En caso de que llegue Juan, dile que ya salí.
In case Juan arrives, tell him that I already left.

Ways to love 1. Here you have the credit card, but use it only in case there is an emergency, OK? **2.** Listen to me well. You are not going out until you finish your homework. **3.** I want to marry you so that we are always together and so you don't go out with Raúl any more.

UN POCO DE TODO

Answers: Un poco de todo
1. *llegado* 2. *Estoy* 3. *descansar* 4. *salgamos* 5. *también* 6. *haya* 7. *te preocupes* 8. *hecho* 9. *Cálmate* 10. *nada* 11. *perdió* 12. *prometió* 13. *la* 14. *este* 15. *salido* 16. *bonita* 17. *tuvimos* 18. Había 19. *esperábamos* 20. *se divirtieron* 21. *guste* 22. *podamos* 23. *de la* 24. *agüe* 25. *tampoco*

Follow-up: Un poco de todo
To personalize the topic, ask: *¿Cuál es la mejor boda a la que Ud. ha asistido? Dé todos los detalles que recuerde.* Encourage students to ask each other questions about weddings they describe.

In the *Capítulo 15* segment of "Chapter-by-Chapter Supplementary Materials" in the IM, you will find a chapter-culminating activity. You can use this activity to consolidate and review the vocabulary and grammar skills students have acquired.

La luna de miel. Complete the following dialogues with the correct form of the words in parentheses, as suggested by the context. When two possibilities are given in parentheses, select the correct one. **¡OJO!** You will use indicative, present subjunctive, and command forms. *P* and *I* stand for *preterite* and *imperfect*, respectively. Use the past participle of infinitives in italics.

En el aeropuerto

MUJER: ¡Por fin hemos (*llegar*[1])! ¡Qué vuelo más largo!
MARIDO: Sí. (Soy/Estoy[2]) bastante cansado. Quiero (descansar[3]) un rato antes de que (*nosotros:* salir[4]) a ver la ciudad.
MUJER: Yo (también/tampoco[5]). Vamos a recoger[a] el equipaje. ¡Ojalá que no se nos (ha/haya[6]) perdido!
MARIDO: No (preocuparte[7]). Todo saldrá bien.[b] Vamos.

[a]*pick up* [b]saldrá... *will turn out all right*

En el hotel

MARIDO: Ay, ¡qué desgracia! ¿Qué hemos (*hacer*[8]) nosotros para merecer[a] esto?
MUJER: (Calmarte[9]), mi amor. No pasa (nunca/nada[10]). Si sólo[b] se nos (*P:* perder[11]) una maleta. Y la empleada de la aerolínea nos (*P:* prometer[12]) que (lo/la[13]) vamos a tener para mañana.
MARIDO: Sí, tienes razón. Verdad que hasta (este/esto[14]) momento, todo ha (*salir*[15]) muy bien. ¡Qué boda más (bonito[16]) (*P, nosotros:* tener[17])! (*I:* Haber[18]) muchas más personas de lo que (*I, nosotros:* esperar[19]). Pero creo que todos (*P:* divertirse[20]).
MUJER: Creo que sí. En mi opinión, no hay nadie a quien no le (gustar[21]) una fiesta de bodas...
MARIDO: Bueno, descansemos[c] un poco para que (*nosotros*: poder[22]) disfrutar del[d] resto (del / de la[23]) noche. No quiero que una maleta perdida (aguar[e] [24]) la luna de miel.
MUJER: ¡Ni yo (también/tampoco[25])!

[a]*deserve* [b]Si... *Only* [c]*let's rest* [d]disfrutar... *enjoy the* [e]*to spoil*

Comprensión: ¿Cierto, falso o no lo dice?

1. Las dos personas son recién casadas.
2. La fiesta de bodas tuvo lugar en casa de los padres de la mujer.
3. Los esposos perdieron dos maletas.
4. Fueron a Cancún en su luna de miel.
5. La boda fue bonita y muy divertida.

Paso 4: Un paso más
Optional section

See IM for suggestions and follow-up activities to accompany the video segment.

VIDEOTECA: En contexto

In this video segment, Mariela makes an appointment to see the university's career counselor. As you watch the segment, pay attention to the exchange between Mariela and the receptionist and how they decide upon a time that suits both Mariela and the counselor. Does your university or college provide a similar service?

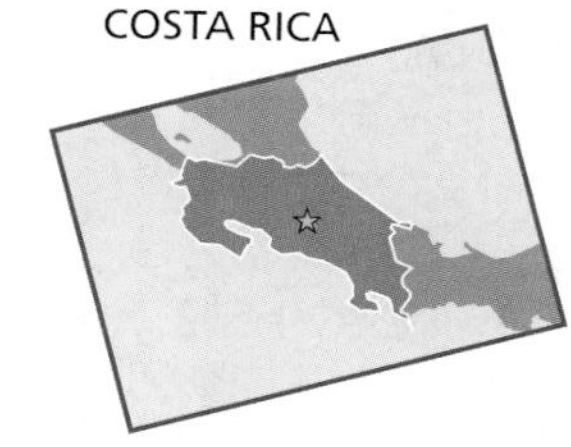

Suggestion A
Remind students that *cita* is used for professional appointments as well as dates.

A. Lluvia de ideas

- Aparte de (*Aside from*) sus clases, ¿tiene Ud. muchos compromisos sociales y citas? ¿Cómo recuerda Ud. cuándo tiene sus compromisos? ¿Usa una agenda o un calendario?
- ¿Cuándo tiene sus próximas citas? ¿Puede decir con quién las tiene o prefiere que no se sepa?

B. Dictado

A continuación aparece un fragmento del diálogo entre Mariela y la recepcionista de la consejera Valenzuela. Complete la explicación con las palabras o frases que faltan.

RECEPCIONISTA: Buenos días, oficina de la consejera Valenzuela. ¿En qué __le__[1] puedo servir?

MARIELA: Muy buenos días. ¿__Me__[2] comunica con la consejera Valenzuela, por favor?

RECEPCIONISTA: Disculpe.[a] ¿De parte de[b] __quién__[3]? [...] __Lo__[4] siento pero la consejera está con un __cliente__[5] en este momento. ¿Quiere dejar un recado?

MARIELA: Bueno, lo que quiero es hacer una __cita__.[6]

[a]*Excuse me.* [b]¿De... *On behalf of*

C. Un diálogo original

Opción 1. Con un compañero / una compañera, dramatice el diálogo entre Mariela y la recepcionista.

Opción 2. Una cita para ir a tomar una lección de baile. Imagine que Ud. y su amigo/a han decidido tomar juntos unas lecciones de baile (rumba, merengue, tango, flamenco, etcétera). Tienen que escoger el día y la hora más convenientes para los dos. Si uno/a de Uds. tiene alguna experiencia en este tipo de baile, no se olvide de darle recomendaciones a la persona que no tenga experiencia (decirle, por ejemplo, qué tipo de ropa y zapatos debe llevar).

Suggestions B
- Point out that *el recado* is another word for *el mensaje.*
- Use the following questions to check comprehension: **1.** *¿Para cuándo hace Mariela la cita con la consejera?* **2.** *¿De qué quiere hablar Mariela con la consejera?* **3.** *¿Qué le recomienda a Mariela la recepcionista?*

FUNCTION

Making an appointment

Cultura en contexto
Lo social en el mundo de los negocios

En el mundo hispano, lo social y lo afectivo hacen un papel[a] muy importante en los negocios. En casi toda interacción, como la búsqueda de trabajo o un acuerdo entre los representantes de dos empresas, lo social tiene mucha importancia. Conocerse en persona y establecer relaciones cordiales es imprescindible para llevar a cabo[b] un acuerdo o una negociación.

[a]hacen... *play a role* [b]es... *is essential for carrying out*

PASO FINAL

A LEER

Estrategia: Using Graphics to Get Information

Sobre la lectura... La lectura, o mejor dicho, el gráfico, a continuación es del periódico *El País,* de España. Es parte de un artículo más largo sobre el divorcio en España. Como Ud. puede ver, el uso de elementos visuales, como este gráfico, sirve para presentar la información de una manera más organizada para el lector.

Reading graphics such as tables and pie charts requires as much concentration as, if not more than, any other reading since a lot of information is often summarized in a compact space. Paying attention to the heading of a section as well as to the categories within the graphic can help you to focus your attention on important parts of the information presented.

The following chart offers a visual snapshot of statistical information pertaining to marriage and divorce in Spain since 1981. As you read and analyze the information in the chart, remember to rely on all of the visual clues that you can to facilitate your comprehension. Maybe you'll be surprised by what you read!

Las separaciones y los divorcios han aumentado el 66% en los últimos diez años

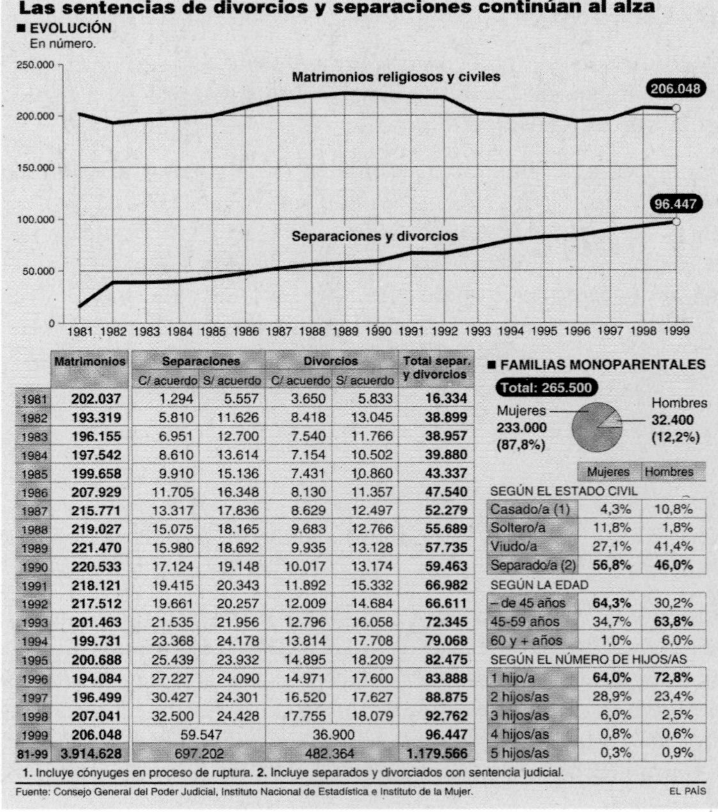

Las sentencias de divorcios y separaciones continúan al alza

■ EVOLUCIÓN

En número.

	Matrimonios	Separaciones		Divorcios		Total separ. y divorcios
		C/ acuerdo	S/ acuerdo	C/ acuerdo	S/ acuerdo	
1981	**202.037**	1.294	5.557	3.650	5.833	**16.334**
1982	**193.319**	5.810	11.626	8.418	13.045	**38.899**
1983	**196.155**	6.951	12.700	7.540	11.766	**38.957**
1984	**197.542**	8.610	13.614	7.154	10.502	**39.880**
1985	**199.658**	9.910	15.136	7.431	10.860	**43.337**
1986	**207.929**	11.705	16.348	8.130	11.357	**47.540**
1987	**215.771**	13.317	17.836	8.629	12.497	**52.279**
1988	**219.027**	15.075	18.165	9.683	12.766	**55.689**
1989	**221.470**	15.980	18.692	9.935	13.128	**57.735**
1990	**220.533**	17.124	19.148	10.017	13.174	**59.463**
1991	**218.121**	19.415	20.343	11.892	15.332	**66.982**
1992	**217.512**	19.661	20.257	12.009	14.684	**66.611**
1993	**201.463**	21.535	21.956	12.796	16.058	**72.345**
1994	**199.731**	23.368	24.178	13.814	17.708	**79.068**
1995	**200.688**	25.439	23.932	14.895	18.209	**82.475**
1996	**194.084**	27.227	24.090	14.971	17.600	**83.888**
1997	**196.499**	30.427	24.301	16.520	17.627	**88.875**
1998	**207.041**	32.500	24.428	17.755	18.079	**92.762**
1999	**206.048**	59.547		36.900		**96.447**
81-99	**3.914.628**	697.202		482.364		**1.179.566**

■ **FAMILIAS MONOPARENTALES**

Total: 265.500

	Mujeres	Hombres
SEGÚN EL ESTADO CIVIL		
Casado/a (1)	4,3%	10,8%
Soltero/a	11,8%	1,8%
Viudo/a	27,1%	41,4%
Separado/a (2)	**56,8%**	**46,0%**
SEGÚN LA EDAD		
– de 45 años	**64,3%**	30,2%
45-59 años	34,7%	**63,8%**
60 y + años	1,0%	6,0%
SEGÚN EL NÚMERO DE HIJOS/AS		
1 hijo/a	**64,0%**	**72,8%**
2 hijos/as	28,9%	23,4%
3 hijos/as	6,0%	2,5%
4 hijos/as	0,8%	0,6%
5 hijos/as	0,3%	0,9%

1. Incluye cónyuges en proceso de ruptura. **2.** Incluye separados y divorciados con sentencia judicial.

Fuente: Consejo General del Poder Judicial, Instituto Nacional de Estadística e Instituto de la Mujer.

EL PAÍS

Comprensión

A. ¿Qué significa el título? Utilice el gráfico para determinar el equivalente en inglés de la frase «han aumentado» del título.

☐ have decreased ☐ have increased ☐ have remained unchanged

B. ¿Cierto o falso? Conteste según el gráfico. Corrija las oraciones falsas.

1. En 1999 hay más divorcios en España que matrimonios.
2. El porcentaje de hogares (*households*) monoparentales encabezados por (*headed by*) madres y padres es igual.

C. A contestar. Conteste según el gráfico.

1. ¿En qué año se nota el mayor (*greatest*) número de matrimonios en España?
2. ¿Entre qué años se ve el aumento más profundo en el número total de divorcios y separaciones?

A ESCRIBIR

Según el gráfico, el número de separaciones y divorcios en España va aumentando constantemente desde 1981, año en que se legalizó el divorcio en dicho (*that*) país. Una consecuencia de este cambio social es el aumento en alternativas fuera del matrimonio. Por ejemplo, muchas personas prefieren convivir (*to live together*) en vez de contraer matrimonio (*getting married*). Esta decisión puede traer ventajas y desventajas.

Paso 1. Imagine que un amigo suyo / una amiga suya (*friend of yours*) le pide consejos respecto al asunto (*about this question*). ¿Qué le va a recomendar? Haga una lista de tres de las ventajas y tres de las desventajas de convivir sin casarse.

Ventajas

1. ________ **2.** ________ **3.** ________

Desventajas

1. ________ **2.** ________ **3.** ________

Paso 2. Ahora, escríbale una carta a su amigo/a, presentándole una de las dos perspectivas. Intente formular un buen argumento para persuadirle de que siga sus consejos. Puede empezar su carta así:

Querido/a: ________.

He pensado mucho en tu situación y creo que…

En resumen

GRAMÁTICA

To review the grammar points presented in this chapter, refer to the indicated grammar presentations. You'll find further practice of these structures in the Workbook/Laboratory Manual, on the CD-ROM, and on the website.

40. Subjunctive after Nonexistent and Indefinite Antecedents

You should know how to use the subjunctive in two-clause sentences when the antecedent is nonexistent or indefinite.

41. Subjunctive after Conjunctions of Contingency and Purpose

You should know how and when to use the subjunctive after certain conjunctions of contingency and purpose.

VOCABULARIO

Las relaciones sentimentales

amar	to love
casarse (con)	to marry
divorciarse (de)	to get divorced (from)
enamorarse (de)	to fall in love (with)
llevarse bien/mal (con)	to get along well/poorly (with)
pasar tiempo (con)	to spend time (with)
querer (ie)	to love
romper (con)	to break up (with)
salir (salgo) (con)	to go out (with)
separarse (de)	to separate (from)

la amistad	friendship
el amor	love
la boda	wedding (*ceremony*)
la cita	date
el divorcio	divorce
la luna de miel	honeymoon
el marido	husband
el matrimonio	marriage; married couple
la mujer	wife
el noviazgo	engagement
la pareja	(married) couple; partner

Rapaso: el/la amigo/a, el/la esposo/a, el/la novio/a

amistoso/a	friendly

Repaso: cariñoso/a, casado/a, soltero/a

Etapas de la vida

la adolescencia	adolescence
la infancia	infancy
la juventud	youth
la madurez	middle age
la muerte	death
el nacimiento	birth
la vejez	old age

Repaso: la niñez

crecer	to grow
nacer	to be born

Repaso: morir (ue, u)

Otras palabras y expresiones útiles

la gente	people
a primera vista	at first sight
bastante	rather, sufficiently; enough
juntos/as	together
propio/a	own

Conjunciones

a menos que	unless
antes (de) que	before
con tal (de) que	provided (that)
en caso de que	in case
para que	so that

Suggestions: Vocabulario

- Point out that the first person singular of *crecer* is *crezco* and for *nacer* is *nazco*.
- Have students describe a relationship in their family, for example, that of their parents, and tell when and how they met, how long they dated, and so on. Model a description for them.
- Write the stages of life in Spanish on the board. Have students write at least two sentences for each stage of life. Have them write sentences describing a typical activity for the stages of life, for example, *Llora a menos que esté cerca de su mamá* (*infancia*) or *Está muy sólo y deprimido porque ya no trabaja y sus hijos estan muy ocupados con sus familias* or *Está muy feliz porque por fin tiene tiempo para viajar y trabajar en el jardín* (*vejez*). Have students read sentences to the class. The class should identify the stage of life.

¿Trabajar para vivir o vivir para trabajar?

Suggestion: Chapter Opening photo
Point out chapter opening photo. Have students talk about this business area and the people in it. What kinds of professions do they think the 2 women in the foreground have? What kinds of offices would they expect to find in these buildings? Also, have students compare the architecture in this area. Ask if they see contrasting architectural periods in many cities in this country.

CAPÍTULO 16

Resources: For a list of resources for Capítulo 16, please see page 382.

VOCABULARIO

- Professions and trades
- The working world

GRAMÁTICA

42 Future Verb Forms
43 Subjunctive and Indicative after Conjunctions of Time

CULTURA

- **Enfoque cultural:** el Uruguay y el Paraguay
- **Nota cultural:** Los nombres de las profesiones
- **En los Estados Unidos y el Canadá:** El creciente mercado hispano
- **Cultura en contexto:** Los cajeros automáticos

Multimedia

You will learn about opening a bank account in the **En contexto** video segment.

Review vocabulary and grammar and practice language skills with the interactive CD-ROM.

Get connected to the Spanish-speaking world with the *¿Qué tal?* Online Learning Center: **www.mhhe.com/quetal**.

◀ Estas mujeres profesionales caminan por la Puerta de la Ciudadela en Montevideo, Uruguay.

CAPÍTULO 16 Vocabulario PASO 1

Paso 1: Vocabulario

See detailed supplementary materials and exercises for this section and a model for vocabulary presentation and other material in the *Capítulo 16 Paso 1: Vocabulario* section of "Chapter-by-Chapter Supplementary Materials," IM.

Profesiones y oficios°

°trades

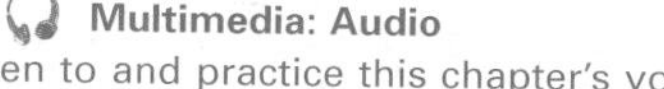

Multimedia: Audio

Students can listen to and practice this chapter's vocabulary on their Listening Comprehension Audio CD.

LUEGO DE PENSARLO MUCHO LLEGUÉ A LA CONCLUSIÓN DE QUE CUANDO SEA GRANDE VOY A SER ESPECIALISTA
¿ESPECIALISTA EN QUÉ, MIGUELITO?

Profesiones

el/la abogado/a lawyer
el/la bibliotecario/a librarian
el/la consejero/a counselor
el/la contador(a) accountant
el/la enfermero/a nurse
el hombre / la mujer de negocios businessperson
el/la ingeniero/a engineer
el/la maestro/a schoolteacher
el/la médico/a doctor
el/la periodista journalist
el/la trabajador(a) social social worker
el/la traductor(a) translator

Oficios

el/la cajero/a cashier; teller
el/la cocinero/a cook; chef
el/la comerciante merchant, shopkeeper
el/la criado/a servant
el/la dependiente/a clerk
el/la obrero/a worker, laborer
el/la peluquero/a hairstylist
el/la plomero/a plumber
el soldado / la mujer soldado soldier
el/la vendedor(a) salesperson

Cognados

el/la analista de sistemas, el/la dentista, el/la electricista, el/la fotógrafo/a, el/la mecánico/a, el/la profesor(a), el/la programador(a), el/la secretario/a, el/la sicólogo/a, el/la siquiatra, el/la técnico/a, el/la veterinario/a

In the preceding chapters of *¿Qué tal?* you have learned to use a number of the words for professions and trades that are listed here. You will practice all of these words in the following activities. However, you will probably want to learn only those new terms that are particularly important or interesting to you. If the vocabulary needed to describe your career goal is not listed here, look it up in a dictionary or ask your instructor.

National Standards: Communication

Have students interview each other about professions in their families. Have them find out what they do or want to do professionally, what their parents or children do, and if they have any relatives that have interesting or unique professions. Have students report their findings to the class and use information to make generalizations about class.

Variations A

- Have students give definitions of professions, following models.
- Have students tell who they would need: 1. *La tubería* (plumbing) *de la cocina no funciona bien.* 2. *Ud. acaba de tener un accidente automovilístico; el otro conductor dice que Ud. tuvo la culpa* (blame). 3. *Por las muchas tensiones y presiones de su vida profesional y personal, Ud. tiene serios problemas afectivos* (emotional). 4. *Ud. está en el hospital y quiere que alguien le dé una aspirina.* 5. *Ud. quiere que alguien lo/la ayude con las tareas domésticas porque no tiene mucho tiempo para hacerlas.* 6. *Ud. quiere que alguien le construya un muro* (wall) *en el jardín.* 7. *Ud. conoce todos los detalles de un escándalo en el gobierno de su ciudad y quiere divulgarlos.*

Extension A

Have students tell what professions they associate with each: *¿Qué profesión asocia Ud. con cada descripción?* 1. *Recibe muchas invitaciones para comer en buenos restaurantes. Es muy susceptible a los ataques al corazón. Viaja mucho.* 2. *Compra y vende cosas. Pone anuncios de sus productos en la televisión, en los periódicos, etcétera. Está contento cuando los empleados venden mucho.* 3. *Tiene que leer mucho. Tiene un puesto de mucho prestigio. A veces no sabe si su cliente es inocente o no.*

Suggestions B

- Model recommendations before allowing students to begin activity. Demonstrate use of subjunctive syntax in model.
- Have students work in pairs to role-play advisor and student who is seeking advice about his/her future. Have students discuss variety of topics including summer jobs, time management, experience, preferences, and money. Have students report findings to class.

Follow-up B

Have students talk about the following: 1. *lo que hacían sus abuelos* 2. *la profesión u oficio de sus padres* 3. *si tiene un amigo o pariente que tenga una profesión extraordinaria o interesante y el nombre de esa profesión* 4. *lo que sus padres* (*su esposo/a*) *quiere(n) que Ud. sea* (*lo que Ud. quiere que sean sus hijos*) 5. *lo que Ud. quiere ser* (*lo que sus hijos quieren ser*) 6. *la carrera para la cual* (which) *se preparan muchos de sus amigos* (*los hijos de sus amigos*)

Conversación

A. Asociaciones. ¿Qué profesiones u oficios asocia Ud. con estas frases? Consulte la lista de profesiones y oficios y use las siguientes palabras también. Haga asociaciones rápidas. ¡No lo piense demasiado!

1. creativo/rutinario
2. muchos/pocos años de preparación
3. mucho/poco salario
4. mucha/poca responsabilidad
5. mucho/poco prestigio
6. flexibilidad/«de nueve a cinco»
7. mucho/poco tiempo libre
8. peligroso (*dangerous*)/seguro
9. en el pasado, sólo para hombres/mujeres
10. todavía, sólo para hombres/mujeres

actor/actriz
arquitecto/a
asistente de vuelo
barman
camarero/a
carpintero/a
chófer
consejero/a
cura/pastor(a)/rabino/a

detective
niñero/a
pintor(a)
poeta
policía/mujer policía
político/a
presidente/a
senador(a)

B. ¿Qué preparación se necesita para ser… ? Imagine que Ud. es consejero universitario / consejera universitaria. Explíquele a un estudiante qué cursos debe tomar para prepararse para las siguientes carreras. Consulte la lista de cursos académicos del **Capítulo 1** y use la siguiente lista. Piense también en el tipo de experiencia que debe obtener.

Vocabulario útil

las comunicaciones
la contabilidad (*accounting*)
el derecho (*law*)
la gerontología
la ingeniería
el *marketing*/mercadeo
la organización administrativa
la pedagogía/enseñanza
la retórica (*speech*)
la sociología

1. traductor(a) en la ONU (Organización de las Naciones Unidas)
2. reportero/a en la televisión, especializado/a en los deportes
3. contador(a) para un grupo de abogados
4. periodista en la redacción (*editorial staff*) de una revista de ecología
5. trabajador(a) social, especializado/a en los problemas de los ancianos
6. maestro/a de primaria, especializado/a en la educación bilingüe

National Standards: Community

If you teach in area with high percentage of Hispanics, invite guest speaker to class to talk about his/her profession. Have students prepare questions they can ask in Spanish before visit. Encourage them to find out how important being bilingual has been for guest in workplace and in community.

Note: Nota cultural

This change of professional roles is also occurring in inverse: professions that were once reserved for women are now being exercised by men as well: *enfermero, amo de casa, secretario,* and so on.

NOTA CULTURAL

Los nombres de las profesiones

En el mundo de habla española hay poco acuerdo sobre las palabras que deben usarse para referirse a las mujeres que ejercen ciertas profesiones. En gran parte, eso se debe al hecho de que, en muchos de estos países, las mujeres acaban de empezar a ejercer esas profesiones; por eso el idioma todavía está cambiando para acomodarse a esa nueva realidad. En la actualidad se emplean, entre otras, las siguientes formas:

¿Qué representan los sombreros que lleva la mujer?

- Se usa el artículo **la** con los sustantivos que terminan en **-ista**.

  el dentista → **la** dent**ista**

- En otros casos se usa una forma femenina.

  el médico → **la** médic**a**
  el trabajador → **la** trabajador**a**

- Se usa la palabra **mujer** con el nombre de la profesión.

  el policía → **la mujer** policía
  el soldado → **la mujer** soldado

Escuche lo que dice la persona con quien Ud. habla para saber las formas que él o ella usa. No se trata de[a] formas correctas o incorrectas, sólo de usos y costumbres locales.

[a]No... *It's not a question of*

El mundo del trabajo

❖ **Transparencias 82, 83**

Transparency 83 offers model sentences using work vocabulary.

caerle bien/mal a alguien — to make a good/bad impression on someone
dejar — to quit
llenar — to fill out (*a form*)
renunciar (a) — to resign (from)

el/la aspirante — candidate, applicant
el currículum — resumé
la dirección de personal — personnel office, employment office
el/la director(a) de personal — personnel director
la empresa — corporation, business
el puesto — job, position
la solicitud — application (*form*)

Graduarse

Llenar solicitudes

la directora de personal

escribir a máquina y contestar el teléfono

renunciar al puesto

PASO 1

Una cuestión de dinero

el banco	bank
el cajero automático	automatic teller machine
el cheque	check (*bank*)
la cuenta / la factura	bill
la cuenta corriente	checking account
la cuenta de ahorros	savings account
el efectivo	cash
el préstamo	loan
el presupuesto	budget
el salario / el sueldo	salary
la tarjeta de crédito	credit card
ahorrar	to save (*money*)
cargar (a la cuenta de uno)	to charge (to someone's account)
depositar/sacar	to deposit/withdraw (*money*)
devolver (ue)	to return (*something*)
economizar	to economize
ganar	to earn
pagar a plazos / con cheque	to pay in installments / by check
pagar en efectivo / al contado	to pay in cash
pedir (i, i) prestado/a	to borrow
prestar	to lend

Suggestion A
Encourage students to read all items before beginning activity.

National Standards: Communication
Have students work together to prepare their own *currículum vitae* in Spanish. Encourage them to include information about education, previous employment, and so on.

Conversación

A. En busca de un puesto. Imagine que Ud. solicitó un puesto recientemente. Usando los números del 1 al 14, indique en qué orden ocurrió lo siguiente. El número 1 ya está indicado.

a. __13__ Se despidió de Ud. cordialmente, diciendo que lo/la iba a llamar en una semana.

b. __2__ Fue a la biblioteca para informarse sobre la empresa: su historia, dónde tiene sucursales (*branches*), etcétera.

c. __5__ Ud. llenó la solicitud tan pronto como la recibió y la mandó, con el currículum, a la empresa.

d. __9__ Por fin, el secretario le dijo que Ud. se iba a entrevistar con la directora de personal.

e. __1__ En la oficina de empleos de su universidad, Ud. leyó un anuncio para un puesto en su especialización.

f. __4__ Le dijo que le iba a mandar una solicitud para que la llenara (*you could fill it out*) y también le pidió que mandara (*you send*) su currículum.

g. __14__ Cuando por fin lo/la llamó la directora, ¡fue para ofrecerle el puesto!

h. __8__ Mientras esperaba en la dirección de personal, Ud. estaba nerviosísimo/a.

i. __11__ La directora le hizo una serie de preguntas: cuándo se iba a graduar, qué cursos había tomado, etcétera.

j. __3__ Llamó al teléfono que daba el anuncio y habló con un secretario en la dirección de personal.

k. __7__ La mañana de la entrevista, Ud. se levantó temprano, se vistió con cuidado y salió temprano para la empresa para llegar puntualmente.

l. __10__ Al entrar en la oficina de la directora, Ud. la saludó con cortesía, tratando de caerle bien desde el principio.

m. __12__ También le pidió que hablara (*you speak*) un poco en español, ya que la empresa tiene una sucursal en Santiago, Chile.

n. __6__ En una semana lo/la llamaron para arreglar una entrevista.

National Standards: Communication
Have students work in pairs to write the following types of questions. Have them imagine that interviewer would be from international computer company with offices and branches in Latin America and Europe: **1.** *preguntas que un entrevistador tiende a* (tends to) *hacer* **2.** *preguntas que un entrevistador no debe hacerle al aspirante* **3.** *preguntas que el aspirante puede o debe hacer.* Have each pair of students exchange questions with another pair of students. Then have original partners role-play interview using questions they received.

B. Diálogos

Paso 1. Empareje las preguntas de la izquierda con las respuestas de la derecha.

1. _____ ¿Cómo prefiere Ud. pagar?
2. _____ ¿Hay algún problema?
3. _____ Me da su pasaporte, por favor. Necesito verlo para que pueda cobrar (*cash*) su cheque.
4. _____ ¿Quisiera (*Would you like*) usar su tarjeta de crédito?
5. _____ ¿Va a depositar este cheque en su cuenta corriente o en su cuenta de ahorros?
6. _____ ¿Adónde quiere Ud. que mandemos la factura?

a. En la cuenta de ahorros, por favor.
b. Me la manda a la oficina, por favor.
c. No, prefiero pagar al contado.
d. Sí, señorita. Ud. me cobró demasiado por el jarabe.
e. Aquí lo tiene Ud. Me lo va a devolver pronto, ¿verdad?
f. Cárguelo a mi cuenta, por favor.

Suggestion B
Have students role-play this activity. You or a native speaker can take role of Spanish-speaking clerk (left-hand column).

Answers B
1. f **2.** d **3.** e **4.** c **5.** a **6.** b

Paso 2. Ahora invente un contexto posible para cada diálogo. ¿Dónde están las personas que hablan? ¿En un banco? ¿en una tienda? ¿Quiénes son? ¿Clientes? ¿cajeros? ¿dependientes?

C. Situaciones. Describa lo que pasa en los siguientes dibujos. Use las preguntas a continuación como guía.

¿Quiénes son estas personas?
¿Dónde están?
¿Qué van a comprar?
¿Cómo van a pagar?
¿Qué van a hacer después?

Variation C
Have students do this as a written activity.

❖ **Transparency 84**

1. 

2. 

3. 

4. 

PASO 2 Gramática

Paso 2: Gramática
See detailed supplementary materials for this grammar section in IM.

42 Talking about the Future • Future Verb Forms

[a]tareas [b]futuro [c]*prayers*

Suggestion: Future
Point out that Mafalda uses a play on words: *oración* can mean *prayer* as well as *sentence.* Another word for *prayer* in Spanish is *plegaria.*

¿Cómo será su vida dentro de diez años? Conteste sí o no a las primeras cinco oraciones. Complete las últimas dos con información verdadera —¡o por lo menos deseable!

1. Viviré en otra ciudad / otro país.
2. Estaré casado/a.
3. Tendré uno o más hijos (nietos).
4. Seré dueño/a de mi propia casa.
5. Llevaré una vida más tranquila.
6. Trabajaré como _____ (nombre de profesión).
7. Ganaré por lo menos _____ dólares al año.

Note: Future
The future perfect is presented only in the footnote on page 364. Active production is not required in the activities.

Follow-up: Future
- Ask students: *¿Por qué pregunta Mafalda si las oraciones de tarea deben ser plegarias?*
- Read the following about Quino characters and have students follow the instructions at the end: *Mafalda es bastante realista y tiene una gran conciencia social. En cambio, Susanita es muy materialista y tradicional en cuanto al papel de la mujer: la mujer como esposa, mamá y subordinada al marido. Usando las oraciones en la presentación gramatical, den algunas oraciones que podrían* (could) *decir Mafalda y Susanita acerca del futuro de cada una.*

A. You have already learned to talk about the future in a number of ways. The forms of the present can be used to describe the immediate future, and the **ir** + **a** + *infinitive* construction (Grammar 10) is very common in both spoken and written Spanish. The future can also be expressed, however, with future verb forms.

hablar		**comer**		**vivir**	
hablar**é**	hablar**emos**	comer**é**	comer**emos**	vivir**é**	vivir**emos**
hablar**ás**	hablar**éis**	comer**ás**	comer**éis**	vivir**ás**	vivir**éis**
hablar**á**	hablar**án**	comer**á**	comer**án**	vivir**á**	vivir**án**

B. In English, the future is formed with the auxiliary verbs *will* or *shall: I* ***will/shall*** *speak.* In Spanish, the *future* (**el futuro**) is a simple verb form (only one word). It is formed by adding future endings to the infinitive. No auxiliary verbs are needed.

Future verb endings:

-é	**-emos**
-ás	**-éis**
-á	**-án**

W. Multimedia: Internet
Have students search the Internet for a Spanish-language horoscope site. Students should print out and bring in their horoscope to share with class. Have students rewrite horoscope in future tense if it is not already so.

C. In a subordinate clause after these conjunctions of time, the subjunctive is used to express a future action or state of being—that is, one that is still pending or has not yet occurred from the point of view of the main verb. This use of the subjunctive is very frequent in conversation in phrases such as the examples on the right.

The events in the subordinate clause are imagined—not real-world—events. They haven't happened yet.

Cuando sea grande/mayor...
When I'm older . . .

Cuando tenga tiempo...
When I have the time . . .

Cuando me gradúe...
When I graduate . . .

D. When the present subjunctive is used in this way to express pending actions, the main-clause verb is in the present indicative or future.

PENDING ACTION (SUBJUNCTIVE):

Pagaré las cuentas **en cuanto reciba** mi cheque.
I'll pay the bills as soon as I get my check.

Debo depositar el dinero **tan pronto como** lo **reciba**.
I should deposit money as soon as I get it.

E. However, the indicative (not the present subjunctive) is used after conjunctions of time to describe a habitual action or a completed action in the past. Compare the following.

HABITUAL ACTIONS (INDICATIVE):

Siempre **pago** las cuentas **en cuanto recibo** mi cheque.
I always pay bills as soon as I get my check.

Deposito el dinero **tan pronto como** lo **recibo**.
I deposit money as soon as I receive it.

COMPLETED PAST ACTION (INDICATIVE):

El mes pasado **pagué** las cuentas **en cuanto recibí** mi cheque.
Last month I paid my bills as soon as I got my check.

Deposité el dinero **tan pronto como** lo **recibí**.
I deposited the money as soon as I got it.

OJO The subjunctive is always used with **antes (de) que**. (See **Capítulo 15**.)

Práctica

Preliminary exercise A
Have students tell whether the following express future uncompleted, habitual, or past actions: **1.** I'll do it when he gets here. **2.** They always write when they are abroad. **3.** We'll study until they arrive. **4.** As soon as I have the time, I'll do it. **5.** He studied until he fell asleep. **6.** She'll give us the answers after we hand in the test. **7.** We turn off the lights when we leave the house.

Note A
Students need to focus on habitual (indicative) vs. future (subjunctive) actions.

Answers A
1. a **2.** b **3.** b **4.** a **5.** a

A. Decisiones económicas. Lea las siguientes oraciones sobre Rigoberto y decida si se trata de una acción habitual o de una acción que no ha pasado todavía. Luego indique la frase que mejor complete la oración.

1. Rigoberto se va a comprar una computadora en cuanto...
   a. el banco le dé el préstamo **b.** el banco le da el préstamo
2. Siempre usa su tarjeta de crédito cuando...
   a. no tenga efectivo **b.** no tiene efectivo
3. Cada mes saca el saldo de su cuenta corriente después de que...
   a. reciba el estado de cuentas (*statement*)
   b. recibe el estado de cuentas
4. Piensa abrir una cuenta de ahorros tan pronto como...
   a. consiga un trabajo **b.** consigue un trabajo
5. No puede pagar sus cuentas este mes hasta que...
   a. su hermano le devuelva el dinero que le prestó
   b. su hermano le devuelve el dinero que le prestó

Suggestion B
Personalize each set of activity items by asking questions of individual students. Encourage detailed answers only if students are comfortable revealing this kind of information.

Answers B
1. *me den / deje* **2.** *tenga / sea* **3.** *cobre / me mande* **4.** *saque / deposite* **5.** *terminen / se casen*

B. Hablando de dinero: Planes para el futuro. Complete las siguientes oraciones con el presente del subjuntivo de los verbos indicados.

1. Voy a ahorrar más en cuanto... (darme [ellos] un aumento de sueldo [*raise*]; dejar [yo] de gastar tanto)
2. Pagaré todas mis cuentas tan pronto como... (tener el dinero para hacerlo; ser absolutamente necesario)
3. El semestre/trimestre que viene, pagaré la matrícula después de que... (cobrar mi cheque en el banco; mandarme [¿quién?] un cheque)
4. No podré pagar el alquiler hasta que... (sacar dinero de mi cuenta de ahorros; depositar el dinero en mi cuenta corriente)
5. No voy a jubilarme (*retire*) hasta que mis hijos... (terminar sus estudios universitarios; casarse)

Note C
This activity reviews use of many tenses and moods.

Follow-up C
Have students respond *cierto* or *falso:* **1.** *Mariana estudia en la universidad ahora.* **2.** *En la universidad, ha seguido muchos cursos de matemáticas.* **3.** *Mariana es muy responsable en cuanto a sus finanzas.*

Answers C
1. *se graduó, le dieron, se gradúe, le darán* **2.** *era, quería, tenía, decidió, termine, podrá* **3.** *escribe, tiene, va, llegue*

C. Algunos momentos en la vida. Las siguientes oraciones describen algunos aspectos de la vida de Mariana en el pasado, en el presente y en el futuro. Lea cada grupo de oraciones para tener una idea general del contexto. Luego dé la forma apropiada de los infinitivos.

1. Hace cuatro años, cuando Mariana (graduarse) en la escuela secundaria, sus padres (darle) un reloj. El año que viene, cuando (graduarse) en la universidad, (darle) un coche.
2. Cuando (ser) niña, Mariana (querer) ser enfermera. Luego, cuando (tener) 18 años, (decidir) que quería estudiar computación. Cuando (terminar) su carrera este año, yo creo que (poder) encontrar un buen trabajo como programadora.
3. Generalmente Mariana no (escribir) cheques hasta que (tener) los fondos en su cuenta corriente. Este mes tiene muchos gastos, pero no (ir) a pagar ninguna cuenta hasta que le (llegar) el cheque de su trabajo de tiempo parcial.

Follow-up: En los Estados Unidos y el Canadá…
- Ask students if they have seen ads in Spanish for any famous business in this country.
- Bring some ads in Spanish from U.S. or Canadian Spanish-language magazines. Have students name the types of people ads address, and ask what they think is the slant for the Hispanic market (versus the North American market at large).

En los Estados Unidos y el Canadá…

El creciente mercado hispano

¿Qué tienen en común Ford, Toyota, Sprint, Dockers, United Health y Toys "Я" Us? Pues que, como muchas compañías norteamericanas, tienen activas **campañas publicitarias** para atraer al **mercado hispano nacional**. Con más de 35 millones de hispanos, según el censo estadounidense del año 2000, los Estados Unidos ocupan **el cuarto puesto**[a] entre las naciones que tienen una población hispanohablante (se calcula que podría[b] ser **la segunda** o **tercera nación** en los próximos quince años, por delante de España). La población hispana de los Estados Unidos se traduce en[c] un mercado de más de 600.000 millones de dólares.

CNN en español, HBO Latino y *People en español* se dirigen a[d] la variada comunidad hispana de los Estados Unidos. Muchos programas y publicaciones se originan en Florida, entre ellos *Latin Trade*, una **revista mensual**[e] de **negocios** y **economía** referente a Norteamérica en relación con todos los países latinos. El ámbito de lectores[f] de *Latin Trade* incluye a latinos de todo el mundo, un grupo de más de 400 millones de personas.

Desgraciadamente,[g] la importancia numérica de los hispanoamericanos, un 12 por ciento de la población de los Estados Unidos, no se ve reflejada[h] en el mundo de **la comunicación**, de **la política** ni de los negocios. Es este el gran reto[i] para los hispanos de este país.

[a]*position* [b]*it could* [c]se… *translates into* [d]se… *target* [e]*monthly* [f]ámbito… *readership* [g]*Unfortunately* [h]no… *is not reflected* [i]*challenge*

- Have students search the Internet for information about the Hispanic market in North America.

Conversación

A. Descripciones. Describa Ud. los dibujos, completando las oraciones e inventando un contexto para las escenas. Luego describa su propia vida.

1. Pablo va a estudiar hasta que ______.

   Esta noche yo voy a estudiar hasta que ______.
   Siempre estudio hasta que ______.
   Anoche estudié hasta que ______.

1.

❖ **Transparency 87**

Note A
The drawing on the right of each paired set indicates a future uncompleted action.

Extension A
Have students complete the following sentences with personal information:
1. *Voy a… en cuanto…* 2. *Siempre… en cuanto…* 3. *De niño/a,… en cuanto…*

2. Los señores Castro van a cenar tan pronto como ____.

   Esta noche voy a cenar tan pronto como ____.
   Siempre ceno tan pronto como ____.
   Anoche cené tan pronto como ____.

2.

3. Lupe va a viajar al extranjero en cuanto ____.

   En cuanto gane la lotería, yo voy a ____.
   En cuanto tengo el dinero, siempre ____.
   De niño/a, ____ en cuanto tenía el dinero.

3.

Extension B
7. *Antes de graduarme,...* **8**. *Después de conseguir mi primer/próximo trabajo,...* **9**. *En cuanto tenga suficiente dinero,...* **10**. *Antes de tener hijos...*

B. Reacciones. ¿Cómo reaccionará o qué hará cuando ocurran los siguientes acontecimientos? Complete las oraciones con el futuro.

1. Cuando colonicemos otro planeta, ____.
2. Cuando descubran una cura para el cáncer, ____.
3. Cuando haya una mujer presidenta, ____.
4. Cuando me jubile, ____.
5. Cuando yo sea anciano/a, ____.
6. Cuando me gradúe, ____.

UN POCO DE TODO

¿Cómo se ganan la vida (*earn a living*) **los estudiantes?** Complete the following paragraphs with the correct form of the words in parentheses, as suggested by the context. When two possibilities are given in parentheses, select the correct word. Use an adverb derived from the adjectives in italics.

La preocupación por el dinero es (algo/alguien[1]) compartido[a] por los estudiantes en todo el mundo. En (el/la[2]) mayor parte de los países de habla española, (el/la[3]) sistema universitario es gratuito.[b] Sin embargo, hay (de/que[4]) tener dinero para los (gastar/gastos[5]) personales y también para (los/las[6]) cines y otras diversiones.

Aquí, algunos estudiantes hispánicos contestan la pregunta: ¿Cómo (te/se[7]) ganaba Ud. la vida cuando era estudiante?

Una joven de México: A los trece años, (*yo:* empezar[8]) a trabajar en una oficina. Así (*yo:* poder[9]) pagar la colegiatura[c] de mis estudios. (*Yo:* Trabajar[10]) de día y (estudiar[11]) de noche.

Un joven uruguayo: Cuando (*yo:* ser/estar[12]) estudiante, me (ganar[13]) la vida como fotógrafo. (*Yo:* Sacar[14]) fotos de bodas, bautismos, fiestas de cumpleaños. (*Yo:* Trabajar[15]) en cualquier ocasión y en cualquier sitio.

Una mujer española: (*Yo:* Ayudar[16]) a enseñar a párvulos.[d]

Algunos estudiantes (ofrecer[17]) los siguientes comentarios adicionales.

Una joven chilena: Los padres (*normal*[18]) mantienen a sus hijos (*económico*[19]). Pero muchos chicos (trabajar[20]) de todas maneras. Las chicas (cuidar[21]) a niños o (ayudar[22]) en casa y los chicos (trabajar[23]) en talleres. Si los padres tienen dinero, es raro que los hijos (trabajar[24]) hasta que no (terminar[25]) su carrera.[e]

Un joven argentino: En la Argentina, la enseñanza universitaria (ser/estar[26]) gratuita. De todos modos, los estudiantes siempre (necesitar[27]) tener más de un trabajo y los padres los ayudan con (que / lo que[28]) pueden. Muchos estudiantes no (irse[29]) a otras ciudades a (estudiar[30]). (*Ellos:* Vivir[31]) con (su[32]) padres y estudian en (el/la[33]) universidad más cercana.

[a]*shared* [b]*free* [c]*fees* [d]*tots* [e]*studies*

Comprensión: ¿Cierto o falso?

Corrija las oraciones falsas.

1. El sistema universitario es gratuito en muchos países hispánicos.
2. Los estudiantes hispánicos nunca tienen que trabajar.
3. Generalmente los padres mantienen a sus hijos mientras estos son estudiantes.

Follow-up: Un poco de todo

- Ask students: *¿Qué harán Uds. para buscar trabajo este verano? ¿y cuando se gradúen?*
- Have students discuss similarities and differences between U.S. and Canadian systems and Hispanic system regarding student life. Ask: *¿Qué hacen Uds. para pagar sus estudios?*

Answers: Un poco de todo

1. *algo* **2.** *la* **3.** *el* **4.** *que* **5.** *gastos* **6.** *los* **7.** *se* **8.** *empecé* **9.** *podía* **10.** *Trabajaba* **11.** *estudiaba* **12.** *era* **13.** *ganaba* **14.** *sacaba* **15.** *Trabajaba* **16.** *Ayudaba* **17.** *ofrecen* **18.** *normalmente* **19.** *económicamente* **20.** *trabajan* **21.** *cuidan* **22.** *ayudan* **23.** *trabajan* **24.** *trabajen* **25.** *terminen* **26.** *es* **27.** *necesitan* **28.** *lo que* **29.** *se van* **30.** *estudiar* **31.** *Viven* **32.** *sus* **33.** *la*

In the *Capítulo 16* segment of "Chapter-by-Chapter Supplementary Materials" in the IM, you will find a chapter-culminating activity. You can use this activity to consolidate and review the vocabulary and grammar skills students have acquired.

PASO 4 Un paso más

Paso 4: Un paso más
Optional section

See IM for suggestions and follow-up activities to accompany the video segment.

VIDEOTECA: En contexto

FUNCTION

Opening a bank account

In this video segment, Juan Carlos opens an account at the bank. As you watch, pay attention to the vocabulary Juan Carlos and the bank employee use for opening an account. Do you have a bank account? Was your experience similar when you went to open it?

A. Lluvia de ideas

- ¿Es Ud. bueno/a para manejar el dinero? ¿Por qué? ¿Sabe Ud. ahorrar o se le va el dinero como agua en las manos?
- ¿Cuántas cuentas tiene Ud.? ¿De qué tipo son? ¿Cuándo las abrió? ¿Por qué razón eligió ese banco?

Suggestion A
Offer students the following expressions: *ser ahorrador(a), ser manirroto/a.*

B. Dictado

A continuación aparece un fragmento del diálogo entre Juan Carlos y el empleado del banco. Complete el diálogo con las palabras o frases que faltan.

EMPLEADO: ¿Y qué tipo de __cuenta__[1] quiere Ud. abrir?
JUAN CARLOS: Necesito una cuenta __corriente__[2] y una cuenta de __ahorros__.[3] ¿Ganan intereses sus cuentas corrientes?
EMPLEADO: Depende del tipo de cuenta corriente. Si Ud. elige esta cuenta, __gana__[4] interés mensualmente, con __tal__[5] de que mantenga un mínimo de cien soles en la cuenta.
JUAN CARLOS: [...] ¿Tiene este __banco__[6] cajeros automáticos?
EMPLEADO: Sí, claro. Tenemos un __cajero__[7] automático afuera, y también puede utilizar, sin __pagar__,[8] los cajeros __automáticos__[9] de las otras __sucursales__[10] del banco.

Cultura en contexto
Los cajeros automáticos

Los cajeros automáticos, disponibles[a] en casi todas los pueblos y las ciudades de Latinoamérica, han facilitado[b] el turismo al ofrecer una manera fácil de conseguir la moneda nacional. Por ejemplo, un turista en el Perú puede sacar dinero de su cuenta personal y recibirlo del cajero automático en soles, la moneda nacional del Perú. De esta manera, ya no es necesario ir a una casa de cambio[c] o a un banco.

[a]*available* [b]han... *have made easier* [c]casa... *money exchange office*

Suggestion B
To check comprehension, ask: **1.** *¿Qué tipo de cuenta corriente escoge Juan Carlos? ¿Por qué?* **2.** *¿Qué otra cosa le parece importante a Juan Carlos?* **3.** *¿Cómo abre sus cuentas Juan Carlos?*

C. Un diálogo original

Follow-up C
Ask students: *¿Qué harán Uds. para buscar trabajo este verano? ¿Y cuando se gradúen?*

Opción 1. Con un compañero / una compañera, dramatice el diálogo entre Juan Carlos y el empleado del banco.

Opción 2. También dramatice la siguiente situación.

E1: Ud. habla con un amigo / una amiga que entiende mucho de finanzas personales. Ud. necesita algún tipo de cuenta, pero no sabe exactamente cuál.

E2: Ud. actúa de consejero de finanzas. Si su amigo/a no le da suficiente información, hágale preguntas para poder darle consejos mejores.

PASO FINAL

National Standards: Communication
Have students interview each other or students from another Spanish class about whether or not they work, and why, where, and how many hours per week they work. Whole class can brainstorm possible questions. Have them conduct interviews outside of class if possible and summarize findings in brief paragraph. In class, have them share results in small groups. Then discuss results as a class. Encourage them to characterize students at your university based on findings and have them debate whether or not student body is typical compared to other universities in the country.

A CONVERSAR

Un futuro imaginado

Paso 1. En una hoja de papel aparte, prepare un cuadro como el siguiente. Apunte brevemente sus respuestas en los espacios en blanco. Si el nombre de la profesión que a Ud. le interesa no está en este capítulo, búsquelo en un diccionario. Use su imaginación: ¡el futuro está lleno de posibilidades!

MODELO:

	Mi trabajo	Mi vivienda / El lugar	Mis vacaciones
En cinco años...	cocinera	apartamento/Nueva York	ninguna
En diez años...	dueña de un restaurante elegante	casa/California	una isla en el Caribe
En quince años...			

Paso 2. Con un compañero / una compañera, hable de su futuro. Deben hacer las predicciones indicadas (hasta quince años), pero pueden hablar de un futuro aun más distante si quieren. Utilicen verbos en el futuro en sus preguntas y respuestas.

MODELO: E1: ¿Qué trabajo tendrás en cinco años?
E2: Seré cocinera, pero sólo de tiempo parcial. Trabajaré por la noche mientras estudio para la maestría (*Master's*) en negocios. Quiero ser dueña de un restaurante. Será bueno tener experiencia en restaurantes, pero también será importante saber mucho de los negocios. ¿Y tú?
E1: Me graduaré en dos años, así que en cinco años ya seré trabajador social. Trabajaré con jóvenes delincuentes en Los Ángeles. Muchos de mis familiares son de esa área. ¿Y tú? ¿Dónde vivirás?
E2: Viviré en un apartamento en Nueva York, cerca de la universidad…

Paso 3. Entre todos, hablen de los planes de sus compañeros. Pueden comparar los planes de sus compañeros con sus propios planes. Usen verbos en el futuro para describir los planes. Deben marcar la información en la pizarra en un cuadro como el del **Paso 1**.

MODELO: E1: En cinco años, Marsha será cocinera de tiempo parcial. Vivirá en un apartamento en Nueva York, cerca de la universidad donde estudiará para su maestría en negocios. Quiere ser dueña de un restaurante y necesitará la experiencia en restaurantes y la preparación en negocios.

Paso 4. Después de apuntar la información en la pizarra, comparen los planes y las carreras. Traten de hacer algunas generalizaciones sobre la clase, pero hablen también de puntos específicos. ¿Quiénes tendrán las carreras más interesantes? ¿más exigentes (*demanding*)? ¿Quiénes tendrán que pasar más tiempo estudiando y preparándose para su profesión? ¿En qué partes del país (del mundo) vivirá la mayoría de Uds.? ¿Quiénes tendrán las vacaciones más divertidas? ¿originales? Deben expresar sus opiniones y defenderlas si no están de acuerdo.

MODELO: E1: Marsha tendrá una carrera exigente porque en diez años será dueña de un restaurante. Los restaurantes representan mucho trabajo y Marsha no tendrá mucho tiempo para vacaciones.
E2: Bill tendrá la carrera más exigente porque será trabajador social y trabajará con jóvenes delincuentes…

Follow-up: A conversar
Ask follow-up questions that require third person plural responses: *¿Cuántas personas vivirán en Nueva York en cinco años? ¿Cuántas personas irán de vacaciones a Italia en diez años?* Students who would like to do those things raise their hands, then another student can respond to your question: *Tres personas vivirán en Nueva York en cinco años. Cuatro personas irán de vacaciones a Italia en diez años.*

En resumen

GRAMÁTICA

To review the grammar points presented in this chapter, refer to the indicated grammar presentations. You'll find further practice of these structures in the Workbook/Laboratory Manual, on the CD-ROM, and on the website.

42. Future Verb Forms

You should know how to form and when to use the future tense, including all irregular forms.

43. Subjunctive and Indicative after Conjunctions of Time

Do you know how to express actions that will take place only after something else takes place? What are the conjunctions that you can use for this?

VOCABULARIO

Los verbos

jubilarse to retire
mudarse to move (*residence*)

Profesiones y oficios

el/la abogado/a lawyer
el/la cajero/a cashier; teller
el/la cocinero/a cook; chef
el/la comerciante merchant, shopkeeper
el/la contador(a) accountant
el/la criado/a servant
el hombre / la mujer de negocios businessperson
el/la ingeniero/a engineer
el/la maestro/a schoolteacher
el/la obrero/a worker, laborer
el/la peluquero/a hairstylist
el/la periodista journalist
el/la plomero/a plumber
el soldado / la mujer soldado soldier
el/la trabajador(a) social social worker
el/la traductor(a) translator
el/la vendedor(a) salesperson

Cognados: el/la analista de sistemas, el/la electricista, el/la fotógrafo/a, el/la programador(a), el/la sicólogo/a, el/la siquiatra, el/la técnico/a, el/la veterinario/a

Repaso: el/la bibliotecario/a, el/la consejero/a, el/la dentista, el/la dependiente/a, el/la enfermero/a, el/la mecánico/a, el/la médico/a, el/la profesor(a), el/la secretario/a

En busca de un puesto

el/la aspirante candidate; applicant
el currículum resumé
la dirección de personal personnel office, employment office
el/la director(a) de personal personnel director
la empresa corporation; business
el/la entrevistador(a) interviewer
la solicitud application (*form*)
la sucursal branch (*office*)

Repaso: el teléfono

caerle bien/mal a alguien to make a good/bad impression on someone
dejar to quit
entrevistar to interview
escribir a máquina to type
graduarse (en) to graduate (from)

llenar to fill out (*a form*)
renunciar (a) to resign (from)

Repaso: contestar

Una cuestión de dinero

el aumento de sueldo raise
el banco bank
el cajero automático automatic teller machine
el cheque check
la cuenta corriente checking account
la cuenta de ahorros savings account
el efectivo cash
la factura bill
el préstamo loan
el presupuesto budget
el salario salary

Repaso: la cuenta, el sueldo, la tarjeta de crédito

ahorrar to save (*money*)
cargar to charge (*to an account*)
cobrar to cash (*a check*); to charge (*someone for an item or service*)
depositar to deposit
devolver (ue) to return (*something*)
economizar to economize
pedir (i, i) prestado/a to borrow
sacar to withdraw, take out
  sacar el saldo to balance a checkbook

Repaso: ganar, pagar, prestar

a plazos in installments
al contado / en efectivo in cash
con cheque by check

Conjunciones

después (de) que after
en cuanto as soon as
hasta que until
tan pronto como as soon as

Repaso: antes (de) que, cuando

Palabras adicionales

al principio de at the beginning of
en vez de instead of

Suggestions: Vocabulario

- Play game to identify professions. Make individual cards with names of professions in Spanish. Tape card on each student's back without allowing him/her to see it. Have students circulate to ask *sí/no* questions about themselves. After each question, they should move to another classmate. Classmates may only respond *sí* or *no;* they should not elaborate. First student to figure out what he/she is wins. Continue until everyone is successful. Model exchanges before they begin: *¿Trabajo en una oficina?* → *No. ¿Manejo mucho?* → *No. ¿Enseño?* → *Sí. ¿Soy maestro/a?* → *Sí.*
- Point out that first person singular of *caerle* is *le(s)* (*te*) *caigo.* The first person singular of *graduarse* is *me gradúo.* Remind them of the spelling changes for *cargar* (*gu*), *economizar* (*c*), and *sacar* (*qu*).
- Have students list on board different work-related and bank-related situations, for example, office manager giving employee a bad work review, student asking for loan. Have students take turns role-playing different situations without indicating which one. Class should guess situation.

Resources

You and your students may find the following *¿Qué tal?* supplements helpful as you teach this chapter:

For the Instructor

- *Instructor's Manual and Resource Kit,* "Chapter-by-Chapter" Supplementary Materials
- Testing Program
- Overhead Transparencies 82–87
- Video (VHS or CD)
- *¿Qué tal?* Online Learning Center Website
- Audioscript
- Instructor's Resource CD

For Students

- Workbook/Laboratory Manual and Audio Program or Electronic Workbook/Laboratory Manual
- Video or CD
- Interactive CD-ROM
- *¿Qué tal?* Online Learning Center Website
- Listening Comprehension Audio CD
- McGraw-Hill Electronic Language Tutor (MHELT)

CAPÍTULO 17

Suggestions: Chapter Opening photo

- Point out chapter opening photo. Have students describe the campaign sign and speculate about the politics of this particular candidate. They should include comments about the colors chosen, as well as the text. Ask how this sign compares to political campaign signs in this country.

En la actualidad

- Introduce the words *noticias* and *periódico*. Then ask students what type of news is most interesting to them. *Cuando Uds. abren el periódico, ¿qué tipo de noticias leen primero? ¿Las noticias internacionales? ¿las nacionales? ¿las locales? ¿las deportivas? ¿las sociales y culturales? ¿O prefieren leer la sección de negocios? ¿la sección humorística y las tiras cómicas?*

Resources

You and your students may find the following *¿Qué tal?* supplements helpful as you teach this chapter:

For the Instructor

- *Instructor's Manual and Resource Kit,* "Chapter-by-Chapter" Supplementary Materials
- Testing Program
- Overhead Transparency 88
- Video (VHS or CD)
- *¿Qué tal?* Online Learning Center Website
- Audioscript
- Instructor's Resource CD

For Students

- Workbook/Laboratory Manual and Audio Program or Electronic Workbook/ Laboratory Manual
- Video on CD
- Interactive CD-ROM
- *¿Qué tal?* Online Learning Center Website
- Listening Comprehension Audio CD
- McGraw-Hill Electronic Language Tutor (MHELT)

Antes de las elecciones presidenciales hay mucha propaganda política, como esta en Santo Domingo, la capital de la República Dominicana.

VOCABULARIO

- The news
- Government and civic responsibility

GRAMÁTICA

44 Past Subjunctive

CULTURA

- **Enfoque cultural:** la República Dominicana
- **Nota cultural:** La mayoría de edad en los países hispanos
- **En los Estados Unidos y el Canadá:** Tres hispanos del mundo de la televisión
- **Cultura en contexto:** El periódico

Multimedia

You will learn about purchasing a newspaper in the **En contexto** video segment.

Review vocabulary and grammar and practice language skills with the interactive CD-ROM.

Get connected to the Spanish-speaking world with the *¿Qué tal?* Online Learning Center: **www.mhhe.com/quetal**.

PASO 1 Vocabulario

CAPÍTULO 17

Paso 1: Vocabulario

See detailed supplementary materials and exercises for this section and a model for vocabulary presentation and other material in the *Capítulo 17 Paso 1: Vocabulario* section of "Chapter-by-Chapter Supplementary Materials," IM.

Las noticias

el acontecimiento event
el medio de comunicación means of communication
la prensa press; news media
el/la reportero/a reporter
el/la testigo witness

el choque collision
el desastre disaster
la esperanza hope
la paz peace

comunicarse (con) to communicate (with)
enterarse (de) to find out, learn (about)
informar to inform
ofrecer to offer

❖ **Transparency 88**

National Standards: Communication

- Give students 5–10 minutes to prepare news reports. Assign specific topics to different students or groups: headlines, weather, local, international, sports, and so on. Have students select an order of presentation, and begin news program. If possible, videotape presentation.
- Have students watch evening television newscast on Spanish-language channel and hand in report of 2–3 paragraphs.

Heritage speakers

Pregúnteles a los hispanohablantes de la clase si prefieren escuchar las noticias en español o inglés. Si las escuchan en español, pregúnteles en qué canal de televisión o estación de radio. Pídales que comparen los noticieros hispanos con los noticieros norteamericanos. ¿Cómo son diferentes? ¿En qué aspectos son iguales?

Multimedia: Audio

Students can listen to and practice this chapter's vocabulary on their Listening Comprehension Audio CD.

Y ahora, el canal 45 les ofrece a Uds. el NOTICIERO 45 con los últimos eventos del mundo…

Nuestro reportero en el Oriente Medio nos informa sobre la guerra: Bombas en el desierto

Huelga de obreros en España

Otro asesinato en la ciudad. Dos testigos cuentan lo que vieron.

Desastre en Centroamérica: erupción de un volcán

Conversación

Follow-up A

Use activity to find out favorite newspapers, magazines, Net servers, and so on of students in class.

A. **¿Cómo se entera Ud.?** El público utiliza diferentes medios para enterarse de los acontecimientos locales, nacionales e internacionales. ¿Cómo se entera Ud. de las noticias? Indique con qué frecuencia utiliza los medios en la página 385. Luego, compare sus respuestas con las de sus compañeros. ¿Cuál es el medio preferido?

Follow-up B
Have students contrast what ultraconservative and ultraliberal people might say about the following: **1.** *la libertad de prensa* **2.** *una dictadura en Centroamérica* **3.** *la pena de muerte* (describe) **4.** *la obediencia a las leyes* **5.** *las huelgas*

	TODOS LOS DÍAS	DE 3 A 5 VECES POR SEMANA	CASI NUNCA
1. Leo un periódico local.	☐	☐	☐
2. Leo un periódico nacional.	☐	☐	☐
3. Leo una revista.	☐	☐	☐
4. Leo las noticias en el Internet.	☐	☐	☐
5. Miro el telediario (*newscast*) local.	☐	☐	☐
6. Miro el telediario nacional.	☐	☐	☐
7. Miro CNN.	☐	☐	☐
8. Escucho la radio.	☐	☐	☐

Variation B
Have students respond *Estoy de acuerdo* or *No estoy de acuerdo:* **1.** *Los reporteros de la televisión nos informan imparcialmente de los acontecimientos.* **2.** *Por lo general ofrecen los programas más interesantes en el canal de televisión pública.* **3.** *En este país la prensa es irresponsable. Nos da sólo los detalles que apoyan sus ideas políticas.* **4.** *Las telenovelas* (soap operas) *reflejan la vida tal* (just) *como es.* **5.** *Los anuncios son sumamente* (extremely) *informativos y más interesantes que muchos programas.* **6.** *Me gusta que los reporteros y meteorólogos cuenten chistes durante el noticiero.*

B. Definiciones. ¿Qué palabra se asocia con cada definición?

1. __a__ un programa que nos informa de lo que pasa en nuestro mundo
2. __f__ la persona que está presente durante un acontecimiento y lo ve todo
3. __i__ un medio importantísimo de comunicación
4. __g__ la persona que nos informa de las novedades
5. __d__ la persona que gobierna un país de una forma absoluta y que no apoya (*supports*) los derechos civiles
6. __c__ la persona que emplea la violencia para cambiar el mundo
7. __h__ cuando los obreros se niegan a (*refuse*) trabajar
8. __e__ la frecuencia en que se transmiten y se reciben los programas de televisión
9. __b__ la confrontación armada entre dos o más países

a. el noticiero
b. la guerra
c. el/la terrorista
d. el/la dictador(a) (*dictator*)
e. el canal
f. el/la testigo
g. el/la reportero/a
h. la huelga
i. la prensa

El gobierno y la responsabilidad cívica

[a]un... *not at all*
[b]¡Justo... *That's all I'd need!*

el/la ciudadano/a	citizen	**la ley**	law
el deber	responsibility, obligation	**la política**	politics
los/las demás	others, other people	**el/la político/a**	politician
el derecho	right	**el rey / la reina**	king/queen
la (des)igualdad	(in)equality	**el servicio militar**	military service
la dictadura	dictatorship	**durar**	to last
la discriminación	discrimination	**obedecer**	to obey
el ejército	army	**votar**	to vote

PASO 1

NOTA CULTURAL

La mayoría de edad en los países hispanos

En el mundo hispano los jóvenes se consideran legalmente adultos, es decir, alcanzan[a] **la mayoría de edad**, a los 18 años. Al cumplir los 18 años, los jóvenes hispanos pueden participar en la política y pueden votar. En varios países los hombres de 18 años también tienen la responsabilidad de inscribirse[b] en **el servicio militar**. En Colombia, los jóvenes pueden inscribirse en el servicio militar a los 16 años. La selección de los conscriptos[c] generalmente se hace mediante una lotería. Recientemente, las mujeres mexicanas y argentinas también pueden inscribirse en el servicio militar, un hecho sin precedentes en Latinoamérica.

A los 18 años, los jóvenes hispanos pueden obtener su **licencia de manejar**. Sin embargo, muchos jóvenes hispanos no esperan hasta los 18 años. A los 16 años solicitan un **permiso especial** para menores de edad para operar un vehículo.

Otro aspecto importante al llegar a la mayoría de edad es el consumo de alcohol. **La edad límite** para tomar bebidas alcohólicas varía entre los 18 y 21 años. En Ecuador, por ejemplo, la edad límite es de 21 años. En algunos países hay menos restricciones sociales sobre el alcohol.

[a]*they reach* [b]de… *of registering* [c]*draftees*

Suggestion A
To personalize, ask: **1.** *¿Qué canal de televisión prefiere Ud. para enterarse de las noticias? ¿Cree Ud. que en ese canal le informan mejor? ¿O es que le gusta el locutor / la locutora que se las ofrece? ¿Le interesan a Ud. mucho o poco las noticias del estado o de la provincia de* (your state/province)*? ¿Por qué sí o por qué no?* **2.** *¿Le importan más a Ud. su autonomía e individualismo o los sentimientos de los demás? En una tienda, ¿hace cola con paciencia o primero trata de atraer la atención del dependiente? En una parada de autobús, ¿hace cola o trata de subir primero?* **3.** *Para Ud., ¿cuáles son los derechos más básicos de que todos debemos gozar? ¿Cuáles son los deberes de un buen ciudadano? ¿Es importante que todos votemos en todas las elecciones, sean nacionales o locales? ¿Por qué cree Ud. que muchas personas no votan?*

Follow-up B
Have students work in groups to write 4–5 questions to quiz the rest of class.

Conversación

A. Asociaciones. ¿Qué cosas, personas o ideas asocia Ud. con las siguientes palabras?

1. el deber
2. el ejército
3. la política
4. la ley
5. la monarquía
6. la dictadura

B. ¡Peligro! (*Jeopardy!*) ¿Cuánto sabe Ud. de la historia y la política? Conteste con la información necesaria y en forma de pregunta.

1. Fue un dictador argentino que tenía una esposa famosa.
2. Se llama Elizabeth y vive en Buckingham Palace.
3. Es una película de Orson Welles, y su protagonista se llama Kane.
4. Fue un presidente estadounidense que se opuso a (*opposed*) la esclavitud de los negros.
5. En algunos países, es un deber de los hombres de cierta edad. Generalmente, tienen que entrar en el ejército por dos años.
6. Es la forma de gobierno que existe en España.
7. Existe cuando muchas personas no tienen los mismos derechos que los demás.
8. Es un deber de los ciudadanos en una democracia.

Paso 2: Gramática
See detailed supplementary materials for this grammar section in IM.

¿Recuerda Ud.?

In Grammar Section 44, you will learn about and begin to use the forms of the past subjunctive. As you learn this new tense, you will be continually using the past tense forms you have already learned along with the new material, so this section presents many opportunities for review. The following brief exercises will help you get started.

A. To learn the forms of the past subjunctive, you will need to know the forms of the preterite well, especially the third person plural. Regular **-ar** verbs end in **-aron** and regular **-er/-ir** verbs in **-ieron** in the third person plural of the preterite. Stem-changing **-ir** verbs show the second change in the third person: **servir (i, i) → sirvieron; dormir (ue, u) → durmieron**. Verbs with a stem ending in a vowel change the **i** to **y: leyeron, cayeron, construyeron**. Many common verbs have irregular stems in the preterite: **quisieron, hicieron, dijeron**, and so on. Four common verbs are totally irregular in this tense: **ser/ir → fueron, dar → dieron, ver → vieron**.

Give the third person plural of the preterite for these infinitives.

1. hablar
2. comer
3. vivir
4. jugar
5. perder
6. dormir
7. reír
8. leer
9. estar
10. tener
11. destruir
12. mantener
13. traer
14. dar
15. saber
16. vestirse
17. decir
18. creer
19. ir
20. poder

B. The forms of the imperfect are relatively regular. Only three verbs have irregular imperfect forms: **ir, ser,** and **ver**. Give their first person singular and plural forms.

44 ¡No queríamos que fuera así! • Past Subjunctive

¡Qué pena que no nos lleváramos bien!

MARÍA: ¿No recuerdas? ¡Qué mala memoria!
ELISA: Pero, mamá, ¿tú permitías que yo *hablara* así? ¡Qué falta de respeto hacia ti!
MARÍA: Eras muy cabezuda. No había nadie que *pudiera* contigo. ¡Cómo discutíamos! Tú creías que siempre tenías razón. Era imposible que *te equivocaras*. Tampoco querías que te *dijeran* lo que debías hacer.
ELISA: Bueno, por lo menos ahora no soy así. Digo, no tanto…
MARÍA: Sí, pero de todos modos, es necesario que una buena periodista sea un poco terca.
ELISA: Estoy de acuerdo. Es probable que, sin esa cualidad mía, yo no hubiera obtenido ese puesto.

Hace diez años…

1. ¿era difícil que Ud. hablara con sus padres sobre algún tema? ¿Cuál?
2. ¿con quién era imposible que Ud. se pusiera de acuerdo?
3. ¿con quién era imposible que Ud. se comunicara?
4. ¿contra qué orden de sus padres era común que Ud. protestara?

Cuando Ud. era niño/a…

5. ¿era probable que discutiera con alguien en la escuela primaria o en el barrio? ¿Con quién?
6. ¿dónde le prohibían sus padres que jugara?
7. ¿qué era obligatorio que comiera o bebiera?
8. ¿de qué temía que sus padres se enteraran?

Suggestion: Past Subjunctive
Teach this grammar topic for recognition only. Most first-year students will not acquire productive control of past subjunctive.

Follow-up: Past Subjunctive
To personalize, ask: **1.** *¿A quién es posible que Ud. le dijera «Uds. no entienden», a sus padres, a sus hermanos, a sus hijos o a sus amigos?* **2.** *¿Qué le molestaba más que le dijeran los adultos cuando era Ud. más joven: «Tú eres demasiado joven para saberlo» o «Tú eres demasiado mayor para esto»?*

Although Spanish has two simple indicative past tenses (preterite and imperfect), it has only one simple subjunctive past tense, the *past subjunctive* (**el imperfecto del subjuntivo**). Generally speaking, this tense is used in the same situations as the present subjunctive but, of course, when talking about past events. The exact English equivalent depends on the context in which it is used.

It's a shame we didn't get along! MARÍA: You don't remember? What a bad memory! ELISA: But Mom, did you allow me to speak in that way? What a lack of respect towards you! MARÍA: You were very stubborn. No one could change your mind. How we used to argue! You thought you were always right. It was impossible that you could ever make a mistake. Nor did you want anyone to tell you what to do. ELISA: Well, at least I'm not like that now. I mean, not as much… MARÍA: Yes, but, in any case, it's necessary for a good journalist to be a little bit stubborn. ELISA: I agree. It's probable that, without that quality of mine, I wouldn't have gotten that job.

FORMS OF THE PAST SUBJUNCTIVE

Past Subjunctive of Regular Verbs*

hablar:	**hablar~~on~~**	**comer:**	**comier~~on~~**	**vivir:**	**vivier~~on~~**
habla**ra**	hablá**ramos**	comie**ra**	comié**ramos**	vivie**ra**	vivié**ramos**
habla**ras**	habla**rais**	comie**ras**	comie**rais**	vivie**ras**	vivie**rais**
habla**ra**	habla**ran**	comie**ra**	comie**ran**	vivie**ra**	vivie**ran**

A. The past subjunctive endings **-a, -as, -a, -amos, -ais, -an** are identical for **-ar**, **-er**, and **-ir** verbs. These endings are added to the third person plural of the preterite indicative, minus its **-on** ending. For this reason, the forms of the past subjunctive reflect the irregularities of the preterite.

PAST SUBJUNCTIVE ENDINGS

-ar → -ara
-er, -ir → -iera

B. Stem-changing verbs

-Ar and **-er** verbs: no change

-Ir verbs: all persons of the past subjunctive reflect the vowel change in the third person plural of the preterite.

empezar (ie): empezar~~on~~ → **empezara, empezaras,...**
volver (ue): volvier~~on~~ → **volviera, volvieras,...**
dormir (ue, u): durmier~~on~~ → **durmiera, durmieras,...**
pedir (i, i): pidier~~on~~ → **pidiera, pidieras,...**

C. Spelling changes

All persons of the past subjunctive reflect the change from **i** to **y** between two vowels.

i → y (caer, construir, creer, destruir, leer, oír)

creer: creyer~~on~~ → **creyera, creyeras, creyera, creyéramos, creyerais, creyeran**

D. Verbs with irregular preterites

dar: dier~~on~~ → **diera, dieras, diera, diéramos, dierais, dieran**

decir:	dijer~~on~~ → **dijera**	poner:	pusier~~on~~ → **pusiera**
estar:	estuvier~~on~~ → **estuviera**	querer.	quisier~~on~~ → **quisiera**
haber:	hubier~~on~~ → **hubiera**	saber:	supier~~on~~ → **supiera**
hacer:	hicier~~on~~ → **hiciera**	ser:	fuer~~on~~ → **fuera**
ir:	fuer~~on~~ → **fuera**	tener:	tuvier~~on~~ → **tuviera**
poder:	pudier~~on~~ → **pudiera**	venir:	vinier~~on~~ → **viniera**

*An alternative form of the past subjunctive ends in **-se: hablase, hablases, hablase, hablásemos, hablaseis, hablasen**. This form will not be practiced in *¿Qué tal?*

USES OF THE PAST SUBJUNCTIVE

A. The past subjunctive usually has the same applications as the present subjunctive, but it is used for past events. Compare these pairs of sentences.

Quiero que **jueguen** esta tarde.
I want them to play this afternoon.

Quería que **jugaran** por la tarde.
I wanted them to play in the afternoon.

Siente que no **estén** allí esta noche.
He's sorry (that) they aren't there tonight.

Sintió que no **estuvieran** allí anoche.
He was sorry (that) they weren't there last night.

Dudamos que se **equivoquen**.
We doubt that they will make a mistake.

Dudábamos que se **equivocaran**.
We doubted that they would make a mistake.

B. Remember that the subjunctive is used after (1) expressions of *influence, emotion*, and *doubt;* (2) *nonexistent* and *indefinite antecedents;* and (3) *conjunctions* of *contingency and purpose*, as well as those of *time*.

(1) ¿**Era necesario** que **regatearas**?
Was it necessary for you to bargain?

(1) **Sentí** que no **tuvieran** tiempo para ver Granada.
I was sorry that they didn't have time to see Granada.

(2) **No había nadie** que **pudiera** resolverlo.
There wasn't anyone who could (might have been able to) solve it.

(3) Los padres **trabajaron para que** sus hijos **asistieran** a la universidad.
The parents worked so that their children could (might) go to the university.

(3) Anoche, **íbamos** a salir **en cuanto llegara** Felipe.
Last night, we were going to leave as soon as Felipe arrived.

C. The past subjunctive of the verb **querer** is often used to make a request sound more polite.

Quisiéramos hablar con Ud. en seguida.
We would like to speak with you immediately.

Quisiera un café, por favor.
I would like a cup of coffee, please.

Práctica

A. Si pudiera regresar... ¿Le gusta la idea de volver a la escuela secundaria? ¿O prefiere la vida de la universidad?

Paso 1. Lea las siguientes oraciones e indique las que son verdaderas para Ud. Cambie las oraciones falsas para que expresen su propia experiencia.

En la escuela secundaria...

1. ☐ era obligatorio que yo asistiera a todas mis clases.
2. ☐ mis padres insistían en que yo estudiara mucho.
3. ☐ era necesario que yo trabajara para que pudiera asistir a la universidad algún día.
4. ☐ no había ninguna clase que me interesara.
5. ☐ tenía que sacar buenas notas para que mis padres me dieran dinero.
6. ☐ era necesario que volviera a casa a una hora determinada, aun (*even*) en los fines de semana.
7. ☐ mis padres me exigían que limpiara mi cuarto cada semana.
8. ☐ mis padres no permitían que saliera con alguna persona o con los miembros de ciertos grupos.

Paso 2. Ahora considere sus respuestas. ¿Realmente era mejor la vida en la escuela secundaria? ¿Le gustaría regresar a esa época? ¿Por qué sí o por qué no?

B. Y ahora, la niñez

Paso 1. ¿Qué quería Ud. de la vida cuando era niño/a? ¿Y qué querían los demás que Ud. hiciera? Conteste, haciendo oraciones con una frase de cada grupo.

1. Mis padres (no) querían que yo...
2. Mis maestros me pedían que...
3. Yo buscaba amigos que...
4. Me gustaba mucho que nosotros...

ir a la iglesia / al templo con ellos
portarse bien, ser bueno/a
estudiar mucho, hacer la tarea todas las noches, sacar buenas notas
ponerse ropa vieja para jugar, jugar en la calle, pelear con mis amigos
mirar mucho la televisión, leer muchas tiras cómicas, comer muchos dulces
vivir en nuestro barrio, asistir a la misma escuela, tener muchos juguetes, ser aventureros
ir de vacaciones en verano, pasar todos juntos los días feriados, tener un árbol de Navidad muy alto

Preliminary exercise A
Use chain drill to practice forms. *Dé oraciones nuevas según las indicaciones. Cuando Ud. estudiaba en secundaria, ¿qué le gustaba? Me gustaba que nosotros... (estudiar idiomas, leer libros interesantes, ver películas en la clase de historia, hacer experimentos en la clase de física, bailar después de los partidos, divertirnos después de clase, ¿ ?)*

Suggestion A, B
If you have multigenerational class, compare answers of students of different generations.

Extension B
Have students describe a friend from their youth: *Yo tenía un amigo / una amiga que...* ¡**OJO!** Students will need the indicative in this initial sentence.

En los Estados Unidos y el Canadá...

Tres hispanos del mundo de la televisión

Ray Rodríguez, María Hinojosa y Jim Ávila son tres hispanos cuyos[a] nombres se destacan[b] en **el mundo de la televisión** y **los noticieros**. Ray Rodríguez, quien ahora vive en Miami, es contador de profesión y por varios años fue *manager* de Julio Iglesias. En 1992 llegó a ser presidente de Univisión, una **cadena** en español que, según los cálculos, se ve en el 95 por ciento de los hogares hispanos en los Estados Unidos. Junto con Galavisión y Telefutura, la cadena Univisión forma parte de la **compañía de difusión**[c] en español más importante de los Estados Unidos: Univisión Networks. Rodríguez es ahora presidente de esta poderosa[d] empresa.

Ray Rodríguez, presidente de Univisión

Una hispana que también se distingue en el mundo de la información es María Hinojosa. Hinojosa nació en la Ciudad de México. Estudió en los Estados Unidos, y por varios años trabajó para NPR (*National Public Radio*) en el área de Nueva York. Desde 1997 es **corresponsal**[e] de la CNN (*Cable News Network*), donde se especializa en **cuestiones urbanas**. Es autora de dos libros y ha recibido varios **premios periodísticos**, entre ellos el Premio Rubén Salazar, otorgado[f] por el **Consejo Nacional de la Raza**,[g] una prestigiosa institución de los hispanos estadounidenses.

Jim Ávila tiene una larga y distinguida carrera periodística. Es **reportero** de NBC y reporta **acontecimientos** importantes dentro y fuera de los Estados Unidos. Tiene el récord más alto de reportajes en televisión sobre las minorías. La **Asociación Nacional de Periodistas Hispanos** lo premió[h] en 1999 junto con Hugo Pérez por «*Fire Racism*», una pieza sobre el racismo entre los bomberos[i] de Chicago.

[a]*whose* [b]se... *stand out* [c]*media* [d]*powerful* [e]*correspondent* [f]*awarded* [g]Consejo... *National Council of La Raza* [h]*awarded a prize* [i]*firefighters*

Suggestion C

Bring Spanish-language newspaper or have students look for one on Internet. Have them identify instances of past subjunctive. Then have them explain why past subjunctive was used in each case. ¡OJO! Reassure students that they may not understand enough of context to explain use of this tense.

Suggestions: En los Estados Unidos y el Canadá...

- Have students search Internet for information about Hispanics in TV programs and movies.
- Point out that there are 35 million Hispanics in the U.S., about 12.5% of the total population, but that only 2% of the TV characters represent this group.

Paso 2. Ahora, conteste las siguientes preguntas. ¿Qué no le gustaba nada cuando era niño/a? ¿Qué quería Ud. que sus padres (sus hermanos) hicieran?

C. El noticiero de las seis. En las noticias los reporteros nos informan de los acontecimientos del día, pero a veces también ofrecen sus propias opiniones.

Paso 1. Lea las siguientes oraciones y cámbielas al pasado. Debe usar el imperfecto del primer verbo en cada oración y luego el imperfecto del subjuntivo en la segunda parte.

1. «Los obreros quieren que les den un aumento de sueldo.»
2. «Es posible que los trabajadores sigan en huelga hasta el verano.»
3. «Es necesario que las víctimas reciban atención médica en la Clínica del Sagrado Corazón.»
4. «Es una lástima que no haya espacio para todos allí.»
5. «Los terroristas piden que los oficiales no los persigan.»

6. «Parece imposible que el gobierno acepte sus demandas.»
7. «Es necesario que el gobierno informe a todos los ciudadanos del desastre.»
8. «Dudo que la paz mundial esté fuera de nuestro alcance (*reach*).»
9. «El presidente y los directores prefieren que la nueva fábrica se construya en México.»
10. «Temo que el número de votantes sea muy bajo en las próximas elecciones.»

Paso 2. Ahora indique si las oraciones representan un hecho o si son una opinión del reportero o de la persona citada (*quoted*).

Conversación

A. Los consejos se dan gratis (*free*). Sin duda, varias personas le dieron a Ud. muchos consejos o recomendaciones antes de que Ud. empezara a estudiar en la universidad. ¿Qué le recomendaron las siguientes personas? Indique las oraciones que son apropiadas para Ud. Luego dé por lo menos otro consejo o recomendación más que cada persona o grupo de personas le ofreció a Ud.

1. Mis amigos me recomendaron que viviera en una residencia en vez de en un apartamento.
2. Mis padres me aconsejaron que estudiara mucho.
3. Mi mejor amigo/a me pidió que le escribiera de vez en cuando.
4. Mi consejero/a me recomendó que me especializara en una carrera práctica y útil.

Frases útiles: tomar muchas clases diferentes, hacerme socio/a (*member*) de un(a) *fraternity/sorority*, graduarme dentro de cuatro años, participar en muchas actividades extracurriculares, llamar con frecuencia, evitar el alcohol y las drogas

Suggestion A
Encourage students to use clauses with *para que, con tal de que,* and so on.

B. Preguntas

1. ¿A qué le tenía miedo Ud. cuando era pequeño/a? ¿Era probable que ocurrieran las cosas que Ud. temía? ¿Temía a veces que sus padres lo/la castigaran (*punish*)? ¿Lo merecía a veces? ¿Era necesario que Ud. siempre los obedeciera? ¿Qué le prohibían a Ud. que hiciera?
2. ¿Qué tipo de clases buscaba Ud. para este semestre/trimestre? ¿Clases que fueran fáciles? ¿interesantes? ¿Las encontró? ¿Han sido las clases tal como Ud. las esperaba? ¿Qué tipo de clases va a buscar para el semestre/trimestre que viene?
3. ¿Qué buscaban los primeros inmigrantes que vinieron a los Estados Unidos? ¿Buscaban un lugar donde pudieran practicar su religión? ¿un lugar donde hubiera abundancia de recursos naturales? ¿menos restricciones? ¿más libertad política y personal? ¿más respeto por los derechos humanos? ¿menos gente? ¿más espacio?

Suggestion C

Practice comprehension of past subjunctive using context: *Imagine que su tía Laura, quien asistió a la universidad en los años cincuenta, le ha explicado a Ud. las normas de conducta de esa época. ¿Qué es diferente hoy día? ¿Hay algunas normas antiguas que a Ud. le parezcan mejores que las modernas? ¿Por qué?* 1. *Era obligatorio que los hombres y las mujeres vivieran en residencias apartes.* 2. *Todos cenaban a la misma hora. Para entrar en el comedor, era necesario que los hombres llevaran corbata y las mujeres, falda.* 3. *Había «hora de visita» en las residencias. Los hombres sólo podían visitar a sus amigas durante esas horas y viceversa.* 4. *Era necesario que las mujeres estuvieran en su residencia a una hora determinada de la noche. Pero no había ninguna restricción semejante para los hombres.*

—Verás, quisiera un vaso de agua. Pero no te molestes, porque ya no tengo sed. Sólo quisiera saber si, en el caso de que tuviese otra vez sed, podría (*I could*) venir a pedirte un vaso de agua.

Follow-up C

Have students tell what they would say in the following situations, using the past subjunctive whenever possible. *¿Qué diría Ud. en las siguientes situaciones?* 1. *Ud. ha llamado a un amigo a las diez de la noche para invitarlo a salir, pero ya estaba dormido y Ud. lo ha despertado.* 2. *Ud. llega a casa muy enfermo/a, con tos y fiebre. El médico le ha aconsejado guardar cama* (stay in bed) *para descansar. Pero su compañero/a de cuarto (esposo/a, etcétera) le ha preparado una fiesta sorpresa de cumpleaños. Todos los amigos lo/la saludan cuando entra.*

Suggestion: Nota comunicativa

Remind students that *Ojalá* + present subjunctive means *I hope (something will happen)*. *Ojalá* + past subjunctive means *I wish*. Wishes with the past subjunctive are unlikely or impossible to happen.

C. Situaciones. El niño del dibujo sabe que está molestando a sus padres cuando los despierta pidiendo ahora un vaso de agua que no quiere pero que podría querer más tarde. Por eso les habla de una forma muy cortés: «quisiera un vaso de agua… quisiera saber… ». ¿Cómo podría Ud. pedir de una forma muy cortés lo que necesita en las siguientes situaciones? ¿Qué diría para conseguirlo?

1. Ud. quiere tener el número de teléfono de un chico / una chica que acaba de conocer. Habla con un amigo de él / una amiga de ella.
2. En un restaurante, el camarero no lo/la atiende como debe. Ud. no quiere perder la paciencia con él, pero quiere la taza de café que le pidió hace diez minutos… y la cuenta.
3. Uds. quieren saber cuándo es el examen final en esta clase y qué va a incluir.
4. Ud. necesita una extensión para el próximo examen de español.
5. Ud. piensa que va a necesitar una extensión para el próximo proyecto.
6. Ud. necesita una carta de recomendación del profesor / de la profesora.
7. Ud. quiere hablar con el rector / la rectora de la universidad para invitarlo/la a cenar en su residencia con motivo de algo especial.

NOTA COMUNICATIVA

I wish I could . . . I wish they would . . .

There are many ways to express wishes in Spanish. As you know, one of the most common is **ojalá (que)** with the subjunctive. The past subjunctive following **ojalá** is one of the most frequent uses of those verb forms.

Ojalá (que) pudiera acompañarlos, pero no es posible.	*I wish I could go with you, but it's not possible.*
Ojalá inventaran una máquina que hiciera todas las tareas domésticas.	*I wish they would invent a machine that would do all the household chores.*

D. ¡Ojalá! Complete las oraciones lógicamente.

1. Ojalá que (yo) tuviera ____.
2. Ojalá que pudiera ____.
3. Ojalá inventaran una máquina que ____.
4. Ojalá solucionaran el problema de ____.
5. Ojalá que en esta universidad fuera posible ____.

Enfoque cultural

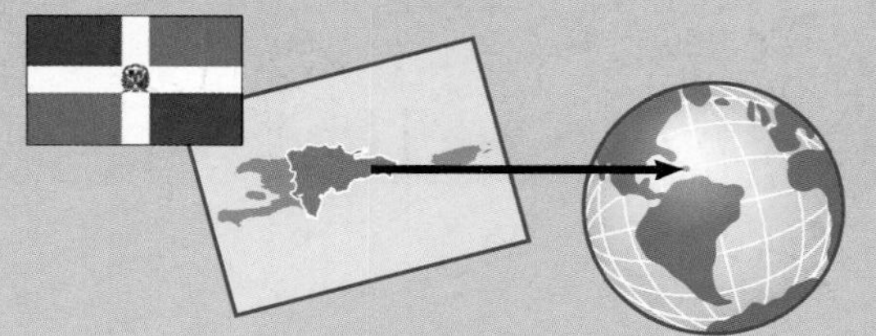

Enfoque cultural
See follow-up activities for this section in chapter-by-chapter materials in IM.

la República Dominicana

Datos esenciales

Nombre oficial: República Dominicana

Capital: Santo Domingo

Población: 8.000.000 de habitantes

Moneda: el peso

Idiomas: el español (oficial), el francés criollo

¡Fíjese!

- Santo Domingo fue fundada en 1496 por Bartólome Colón, hermano de Cristóbal Colón. Esta población en lo que entonces se llamaba la isla de La Española fue la primera colonia europea en el Nuevo Mundo.
- En el siglo XV, bucaneros franceses, que en realidad no eran más que piratas, fundaron la colonia de Sant Domingue en el oeste de la isla. Dentro de poco tiempo, se estableció un sistema de plantaciones basado en la labor de esclavos africanos.
- España le cedió[a] a Francia, en 1697, el tercio occidental[b] de La Española. Por esta razón, este territorio, el actual país de Haití, tiene una cultura y un idioma diferentes a los de la República Dominicana.
- Muchos atletas dominicanos han tenido gran éxito[c] en las Grandes Ligas de los Estados Unidos. Entre los que se han destacado[d] recientemente han sido Sammy Sosa, Juan Marichal y Roberto y Sandy Alomar.

[a]*ceded* [b]tercio... *western third* [c]*success* [d]se... *have stood out*

Multimedia: Internet
Encourage students to look for the official website of Julia Álvarez to find more information on her and her writing.

Conozca a... Julia Álvarez

Julia Álvarez

Aunque la novelista Julia Álvarez (1950–) nació en la ciudad de Nueva York y ahora es profesora de inglés en Middlebury College en Vermont, pasó su niñez en la República Dominicana. Cuando tenía apenas[a] 10 años, su padre tuvo que exiliarse con la familia después de tratar de derrotar[b] el régimen del dictador Trujillo. Al llegar a la madurez, se destacó como[c] poeta y ganó su primer premio de importancia en 1974, el mismo año en que publicó su primer libro de poesíe, *Homecoming.* Pero cuando, en 1991, publicó su primera novela *How the García Girls Lost their Accents* —en verdad, una serie de cuentos entrelazados[d]— recibió atención crítica y pública del mundo entero. Esta obra, como las que la han seguido, refleja su múltiple existencia como mujer, como latina y como americana.

[a]*barely* [b]*defeat* [c]se... *she distinguished herself as a* [d]*linked*

Capítulo 17 of the video to accompany *¿Qué tal?* contains cultural footage of the Dominican Republic.

Visit the *¿Qué tal?* website at www.mhhe.com/quetal.

UN POCO DE TODO

¿Qué lees? Complete the following dialogue with the correct form of the words in parentheses, as suggested by the context. When two possibilities are given in parentheses, select the correct word.

EDUARDO: ¿De quién (ser/estar[1]) esta revista?
LINDA: Es mío.[a] Te (lo/la[2]) puedo prestar si quieres.
EDUARDO: Pues me gustaría que me la (dejar[3]). La he (hojear[b4]) y me (haber[5]) gustado.
LINDA: Para (yo/mí[6]) también ha sido una sorpresa. No pensaba que (ser/estar[7]) (tan/tanto[8]) buena. Tiene un poco de todo. Aunque yo temía que (resultar[c9]) superficial, no es así.
EDUARDO: (*Yo:* Ser/Estar[10]) de acuerdo. Trae artículos de política internacional (muy/mucho[11]) interesantes. Quiero terminar de (leer[12]) ese artículo sobre la situación de las antiguas[d] repúblicas soviéticas.
LINDA: (*Tú:* Leer[13]) también el reportaje sobre África. Hace un análisis muy interesante sobre (el/la[14]) relación entre el hambre, la guerra y (el/la[15]) desertización. Pero también habla de la política nacional, de ciencia…
EDUARDO: Sí, y ya (*yo:* ver[16]) que además trae (un/una[17]) reportaje sobre mi actor favorito.
LINDA: (Es/Está[18]) cierto. Trae bastantes comentarios sobre el cine. También puedes (enterarse[19]) de las últimas novedades, tanto sobre libros (que/como[20]) sobre música.
EDUARDO: Y también me imagino[e] que tiene secciones sobre viajes, salud, deportes…
LINDA: Tienes (suerte/razón[21]). Es una buena forma de enterarse de todo lo actual.

[a]*mine* [b]*to look over* [c]*to turn out* [d]*former* [e]me… *I imagine*

Comprensión: ¿Cierto o falso?

1. A Linda le gusta leer más que a Eduardo.
2. La revista de que hablan se publica una vez al año.
3. Es posible que tenga también una sección sobre viajes.

Follow-up: Un poco de todo
Ask students the following questions: *¿Lee Ud. revistas o periódicos? ¿Qué tipo de prensa prefiere? ¿Está suscrito/a a algo? ¿Cómo se informa Ud.?*

In the *Capítulo 17* segment of "Chapter-by-Chapter Supplementary Materials" in the IM, you will find a chapter-culminating activity. You can use this activity to consolidate and review the vocabulary and grammar skills students have acquired.

Answers: Un poco de todo
1. *es* **2.** *la* **3.** *dejaras* **4.** *hojeado* **5.** *ha* **6.** *mí* **7.** *fuera* **8.** *tan* **9.** *resultara* **10.** *Estoy* **11.** *muy* **12.** *leer* **13.** *Leíste / Has leído* **14.** *la* **15.** *la* **16.** *he visto* **17.** *un* **18.** *Es* **19.** *enterarte* **20.** *como* **21.** *razón*

Paso 4: Un paso más
Optional section

See IM for suggestions and follow-up activities to accompany the video segment.

VIDEOTECA: En contexto

Suggestion A
Ask: *¿Lee Ud. las noticias en el Internet? ¿Sabía Ud. que puede conseguir noticias de todos los países hispánicos a través del Internet?*

FUNCTION
Purchasing a newspaper

A. Lluvia de ideas

- En su opinión, ¿qué medios de información debe leer una persona que quiere estar bien informada de lo que pasa en el país o en el mundo? ¿Se considera Ud. una persona bien informada? ¿Por qué?
- ¿Está Ud. suscrito/a a alguna revista o algún periódico? ¿Cuáles? Si Ud. compra alguna revista o algún periódico, ¿dónde los compra? ¿Los compra a menudo (*often*)? ¿Qué calidades o valores espera encontrar en una revista o un periódico?
- ¿Sabía Ud. que en los países hispánicos no es tan común como en este país estar suscrito a los periódicos y a las revistas? ¿Qué prefiere Ud., suscribirse a una publicación o comprarla en un quiosco (o puesto de periódicos)? ¿Por qué?

B. Dictado

A continuación aparece un fragmento del diálogo entre Roberto y la vendedora de periódicos. Complete el diálogo con las palabras o frases que faltan.

DOÑA BEATRIZ: ¡Roberto! Hijo, ¿cómo estás? Estaba ___preocupada___[1] porque no ___viniste___[2] ayer.

ROBERTO: Doña Beatriz, no debe preocuparse. Me ___levanté___[3] tarde ayer y tuve que apurarme[a] para llegar al trabajo.

DOÑA BEATRIZ: Tuve mucho ___miedo___[4] ayer. ¿No sabes cuántos ___crímenes___[5] hay hoy en día?

ROBERTO: Lo ___siento___,[6] doña Beatriz. Fue sin querer. A ver… ¿Qué necesito hoy? Un ___periódico___[7] liberal… un periódico conservador… una revista internacional… dos revistas ___políticas___[8]…

DOÑA BEATRIZ: ¡Cuántas ___revistas___[9] y periódicos! ¿Qué pasa, Roberto? ¿Vendes en otra esquina? ¿Tienes tu propio puesto[b]?

ROBERTO: Es importante ___informarse___,[10] doña Beatriz.

[a]*hurry* [b]*stand*

Cultura en contexto
El periódico

El periodismo tiene una larga tradición en Latinoamérica y España. Varios escritores famosos, entre ellos Gabriel García Márquez, el novelista colombiano y ganador del premio Nóbel de Literatura en 1981, fueron periodistas antes de dedicarse a escribir ficción. En los países hispanos, la gran mayoría de la gente educada lee por lo menos un periódico al día. En las grandes ciudades, algunos periódicos tienen asociaciones políticas y se puede encontrar un periódico para cada filosofía política, desde el más conservador (derechista) hasta el más liberal (izquierdista).

Note A
- In Hispanic countries, magazine and newspaper subscriptions are less common than in the U.S. and Canada. Most people buy them in the *quioscos* or *tiendas de prensa*, which are found everywhere in large cities.
- In Spanish-speaking countries it is unusual to find local newspapers in small towns, as in the U.S. and Canada. Only the most important cities have their own local paper. There are, of course, national papers which often have special daily sections for the capital and other major cities.

Suggestion B
To check comprehension, ask: **1.** *¿Qué compró Roberto?* **2.** *¿Por qué no fue Roberto a comprar periódicos al quiosco de doña Beatriz ayer?* **3.** *¿Por qué se puso doña Beatriz tan preocupada?*

C. Un diálogo original

Opción 1. Con un compañero / una compañera, dramatice el diálogo entre Roberto y doña Beatriz.

Opción 2. ¡Qué desesperación! En esta dramatización uno/a de Uds. hace el papel de una persona que está desesperada por comprar un periódico del extranjero. El otro / La otra es el dueño / la dueña de un quiosco de periódicos.

E1: Ud. tiene un buen amigo que está en un país del Oriente Medio, en un área donde ha estallado (*has broken out*) una guerra. Quiere un periódico de ese país para averiguar (*find out*) más acerca de los acontecimientos. Pero el periódico tiene que ser en inglés o en español, ya que Ud. no sabe leer ni árabe ni hebreo.

E2: Aunque Ud. vende periódicos del extranjero, ninguno de los periódicos del Oriente Medio que tiene es en inglés o en español. Pero Ud. conoce a una reportera árabe en su ciudad que está enterada sobre la guerra. Ud. ofrece comunicarse con ella para que su cliente se pueda informar sobre su amigo.

PASO FINAL

Sobre el autor... Gustavo Pérez Firmat (1949–) nació en La Habana, Cuba, y se crió en Miami, Florida. Su poesía tiene una variedad de temas, entre los que se incluyen las relaciones de familia y la experiencia cubano-americana en los Estados Unidos. Pérez Firmat recibió un doctorado de la Universidad de Michigan y ahora enseña en la Universidad de Columbia. El poema que aquí se presenta, «Cubanita descubanizada», es de una colección que se titula *Bilingual Blues*.

Suggestions: A leer
- Do *Estrategia* in class before assigning poem.
- Have volunteers read poem out loud for class.

A LEER

Estrategia: Using Language Cues to Understand Poetry

Much of the information you get in a poem is conveyed through the use of particular grammatical forms. These forms may also contribute to a poem's unique mood. For example, a poem written primarily in the imperfect may convey a sense of timelessness or of things recurring in the poet's personal history. The use of the preterite may give you the feeling that the moment was fleeting, perhaps all too fleeting.

As you read the following poem, note the instances of the past subjunctive that you have learned in this chapter. Why do you think the poet chose this form? What or how does it make you feel? Do you think the poem would be different if the poet had chosen a different grammatical form?

WWW Multimedia: Internet
- Encourage students to look for online bookstores that sell works by Cuban and Cuban-American authors. These websites often include biographical and literary information on the authors they feature.
- Have students search the Internet for information on the popular Cuban dance *El son*.

Cubanita descubanizada

Cubanita descubanizada
quién te pudiera recubanizar.
Quién supiera devolverte
el ron[a] y la palma,[b]
el alma y el son.[c]

Cubanita descubanizada,
tú que pronuncias todas las eses*
y dices ómnibus[d] y autobús
quién te pudiera
quién te supiera
si te quisieras recubanizar.

[a]*rum* [b]*palm tree* [c]el... *the soul and the sound* (*the* **son** *is also a popular Cuban dance*) [d]*synonym for* **autobús** (*the author is referring to the rich lexical variety that exists in Cuban Spanish, but that in this case signals a departure from its local, rural roots*).

Suggestion: A leer
Have students talk about image that Pérez Firmat presents of Cuba. Ask, for instance: *¿Por qué se mencionan el ron y el son en el poema? ¿y la palma? Según el poeta, ¿qué implica* (implies) *el hecho de que la cubanita haya perdido el alma? ¿Qué perdió la cubanita exactamente? ¿Qué otros elementos no mencionados en el poema creen Uds. que son típicamente cubanos?*

Comprensión

A. Definiciones. El autor toma libertades poéticas en su poema e inventa palabras que sirven para expresar sus ideas. Con un compañero / una compañera, trate de definir las siguientes palabras inventadas por Pérez Firmat. Comparen sus definiciones con las de otra persona en la clase.

- descubanizada
- recubanizar

B. Interpretación. ¿Cuál cree Ud. que es el punto de vista del narrador del poema? ¿Tiene una actitud positiva hacia la vida en el extranjero? ¿Qué mensaje intenta expresar? ¿Qué elementos de la poesía comunican este mensaje?

A ESCRIBIR

El tema de la inmigración es uno que provoca mucha reacción en este país. A continuación hay dos puntos de vista contrarios. Escoja una de estas posturas y escriba un breve informe en el que presenta y apoya su opinión.

- El bilingüismo y el biculturalismo enriquecen la vida de este país.
- Los inmigrantes a este país deben asimilarse por completo a la lengua, la vida y la cultura.

Variations: A escribir
- Have students write brief compositions about immigration experience. Students who are from this country can write about family member, friend, or imaginary character. Have them address when, why, and with whom they or their subject immigrated, as well as where they first arrived, what they felt at first, and what they feel now.
- Have students find or hand out other poems from *Bilingual Blues* and have students write several paragraphs comparing one to *Cubanita descubanizada.*

*In general, Cuban Spanish is characterized by a lack of pronunciation of the letter **s** when found in certain positions within a word.

PASO 1 Vocabulario

Paso 1: Vocabulario
See detailed supplementary materials and exercises for this section and a model for vocabulary presentation and other material in the *Capítulo 18 Paso 1: Vocabulario* section of "Chapter-by-Chapter Supplementary Materials," IM.

Lugares y cosas en el extranjero°

en... *abroad*

Multimedia: Audio
Students can listen to and practice this chapter's vocabulary on their Listening Comprehension Audio CD.

❖ **Transparencias 89–91**

Más cosas

el champú	shampoo
el jabon	soap
la pasta dental	toothpaste
el correo	mail
el papel para cartas	stationery
el paquete	package
la revista	magazine
el sobre	envelope
el batido	*drink similar to a milkshake*
una copa / un trago	(*alcoholic*) drink
el pastelito	small pastry

Variation A
Have students practice circumlocution for communicating. Have each student list things he/she needs when traveling abroad. Students should try to list things they don't know how to say in Spanish. Then have them work in pairs to explain their lists to each other. Suggest following items: hair dryer, batteries, shaver, comb, aftershave, hanger, motion sickness pills, sanitary pads, needle and thread, button, dental floss, faucet, sink, light switch.

Conversación

A. En el extranjero. Conteste con oraciones completas.

1. ¿Dónde se compra el champú? ¿el jabón?
2. ¿Cuál es la diferencia entre una farmacia de este país y una farmacia en el extranjero?
3. ¿Dónde se puede comprar sellos? (dos lugares)
4. Si se necesitan cigarrillos o fósforos, ¿adónde se va?
5. ¿Qué es un quiosco? ¿Qué cosas se venden allí?
6. ¿Qué venden en una papelería?

NOTA CULTURAL

De compras en el extranjero

Aunque los nombres de muchos lugares y tiendas del mundo hispánico se parecen a los de este país, no siempre son iguales los productos que en ellos se venden. Tomen en cuenta sobre todo las siguientes diferencias.

- En **las farmacias** no venden la variedad de cosas —dulces, tarjetas postales, etcétera— que se venden en las farmacias de los EE.UU.* y el Canadá. Por lo general, sólo se venden medicinas y productos para **la higiene personal** como jabón, pasta dental, champú…
- En **los estancos**, además de productos tabacaleros, se venden **sellos**, así que[a] uno no tiene que ir a una oficina de correos para comprarlos. También se venden **sobres** y **tarjetas postales** en los estancos.
- En **los quioscos** se vende una **gran variedad** de cosas: periódicos, revistas, libros, etcétera, pero también lápices, papel para cartas…

[a]así… *so*

Madrid, España

B. **¿Cierto o falso?** Corrija las oraciones falsas.

1. Se puede comprar batidos y pastelitos en una pastelería.
2. Si yo quisiera tomar una copa, iría (*I would go*) a un quiosco.
3. Se va a un quiosco para mandar paquetes.
4. Es más rápido ir a pie que tomar el metro.
5. Se va a un café a comprar champú.
6. Si yo necesitara pasta dental, iría a la oficina de correos.
7. Se puede comprar fósforos en un estanco.
8. Un batido se hace con vino.

---

*__EE.UU.__ is one way to abbreviate **Estados Unidos**. **E.U.** and **USA** are also used.

PASO 1

CAPÍTULO 18

En un viaje al extranjero

❖ Transparency 92

viajar al/en el extranjero to travel abroad

la aduana customs
los derechos de aduana customs duty
la multa fine, penalty
la nacionalidad nationality
el pasaporte passport

El alojamiento°

El... *Lodging*

alojarse/quedarse to stay (*in a place*)
hacer (*irreg.*)**/confirmar las reservas/reservaciones*** to make / to confirm reservations
la criada maid

la habitación room (*in a hotel*)
  individual/doble single/double
  con/sin baño/ducha with/without bath/shower

el hotel (de lujo) (luxury) hotel
el/la huésped(a) (*hotel*) guest
el mozo/botones bellhop
la pensión boardinghouse
  pensión completa room and full board
  media pensión room with breakfast and one other meal
la propina tip (*to an employee*)
la recepción front desk

completo/a full, no vacancy
con anticipación ahead of time
desocupado/a vacant, unoccupied

Conversación

Variation A
Have students give opinions about statements in activity, beginning with phrases such as *Es bueno...* , *Es buena idea...* , and so on.

Follow-up A
Have students explain why particular actions could cause problems.

A. En la aduana. ¿Ha viajado Ud. al extranjero? ¿Sabe Ud. cómo portarse al pasar por la aduana? Use el sentido común para explicar cuáles de las siguientes acciones pueden causar problemas en la aduana.

1. ser cortés con el inspector
2. escribir información falsa en el formulario de inmigración
3. no tener el pasaporte (o el visado necesario)
4. declarar todas sus compras
5. llevar gafas oscuras y parecer que está nervioso/a
6. esconder (*hiding*) artículos de contrabando en su equipaje
7. pagar los derechos (o la multa) sin quejarse
8. intentar cruzar la frontera con un pasaporte falsificado
9. tratar de distraer al inspector mientras este (*he*) registra sus maletas

*__La reserva__ is used in Spain for a reservation (for accommodations). **La reservación** is widely used in other parts of the Spanish-speaking world.

B. ¿Quiénes son? Empareje las personas con la descripción apropiada.

1. el huésped
2. el recepcionista
3. el botones
4. la turista
5. la inspectora de aduanas
6. el viajero

a. la persona que nos ayuda con el equipaje en un hotel
b. la persona que se aloja en un hotel o una pensión
c. una persona que va de un lugar a otro
d. alguien que viaja para ver otros lugares
e. la persona que nos registra las maletas y toma la declaración en la aduana
f. la persona que nos atiende en la recepción de un hotel

Suggestion B
Have students define in Spanish: **1.** *la aduana* **2.** *el pasaporte* **3.** *los derechos de aduana* **4.** *la frontera* **5.** *la multa* **6.** *el formulario de inmigración*

Follow-up B
Have students describe other things done by people named in activity.

C. Cuando Ud. viaja...

Paso 1. A continuación hay una lista de acciones que son típicas de los viajeros. ¿Hace Ud. lo mismo cuando viaja? Indique las acciones que son verdaderas para Ud.

1. ☐ Hago una reserva en un hotel (motel) o en una pensión con un mes de anticipación.
2. ☐ Confirmo la reserva antes de salir de viaje.
3. ☐ Voy al banco a conseguir cheques de viajero.
4. ☐ Alquilo un coche.
5. ☐ Me alojo en un hotel de lujo.
6. ☐ Pido que el mozo me suba las maletas.
7. ☐ Llamo al servicio de cuartos en vez de comer en el restaurante.
8. ☐ Le dejo una propina a la criada el último día de mi estancia (*stay*) en la habitación.

Suggestion C
Role-play each *paso* with at least 1 student before letting students do role play on their own.

D. Situaciones. Con un compañero / una compañera, improvise una escena. Hagan los papeles de un viajero / una viajera y del / de la recepcionista de un hotel.

Paso 1. El/La recepcionista le pregunta al viajero / a la viajera, que acaba de llegar:

- si tiene una reserva.
- cuánto tiempo piensa quedarse.
- el tipo de habitación reservada (o deseada).
- la forma de pago.

Paso 2. El/la huésped(a) pide los siguientes servicios:

- el desayuno en su cuarto.
- más toallas (*towels*) / jabón.
- información sobre lugares turísticos de interés.

Paso 3. Por fin, el huésped / la huéspeda pasa por la recepción para pagar la cuenta. Encuentra los siguientes errores en su cuenta.

- Le cobraron (*they charged*) por un desayuno que no tomó.
- Le cobraron por cuatro noches en vez de tres.
- Le cobraron por una llamada a larga distancia que nunca hizo.

National Standards: Communication
Have students imagine that they have an appointment with a travel agent in order to plan a trip to some exotic country. Have them prepare questions on index cards to ask the agent. Then have volunteers role-play situations between an agent and client. The travel agents will not know where the person wants to go or what he/she wants to do until the client arrives!

 **Paso 2: Gramática**
See detailed supplementary materials for this grammar section in IM.

45 Expressing What You Would Do • Conditional Verb Forms

La fantasía de la maestra de Mafalda

«¡Ya no aguanto este puesto! Creo que me *gustaría* ser abogada... *Pasaría* todo el día con tipos interesantes... *Ganaría* mucho dinero... *Viajaría* mucho, pues *tendría* clientes en todas partes del país... Me *llamarían* actores, actrices, políticos, hombres y mujeres de negocios para consultar conmigo... También *haría* viajes internacionales para investigar casos en el extranjero... Todo el mundo me *respetaría* y me *escucharía*... »

Y Ud., siendo la maestra / el maestro de Mafalda, ¿cómo sería? Use **no** cuando sea necesario.

- estar contento/a → *Estaría* contento/a.
- ser un tipo / una tipa coherente
- desorientar a los estudiantes
- mirarlos con ojos furiosos
- hacerlos morir de miedo (**¡OJO! har-**)
- ponerles cara de poco sueldo (**¡OJO! pondr-**)
- hacer a los estudiantes llorar de lástima

Suggestions: Conditional
- Before beginning Grammar 45, lead into *minidiálogo* with *le gustaría* + infinitive questions, which have been active since *Capítulo 7*.
- Preview section by asking following kinds of questions: *Si Ud. tuviera un millón de dólares, ¿qué haría? Si Ud. pudiera hacerle una sola pregunta al presidente de los Estados Unidos / al primer ministro del Canadá, ¿qué le preguntaría? Si pudiera cambiar cualquier cosa en el mundo, ¿qué cambiaría?*

Note: Conditional
Tipa coherente is very colloquial expression.

You have been using the phrase **me gustaría...** for some time to express what you *would like* (to do, say, and so on). **Gustaría** is a conditional verb form, part of a system that will allow you to talk about what you and others would do (say, buy, and so on) in a given situation.

The fantasy of Mafalda's teacher I can't bear this job anymore! I think I would like to be a lawyer . . . I would spend all day with interesting people . . . I would earn a lot of money . . . I would travel a lot, since I would have clients all over the country . . . Actors, actresses, politicians, businesspeople would call me to consult with me . . . I would also travel internationally to investigate cases abroad . . . Everyone would respect me and listen to me . . .

hablar		comer		vivir	
hablaría	hablaríamos	comería	comeríamos	viviría	viviríamos
hablarías	hablaríais	comerías	comeríais	vivirías	viviríais
hablaría	hablarían	comería	comerían	viviría	vivirían

A. Like the English future, the English conditional is formed with an auxiliary verb: *I **would** speak, I **would** write.* The Spanish *conditional* (**el condicional**), like the Spanish future, is a simple verb form (only one word). It is formed by adding conditional endings to the infinitive. No auxiliary verbs are needed.

CONDITIONAL ENDINGS

-ía, -ías, -ía, -íamos, íais, -ían

B. Verbs that form the future on an irregular stem use the same stem to form the conditional.

The conditional of **hay (haber)** is **habría** (*there would be*).*

decir: diría, dirías, diría, diríamos, diríais, dirían

decir:	**dir-**	
hacer:	**har-**	**-ía**
poder:	**podr-**	**-ías**
poner:	**pondr-**	**-ía**
querer:	**querr-**	**-íamos**
saber:	**sabr-**	**-íais**
salir:	**saldr-**	**-ían**
tener:	**tendr-**	
venir:	**vendr-**	

C. The conditional expresses what you would do in a particular situation, given a particular set of circumstances.

—¿**Hablarías** español en el Brasil?
Would you speak Spanish in Brazil?

—No. **Hablaría** portugués.
No. I would speak Portuguese.

OJO When *would* implies *used to* in English, Spanish uses the imperfect.

Íbamos a la playa todos los veranos.
We would go (used to go) to the beach every summer.

*The conditional forms of the verb **haber** are used to form the *conditional perfect tense* (**el condicional perfecto**), which expresses what *would have* occurred at some point in the past.

Habríamos tenido que buscarla en el aeropuerto. — *We would have had to pick her up at the airport.*

You will find a more detailed presentation of these forms in Appendix 3, Additional Perfect Forms (Indicative and Subjunctive).

Preliminary exercise A

Use rapid response drill to practice forms: *Dé el condicional.* ***yo:*** *mandar, necesitar, aprender, decir;* ***tú:*** *llevar, viajar, leer, hacer;* ***Ud./él/ella:*** *entrar, comprar, vivir, poner;* ***nosotros:*** *celebrar, comprender, ir, poder;* ***Uds./ellos/ellas:*** *regresar, creer, tener, venir*

Suggestion A

To contextualize the conditional, ask: **1.** *¿Qué lengua hablaría una persona de Pekín? ¿Cuál sería su nacionalidad? ¿Y una persona de Moscú? ¿del Canadá? ¿de Lisboa? ¿de Guadalajara? ¿Podría Ud. hablar con todos ellos? ¿Qué lengua(s) tendría que aprender?* **2.** *¿Qué haría Ud. para obtener mucho dinero? ¿Y para ahorrar mucho dinero? ¿Y para gastar mucho dinero? ¿Siempre ha tenido Ud. mucho dinero? Como consecuencia, ¿qué tipo de vida ha llevado Ud. en cuanto al aspecto económico?*

Variation A

Assign *Pasos 1* and *2* as homework, allowing students to complete paragraphs about any Spanish-speaking country of interest to them.

Suggestions B

- Have students retell passage using *los trabajadores sociales.*
- Use conditional verb forms in personalized questions to students about what they would do on vacation in Puerto Rico.
- Ask students: *¿Adónde irían Uds. (si pudieran) este fin de semana? ¿Qué pasaría después de su escapada?*

Answers B

1. *gustaría* **2.** *trabajaría* **3.** *Podría* **4.** *Tomaría* **5.** *comería* **6.** *Vería* **7.** *sería* **8.** *tendría* **9.** *Podría* **10.** *tendría*

Práctica

A. ¿Qué haría Ud.?

Paso 1. Imagine que hace un viaje a España. Complete las siguientes oraciones de manera que corresponda a la realidad y a lo que a Ud. le gustaría hacer. ¡Es una gran oportunidad de demostrarles a sus compañeros y a su profesor(a) su conocimiento (*knowledge*) sobre la vida y la cultura españolas!

1. Hablaría _____.
2. Comería _____ y bebería _____.
3. Iría a _____ y allí vería _____.
4. No podría irme sin antes visitar _____.
5. Me compraría _____.
6. Me divertiría mucho _____ (**¡OJO!** Se necesita un gerundio: **-iendo** o **-ando**).

Paso 2. Claro que durante un viaje no sólo se hacen actividades culturales. Las oraciones a continuación muestran actividades típicas durante un viaje, pero Ud. debe completarlas con algunos detalles.

1. Yo haría el viaje a España con _____.
2. Tendría que sacar muchas fotos para mostrárselas a _____.
3. Le(s) mandaría tarjetas postales a _____.
4. Querría _____ durante el viaje, pero probablemente no lo haría.
5. Conocería a _____.

Paso 3. Ahora con un compañero / una compañera, haga una lista similar a las del **Paso 1** y el **Paso 2**, pero sobre otro país hispánico.

B. ¿Es posible escapar?

Cuente Ud. la fantasía de esta trabajadora social, dando la forma condicional de los verbos.

Necesito salir de todo esto… Creo que me (gustar[1]) ir a Puerto Rico o a algún otro lugar exótico del Caribe… No (trabajar[2])… (Poder[3]) nadar todos los días… (Tomar[4]) el sol en la playa… (Comer[5]) platos exóticos… (Ver[6]) bellos lugares naturales… El viaje (ser[7]) ideal…

Pero… , tarde o temprano, (tener[8]) que volver a lo de siempre… a los rascacielos de la ciudad… al tráfico… al medio ambiente contaminado… al mundo del trabajo… (Poder[9]) usar mi tarjeta de crédito, como dice el anuncio —pero ¡(tener[10]) que pagar después!

Comprensión: ¿Cierto, falso o no lo dice? Corrija las oraciones falsas.

1. Esta persona trabaja en una ciudad grande.
2. No le interesan los deportes acuáticos.
3. Puede pagar este viaje de sueños (*dreams*) al contado.
4. Tiene un novio con quien quisiera hacer el viaje.

C. **¿Qué harías?** Con un compañero / una compañera, haga y conteste las preguntas según el modelo. Pueden cambiar los detalles, si quieren. Para números 9–12, inventen las respuestas.

MODELO: estudiar árabe/japonés →
E1: ¿Estudiarías árabe?
E2: No. Estudiaría japonés.

1. estudiar italiano / chino
2. renunciar un puesto sin avisar / con dos semanas de anticipación
3. hacer un viaje a España / la Argentina
4. salir de casa sin apagar el estéreo / las luces
5. seguir un presupuesto rígido / flexible
6. gastar menos en ropa / libros
7. poner el aire acondicionado en invierno / verano
8. alquilar un coche de lujo / económico
9. dejar de estudiar / ¿ ?
10. vivir en otra ciudad / ¿ ?
11. ser presidente/a de los Estados Unidos / primer ministro (primera ministra) del Canadá / ¿ ?
12. gustarle conocer a una persona famosa / ¿ ?

Suggestions C

- Have students complete the items in the future. Contrast the difference in meaning when the future is used.
- Have students add two questions of their own to each group.

Conversación

Suggestions A

- Ask students about New Year's resolutions. *¿Cuáles son algunas de las promesas del Año Nuevo que Ud. hace todos los años? ¿Qué promesas hizo Ud. el enero pasado?* Model answer for them. *Dije que dejaría de fumar.* Follow up with present perfect questions, using object pronouns whenever possible, for example, *¿Lo ha hecho Ud.? ¿Ha dejado de fumar?*
- This is good activity to introduce use of conditional to express future in past.
- Present and practice *el condicional de probabilidad.* Have students make conjectures about where you and other students were at certain times (last night at 11:00 / last July / in 1985): *¿Dónde estaría Susie ayer a las 11 de la noche?* Bring in personal photos or magazine clippings and have students invent details about people and events pictured, for example, *La mujer estaría riéndose porque estaría oyendo algo divertido.* Have different groups work with same images, then compare results.

Follow-up A

Have students write 2 questions that use future tense and 2 that use conditional. Have them ask their classmates these questions.

A. Entrevista. ¿Cómo será su futuro? ¿Qué hará? ¿Qué haría? Con un compañero / una compañera, haga y conteste las siguientes preguntas.

MODELO: E1: ¿Dejarás de fumar algún día? →
E2: No. No dejaré de fumar nunca. No puedo. (Creo que sí. Dejaré de fumar algún día.)

PREGUNTAS CON EL FUTURO

1. ¿Te graduarás en esta universidad (o en otra)?
2. ¿Vivirás en esta ciudad después de graduarte?
3. ¿Buscarás un puesto aquí?
4. ¿Te casarás (¿Te divorciarás) después de graduarte?
5. ¿Cuántos niños (nietos) crees que tendrás algún día?
6. ¿Serás famoso/a algún día?

PREGUNTAS CON EL CONDICIONAL

1. ¿Te casarías con una persona de otro país?
2. ¿Podrías estar contento/a sin la televisión?
3. ¿Serías capaz de (*capable of*) ahorrar el 10 por ciento de tu salario?
4. ¿Te gustaría ayudar a colonizar otro planeta?
5. ¿Podrías vivir sin las tarjetas de crédito?
6. ¿Renunciarías tu trabajo para viajar por el mundo?

Note: Nota comunicativa

- Point out that, like *if* in English, *si* can mean *cuando* if it is a recurrent situation: *Si mi mejor amiga me llama por teléfono, cierro la puerta para que nadie me oiga.*
- Stress similarity between English and Spanish. Point out that past tense form after *if,* as in *If I had a million dollars . . . ,* does not necessarily mean past action. It is the equivalent to meaning of imperfect subjunctive in Spanish.

NOTA COMUNICATIVA

If I were you, I would . . .

Both English and Spanish use clauses to speculate about likely or unlikely situations. These are called *if* or **si** clauses.

- The present indicative after **si** presents a situation that is likely to occur. It is followed or preceded by a clause in the indicative or by a command.

LIKELY

Si **ahorro** suficiente dinero, **iré** de vacaciones a España.	*If I save enough money, I will go to Spain on vacation.*

- The imperfect subjunctive after **si** introduces an unlikely event. The preceding or following clause includes a verb in the conditional.

UNLIKELY

Si **tuviera** dinero suficiente, le **daría** la vuelta al mundo.	*If I had enough money, I would go around the world.*

B. Circunstancias

Paso 1. ¿Qué hace Ud. si le ocurren estas cosas?

1. Si su primera clase es a las 9:00 de la mañana y Ud. se despierta a las 8:50.
2. Si su mejor amigo/a (novio/a, esposo/a, hijo/a) tiene un resfriado muy fuerte.
3. Si es viernes por la noche y no tiene ningún plan para divertirse esa noche.
4. Si se le pierde la llave de su cuarto/casa.

Paso 2. ¿Qué haría Ud. en estas situaciones?

1. Si le dejaran una herencia (*inheritance*) de dos millones de dólares.
2. Si pudiera hacer lo que quisiera en este momento.
3. Si tuviera un solo (*single*) deseo para todo el mundo.
4. Si pudiera dar la fiesta de sus sueños.

Suggestions B

- Have students invent context for each *paso* and poll classmates.
- Assign as homework.

Suggestion: En los Estados Unidos y el Canadá...
Use the following questions to check comprehension: **1.** *¿Qué tipos de platos ofrecen los dos restaurantes?* **2.** *¿Desde cuándo hay un restaurante con comida española en Ottawa?* **3.** *¿Qué cosa no es típicamente española en los restaurantes ibéricos de Ottawa?*

En los Estados Unidos y el Canadá...

Manjares[a] hispanocanadienses

Los que han viajado por la Península Ibérica ya conocen **los sabores[b] de los platos españoles y portugueses**. En la capital canadiense, Ottawa, tanto los turistas como los nativos disfrutan de[c] estos mismos platos en dos restaurantes que sirven **auténticas recetas de los países ibéricos. El Mesón**, que se encuentra en una casa al estilo victoriano, provee una cocina para satisfacer al cliente más exigente.[d] Desde 1987 José Alves ofrece un **menú de platos típicos regionales** de España y de Portugal que incluye calamares al ajillo, mejillones marineros, vieia a la gallega[e] y tres variedades de paella, el sabroso[f] plato a base de arroz y azafrán. También se ofrece un menú especial para vegetarianos. Para complementar sus platos, El Mesón tiene una impresionante lista de vinos españoles y una selección de los famosos «vinhos verdes»* de Portugal.

Una paella tipo español

Lejos de la vecindad de El Mesón y más cerca del centro de la capital, Ud. puede encontrar un ambiente acogedor[g] y relajado en donde hablar y tomar una copa de vino tinto mientras Alfonso Pérez, del restaurante **Don Alfonso,** le prepara uno de sus famosos platos. Nativo de Galicia, el Sr. Pérez vivió en Venezuela antes de emigrar al Canadá adonde vino primero con el propósito de aprender inglés. Hace más de veinticinco años que los ciudadanos de Ottawa y sus muchos turistas del extranjero disfrutan de los mariscos y los sabrosos platos a la plancha[h] preparados por don Alfonso. Entre muchos, se ofrecen escalopines[i] Tío Pepe, una zarzuela de mariscos y gazpacho andaluz[j].

[a]*Delicacies* [b]*flavors* [c]disfrutan... *enjoy* [d]*demanding* [e]calamares... *squid in garlic sauce, mussels cooked sailor-style, scallops Galician-style* [f]*tasty* [g]*welcoming* [h]a... *grilled* [i]*breaded cutlets* [j]zarzuela... *seafood stew, and a cold vegetable soup from Andalucía*

---

*__Vinho verde__ (*Young wine*) is produced in the Minho region of northwest Portugal. Slightly sparkling, it can be either red or white.

WWW. Multimedia: Internet
Encourage students to look for restaurants in Spanish-speaking countries or Hispanic restaurants in the U.S. and Canada online. Students can also find Spanish and Hispanic recipes online.

Enfoque *cultural*

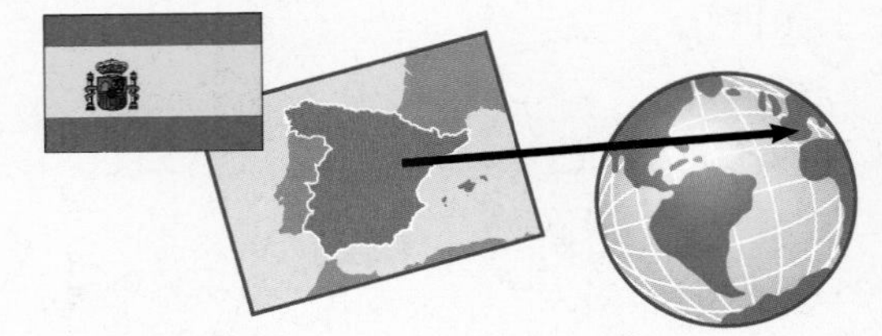

 **Enfoque cultural**
See follow-up activities for this section in chapter-by-chapter materials in IM.

España

Datos esenciales

Nombre oficial: Reino de España

Capital: Madrid

Población: 39.000.000 de habitantes

Moneda: el euro

Idiomas: el español, el catalán, el gallego y el vasco*

Conozca a... Pedro Almodóvar

Las películas del cineasta[a] Pedro Almodóvar (1951–) han tenido y siguen teniendo un éxito enorme dentro y fuera de España, y Almodóvar es el director de cine español más conocido de las últimas décadas. Con temas que satirizan actitudes tradicionales respecto a la familia, la religión, el machismo y la moralidad convencional, sus películas presentan una sociedad española moderna y cambiante.[b]

Muchas de sus películas se pueden conseguir en las bibliotecas públicas y universitarias, así como en los videoclubs de este país: *Mujeres al borde de un ataque de nervios, La ley del deseo, ¿Qué he hecho yo para merecer esto?, ¡Átame!,*[c] *Kika, La flor de mi secreto* y *Todo sobre mi madre,* esta última de 1999 y ganadora del Óscar para la mejor película extranjera.

[a]director de cine [b]*changing* [c]*Tie Me Up! Tie Me Down!*

¡Fíjese!

- España es una país donde muchas culturas se han encontrado a través de[a] la historia. Sin embargo fueron los romanos los que marcaron el principio de la historia de la España que hoy conocemos, pues ellos introdujeron el latín a la península durante su dominio (desde el año 200 a.C.[b] hasta la invasión de los visigodos, un pueblo germánico, en el 419 d.C.[c]).
- El latín es la lengua madre del español y también del catalán, el gallego y el portugués. La otra lengua que se habla en la península, el vasco, es una lengua ancestral de origen desconocido: ni siquiera es[d] una lengua indoeuropea.
- España no fue siempre un solo país. De hecho,[e] España se unificó en el siglo XV cuando los Reyes Católicos, Isabel y Fernando, monarcas de dos reinos[f] independientes, se casaron. Su campaña[g] de unificación terminó en 1492 con la conquista del reino musulmán[h] de Granada.
- Los árabes vivieron en España durante ocho siglos, hasta su expulsión, junto con los judíos, en el año 1492.

[a]a... *throughout* [b]a.C.... antes de Cristo [c]d.C.... después de Cristo [d]ni... *it is not even* [e]De... *In fact* [f]*kingdoms* [g]*campaign* [h]*Muslim*

El escudo (*shield*) de Fernando e Isabel

 **Capítulo 18** of the video to accompany *¿Qué tal?* contains cultural footage of Spain.

WWW. Visit the *¿Qué tal?* website at www.mhhe.com/quetal.

*El español es el lenguaje oficial de todo el país; el catalán, el gallego y el vasco también son lenguas oficiales en Cataluña, Galicia y el País Vasco, respectivamente.

Suggestions: Enfoque cultural
- Have students research and report to the class about famous Spanish historic and literary figures, such as *el Cid Campeador, el Lazarillo de Tormes, Isabel la Católica* and *Fernando de Aragón, Don Quijote* and *Sancho Panza, la Celestina,* and *don Juan Tenorio.* You may wish to invite students to dress up as these characters at an end-of-class party.
- If the class is composed of mature students, show Almodóvar's *Todo sobre mi madre* as an end-of-term activity.

UN POCO DE TODO

En busca de alojamiento. Complete the following dialogue with the correct form of the words in parentheses, as suggested by the context. When two possibilities are given in parentheses, select the correct word.

ALFONSO: Yo no (saber/conocer[1]) cómo vamos a encontrar alojamiento. No tenemos (mucho/muy[2]) dinero, y ya (ser/estar[3]) un poco tarde.
ELENA: Y (el/la[4]) equipaje pesa[a] mucho. No podemos (ir[5]) muy lejos.
ALFONSO: (*Tú:* Mirar[6]), en esa oficina parece que dan información.
EMPLEADO: ¿Qué (*Uds.:* desear[7])?
ALFONSO: Pues quisiéramos una habitación (por/para[8]) los dos. Sólo (por/para[9]) esta noche, pues solamente estamos (hacer[10]) escala aquí y mañana (*nosotros:* seguir[11]) con nuestro viaje.
ELENA: (Por/Para[12]) favor, no queremos que (ser/estar[13]) muy cara. Hemos (cambiar[14]) muy poca moneda. Tampoco queremos que (ser/estar[15]) muy lejos.
EMPLEADO: Bien, (*Uds.:* esperar[16]) un momento. Voy a llamar a una pensión (mucho/muy[17]) agradable que no (ser/estar[18]) muy lejos.

Pocos minutos después…

EMPLEADO: Me dicen que (haber[19]) una habitación doble disponible[b].
ALFONSO: ¡Qué bien! ¿Pagamos ahora?
EMPLEADO: No (ser/estar[20]) necesario. Aquí tienen los datos. (Este/Esta[21]) papel sirve como reserva. También (los/les[22]) he anotado el precio. Pero no tarden mucho en (llegar[23]).
ELENA: Muy bien. ¿Podría Ud. indicarnos cómo llegar allí?
EMPLEADO: (*Uds.:* Mirar[24]). Estamos aquí y la pensión (ser/estar[25]) en esta plaza. Se lo marco en (el/la[26]) mapa.
ELENA: ¿Sabe si (ser/estar[27]) incluido el desayuno en el precio?
EMPLEADO: Sí, lo que Uds. (llamar[28]) desayuno continental.
ALFONSO: Y otra cosa. ¿(Ser/Estar[29]) posible dejar parte de nuestro equipaje en la estación? Mañana tenemos (de/que[30]) volver a la estación.
EMPLEADO: Sí. Cuando salgan de la oficina, a mano derecha (*Uds.:* ver[31]) la consigna.[c] Pueden dejar(lo/la[32]) allí.
ALFONSO: Adiós y gracias (por/para[33]) todo.

[a]*weighs* [b]*available* [c]*baggage check*

Comprensión: ¿Quién lo dice?

1. Sí, todavía tenemos una habitación para esta noche.
2. ¡Qué suerte hemos tenido! Una habitación barata y cerca.
3. A ver qué quieren estos dos jóvenes.
4. Sí, señor. El empleado de la estación nos dio este papel como reserva.

In the *Capítulo 18* segment of "Chapter-by-Chapter Supplementary Materials" in the IM, you will find a chapter-culminating activity. You can use this activity to consolidate and review the vocabulary and grammar skills students have acquired.

Answers: Un poco de todo
1. *sé* **2.** *mucho* **3.** *es* **4.** *el* **5.** *ir* **6.** *Mira* **7.** *desean* **8.** *para* **9.** *para* **10.** *haciendo.* **11.** *seguimos/seguiremos* **12.** *Por* **13.** *sea* **14.** *cambiado* **15.** *esté* **16.** *esperen* **17.** *muy* **18.** *está* **19.** *hay* **20.** *es* **21.** *Este* **22.** *les* **23.** *llegar* **24.** *Miren* **25.** *está* **26.** *el* **27.** *está* **28.** *llaman* **29.** *Es* **30.** *que* **31.** *verán* **32.** *lo* **33.** *por*

PASO 4 Un paso más

Paso 4: Un paso más
Optional section

 See IM for suggestions and follow-up activities to accompany the video segment.

VIDEOTECA: En contexto

Note A
In Costa Rica the word for stamp is *estampilla* and to express *mandar,* the verb *enviar* is used.

FUNCTION

Mailing letters and packages

Cultura en contexto *Los paquetes al extranjero*

En los países hispanos, como en los Estados Unidos, hay que llenar una declaración de aduanas cuando se envía un paquete al extranjero. En la declaración, hay que describir el contenido del paquete. Después, se indica si se quiere mandar el paquete por correo aéreo o por superficie.[a] El precio del franqueo[b] depende del modo de transporte. Claro, mandar un paquete por vía aérea es más caro que mandarlo por superficie.

[a]por... *by surface (mail)* [b]*postage*

A. Lluvia de ideas

COSTA RICA

- ¿Para qué tipo de cartas o paquetes usa Ud. el correo? ¿Con cuánta frecuencia?
- ¿Cuánto cuesta actualmente en este país mandar una carta por correo doméstico? ¿y una tarjeta postal al extranjero?

Suggestion A
Ask students: *¿Qué usa Ud. más para comunicarse con familiares y amigos, el correo postal o el correo electrónico? ¿Por qué?*

B. Dictado

A continuación aparece un fragmento del diálogo entre Mariela y el empleado de la oficina de correos. Complete el diálogo con las palabras o frases que faltan.

MARIELA: Buenos días, señor. Necesito estampillas[a] para tarjetas ___postales___.[1]

EMPLEADO: ¿Son postales para correo doméstico o correo ___internacional___[2]?

MARIELA: Esta ___tarjeta___[3] es para correo doméstico. [...]

EMPLEADO: Muy bien. ¿Hay algo más?

MARIELA: Sí. Quisiera mandar este ___paquete___[4] a Francia. ¿Cuánto cuesta?

EMPLEADO: Eso depende de cómo quiera mandarlo, señorita. Por ___correo___[5] aéreo le cuesta 1.230 colones, pero llega en dos semanas. Si desea mandarlo por barco, sólo le cuesta 780 colones.

MARIELA: Es un ___regalo___[6] navideño[b] [...]. Por barco está bien.

EMPLEADO: Cómo no, señorita. Por favor, ___escriba___[7] aquí el contenido del paquete y el valor. Es para la ___aduana___.[8]

[a]sellos [b]*Christmas*

Suggestion B
To check comprehension, ask: **1.** *¿Por qué tipo de correo decide Mariela mandar el paquete? ¿Por qué?* **2.** *¿Qué tiene que escribir Mariela en el papel? ¿Por qué?* **3.** *¿Cuánto paga Mariela en total?*

C. Un diálogo original

Opción 1. Con un compañero / una compañera, dramatice el diálogo entre Mariela y el empleado de la oficina de correos.

Opción 2. ¿Vale la pena? (*Is it worthwhile?*) Dos amigos han comprado un regalo de cumpleaños para otro amigo que vive en otro estado. El problema es que el libro que mandan es grande y pesado (*heavy*), y el correo resulta más caro que el libro mismo. Por otro lado, el cumpleaños es pasado mañana (*the day after tomorrow*) y tendrían que mandar el regalo por correo urgente para que llegara a tiempo.

Con un compañero / una compañera, represente una escena entre los amigos y solucionen el problema de cómo mandar el regalo.

PASO FINAL

A CONVERSAR

Improvisación turística

Si Ud. viaja a un país hispanohablante algún día, tendrá la oportunidad de hablar español. Imagine que Ud. es turista en un país hispanohablante. ¿Qué diría en las siguientes situaciones?

Paso 1. Formen grupos de tres o cuatro personas. Escojan una de las siguientes situaciones para improvisar. Lean la situación y escriban en una hoja de papel aparte un esquema (*outline*) de la improvisación.

MODELO: en el aeropuerto → saludarse; pedir los pasaportes; preguntar y contestar por qué vienen a este país…

Suggestion: A conversar, Paso 1
For students without experience in these situations, write suggestions on board: *En el hotel: preguntar si la persona tiene una reservación; preguntar si la persona quiere una habitación sencilla o doble; pedir una tarjeta de crédito*

Lugar	Situación	Personajes
En el aeropuerto	pasar por el control de pasaportes y por la aduana	uno o dos turistas, el/la agente que revisa los pasaportes, el/la agente de aduana
En el hotel	pedir una habitación y pedirle al botones que lleve las maletas a la habitación	uno o dos turistas, el/la recepcionista del hotel, el botones
En la calle	pedirles direcciones a algunas personas	uno o dos turistas, las personas del grupo

Paso 2. Cada miembro del grupo debe escoger un personaje y prepararse para la improvisación, haciendo apuntes sobre las posibles preguntas que necesitará hacer y contestar.

MODELO: agente de aduana → preguntarles si tienen algo que declarar; preguntarles si llevan plantas o productos orgánicos…

Paso 3. Improvisen la escena varias veces, modificándola si es necesario. Luego, presenten su improvisación a la clase.

MODELO: E1: Sus pasaportes, por favor. Gracias. ¿De dónde vienen?
E2: Venimos de los Estados Unidos.
E1: ¿Y por qué vienen a México?
E3: Estamos de vacaciones. Vamos a ir a la playa…

Suggestion: A conversar, Paso 3
For students without experience in these situations, model each improvisation with volunteers. Then have students practice their own improvisations. Observe each group of students as they practice and offer suggestions if they are uncertain of what should occur.

Optional: A conversar
After students perform their improvisations for the class, mix up groups and have them do new improvisations for class, based on ones they have just performed and watched. They will not have opportunity to take notes and practice; rather, they will be relying on what they recall from performances they have just seen.

En resumen

GRAMÁTICA

To review the grammar point presented in this chapter, refer to the indicated grammar presentation. You'll find further practice of this structure in the Workbook/Laboratory Manual, on the CD-ROM, and on the website.

45. Conditional Verb Forms

Do you know how to form the conditional tense?
When is the conditional used in Spanish?

VOCABULARIO

Cosas y lugares en el extranjero

el batido	*drink similar to a milkshake*
el café	café
el champú	shampoo
una copa / un trago	(*alcoholic*) drink
el correo	mail
la oficina de correos	post office
la estación del metro	subway stop
el estanco	tobacco stand/shop
los fósforos	matches
el jabón	soap
el papel para cartas	stationery
la papelería	stationery store
el paquete	package
la parada del autobús	bus stop
la pasta dental	toothpaste
la pastelería	pastry shop
el pastelito	small pastry
el quiosco	kiosk
el sello	stamp
el sobre	envelope

Repaso: la farmacia, la revista, la tarjeta postal

Ir al extranjero

cruzar	to cross
declarar	to declare
registrar	to search, examine

Repaso: pagar, viajar

la aduana	customs
el cheque de viajero	traveler's check
los derechos (de aduana)	(customs) duty
el extranjero	abroad
el formulario	form (*to fill out*)
la frontera	border
la inmigración	immigration
el/la inspector(a) (de aduanas)	(customs) inspector
la multa	fine, penalty
el pasaporte	passport
el/la viajero/a	traveler

Repaso: las compras, la maleta, la nacionalidad

El alojamiento

alojarse	to stay (*in a place*)
confirmar	to confirm
el botones/mozo	bellhop
la criada	maid
la estancia	stay (*in a hotel*)
la habitación	room (*in a hotel*)
individual/doble	single/double
con/sin baño/ducha	with(out) bath/shower
el hotel (de lujo)	(luxury) hotel
el/la huésped(a)	(hotel) guest
la pensión	boardinghouse
pensión completa	room and full board
media pensión	room with breakfast and one other meal

la propina	tip (to an employee)
las reservaciones / las reservas	reservations
recepción	front desk

Repaso: quedarse

completo/a	full, no vacancy
con anticipación	ahead of time
desocupado/a	vacant, unoccupied

Suggestion: Vocabulario

Read the following passage to contextualize vocabulary. Pause from time to time to ask comprehension questions.

Cuando uno viaja a otro país, su primer encuentro cultural puede ser en la aduana, antes de salir ni siquiera del aeropuerto. Puede haber problemas en la aduana de todos los países, pero por lo general esta experiencia es muy rutinaria. Para pasar por la aduana sin problema, lo único importante es no llevar nada que esté prohibido: cierto tipo de alimentos, plantas, ciertas sustancias químicas, etcétera. Si Ud. tiene alguna duda, es buena idea que se entere de cuáles son las cosas prohibidas en el país que va a visitar antes de entrar en él.

Glossary of Grammatical Terms

ADJECTIVE A word that describes a noun or pronoun.

una casa **grande**
*a **big** house*

Ella es **inteligente.**
*She is **smart.***

Demonstrative adjective An adjective that points out a particular noun.

este chico, **esos** libros, **aquellas** personas
***this** boy, **those** books, **those** people (over there)*

Interrogative adjective An adjective used to form questions.

¿**Qué** cuaderno?
***Which** notebook?*

¿**Cuáles** son los carteles que buscas?
***What (Which)** posters are you looking for?*

Possessive adjective (unstressed) An adjective that indicates possession or a special relationship.

sus coches
***their** cars*

mi hermana
***my** sister*

Possessive adjective (stressed) An adjective that more emphatically describes possession.

Es **una** amiga **mía.**
*She's **my** friend / She's a friend **of mine.***

Es **un** coche **suyo.**
*It's **her** car / It's a car **of hers.***

ADVERB A word that describes an adjective, a verb, or another adverb.

Él es **muy** alto.
*He is **very** tall.*

Ella escribe **bien.**
*She writes **well.***

Van **demasiado** rápido.
*They are going **too** quickly.*

ARTICLE A determiner that sets off a noun.

Definite article An article that indicates a specific noun.

el país
***the** country*

la silla
***the** chair*

las mujeres
***the** women*

Indefinite article An article that indicates an unspecified noun.

un chico
***a** boy*

una ciudad
***a** city*

unas zanahorias
*(**some**) carrots*

CLAUSE A construction that contains a subject and a verb.	
Main (Independent) clause A clause that can stand on its own because it expresses a complete thought.	**Busco una muchacha.** ***I'm looking for a girl.*** Si yo fuera rica, **me compraría una casa.** *If I were rich,* ***I would buy a house.***
Subordinate (Dependent) clause A clause that cannot stand on its own because it does not express a complete thought.	Busco a la muchacha **que juega al tenis.** *I'm looking for the girl* ***who plays tennis.*** **Si yo fuera rico,** me compraría una casa. ***If I were rich,*** *I would buy a house.*
COMPARATIVE The form of adjectives and adverbs used to compare two nouns or actions.	Luis es **menos hablador** que Julián. *Luis is* ***less talkative*** *than Julián.* Él corre **más rápido** que Julián. *He runs* ***faster*** *than Julián.*
CONJUGATION The different forms of a verb for a particular tense or mood. A present indicative conjugation:	(yo) hablo — (nosotros/as) hablamos (tú) hablas — (vosotros/as) habláis (Ud., él/ella) habla — (Uds., ellos/as) hablan *I speak* — *we speak* *you (fam. sing.) speak* — *you (fam. pl.) speak* *you (form. sing.) speak* — *you (pl. fam. & form.) speak* *he/she speaks* — *they speak*
CONJUNCTION An expression that connects words, phrases, or clauses.	Cristóbal **y** Diana *Cristóbal* ***and*** *Diana* Hace frío, **pero** hace buen tiempo. *It's cold,* ***but*** *it's nice out.*
DIRECT OBJECT The noun or pronoun that receives the action of a verb.	Veo **la caja.** *I see* ***the box.*** **La** veo. *I see* ***it.***
GENDER A grammatical category of words. In Spanish there are two genders: masculine and feminine. Here are a few examples.	(see table below)

	MASCULINE	FEMININE
ARTICLES AND NOUNS:	**el** disco compacto	**la** cinta
PRONOUNS:	**él**	**ella**
ADJECTIVES:	bonit**o**, list**o**	bonit**a**, list**a**
PAST PARTICIPLES:	El informe está **escrito.**	La composición está **escrita.**

IMPERATIVE *See* Mood.	
IMPERFECT (*IMPERFECTO*) In Spanish, a verb tense that expresses a past action with no specific beginning or ending.	**Nadábamos** con frecuencia. *We* ***used to swim*** *often.*
IMPERSONAL CONSTRUCTION One that contains a third-person singular verb but no specific subject in Spanish. The subject of English impersonal constructions is generally *it.*	**Es importante** que... ***It is important*** *that . . .* **Es necesario** que... ***It is necessary*** *that . . .*

INDICATIVE *See* Mood.

INDIRECT OBJECT The noun or pronoun that indicates for whom or to whom an action is performed. In Spanish, the indirect object pronoun must always be included. The noun that the pronoun stands for may be included for emphasis or clarification.

Marcos **le** da el suéter a **Raquel**. / Marcos **le** da el suéter.
Marcos gives the sweater ***to Raquel.*** */ Marcos gives* ***her*** *the sweater.*

INFINITIVE The form of a verb introduced in English by *to: to play, to sell, to come.* In Spanish dictionaries, the infinitive form of the verb appears as the main entry.

Luisa va a **comprar** un periódico.
Luisa is going ***to buy*** *a newspaper.*

MOOD A set of categories for verbs indicating the attitude of the speaker towards what he or she is saying.

Imperative mood A verb form expressing a command.

¡**Ten** cuidado!
Be *careful!*

Indicative mood A verb form denoting actions or states considered facts.

Voy a la biblioteca.
I am going *to the library.*

Subjunctive mood A verb form, uncommon in English, used primarily in subordinate clauses after expressions of desire, doubt, or emotion. Spanish constructions with the subjunctive have many possible English equivalents.

Quiero que **vayas** inmediatamente.
I want you to go immediately.

NOUN A word that denotes a person, place, thing, or idea. Proper nouns are capitalized names.

abogado, ciudad, periódico, libertad, Luisa
lawyer, city, newspaper, freedom, Luisa

NUMBER

Cardinal number A number that expresses an amount.

una silla, **tres** estudiantes
one *chair,* ***three*** *students*

Ordinal number A number that indicates position in a series.

la **primera** silla, el **tercer** estudiante
the ***first*** *chair, the* ***third*** *student*

PAST PARTICIPLE The form of a verb used in compound tenses (*see* Perfect Tenses). Used with forms of *to have* or *to be* in English and with **ser, estar,** or **haber** in Spanish.

comido, terminado, perdido
eaten, finished, lost

PERFECT TENSES Compound tenses that combine the auxiliary verb **haber** with a past participle.

Present perfect indicative This form uses a present indicative form of **haber.** The use of the Spanish present perfect generally parallels that of the English present perfect.

No **he viajado** nunca a México.
I've *never* ***traveled*** *to Mexico.*

Past perfect indicative This form uses **haber** in the imperfect tense to talk about something that had or had not been done before a given time in the past.

Antes de 1997, **no había estudiado** español.
Before 1997, ***I hadn't studied*** *Spanish.*

Present perfect subjunctive This form uses the present subjunctive of **haber** to express a present perfect action when the subjunctive is required.	¡Ojalá que Marisa **haya llegado** a su destino! *I hope Marisa **has arrived** at her destination!*
PERSON The form of a pronoun or verb that indicates the person involved in an action.	SINGULAR / PLURAL FIRST PERSON *I* / yo — *we* / nosotros/as SECOND PERSON *you* / tú, Ud. — *you* / vosotros/as, Uds. THIRD PERSON *he, she* / él, ella — *they* / ellos, ellas
PREPOSITION A word or phrase that specifies the relationship of one word (usually a noun or pronoun) to another. The relationship is usually spatial or temporal.	**a** la escuela ***to** school* **cerca de** la biblioteca ***near** the library* **con** él ***with** him* **antes de** la medianoche ***before** midnight*
PRETERITE (*PRETÉRITO*) In Spanish, a verb tense that expresses a past action with a specific beginning and ending.	**Salí** para Roma el jueves. ***I left** for Rome on Thursday.*
PRONOUN A word that refers to a person (I, you) or that is used in place of one or more nouns.	
Demonstrative pronoun A pronoun that singles out a particular person or thing.	Aquí están dos libros. **Este** es interesante, pero **ese** es aburrido. *Here are two books. **This one** is interesting, but **that one** is boring.*
Interrogative pronoun A pronoun used to ask a question.	¿**Quién** es él? ***Who** is he?* ¿**Qué** prefieres? ***What** do you prefer?*
Object pronoun A pronoun that replaces a direct object noun or an indirect object noun. Both direct and indirect object pronouns can be used together in the same sentence. However, when the pronoun **le** is used with **lo** or **la,** it changes to **se.**	Veo a **Alejandro. Lo** veo. *I see **Alejandro.** I see **him.*** **Le** doy el libro (**a Juana**). *I give the book **to Juana.*** **Se lo** doy (**a ella**). *I give **it** to **her.***
Reflexive pronoun A pronoun that represents the same person as the subject of the verb.	**Me** miro en el espejo. *I look at **myself** in the mirror.*
Relative pronoun A pronoun that introduces a dependent clause and denotes a noun already mentioned.	El hombre con **quien** hablaba era mi vecino. *The man with **whom** I was talking was my neighbor.* Aquí está el bolígrafo **que** buscas. *Here is the pen (**that**) you are looking for.*
Subject pronoun A pronoun representing the person or thing performing the action of a verb.	**Lucas y Julia** juegan al tenis. ***Lucas and Julia** are playing tennis.* **Ellos** juegan al tenis. ***They** are playing tennis.*

SUBJECT The word(s) denoting the person, place, or thing performing an action or existing in a state.	**Sara** trabaja aquí. *Sara works here.* ¡**Buenos Aires** es una ciudad magnífica! *Buenos Aires is a great city!* Mis **libros** y mi **computadora** están allí. *My **books** and my **computer** are over there.*
SUBJUNCTIVE *See* Mood.	
SUPERLATIVE The form of adjectives or adverbs used to compare three or more nouns or actions. In English, the superlative is marked by *most, least,* or *-est.*	Escogí el vestido **más caro.** *I chose **the most expensive** dress.* Ana es la persona **menos habladora** que conozco. *Ana is **the least talkative** person I know.*
TENSE The form of a verb indicating time: present, past, or future.	Raúl **era**, **es** y siempre **será** mi mejor amigo. *Raúl **was**, **is**, and always **will be** my best friend.*
VERB A word that reports an action or state.	Ella **llegó.** *She **arrived.*** Ella **estaba** cansada. *She **was** tired.*
Auxiliary verb A verb in conjunction with a participle to convey distinctions of tense and mood. In Spanish, this auxiliary verb is **haber.**	**Han** viajado por todas partes del mundo. *They **have** traveled everywhere in the world.*
Reflexive verb A verb whose subject and object are the same.	Él **se corta** la cara cuando **se afeita.** *He **cuts himself** when he **shaves (himself).***

APPENDIX 2

Using Adjectives as Nouns

Nominalization means using an adjective as a noun. In Spanish, adjectives can be nominalized in a number of ways, all of which involve dropping the noun that accompanies the adjective, then using the adjective in combination with an article or other word. One kind of adjective, the demonstrative, can simply be used alone. In most cases, these usages parallel those of English, although the English equivalent may be phrased differently from the Spanish.

Article + Adjective

Simply omit the noun from an *article + noun + adjective* phrase.

el **libro** azul → **el azul** (*the blue one*)
la **hermana** casada → **la casada** (*the married one*)
el **señor** mexicano → **el mexicano** (*the Mexican one*)
los **pantalones** baratos → **los baratos** (*the inexpensive ones*)

You can also drop the first noun in an *article + noun +* **de** *+ noun* phrase.

la **casa** de Julio → **la de Julio** (*Julio's*)
los **coches** del Sr. Martínez → **los del Sr. Martínez** (*Mr. Martínez's*)

In both cases, the construction is used to refer to a noun that has already been mentioned. The English equivalent uses *one* or *ones,* or a possessive without the noun.

—¿Necesitas el libro grande?
—No. Necesito **el pequeño.**
—Do you need the big book?
—No. I need the small one.

—¿Usamos el coche de Ernesto?
—No. Usemos **el de Ana.**
—*Shall we use Ernesto's car?*
—*No. Let's use Ana's.*

Note that in the preceding examples the noun is mentioned in the first part of the exchange (**libro, coche**) but not in the response or rejoinder.

Note also that a demonstrative can be used to nominalize an adjective: **este rojo** (*this red one*), **esos azules** (*those blue ones*).

Lo + Adjective

As seen in **Capítulo 10, lo** combines with the masculine singular form of an adjective to describe general qualities or characteristics. The English equivalent is expressed with words like *part* or *thing.*

lo mejor *the best thing* (*part*), *what's best*
lo mismo *the same thing*
lo cómico *the funny thing* (*part*), *what's funny*

Article + Stressed Possessive Adjective

The stressed possessive adjectives—but not the unstressed possessives—can be used as possessive pronouns: **la maleta suya** → **la suya.** The article and the possessive form agree in gender and number with the noun to which they refer.

Este es mi **banco.** ¿Dónde está **el suyo**?
This is my bank. Where is yours?

Sus **bebidas** están preparadas; **las nuestras,** no.
Their drinks are ready; ours aren't.

No es la **maleta** de Juan; es **la mía.**
It isn't Juan's suitcase; it's mine.

Note that the definite article is frequently omitted after forms of **ser: ¿Esa maleta? Es suya.**

Demonstrative Pronouns

The demonstrative adjective can be used alone, without a noun. An accent mark can be added to the demonstrative pronoun to distinguish it from the demonstrative adjectives (**este, ese, aquel**).

Necesito este diccionario y **ese** (**ése**).
I need this dictionary and that one.

Estas señoras y **aquellas** (**aquéllas**) son las hermanas de Sara, ¿no?
These women and those (over there) are Sara's sisters, aren't they?

It is acceptable in modern Spanish, per the **Real Academia Española,** to omit the accent on demonstrative pronouns when context makes the meaning clear and no ambiguity is possible.

APPENDIX 3

Additional Perfect Forms (Indicative and Subjunctive)

Some indicative verb tenses have corresponding perfect forms in the indicative and subjunctive moods. Here is the present tense system.

el presente:	yo hablo, como, pongo
el presente perfecto:	yo he hablado, comido, puesto
el presente perfecto de subjuntivo:	yo haya hablado, comido, puesto

Other indicative forms that you have learned also have corresponding perfect indicative and subjunctive forms. Here are the most important ones, along with examples of their use. In each case, the tense or mood is formed with the appropriate form of **haber.**

El pluscuamperfecto del subjuntivo

yo:	hubiera hablado, comido, vivido, *etc.*
tú:	hubieras hablado, comido, vivido, *etc.*
Ud./él/ella:	hubiera hablado, comido, vivido, *etc.*
nosotros:	hubiéramos hablado, comido, vivido, *etc.*
vosotros:	hubierais hablado, comido, vivido, *etc.*
Uds./ellos/ellas:	hubieran hablado, comido, vivido, *etc.*

These forms correspond to **el presente perfecto del indicativo** (**Capítulo 14**). They are most frequently used in **si** clause sentences, along with the conditional perfect. See examples below. (***Si*** Clause).

El futuro perfecto

yo: habré hablado, comido, vivido, *etc.*
tú: habrás hablado, comido, vivido, *etc.*
Ud./él/ella: habrá hablado, comido, vivido, *etc.*
nosotros: habremos hablado, comido, vivido, *etc.*
vosotros: habréis hablado, comido, vivido, *etc.*
Uds./ellos/ellas: habrán hablado, comido, vivido, *etc.*

These forms correspond to **el futuro** (**Capítulo 16**) and are most frequently used to tell what *will have already happened* at some point in the future. (In contrast, the future is used to tell what *will happen.*)

Mañana **hablaré** con Miguel.
I'll speak with Miguel tomorrow.

Para las tres, ya **habré hablado** con Miguel.
By 3:00, I'll already have spoken to Miguel.

El año que viene **visitaremos** a los nietos.
We'll visit our grandchildren next year.

Para las Navidades, ya **habremos visitado** a los nietos.
We'll already have visited our grandchildren by Christmas.

El condicional perfecto

yo: habría hablado, comido, vivido, *etc.*
tú: habrías hablado, comido, vivido, *etc.*
Ud./él/ella: habría hablado, comido, vivido, *etc.*
nosotros: habríamos hablado, comido, vivido, *etc.*
vosotros: habríais hablado, comido, vivido, *etc.*
Uds./ellos/ellas: habrían hablado, comido, vivido, *etc.*

These forms correspond to **el condicional** (**Capítulo 18**). They are frequently used to tell what *would have happened* at some point in the past. (In contrast, the conditional tells what one *would do.*)

Yo **hablaría** con Miguel.
I would speak with Miguel (if I were you, at some point in the future).

Yo **habría hablado** con Miguel.
I would have spoken with Miguel (if I had been you, at some point in the past).

***Si* Clause: Sentences About the Past**

You have learned (**Capítulo 18**) to use the past subjunctive and conditional to speculate about the present in **si** clause sentences: what *would happen* if a particular event *were* (or *were not)* to occur.

Si **tuviera** el tiempo, **aprendería** francés.
If I had the time, I would learn French (in the present or at some point in the future).

The perfect forms of the past subjunctive and the conditional are used to speculate about the past: what *would have happened* if a particular event *had* (or *had not)* occurred.

En la escuela superior, si **hubiera tenido** el tiempo, **habría aprendido** francés.
In high school, if I had had the time, I would have learned French.

APPENDIX 4

Verbs

A. Regular Verbs: Simple Tenses

Infinitive Present Participle Past Participle	INDICATIVE					SUBJUNCTIVE		IMPERATIVE
	Present	Imperfect	Preterite	Future	Conditional	Present	Imperfect	
hablar hablando hablado	hablo hablas habla hablamos habláis hablan	hablaba hablabas hablaba hablábamos hablabais hablaban	hablé hablaste habló hablamos hablasteis hablaron	hablaré hablarás hablará hablaremos hablaréis hablarán	hablaría hablarías hablaría hablaríamos hablaríais hablarían	hable hables hable hablemos habléis hablen	hablara hablaras hablara habláramos hablarais hablaran	habla tú, no hables hable Ud. hablemos hablen
comer comiendo comido	como comes come comemos coméis comen	comía comías comía comíamos comíais comían	comí comiste comió comimos comisteis comieron	comeré comerás comerá comeremos comeréis comerán	comería comerías comería comeríamos comeríais comerían	coma comas coma comamos comáis coman	comiera comieras comiera comiéramos comierais comieran	come tú, no comas coma Ud. comamos coman
vivir viviendo vivido	vivo vives vive vivimos vivís viven	vivía vivías vivía vivíamos vivíais vivían	viví viviste vivió vivimos vivisteis vivieron	viviré vivirás vivirá viviremos viviréis vivirán	viviría vivirías viviría viviríamos viviríais vivirían	viva vivas viva vivamos viváis vivan	viviera vivieras viviera viviéramos vivierais vivieran	vive tú, no vivas viva Ud. vivamos vivan

B. Regular Verbs: Perfect Tenses

INDICATIVE					SUBJUNCTIVE	
Present Perfect	Past Perfect	Preterite Perfect	Future Perfect	Conditional Perfect	Present Perfect	Past Perfect
he has ha hemos habéis han } hablado, comido, vivido	había habías había habíamos habíais habían } hablado, comido, vivido	hube hubiste hubo hubimos hubisteis hubieron } hablado, comido, vivido	habré habrás habrá habremos habréis habrán } hablado, comido, vivido	habría habrías habría habríamos habríais habrían } hablado, comido, vivido	haya hayas haya hayamos hayáis hayan } hablado, comido, vivido	hubiera hubieras hubiera hubiéramos hubierais hubieran } hablado, comido, vivido

Infinitive Present Participle Past Participle	INDICATIVE					SUBJUNCTIVE		IMPERATIVE
	Present	Imperfect	Preterite	Future	Conditional	Present	Imperfect	
andar andando andado	ando andas anda andamos andáis andan	andaba andabas andaba andábamos andabais andaban	anduve anduviste anduvo anduvimos anduvisteis anduvieron	andaré andarás andará andaremos andaréis andarán	andaría andarías andaría andaríamos andaríais andarían	ande andes ande andemos andéis anden	anduviera anduvieras anduviera anduviéramos anduvierais anduvieran	anda tú, no andes ande Ud. andemos anden
caer cayendo caído	caigo caes cae caemos caéis caen	caía caías caía caíamos caíais caían	caí caíste cayó caímos caísteis cayeron	caeré caerás caerá caeremos caeréis caerán	caería caerías caería caeríamos caeríais caerían	caiga caigas caiga caigamos caigáis caigan	cayera cayeras cayera cayéramos cayerais cayeran	cae tú, no caigas caiga Ud. caigamos caigan
dar dando dado	doy das da damos dais dan	daba dabas daba dábamos dabais daban	di diste dio dimos disteis dieron	daré darás dará daremos daréis darán	daría darías daría daríamos daríais darían	dé des dé demos deis den	diera dieras diera diéramos dierais dieran	da tú, no des dé Ud. demos den
decir diciendo dicho	digo dices dice decimos decís dicen	decía decías decía decíamos decíais decían	dije dijiste dijo dijimos dijisteis dijeron	diré dirás dirá diremos diréis dirán	diría dirías diría diríamos diríais dirían	diga digas diga digamos digáis digan	dijera dijeras dijera dijéramos dijerais dijeran	di tú, no digas diga Ud. digamos digan
estar estando estado	estoy estás está estamos estáis están	estaba estabas estaba estábamos estabais estaban	estuve estuviste estuvo estuvimos estuvisteis estuvieron	estaré estarás estará estaremos estaréis estarán	estaría estarías estaría estaríamos estaríais estarían	esté estés esté estemos estéis estén	estuviera estuvieras estuviera estuviéramos estuvierais estuviera	está tú, no estés esté Ud. estemos estén
haber habiendo habido	he has ha hemos habéis han	había habías había habíamos habíais habían	hube hubiste hubo hubimos hubisteis hubieron	habré habrás habrá habremos habréis habrán	habría habrías habría habríamos habríais habrían	haya hayas haya hayamos hayáis hayan	hubiera hubieras hubiera hubiéramos hubierais hubieran	
hacer haciendo hecho	hago haces hace hacemos hacéis hacen	hacía hacías hacía hacíamos hacíais hacían	hice hiciste hizo hicimos hicisteis hicieron	haré harás hará haremos haréis harán	haría harías haría haríamos haríais harían	haga hagas haga hagamos hagáis hagan	hiciera hicieras hiciera hiciéramos hicierais hicieran	haz tú, no hagas haga Ud. hagamos hagan

C. Irregular Verbs (continued)

Infinitive Present Participle Past Participle	INDICATIVE					SUBJUNCTIVE		IMPERATIVE
	Present	Imperfect	Preterite	Future	Conditional	Present	Imperfect	
ir yendo ido	voy vas va vamos vais van	iba ibas iba íbamos ibais iban	fui fuiste fue fuimos fuisteis fueron	iré irás irá iremos iréis irán	iría irías iría iríamos iríais irían	vaya vayas vaya vayamos vayáis vayan	fuera fueras fuera fuéramos fuerais fueran	ve tú, no vayas vaya Ud. vayamos vayan
oír oyendo oído	oigo oyes oye oímos oís oyen	oía oías oía oíamos oíais oían	oí oíste oyó oímos oísteis oyeron	oiré oirás oirá oiremos oiréis oirán	oiría oirías oiría oiríamos oiríais oirían	oiga oigas oiga oigamos oigáis oigan	oyera oyeras oyera oyéramos oyerais oyeran	oye tú, no oigas oiga Ud. oigamos oigan
poder pudiendo podido	puedo puedes puede podemos podéis pueden	podía podías podía podíamos podíais podían	pude pudiste pudo pudimos pudisteis pudieron	podré podrás podrá podremos podréis podrán	podría podrías podría podríamos podríais podrían	pueda puedas pueda podamos podáis puedan	pudiera pudieras pudiera pudiéramos pudierais pudieran	
poner poniendo puesto	pongo pones pone ponemos ponéis ponen	ponía ponías ponía poníamos poníais ponían	puse pusiste puso pusimos pusisteis pusieron	pondré pondrás pondrá pondremos pondréis pondrán	pondría pondrías pondría pondríamos pondríais pondrían	ponga pongas ponga pongamos pongáis pongan	pusiera pusieras pusiera pusiéramos pusierais pusieran	pon tú, no pongas ponga Ud. pongamos pongan
querer queriendo querido	quiero quieres quiere queremos queréis quieren	quería querías quería queríamos queríais querían	quise quisiste quiso quisimos quisisteis quisieron	querré querrás querrá querremos querréis querrán	querría querrías querría querríamos querríais querrían	quiera quieras quiera queramos queráis quieran	quisiera quisieras quisiera quisiéramos quisierais quisieran	quiere tú, no quieras quiera Ud. queramos quieran
saber sabiendo sabido	sé sabes sabe sabemos sabéis saben	sabía sabías sabía sabíamos sabíais sabían	supe supiste supo supimos supisteis supieron	sabré sabrás sabrá sabremos sabréis sabrán	sabría sabrías sabría sabríamos sabríais sabrían	sepa sepas sepa sepamos sepáis sepan	supiera supieras supiera supiéramos supierais supieran	sabe tú, no sepas sepa Ud. sepamos sepan
salir saliendo salido	salgo sales sale salimos salís salen	salía salías salía salíamos salíais salían	salí saliste salió salimos salisteis salieron	saldré saldrás saldrá saldremos saldréis saldrán	saldría saldrías saldría saldríamos saldríais saldrían	salga salgas salga salgamos salgáis salgan	saliera salieras saliera saliéramos salierais salieran	sal tú, no salgas salga Ud. salgamos salgan
ser siendo sido	soy eres es somos sois	era eras era éramos erais	fui fuiste fue fuimos fuisteis	seré serás será seremos seréis	sería serías sería seríamos seríais	sea seas sea seamos seáis	fuera fueras fuera fuéramos fuerais	sé tú, no seas sea Ud. seamos sean

Infinitive Present Participle Past Participle	INDICATIVE					SUBJUNCTIVE		IMPERATIVE
	Present	Imperfect	Preterite	Future	Conditional	Present	Imperfect	
tener teniendo tenido	tengo tienes tiene tenemos tenéis tienen	tenía tenías tenía teníamos teníais tenían	tuve tuviste tuvo tuvimos tuvisteis tuvieron	tendré tendrás tendrá tendremos tendréis tendrán	tendría tendrías tendría tendríamos tendríais tendrían	tenga tengas tenga tengamos tengáis tengan	tuviera tuvieras tuviera tuviéramos tuvierais tuvieran	ten tú, no tengas tenga Ud. tengamos tengan
traer trayendo traído	traigo traes trae traemos traéis traen	traía traías traía traíamos traíais traían	traje trajiste trajo trajimos trajisteis trajeron	traeré traerás traerá traeremos traeréis traerán	traería traerías traería traeríamos traeríais traerían	traiga traigas traiga traigamos traigáis traigan	trajera trajeras trajera trajéramos trajerais trajeran	trae tú, no traigas traiga Ud. traigamos traigan
venir viniendo venido	vengo vienes viene venimos venís vienen	venía venías venía veníamos veníais venían	vine viniste vino vinimos vinisteis vinieron	vendré vendrás vendrá vendremos vendréis vendrán	vendría vendrías vendría vendríamos vendríais vendrían	venga vengas venga vengamos vengáis vengan	viniera vinieras viniera viniéramos vinierais vinieran	ven tú, no vengas venga Ud. vengamos vengan
ver viendo visto	veo ves ve vemos veis ven	veía veías veía veíamos veíais veían	vi viste vio vimos visteis vieron	veré verás verá veremos veréis verán	vería verías vería veríamos veríais verían	vea veas vea veamos veáis vean	viera vieras viera viéramos vierais vieran	ve tú, no veas vea Ud. veamos vean

D. Stem-Changing and Spelling Change Verbs

Infinitive Present Participle Past Participle	INDICATIVE					SUBJUNCTIVE		IMPERATIVE
	Present	Imperfect	Preterite	Future	Conditional	Present	Imperfect	
pensar (ie) pensando pensado	pienso piensas piensa pensamos pensáis piensan	pensaba pensabas pensaba pensábamos pensabais pensaban	pensé pensaste pensó pensamos pensasteis pensaron	pensaré pensarás pensará pensaremos pensaréis pensarán	pensaría pensarías pensaría pensaríamos pensaríais pensarían	piense pienses piense pensemos penséis piensen	pensara pensaras pensara pensáramos pensarais pensaran	piensa tú, no pienses piense Ud. pensemos piensen
volver (ue) volviendo vuelto	vuelvo vuelves vuelve volvemos volvéis vuelven	volvía volvías volvía volvíamos volvíais volvían	volví volviste volvió volvimos volvisteis volvieron	volveré volverás volverá volveremos volveréis volverán	volvería volverías volvería volveríamos volveríais volverían	vuelva vuelvas vuelva volvamos volváis vuelvan	volviera volvieras volviera volviéramos volvierais volvieran	vuelve tú, no vuelvas vuelva Ud. volvamos vuelvan

D. Stem-Changing and Spelling Change Verbs (continued)

Infinitive Present Participle Past Participle	INDICATIVE					SUBJUNCTIVE		IMPERATIVE
	Present	Imperfect	Preterite	Future	Conditional	Present	Imperfect	
dormir (ue, u) durmiendo dormido	duermo duermes duerme dormimos dormís duermen	dormía dormías dormía dormíamos dormíais dormían	dormí dormiste durmió dormimos dormisteis durmieron	dormiré dormirás dormirá dormiremos dormiréis dormirán	dormiría dormirías dormiría dormiríamos dormiríais dormirían	duerma duermas duerma durmamos durmáis duerman	durmiera durmieras durmiera durmiéramos durmierais durmieran	duerme tú, no duermas duerma Ud. durmamos duerman
sentir (ie, i) sintiendo sentido	siento sientes siente sentimos sentís sienten	sentía sentías sentía sentíamos sentíais sentían	sentí sentiste sintió sentimos sentisteis sintieron	sentiré sentirás sentirá sentiremos sentiréis sentirán	sentiría sentirías sentiría sentiríamos sentiríais sentirían	sienta sientas sienta sintamos sintáis sientan	sintiera sintieras sintiera sintiéramos sintierais sintieran	siente tú, no sientas sienta Ud. sintamos sientan
pedir (i, i) pidiendo pedido	pido pides pide pedimos pedís piden	pedía pedías pedía pedíamos pedíais pedían	pedí pediste pidió pedimos pedisteis pidieron	pediré pedirás pedirá pediremos pediréis pedirán	pediría pedirías pediría pediríamos pediríais pedirían	pida pidas pida pidamos pidáis pidan	pidiera pidieras pidiera pidiéramos pidierais pidieran	pide tú, no pidas pida Ud. pidamos pidan
reír (i, i) riendo reído	río ríes ríe reímos reís ríen	reía reías reía reíamos reíais reían	reí reíste rió reímos reísteis rieron	reiré reirás reirá reiremos reiréis reirán	reiría reirías reiría reiríamos reiríais reirían	ría rías ría riamos riáis rían	riera rieras riera riéramos rierais rieran	ríe tú, no rías ría Ud. riamos rían
seguir (i, i) (g) siguiendo seguido	sigo sigues sigue seguimos seguís siguen	seguía seguías seguía seguíamos seguíais seguían	seguí seguiste siguió seguimos seguisteis siguieron	seguiré seguirás seguirá seguiremos seguiréis seguirán	seguiría seguirías seguiría seguiríamos seguiríais seguirían	siga sigas siga sigamos sigáis sigan	siguiera siguieras siguiera siguiéramos siguierais siguieran	sigue tú, no sigas siga Ud. sigamos sigan
construir (y) construyendo construido	construyo construyes construye construimos construís construyen	construía construías construía construíamos construíais construían	construí construiste construyó construimos construisteis construyeron	construiré construirás construirá construiremos construiréis construirán	construiría construirías construiría construiríamos construiríais construirían	construya construyas construya construyamos construyáis construyan	construyera construyeras construyera construyéramos construyerais construyeran	construye tú, no construyas construya Ud. construyamos construyan
producir (zc) produciendo producido	produzco produces produce producimos producís producen	producía producías producía producíamos producíais producían	produje produjiste produjo produjimos produjisteis produjeron	produciré producirás producirá produciremos produciréis producirán	produciría producirías produciría produciríamos produciríais producirían	produzca produzcas produzca produzcamos produzcáis produzcan	produjera produjeras produjera produjéramos produjerais produjeran	produce tú, no produzcas produzca Ud. produzcamos produzcan

This **Spanish-English Vocabulary** contains all the words that appear in the text, with the following exceptions: (1) most close or identical cognates that do not appear in the chapter vocabulary lists; (2) most conjugated verb forms; (3) diminutives ending in **-ito/a**; (4) absolute superlatives in **-ísimo/a**; and (5) most adverbs ending in **-mente**. Active vocabulary is indicated by the number of the chapter in which a word or given meaning is first listed (P–Preliminar); vocabulary that is glossed in the text is not considered to be active vocabulary and is not numbered. Only meanings that are used in the text are given. The **English-Spanish Vocabulary** is based on the chapter lists of active vocabulary.

The gender of nouns is indicated, except for masculine nouns ending in **-o** and feminine nouns ending in **-a**. Stem changes and spelling changes are indicated for verbs: **dormir** (**ue, u**); **llegar** (**gu**). Because **ch** and **ll** are no longer considered separate letters, words beginning with **ch** and **ll** are found as they would be found in English. The letter **ñ** follows the letter **n: añadir** follows **anuncio**, for example. The following abbreviations are used:

abbrev.	abbreviation	*inf.*	infinitive	*pl.*	plural
adj.	adjective	*interj.*	interjection	*poss.*	possessive
adv.	adverb	*inv.*	invariable	*p.p.*	past participle
coll.	colloquialism	*i.o.*	indirect object	*P.R.*	Puerto Rico
conj.	conjunction	*irreg.*	irregular	*prep.*	preposition
d.o.	direct object	*L.A.*	Latin America	*pron.*	pronoun
f.	feminine	*m.*	masculine	*refl. pron.*	reflexive pronoun
fam.	familiar	*Mex.*	Mexico	*s.*	singular
fig.	figurative	*n.*	noun	*sl.*	slang
form.	formal	*obj. of a prep.*	object of a preposition	*Sp.*	Spain
gram.	grammatical term	*pers.*	personal	*sub. pron.*	subject pronoun

Spanish-English Vocabulary

A

a to (P); at (*with time*) (P); **a base de** by, based on; **a bordo de** on board; **a consecuencia de** as a result of; **a continuación** following, below; **a diferencia de** unlike; **a esas horas** at that hour; **a finales de** at the end of; **a la(s)...** at (*time*) (P); **a la derecha (de)** to the right (of) (5); **a la izquierda (de)** to the left (of) (5); **a la vez** at the same time; **a menos que** *conj.* unless (15); **a menudo** often; **a partir de** starting from; **a pesar de** in spite of; **a plazos** in installments (16); **a primera vista** at first sight (15); **a principios de** at the beginning of; **a punto de** just about to; **¿a qué hora... ?** (at) what time . . . ? (P); **a solas** alone; **a su gusto** to taste (*cooking*); **a tiempo** on time (7); **a través de** through; throughout; across; **a veces** sometimes (2); **a ver** let's see

a. C. (*abbrev. for* **antes de Cristo**) B.C. (*Before Christ*)

abajo below, underneath

abalanzarse (c) sobre to pounce on

abandonar to abandon; to leave

abandono abandonment

abierto/a *p.p.* open(ed) (5)

abogado/a lawyer (16)

abrazar (c) to embrace, hug

abrigo coat (3)

abril *m.* April (5)

abrir (*p.p.* **abierto**) to open (2)

absoluto/a absolute

absorbente absorbing

abstracto/a abstract

abuelo/a grandfather/grandmother (2); **abuelos** *m., pl.* grandparents (2)

abundancia abundance

aburrido/a bored (5); boring

aburrimiento boredom
aburrir to bore (13); **aburrirse** to get bored (9)
acabar to finish (11); to run out, use up completely (14); **acabarse** to run out of (11); **acabar de** + *inf.* to have just (*done something*) (6)
academia: Real Academia Española Royal Spanish Academy
académico/a *adj.* academic
acaso: por si acaso just in case (11)
acceso access
accidente *m.* accident (11)
acción *f.* action; **Día** (*m.*) **de Acción de Gracias** Thanksgiving
aceite *m.* oil (14); **aceite de oliva** olive oil; **filtro de aceite** oil filter
aceituna olive
acelerado/a fast, accelerated (14)
acelerar to accelerate, speed up
acento accent
aceptable acceptable
aceptar to accept
acerca de *prep.* about, concerning
aclarar to clarify
acomodarse (a) to adapt oneself (to)
acompañar to go with; to accompany
acondicionado/a: aire (*m.*) **acondicionado** air conditioning
aconsejable advisable
aconsejar to advise
acontecimiento event, happening (17)
acordarse (ue) (de) to remember (11)
acordeón *m.* accordion
acostar (ue) to put to bed; **acostarse** to go to bed (4)
acostumbrado/a (a) accustomed (to), used (to)
acostumbrar to be accustomed to
acreedor: hacerse (*irreg.*) **acreedor(a)** to be deemed worthy of
acrílico/a acrylic
actitud *f.* attitude
activar to activate
actividad *f.* activity
activo/a active
acto act
actor *m.* actor (13)
actriz *f.* (*pl.* **actrices**) actor, actress (13)
actual *adj.* current, up to date
actualidad *f.* present time
actualmente currently
actuar (actúo) to act
acuario/a Aquarius (*zodiac sign*)
acuático/a *adj.* water
acuerdo agreement; **acuerdo de paz** peace agreement; **de acuerdo** agreed, O.K..; **de acuerdo con** in accordance with; **(no) estoy de acuerdo** I (don't) agree (2); **ponerse** (*irreg.*) **de acuerdo** to reach an agreement
adaptación *f.* adaptation
adaptarse (a) to adapt (to)
adecuado/a appropriate
¡adelante! come in!
adelanto advance
adelgazar (c) to lose weight
además *adv.* moreover; **además de** *prep.* besides
adicional additional (P)
adiós good-bye (P)
adivinar to guess
adjetivo adjective (2); **adjetivo demostrativo** *gram.* demonstrative adjective; **adjetivo posesivo** *gram.* possessive adjective (2)
adjuntar to enclose, attach
administración *f.* administration; **administración de empresas** business administration (1); **administración de negocios** business administration
administrativo/a administrative
admirar to admire
adolescencia adolescence (15)
¿adónde? where (to)? (3)
adopción *f.* adoption
adoquinado/a *adj.* cobblestone
adorado/a adored
adorno ornament, decoration
aduana *s.* customs (18); **agente** (*m., f.*) **de aduana** customs agent; **derechos** (*m. pl.*) **de aduana** customs duty (18); **inspector(a) de aduanas** customs inspector (18)
adulto/a *n., adj.* adult
adverbio adverb
aéreo/a *adj.* air; **correo aéreo** airmail; **por vía aérea** by air; by airmail
aeróbico/a aerobic; **hacer** (*irreg.*) **ejercicios aeróbicos** to do aerobics (10)
aerolínea airline
aeropuerto airport (7)
afectar to affect
afectivo/a emotional
afectuoso/a affectionate
afeitarse to shave (4)
afición *f.* hobby (9)
aficionado/a (a) fan (of) (9); **ser** (*irreg.*) **aficionado/a (a)** to be a fan (of) (9)
afirmación *f.* statement
afirmar to affirm
afirmativo/a affirmative
África Africa
africano/a *adj.* African
afrocaribeño/a *adj.* Afro-Caribbean
afrocubano/a *adj.* Afro-Cuban
afuera *adv.* outside; outdoors (5); **afueras** *n. pl.* outskirts (12); suburbs (12)
agencia agency; **agencia de viajes** travel agency (7)
agenda agenda; date book
agente *m., f.* agent; **agente de aduana** customs agent; **agente de billetes** ticket agent; **agente de inmobiliaria** real estate agent; **agente de pasaportes** passport agent; **agente de viajes** travel agent (7)
agosto August (5)
agradable pleasant
agradar to please (13)
agravar to worsen
agresivo/a aggressive
agrícola *m., f.* agricultural; **trabajador(a) agrícola** agricultural worker
agricultor(a) farmer (14)
agua *f.* (*but* **el agua**) water; **agua mineral** mineral water (6); **cama de agua** water bed (4)
aguacate *m.* avocado

aguar (gü) to spoil (*a party*)
agujero hole
ahí there
ahora now (1); **ahora mismo** right now; at once
ahorrar to save (*money*) (16)
ahorros *m. pl.* savings; **cuenta de ahorros** savings account (16)
aimará *m.* Aymara (*indigenous language*)
aire *m.* aire (14); **aire acondicionado** air conditioning; **al aire libre** outdoors
aislamiento isolation (14)
ajedrez *m.* chess (4); **jugar (ue) (gu) al ajedrez** to play chess (9)
ajo garlic; **diente** (*m.*) **de ajo** garlic clove
al (*contraction of* **al** + **el**) to the (3); **al** + *inf.* upon, while, when + *verb form*; **al aire libre** outdoors; **al borde de** on the verge of; **al contado** in cash (16); **al final de** at the end of; **al fondo** in the background; **al lado de** next to (5); **al otro lado** on the other side; **al principio (de)** at the beginning (of) (16)
alabarse to congratulate oneself
álbum *m.* album
alcance *m.* reach
alcanzar (c) to reach
alce *m.* elk, moose
alcoba bedroom (4)
alcohol *m.* alcohol
alcohólico/a alcoholic
alegrarse (de) to be happy (about) (12)
alegre happy (5)
alegría happiness
alemán *m.* German (*language*) (1)
alemán, alemana *n., adj.* German (2); **pastor alemán** German shepherd (*dog*)
Alemania Germany
alergia allergy
alérgico/a allergic
alerta: ojo alerta be alert, watch out
alfabetización *f.* literacy
alfabetizado/a alphabetized
alfabeto alphabet
alfombra rug (4)
algo something (3)
algodón *m.* cotton (3); **es de algodón** it's made of cotton (3)
alguien someone, anyone (6)
algún, alguno(s)/a(s) some, any (6); **algún día** some day; **alguna vez** once; ever
alimento food
aliviar to relieve
alivio relief
allá over there; **más allá** beyond
allí (over) there (3)
alma *f.* (*but* **el alma**) soul
almacén *m.* department store (3)
almorzar (ue) (c) to have lunch (4)
almuerzo lunch (6)
alojamiento lodging (18)
alojarse to stay (*as a guest*) (18)
alquilar to rent (12)
alquiler *m.* rent (12)
alrededor de *prep.* around; **alrededores** *m. pl.* outskirts, environs
alternarse to alternate
alternativa alternative; choice
altitud *f.* altitude
alto/a tall (2); high
altura height, altitude
aluminio aluminum
amable kind, nice (2)
amado/a *adj.* beloved
amante *adj.* loving
amar to love (15)
amarillo/a yellow (3)
Amazonas *m. s.* Amazon (*river*)
ambiental environmental
ambiente *m.* environment, atmosphere; **medio ambiente** environment (14)
ámbito de lectores readership
amenazador(a) threatening
América America
americano/a *adj.* American; **fútbol** (*m.*) **americano** football (9)
amigo/a friend (1)
amistad *f.* friendship (15)
amistoso/a friendly (15)
amor *m.* love (15)
amueblado furnished; **semiamueblado/a** partly furnished
analfabetismo illiteracy
análisis *m. s., pl.* analysis
analista (*m., f.*) **de sistemas** systems analyst (16)
analizar (c) to analyze
anaranjado/a *adj.* orange (*color*) (3)
ancho/a wide; **de ancho** in width
anciano/a *n.* old person; *adj.* old
andar (*irreg.*) **en bicicleta** to ride a bicycle
andino/a *adj.* Andean
anémico/a anemic
anfitrión, anfitriona host, hostess (8)
ángel *m.* angel
anglohablante *m., f.* English speaker
animado/a lively; **dibujo animado** (film) cartoon
animarse to cheer up
ánimo: dar (*irreg.*) **ánimo** to cheer, encourage; **estado de ánimo** state of mind
anoche *adv.* last night
anotar to make a note of
ansiedad *f.* anxiety
ante before; **ante todo** first of all
anteayer the day before yesterday
antecedente *m. gram.* antecedent
antemano: de antemano beforehand
anterior previous, preceding
antes *adv.* before; **antes de** *prep.* before (4); **antes de Cristo** Before Christ (B.C.); **antes (de) que** *conj.* before (15)
antibiótico antibiotic (10)
anticipación *f.* anticipation; **con anticipación** ahead of time (18)
anticuado/a antiquated, old-fashioned
antiguo/a old, ancient
antipático/a unpleasant (2)
antónimo antonym
antropología anthropology
anualmente yearly, annually
anunciar to announce (7)
anuncio advertisement; announcement

añadir to add
año year (5); **cumplir años** to have a birthday (8); **Día** (*m.*) **de Año Nuevo** New Year's Day; **el año pasado** last year; **Feliz Año Nuevo** Happy New Year; **Prospero Año Nuevo** Happy New Year; **tener** (*irreg.*) **... años** to be . . . years old (2)
apagar (gu) to turn off (*light*)
aparato appliance (9); **aparato doméstico** home appliance (9); **aparato electrónico** electronic device
aparcamiento parking
aparcar (qu) to park
aparecer (zc) to appear
aparentemente apparently
apariencia appearance
apartamento apartment (1); **casa (bloque** [*m.*]**) de apartamentos** apartment building (12)
aparte *adv.* apart; **aparte de** aside from
apasionado/a passionate
apellido last name, surname
apenas hardly any; barely
apendicitis *f. s.* appendicitis
aperitivo appetizer; aperitif
apiñado/a crammed or packed together
aplazado/a postponed
aplicar (qu) to apply
apoyar to support (17)
apoyo support; **fondos** (*m. pl.*) **de apoyo** economic support
apreciar to appreciate (13)
aprecio: hacer (*irreg.*) **aprecio de** to appreciate
aprender to learn (2)
apropiado/a appropriate
aprovechar to make use of, take advantage of
aproximadamente approximately
apuntar to write down
apunte *m.* note; **tomar apuntes** to take notes
apurarse to hurry
aquel, aquella *adj.* that (*over there*) (3)
aquél, aquélla *pron.* that one (*over there*)
aquello that (*thing*) (over there) (3)
aquellos/as *adj.* those (*over there*) (3)
aquéllos/as *pron.* those (ones) (*over there*)
aquí here (1)
árabe *m.* Arabic (*language*); **árabe** *m., f. n.* Arab; *m., f. adj.* Arabic
Arabia Saudita Saudi Arabia
árbol *m.* tree (14)
archivo (computer) file (12)
ardilla squirrel
área *f.* (*but* **el área**) area (12)
arena sand
arete *m.* earring (3)
argentino/a *n., adj.* Argentinian
argumento reasoning; argument
árido/a arid, dry
armado/a armed
armario closet (4)
arqueológico/a archeological
arqueólogo/a archeologist
arquitecto/a architect (13)
arquitectónico/a architectural
arquitectura architecture (13)
arrancar (qu) to start (*a motor*) (14)
arreglar to straighten (up) (12); to fix, repair (12)
arrogante arrogant
arrollador(a) overwhelming
arroz *m.* rice (6)
arruinado/a ruined
arte *f.* (*but* **el arte**) art (1); **obra de arte** work of art (13)
artesanía arts and crafts (13)
artesano/a artisan, craftsperson
artículo article; **artículo definido** *gram.* definite article
artificial artificial; **fuegos** (*m. pl.*) **artificiales** fireworks
artista *m., f.* artist (13)
artístico/a artistic (13)
arveja pea (6)
arzobispo archbishop
asado/a roast(ed) (6)
ascensor *m.* elevator
asco: dar (*irreg.*) **asco** to make sick
asegurar to assure; **asegurarse** to make sure
asequible available
asesinado/a assassinated
asesinato assassination (17)
así thus, so; **así como** as well as; like; **así que** therefore, consequently
asiático/a *adj.* Asian
asiento seat (7)
asimilarse to assimilate
asistente *m., f.* assistant; **asistente de vuelo** flight attendant (7)
asistir (a) to attend, go to (*a function*) (2)
asma *f.* (*but* **el asma**) asthma
asociación *f.* association
asociado/a associated; **estado libre asociado** free associated state
asociar to associate
aspecto appearance; aspect
aspiradora vacuum cleaner (9); **pasar la aspiradora** to vacuum (9)
aspirante *m., f.* candidate (16); applicant (16)
aspirina aspirin
astronauta *m., f.* astronaut
asumir to assume
asunto matter, question
atacar (qu) to attack
ataque *m.* attack
atar to tie
atención *f.* attention
atender (ie) to attend to; to serve
atlántico: Océano Atlántico Atlantic Ocean
atleta *m., f.* athlete
atracción *f.* attraction; **parque** (*m.*) **de atracciones** amusement park
atractivo/a attractive
atraer (*like* **traer**) to attract
atrasado/a: estar (*irreg.*) **atrasado** to be late (7)
atrevido/a daring
atribuir (y) (a) to attribute (to)
atún *m.* tuna (6)
audición (*f.*) **de reparto** casting call
aumentar to increase, raise
aumento increase; raise (12); **aumento de sueldo** raise (16)
aun *adv.* even
aún *adv.* still, yet

aunque although
auscultar to listen (*medical*)
australiano/a *adj.* Australian
auténtico/a authentic
auto car
autobiografía autobiography
autobiográfico/a autobiographical
autobús *m.* bus (7); **estación** (*f.*) **de autobuses** bus station (7); **ir** (*irreg.*) **en autobús** to go by bus; **parada de autobús** bus stop (18)
autocontrol *m.* self-control
autoestima self-esteem
automático/a: cajero automático automatic teller machine (16); **contestador** (*m.*) **automático** answering machine (12)
automóvil *m.* automobile
automovilístico/a *adj.* automobile
autopista freeway; highway (14)
autor(a) author
autoridad *f.* authority
autostop: hacer (*irreg.*) **autostop** to hitchhike
avance *m.* advance
avanzado/a advanced
ave *m.* bird
avenida avenue (12)
aventura adventure
aventurero/a adventurous
avergonzado/a embarrassed (8)
averiguar (gü) to find out
avestruz *m.* (*pl.* **avestruces**) ostrich
avión *m.* airplane (7); **ir** (*irreg.*) **en avión** to go by plane
avisar to warn
aviso warning
ayer yesterday; **ayer fue (miércoles)** yesterday was (Wednesday) (4)
ayuda help
ayudar to help (6)
azteca *m., f. n., adj.* Aztec
azúcar *m.* sugar
azul blue (3)

B

bacán: ¡qué bacán! *sl.* cool!
bailable danceable
bailar to dance (1)
bailarín, bailarina dancer (13)
baile *m.* dance (13)
bajar to carry down; **bajar (de)** to get down (from) (7); to get off (of) (7)
bajo *prep.* under; **bajo/a** *adj.* short (*height*) (2); low; **planta baja** ground floor (12)
balancear to balance
balboa *unit of currency of Panama*
ballet *m.* ballet (13)
banana banana (6)
bancarrota bankruptcy
banco bank (16)
bandoneón *m.* large concertina (*music*)
bañar to bathe; **bañarse** to take a bath (4)
bañera bathtub (4)
baño bathroom (4); **habitación** (*f.*) **con/sin baño** room with(out) bath (18); **traje** (*m.*) **de baño** swimsuit (3)
bar *m.* bar; **ir** (*irreg.*) **a un bar** to go to a bar (9)
barato/a inexpensive, cheap (3)
barbacoa barbecue
barbería barbershop
barbero barber
barcaza barge, ship
barco boat, ship (7); **ir** (*irreg.*) **en barco** to go by boat
barrer (el piso) to sweep (the floor) (9)
barrera barrier
barrio neighborhood (12); **fiesta de barrio** neighborhood (block) party
basado/a en based on
base *f.* base, foundation; **a base de** by, based on
basquetbol *m.* basketball (9)
bastante *adv.* rather, sufficiently (15); enough (15)
basura trash; **sacar (qu) la basura** to take out the trash (9)
bata robe, bathrobe
batalla battle
batería battery (14)
batido *drink similar to a milkshake* (18)
bautismo baptism
bebé *m.* baby
beber to drink (2)
bebida drink, beverage (6)
béisbol *m.* baseball (9)
beisbolista *m., f.* baseball player
Bélgica Belgium
Belice *m.* Belize
belleza beauty
bello/a beautiful (14)
berenjena eggplant
biblioteca library (1)
bibliotecario/a librarian (1)
bicicleta (de montaña) (mountain) bicycle (12); **montar/andar** (*irreg.*) **en bicicleta** to ride a bicycle; **pasear en bicicleta** to ride a bicycle (9)
biculturalismo biculturalism
bien *adv.* well (P); **caerle** (*irreg.*) **bien a alguien** to make a good impression on someone (16); **estar** (*irreg.*) **bien** to be comfortable (*temperature*) (5); **llevarse bien (con)** to get along well (with) (15); **muy bien** very well, fine (P); **pasarlo bien** to have a good time (8); **salir** (*irreg.*) **bien** to turn out well
bienestar *m.* well-being (10)
bilingüe bilingual
bilingüismo bilingualism
billete *m.* ticket (7); **agente** (*m., f.*) **de billetes** ticket agent; **billete de ida** one-way ticket (7); **billete de ida y vuelta** round-trip ticket (7)
billón trillion
biodiversidad *f.* biodiversity
biología biology
biólogo/a biologist
bisonte *m.* bison
bistec *m.* steak (6)
blanco/a white (3); **vino blanco** white wine (6)
bloque (*m.*) **de apartamentos** apartment building (12)
blusa blouse (3)
bobo/a dumb, stupid
boca mouth (10)
boda wedding (15)
boicoteo boycott, boycotting

boleto ticket (7); **boleto de ida** one-way ticket (7); **boleto de ida y vuelta** round-trip ticket (7)
bolígrafo ballpoint pen (1)
bolívar *m. monetary unit of Venezuela*
boliviano/a *adj.* Bolivian
bolsa purse (3)
bolsillo pocket
bomba light bulb; **la bomba y la plena** *dance and music from the Caribbean*
bombardeo bombardment
bombero/a firefighter
bondadoso/a kind; good-hearted
bonito/a pretty (2)
borde (*m.*)**: al borde de** on the verge of
bordo: a bordo de on board
boricua *m., f. n.* Puerto Rican (*from the indigenous language of Puerto Rico*)
Borinquen *f. indigenous name for Puerto Rico*
bosque *m.* forest (14)
bota boot (3)
botella bottle
botones *m. s., pl.* bellhop (18)
brasileño/a *adj.* Brazilian
bravo/a brave; fierce
bravura bravery; fierceness
brazo arm (11)
breve *adj.* brief
brindar to offer (*a toast*)
bronce *m.* bronze
bronceado/a tanned
bronquitis *f.* bronchitis
bruja witch
brujo magician
bucanero/a buccaneer, pirate
bucear to scuba dive; to snorkel
buen, bueno/a *adj.* good (2); **buen viaje** have a good trip (7); **buenas noches** good evening/night (P); **buenas tardes** good afternoon (P); **buenos días** good morning (P); **de buen gusto** in good taste; **hace buen tiempo** it's good weather (5); **lo bueno** the good thing, news (10); what's good; **muy buenas** good afternoon/evening (P); **sacar (qu) buenas notas** to get good grades
bueno *interj.* well (2)
bullicioso/a lively
burbuja bubble
burocracia bureaucracy
burocrático/a bureaucratic
burro burro, donkey
busca: en busca de in search of (16)
buscar (qu) to look for (1)
búsqueda search
butaca seat (*in a theater*)

C

caballo horse; **montar a caballo** to ride a horse (9)
cabeza head (10); **dolor** (*m.*) **de cabeza** headache
cabezota *m., f. adj., n.* stubborn
cabezudo/a stubborn
cabina cabin (*on a ship*) (7); **cabina telefónica** telephone booth
cabo: llevar a cabo to carry out
cacique *m.* chief
cada *inv.* each, every (4)
cadena chain
cadera hip (*anatomy*)
caer *irreg.* to fall (11); **caerle bien/mal a alguien** to make a good/bad impression (16); **caerse** to fall down (11)
café *m.* café (18); coffee (1)
cafeína caffeine
cafetera coffeepot (9)
cafetería cafeteria (1)
caída fall
caja box
cajero/a cashier (16); teller (16); **cajero automático** automatic teller machine (16)
cajón *m.* drawer
cakchiquel *m. indigenous language*
calcetín *m.* (*pl.* **calcetines**) sock (3)
calculadora calculator (1)
cálculo calculus; calculation
calendario calendar (11)
calentar (ie) to heat up
calidad *f.* quality
cálido/a hot
caliente hot
calificación *f.* grade (11)
calle *f.* street (12)
calma calm
calmarse to calm down
calor *m.* heat; **hace calor** it's hot (*weather*) (5); **tener** (*irreg.*) **(mucho) calor** to be (very) warm, hot (*feeling*) (5)
caloría calorie
cama (de agua) (water) bed (4); **guardar cama** to stay in bed (10); **hacer** (*irreg.*) **la cama** to make the bed (9)
cámara (de video) (video) camera (12)
camarero/a waiter/waitress (6)
camarón *m.* (*pl.* **camarones**) shrimp (6)
cambiante *adj.* changing
cambiar (de) to change (12)
cambio change; **en cambio** on the other hand
caminar to walk (10)
camino street, road (14); **en camino** on the way
camioneta station wagon (7)
camisa shirt (3)
camiseta T-shirt (3)
campaña campaign; **tienda de campaña** tent (7)
campeonato championship
campesino/a farm worker (14); peasant (14)
camping *m.* campground (7); **hacer** (*irreg.*) ***camping*** to go camping (7)
campo countryside (12)
campus *m. s.* (university) campus (12)
Canadá *m.* Canada
canadiense *m., f. n.* Canadian
canal *m.* canal; channel (12)
cancelar to cancel
cáncer *m.* cancer
cancha court (*sports*); field (*sports*)
canción *f.* song (13)
candidato/a candidate
cansado/a tired (5)

cansarse to tire, get tired
cantante *m., f.* singer (13)
cantar to sing (1)
capa de ozono ozone layer (14)
capaz (*pl.* **capaces**) able, capable
capital *f.* capital city (5)
capítulo chapter
capricornio Capricorn
cara face
característica *n.* characteristic
caracterizar (c) to characterize
cardinal: punto cardinal cardinal direction (5)
cargar (gu) to charge (*to an account*) (16)
cargo post; charge; **estar** (*irreg.*) **a cargo de** to be in control of, be in charge of
Caribe *m. n.* Caribbean
caribeño/a *adj.* Caribbean
cariño affection
cariñoso/a affectionate (5)
carne *f.* meat (6)
carnet (*m.*) **de conducir/chofer** driver's license
caro/a expensive (3)
carpintero/a carpenter
carrera career; major (*academic*); studies
carretera highway (14)
carro (descapotable) (convertible) car (12)
carta letter (2); **jugar (ue) (gu) a las cartas** to play cards (9); **papel** (*m.*) **para cartas** stationery (18)
cartel *m.* poster
cartera wallet (3)
cartón *m.* cardboard
casa house, home (2); **casa de apartamentos** apartment building (12); **en casa** at home (1); **limpiar la casa (entera)** to clean the (whole) house (9); **regresar a casa** to go home (1)
casado/a married (2)
casarse (con) to marry (15)
cascanueces *m. s., pl.* nutcracker
casi almost; **casi nunca** almost never; hardly ever (2)
caso case; **en caso de que** *conj.* in case (15)
castellano/a Castilian
castigar (gu) to punish (17)
catalán *m.* Catalan (*language spoken in northeastern Spain*)
catálogo catalogue
Cataluña Catalonia (*region of northeastern Spain*)
catarata waterfall
catastrófico/a catastrophic
catedral *f.* cathedral
categoría category
católico/a *n., adj.* Catholic
catorce fourteen (P)
causa cause
causar to cause
cazador(a) hunter
CD-ROM *m.* CD-ROM (12)
cebiche *m. raw fish marinated in lemon juice*
cebolla onion
cebra zebra
ceder to cede
celebración *f.* celebration
celebrar to celebrate (5)
celular: teléfono celular cellular telephone (12)
cementerio cemetery
cena supper, dinner (6)
cenar to have (eat) dinner (6)
censo census
centavo cent
centrico/a central
centro center; downtown (3); **centro comercial** shopping mall (3)
Centroamérica Central America
centroamericano/a *n., adj.* Central American
cepillarse los dientes to brush one's teeth (4)
cerámica pottery, ceramics (13)
cerca de *prep.* close to (5)
cercano/a close, near
cerdo pork; **chuleta de cerdo** pork chop (6)
cereales *m. pl.* cereal (6)
cerebro brain (10)
ceremonia ceremony
cerilla match (*for lighting things*)
cero zero (P)
cerrado/a closed (5)
cerrar (ie) to close (4)
cerro hill
cervantino/a *pertaining to Cervantes*
cerveza beer (1)
césped: cortar el césped to cut the grass
ceta *the letter z*
ceviche *m. raw fish marinated in lemon juice*
champán *m.* champagne
champiñón *m.* mushroom (6)
champú *m.* shampoo (18)
chaqueta jacket (3)
charlar to chat
cheque *m.* (bank) check (16); **cheque de viajero** traveler's check (18); **con cheque** by check (16)
chequeo check-up (10)
¡chévere! *coll.* cool!, great! (*Caribbean*)
chico/a boy/girl
chileno/a *n., adj.* Chilean
chimpancé *m.* chimpanzee
chino *n.* Chinese (*language*)
Chipre *m.* Cyprus
chiste *m.* joke (8)
chistoso/a amusing
chocar (qu) (con) to run into, collide (with) (14)
chocolate *m.* chocolate
chofer *m.* driver, chauffeur; **carnet** (*m.*) **de chofer** driver's license
choque *m.* collision (17)
chuleta (de cerdo) (pork) chop (6)
ciberespacio cyberspace
ciclismo bicycling (9)
ciego/a blind
cielo sky; *fig.* dear
cien, ciento one hundred (2); **por ciento** percent
ciencia science (1)
científico/a *n.* scientific
cierto/a certain (13); true
cigarillo cigarette
cilantro cilantro, fresh coriander
cinco five (P); **Cinco de Mayo** Cinco de Mayo

cincuenta fifty (2)
cine *m.* movies (4); movie theater (4); **ir** (*irreg.*) **al cine** to go to the movies (9)
cineasta *m., f.* film producer, film maker
cinta tape (3)
cinturón *m.* (*pl.* **cinturones**) belt (3)
circo circus
circulación *f.* traffic (14)
circular to circulate
circunstancia circumstance
cisne *m.* swan
cita date, appointment (15)
citado/a quoted
ciudad *f.* city (2)
ciudadano/a citizen (17)
ciudadela citadel
cívico/a civic (17)
civilización *f.* civilization
clarinete *m.* clarinet
claro/a clear; **claro (que sí)** *interj.* of course
clase *f.* class (1); **clase turística** tourist class (7); **compañero/a de clase** classmate (1); **primera clase** first class (7); **sala de clase** classroom
clásico/a classic(al) (13)
cláusula *gram.* clause
cliente *m., f.* client, customer (1)
clima *m.* climate (5)
climatología climatology
clínica clinic
club *m.* club
cobrar to cash (*a check*) (16); to charge (*someone for an item or service*) (16)
coche (*m.*) **(descapotable)** (convertible) car (2); **teléfono de coche** car phone (12)
cochera one- or two-car garage
cocina kitchen (4); cuisine
cocinar to cook (6)
cocinero/a cook; chef (16)
coctel *m.* cocktail
cognado *gram.* cognate (6)
coherente coherent
coincidir to coincide
cola line (*of people*); **hacer** (*irreg.*) **cola** to stand in line (7)
colección *f.* collection
colegio secondary school
colesterol *m.* cholesterol
colgar (ue) (gu) to hang
colombiano/a *n., adj.* Colombian
colón *m. monetary unit of Costa Rica*
colonia colony
colonialismo colonialism
colonización *f.* colonization
colonizar (c) to colonize
color *m.* color (3)
columna column
columnista *m., f.* columnist
combatir to fight
combinar to combine
comedor *m.* dining room (4)
comentar to comment on
comentario comment, commentary
comenzar (ie) (c) to begin
comer to eat (2); **comérselo** to eat something up
comercial commercial; **centro comercial** shopping mall (3)
comerciante *m., f.* merchant, shopkeeper (16)
cómico/a funny; **tira cómica** cartoon strip
comida food (6); meal (6)
comisión *f.* commission
comité *m.* committee
como like; as; **así como** as well as; **tal(es) como** such as; **tan... como** as . . . as (5); **tan pronto como** as soon as (16); **tanto como** as much as (5); **tanto/a(s)... como** as much/many . . . as (5)
¿cómo? how? (P); what? (P); **¿cómo es usted?** what are you like? (P); **¿cómo está(s)?** how are you? (P); **¿cómo te llamas?/¿cómo se llama usted?** what's your name? (P)
cómoda dresser, bureau (4)
cómodo/a comfortable (4)
compacto: disco compacto compact disk (12)
compañero/a friend; companion; **compañero/a de clase** classmate (1); **compañero/a de cuarto** roommate (1)
compañía company; **compañía de difusión** broadcasting company
comparación *f.* comparison (5)
comparar to compare
comparativo *n. gram.* comparative
compartir to share
compasión *f.* compassion
compendio de datos summary file
compensar to compensate, make up for
competición *f.* competition
complejo/a complex
complementario/a complementary
complemento directo *gram.* direct object pronoun; **complemento indirecto** indirect object pronoun
completar to complete
completo/a complete; full, no vacancy (18); **de tiempo completo** full-time (job) (11); **pensión** (*f.*) **completa** room and full board (18); **por completo** completely
complicar (qu) to complicate
componer (*like* **poner**) to compose
comportamiento behavior
composición *f.* composition
compositor(a) composer (13)
compra: hacer (*irreg.*) **la compra** to shop
comprar to buy (1)
compras: de compras shopping (3); **ir** (*irreg.*) **de compras** to go shopping (3)
comprender to understand (2)
comprensión *f.* comprehension
comprensivo/a *adj.* understanding
compromiso commitment
computación *f.* computer science (1)
computadora computer (*L.A.*) (12); **computadora portátil** laptop computer; **disco de computadora** computer disk (12)
común common; **sentido común** common sense
comunicación *f.* communication; *pl.* communications (1); **medio de**

disco disk; **disco compacto** compact disk (12); **disco de computadora** computer disk (12); **disco duro** hard drive (12)
discoteca discotheque; **ir** (*irreg.*) **a una discoteca** to go to a disco (9)
discriminación *f.* discrimination (17)
disculpa: pedir (i, i) disculpas to apologize (11)
discúlpame pardon me, I'm sorry (11)
discutir (sobre) (con) to argue (about) (with) (8)
diseñador(a) designer
diseñar to design
diseño design
disfraz (*m.*)**: fiesta de disfraz** costume party
disfrutar (de) to enjoy
disminuir (y) to diminish, lessen
disparar to shoot
disponible available
disputa dispute
distancia distance
distante distant
distinguido/a distinguished
distinto/a different
distraer (*like* **traer**) to distract
distraído/a absentminded (11)
distrito district
diversidad *f.* diversity
diversión *f.* entertainment, amusement (9)
diverso/a diverse; *pl.* various
divertido/a fun; **ser** (*irreg.*) **divertido/a** to be fun (9)
divertir (ie) to entertain; **divertirse** to enjoy oneself, have a good time (4)
divorciado/a divorced
divorciarse (de) to get divorced (from) (15)
divorcio divorce (15)
divulgar (gu) to divulge, disclose
doblar to dub; to bend; to turn (14)
doble double (18); **habitación** (*f.*) **doble** double room (18)
doce twelve (P)
docena dozen
doctor(a) doctor
doctorado doctorate
documentar to document
documento document
dólar *m.* dollar
doler (ue) to hurt, ache (10)
dolor *m.* pain, ache (10); **dolor de cabeza, estómago, muela** headache, stomachache, toothache; **tener** (*irreg.*) **dolor (de)** to have a pain (in) (10)
doméstico/a domestic; **aparato doméstico** home appliance (9); **quehacer** (*m.*) **doméstico** household chore (9); **tarea doméstica** household chore
domingo Sunday (4)
dominicano/a *n., adj.* Dominican
dominio power; control
don *m. title of respect used with a man's first name*
donde where
¿dónde? where? (P); **¿de dónde es Ud.?** where are you from? (2)
dondequiera wherever
doña *f. title of respect used with a woman's first name*
dormir (ue, u) to sleep (4); **dormir la siesta** to take a nap (4); **dormirse** to fall asleep (4)
dormitorio bedroom
dos two (P); **dos veces** twice (10)
doscientos/as two hundred (3)
drama *m.* drama (13)
dramatizar (c) to dramatize
dramaturgo/a playwright (13)
droga drug
dromedario dromedary, camel
dualidad *f.* duality
ducha shower (18); **habitación** (*f.*) **con/sin ducha** room with(out) a shower (18)
ducharse to take a shower (4)
duda doubt; **no hay duda** there is no doubt; **sin duda** without a doubt
dudar to doubt (12)
dudoso/a doubtful
dueño/a landlord/landlady (12); owner (6)
dulce *m.* sweet, candy (6); *adj.* sweet
durante during (4)
durar to last (17)
duro/a hard; **disco duro** hard drive (12)

E

e and (*used instead of* **y** *before words beginning with stressed* **i** *or* **hi**)
ecología ecology
ecológico/a ecological
economía economy (1)
económico/a economical, economic
economizar (c) to economize (16)
ecoturismo ecoturism
ecuatoriano/a *n., adj.* Ecuadorian
edad *f.* age; **edad límite** minimum age; **menor** (*m., f.*) **de edad** minor
edificio building (1)
editor(a) editor
educación *f.* education
educativo/a educational
efectivo cash (16); **en efectivo** in cash (16)
efecto effect
eficiencia efficiency
eficiente efficient
Egipto Egypt
egocéntrico/a egocentric
egoísta *m., f.* selfish
ejemplar *m.* issue (*of a magazine*)
ejemplicar (qu) to exemplify
ejemplo example; **por ejemplo** for example (11)
ejercer (z) to practice (*a profession*)
ejercicio exercise (3); **hacer** (*irreg.*) **ejercicios** to exercise (4); **hacer** (*irreg.*) **ejercicios aeróbicos** to do aerobics (10)
ejército army (17)
el *def. art. m.* the; **el hecho de que** the fact that; **el primero de** first of (*the month*) (5)
él *sub. pron.* he (1); *obj. of a prep.* him
elaborar to make, craft
elección *f.* election
electricidad *f.* electricity
electricista *m., f.* electrician (16)
eléctrico/a electric (14)

estimulante stimulating
estimular to stimulate
esto *dem. pron. neuter* this (3)
estómago stomach (10); **dolor** (*m.*) **de estómago** stomachache
estos/as *dem. adj.* these (2)
éstos/as *dem. pron.* these (ones)
estoy de acuerdo I agree (2); **no estoy de acuerdo** I don't agree (2)
estrategia strategy
estrecho/a narrow
estrés *m.* stress (11)
estricto/a strict
estudiante *m., f.* student (1)
estudiantil *adj.* student (11)
estudiar to study (1)
estudio study; **estudios graduados** graduate studies
estudioso/a studious
estufa stove (9)
estupendo/a stupendous
etapa stage (15)
étnico/a ethnic
euro euro (*unit of currency for countries in the European Union*)
Europa Europe
europeo/a *n., adj.* European
evento event (17)
evitar to avoid (14)
evolución *f.* evolution
exacto/a exact
examen *m.* test, exam (3)
examinar to examine (10)
exceder to exceed
excelente excellent
excepción *f.* exception
excepto *prep.* except
exceso excess
exclusivo/a exclusive
excursión *f.* excursion
excusa excuse
exhibición *f.* exhibition
exigente *adj.* demanding
exigir (j) to demand
exiliarse to be exiled
existencia existence
existir to exist
éxito success
exitoso/a successful
éxodo exodus
exótico/a exotic
expectativa expectation
experiencia experience
experimento experiment
experto/a *n., adj.* expert
explicación *f.* explanation
explicar (qu) to explain (7)
explorar to explore
explotación *f.* exploitation
exportación *f.* export
exposición *f.* exhibition
expresar to express
expresión *f.* expression; **saludos y expresiones de cortesía** greetings and expressions of courtesy (P)
expreso/a precise; clear
expuesto/a (*p.p. of* **exponer**) exposed
expulsar to expel
expulsión *f.* expulsion
extendido/a extended
extenso/a spacious
extranjero *n.* abroad (18); **ir** (*irreg.*) **al extranjero** to go abroad, overseas (18); **extranjero/a** *n.* foreigner (1); *adj.* foreign; **lenguas extranjeras** foreign languages (1)
extraño/a strange (13); **es extraño** it's strange (13); **¡qué extraño!** how strange! (13)
extraordinario/a extraordinary
extravagante extravagant
extremo end, tip
extroversión *f.* extroversion
extrovertido/a extroverted
exuberancia exuberance
exuberante exuberant

F

fábrica factory (14)
fabuloso/a fabulous
fácil easy (5)
facilidad *f.* ease; facility
facilitar to facilitate
factible feasible
factura bill, invoice (16)
facturar to check (*baggage*) (7)
facultad *f.* faculty; campus; department (*of a university*)
facultado/a authorized
falda skirt (3)
fallar to "crash" (*computer*) (12)
falsificado/a forged
falso/a false
falta lack, absence (14); **falta de flexibilidad** lack of flexibility (11); **sin falta** without fail
faltar to be absent, lacking (8)
familia family (2)
familiar *m., f. n.* relative, family member; *adj.* family, *pertaining to the family*
famoso/a famous
fantasía fantasy
fantástico/a fantastic
farmacéutico/a pharmacist (10)
farmacia pharmacy (10)
farmacología pharmacology
faro lighthouse
fascinante fascinating
fatal fateful
fatiga fatigue
favor *m.* favor; **por favor** please (P)
favorecer (zc) to favor
favorito/a favorite
fax *m. s., pl.* fax (12)
febrero February (5)
fecha date (*calendar*) (5); **¿cuál es la fecha de hoy?** what is the date today? (5); **fecha límite** deadline (11)
¡felicitaciones! *f. pl.* congratulations! (8)
feliz (*pl.* **felices**) happy (8); **Feliz Año Nuevo** Happy New Year; **feliz cumpleaños** happy birthday; **Feliz Navidad** Merry Christmas
femenino/a feminine
feminidad *f.* femininity
fenómeno phenomenon
feo/a ugly (2)
feriado/a: día (*m.*) **feriado** holiday
feroz (*pl.* **feroces**) fierce
ferroviario/a *adj.* railroad
fértil fertile
festividad *f.* festivity
festivo/a: día (*m.*) **festivo** holiday (8)
ficción *f.* fiction

ficticio/a fictional
fiebre *f.* fever (10); **tener** (*irreg.*) **fiebre** to have a fever
fiel faithful (2)
fiesta party (1); **dar** (*irreg.*)/**hacer** (*irreg.*) **una fiesta** to give/have a party (8); **fiesta de barrio** neighborhood (block) party; **fiesta de disfraz** costume party; **Fiesta de las Luces** Hanukkah
figura figure
fijarse en to take note of, notice
fijo/a: precio fijo fixed (set) price (3)
filmación *f.* filming
filmar to film
filosofía philosophy (1)
filtro filter; **filtro de aceite** oil filter
fin *m.* end; **en fin** in short; **fin de semana** weekend (1); **por fin** finally, at last (4); **sin fines de lucro** not-for-profit; **sin fines lucrativos** non-profit
final *m.* end; **a finales de** at the end of; **al final de** at the end of; *adj.* final; last
financiación *f.* financing
financiero/a financial
finanza finance
finca farm (14)
Finlandia Finland
fino/a fine, elegant
firmar to sign
física *f. s.* physics (1)
físico/a physical
flan *m.* baked custard (6)
flauta flute
flexibilidad *f.* flexibility (11); **falta de flexibilidad** lack of flexibility (11)
flexible flexible (11); **ser** (*irreg.*) **flexible** to be flexible (11)
flor *f.* flower (7)
florecer (zc) to flourish
flota fleet
folclore *m.* folklore
folklórico/a folkloric (13)
fondo bottom, back; *pl.* funds; **al fondo** in the background; **fondos de apoyo** economic support
fontanero/a plumber (*Sp.*)
forjar to forge
forma form (3); shape
formación *f.* formation
formar to form; **formar parte** to make up
formular to formulate
formulario form (*to fill out*) (18)
fósforo match (*for lighting things*) (18)
foto(grafía) *f.* photo(graph) (7); **sacar (qu) fotos** to take pictures
fotografía photography
fotográfico/a: equipo fotográfico photography equipment (12)
fotógrafo/a photographer (16)
frágil fragile
fragmento fragment
francés *m. n.* French (*language*) (1); **francés, francesa** *n., adj.* French (2)
Francia France
franqueo postage
frase *f.* phrase
frecuencia frequency; **con frecuencia** frequently (1)
frecuente frequent
freno brake (14)
fresco/a fresh (6); cool; **hace fresco** it's cool (*weather*) (5)
frialdad *f.* coldness
frigidez *f.* frigidity
frijol *m.* bean (6)
frío *n.* cold(ness); **hace frío** it's cold (*weather*) (5); **tener** (*irreg.*) **(mucho) frío** to be (very) cold (5); **frío/a** *adj.* cold
frito/a fried (6); **patata frita** French-fried potato (*Sp.*) (6)
frontera *n.* border (18)
fronterizo/a *adj.* border
frustrado/a frustrated
fruta fruit (6); **jugo de fruta** fruit juice (6)
fue: ayer fue yesterday was (4); **fue sin querer** it was unintentional (11)
fuegos artificiales *m. pl.* fireworks
fuente *f.* source
fuera *adv.* outside; **fuera de** *prep.* outside of
fuerte strong (6); heavy (*meal, food*) (6)
fuerza strength; force
fumar to smoke (7); **sección** (*f.*) **de (no) fumar** (no) smoking section (7)
función *f.* function
funcionar to work, function (12); to run (*machine*) (12)
fundación *f.* foundation
fundar to found
furioso/a furious, angry (5)
furtivamente furtively
fútbol *m.* soccer (9); **fútbol americano** football (9)
futuro *n.* future
futuro/a *adj.* future

G

gafas *f. pl.* (eye)glasses (10)
gallego Galician (*language spoken in the northwest of Spain*)
galleta cookie (6)
gana: dar (*irreg.*) **la gana** to feel like; **tener** (*irreg.*) **ganas de** + *inf.* to feel like (*doing something*) (3)
ganador(a) winner
ganar to win (9); to earn
ganga bargain (3)
garaje *m.* garage (4)
garganta throat (10)
gas *m.* gas (12); heat (12)
gasolina gasoline (14); **estación** (*f.*) **de gasolina** gas station (14)
gasolinera gas station (14)
gastar to spend (*money*) (8); to use, expend (14)
gasto expense (12)
gato/a cat (2)
Géminis *m.* Gemini
generación *f.* generation
general general; **en general** in general; **por lo general** generally, in general (4)
generalización *f.* generalization
generoso/a generous
génesis *m.* genesis; beginning(s)
genio/a genius
gente *f. s.* people (15)

mil one thousand (3); **mil millón** one billion
milagro miracle
milenio millennium
militar: servicio militar military service (17)
millón one million (3); **mil millón** one billion
mineral: agua (*f., but* **el agua**) **mineral** mineral water (6)
minero/a *adj.* mining
minidiálogo minidialogue
minifalda miniskirt
mínimo minimum
ministro/a minister; **primer(a) ministro/a** prime minister
minoría minority
minuto *n.* minute (*time*)
mío/a(s) *poss. adj.* my, (of) mine
mirar to look at, watch (2); **mirar la televisión** to watch television (2)
misa mass (*church service*); **oficiar una misa** to celebrate mass
misión *f.* mission
mismo/a self; same (10); **ahora mismo** right now; **lo mismo** the same thing
misquito *indigenous language spoken in Nicaragua*
misterioso/a mysterious
mitad *f.* half
mito myth
mitología mythology
mixteca *m., f. n.* Mixtec (*person*); **mixteca** *n. m.* Mixtec (*language*)
mochila backpack (1)
moda fashion; **de última moda** the latest style (3)
modelo *n.* model
módem *m.* modem (12)
moderado/a moderate
moderno/a modern (13)
módico/a moderate, reasonable
modificar (qu) to modify
modismo idiom
modo way, means; *gram.* mood; **de modo** in such a way; **de todos modos** anyway
molestar to bother, annoy; **me (te, le, ...) molesta** it bothers me (you, him, . . .) (13)
molestia bother, annoyance
momento moment; **por el momento** at this time
monarquía monarchy
moneda currency; coin
monoparental *adj.* single-parent
monopatín *m.* skateboard (12)
monstruo monster
montaña mountain (7); **bicicleta de montaña** mountain bicycle (12)
montar to set up; **montar a caballo** to ride a horse (9); **montar en bicicleta** to ride a bicycle; **montar en tabla de vela** to windsurf
montón *m.* bunch
monumento monument
morado/a purple (3)
moralidad *f.* morality
moreno/a brunet(te) (2)
morir(se) (ue, u) (*p.p.* **muerto**) to die (8)
mosca fly
mostrador *m.* counter
mostrar (ue) to show (7)
motivo motive
moto(cicleta) *f.* motorcycle (12)
motor *m.* motor
movimiento movement
mozo bellhop (18)
muchacho/a boy/girl (4)
mucho *adv.* much (1); a lot (1); **mucho/a** *adj.* a lot (2); *pl.* many (2); **muchas gracias** thank you very much (P); **mucho gusto** nice to meet you (P)
mudarse to move (*residence*) (16)
muebles *m., pl.* furniture (4); **sacudir los muebles** to dust the furniture (9)
muela: dolor (*m.*) **de muela** toothache; **sacar (qu) una muela** to extract a tooth (10)
muerte *f.* death (15)
muerto/a *n.* dead person; **Día** (*m.*) **de los Muertos** Day of the Dead; *adj.* (*p.p. of* **morir**) dead
muestra sample
mujer *f.* woman (1); wife (15); **mujer de negocios** businesswoman (16); **mujer policía** policewoman; **mujer soldado** (female) soldier (16)
multa fine, penalty (18)
mundial *adj.* world; **Copa Mundial** World Cup; **Segunda Guerra Mundial** World War II
mundo *n.* world (7)
muralismo muralism
muralista *m., f.* muralist
músculo muscle
museo museum; **visitar un museo** to visit a museum (9)
música music (13)
músico/a musician (13)
musulmán, mulsulmana *n., adj.* Moslem
mutuo/a mutual
muy very (1); **muy bien** very well (P); **muy buenas** good afternoon/evening (P)

N

nacer (zc) to be born (15)
nacimiento birth (15)
nación *f.* nation; **Naciones Unidas** United Nations
nacional national
nacionalidad *f.* nationality (2)
nada nothing, not anything (6); **de nada** you're welcome (P)
nadar to swim (7)
nadie no one, not anybody, nobody (6)
nahuatl *m. indigenous language from Central America*
naranja orange (*fruit*) (6)
nariz *f.* (*pl.* **narices**) nose (10)
narración *f.* narration
narrador(a) narrator
narrar to narrate
natación *f.* swimming (9)
nativo/a *adj.* native
natural natural; **recursos** (*m. pl.*) **naturales** natural resources (14)
naturaleza nature (14)
náuseas *f. pl.* nausea

navegable navigable
navegante *m., f.* sailor
navegar (gu) to sail; **navegar la red** to surf the net (12)
Navidad *f.* Christmas (8); **Feliz Navidad** Merry Christmas
navideño/a *adj. pertaining to Christmas*
necesario/a necessary (2)
necesidad *f.* necessity
necesitar to need (1)
negación *f.* negation; denial
negar (ie) (gu) to deny (13)
negativo/a negative (6)
negociación *f.* negotiation
negocio business (*company*); *pl.* business (*general*); **administración** (*f.*) **de negocios** business administration; **hombre** (*m.*)/**mujer** (*f.*) **de negocios** businessperson (16)
negro/a black (3)
neoyorquino/a *adj. of or from New York*
nervio nerve
nervioso/a nervous (5)
neutro/a neutral
nevar (ie) to snow (5); **nieva** it's snowing (5)
ni neither; nor; **ni siquiera** not even
nicaragüense *m., f. n.* Nicaraguan
nieto/a grandson/granddaughter (2); *m. pl.* grandchildren
nieva it's snowing (5)
ningún, ninguno/a no, none, not any (6); neither; **ningún lugar** nowhere
niñero/a babysitter (9)
niñez *f.* childhood (9)
niño/a small child (2); boy/girl (2); **de niño/a** as a child (9)
nivel *m.* level (14)
no no (P); not; **¿no?** right? (3); **no creer** *irreg.* to disbelieve; **no hay de que** you're welcome (P); **no hay duda** there is no doubt; **no me diga** *interj.* you don't say; **no, no me gusta...** no, I don't like . . . (P)
Nóbel: Premio Nóbel Nobel Prize
noche *f.* night; **buenas noches** good evening (P); good night (P); **de la noche** p.m., in the evening (P); **esta noche** tonight (5); **Noche Vieja** New Year's Eve (8); **por la noche** at night (1)
Nochebuena Christmas Eve (8)
nombrar to name
nombre *m.* name
nominado/a nominated
noreste *m.* northeast
norte *m.* north (5)
Norteamérica North America
norteamericano/a *n., adj.* North American (2)
nos *d.o. pron.* us; *i.o. pron.* to/for us; *refl. pron.* ourselves; **nos vemos** see you around (P)
nosotros/as *sub. pron.* we (1); *obj. of a prep.* us
nota note; grade (*in a class*) (11); **sacar (qu) buenas/malas notas** to get good/bad grades
notar to notice
noticia piece of news (8); *pl.* news
noticiero newscast (17)
novato/a *n.* novice
novecientos/as nine hundred (3)
novedades *f. pl.* news (17)
novela novel
novelista *m., f.* novelist
noveno/a ninth (13)
noventa ninety (2)
noviazgo engagement (15)
noviembre *m.* November (5)
novio/a boyfriend/girlfriend (5)
nublado/a cloudy; **está (muy) nublado** it's (very) cloudy, overcast (5)
nuclear nuclear (14)
nuera daughter-in-law
nuestro/a(s) *poss. adj.* our (2); our, of ours
nueve nine (P)
nuevo/a new (2); **de nuevo** again; **Día** (*m.*) **de Año Nuevo** New Year's Day; **Feliz/Próspero Año Nuevo** Happy New Year
numérico/a numerical
número number (P)
numeroso/a numerous
nunca never (2); **casi nunca** almost never (2)

O

o or (P)
obedecer (zc) to obey (14)
objetivo objective
objeto object
obligación *f.* obligation
obligatorio/a obligatory, compulsory
obra work (13); **manos a la obra** let's get to work; **obra de arte** work of art (13); **obra maestra** masterpiece (13)
obrero/a worker, laborer (16)
obstáculo obstacle
obtener (*like* **tener**) to get, obtain (12)
obvio/a obvious
ocasión *f.* occasion
ocasionar to bring about
occidental western
océano ocean (7); **Océano Atlántico** Atlantic Ocean
ochenta eighty (2)
ocho eight (P)
ochocientos/as eight hundred (3)
ocio leisure time
octavo/a *adj.* eighth (13)
octubre *m.* October (5)
ocular *adj. of the eye,* ocular
ocupado/a busy (5)
ocupar to occupy
ocurrir to occur
odiar to hate (7)
odio hatred
oeste *m.* west (5)
ofenderse to be offended
oferta sale; offer
oficial *m. n., adj.* official
oficiar una misa to celebrate mass
oficina office (1); **oficina de correos** post office (18); **oficina de empleos** employment office
oficio trade (16)
ofrecer (zc) to offer (7)
oído inner ear (10)
oír *irreg.* to hear (4)

sé I know
secadora clothes dryer (9)
secar (qu) to dry
sección *f.* section; **sección de (no) fumar** (no) smoking section (7)
secretario/a secretary (1)
secreto *n.* secret
secuencia sequence
secundario/a secondary
sed *f.* thirst; **tener** (*irreg.*) **(mucha) sed** to be (very) thirsty (6)
seda silk (3); **es de seda** it's made of silk (3)
sede *f.* seat; site
segmento segment
seguida: en seguida right away
seguir (i, i) (g) to continue (14); to follow; **seguir todo derecho** to go straight ahead
según according to (2)
segundo/a *adj.* second (13); **de segunda mano** second hand; **Segunda Guerra Mundial** World War II
seguro/a *adj.* sure, certain (5); **es seguro** it's a sure thing (13); **seguro social** *n.* Social Security
seis six (P)
seiscientos/as six hundred (3)
selección *f.* selection
sello stamp (*postage*) (18)
selva jungle
semáforo traffic signal (14)
semana week; **fin** (*m.*) **de semana** weekend (1); **la semana que viene** next week (4); **Semana Santa** Holy Week; **una vez a la semana** once a week (2)
sembrar (ie) to plant, sow
semejante similar
semejanza similarity
semestre *m.* semester
semi-amueblado/a partly furnished
senado senate
senador(a) senator
sencillo/a simple
sendero path
sensación *f.* sensation
sensible sensitive
sentarse (ie) to sit down (4)
sentido meaning; sense; **sentido común** common sense
sentimiento feeling
sentir (ie, i) to regret (13); to feel sorry (13); **lo siento (mucho)** I'm (very) sorry (11); **sentirse** to feel (8)
señor *m.* man; Mr. (P)
señora *f.* woman; Mrs. (P)
señorita *f.* young woman; Miss (P)
separación *f.* separation
separado: por separado separately
separarse (de) to separate (from) (15)
septiembre *m.* September (5)
séptimo/a seventh (13)
ser *irreg.* to be (2); **fue sin querer** it was unintentional (11); **ser aficionado/a (a)** to be a fan (of) (9); **ser divertido/a** to be fun (9); **ser en** + *place* to take place in/at (*place*) (8); **ser flexible** to be flexible (11)
ser *m.* being
serio/a serious
serpenteante winding
serpiente *f.* snake
servicio service (14); **servicio militar** military service (17)
servilleta (dinner) napkin
servir (i, i) to serve (4)
sesenta sixty (2)
sesión *f.* session
setecientos/as seven hundred (3)
setenta seventy (2)
severo/a severe
sevillano/a *n. person from Seville*
sexo sex
sexto/a sixth (13)
si if (2)
sí yes (P); **sí, me gusta...** yes, I like . . . (P)
siamés *adj.* Siamese
sicoanálisis *m.* psychoanalysis
sicología psychology (1)
sicólogo/a psychologist (16)
SIDA *m.* AIDS
siempre always (2)
siesta nap; **dormir (ue, u) la siesta** to take a nap (4)
siete seven (P)
siglo century
significar (qu) to mean
signo sign
siguiente *adj.* following (5)
sílaba syllable
silencio silence
silla chair (1)
sillón *m.* armchair (4)
simbólico/a symbolic
simbolizar (c) to symbolize
símbolo symbol
simpático/a nice (2); likeable (2)
sin without (4); **sin baño/ducha** without bath/shower (18); **sin duda** without a doubt; **sin embargo** however; **sin falta** without fail; **sin fines de lucro** not-for-profit; **sin fines lucrativos** non-profit; **sin intromisiones** without intrusions
sinceridad *f.* sincerity
sincero/a sincere
sindical *adj.* union, *pertaining to a labor/trade union*
sindicato union (*labor, trade*)
sinfin *m.* endless number
sino but (rather)
sintético/a synthetic
síntoma *m.* symptom (10)
siquiatra *m., f.* psychiatrist (16)
siquiera: ni siquiera not even
sistema *m.* system; **analista** (*m., f.*) **de sistemas** systems analyst (16)
sitio place; site; **sitio *web*** web site
situación *f.* situation
situado/a situated, located
sobre *m.* envelope (18); **sobre** *prep.* on; over; about; **sobre todo** above all
sobrepasar to surpass
sobrino/a nephew/niece (2)
social: seguro social Social Security; **trabajador(a) social** social worker (16)
socialista *m., f. adj.* socialist
sociedad *f.* society
socio/a member
socioeconómico/a socioeconomic
sociología sociology (1)
sociólogo/a sociologist

socorro *n.* help
sofá *m.* sofa (4)
sofisticado/a sophisticated
software *m.* software
sol *m.* sun; *monetary unit of Peru;* **hace sol** it's sunny (5); **tomar el sol** to sunbathe (7)
solamente only
solar solar (14)
solas: a solas alone
soldado soldier (16); **mujer** (*f.*) **soldado** female soldier (16)
soledad *f.* solitude
soler (ue) to be in the habit of
solicitar to ask for
solicitud *f.* application (*form*) (16)
solitario/a solitary
solo/a single; alone (7)
sólo *adv.* only (1)
soltero/a single (*unmarried*) (2)
solución *f.* solution
solucionar to solve
sombra shadow
sombrero hat (3)
sombrilla umbrella
somozista *m., f. follower of Somoza*
son las... it's . . . (*time*) (P)
sonar (ue) to ring (9); to sound (9)
sonreír(se) (i, i) to smile (8)
soñar (ue) (con) to dream (about)
sopa soup (6)
sorprendente surprising
sorprender to surprise; **me (te, le...) sorprende** it surprises me (you, him, . . .) (13)
sorpresa surprise (8)
soviético/a Soviet
soy I am (P)
Sr. (*abbrev. of* **señor**) Mr. (P)
Sra. (*abbrev. of* **señora**) Mrs. (P)
Srta. (*abbrev. of* **señorita**) Miss (P)
su(s) *poss. adj.* his, her, its, your (*form. s.*) (2); their, your (*form. pl.*) (2)
subir (a) to go up (7); to get on (*a vehicle*) (7)
subjuntivo *gram.* subjunctive
subordinado/a subordinate
subrayado/a underlined
subsistir to subsist
subtítulo subtitle
subtropical subtropical
sucio/a dirty (5)
sucre *m. former monetary unit of Ecuador*
sucursal *f.* branch (*office*) (16)
Sudamérica South America
sudamericano/a *n., adj.* South American
Suecia Sweden
suegro/a father-in-law/mother-in-law
sueldo salary (12); **aumento de sueldo** salary raise (16)
suelo floor
suelto/a *adj.* free
sueño sleep; dream; **tener** (*irreg.*) **sueño** to be sleepy (3)
suerte *f.* luck; **¡qué mala suerte!** what bad luck! (11); **tener** (*irreg.*) **suerte** to be lucky
suéter *m.* sweater (3)
suficiente enough; **lo suficiente** enough (10)
sufijo *gram.* suffix
sufrimiento suffering
sufrir to suffer (11); **sufrir (muchas) presiones** to be under (a lot) of pressure (11)
sugerencia suggestion
sugerir (ie, i) to suggest (8)
suicidio suicide
Suiza Switzerland
sujeto subject
sumo *indigenous people of Nicaragua*
superar to overcome
supercarretera superhighway
superficie *f.* surface
superior higher
superlativo *gram.* superlative
supermercado supermarket
suponer (*like* **poner**) to suppose
supuesto: por supuesto of course (11)
sur *m. n.* south (5); *adj.* southern
surgir (j) to spring up, arise
surrealista *m., f. adj.* surrealistic
suscribirse (*p.p.* **suscrito**) to subscribe
suscrito/a (*p.p. of* **suscribirse**) subscribed
suspender to suspend, cut off
sustancioso/a heavy
sustantivo *gram.* noun (1)
sustituir (y) to substitute
suyo(s)/a(s) *poss. adj.* his, (of) his, her, (of) hers, your, (of) yours (*form.*)

T

tabacalero/a *adj.* tobacco, *pertaining to tobacco*
tabaco tobacco
tabla: montar en tabla de vela to windsurf
tailandés, tailandesa *adj.* Thai
taíno *indigenous group of the Caribbean*
tal such (a); just; **con tal (de) que** *conj.* provided (that) (15); **¿qué tal?** how are you (*doing*)? (P); **tal(es) como** such as; **tal vez** perhaps
talento talent
talentoso/a talented
taller *m.* (repair) shop (14)
también also (P)
tamborista *m., f.* drummer
tampoco neither, not either (6)
tan so; as; **tan... como** as . . . as (5); **tan pronto como** *conj.* as soon as (16)
tanque *m.* tank (14)
tanto *adv.* so much; **tanto/a** *adj.* so much; such; *pl.* so many; **estar** (*irreg.*) **al tanto** to be up-to-date; **tanto como** as much as (5); **tantos/as... como** as much/many . . . as (5)
tarde *adv.* late (1); **llegar (gu) tarde** to arrive late (11); **tarde** *f. n.* afternoon; **buenas tardes** good afternoon (P); **de la tarde** p.m., in the afternoon (P); **por la tarde** in the afternoon (1)
tarea homework (4); task; **tarea doméstica** household chore
tarjeta card (7); **tarjeta de crédito** credit card (6); **tarjeta de identificación** identification card (11); **tarjeta postal** postcard (7)

clumsy **torpe** (11)
coat **abrigo** (3)
coffee **café** *m.* (1)
coffee pot **cafetera** (9)
cognate **cognado** (6)
cold (*illness*) **resfriado** (10); to be cold **tener** (*irreg.*) **frío** *n.* (5); to catch a cold **resfriarse** (10); it's cold (*weather*) **hace frío** (5); very cold **congelado/a** (5)
collect **recoger (j)** (11)
collide (with) **chocar (qu) (con)** (14)
collision **choque** *m.* (17)
color **color** *m.* (3)
comb one's hair **peinarse** (4)
come **venir** (*irreg.*) (3)
comfortable **cómodo/a** (4); to be comfortable (*temperature*) **estar** (*irreg.*) **bien** (5)
communicate (with) **comunicarse (qu) (con)** (17)
communication (*major*) **comunicación** *f.* (1); means of communication **medio de comunicación** (17)
community **comunidad** *f.* (12)
compact disc **disco compacto** (12)
comparison **comparación** *f.* (5)
complain (about) **quejarse (de)** (8)
composer **compositor(a)** (13)
computer **computadora** (*L.A.*) (12); **ordenador** *m.* (*Sp.*) (12); computer disk **disco de computadora** (12); computer file **archivo** (12); computer science **computación** *f.* (1); laptop computer **computadora/ ordenador portátil** (12)
concert **concierto** (9); to go to a concert **ir** (*irreg.*) **a un concierto** (9)
confirm **confirmar** (18)
congested **congestionado/a** (10)
congratulations **felicitaciones** *f. pl.* (8)
conjunction **conjunción** (*f.*) *gram.* (15)
conserve **conservar** (14)
contact lenses **lentes** (*m. pl.*) **de contacto** (10)
content *adj.* **contento/a** (5)
continue **seguir (i, i) (g)** (14); to continue straight ahead **seguir (i, i) derecho** (14)
control: remote control **control** (*m.*) **remoto** (12)
convertible (*car*) **descapotable** (12)
cook *v.* **cocinar** (6); *n.* cook **cocinero/a** (16)
cookie **galleta** (6)
cool: it's cool (*weather*) **hace fresco** (5)
copy **copia** (12); to copy **hacer** (*irreg.*) **copia** (12)
corn **maíz** *m.* (5)
corner (*street*) **esquina** (14)
corporation **empresa** (16)
cost: how much does it cost? **¿cuánto cuesta?** (3)
cotton **algodón** *m.* (3); it is made of cotton **es de algodón** (3)
cough **tos** *f.* (10); to cough **toser** (10); cough syrup **jarabe** *m.* (10)
count **contar (ue)** (17)
country **país** *m.* (2)
countryside **campo** (12)
couple (*married*) **matrimonio** (15), **pareja** (15)
course (*of a meal*) **plato** (6); of course **por supuesto** (11)
courtesy **cortesía** (P)
cousin **primo/a** (2)
cover **cubrir** (*pp.* **cubierto/a**) (14)
crafts: arts and crafts **artesanía** (13)
crash (*computer*) **fallar** (12)
crazy **loco/a** (5)
create **crear** (13)
credit card **tarjeta de crédito** (16)
crime **delito, crimen** *m.* (14)
cross **cruzar (c)** (18)
cry **llorar** (8)
custard: baked custard **flan** *m.* (6)
custom **costumbre** *f.* (9)
customs **aduana** *s.* (18); (customs) duty **derechos** (*m. pl.*) **(de aduana)** (18); (customs) inspector **inspector(a) (de aduanas)** (18)

D

dad **papá** *m.* (2)
daily routine **rutina diaria** (4)
dance **baile** *m.* (13); **danza** (13); to dance **bailar** (1)
dancer **bailarín, bailarina** (13)
date (*calendar*) **fecha** (5); (*social*) **cita** (15); what's today's date? **¿cuál es la fecha de hoy?** (5)
daughter **hija** (2)
day **día** *m.* (1); day after tomorrow **pasado mañana** (4); every day **todos los días** (1)
deadline **fecha límite** (11)
dear **querido/a** *n., adj.* (5)
death **muerte** *f.* (15)
December **diciembre** *m.* (5)
declare **declarar** (18)
delay *n.* **demora** (7)
delighted **encantado/a** (P)
deluxe **de lujo** (18)
demonstrative **demostrativo** (3)
dense **denso/a** (14)
dentist **dentista** *m., f.* (10)
deny **negar (ie) (gu)** (13)
department store **almacén** *m.* (3)
departure **salida** (7)
deposit **depositar** (16)
desk **escritorio** (1); front desk **recepción** *f.* (18)
dessert **postre** *m.* (6)
destroy **destruir (y)** (14)
detail **detalle** *m.* (6)
develop **desarrollar** (14)
dictator **dictador(a)** (17)
dictatorship **dictadura** (17)
dictionary **diccionario** (1)
die **morir (ue, u)** (*p.p.* **muerto/a**); to be dying **morir(se)** (8)
difficult **difícil** (5); **pesado/a** (9)
dining room **comedor** *m.* (4)
dinner **cena** (6); to have dinner **cenar** (6)
directions: cardinal directions **puntos** (*m. pl.*) **cardinales** (5)
director **director(a)** (13); personnel director **director(a) de personal** (16)
dirty **sucio/a** (5)
disadvantage **desventaja** (10)
disaster **desastre** *m.* (17)
disc: compact disc **disco compacto** (12)
discotheque, disco **discoteca** (9)

discover **descubrir** (*pp.* **descubierto**) (14)
discrimination **discriminación** *f.* (17)
dish (prepared) **plato** (4)
dishwasher **lavaplatos** *m. s., pl.* (9)
disk: computer disk **disco de computadora** (12)
divorce **divorcio** (15)
divorced: to get divorced (from) **divorciarse (de)** (15)
dizzy **mareado/a** (10)
do **hacer** (*irreg.*) (4); (*do something*) again **volver a** + *inf.* (4); to do aerobics **hacer** (*irreg.*) **ejercicios aeróbicos** (10); to do exercise **hacer** (*irreg.*) **ejercicio** (4)
doctor (*medical*) **médico/a** (2)
dog **perro/a** (2)
don't they (you, etc.)? **¿no?, ¿verdad?** (3)
door **puerta** (1)
doorman **portero/a** (12)
dormitory **residencia** (1)
double **doble** (18); double room **habitación** (*f.*) **doble** (18)
doubt **dudar** (12)
downtown **centro** (3)
drama **drama** *m.* (13)
draw **dibujar** (13)
dress **vestido** (3)
dressed: to get dressed **vestirse (i, i)** (4)
dresser (*furniture*) **cómoda** (4)
drink **bebida** (6); **copa, trago** (*alcoholic*) (18); *drink similar to a milkshake* **batido** (18); to drink **tomar** (1); **beber** (2); soft drink **refresco** (6)
drive (*a vehicle*) **conducir** (*irreg.*) (14); **manejar** (12); hard drive **disco duro** (12)
driver **conductor(a)** (14); driver's license **licencia de manejar/conducir** (14)
dryer: clothes dryer **secadora** (9)
during **durante** (4); **por** (4)
dust the furniture **sacudir los muebles** (9)
duty: (customs) duty **derechos** (*m. pl.*) **(de aduana)** (18)

E

each **cada** *inv.* (4)
ear (inner) **oído** (10); (outer) **oreja** (10)
early **temprano** *adv.* (1)
earn **ganar** (9)
earring **arete** *m.* (3)
east **este** *m.* (5)
Easter **Pascua (Florida)** (8)
easy **fácil** (5)
eat **comer** (2); eat breakfast **desayunar** (6); eat dinner **cenar** (6)
economics **economía** (1)
economize **economizar (c)** (16)
egg **huevo** (6)
eight **ocho** (P)
eight hundred **ochocientos/as** (3)
eighteen **dieciocho** (P)
eighth **octavo/a** *adj.* (13)
eighty **ochenta** (2)
either: not either **tampoco** (6)
electric **eléctrico/a** (14)
electrician **electricista** *m., f.* (16)
electricity **luz** *f.* (*pl.* **luces**) (11)
electronic mail **correo electrónico** (12)
electronics **electrónica** (12)
eleven **once** (P)
e-mail **correo electrónico** (12)
embarrassed **avergonzado/a** (8)
emergency room **sala de emergencias/urgencia** (10)
emotion **emoción** *f.* (8)
employment office **dirección** (*f.*) **de personal** (16)
end table **mesita** (4)
energy **energía** (14)
engagement **noviazgo** (15)
engineer **ingeniero/a** (16)
English (*language*) **inglés** *m.* (1); *n., adj.* **inglés, inglesa** (2)
enjoy oneself, have a good time **divertirse (ie, i)** (4)
enough **bastante** *adv.* (15); **lo suficiente** (10)
entertainment **diversión** *f.* (9)
entire **entero/a** (9)
envelope **sobre** *m.* (18)
environment **medio ambiente** *m.* (14)
equality **igualdad** *f.* (17)
equipment: stereo equipment **equipo estereofónico** (12); photography equipment **equipo fotográfico** (12)
era **época** (9)
evening **tarde** *f.* (1); good evening **buenas tardes** (P); in the afternoon, evening **de la tarde** (P); in the evening **por la tarde** (1)
event **acontecimiento** (17); **evento** (17); **hecho** (8)
every **cada** *inv.* (4); **todo(s)/a(s)** *adj.* (2); every day **todos los días** (1)
everything **de todo** (3)
everywhere **por todas partes** (11)
exactly, on the dot (*time*) **en punto** (P)
exam **examen** *m.* (3)
examine **examinar** (10); **registrar** (18)
example: for example **por ejemplo** (11)
excuse me **con permiso, perdón** (P); **discúlpeme** (11)
exercise **ejercicio** (3); **hacer** (*irreg.*) **ejercicio** (4)
expect **esperar** (6)
expend **gastar** (8)
expense **gasto** (12)
expensive **caro/a** (3)
explain **explicar (qu)** (7)
expressions: greetings and expressions of courtesy **saludos** (*m. pl.*) **y expresiones** (*f. pl.*) **de cortesía** (P)
extract **sacar (qu)** (10); extract a tooth **sacar una muela** (10)
eye **ojo** (10)
eyeglasses **gafas** *f. pl.* (10)

F

fact **hecho** *n.* (8)
factory **fábrica** (14)
faithful **fiel** (2)
fall (*season*) **otoño** (5)

postcard **tarjeta postal** (7)
potato **patata** (*Sp.*) (6); French fried potato **patata frita** (*Sp.*) (6)
pottery **cerámica** (13)
practical **práctico/a** (2)
practice **practicar (qu)** (1); **entrenar** (9)
prefer **preferir (ie, i)** (3)
preferable **preferible** (13)
preference **gusto, preferencia** (P)
prepare **preparar** (6)
preposition **preposición** *f. gram.* (4)
prescription **receta** (10)
present (*gift*) **regalo** *n.* (2)
press *n.* **prensa** (17)
pressure: to be under pressure **sufrir presiones** *f. pl.* (11)
pretty **bonito/a** (2)
price **precio** (3); fixed price **precio fijo** (3)
print **imprimir** (12)
printer **impresora** (12)
profession **profesión** *f.* (16)
professor **profesor(a)** (1)
programmer **programador(a)** (16)
prohibit **prohibir (prohíbo)** (12)
promise *v.* **prometer** (7)
pronoun **pronombre** *m. gram.* (1)
protect **proteger (j)** (14)
provided (that) **con tal (de) que** (15)
psychiatrist **siquiatra** *m., f.* (16)
psychologist **sicólogo/a** (16)
psychology **sicología** (1)
public **público/a** *adj.* (14)
punish **castigar (gu)** (17)
purchases **compras** (*f. pl.*) (3)
pure **puro/a** (14)
purple **morado/a** (3)
purse **bolsa** (3)
put **poner** (*irreg.*) (4); to put on (*clothing*) **ponerse** (*irreg.*) (4)

Q

quarter past (*with time*) **y cuarto** (P)
queen **reina** (17)
question: ask a question **hacer una pregunta** (4); **preguntar** (6); (*issue*) **cuestión** (16)
quit **dejar** (16); (*doing something*) **dejar de** + *inf.* (10)
quiz **prueba** (11)

R

radio **radio** *m.* (*set*); portable radio **radio portátil** (12); radio (*medium*) (12) **radio** *f.*
rain **llover (ue)** (5); it's raining **llueve** (5)
raincoat **impermeable** *m.* (3)
raise **aumento** (12); (in salary) **aumento de sueldo** (16)
rare **raro/a** (8)
rather **bastante** *adv.* (15)
react **reaccionar** (8)
read **leer (y)** (2)
reader **lector(a)** (13)
reason **razón** *f.* (3)
receive **recibir** (2)
recommend **recomendar (ie)** (7)
record **grabar** (12)
recorder: tape recorder **grabadora** (12); videocassette recorder (VCR) **videocasetera** (12)
recycle **reciclar** (14)
red **rojo/a** (3); red wine **vino tinto** (6)
reduction **rebaja** (3)
refreshment **refresco** (8)
reflexive **reflexivo** (4)
refrigerator **refrigerador** *m.* (9)
regret **sentir (ie, i)** (13)
relationship **relación** (*f.*) **sentimental** (15)
relative **pariente** *m., f.* (2)
remain (*in a place*) **quedar(se)** (5); to remain, stay (*as a guest*) **alojarse** (18)
remember **recordar (ue)** (8); **acordarse (ue) (de)** (11)
remote control **control** (*m.*) **remoto** (12)
rent **alquiler** *m.* (12); to rent *v.* **alquilar** (12)
renter **inquilino/a** (12)
repair **arreglar** (12); (repair) shop **taller** *m.* (14)
report **informe** *m.*; **trabajo** (11)
reporter **reportero/a** (17)
represent **representar** (13)
reservation **reserva, reservación** (*f.*) (18)
resign (from) **renunciar (a)** (16)
resolve **resolver (ue)** (*p.p.* **resuelto/a**) (14)
resource **recurso**; natural resources **recursos naturales** (14)
responsibility **responsabilidad** *f.*; **deber** *m.* (17)
rest **descansar** (4); the rest **los/las demás** (12)
restaurant **restaurante** *m.* (6)
résumé **currículum** *m.* (16)
retire **jubilarse** (16)
return (*to a place*) **regresar** (1); **volver (ue)** (*p.p.* **vuelto/a**) (4); (*something*) **devolver (ue)** (*pp.* **devuelto/a**) (16)
rhythm **ritmo** (14)
rice **arroz** *m.* (6)
rich **rico/a** (2)
ride a bicycle **pasear en bicicleta** (9); to ride horseback **montar a caballo** (9)
right (*legal*) **derecho** *n.* (17); (*direction*) **derecha** *n.* (5); right? **¿verdad?** (3); to be right **tener** (*irreg.*) **razón** (3); to the right (of) **a la derecha (de)** (5)
ring **sonar (ue)** (9)
road **camino** (14)
roast chicken **pollo asado** (6)
role **papel** *m.* (13)
roller skates **patines** *m. pl.* (12)
rollerblade *v.* **patinar en línea** (9)
room **cuarto** (1); room (*in a hotel*) **habitación** *f.* (18); dining room **comedor** *m.* (4); double room **habitación** (*f.*) **doble** (18); emergency room **sala de emergencias/urgencia** (10); living room **sala** (4); room and full board (all meals) **pensión** (*f.*) **completa** (18); room with(out) bath/shower **habitación** (*f.*) **con/sin baño/ducha** (18); single room **habitación** (*f.*) **individual**

(18); waiting room **sala de espera** (7)
roommate **compañero/a de cuarto** (1)
round-trip ticket **billete** (*m.*)**/boleto de ida y vuelta** (7)
routine: daily routine **rutina diaria** (4)
rug **alfombra** (4)
ruin *n.* **ruina** (13)
rule **gobernar (ie)** (17)
run **correr** (9); (*machines*) **funcionar** (12); to run into **darse** (*irreg.*) **con, pegarse (gu) en/contra** (11); **chocar (qu) (con)** (14); to run out of **acabar(se)** (11)

S

sad **triste** (5)
sake: for God's sake **por Dios** (12)
salad **ensalada** (6)
salary **sueldo** (12); **salario** (16); raise in salary **aumento de sueldo** (16)
sale **rebaja** (3)
salesperson **dependiente/a** (1); **vendedor(a)** (16)
salmon **salmón** *m.* (6)
same **mismo/a** (10); same here **igualmente** (P)
sandal **sandalia** (3)
sandwich **sándwich** *m.* (6)
Saturday **sábado** (4)
sausage **salchicha** (6)
save (*a place/documents*) **guardar** (7); **conservar** (14); (*money*) **ahorrar** (16)
savings **ahorros** *m. pl.*; savings account **cuenta de ahorros** (16)
say **decir** (*irreg.*) (7); to say good-bye (to) **despedirse (i, i) (de)** (8)
schedule **horario** (11)
school **escuela** (9)
schoolteacher **maestro/a** (16)
science **ciencia** (1); computer science **computación** *f.* (1)
script **guión** *m.* (13)
sculpt **esculpir** (13)
sculptor **escultor(a)** (13)
sculpture **escultura** (13)
sea **mar** *m., f.* (7)
seaport **puerto** (7)
search **registrar** (18); in search of **en busca de** (16)
season **estación** *f.* (5)
seat *n.* **asiento** (7)
second **segundo/a** *adj.* (13)
secretary **secretario/a** (1)
section: (non)smoking section **sección** (*f.*) **de (no) fumar** (7)
see **ver** (*irreg.*) (4); see you around **nos vemos** (P); see you later **hasta luego** (P); see you tomorrow **hasta mañana** (P)
seem **parecer (zc)** (13)
self **mismo/a** (10)
sell **vender** (2)
send **mandar** (7)
separate (from) *v.* **separarse (de)** (15)
September **septiembre** *m.* (5)
servant **criado/a** (16)
serve **servir (i, i)** (4)
service **servicio** (14); military service **servicio militar** (17)
set: television set **televisor** *m.* (4); set the table **poner** (*irreg.*) **la mesa** (9)
seven **siete** (P)
seven hundred **setecientos/as** (3)
seventeen **diecisiete** (P)
seventh **séptimo/a** *adj.* (13)
seventy **setenta** (2)
shame **lástima** (13); it is a shame **es lástima** (13); what a shame! **¡qué lástima!** (13)
shampoo **champú** *m.* (18)
shave oneself **afeitarse** (4)
she **ella** (1)
shellfish **marisco** (6)
ship **barco** (7)
shirt **camisa** (3)
shoe **zapato** (3); tennis shoe **zapato de tenis** (3)
shop **tienda** (3); (repair) **taller** *m.* (14); pastry shop **pastelería** (18); tobacco shop **estanco** (18)
shopkeeper **comerciante** *m., f.* (16)
shopping **de compras** (3); shopping mall **centro comercial** (3); to go shopping **ir** (*irreg.*) **de compras** (3)
short (*in height*) **bajo/a** (2); (*in length*) **corto/a** (2)
shortage **escasez** *f.* (*pl.* **escaseces**) (14)
shot **inyección** *f.* (10)
should (*do something*) **deber** (+ *inf.*) (2)
show **mostrar (ue)** (7)
shower **ducha** (18); to take a shower **ducharse** (4)
shrimp **camarón** *m.* (6)
sick **enfermo/a** *adj.* (5); to get sick **enfermarse** (8)
sickness **enfermedad** *f.* (10)
side: to get up on the wrong side of the bed **levantarse con el pie izquierdo** (11)
sight: at first sight **a primera vista** (15)
signal: traffic signal **semáforo** (14)
silk **seda** (3); it is made of silk **es de seda** (3)
silly **tonto/a** (2)
since: it's been (*time*) since... **hace** + *time* + **que...** + *present* (11)
sing **cantar** (1)
singer **cantante** *m., f.* (13)
single (*not married*) **soltero/a** (2); single room **habitación** (*f.*) **individual** (18)
sink (bathroom) **lavabo** (4)
sir **señor (Sr.)** *m.* (P)
sister **hermana** (2)
sit down **sentarse (ie)** (4)
six **seis** (P)
six hundred **seiscientos/as** (3)
sixteen **dieciséis** (P)
sixth **sexto/a** *adj.* (13)
sixty **sesenta** (2)
skate *v.* **patinar** (9)
skateboard **monopatín** *m.* (12)
skates: roller skates **patines** *m. pl.* (12)
ski **esquiar (esquío)** (9)
skirt **falda** (3)
skyscraper **rascacielos** *m. s.* (14)
sleep **dormir (ue, u)** (4)
sleepy: to be sleepy **tener** (*irreg.*) **sueño** (3)

tourist **turístico/a** *adj.*; tourist class **clase** (*f.*) **turística** (7)
trade (*job*) **oficio** (16)
tradition **tradición** *f.* (13)
traffic **tránsito**; **circulación** *f.* (14); traffic signal **semáforo** (14)
train **tren** *m.* (7); train station **estación** (*f.*) **de trenes** (7); to go by train **ir** (*irreg.*) **en tren** (7); to train **entrenar** (9)
translator **traductor(a)** (16)
transportation (means of) transportation **transporte** *m.* (14)
trash: to take out the trash **sacar (qu) la basura** (9)
travel **viajar** (7); travel agency **agencia de viajes** (7); travel agent **agente** (*m. f.*) **de viajes** (7)
traveler **viajero/a** (18); traveler's check **cheque** (*m.*) **de viajero** (18)
treatment **tratamiento** (10)
tree **árbol** *m.* (14)
trip **viaje** *m.* (7); have a good trip **buen viaje** (7); on a trip **de viaje** (7); round-trip ticket **billete** (*m.*)**/boleto de ida y vuelta** (7); to go on a trip **ir** (*irreg.*) **de viaje** (10); to take a trip **hacer** (*irreg.*) **un viaje** (4)
try **intentar** (13); try to (*do something*) **tratar de** + *inf.* (13)
Tuesday **martes** *m. s., pl.* (4)
tuition **matrícula** (1)
tuna **atún** *m.* (6)
turkey **pavo** (6)
turn **doblar** (14); to turn in **entregar (gu)** (11); to be someone's turn **tocarle (qu) a uno** (9)
twelve **doce** (P)
twenty **veinte** (P)
twice **dos veces** (10)
two **dos** (P)
two hundred **doscientos/as** (3)
type **escribir** (*pp.* **escrito/a**) **a máquina** (16)

U

ugly **feo/a** (2)
unbelievable **increíble** (13)
uncle **tío** (2)
under: to be under pressure **sufrir presiones** (11)
understand **comprender** (2); **entender (ie)** (4)
underwear **ropa interior** (3)
unintentional: it was unintentional **fue sin querer** (11)
university **universidad** *f.* (1); (of the) university **universitario/a** (11); university campus ***campus*** *m. s.* (12)
unless **a menos que** (15)
unoccupied **desocupado/a** (18)
unpleasant **antipático/a** (2)
until **hasta** *prep.* (4); **hasta que** *conj.* (16); until tomorrow **hasta mañana** (P)
urgent **urgente** (13)
us **nos** *d.o.*; *i.o.* to/for us; *refl. pron.* ourselves; see you around **nos vemos** (P)
use **usar** (3); **gastar** (8); to use up completely **acabar (se)** (14)
useful **útil** (15)

V

vacancy: no vacancy **completo/a** (18)
vacant **desocupado/a** (18)
vacation **vacación** *f.* (7); to be on vacation **estar** (*irreg.*) **de vacaciones** (7); to go on vacation **ir** (*irreg.*) **de vacaciones** (7)
vacuum cleaner **aspiradora** (9); to vacuum **pasar la aspiradora** (9)
vegetable **verdura** (6)
vehicle **vehículo** (12)
verb **verbo** *gram.* (1)
very **muy** (1); very well **muy bien** (P)
veterinarian **veterinario/a** (16)
video camera **cámara de video** (12)
videocassette recorder (VCR) **videocasetera** (12)
view **vista** (12)
violence **violencia** (14)
visit a museum **visitar un museo** (9)
volleyball **vólibol** *m.* (9)
vote **votar** (17)

W

wagon: station wagon **camioneta** (7)
wait (for) **esperar** (6)
waiter **camarero** (6)
waiting room **sala de espera** (7)
waitress **camarera** (6)
wake up **despertarse (ie)** (4)
walk **caminar** (10); to take a walk **dar** (*irreg.*) **un paseo** (9); to walk (go on foot) **ir** (*irreg.*) **a pie** (10)
walkman ***walkman*** (12)
wall **pared** *f.* (4)
wallet **cartera** (3)
want **desear** (1); **querer** (*irreg.*) (3)
war **guerra** (17)
warm: to be (feel) warm, hot **tener** (*irreg.*) **calor** (5)
wash **lavar** (9); to wash (the windows, the dishes, clothes) **lavar (las ventanas, los platos, la ropa)** (9); to wash (oneself) **lavar(se)**
washing machine **lavadora** (9)
waste **desperdiciar** (14)
watch **reloj** *m.* (3); to watch **mirar** (2); to watch television **mirar la televisión** (2)
water **agua** *f.* (*but* **el agua**); mineral water **agua** *f.* (*but* **el agua**) **mineral** (6); waterbed **cama de agua** (4)
way: one-way ticket **billete/boleto de ida** (7)
we **nosotros/as** (1)
wear (clothing) **llevar, usar** (3)
weather **tiempo** (5); it's good/bad weather **hace buen/mal tiempo** (5); what's the weather like? **¿qué tiempo hace?** (5)
weave **tejer** (13)
wedding **boda** (15)
Wednesday **miércoles** *m. s., pl.* (4)
week **semana** (4); next week **la semana que viene** (4); once a week **una vez a la semana** (2)
weekend **fin** (*m.*) **de semana** (1)
welcome: you're welcome **de nada, no hay de qué** (P)

well **bien** *adv.* (P); well . . . *interj.* **bueno...** (2)
well-being **bienestar** *m.* (10)
west **oeste** *m.* (5)
what **lo que** (7)
what . . . ! **¡qué... !**; what a shame! **¡qué lástima!** (13)
what? which? **¿qué? ¿cuál(es)?** (P); what are you like? **¿cómo es usted?** (P); what is the date today? **¿cuál es la fecha de hoy?** (5); what time is it? **¿qué hora es?** (P); what's your name? **¿cómo te llamas? / ¿cómo se llama usted?** (P)
when? **¿cuándo?** (P)
where (to)? **¿adónde?** (3)
where? **¿dónde?** (P); where are you from? **¿de dónde es Ud.?** (2)
which **que** (2); **¿cuál (es)?** (P); that which **lo que** (7)
while **mientras** (9); **rato** *n.* (9)
white **blanco/a** (3); white wine **vino blanco** (6)
who **que** (2)
who? whom? **¿quién(es)?** (P)
whole **entero/a** (9)
whose? **¿de quién?** (2)
why? **¿por qué?** (2)
wife **esposa** (2); **mujer** *f.* (15)
win **ganar** (9)
wind *n.* **viento** (5); *adj.* **eólico/a** (14)
window **ventana** (1)
windshield **parabrisas** *m. s.* (14)
windy: it's windy **hace viento** (5)
wine (white, red) **vino (blanco, tinto)** (6)
winter **invierno** (5)
wish **deseo** (8); **esperanza** (17); I wish **ojalá (que)** (13)
with **con** (1)
withdraw (*money*) **sacar (qu)** (16)
without **sin** (4)
witness **testigo** *m., f.* (17)
woman **señora (Sra.)** (P); **mujer** *f.* (1)
wool **lana** (3); it is made of wool **es de lana** (3)
word **palabra** (P)
work (of art) **obra (de arte)** (13); *n.* **trabajo** (11); to work **trabajar** (1); (*machine*) **funcionar** (12)
worker **obrero/a** (16); social worker **trabajador(a) social** (16)
world **mundo** (7)
worried **preocupado/a** (5)
worse **peor** (5)
woven goods **tejidos** *m. pl.* (13)
write **escribir** (*p.p.* **escrito/a**) (2)
writer **escritor(a)** (13)
written **escrito/a** *p.p.* (11); written report **informe** (*m.*) **escrito** (11)
wrong: to be wrong **no tener** (*irreg.*) **razón** (3); **equivocarse (qu)** (11); to get up on the wrong side of the bed **levantarse con el pie izquierdo** (11)

Y

yard, **patio** (4); **jardín** *m.* (4)
year **año** (5); (*in school*) **grado** (9); to be . . . years old **tener** (*irreg.*)**... años** (2)
yellow **amarillo/a** (3)
yes **sí** (P); yes, I like . . . **sí, me gusta...** (P)
yesterday **ayer** (4); yesterday was (Wednesday) **ayer fue (miércoles)** (4)
yet **todavía** (5)
yogurt **yogur** *m.* (6)
you *sub. pron.* **tú** (*fam. s.*) (P); **usted (Ud., Vd.)** (*form. s.*) (P); **vosotros/as** (*fam. pl., Sp.*); **ustedes (Uds., Vds.)** (*pl.*); *d.o.* **te, os, lo/la, los, las**; to/for you *i.o.* **te, os, le, les**; *obj.* (*of prep.*) **ti, Ud., Uds., vosotros/as** (5)
you're welcome **de nada, no hay de qué** (P)
young **joven** (2)
young woman **señorita (Srta.)** (P)
younger **menor** (5)
your *poss.* **tu** (*fam. s.*) (2); **su(s)** (*form.*) (2); **vuestro/a(s)** (*fam. pl., Sp.*) (2)
youth **joven** *n. m., f.* (2); *adj.* young (2); as a youth **de joven** (9); (*young adulthood*) **juventud** *f.* (15)

Z

zero **cero** (P)

INDEX

In this Index, cultural notes, reading strategies, and vocabulary topic groups are listed by individual topic as well as under those headings.

D

E

CREDITS

Grateful acknowledgment is made for use of the following:

Photographs: *Page 1* © Wartenberg/Picture Press/Corbis; *2* Marty Granger; *7* (*from left*) Stephanie Cardinale/Corbis Sygma, AP/Wide World Photos, Mitchell Gerber/Corbis, Gregory Pace/Corbis Sygma; *10* © Stuart Cohen; *16* SuperStock; *24* (*left*) Pictor/Uniphoto, (*right*) © Antonio Mendoza/Stock Boston; *25* (*clockwise from left*) SuperStock, © Ulrike Welsch, © Peter Menzel; *27* Marty Granger; *29* Peter Vandermark/Stock Boston; *31* Steve Vidler/SuperStock; *32* A.G.E. Fotostock; *39* © Bettman/Corbis; *40* Susan Casarin; *44* AP/Wide World Photos; *49* © Ulrike Welsch; *53* © Vince Dewitt/D. Donne Bryant Stock; *64* © Museo del Prado, Madrid, Spain/Giraudon, Paris/SuperStock; *66* Commissioned by the Trustees of Dartmouth College; *67* © Llewellyn/Uniphoto; *71* Susan Casarin; *75* © Trapper Frank/Corbis Sygma; *80* © Larry Luxner 2000; *83* (*top*) © Reuters NewMedia Inc./Corbis, (*bottom*) © Gonzalo Endara Crow; *89* Marty Granger; *93* © Corbis-Bettman; *96* © Topham/The Image Works; *97* Marty Granger; *102* Martin Rogers/Corbis; *106* © Ric Ergenbright; *113* © Bill Gentile/Corbis; *117* Vincente Wolf Associates, Inc.; *119* Marty Granger; *128* © Vince Streano/Corbis; *131* (*top and bottom*) *A logo for America* by Alfredo Jaar; *137* © Rob Crandall/The Image Works; *138* (*top*) Uniphoto, (*bottom*) © Ulrike Welsch; *144* Marty Granger; *146* © Frans Lating/Getty Images/Stone; *149* Richard Lord/PhotoEdit; *152* (*left*) © FoodPix, (*right*) © Peter Guttman/Corbis; *154* Marty Granger; *161* Courtesy of Oswaldo & Alice Arana; *162* SuperStock; *168* Marty Granger; *173* © Suzanne Murphy-Larronde/D. Donne Bryant Stock; *175* © Alfred Buellesbach/Plus 49/The Image Works; *176* © Stuart Cohen; *185* © Stephen and Donna O'Meara/Photo Researchers, Inc.; *186* Marty Granger; *189* © Corbis; *192* Marty Granger; *194* SuperStock; *197* © AFP/Corbis; *200* © Jack Kurtz/The Image Works; *208* © Prensa Latina/Getty Images; *211* © Bob Riha/Getty Images; *213* Marty Granger; *217* © Robert Frerck/Odyssey/Chicago; *219* (*top*) Corbis-Bettmann, (*bottom*) AP/Wide World Photos; *226* (*left*) © Stephanie Cardinale/Corbis Sygma, (*right*) Associated Press; *228* © George Holton/Photo Researchers, Inc.; *231* © Monica Graff/The Image Works; *232* Marty Granger; *234* Joe Viesti/Viesti Collection; *237* © D. Donne Bryant Stock; *242* Marty Granger; *248* © Ken Fisher/Getty Images/Stone; *250* AP/Wide World Photos; *253* Marty Granger; *257* © Suzanne Murphy-Larronde/D. Donne Bryant Stock; *265* © Dalle Luche/Sestini/Grazia Neri/Corbis Sygma; *268* © Ulrike Welsch; *273* Marty Granger; *275* Pictor/Uniphoto; *279* © Corbis; *288* Marty Granger; *292* David Young-Wolfe/PhotoEdit; *293* © Robert Frerck/Odyssey/Chicago; *298* Marty Granger; *302* © Craig Duncan/D. Donne Bryant Stock; *305* © Charles Kennard/Stock Boston; *307* © Joe Sohm/The Image Works; *311 Madre y niño* by Oswaldo Guayasamín, Oleo sobre tela 80 x 80 cm, Fundacion Guayasamín, Quito, Ecuador; *312* Collection of the Art Museum of the Americas, Organization of American States, Gift of IBM; *315* © Susana Gonzalez/Getty Images; *316* The Granger Collection; *317* Marty Granger; *322* © Terry Whittaker/Photo Researchers, Inc.; *325* © David Simpson/Stock, Boston; *331* © Robert Frerck/Odyssey; *336* AP/Wide World Photos; *338* Marty Granger; *342* © D. Donne Bryant Stock; *350* © Mathias Opperdorff/Photo Researchers, Inc.; *353* © AP/Wide World Photos; *355* Marty Granger; *360* © Matthew Bryant/D. Donne Bryant Stock; *363* Marty Granger; *371* © Chip and Rosa Maria Peterson; *378* Marty Granger; *383* © John Mitchel/D. Donne Bryant Stock; *392* © Getty Images; *395* Courtesy of Algonquin Books; *397* Marty Granger *401* © George Holton/Photo Researchers, Inc.; *403* © Stuart Cohen; *411* © Stuart Cohen; *412* © Peter Menzel/Stock Boston; *414* Marty Granger

Realia: *Page 11* © Joaquín S. Lavado, Quino, Toda Mafalda, Ediciones de la Flor, 1997; *13* Ansa International; *85 Quo*, HF Revistas; *166* © Goya Foods, Inc.; *209* © Joaquín S. Lavado, Quino, Toda Mafalda, Ediciones de la Flor, 1997; *219 Cambio 16*; *249* © Green Comics; *318 Diario EL PAÍS*; Architect Eduardo Scheck, President of MUVA, *Museo Virtual de Artes EL PAÍS*; Professor Alicia Haber, Director of *Museo Virtual de Artes EL PAÍS*; Guillermo Pérez Rosell, General Coordinator, Digital Department of *Diario EL PAÍS*; *335* (*left*) © Joaquín S. Lavado, Quino, Toda Mafalda, Ediciones de la Flor, 1997, (*right*) © ALI, Brussels; *346* © Joaquín S. Lavado, Quino, Toda Mafalda, Ediciones de la Flor, 1997; *356* Consejo General del Poder Judicial, Instituto Nacional de Estadística e Instituto de la Mujer, from *EL PAÍS*; *361* © Joaquín S. Lavado, Quino, Toda Mafalda, Ediciones de la Flor, 1997; *366* © Joaquín S. Lavado, Quino, Toda Mafalda, Ediciones de la Flor, 1997; *375 People en español*, September 1998. Used by permission of Time Inc.; *385* © Joaquín S. Lavado, Quino, Toda Mafalda, Ediciones de la Flor, 1997; *394* Antonio Mingote; *406* © Joaquín S. Lavado, Quino, Toda Mafalda, Ediciones de la Flor, 1997.

Readings: *Page 98 Quo*, no. 31, April 1998; *145* Courtesy of *Muy Interesante*; *193 GeoMundo*; *208 Poema con niños* by Nicolás Guillén. Used by permission of the heirs of Nicolás Guillén and the Agencia Literaria Latinoamericana; *233 Quo*, 1997; *275 GeoMundo*; *318 Museo Virtual de Artes*. Courtesy of *GeoMundo*; *356* El País; *350* Reprinted with permission of Provincia Franciscana de la Santisima Trinidad, Santiago de Chile; *399 Cubanita descubanizada*, in *Bilingual Blues* by Gustavo Pérez Firmat, *Bilingual Review Press*, Arizona State University, Tempe, AZ, 1995.

ABOUT THE AUTHORS

Thalia Dorwick is Editor-in-Chief of Humanities, Social Sciences, and Languages for McGraw-Hill. She is in charge of the World Languages college list in Spanish, French, Italian, German, Japanese, and Russian. She has taught at Allegheny College, California State University (Sacramento), and Case Western Reserve University, where she received her Ph.D. in Spanish in 1973. Dr. Dorwick is the coauthor of several textbooks and the author of several articles on language teaching issues. She was recognized as an Outstanding Foreign Language Teacher by the California Foreign Language Teachers Association in 1978.

Ana María Pérez-Gironés is an Adjunct Assistant Professor of Spanish at Wesleyan University, Middletown, Connecticut, where she teaches and coordinates Spanish language courses. She received a Licenciatura en Filología Anglogermánica from the Universidad de Sevilla in 1985, and her M.A. in General Linguistics from Cornell University in 1988. She is a coauthor of *¿Qué tal?*, Fourth Edition.

Marty Knorre was formerly Associate Professor of Romance Languages and Coordinator of basic Spanish courses at the University of Cincinnati, where she taught undergraduate and graduate courses in language, linguistics, and methodology. She received her Ph.D. in foreign language education from The Ohio State University in 1975. Dr. Knorre is coauthor of *Cara a cara* and *Reflejos* and has taught at several NEH Institutes for Language Instructors. She received a Master of Divinity at McCormick Theological Seminary in 1991.

William R. Glass is the Publisher for World Languages at McGraw-Hill. He was formerly an Assistant Professor of Spanish at The Pennsylvania State University, where he taught both undergraduate and graduate courses in language and applied linguistics. He received his Ph.D. from the University of Illinois at Urbana-Champaign in Spanish Applied Linguistics with a concentration in Second Language Acquisition and Teacher Education (SLATE). Dr. Glass' research interests include second language reading theory and second language acquisition in tutored contexts. He is also a coauthor of *Puntos de partida*, Sixth Edition and the *Manual que acompaña ¿Sabías que... ?*, both by McGraw-Hill.

Hildebrando Villarreal is Professor of Spanish at California State University, Los Angeles, where he teaches undergraduate and graduate courses in language and linguistics. He received his Ph.D. in Spanish with an emphasis in Applied Linguistics from UCLA in 1976. Professor Villarreal is the author of several reviews and articles on language, language teaching, and Spanish for Native Speakers of Spanish. He is the author of *¡A leer! Un paso más*, an intermediate textbook that focuses on reading skills.

Los hispanos en los Estados Unidos	**1500–1600** Exploraciones españolas	**1700–1776** Establecimiento de misiones en Arizona y California	**1835–1836** Guerra de la independencia tejana	**1846–1848** Guerra entre México y los Estados Unidos
México y Centroamérica	**a.C.[a] 800–400** Civilización olmeca	**d.C.[b] 300–900** Civilización maya	**1200–1521** Civilización azteca florece hasta la conquista de Tenochtitlán por Hernán Cortés	**1821** Independencia de México y Centroamérica
Las naciones caribeñas	**d.C. 25–600** Civilización igneri y fundación del pueblo de Tibes en Puerto Rico	**1492–1498** Viajes de Cristóbal Colón al Caribe y a Venezuela	**1500–1512** Colonización española de Venezuela, Puerto Rico y Cuba	**1821** Independencia de Venezuela y Colombia
Las naciones andinas	**1000–1500** Civilización nasca en el Perú	**1200–1532** Imperio incaico	**1532** Francisco Pizarro conquista a los incas	**1821** Independencia del Perú
Las naciones del Cono Sur	**1536** Primera fundación de Buenos Aires	**1724** Expulsión de los portugueses del Uruguay	**1816** Independencia de la Argentina, el Paraguay, el Uruguay	**1818** Independencia de Chile
España	**a.C. 200** Llegada de los romanos a la Península	**711–1492** Establecimiento del imperio moro en la Península	**1492** Reconquista de Granada; expulsión de los judíos de España; primer viaje de Cristóbal Colón	**1500–1700** El Siglo de Oro
Los Estados Unidos y el Canadá	**a.C. 800–d.C. 1600** Varias culturas indígenas	**1534** Jacques Cartier reclama el Canadá en nombre de Francia	**1600–1750** Fundación de las colonias británicas	**1776–1789** Guerra de la Independencia en los Estados Unidos

[a]antes de Cristo [b]después de Cristo